C000215339

DAVID BOWIE
RAINBOWMAN

Jérôme Soligny

DAVID BOWIE
RAINBOWMAN

1967–1980

Interviews transcribed by
Sophie Soligny

English translation prepared for publication
by Clifford Slapper

monoray

Dandy

IAN HUNTER

Something is happening – Mr Jones
My brother says you're better than the Beatles 'n' the Stones
Saturday nite 'n' Sunday morning
You turned us into 'Heroes' – can you hear the heroes sing?

Dandy – you're the prettiest star
There ain't no life on Mars
But we always thought there might be
Dandy – you opened up the door
You left us wanting more
And then we took the last bus home

Who let the Genie outta the lamp?
And Little Lord Fauntleroy – who let him outta his amp?
Saturday nite 'n' Sunday morning
Trevor's gettin' bolder – 'n' Woody loves to hit things

Dandy – the world was black 'n' white
You showed us what it's like
To live inside a rainbow
Dandy – you thrilled us to the core
You left us wanting more
And then we took the last bus home

You beat up Goliath – you had it all
The voice, the look, the songs that shook
The gift of the gab 'n' the gall
Saturday nite 'n' Sunday morning
All we had to look forward to was the weekend
You made our lives worth living

Dandy – you're still the prettiest star
There ain't no life on Mars
But we always thought there might be
Dandy – you took us to the fair
Cabaret Voltaire – and then we caught the last bus home

Dandy – we've waited long enough
They should put a statue up
In Piccadilly Circus
Dandy – you blew us all away
Outta the drab 'n' the grey
And then we caught the last bus home

Dandy – the keeper of the flame
We won't see your like again
No, Dandy was a one-off
Dandy – look what you've become
I guess I owe you one
So thanks for the memories

'The day David Bowie died, I witnessed something I'd never seen over Manhattan: a double rainbow. I knew it was him, sending us a message. The weather was beautiful, and there was this huge rainbow with another one inside it.'
CATHERINE RUSSELL

CONTENTS

PROLOGUE

by Jérôme Soligny

'Planet Earth is blue and there's nothing I can do'

The black and white pictures appearing on our bulky television set were grainy back then. It was the middle of the night, and my parents had woken me up. I vaguely remember flannel pyjamas, a cup of Nesquik. I'd turned ten the month before and, sitting all the way back in my seat, my feet didn't touch the ground. I'd grown up playing with Mattel astronauts and building Revell model rockets, sometimes with the help of my grandfather. I'd collected the cards about space conquest that came in camembert boxes. It was the end of the 1960s – another time, the world before. I was the son of a teacher – well brought up and sensible – but already I'd been swept up by pop music including, of course, The Beatles. And there I was, at four in the morning, along with millions of other children, watching men walk on the moon. For the first time. It was two Americans, of course, because to do such a thing you had to have been born in the United States or at least be able to speak English. English was the language of Shakespeare, although I didn't know anything about him, but I thought it was better than French because it was also the language of the songs I loved. Our memories play tricks on us because, before writing this, I could have sworn I'd discussed the moon walk early the next morning at school with my best friend, before the bell rang, before lining up and heading to class. But Neil Armstrong and Edwin 'Buzz' Aldrin set foot on lunar soil on 21 July 1969. Which means it was the summer holidays and, if I saw Thierry at all, it would have been later in the day.

David Gilmour's memories of the summer of 1969 are equally confused.

He'd joined Pink Floyd as a guitarist after Syd Barrett's inevitable departure the year before, and remembers being with the band on the set of *Apollo 11* when the moon walk happened. *Apollo 11* was the generic title given to a series of television programmes celebrating the mission by BBC1 and BBC2, which had started airing in colour just a few months before. No one can quite recall anymore, but it seems that at the moment the Lunar Excursion Model (LEM) landed on the moon, Pink Floyd were playing 'Moonhead' – a partly improvised instrumental piece that was never officially released, but contained elements of the future 'Money' – to accompany the historic images. The actors Ian McKellen, Judi Dench and Michael Hordern recited passages and poems about the moon, and the Dudley Moore Trio performed live, along with Marion Montgomery, an American jazz singer who lived in England. Finally came the music of David Bowie, his single 'Space Oddity', which had been released a few days before and accompanied the images of the lunar soil, probably with men in white bouncing around on it. David wasn't on set that day, but he watched the programme from a friend's house somewhere in London.

This book, the first volume of *Rainbowman*, was first published in France on the 50th anniversary of 'Space Oddity', the ballad of Major Tom (whom I got to know after Major Matt Mason, my Mattel toy astronaut). It was a coincidence. The book's release date had been pushed back at least twice – I'd underestimated the amount of work the project demanded, or perhaps I wasn't ready to write it, or in no hurry to finish it. I know it helped me to turn a page, to close a personal chapter.

When Éditions Gallimard approached me in February 2016, I saw an opportunity to do something different with this book. At the time, I'd just turned down a request to update – for the third time (!) – a David Bowie biography I wrote in the mid-80s at the request of Christian Lebrun. With this new book I could pay tribute to Bowie the musician, by focusing only on this talent because, after (and before) all, his music is what made him famous, what enriched our lives and what survives him today. Survive? He got that right in 1999.

I really wanted to explore and recount the stories behind the creation and recording of David Bowie's albums – and his tours and musical collaborations –

in as much depth as possible, but I knew I couldn't do it alone. As a musician myself, I knew I had to give the stage to those who had helped Bowie build and refine his work. So I spent more than three and a half years interviewing musicians, producers, recording engineers, assistants and technicians who had been with David Bowie in the studio or on stage as he created his songs and performed them live. I spoke to the well-known characters in his story, but I also sought out those who hadn't spoken much before and even those who have never recounted their memories until now. I spoke to the designers who created the sleeves for his records, to set designers, photographers and even long-time fans. I gathered the words of the musicians who were with him in the beginning, others who loved his music or influenced it, and people with whom he simply rehearsed or recorded demos. I also spoke to two or three fellow musicians he reached out to, but never played with. To all this I've added reflections and opinions from people I've met during my three decades in rock journalism. Mick Ronson and The Spiders From Mars speak in *Rainbowman*. But it's not enough to simply collect words. Memory is fallible and oral history can become distorted over the years, so out of respect for my interviewees I decided to correct a few facts here and there, with their permission and even at their request.

Each of the chapters of this first volume of *Rainbowman* is named after a studio album David Bowie released between 1967 and 1980. They are divided into two distinct parts – first comes the narrative, then follows a selection of interviews (dated) from this galaxy of nearly 300 collaborators (for both volumes) and those with a story to tell. To avoid repetition, the information they provided doesn't appear in the narrative section and vice versa.

I've also made a point of almost exclusively including material from conversations I had with people personally. Even at my humble level, I have been a victim of the common practice among certain journalists and writers of supporting their work with large sections of interviews conducted by others (sometimes without citing the source). I didn't want to lower myself to that here. But because this story is a bit of a family affair, I did include a few excerpts from interviews with David Bowie, Nile Rodgers and Philip Glass offered to me by my friends, the eminent journalists Philippe Manoeuvre and Eric Dahan. Their contributions are acknowledged in the footnotes. Lastly, having read (or rather skimmed through) many pieces of writing made unintelligible by the sheer volume of names – of people, places, studios, concert venues and works known to the authors but not necessarily to the readers – I have provided, especially in the footnotes, historical and geographical clarification where I felt it was necessary.

Tony Visconti – a friend of mine for more than 30 years, who has made a priceless contribution to David Bowie's work by producing and co-producing many of his albums – has written the foreword for this book. Tony helped me, supported me, advised me and was always available as I was writing. The support of Mike Garson, whom I've known for even longer, was equally valuable. Craig San Roque, who met David as he rose to fame, has had less recognition than Tony or Mike by even the keenest of Bowie fans, but his interview, which Chris Haskett urged me to do, is a major contribution to this book. As I progressed through my work, other key players came forward to tell their story, either contacting me directly or through one of the people I'd already interviewed. The interview sections act as a human counterbalance to the historical narrative – alive and bursting with memories from the time.

 Some statements in *Rainbowman*, especially by people who have spoken a lot about David Bowie (and even more so since his death on 10 January 2016), appear in other books or articles. My intention was not to gather gossip (even though there is some here), but to weave a gigantic web with the help of this brotherhood of colleagues and lovers of Bowie's music – not to conform to the stereotype the media and public have constructed over the decades, but to paint a portrait of the active music-lover he was by those who knew him. I'm very grateful to the people (in addition to Tony and Mike) I spoke to – Reeves Gabrels, Hermione Farthingale, Mark Plati and Dana Gillespie are the first that come to mind, but there are many, many more.

 There may be rock and roll in these pages, but there's no sex and there are very few drugs. No money either. People who want to read about these subjects can find them in just about any of the other books written about David Bowie. And to avoid stretching myself too thin – and for practical reasons too (the complete *Rainbowman* manuscript exceeds three and a half million characters) – I didn't delve into the other arts (acting and painting) Bowie practised. The publisher suggested *Rainbowman* should come out in two volumes – volume one was first published in French in 2019 and the second in 2020. The cover photo for this first volume of *Rainbowman* was taken by Mick Rock, another legend in his own field who recently passed away. We had known each other for many years and it was an honour that he agreed to allow one of his legendary shots to illustrate the work. At the start of the 1970s, the first David Bowie songbook I bought with my own money contained only Mick's photos. We chose one of those.

Like the majority of Bowie's albums, this book had a different title for a good part of the writing stage. I chose the title *Rainbowman* at the beginning because it's the name David Bowie adopted at the end of February 1970 for the famous concert at the Roundhouse with Mick Ronson, Tony Visconti and John Cambridge. Two years before becoming Ziggy Stardust, David had already adopted a stage name – he picked Rainbowman because of his multicoloured outfit. I then decided to change it to a title with a more musical connotation. But during my interview with Catherine Russell, a backing vocalist and keyboardist on A Reality tour, she told me that the day David Bowie died, she witnessed a strange meteorological phenomenon – a double rainbow in the sky above Manhattan. So I decided perhaps *Rainbowman* was the right title after all. What really convinced me, though, was 'Dandy', the tribute song Ian Hunter released in the summer of 2016 about Bowie, the man who gave 'All The Young Dudes' to Mott The Hoople. The lyrics are nothing short of magnificent and contain the most beautiful sentence written about David since his death: 'You showed us what it's like to live inside a rainbow.' I took that as a sign and decided to call the book *Rainbowman*. I asked Ian for permission to publish the lyrics to 'Dandy' and he agreed (see pages 4–5).

The last time I spoke to David Bowie in person, I found him cheerful and passionate, but angry. All fired up. He was up in arms against the mediocrity of teaching, the loss of moral values, the way 'earthlings' were using the internet (already), the lack of curiosity among young people, the situation in the Middle East. All of it obscured by quite a dark sense of humour. That day, David talked a lot about his children. He showed me photographs of Alexandria (his youngest) and asked me about mine (all grown up now). He told me that all he had to do was put on a cap and he could walk down the street and take his daughter to the park without being recognized. He asked which singers my children liked and then warned me, 'Youth must forge ahead. It's especially important that children do not listen to the same music their parents did!'

The conversation turned to *Toy Story* and the sequel, also directed by John Lasseter that had come out three or four years before. I told him I'd explained to my children that Buzz Lightyear was named after Buzz Aldrin, the second man to set foot on the moon, in 1969. He asked me what I had been doing that night. I described the scene as I did at the start of this prologue (except for the bit about flannel pyjamas – I didn't know how to say that in English). He laughed and said he only had vague memories of that night in July, but remembered he'd been thrilled to hear 'Space Oddity' on television. Then he told me he never really understood why Tony Visconti hadn't wanted to produce the song, but that Gus Dudgeon had done a terrific job. He recalled his attachment to Major Tom, one of his first characters, and commented on pollution which, along with the melting glaciers and the devastating effects of deforestation, is now visible from space. Then he turned towards the window and raised his arms slowly, like a child pretending to be an aeroplane, and said, in a voice deeper than on the record, 'Planet Earth is blue and there's nothing I can do.'

Le Havre, March 2023

FOREWORD

Tony Visconti

érôme Soligny and I have been friends for more than three decades. Our friendship has strengthened over the years, thanks to email and the double-edged sword of social media. Actually, I'm friends with the whole Soligny family!

Although we live in two different countries, Jérôme and I are pretty close, and we often meet in New York, London or Paris, sometimes when he's interviewing me for French music magazine *Rock&Folk* or, recently, for this book. And of course we had a mutual friend – David Bowie. In 2013, Jérôme and I travelled together from Paris to London for the launch of the David Bowie Is exhibition at the Victoria and Albert Museum. Two years later, he translated the exhibition material into French when it appeared in Paris. Jérôme also translated my autobiography, *Bowie, Bolan and the Brooklyn Boy*, into French. He spotted more than a hundred factual errors that I asked him to correct for the French edition. If my book ever gets another printing in English, I'll make sure they translate Jérôme's version.

I'm lucky to have worked with Jérôme on his music as well. I wrote some string arrangements for his next album and I mixed the song that he and Catherine Ringer wrote to celebrate the 500th anniversary of the founding of the city of Le Havre.

But how does Jérôme know so much about the history of rock (including my modest contribution)? Because he's a responsible journalist who has done what all the others should do as well – he has mastered the art of research. Before the internet, Jérôme always had his nose buried in some insightful book about music, or in an article by a respected journalist from a previous generation, one who also took the history of rock seriously. In the 70s and 80s, being published in *Rolling Stone* or *Creem* magazine was like contributing to the Bible!

One major rock star also recognized these qualities in Jérôme Soligny – David Bowie. Right away he saw that Jérôme was responsible and capable. When in France,

Bowie often communicated through Jérôme. He appreciated his point of view. When David and I worked together again at the beginning of the 2000s, when the music world was grappling with the internet revolution, Jérôme's name came up often – we talked about things he'd told us or that he'd written about. I've been in the room with them together and I know that Bowie the artist has always trusted Soligny the writer.

I wanted to contribute to *Rainbowman* because Jérôme's approach – David Bowie's music as told by those who helped him make it – is the right one. I haven't read all the interviews yet, but I know this book contains more information than any other on the subject, and that Jérôme spoke to people who have never told their story until now. I'm looking forward to reading it.

New York, May 2019

FOR THE WINGS

Mike Garson

About 25 or 30 years ago – I'm not very good with dates – I received a phone call from France. It was a gentleman called Jérôme Soligny. At the time I was playing jazz with local bands in California and teaching piano. I hadn't seen David Bowie in over 15 years. Jérôme asked me about my time working with him in the 70s, which brought back old memories, things I'd almost forgotten. Between 1975 and that phone call, I don't think I'd even listened to *Aladdin Sane*. But that call made me wake up a bit, made me feel something come alive in me again, and I said to myself, 'Something's going on!' I guessed Jérôme wanted me to play with David again – and I, too, felt that perhaps it was my destiny.

I forget the details, but I know Jérôme spoke to Bowie about me, planted a seed in his mind. Apparently Reeves Gabrels also helped, as did my wife, Susan. These three lovely people all played a part but Jérôme was particularly insistent and persuasive – David was very clear about that! And the rest is history. I got back together with Bowie at the start of the 90s – I think it was for *Black Tie White Noise*.

Jérôme came to Los Angeles once. We spent a lot of time together and became like brothers. He'd written some nice things about me in a book he was finishing and that seemed amazing, even though, as the ignorant American I am, I couldn't read French. But he explained it to me and the nature of his work gave me a good feeling. He only talked about music, producers, musicians – about how records were made, where and when. One day I went to pick him up at the Sunset Marquis and we drove all the way to Santa Monica because he wanted to see the Civic Auditorium where I'd played with David and The Spiders From Mars. Then we headed over to Malibu and had lunch by the beach. It was a really nice moment and I felt his connection with the ocean, which he explained to me 20 years later, before recording 'She's Ocean', a song on his next album. He probably would have finished the album a long time ago had he not agreed to write *Rainbowman*.

Jérôme never saw this book as just another biography, more a study of David Bowie's musical career as seen by those who contributed to it – all the while trying to remain as true as possible to historical facts. I know Tony Visconti agrees with me: Jérôme is the only journalist in the world who can reach out to us at any time of the day or night with a question he doesn't know the answer to, but he only asks after scouring for it elsewhere first. I can't usually help him much because he knows a lot more than I do! When we were in France, David often said, 'No one remembers that? We have to ask Jérôme!'

The thing about Jérôme is that he's also a singer-songwriter, which made it easier for him to get close to us, David Bowie's musicians. I played on his album *Thanks For The Wings* – the title is a reference to *It's A Wonderful Life*, one of our favourite movies. While we were in the studio, in Paris and Brussels, we would play all night. A year later, he composed the soundtrack for a French film and he asked me to play again. During the time we spent together, we conjured up a lot of plans and we did some great things. Jérôme was the one who pushed me to record my cover album, *The Bowie Variations*, with just piano. David wasn't surprised!

Before Bowie stopped touring, Jérôme and I saw each other regularly at his concerts. Jérôme, sometimes with his friend Eric Dahan, went everywhere Bowie played – France, London, New York, and even Hartford, Connecticut! Those two always gave me the impression that they knew everything, or almost everything, about David Bowie. But the most important thing was that they loved his music.

Jérôme worked on this book for over three years. He interviewed a slew of musicians, producers and recording engineers – the famous ones, but also the lesser-known people that he rightly thought had equally valuable opinions and memories. *Rainbowman* is only about music. No gossip or anything of that nature. Most of the people interviewed really did contribute to Bowie's work.

What's incredible is that David, always open, wasn't just a sponge or a chameleon. He attracted talented people who went on to exceed even their own expectations of themselves after coming into contact with him. Not long ago, Jérôme said something that I think is very true: 'David Bowie played saxophone, guitar and a bit of piano, but above all, he played musicians!' I think he really hit the nail on the head with that comment. It's exactly that. He borrowed, he took possession of things, he rejected whatever didn't interest him, he appropriated what really fascinated him and all this art, recycled in this way, became his own, in his own voice. This book isn't going to tell you that David Bowie was a genius. We already know that. *Rainbowman* allows us to see the extent of his magnetism and how much he was able to galvanize his team.

Honestly, I couldn't wait to read this book – I even interviewed my friend Earl Slick for it! Many people in these pages are dear friends, people I've worked with. I'm curious to see what everyone has to say about David. Jérôme really was the best person for this job. We all spoke to him with complete trust. If we got a date wrong, or the location of a recording or the title of a song, he'd correct it!

I want to thank Jérôme personally, 'for the wings' of course, but also for his devotion to David Bowie and his music, and I hope that you'll love this book as much as I do. I already adore it.

Los Angeles, April 2019

And these children that you spit on
As they try to change their worlds
Are immune to your consultations
They're quite aware of what they're going through

DAVID BOWIE, 'CHANGES', 1971

In memory of Mick Rock,

Jeff Beck,
Paul Buckmaster,
Ricky Gardiner,
John Hutchinson,
Phil May,
Robin Mayhew,
Terry O'Neill,
Matthew Seligman,
Joe Tarsia,
Lloyd Watson
and Roy Young

INTRODUCTION

I n March 2003, the messages started – bottles thrown into the sea, skimming the waves between Le Havre and his management. Emails to and from the magazine. A few calls to the record label, Sony. What could David Bowie offer *Rock&Folk*, the most prominent French rock magazine, to get them to put him on the cover? It had only been a year since he made the front page, for the release of *Heathen*. Back then it was normal for the editor-in-chief of a music magazine to commit to putting a musician on the cover, even before listening to a single note of their upcoming album. But *Rock&Folk* never agreed to this, regardless of the artist or how famous they were. Even just three days before going to press, I'd seen them discarding covers they'd long since planned, that the record companies thought were in the bag.

After discussing covers again and again, we came up with the idea of asking David Bowie to comment on all the front pages the magazine had dedicated to him since the first, three decades before. Sony warned that while Bowie could spare a bit of time, he could only talk about *Reality*, his new album, which was coming out just a year and a half after the last. This was madness back then, when great time lapses between records were common. But people wanted more.

Finally, after a last-minute email exchange, the concept of an 'expert witness' was raised and everyone agreed that David Bowie could do as he pleased with the September issue of *Rock&Folk*: choose which articles to comment on, which columns, give his opinions on the music, talk about the latest gigs he'd been to, recommend a book. That he could do. But only talk about *Reality*? No thanks. I received an email from the magazine: 'Hey! Big J! Bowie editor-in-chief of the issue – huge news. You'll figure it out, we'll send you the brief, he's going to contribute what he wants. Call us when you're back. Ha ha! You lucky devil!' It was easier said than done and the editor Philippe Manoeuvre knew it. He'd set me up; made his own little merry-go-round.

The night before I left for New York, even management wished me good luck. 'You'll have more than enough time. But we submitted your proposal to him and he hasn't responded yet. You should receive an email soon.' Ten minutes before getting on the plane, I checked my inbox on my mobile at an exorbitant price – it was still empty: no more emails than there were hairs on Aladdin Sane's chest. It seemed all too risky.

'What, again?!' is what everyone had said when, in January, they'd caught wind of another Bowie album, planned for the end of summer. 'And a world tour on top of that? His biggest one in ten years?' The man was definitely full of surprises. That spring, news had travelled around at the speed of light: Tony Visconti was in charge of the record. The Matrix, a team of young British producers who'd risen to fame after working with Liz Phair and Avril Lavigne, had been approached to take care of a couple of songs. The album would feature two cover songs ('Pablo Picasso' and 'Try Some, Buy Some') and a reinterpretation of an unreleased track, 'Bring Me The Disco King'. Word on the street was that it was a commercial album meant to boost the tour. But actually, *Reality* didn't turn out to be a sequel to *Let's Dance* or to *Heathen*. The album was presented to the press in New York, the day before my interview with Bowie, at Philip Glass's studios on Broadway, where Tony Visconti was working at the time. In that overheated glass box, where no one was allowed to bring in a bag (or recording device), an assortment of journalists from all over the world gathered. Over the loudspeakers, *Reality* sounded like New York itself – electric, a low shriek. More precisely, it sounded like the very essence of the city we love.

David Bowie gave me his interview, his last for *Rock&Folk*, on 26 June 2003 at around midday. The tarmac was starting to melt as we checked into the Thompson Hotel. Coco Schwab, his PA, enthusiastic and on good form, greeted me with big hugs and said David was excited to see me. She asked if the paper roll I had under my arm contained the twenty-something magazine covers with David's face on them. She confirmed that he would be the editor of issue 433 of *Rock&Folk*. Once again, the interview felt like a real conversation. Sometimes he'd be the one asking questions. As always, he wanted to hear the other person's opinion. Far from wanting to steer conversations, David Bowie let life flow into them; he let them breathe. Throughout our conversation, which lasted more than 90 minutes (we recorded on both sides of the tape), he jumped from subject to subject, lost his temper, offered insights and laughed, a lot. Always in his own style, as usual. Sometimes, when he was going a bit too far, he'd stop the recording. He gave this last interview with total honesty and openness, as if it were the most natural thing in the world. It was a unique moment. Could he comment on the covers? No problem. I placed them on the floor and he danced around them. I can still see him. Could he contribute to the issue by giving his opinion of the artists featured and the columns? He was happy to do it. And he didn't want us to worry about the length of the interview. That year, time was still on his side.

Because I'd just received it, I had a book poking out of my bag that 'explained' Bowie's songs. He hadn't seen it before, so David, with the deftness of a pickpocket, pulled it out. 'Ah! You'll see. We're gonna read here that I wrote this or that song because I had a complicated relationship with my mother. What do these people know?' David read a few lines before bursting out laughing. 'Sure, I was traumatized by this or that. Oh what an unhappy childhood! My youthful waywardness...and what else? Anyone is free to interpret my lyrics as they wish, but to assume they know everything about my life, sometimes better than I do...I'm not a secretive person, but I only talk about my family very rarely: my private life should remain so. Personally, I'm more interested in the work of artists than in the artists themselves.'

According to official records (usually reliable), and his Wikipedia page (laughably inaccurate), David Bowie first came into this world on 8 January 1947 at 40 Stansfield Road in Brixton, South London. But is that so? For a good number of his compatriots and a handful of future musicians, he first came into being on 6 July 1972, when he appeared on *Top Of The Pops* on BBC1, singing 'Starman' in a quilted suit made by his friend Freddie Burretti, with his arm around the neck of a platinum-haired Mick Ronson – his guitarist at the time, his comrade, his battle axe.

Or maybe his beginnings started as far back as the Blitz, the terrible and deafening bombing raids on London during World War II. Bowie was too young to have experienced the bombing, but it shaped the city and its outskirts, probably eliciting in him – and in many children of the post-war period – the will to move at all costs, to get away from the brick dust, red in their hair, to seek salvation in change. With Bowie, this would become a recurring and visceral theme. As soon as young David Jones was old enough to recognize the confines of suburbia – the inspiration for Lou Reed and John Cale's 'Smalltown' (the opening track on

Songs for Drella, their tribute album to Andy Warhol in 1990), intensely grey and beautifully portrayed by the Pet Shop Boys four years earlier – he sought to escape it.

For others, David came into being in 1969, the year a man first walked somewhere other than on Earth. As David Bowie, he'd just written 'Space Oddity', a small song inspired by a photograph of the blue planet taken from the moon, but a giant song for mankind. Others would swear that he first appeared in Berlin, near the Wall, in 1977. That's where he recorded "Heroes", his personal hymn. As legend has it, the lyrics came to him after he looked out of the studio window and saw Tony Visconti kiss a local girl. Well, Bowie wouldn't be Bowie without a few sweet little lies...

Like all plants, from the most beautiful to the wildest, David Bowie started out growing in fertile, well watered soil, and was cultivated by particular tutors. But exactly how he evolved remains more or less a mystery. In the following pages, a prelude to the opening chapter, I chose simply to present the facts and first steps, rather than dissect or over-analyse them. Then it's up to each individual to reach their own opinions about the artist's youth, their own ideas about the repercussions and consequences of certain family events. Some readers will deem such events insignificant, others will see them as crucial. The parameters in the David Bowie equation, from his infancy to his departure, are subject to so many permutations that there are a multitude of explanations of his life. Perhaps one, not necessarily the most obvious, was evident only to him alone, and he has taken that with him. Meanwhile, I also want to point out that for many of today's young lovers of his music, who have the good taste to purchase his records on vinyl (the noble format on which they were first released in the beginning), Bowie, at the eye of the most bewildering media storm they will have witnessed in their lives so far, was born on the second Sunday of January, 2016. Two days after his sixty-ninth birthday and the release of *Blackstar*.

WEDNESDAY'S CHILD

Haywood Stenton Jones was born in Doncaster, Yorkshire, in 1912. His father was killed during World War I and his mother died soon after so Haywood, widely known as John, spends his childhood moving between an orphanage and his aunt's house. When he comes of age, he receives an inheritance from the family business and invests it in a theatrical troupe, but he goes on to lose everything.

John Jones meets Hilda Louise in 1933 and they marry in London. They open a piano bar at 74 Charlotte Street, but this venture is also doomed for failure although the premises are still standing to this day. So Jones goes to work for Dr Barnardo's, a charity that helps disadvantaged children and orphans, where he will eventually become the head of public relations. John and Hilda separate at one point, but get back together after two years, shortly before the birth of Annette, John's illegitimate child from another relationship. He and Hilda go on to adopt Annette.

John serves as a sniper in World War II. After discharge, he meets Margaret Mary Burns (known as Peggy), who is working as a waitress at the Ritz Cinema in Tunbridge Wells. Born in 1913 near Folkestone, Peggy already has two children of her own – Terence (Terry) Guy Adair Burns, who was born in 1937 and whose father was a Frenchman who'd left Peggy before he was born; and Myra Ann, who was born in August 1943 with an unknown father, and who had been given up for adoption. Even though John is still married to Hilda and is in regular contact with her, he moves in with Peggy – first in Kentish Town, then in a house they buy near Brixton, in South London.

This is where, on a Wednesday in 1947[1], on Elvis Presley's twelfth birthday, David Robert Jones opens his eyes for the first time. It is a harsh winter and London is still being rebuilt after the war. People are struggling to recover from the hardships of war and food rationing is still in force – and will remain so until 1954. Life isn't easy for David's parents, but Brixton is a source of wonder for many children of that generation, who use the ruins of Victorian homes as their playground. That same year, John Jones and Hilda are divorced, and he and Peggy Burns get married. John's relationship with David's half-brother Terry is strained, but Terry takes the Jones surname (although he will later revert back to Burns).

David, the baby of the family, adores his father. He'll treasure one of his gifts his whole life – a golden cross[2], which David will wear around his neck for many years. David and Peggy's relationship, however, won't be quite as warm. According to Peggy's sister Pat, Peggy inherited some of their mother's aloofness. Her side of the family struggled with mental illness. David's maternal grandmother suffered with schizophrenia since adolescence, and so did three of her children, including Nora, who will be lobotomized. Peggy seems to have been spared the worst of it, but she has trouble expressing her feelings. Terry, who was raised by Pat in his early years, suffers because of it. He has a shy disposition and feels rejected by his stepfather, which may contribute to the development of his mental illness later on.

In 1951, David starts school in Stockwell, down the road from his house. Two years later, the family moves to 106 Canon Road in Bickley, south of Bromley, where David attends the Raglan Primary School. In the afternoons, he hurries home to watch television, especially his favourite show *The Quatermass Experiment*, a hit sci-fi series on the BBC. His family is one of the first in the area to own a television. In 1954, David's father receives a promotion and the Joneses move again, this time to 22 Clarence Road in Bromley. Although the house is elegant, it is small, but that doesn't stop Annette, David's half-sister, from moving in too. The following year, the family move yet again and finally settle in a townhouse at 4 Plaistow Grove, in Sundridge Park, where they will stay for 15 years. Terry has the bedroom next to David's and although he isn't home much, he has a strong influence on David's cultural education by lending him, most significantly, his copy of *On The Road* by Jack Kerouac.

In 1955, David Jones joins the top class of Burnt Ash Primary School, north of Bromley. There he meets Geoffrey MacCormack, who will remain his lifelong friend. David thrives under Burnt Ash's new educational system, which encourages physical expression and the playing of musical instruments. In November, Terry leaves home for military service in the Royal Air Force. David sees him as a hero, a sort of role model, or at least that's what he will claim most of his life, although he will revise his judgement in later years.

At the age of nine, David discovers Elvis Presley. He also goes to see Tommy Steele playing live, with his cousin Kristina, who is four years older than him. Tommy Steele is idolized by many teenagers at the time, and David manages to get his autograph. The following year he joins the Scouts at St Mary's Church on College Road. That's where he meets George Underwood and the two will remain inseparable for many years. They are both ambidextrous and take up the guitar together. They sing in St Mary's choir, along with Geoff MacCormack, although their interest in religion is limited. That year, *Mister Rock And Roll*, a musical film by Charles S. Dubin is released. David is awestruck when Little Richard appears on the screen, singing the upbeat 'Lucille'. Little Richard, like other rock'n'roll pioneers, is very popular in Britain at the time, but David will have to wait five years before he can see him in concert, at the Granada Cinema in Woolwich. That night he will dream of joining the brass section.

After primary school, David Jones goes on to Bromley Tech, a secondary school for boys on Oakley Road in Keston. He starts to ignore his mother's advice and increasingly turns his back on his studies to focus on music, art and fashion. Unlike his father, who regularly buys him records (and will support him in his artistic endeavours), his mother does not approve of his musical interests. David devours weekly music magazines and starts to write songs. Meanwhile, Terry has moved back in with the family and, confronted with his deteriorating mental health (Terry was showing worrying signs of schizophrenia and would later be diagnosed with bipolar disorder), David writes song lyrics that tackle some very serious subjects for a boy of his age. At Bromley Tech, David Jones and George Underwood are in the same class, with Owen Frampton as their art teacher; they adore him and he will introduce them to many painters and other artists.

By the beginning of the 60s, David and George start to cultivate their look, to notice girls and to go to any local bar that lets minors in. After school, David often hangs out at Medhurst's, a department store on Bromley High Street. The music department specializes in American imports and is run by a couple of gay men with a passion for jazz, something they pass on to David. Terry also encourages the boy, leading him to discover Charles Mingus, Charlie Parker, Roland Kirke and King Curtis. David is inspired by everything around him and in addition to music, he becomes interested in American football (he'd started kicking a ball around at Burnt Ash) and, through the work of Illinois writer Frank Edwards, in aliens (and their spaceships!) and paranormal phenomena. He also never misses a television appearance by Anthony Newley.

George Underwood becomes the singer for The Konrads[3], a local band with Neville Wills and Alan Dobbs on guitar, Rocky Shahan on bass and Dave Crook on drums. Meanwhile, David's interest in Kerouac leads him to become fascinated with bebop and the Beat movement, which were closely related[4]. At the end of 1961, his father offers him a plastic alto saxophone as a Christmas present. It's a Grafton, which he'd bought at A.T. Furlong & Sons, a record and instrument shop in Bromley (where David will later work on Saturday afternoons, and where he'll meet other musicians). He will exchange the instrument a few weeks later for a C.G. Conn Ltd brass tenor sax[5].

In February the following year, David Jones and George Underwood come to blows over a girl at Bromley Tech. David's eye is injured and, despite an operation, his left pupil will never be able to dilate properly again. He is still recovering when in April, George and a few classmates perform at the school fair as George & The Dragons. David is well again by late spring and finally joins The Konrads. On 16 June 1962, David Jones appears on stage in front of an audience for the first time, at a school event organized by parents and teachers – he's happy just to blow his saxophone. The band's repertoire consists of covers of the latest hits – including many by The Shadows – and they will play pubs and small music venues in and around London until the end of the following year. Along the way, The Konrads lose their drummer (replaced by Dave Hadfield) and, when George Underwood also quits, Roger Ferris shares lead vocals with David.

In 1963, David Jones leaves Bromley Tech with O-levels in art and woodwork and gets a job as an illustrator with Nevin D. Hirst, an advertising agency in the West End of London. That same summer, The Konrads, who have been joined by keyboardist Tony Edwards, get an audition with the record label Decca, arranged by the The Rolling Stones' management. The label – which has turned down The Beatles – is impervious to the charms of 'I Never Dreamed'. The song is credited to Ferris and Jones and, ironically, it has a very Merseybeat sound. David is starting to feel too constrained by the Konrads. They no longer suit him – they apparently refused to add 'Can I Get A Witness', written for Marvin Gaye by Lamont Dozier and the Holland Brothers, to their repertoire – so on 31 December he performs with them for the last time.

At the beginning of 1964, David meets some musicians from Fulham who've been playing together for a few months: guitarist Roger Bluck, bassist Dave Howard and drummer Bob Allen. David and George Underwood join the group and they become The King Bees. The name is inspired by 'I'm A King Bee', a classic track by Louisiana blues musician Slim Harpo, covered by The Rolling Stones and Pink Floyd that same year. At the tender age of 17, David already understands that money is the driving force behind the music business, so he takes the initiative to seek financial backing from John Bloom, the washing machine tycoon known for his aggressive business manner. Impressed by the audacity of this young musician, Bloom introduces David to Leslie Conn, a talent scout for music publisher Dick James. James recently joined with Brian Epstein to launch Northern Songs, the company that takes care of The Beatles' publishing. At the same time, Conn is interested in another musician named Mark Feld, who is also itching to be famous. And be famous he will – a few years later he will be the leader of T. Rex, under the name Marc Bolan[6].

That spring, Leslie Conn becomes the manager of The King Bees, and especially of their lead singer. David is still a minor, so at least one of his parents has to sign the contract. Bloom books The King Bees for one of his events, but the audience doesn't much appreciate their rhythm'n'blues, so their performance is cut short. But Conn, still on good terms with Decca, even though the label didn't sign The Konrads the year before, arranges for Davie Jones (his new stage name) and his band to record a single, to be released on 5 June 1964 by the subsidiary label Vocalion Pop.

On the A-side is 'Liza Jane', a thunderous reinterpretation of 'Li'l Liza Jane', an African-American folk song that the crafty manager furtively took credit for writing (he also credited himself as 'musical director' of the sessions). The B-side is 'Louie, Louie Go Home', written by American musicians Paul Revere and Mark Lindsay (from Paul Revere & The Raiders). It isn't as much fun as a song, but David performs it as if his life depends on it. This single gets him on national television (on *Juke Box Jury*, *The Beat Room* and *Ready Steady Go!*) and earns him a few lines in the press. 'Liza Jane' will be a flop, but that doesn't dampen David's resolve. He always seems to be one step ahead.

In July, he walks out of Nevin D. Hirst, leaves The King Bees and successfully auditions as a singer-saxophonist for The Manish Boys, a band from Maidstone. Although he was initially averse to James Brown's soul music – Geoff MacCormack tried to introduce him to it some years before – David Jones can't stop listening to *The Apollo Theatre Presents – In Person! The James Brown Show*, which came out in 1963. The music of The Manish Boys – with Johnny Flux on guitar, organist Bob Solly, Paul Rodriguez and Woolf Byrne on brass, bassist John Watson and Mick White on drums – starts to take on this burgeoning influence, which will turn into a major one a decade later.

Between 25 July (in Sheffield) and 31 December 1964 (in Finchley), The Manish Boys will perform 50 gigs nationwide, often as a support band. They also perform on a joint mini-tour, with American singer Gene Pitney and Liverpudlian band Gerry And The Pacemakers headlining. David is far from being fully satisfied with The Manish Boys (the fact that they don't live in London is a problem), but playing with them he gets better live, notably at the Marquee[7]. The club has opened a few months before in the heart of Soho, and David steps on stage there for the first time on 6 November 1964. This is the night he meets Dana Gillespie. She is beautiful, has a strong personality and is from a well-off family. This future good friend and singer is one of the few objective witnesses of David Jones' rise to glory.

A week later, he gives his first television interview as the founder of The Society for the Prevention of Cruelty to Long-Haired Men. Some of The Manish Boys sport a Keith Relf[8] hairdo, which leads to mockery they could do without.

In 1964, the group recorded three covers for Decca. This company passed on them, but Parlophone, The Beatles' label, released a single on 5 March 1965 with 'I Pity The Fool' on the A-side, backed by 'Take My Tip'. The sessions were produced at IBC Studios at Portland Place in mid-January by Shel Talmy[9], an American whose name will be associated with the success of The Kinks, The Who and The Easybeats over the course of the decade. David Bowie will record songs by these three bands for his 1973 album *Pin Ups*.

'I Pity The Fool' is an unremarkable cover of a blues track recorded by American Bobby 'Blue' Bland for his first album, but 'Take My Tip', the first David Jones song to be etched on vinyl, is much more adventurous on a harmonic and structural level. Jimmy Page, a 21-year-old session guitarist who works with Talmy regularly, plays on the recording.

The Manish Boys single (David's own name appeared only on the centre label as songwriter, which he was very unhappy about) is not Parlophone's marketing priority that spring, so the group stage a publicity stunt with Leslie Conn and Barry Langford, the producer of BBC2 show *Gadzooks! It's All Happening*, on which they are appearing in March for the first time. To create some buzz, the musicians spread a rumour that the length of their hair might hinder their appearance on the show. The media (notably the *Daily Mirror*) takes the bait and blows the whole affair out of proportion, but not enough to keep 'I Pity The Fool' from being another flop.

David doesn't have a good year in 1965 – Terry is starting to spend time at Cane Hill mental hospital in Croydon, south of London. David also resents the interest shown in a single recorded by George Underwood (which Mickie Most has produced and Leslie Conn set up) after he left The King Bees. Conn is struggling to book concerts for The Manish Boys, so David leaves the band in the spring. He will soon meet three musicians from Margate at La Gioconda[10] on Denmark Street (guitarist Denis Taylor, bassist Graham Rivens and drummer Les Mighall). They came to London seeking fame as The Lower Third. They are looking for a singer and David Jones needs a band. They set up auditions at La Discotheque, another club on Wardour Street, and David mostly plays the saxophone. Future frontman of Small Faces Steve Marriott, with whom David will become friends, also tries his luck that day. The Lower Third choose David, who then cheekily asks to audition the band. He invites them to his parents' house, where he is still living most of the time – there they give an informal but conclusive performance.

David and his new band start to perform together at the beginning of June, driving between gigs in a converted ambulance which often doubles up as their hotel on wheels. The following month, their drummer is replaced by Phil Lancaster, who responded to an ad in *Melody Maker*. His audition, which is more of a rambling conversation about music, takes place at La Gioconda. A few weeks before, David and The Lower Third had recorded a handful of tracks at Central Sound Studio, including 'Born Of The Night', a song David had recently written. Unfortunately, Shel Talmy is not interested in it, but he agrees to produce 'You've Got A Habit Of Leaving' and 'Baby Loves That Way' at IBC Studios that July. 'You've Got A Habit Of Leaving' is more complex than it first appears, and the debatable influence of The Who is especially felt in the cacophonous parts. On 20 August, the day of the single's release, Davie Jones and The Lower Third open for the mod group at the Pavilion Theatre in Bournemouth. Pete Townshend, The Who's guitarist, stops by as The Lower Third do their sound check. He stays just long enough to hear the similarities between some of David's songs and his own, and express his displeasure.

Shel Talmy has hired Glyn Johns[11] as recording engineer on the two tracks, and the excellent Nicky Hopkins (whom Talmy has also hired to play with The Who) on piano. Hopkins hammers out the chords of 'Baby Loves That Way' with confidence. For the chorus, David wanted to create a kind of monastic choir sound, demonstrating that his interest in Tibet and Buddhism had begun long before is generally thought. He called on everyone he could find in the studio to join this improvised choir.

The band also recorded five demos during the single's sessions. The booklet notes of *Early On (1964–1966)* – a very good compilation of Bowie's recordings dating from before his first album, released by Rhino in 1991 (some are different from previously released versions) – state that these songs were attributed to Davy Jones on the label, without The Lower Third (which not surprisingly angered the musicians). 'I'll Follow You', 'Glad I've Got Nobody', 'That's Where My Heart Is', 'I Want My Baby Back' and 'Bars Of The Country Jail' are not Bowie's best songs and their lyrics are not his most beautiful. But they do confirm that at 18 years old, he was already developing a number of different strengths and wasn't afraid to take on complicated melodies. These five songs on *Early On* also show Bowie's ability to emulate the stars of the time, including Brian Wilson of The Beach Boys in 'I Want My Baby Back'.

Believing that Leslie Conn isn't doing a good enough job, David turns to Ralph Horton, who is best known for assisting The Moody Blues on the road (they'd had their first hit at the end of 1964 with a cover of 'Go Now'), but is also familiar enough with the club scene to find regular gigs for The Lower Third, especially on the south coast of England. The band opens for The Pretty Things, one of David's favourite bands, in Bournemouth that August. He is impressed by their music and by lead singer Phil May's evident androgyny. Throughout his life, David Bowie described himself as a music-lover first and foremost. During his formative years, he always jumped at the chance to meet his idols and even open for them. Over the course of his career, he will pay tribute to some of them by recording their songs (notably on *Pin Ups*) and by performing snippets (a verse here, a chorus there) of other songs that influenced him. He also often 'quoted' the music of Johnny Kidd & The Pirates, for whom The Lower Third once opened.

At Horton's recommendation, David and his musicians cut their hair and adopt the mod style[12]. In late 1965, worried that 'You've Got A Habit Of Leaving' didn't elicit more interest than its predecessor, The Lower Third record some of David's new songs at R.G. Jones Studios[13]. These include an early version of 'Silly Boy Blue' and 'Baby That's A Promise', whose verse borrows heavily from 'Where Have All The Good Times Gone' by The Kinks. Ralph Horton becomes David's official manager that autumn; the contract doesn't mention any other member of The Lower Third.

Horton is more convinced by David's potential than by his own ability to develop it and decides that a joint management agreement with a big name in the industry could help break him out of his stagnation. His choice is Ken Pitt, a 43-year-old show-business veteran who manages Manfred Mann, the band named after its frontman and keyboardist. A cultured man of fine taste, Pitt has a good thick address book and regularly works with Americans – in 1964, for example, he promoted Bob Dylan's first tour in England.

Ken Pitt is too busy to meet with David, but over the phone he advises Ralph Horton to tell his protégé to adopt a stage name to avoid confusion with Davy Jones, the English actor famous for appearing in Lionel Bart's musical *Oliver!* and singing with The Monkees, the American band whose (fictional) tribulations appeared on a popular television series between 1966 and 1968. In September, David Robert Jones becomes David Bowie as an artist, although on paper and posters he continues to use his real name due to contractual obligations. This name had been knocking around in his head for some time. It appears to be a double tribute, first to Colonel James 'Jim' Bowie, who fought valiantly at the siege of Fort Alamo in San Antonio, Texas, in the winter of 1836. As a teenager, David Jones saw *The Alamo*, John Wayne's dramatic 1960 cinematic depiction of the battle, with Richard Widmark playing the role of Jim Bowie – most likely at the Gaumont Cinema in Bromley, as George Underwood specified for this book. The name might also reference Jim Bowie's talisman, his famous 'Bowie' knife conceived by his brother Rezin, which David considered 'enigmatic' because its blade cut with both edges.

In early November, David and The Lower Third audition for the BBC, where a panel judge which artists are suitable to appear on their music programmes. One of the songs they play is 'Chim Chim Cheree'[14], from the Robert Stevenson musical *Mary Poppins,* released in 1964. It is in fact part of the band's repertoire and demonstrates Bowie's open-mindedness, but it throws off his musicians. During the performance, The Lower Third also plays a shortened version of the instrumental 'Mars, Bringer Of War', one of the seven symphonic movements from *The Planets* by British composer Gustav Holst, which was the theme song to *The Quatermass Experiment* in 1953. That autumn, Ralph Horton tells The Lower Third that the

BBC didn't like their performance (and thought that David Bowie was singing out of tune!), but announces that Tony Hatch has agreed to produce their new single, for Pye Records this time. Hatch is a British musician, composer and songwriter for, among others, Petula Clark and The Searchers. He also worked with Françoise Hardy and is less rock than Shel Talmy, which makes him a good choice because Bowie, after all, is not only rock.

In November, the label arranges a session at its studios at Great Cumberland Place, north of Marble Arch. That's where The Kinks have recorded most of their earlier hits and where, according to Ray Davies, guitar feedback coming from his amp was first caught on tape (it can be heard on 'I Need You'). David wants to record 'Now You've Met The London Boys', planned for the A-side of the next single, and 'You've Got It Made'. Not much is known about the latter – in *At The Birth Of Bowie* (John Blake Publishing, 2019), Phil Lancaster will write he no longer remembers what the song sounded like – but many Bowie fans rate 'Now You've Met The London Boys', which they will hear a year later in a more weighted version, as one of his best early songs. However, Pye doesn't appreciate these semi-autobiographical lyrics about moving to London, especially as pills that you start off trying, then end up taking too many of, are mentioned twice.

The band's disappointment will be short lived and Hatch soon organizes a new session in the same studio. The Lower Third shows up after rehearsing at Regent Sounds. This time, the first track they record is 'Can't Help Thinking About Me', another great song by Bowie. It is decidedly lively and has an even more autobiographical feel as he performs it in the first person. Based on a frenzied rhythm with particularly daring harmonies through the verses, the song is about leaving home and moving on to the big city. Hatch, on piano, will reproach David for his obsession with London.

On the day of the recording, David Bowie forgets to bring the song lyrics with him and rewrites them from memory with whatever comes to mind. He already owns a notebook in which he jots down words and phrases that come to him, according to his moods and whims. Because of the chorus and the fact that he liked to use words to mean whatever he felt they should mean, David will sing

'Can't Help Thinking About Me' again in 1999 on *Storytellers*, and call the song 'a beautiful piece of solipsism'. The B-side of the single is 'And I Say To Myself'; it is lighter, built on a combination of two turnarounds, and more in line with what Tony Hatch expects.

David performs a few more gigs with The Lower Third in 1965, then they cross the Channel on a ferry for three concerts in Paris over the New Year – two at the Golf Drouot (31 December and 1 January) and one at the Bus Palladium (2 January). It is the first time Bowie performs abroad, and the last time the band will. He will have to wait another decade before stepping onto a Parisian stage again, and another two before playing in the same Paris neighbourhood. These gigs are part of a band exchange with the Marquee and there are other artists playing, including Arthur Brown[15] on the first night. According to the local press, the concerts are good, but David seems to have lost faith. Things look like they're working out well for him (a roadie is now accompanying The Lower Third as they travel and a party is planned for the release of their new single), but the gap is widening between him and his musicians, whose living conditions continue to be precarious. After their last concert in Paris, Ralph Horton takes Bowie back to London by plane (another first for David, though for many years afterwards a fear of flying prevented him travelling by air at all) with the excuse that he has to meet the producer of *Ready Steady Go!* as soon as possible. The other members of the band have to make their own way back in their converted ambulance.

'Can't Help Thinking About Me', whose centre label credits 'David Bowie with The Lower Third', is released on 14 January 1966 to the usual indifference. It will make a brief appearance in the *Melody Maker* charts, but all the signs suggest this placement was 'bought', a practice that is as old as the record industry.

On 29 January, Bowie and The Lower Third perform together for the last time at the Marquee, because the concert scheduled for later that day at the Bromel Club, a stone's throw from David's house, will not take place. Horton warns the musicians that he won't be able to pay them that evening, and confirms it as they are unloading their equipment outside the venue. Denis Taylor, Graham Rivens and Phil Lancaster refuse to play and realize there and then that their association with David Bowie is over. A band's breakup is rarely joyful, but this one will leave a particularly bitter taste in the mouths of the musicians because during their final conversation with Bowie, he hardly says a word. His mind is already elsewhere, thinking about the audition he and Ralph Horton have set up at the Marquee to recruit new musicians.

David Bowie first performs with The Buzz on 10 February 1966 at the Mecca Ballroom in Leicester. The band name was suggested by Earl Richmond, a broadcaster with Radio London. The musicians are given nicknames because some of them have similar names; they are John 'Hutch' Hutchinson on guitar, Derek 'Dek' Fearnley on bass, Derrick 'Chow' Boyes on keyboards and John 'Ego' Eager on drums. They were hired just the week before and were warned that they are a singer-songwriter's backing band. They quickly size him up – they find him disconcerting, but like his songs.

Chow, from Yorkshire, has played with The Tennesseans with Hutch, who has recommended him. Hutch has already been around a bit; he's had some success with The Apaches in Gothenburg, Sweden and has crossed paths with the as-yet-unknown American musician Boz Scaggs. At the end of 1965, Hutchinson returned to England to spend Christmas with his parents. After the holidays he realized that his travel documents weren't up to date and, instead of returning to Sweden, he decided to look for work in London. One afternoon, on the first Saturday in February, he walked through the door of the Marquee. The club was empty but its manager, Jack Barrie, gave him the phone number of a certain David Bowie. He was looking for a guitarist to join a band that so far only had a rhythm section.

By November, The Buzz will have performed almost 70 gigs, some of which were scheduled before the breakup of The Lower Third. David Bowie notices that his audience, which includes some long-term fans, is becoming less and less sparse despite his band changes. This year, a fan from Bromley will set up the first Bowie fan club.

In March, The Buzz appears alongside David Bowie on *Ready Steady Go!*, to the great displeasure of members of The Lower Third. Bowie wears a white suit borrowed from John Stephen, the King of Carnaby Street. Stephen owns a dozen clothing stores popular with rock stars and drives from one to another in his Rolls-Royce. Bowie's outfit is so shiny it causes problems on set, but David refuses to wear anything else and the lighting engineer has to deal with it. 'Do Anything You Say' comes out on 1 April as a new single produced by Tony Hatch, with 'Good Morning Girl' on the B-side. Simple, playful and effective, these two tracks were recorded at Pye Studios. They aren't Bowie's best songs of the time, but 'Do Anything You Say' is improved by Hatch's clever arrangements – a pianist himself, he raised Chow's volume in the mix. 'Good Morning Girl' shows that Bowie hasn't left jazz behind. It features a scat vocal/guitar dialogue, a form of improvisation that Alvin Lee, lead singer of the blues-rock band Ten Years After, will master the following year.

From mid-April to the end of June, David and his band will perform every Sunday afternoon at the Marquee and present The Bowie Showboat. The show's name is a reference to the movie *Show Boat*. David has probably seen the George Sydney remake of 1951[16] at the cinema; fans consider it to be the first serious and realistic musical film ever made. Ralph Horton invites Ken Pitt along to the show on Sunday 17 April. He sees Bowie on stage and gets the same feeling that Brian Epstein felt on seeing The Beatles at the Cavern in Liverpool six years before. Pitt immediately recognizes Bowie's talent and potential: his vocal abilities, his confidence on stage, the quality of his songs and the extent and variety of his repertoire. That day, lit by a single spotlight, Bowie ends his performance with 'You'll Never Walk Alone', from the musical *Carousel*[17.] Gerry And The Pacemakers covered the same song successfully and Elvis Presley will record it in 1968. Ken Pitt is in awe of the young man. He seems to have it all. As the lights come back on, he knows he is going to accept the offer and Horton will soon be relegated to the role of road manager. Pitt won't become Bowie's official manager until a little later, but he is soon arranging his affairs, finding him better gigs and giving him precious advice.

At the end of June, John Hutchinson is replaced by Scotsman Billy Gray, who played with The Anteeks and later, in Italy, will join the prog rock group The Trip. He will only perform with The Buzz for a few months and won't play on David

Bowie's third single for Pye Records. A few weeks after a session from which nothing came out, Tony Hatch hires studio musicians to play on 'I Dig Everything' and 'I'm Not Losing Sleep', but their names have been lost to history. As on his two previous singles, Bowie alone is credited on this one, which sounds more professional, but with a 'pop' flavour – Hatch's signature style. While the overall craftsmanship of these songs is respectable, their bridges are especially remarkable – this will be one of Bowie's songwriting strengths throughout his career. 'I Dig Everything', which comes out in mid-August, doesn't cause any more of a stir than any of his other 45s since 'Liza Jane'. A few flattering remarks will be published in the musical press, but none of the radio stations will play the song.

David realizes that Ralph Horton isn't going to perform a miracle and is convinced that his salvation as an artist will come from Ken Pitt. He regularly visits him at his flat on Manchester Street to talk about the future, and they both agree that parting from Pye is inevitable. Pitt agrees to pay for a recording session at R.G. Jones Studios in mid-October and David Bowie and Derek Fearnley are going to act as producers, despite their lack of experience. Instead of letting himself be tossed about by the current, and at the risk of being misunderstood, Bowie decides to take his music into his own hands. He will arrange the songs on his first album with Ego, and then co-produce all of his own records from then until his last. From that moment on, he is going to devise, design and power his own tidal wave.

George Underwood
Dana Gillespie
Kevin Cann
John 'Hutch' Hutchinson
Phil May
Billy Ritchie
John 'Twink' Alder
Marcel Rapp
Roger Glover

GEORGE UNDERWOOD

When I first met David, what struck me most about him was his enthusiasm. We went to Scouts at Bromley together, but music is what really united us. I was listening to Buddy Holly and he to Little Richard, who was definitely his biggest musical hero then. We also loved Lonnie Donegan[18], The Everly Brothers, Dion, Elvis Presley and groups like The Diamonds[19]. Even back then, you could almost feel David buzzing with creativity. You knew he was going to make it sooner or later. He was always working on his musical education, and Terry probably gave him plenty of jazz to listen to. You know, I never felt like he was listening to it just to impress or please Terry. He was motivated by a thirst for culture, which also drove him to read a lot.

I was really mad at myself for injuring David's eye. I never wanted to hurt him like that and it kept him from performing with George & The Dragons, my band in 1962. The following summer, I got him into The Konrads because he played the saxophone, and they let him sing three or four songs. We were in other bands that didn't last, like The Hooker Brothers, and David did some gigs with The Wranglers. Like all the other English bands from the early 60s, we fell in love with the blues and bought all the blues records we could get our hands on. Around that time, David also had a Grundig recorder and we taped quite a lot of things. He put together a sort of home studio in his room. And there was a piano at his house...

Things started to get a bit more serious with The King Bees. David wasn't the frontman at first, but he knew how to scout out musicians. He and I were both very focused on our looks and how we appeared on stage. David was itching to be noticed and when he had the idea to contact John Bloom, his father helped him write the letter. A little later, I joined his famous long-hair society, and we had a laugh when they put us on television for it. At that point, he would have done anything to get people to talk about him.

Making our first record was pretty overwhelming, especially when we found out that Glyn Johns, who'd worked with Georgie Fame[20], was producing the session. I remember it as if it were yesterday, especially because my guitar went out of tune and it took me ages sorting it out! We were more relaxed by the end of the recording, and you can even hear me whistling in the final cut. When David left The King Bees to join The Manish Boys, we were annoyed rather than surprised. He'd started to rehearse with them while he was still with us, which honestly wasn't something musicians did. But he was impatient to move on... We didn't see each other as much in 1965. I released a single under the name Calvin James, produced by Mickie Most, which made David very jealous. Same in 1967... That's around the time I went back to art school and gave up music. (2016)

DANA GILLESPIE

When I was a teenager, to make some pocket money, I delivered newspapers around Soho before school. It made it easier for me to get into places, especially the Marquee. That's where I first met David. He was dressed like Robin Hood and was playing saxophone with The King Bees[21]. I didn't know much about music at the time, but I already loved the blues and I'd seen The Yardbirds perform at the same venue.

That evening, The King Bees were opening for another band – I can't remember who. At the time, I was already big-busted and I dyed my hair peroxide blonde, so I was pretty easy to spot! The back of the Marquee had mirrors on the walls, and towards the end of the evening I went there to brush my hair. All of a sudden, I felt someone take the hairbrush out of my hands and start brushing my hair for me. It was David. We talked for a little and then he asked me, 'Can we stay together tonight?'

I was living with my parents at the time, in a big house next to Harrods. It took us about 20 minutes to walk there. We went up to the top floor, where I spent most of my time, mainly because I had a drum kit there. Music was my raison d'être. I was crazy about my drums and I had a friend who knew Buddy Rich[22] really well, and we'd gone to see him in concert quite a few times. David and I spent the night together, but I'm only telling you because we mainly talked about music and the bands we liked. It was all David could talk about! That's how our friendship started. I got into the habit of taking Robin Hood, who had much longer hair than the other boys, back to mine on a regular basis... Of course, it was always at night, because even if my parents were understanding, we still didn't want them to walk in on us!

One day, I was playing the drums so hard that a piece of ceiling fell on my parents who had the room below. They punished me by relegating me to the basement. But that was an even better spot, because it was huge, with a separate entrance and a garden at the back, and I could make as much noise as I wanted at any hour of the day or night. I threw some pretty memorable rock parties there! From then on I practically lived in the basement and David came to see me there regularly.

We had a very normal relationship. I remember he used to come and pick me up from my dance classes and he'd always insist on carrying the bag with my ballet shoes. Even then when I was a teenager, it pissed me off, as it still does to this day, when I read somewhere that we were 'going out together'. I hate that expression. You know, I soon realized that David wasn't the kind of guy you were supposed to marry; we were just music fanatics who loved to spend time together and up until he recorded his first album, he'd tell me about the bands he was joining and quitting. He always knew what he could get out of people in terms of music. He wasn't necessarily the best musician himself, but he knew how to recognize them and surround himself with them. It's because of them that he was able to create his own style and make his songs so unique and appealing. David was also really interested in the ones I was writing and, in the months after our meeting, he remained so.

One of the things David loved the most was to spend time at La Gioconda, a coffee bar on Denmark Street. He was in his element, because he knew the business of music was done there. It was the type of place where an arranger could pop in out of the blue and say, 'I need backing singers, can anyone here sing?' I vividly remember one time he grabbed me by the hand and took me to a record store and made me go into a booth to listen to 'I Pity The Fool', his single with The Manish Boys. It wasn't his first, but on the B-side was 'Take My Tip', which he'd written himself, and you could see his name on the label. He was so proud that day... His music was by far the most important thing to him, but he wasn't indifferent to the girls who hung around him. I quickly understood what a musician is: someone who lives on the road and who works on the assumption that what happens on tour, stays on tour. And let's not forget that at the time David travelled around and often spent the night in an old ambulance. In the winter, behind the frosted windows, things were happening...

Soon after we met, David insisted on introducing me to his parents. It shocked me, honestly. Not because of them, but because I'd never been to a working-class neighbourhood. We passed these rows of tiny houses and then I met his parents. They were sitting on the sofa watching television. They told David they had to go and see Terry, who was in a mental hospital. They'd barely closed the door behind them when David told me that he only wanted one thing in life: to get away, a long way away, no matter what. His ambition was already really strong and he needed to be in constant motion, so I have as many memories of the concerts we went to as I have of the hours we spent listening to records at his place or mine. And it was mostly blues acts, musicians like John Lee Hooker or Muddy Waters. (2016)

KEVIN CANN

I recently had lunch with Phil Lancaster and Denis Taylor, who usually had his camera with him for interesting band events back in The Lower Third days. I asked him why he didn't take any photos in France or Paris during that trip. He replied, 'I can only think that it was all so absorbing and distracting that I didn't get a chance to get my camera out! We did have a brilliant time there.' Such a shame there is no photographic record of that trip or those first gigs. You would have thought somebody, somewhere, would have a photo of David in Paris in 1965. I do have a postcard from David's mum and dad, sent to David while they were on holiday in Paris in 1967, as well as some colour pics of his parents on that trip. They even visited Decca's Paris office to say hello while they were there! They were always proud of their boy. (2019)

JOHN 'HUTCH' HUTCHINSON

I met David Bowie in February 1966, when I turned up for an audition at the Marquee. He needed some new musicians and I showed up with my guitar, a Telecaster. I messed about a little, strummed a few chords and they hinted to me that David liked my playing. They introduced us that day, but it wasn't until our first rehearsal with the other members of The Buzz, also newly recruited, that we really got to know each other.

What struck me from the start was his professionalism. He already had a manager, people who spoke for him, everything seemed very organized. During rehearsals we all got to know each other better and learned more about him – when a singer-songwriter shows his songs to his musicians, he reveals quite a few things about himself. He came off as experienced even though he'd only started his career two years before. I'd just blown in from Yorkshire, I was quite rough around the edges and didn't spend much time thinking about my appearance. But he was already in control of his image. He'd done the rounds of the London club circuit with his previous bands, The Manish Boys and The Lower Third, and his confidence blew us away. The Buzz musicians' look was pretty clean, elegant and understated. David wasn't about to hire a guy with a 20-inch beard! We looked a bit like mods.

Two other things struck me straight away. First of all, his songs didn't sound anything like what people were doing at the time. They came from another universe – his. And his voice! It was powerful, he could already sing just about anything: the blues, pop, his own songs and certainly anything else. It's something that everyone realized afterwards, but in the beginning, even before his first album came out, he impressed everyone with his vocal skills. He wasn't a great guitar player, but he played well enough to show his songs to the musicians. He was great at describing what he wanted to hear from us.

David was the true leader of The Buzz and he knew exactly where he wanted to go. In those days, managers told artists what they should do. This was absolutely not the case with him. He seemed to have everything planned out in his head and he certainly didn't need anyone to tell him what his band needed to do. Besides, even though Ralph Horton and Ken Pitt did everything they could to launch his career, David seemed to expect something quite different from a manager. In the end, Tony Defries was the one to succeed where others had failed.

In those days, after showing us the chords, David counted on us to play his songs as well as we could. The Buzz was a backing band whose role was to play his music, as well as covers like 'Knock On Wood' or 'The Midnight Hour'. They weren't the easiest songs to sing, but like Georgie Fame or Chris Farlowe, David was more than capable of it. For The Bowie Showboat, our residency at the Marquee in 1966, David wanted to open up the set list. Even though the club was the temple of rock and rhythm'n'blues, he wanted to sing songs with a more pop influence, like 'Monday, Monday' by The Mamas & The Papas. He took pride in the fact that his music was different from everyone else's, and that turned out to be obvious from his first album!

The other members of The Buzz – Chow, Dek and John – certainly hung out a bit with David outside rehearsals and concerts, but I was already a father at the time, and when I wasn't working with the band I tried to spend time with my family. As a general rule, his manager Ralph Horton kept him relatively distanced from us, which was probably the plan. (2016)

PHIL MAY

David Bowie? He was my stalker! From the start, The Pretty Things story fascinated him. He turned up at all our gigs. Dick Taylor was in the band that preceeded The Rolling Stones – when they turned pro, we got them to play at our art school. Until the day they became too expensive for us, way beyond our budget! The only way for us to continue to listen to this music, these covers of songs by Chuck Berry, Bo Diddley, Animals or Muddy Waters, was to play them ourselves. That's how Dick and I started The Pretty Things. Really it was to fill a void!

The crazy thing was that I had absolutely no plans to become a musician, I didn't have the ego for it, the motivation. I wanted to be a painter. The only reason we didn't make it bigger was because we weren't consumed by a thirst for success. Besides, we didn't deal with success very well. When Dick left the band after *SF Sorrow*, it was mainly because he got fed up with being chased down the street, and as he said to me at the time, he wanted his guitar back, he just wanted to play. Likewise, I haven't kept The Pretty Things going all these years in the way Mick Jagger is doing with The Stones. The band is his reason for being alive. I'm convinced that without Mick, Keith Richards and Charlie Watts would have stopped touring a long time ago... But Mick? What would he do without The Stones? He needs them! As soon as he steps on stage, he looks reborn.

I heard Ed Sheeran say the other day that he wanted to become more successful than Adele. What? Is that really coming out of the mouth of a musician? That's what a banker would say, someone with a big capitalist ego! You might think I'm digressing, but I'm not. The blues – the need to succeed despite the fear of having to face yourself, of losing your bearings sometimes – that was David's career, in a way. At the Marquee, for example, he was always in the front row, devouring us with his eyes. That guy from The White Stripes I ran into the other day, who actually reminded me that they'd opened for us in the US, which I didn't remember, makes me think of Bowie. The first thing that kid asked me was how we got the drum sound in 'Livin' In My Skin'. David was the same – like a sponge and obsessed with the details. He wanted to know, to learn. That famous time when he asked me for my phone number, it wasn't just so he could harass me but so he could ask me technical questions. Early on, he set himself up as a sort of historian with an in-depth knowledge of the English music scene, as well as the American one. Remember, he was the first to talk about The Velvet Underground and The Stooges. And believe me, that was a big deal. If Dick changed his guitar strings before they were worn out, David would ask him why! If I picked up another mic, he was curious about that too. He picked up everything, like one of those dogs you throw something for. They just keep coming back. Honestly, it sometimes got to the point where we found him slightly unnerving, but he was different and certainly not a star-struck kid, far from it.

At the same time, he was always out of step. For example, he didn't go to art school like so many musicians of our generation, but he did share their personal approach to music. He didn't know how to read or write it, but he made up a system for jotting it down, with colours and crosses that helped him find his way. This art-school movement wasn't like the Merseybeat thing, the bands from Liverpool, where it was all about music. The kids at art school thought the visual was just as important as the music. We paid attention to how we dressed. And since we didn't have any money, we were getting stuff at jumble sales, which made us look even more unique. David was like that too. He and Bolan would rummage through clothes bins on Carnaby Street to put together an outfit. We were thrifty, crafty... That was part of our education. I designed the cover of *SF Sorrow* myself, because EMI had no idea what we wanted and didn't want to pay for a designer. (2017)

BILLY RITCHIE

In 1966 I played keyboards in a trio, The Premiers, and we were playing in Dundee, Scotland, with David Bowie and The Buzz[23]. I thought he had a lot of style and confidence – he really stood out. He approached me first and said he had never seen a keyboard player like me before, playing the lead role in a rock band. So it was mutual appreciation. We vowed to get in touch when the band came to London.

Later that year, The Premiers became 1-2-3[24]. We left Scotland for London and caused a bit of a sensation at the Marquee. Brian Epstein, The Beatles' manager, signed us up and, when David heard that we were doing one of his songs, 'I Dig Everything', he came to see us at the Marquee and we renewed our acquaintance. From then on, we were close friends for a couple of years. We mainly met in between or after gigs, usually went to the pub together and spoke endlessly about music and the music business. (2017)

JOHN 'TWINK' ALDER

I knew David from about 1964, when we all used to go to La Gioconda. He with his band, me as the drummer for the Fairies. At the time, we were all trying to make it. We shared information, exchanged tips. You know, Bowie was a phenomenal artist from the very beginning. I saw him play with The Buzz at the Marquee, and he was absolutely amazing. The band was really good and he was a real performer. He was determined, committed...

I really knew David from 1964 to 1972. We used to meet at Vince Taylor's Mayfair flat – as you know, Vince was the main inspiration for Ziggy Stardust. That was before he left for Paris and made it big. There was always a crowd at Vince's and the atmosphere was crazy. David was always hanging out there – well, we were fans!

When I was with one of my first bands – Eddie Lee Cooper and The Trappers – we used to play 'Brand New Cadillac' at the 2i's Coffee Bar. Once, Vince was there and I remember he was taken aback when he saw me sing his song from behind my drum kit! (2018)

MARCEL RAPP

I was a big rock fan, so from the early 1960s I spent a lot of time at the Golf Drouot club in Paris. Henri Leproux managed the place and hired me on Saturday and Sunday afternoons as a 'disquaire'. In those days, we didn't use the term DJ. I got to know quite a few of the artists passing through, including David Bowie, when he came to play with The Lower Third. What I remember most about their performance was that it was short and not particularly well received by the audience. But hey, they didn't get thrown out either. Far from it!

On stage, Bowie – this guy we knew nothing about – looked a lot like Mick Jagger. As if he'd copied all his moves. I remember an energetic set, the way rhythm'n'blues was at the time. I can't remember if it was before or after the concert, but I met up with the band at their hotel in Pigalle. Bowie and I had a glass of wine and talked about our musical tastes. He was a charming guy, pretty reserved, but he opened up when he talked about music. (2019)

ROGER GLOVER

In June 1966, Episode Six, the band I played bass in before Deep Purple and whose singer was Ian Gillan, performed at a festival at Brands Hatch in Kent. Small Faces and David Bowie were also on the bill. Steve Marriott and David were friends. He was with his band, The Buzz, but he didn't really make much of an impression on me. On that day, no one could have foreseen that he would become such a huge star! But then again I saw The Rolling Stones in concert twice that same year and thought they were pretty bad... (2017)

1. Of the musicians mentioned in this book, the following were also born in 1947: Ian Anderson, Laurie Anderson, Marc Bolan, Howard Kaylan, Jeff Lynne, Steve Marriott, Brian May, Peter Noone, Ann Peebles, Iggy Pop, Gerry Rafferty, Florian Schneider, George Underwood, Peter Overend Watts, Willie Weeks and Ronnie Wood.

2. The origins of Bowie's cross are much debated. The author goes with the version told by Kevin Cann, writer and world-renowned expert on David Bowie. His book *Any Day Now: The London Years 1947–1974* (Adelita Ltd, 2010) is a chronological reference work focusing on Bowie's childhood and the early years of his career. The author has known Kevin Cann for a long time and asked him a few questions for this book.

3. In 2000, journalist Peter Kane will interview David Bowie for his excellent feature 'Cash For Questions', published in *Q Magazine*. In the interview, David Bowie will set a few records straight. In particular, he will provide the correct spelling for The Konrads, and point out that it looks much better without a hyphen between 'Kon' and 'rads'. Many writers (but not Kevin Cann) will style it wrongly for decades.

4. David took a special interest in jazz because Jack Kerouac had fallen in love with it before him, having been introduced to bebop by his friend Seymour Wyse in the late 1940s. In the mid-60s, David came across some of Kerouac's recordings. Influenced by F. Scott Fitzgerald, who believed that great lyrics should be judged on their musicality and rhythm, and after discovering the spoken-word records of Langston Hughes and Dylan Thomas, Kerouac incorporated bebop into his own art. He also recorded readings and improvisations inspired by the automatic writing method developed by psychologist William James and poet and playwright W.B. Yeats. Throughout his career, Bowie said many times that he attached more importance to the 'music of words' than to their meaning.

5. As legend would have it, David Jones couldn't wait to swap his plexiglass saxophone for another, more professional one. But in reality, the Grafton, an alto sax made by Italian Hector Sommaruga at the end of the 1940s, was no toy – Charlie Parker, Ornette Coleman and some of the other giants of jazz used one.

6. On the music show *Storytellers* on VH1 in 1999, David Bowie will say he'd met Marc Bolan at Leslie Conn's house. They'd both agreed to repaint his office on Denmark Street to make a little pocket money.

7. The Marquee Club, founded by jazz-lover Harold Pendleton, was an institution of the English music scene. During its heyday (which lasted a quarter of a century!), it was located at 90 Wardour Street. With the notable exception of The Beatles, all British musicians who went down in rock history played there at least once. David Bowie (as part of a band or as a soloist) played at the Marquee more than sixty times up until 15 June 1969. He will perform there one last time in 1973, with The Spiders From Mars, for an American television show. He played the Marquee more than any other venue. Many people have said that Davie Jones and The King Bees headlined at the Marquee on 15 May 1964, but that night The Authentics (with John Williams and Jimmy Page) were on stage. Did The King Bees sing a few songs as an opening act? It's not impossible.

8. Keith Relf – singer, harmonicist and founding member of the The Yardbirds – had a fleeting but strong influence on David Bowie in the mid-1960s. Bowie noticed that young women liked Relf's haircut, especially the pretty foreign girls in the London nightclubs, so he adopted it for a while. He will mention his respect for Keith Relf's look and for his 'blues roots' during a promotional event following Tin Machine's interview with *Rock&Folk* in 1991. He will also confirm he'd always identified with the Richmond-born singer more than he did with Brian Jones (with whom journalists sometimes associated him). Relf will die young, in 1976, at home, from electrocution while playing a guitar.

9. Mickie Most and Joe Meek, talented producers in their own right, also crossed paths with The Konrads and the Manish Boys. Meek did audition both bands, but David Jones was not a member then. Most also auditioned The Manish Boys (with David), but nothing came of it. Joe Meek is famous for having turned down The Beatles and David Bowie as a solo artist. David will later confess he would have loved to work with him.

10. La Gioconda was a coffee bar at 9 Denmark Street, a stone's throw from Charing Cross Road in London. It was a meeting place for the big guns in the music industry (or those who aspired to become one). David Bowie was a regular in the 1960s. Denmark Street was nicknamed 'Tin Pan Alley', after the district in New York where music publishers and songwriters had worked for more than half a century (at 28th Street, between 5th and 6th Avenues in Manhattan). Denmark Street was also home to musical instrument shops, music magazines like *Melody Maker* and *New Musical Express*, and legendary music studios – Regent

Sounds, where The Rolling Stones recorded their first album; Peer/Southern Music, where Scottish troubadour Donovan recorded his *Fairytale*; and Central Sound, which adjoined La Gioconda.

11. Interviewed by the author in 1995, after he'd just produced the second album by American band Belly, Glyn Johns will claim he didn't remember recording with David Jones. He won't mention it either in *Glyn Johns – Sound Man* (Penguin), his 2014 autobiography. During the 1960s, Johns will work with The Rolling Stones, The Pretty Things, Small Faces, The Easybeats and even The Beatles, as a recording engineer or producer.

12. The mod style (short for modernist) began in London at the end of the 1950s. It was started by young people who listened to jazz (and American rhythm'n'blues), enjoyed French New Wave cinema, got dressed up to the nines and nipped around London on Italian scooters. The mods were intolerant of other groups (the novel *Absolute Beginners* by Colin MacInnes and its film adaptation by Julien Temple depict the clashes that took place at the start of the movement) and hung around Carnaby Street in the Swinging Sixties. Their musical heroes included The Who, Small Faces and, to a lesser extent, John's Children, a short-lived freakbeat band of crazy mods fronted by Marc Bolan in 1967.

13. Opened in 1943 in Morden in south London, these studios belonged to Ronald Geoffrey Jones, whose sound system company, one of the oldest in the world, is still around today.

14. This track is also on *The John Coltrane Quartet Plays...*, an album the saxophonist released in 1965. 'Nature Boy', which David Bowie will cover 36 years later, can be found on the B-side.

15. At that time, Arthur Brown travels regularly to Paris and appears on the soundtrack of *La Curée*, Roger Vadim's film adaptation of Émile Zola's novel. Brown will make it big in 1968 with The Crazy World Of Arthur Brown. He still brings the house down with the hit song 'Fire' more than half a century later.

16. The musical by Oscar Hammerstein II and Jerome Kern was written in 1927 and was often shown in London, but not between 1928 and 1971.

17. This is also an Oscar Hammerstein II musical, put to music by Richard Rodgers in 1945.

18. Lonnie Donegan was the king of skiffle, a musical genre with American influences, which inspired a lot of British musicians of this generation, especially The Beatles.

19. A Canadian vocal quartet that became successful in the late 1950s, mostly thanks to their covers of rhythm'n'blues hits. The Diamonds still shine to this day, though without any of the original members.

20. A British rhythm'n'blues musician who's still performing today. He mainly plays keyboards and will make the top of the British charts three times in the 1960s. He wrote 'Get Away', the second of his Number 1 songs, but not 'Yeh Yeh', his biggest hit.

21. It's more likely that The Manish Boys were the ones playing with David Jones the night Dana Gillespie met him, which was, most probably, 6 November 1964. They were opening for Gary Farr & The T-Bones. Dana will set the record straight in her own book, *Weren't Born A Man* (Hawksmoor, 2021), four years after this interview.

22. An American giant of jazz drumming who played with the best, including Charlie Parker, Lester Young, Art Tatum and Harry James. Starting in 1966, he directed big bands and toured with them all over the world. He will die in 1987, aged 70.

23. This concert took place on 3 April. The Premiers and David Bowie (with The Buzz, not The Lower Third as some say) opened for Johnny Kidd & The Pirates at the Top 10 Club.

24. 1-2-3, later known as Clouds, is now considered the the most ill-fated band of British prog rock. However, the three musicians (drummer Harry Hughes, bassist Ian Ellis and Billy Ritchie) did influence ELP, Yes, King Crimson, Jethro Tull and The Moody Blues, all of whom will make it big. Clouds will break up at the end of 1971, as told by Billy Ritchie in his memoir, *The ABC Of 1-2-3* (Hillfield, 2016).

DAVID BOWIE

DERAM – 1 JUNE 1967

*'She was the kind of girlfriend God gives you young,
so you'll know loss the rest of your life.'*
(JUNOT DÍAZ, *THE BRIEF WONDROUS LIFE OF OSCAR WAO*, 2007)

'I'm pretty good at imitating singers, especially certain friends or idols of mine. At the time of my first album, I was having fun parodying Anthony Newley, who really let his Cockney accent be heard. I've never denied my roots. Quite the contrary. It's often been said I loved Newley as a singer, but I especially liked him as an actor in the musical *Stop The World – I Want To Get Off* and, of course, in the television series *The Strange World Of Gurney Slade*. What also amazed me was that he was often the driving force behind the songs he performed and helped write them. I would have been fine just being a songwriter. I stepped up because no one else wanted to sing the songs I wrote! So it's partly because of Anthony Newley that very early on I also saw myself as an actor in the service of a musical genre I wanted to dramatize, rather than just as a musician. But I never thought of myself as an intellectual and I don't like people calling me that. I once said that I was a tactile thinker, and I believe I still am, perhaps even more than ever.'

DB (1992)

According to some biographies, the unlikely 'Vaudeville pop' style of David Bowie's first eponymous album, which he released on 1 June in the Summer of Love, was the result of Ken Pitt's influence. It's a hasty deduction. Since childhood, David Jones had been open to anything and everything. He had an insatiable curiosity. He was a voracious reader, more than most boys his age, but more importantly, he was always listening to his half-brother's jazz records and to the pioneers of rhythm'n'blues and rock music. He was also interested in astrology and science fiction, and watched a lot of television. He absorbed anything that could give some colour to the blandness of his suburban life, which was still overshadowed by war at the end of the 1950s. He gulped everything down greedily, indiscriminately. Anything was fair game if it could help him escape what he will later call 'the tyranny of the ordinaire'.

Again, people often say Bowie 'discovered literature' in Ken Pitt's library – Ken was as well read as he was full of good will. But actually, Bowie found a number of works he already knew there, which probably helped them develop their relationship, both friendly and professional. In truth, by introducing him to new authors like Oscar Wilde, André Gide and Antoine de Saint-Exupéry, Ken Pitt is going to further develop David's sense of theatre and cabaret, contributing to his lack of prejudice as a musician. At the end of his life, Bowie will finally be able to create a show based on his songs, a show that can be described as a musical. It will be the dream of a lifetime. He will mention such a project hundreds of times throughout his career, but the germ of the idea probably formed at Pitt's house at 39 Manchester Street, in Marylebone, where Bowie will often stay during the late 1960s.

As Bowie's first real manager, Ken Pitt understood early on that it was better to let him loose than try to squeeze him into a mould, so he will never impose anything on him or take any risks by trying to shape his repertoire. Enthralled with Bowie's talent and personality, Pitt will make a point of helping him develop in any desired direction, all the while steering him gently towards advancing his professional growth. And since David writes prolifically (in all sorts of styles), Ken Pitt has quite a job finding other singers to perform his songs. Oscar Beuselinck is the first singer to perform a David Bowie song – 'Over The Wall We Go' – which Bowie demoed in late 1966 but did not intend for himself. Beuselinck, the son of a famous English entertainment lawyer, will make a foray into pop music under his original name[1] before becoming a stage and musical actor known as Paul Nicholas. The lyrics of 'Over The Wall We Go' were probably inspired, in part, by the London prison break of infamous double-agent George Blake, which was in the papers that year. In the vein of Anthony Newley's comedy songs, 'Over The Wall We Go' would have been great in a musical, but not so much on a pop/rock record[2]. It will be released on the A-side of Oscar's single in January 1967.

Pitt, to his disappointment, will struggle to find performers for Bowie's songs. Some that will appear on his first album will be proposed to Peter, Paul And Mary, Judy Collins or Jefferson Airplane, but three others will be selected by The Beatstalkers, a Scottish band Pitt will manage until the end of the 1960s – 'Silver Treetop School For Boys', 'Everything Is You' and 'When I'm Five' will come out on singles between 1967 and 1969. English rock singer Billy Fury will record a decent version of 'Silly Boy Blue' for one of his 45s in 1968.

David Bowie records three songs with members of The Buzz and a few other musicians in mid-October 1966 at the R.G. Jones Studios – 'Rubber Band', 'The Gravedigger' (provisional title) and 'The London Boys', a track he really cares about, already demoed for Pye. The label weren't keen on the drugs references in 'The London Boys', but they reveal Bowie's difficulties fitting in, finding his place in a London that he is discovering and that fascinates him, yet still eludes him. Whether they are mods, Teddy Boys or just fashion snobs, the cool kids in Swinging London only seem to accept their own people, which goes against what Bowie believes in. He pays attention to fashions and trends, but sees himself mostly as an observer, watching from the sidelines. He inhales various moods, then creates his own style without stooping to imitation. Still feeling London is refusing to let him in, Bowie plants a rough version of himself in the background of 'The London Boys'.

In autumn, with a test pressing[3] of the new songs in hand, Ken Pitt catches the attention of three executives at Decca (which had released 'Liza Jane'): Tony Hall (promotional manager), Hugh Mendl (A&R manager) and Mike Vernon (house producer). David Bowie signs with them at the end of October and his album will be released on Deram[4], a subsidiary label for musicians who can't be easily classified. Decca started Deram to modernize their image and will release records by the likes of Cat Stevens, Ten Years After and Procol Harum.

David Bowie is almost certainly the first English singer-songwriter of his generation to get the chance to record an album before finding success with a single. Sessions for his first LP, produced by Mike Vernon, start in mid-November at the Decca Studios in Broadhurst Gardens, West Hampstead. 'Liza Jane' was recorded there in 1964 and The Konrads auditioned at the same place unsuccessfully a year before. It was where, in February 1962, as the pop revolution was taking off, Dick Rowe, A&R manager for Decca, allegedly told The Beatles that guitar groups were on their way out[5]. To his dying day, he will deny this.

In addition to the three members of The Buzz, several studio musicians play on the sessions: guitarists John Renbourn, Big Jim Sullivan (once a member of Vince Taylor's Playboys) and Pete Hampshire, as well as Bob Michaels on organ and a number of classical orchestral musicians who are often less than cooperative. Between Bowie's occasional public appearances with The Buzz (some concerts are cancelled), recording and mixing carry on until March 1967, with a break from mid-December to the end of January. Only a few years older, band mate Derek Fearnley has little more knowledge of musical theory than David so they make use of *The Observer's Book Of Music* by Freda Dinn to support their undeniable artistic symbiosis and Dek becomes David's arranging partner. Their combined talents will benefit about twenty songs: fourteen of them will be on the album, 'The Laughing Gnome' will only come out as a single, and at least two of them – 'Bunny Thing' and 'Your Funny Smile' – remain unreleased.

When the album comes out, some songs will be unjustly criticized as being rather lightweight. But there's no need to go looking for hidden meanings or obscure references in the lyrics of these songs. The maturity and acerbic tone, combined with themes the songwriter will further develop and delineate later on, clearly stand out. Musically, *David Bowie* is tinged with burlesque and allusions to Phil Spector and Burt Bacharach. Some folk and even a waltz also emerge, as if from a box found in the attic of the early 1960s.

As fate would have it, on 2 December, the day the single 'Rubber Band' is released (with 'The London Boys' on the B-side), The Buzz perform their last concert with David Bowie at the Severn Club in Shrewsbury, Shropshire. 'Rubber Band' is based on a military march rhythm (livened up by Chick Norton's trumpet) and could be called 'Victorian pop'. It is light years away from 'Can't Help Thinking About Me'. The song is about a soldier who returns from war to find his fiancée has run away with an orchestra conductor. The music press will liken David's voice to that of Anthony Newley, but the reviews won't be bad. Unfortunately, this single, the fourth he'd released that year, will hardly air on the radio and won't perform any better than its predecessors.

Bowie, however, doesn't let this get him down. In mid-December, Ken Pitt gives him some records he'd brought back from a business trip to the States and Australia. David is inspired by the psychedelic and political poetry of Ed Sanders and The Fugs. He is speechless with wonder – no exaggeration – every time he hears the test pressing of the first album by a band Pitt hopes will soon play in England: The Velvet Underground. Pitt met Andy Warhol, the band's 'producer', and a certain Lou Reed, the lead singer, at the Factory in New York. Some find the songs on *The Velvet Underground & Nico* repetitive, others find the melodies irresistible, but their raw energy captivates Bowie and the album totally shakes his world. From that moment on, he only wants one thing: to take inspiration from The Velvet Underground's songs and cover at least one of them – 'I'm Waiting For The Man'.

In early 1967, David Bowie and Ralph Horton part ways amicably (and completely), and Ken Pitt draws up a contract that will bind him to Bowie without any third parties. Recording sessions continue at Decca Studios but in March, without telling Pitt or any of his musicians, David starts to rehearse with a new lineup of The Riot Squad, a London band he likes who will benefit from his theatrical touch. After the suicide of Joe Meek, the producer of their most recent single ('Gotta Be A First Time'), the band lost half of its original members. Saxophonist Bob Evans approached Bowie after seeing him in concert at the Marquee (followed by a meeting at La Gioconda) and hired him as singer and harmonicist. Enthusiastic as ever, David suggests expanding their repertoire with two covers – The Fugs' 'Dirty Old Man' (written by Lionel Goldbart and Ed Sanders) and Lou Reed's 'I'm Waiting For The Man' (The Velvet Underground's first album came out that same month). Bowie also gets the band to play some of his new songs, including 'Little Toy Soldier' (or 'Toy Soldier'), in which he recycles the theme of sexual fetishism explored by Lou Reed in 'Venus In Furs'.

Between March and May, Bowie will play around twenty gigs with The Riot Squad. Inspired by both Warhol's pop art and Syd Barrett's Pink Floyd (who he had discovered at the Marquee the year before), Bowie encourages the band to put on more of a show, to dress up and wear make-up. We know that the sinister 'post-skinhead' look worn by the Droogs in the 1971 film *A Clockwork Orange* (the work of costume designer Milena Canonero) will later inspire David Bowie when he creates Ziggy Stardust And The Spiders From Mars, but as proof that influences don't just travel in one direction, Stanley Kubrick actually used photographs of The Riot Squad taken in the spring of 1967 as inspiration for *A Clockwork Orange*, recreating the bowler hats and black make-up around the eyes. On 5 April, without the knowledge of Mike Vernon or anybody else at Decca, David will secretly tape some of The Riot Squad's songs by asking recording engineer Gus Dudgeon to slip them in between sessions for the album[6].

Less than two weeks later, 'The Laughing Gnome' comes out on the A-side of a new single, released by Deram. The gnome voices in the song were created by recording normal voices at a slow tape speed. Many believe it to be David Bowie's most embarassing song – some find it utterly strange, but actually it's just supposed to be a funny song. Like many children of his generation, David devoured Tolkien's *The Lord Of The Rings* and, in the late 1960s, he decided to incorporate supernatural creatures and fairy-tale characters into some of his songs[7]. What's funny is that rhythmically 'The Laughing Gnome', despite its dominant bassoon and oboe, emulates The Velvet Underground's 'I'm Waiting For The Man'. Bowie didn't perform it with The Buzz as some have said (Ken Pitt gave him The Velvet Underground album two weeks after The Buzz's last concert), but that is the song he will cover live most often throughout his career and that will serve as a framework for several others. On the B-side, 'The Gospel According To Tony Day' is a drawn-out blues track with a woodwind section that doesn't really add much. 'The Laughing Gnome' was another commercial failure for Bowie in 1967 and would have been forgotten with his other failed experiments had Deram not reissued it as a single during Bowie-mania in September 1973. The song climbed to Number 6 in the British charts and remained there for twelve weeks[8].

David Bowie is released on 1 June, around the same time as the monumental *Sgt. Pepper's Lonely Hearts Club Band*[9]. One might think that in 1967, The Beatles' revolutionary album would have overshadowed all the rest, but that wasn't the case. Many other pop records released between May and September of that psychedelic year would also be successful and stand the test of time, including *Are You Experienced* by Jimi Hendrix, *Absolutely Free* by Frank Zappa (credited to The Mothers Of Invention), *Flowers* by The Rolling Stones, *The Piper At The Gates*

Of Dawn by Pink Floyd, *Scott* by Scott Walker and Procol Harum's eponymous album. All of these 33s are of their time, but have one eye on the future. *David Bowie*, with its meticulous but dated arrangements, goes against the general tide of experimentation. While The Beatles' album relies in part on George Martin's classic arrangements and orchestrations, it also features electric guitars, a hallucinogenic atmosphere, innovative vocal harmonies and completely new song formats (for example, on 'A Day In The Life'). As for Pink Floyd's album, with Norman Smith, a former recording engineer of The Fab Four, at the helm, its writing is as ground-breaking as its production. Similarly, *The Velvet Underground & Nico*, which was released in March, was relentlessly modern and has remained so ever since. By the 1970s, David Bowie will start to anticipate musical trends, but his first album is staid and polished, even a little retro. Listening to it feels a bit like wandering through a musical flea market, though no trace of the rhythm'n'blues of his first singles can be found. Even his military jacket on the cover (he was photographed for the front by Gerald Fearnley, Dek's brother, and for the back by David Wedgbury), looks drab compared with the multicoloured outfits worn by The Beatles on *Sgt. Pepper*[10].

In 1967, David Bowie is still a long way from being a master in the art of provocation, but it does take some nerve to open his album with 'Uncle Arthur'. Channelling a jig vibe (with wind instruments replacing the violin), he sings about an uncle who is very close to his mother and who goes to live with her again after a breakup. Despite its folk nursery-rhyme chorus and delicate arrangements (similar to those found in Donovan's songs or the work of Simon & Garfunkel), 'Sell Me A Coat' reveals Bowie's lingering self-doubt. Three years have passed since the release of his first single and there are days when success still seems far away, despite the support of his family and Ken Pitt.

When he gets out of bed on the right side, David Bowie writes songs like 'Love You Till Tuesday', a playful pop tune with a rapid tempo (almost 150 beats per minute). Even without Mick Ronson's guitar, it is a precursor to the more upbeat songs of *Hunky Dory*. 'Love You Till Tuesday' could have increased sales of the record if Deram had released it as a single instead of 'Rubber Band'. In the song, Bowie mischievously tells a girl he will commit only three days to their romantic affair.

The first serious track on the album, 'There Is A Happy Land', is a finely orchestrated ballad that lies somewhere between fantasy and reality[11]. It is a song about childhood, seen as a country David doesn't want to leave (he turned 20 in January that year). The title and multiple references in the song come from a novel by English writer Keith Waterhouse, published in the late 1950s, in which a teenager talks about coming into contact with the adult world for a few weeks.

The notion of dystopia was often built into Bowie's songs and became a cornerstone of his work, inspired by the magazines and science fiction novels he read. On *David Bowie* it takes the form of 'We Are Hungry Men'. The tone is farcical – the voices of Mike Vernon and Gus Dudgeon, a dictator and a television news presenter respectively, can be heard – but the suggestion of cannibalism to control overpopulation reflects concerns being discussed in the media at the time.

In 'When I Live My Dream', Bowie portrays a daydreamer as he rides a golden horse and meets a dragon and some giants. To escape his troubles, fuelled by self-suggestion, he projects himself into a utopian future and invites his believers to join him. The chord progression at the end of the song will be echoed five years later in the whirlwind ending of 'Rock'n'roll Suicide'. Throughout his career Bowie will be famous for his bold and unpredictable chord progressions which showcase one of his most amazing musical talents as a songwriter. After 'Rubber Band' and 'Love You Till Tuesday', 'When I Live My Dream' is the third song on the album to feature arrangements by Arthur Greenslade, who was very much in demand at the time.

The first song on the B-side of the album, 'Little Bombardier', has a waltz rhythm and addresses the theme of paedophilia – several news stories on the subject made the front pages of the papers in the 60s. The instrumental part of this surrealist track is truly odd and invites appreciation of the widening gap between Bowie's songs and those of his contemporaries. Since the beginning of the decade, The Beatles have mastered similar time signatures (and seduced a lot more) with the stunning 'This Boy' (which David will later cover on stage), 'Baby's In Black' and 'Norwegian Wood (This Bird Has Flown)'.

The quality of 'Come And Buy My Toys' is primarily down to the fingerpicking of London guitarist John Renbourn, who will form the folk band Pentangle with Bert Jansch in 1968 (the two guitarists had already released *Bert And John*, an excellent album). Of the entire discography of David Bowie, this is the song that gets closest to Donovan's style of folk music. The first verses come straight out of an English nursery rhyme ('A Toyman's Address', a poem published in 1816 in *The Monthly Magazine*, attributed to a certain G.N.). Trickier than it might seem, the melody spans two octaves, and David, with a lot of bucolic images, again contrasts childhood with adulthood.

The only note David Bowie ever sung out of tune on a record can be heard 15 seconds into 'Join The Gang'. It is clearly intentional and meant to enhance the satirical nature of the lyrics. Here Bowie describes a trendy London – he still hasn't tasted fame for himself and he's happy to make fun of those who have. The song features a soulful drum intro, Big Jim Sullivan's sitar playing, a piano part borrowed from 'Let's Spend The Night Together' (the first 1967 single issued by The Rolling Stones) and a direct reference, halfway through, to 'Gimme Some Lovin'' by The Spencer Davis Group. 'Join The Gang' is a real mosaic and, despite the lack of an electric guitar, it's by far the most rock song on the album.

As Nicholas Pegg notes in *The Complete David Bowie* (Titan, 2016), it's highly possible that when writing 'She's Got Medals', David took inspiration from the story of journalist Dorothy Lawrence, who disguised herself as a man so she could fight in the Somme in World War I. Like other songwriters – including his elder, John Lennon – Bowie plucked song ideas from history and from news articles he read. But in his song, Mary (who became Tommy during the war, then Eileen afterwards) has a less tragic fate than did the real-life Dorothy Lawrence, who eventually died in a mental hospital. At the end of the first verse, Bowie sings that Mary wore hobnail boots, also mentioned by Lou Reed in 'Run Run Run' on *The Velvet Underground & Nico*, and again in 1968 by Lennon in The Beatles' 'Happiness Is A Warm Gun'. Harmonically speaking, the song bears an undeniable likeness to 'Hey Joe', the Billy Roberts' song, which was covered by a great many American bands during the 1960s. Jimi Hendrix, one of the most famous people to perform the song, played it in London on 7 May 1967 – the day Bowie first saw him live. However, 'She's Got Medals' had been recorded several months before, so the version of 'Hey Joe' by American band Love, which appeared on their first album released in 1966, was probably the one that had caught Bowie's ear.

In 'Maid Of Bond Street', which, like 'Little Bombardier', features a ternary beat, David Bowie talks about a successful model who appears on the front covers of magazines. Her heart has been broken by her boyfriend, who is jealous of her success because he wants to be a star himself. David Bowie is the only person who could have known which of his lyrics were autobiographical and this is something that makes them even more enticing. An interesting musical detail in this song is the repetition of two major chords separated by a tone, a sort of pendulum that Bowie will use many times again. Back in 1965, Donovan had used this technique in 'Hey Gyp (Dig The Slowness)'. According to David, the idea was inspired by 'The Inch Worm', one of Frank Loesser's songs for *Hans Christian Andersen*, the 1952 Charles Vidor musical loosely based on the life of the Danish storyteller.

The last song on *David Bowie* is the unlikely 'Please Mr Gravedigger', one of the three whose first recording had been financed by Ken Pitt in October 1966. It is another oddity, an a cappella piece enhanced with sound effects. As noted by Paul Trynka in his Bowie biography *Starman* (Sphere, 2011), the song was probably inspired by the Moors murders, the series of child killings by Ian Brady and Myra Hindley in the 1960s[12].

Like the singles that preceded it, David Bowie's first album is going to be a commercial failure. Also released in a few European countries, it will be well received by some inquisitive journalists but, despite Ken Pitt's enthusiastic sleeve notes (he made Bowie a year younger), audiences will largely ignore it[13]. In mid-July, a new version of 'Love You Till Tuesday' comes out as a single, arranged by Ivor Raymonde[14], who is known for his work with The Walker Brothers and London singer Dusty Springfield. The B-side is the playful 'Did You Ever Have A Dream', which despite its apparent superficiality (Big Jim Sullivan plays banjo and Derrick Boyes is on a keyboard that sounds like a mixture of harpsichord and saloon piano), deals with the subjects of space travel and the out-of-body experiences that had interested Bowie since he started reading about Buddhism. If Deram had released this catchy song on the A-side of the single, would it have done better? We'll never know.

Over the following months, Ken Pitt does everything in his power to keep up the spirits of his protégé, who won't take to the stage to promote his new album. Convinced of Bowie's potential, Pitt tries anything to help him find success in a number of different fields – as a theatre or film actor, even a cabaret dancer or a television presenter. With the blessing of David's parents, Ken gives him a room in his flat and, when necessary, some money to meet his needs as a starving artist. That summer, Pitt is starting to worry that Decca will soon lose interest in Bowie as success continues to elude him. Pitt decides to take action, and believes that a change in direction might work. He decides to approach Denny Cordell to produce the songs David continues to write prolifically.

Denny Cordell had been instrumental in the success of The Moody Blues, Procol Harum and Joe Cocker, but he isn't so sure about David Bowie's music. He declines Pitt's offer, but suggests that David Platz, the President of Essex Music with whom Bowie signed the year before, talk to his assistant who has just arrived from New York. This will turn out to be a career-defining meeting. Tony Visconti is just three years older than David, and had played in several orchestras in the United States before he and his first wife started the folk duo Tony and Siegrid. He had then become an in-house songwriter for the Richmond Organization, which managed Essex Music in the United States. Tony had made a few demos for them and met Denny Cordell there at the beginning of the year. Cordell was looking for an assistant and wanted to hire Phil Spector. The producer of The Ronettes refused, so Cordell asked Visconti to come with him and see how the Brits went about making their amazing pop records. In exchange, Cordell expected Tony to bring his experience and American touch to future productions.

It was Platz, as a publisher, who arranged the first meeting between Bowie and Visconti, which marks the beginning of one of the most unique collaborations in the history of rock, both for the quality of their work together, and for the longevity of their relationship. Over the course of half a century, Tony Visconti's name will appear on sixteen of Bowie's albums, from those that ignited his rise to fame, through his more experimental records, to his final masterpiece. Visconti is the producer, arranger and musician who spent the greatest amount of time with David Bowie in the studio and contributed most to the making of his music.

In the summer of 1967, David hears that Lindsay Kemp, who has studied dance with Hilde Holger and Marcel Marceau before working for the Ballet Rambert, is using the songs from his album in *Clowns*, the mime performance that is showing at the Little Theatre in Covent Garden[15]. Flattered, Bowie is also impressed with Kemp, who will encourage him to take mime lessons. They become firm friends (even though the student's approach to his lessons is far from diligent), and will go on to write *Pierrot In Turquoise*[16] together, a new stage show with a contribution from Australian Craig San Roque ('as stage manager', he recently claimed with modesty). The show will open in England that winter and David will sing a few songs from his first album in it. He will play the role of Cloud, alongside Lindsay Kemp and Jack Birkett[17], while dressed in an outfit made by Russian costume designer Natasha Korniloff, with whom he will also become good friends. We now understand just how much David benefited from the time he spent as a mime. Kemp will give him confidence and teach him how to move on stage, how to make an entrance and an exit. The two will talk a lot about Jean Cocteau, Jean Genet, Oscar Wilde and James Joyce, new sources of inspiration for David. Lindsay Kemp will also introduce him to the Theatre of the Absurd, which he will read about extensively and often reference in his work[18].

On 1 September, David Bowie records with Tony Visconti for the first time, at Advision Studios[19]. They tape two new songs which, according to Ken Pitt, David called 'shitty', because he had decided to write hits and that repulsed him. Actually,

'Karma Man' and 'Let Me Sleep Beside You' will be among his best recorded songs that year. Like 'Silly Boy Blue', the first reflects David's infatuation with Tibet. That autumn, perhaps feeling a little disillusioned, and looking for something he could really throw himself into with passionate enthusiasm (he was unable to commit himself to anything lightly), Bowie will express a desire to go to Lhasa, leave everything behind and become a monk. His curiosity about matters of the mind, sparked by his reading (especially *Seven Years in Tibet* by Heinrich Harrer), drove him to visit the Buddhist Society in Eccleston Square, London. Bowie will attend lectures by Christmas Humphreys, a judge who converted to Buddhism, and meets Chime Youngdong Rinpoche, a lama refugee and teacher of Tibetan Dharma. While he also attended some of Rinpoche's lectures and went to the Samye Ling monastery in Eskdalemuir, Scotland, soon after it opened, it's unlikely that David pursued his studies any further. But his commitment to refugees from Tibet (today just another subjugated and polluted Chinese province) will last until the 2000s. Tony Visconti also cares about this cause, and together they will perform three times (between 2001 and 2003) at the Tibet House Benefit Concert, organized in New York by Philip Glass. Later, at 2016's concert in the same series, Iggy Pop will be sure to pay tribute to the friend he has recently lost.

At Advision, Tony Visconti and Andy White[20] play bass and drums, while on guitar are Big Jim Sullivan and John McLaughlin (a session musician from Yorkshire and future leader of the Mahavishnu Orchestra). 'Let Me Sleep Beside You', also recorded that day, is a folk-rock song with orchestral strings and an acrobatic bridge. The song's title might not have been Decca's main reason for refusing to release it as a single – the label had not hesitated to release The Rolling Stones' 'Let's Spend The Night Together' earlier that year – but it certainly didn't help. Less shocking than they might have been, the lyrics reflect David Bowie's rapid emancipation. Addressing his girlfriend, he sings to her: '...lock away your childhood and throw away the key.'

In September, Visconti helps Bowie forge a relationship with Marc Bolan that will eventually lead the two of them to work together. The three friends regularly meet at Visconti's house at 108 Lexham Gardens, between Kensington and Earl's Court. That same month, David finds out that his album and first single released in the US ('Love You Till Tuesday'/'Did You Ever Have A Dream') have been well received by some music journalists there.

September 1967 is also the month David Bowie makes his on-camera acting debut in *The Image*, a horror short directed by Michael Armstrong. Bowie plays

The Boy, a model who climbs out of a canvas, whose artist (The Artist) is played by Michael Byrne. Armstrong had first contacted Pitt when he was creating *A Floral Tale*, a more substantial project for which David was to compose the score, but it eventually fell through; the director would continue to hold on to the pieces written for it, until the present day. In the end, David Bowie will have to wait for more than a quarter of a century to put his name to a soundtrack, the one for the television series *The Buddha Of Suburbia*. Bowie's songs will often be heard in films, but he will never compose an original score for the cinema. The silver lining will be that in 1976, after director Nicolas Roeg and his producers reject the music proposed by Bowie for *The Man Who Fell To Earth*, he will set about making *Low*, the first volume of his famous European Trilogy.

In late 1967, David Bowie continues to write new songs[21], including the ambitious 'C'est La Vie' (he probably played all the instruments himself on the demo) and 'Something I Would Like To Be', written for John Maus, one of The Walker Brothers, who'd started a solo career after the trio broke up earlier that year. Bowie also makes his first overseas television appearance, singing 'Love You Till Tuesday' on the Dutch programme *Fanclub* in November, then takes to the stage for a few moments for a charity event at The Dorchester Hotel in London (the elegant Ziggy Stardust will give a memorable press conference there five years later, in the presence of Lou Reed and Iggy Pop).

In mid-December, the BBC invites David Bowie to play three songs from his album and a new track on the radio show *Top Gear*, accompanied by The Arthur Greenslade Orchestra. This is the first in a long series of sessions David will record up until 2002 (he will appear on the *Dave Lee Travis Show*, the *Sunday Show* with John Peel, *Sounds Of The 70's* and *In Concert*, among others). But while Ken Pitt is trying to make him succeed in any field (nobody showed interest in *The Champion Flower Grower*, a play he wrote for the radio), Bowie is concentrating on mime and *Pierrot In Turquoise*. After a few performances around the country, the London premiere takes place in early March 1968 at the Mercury Theatre (then managed by Frenchman, Jean-Pierre Voos). The show will run there all month.

A few weeks before, while filming an episode of a made-for-television drama series directed by John Gibson, David Bowie met Hermione Farthingale, a classical dancer. They will make music together but, more importantly, they will have an intense year-long romantic relationship. Their eventual breakup will devastate David, who will mention Hermione's name in the title of one of his later songs – as a lover, she alone will be given this honour.

In the spring, Tony Visconti holds new recording sessions at Decca Studios with sound engineer Gus Dudgeon, Mick Wayne[22] on guitar and Andy White on drums. In 'London Bye Ta-Ta', Bowie tackles migration, a subject he will address again 15 years later in the video of 'Let's Dance', but in a very different way. While the term isn't yet used to refer to a musical genre, this song, played to a rhythm with military march accents and enhanced with strings, heralds the glam rock that will ignite the following decade.

Unveiled in late 1967 as part of David's performance on *Top Gear*, 'In The Heat Of The Morning' has an especially daring chord progression (and melody). The guitar and the rhythm section give it a touch of soul to rival the sound of Stax or Motown. Deram's refusal to release 'In The Heat Of The Morning' as a single brings forward David's break with the label, which is made official in April. The following month, he makes a second appearance on *Top Gear* without the support of a record label. His musicians are John McLaughlin, drummer Barry Morgan, Alan Hawkshaw on keyboards and Steve 'Peregrin' Took, the percussionist of Tyrannosaurus Rex, the folk duo formed by Marc Bolan whose first album (recorded at Advision and produced by Visconti) will come out in July. They play five songs, including 'When I'm Five', which The Beatstalkers will cover in 1969. As the title indicates, it's another ode to childhood (sung with a little child's voice), but it has more of a petulant feel than 'There Is A Happy Land'.

That year in London, Tolkien's influence isn't just limited to music. David takes to the stage as a mime in a marathon show at Middle Earth on King Street, in London, with proceeds going to the underground magazine *Gandalf's Garden*. Tyrannosaurus Rex also perform there and, in early June, they will invite David Bowie to open for them as a mime at the Royal Festival Hall. But overall, the summer of 1968 is one of disappointments for Bowie[23]. Apple Corps., The Beatles' label, are not interested in his music, and he can't find any support for the cabaret show he has been trying to put out for a few months. Unresentful, he plans to include in his show a song which might reflect a huge missed opportunity from earlier that year. Ken Pitt had advised him to write English lyrics for a French song that a publisher wanted to release in English-speaking countries. David loved the melody of 'Comme d'Habitude' by Claude François, Gilles Thibault and Jacques Revaux, but he wrote the words in a hurry. The song became 'Even A Fool Learns To Love' and Pitt believed it would make a phenomenal single. But learning that a young nobody was writing the lyrics instead of a known star, the French publisher backed out and 'Comme d'Habitude' was picked up by Paul Anka, who turned it into 'My Way'[24].

What happened next is part of the great history of popular music, and Ken Pitt often wondered what Bowie's career would have looked like had his lyrics been used. Three years later, he will write 'Life On Mars?', in which the chord progression – but not the melody – of the verse cleverly mimics 'My Way'. As Hermione Farthingale points out later in this book, 1968 was a year of trial and error for David Bowie, but not necessarily a wasted one. David might not have released any albums that year (nor did he in 1978, 1988, 1998 or 2008), but the seeds of his unique talent are being blown around in the wind and will soon germinate and bear fruit.

In August, David Bowie, Hermione Farthingale and Tony Hill form a folk trio, which they describe as 'multimedia'. Tony Hill, a British guitarist who played in The Misunderstood, a Californian band who had come to London five years earlier (and were managed by the influential radio DJ John Peel), was recruited by a classified ad in the underground paper *IT (International Times)*. He brings 'Back To Where You've Never Been', one of his own songs, to the couple's repertoire. The trio will play just three performances as Turquoise, the first at the Roundhouse[25] in September. Many acts perform that night, including The Scaffold, a musical comedy trio featuring John Gorman, Roger McGough and Mike McGear (Paul McCartney's younger brother), who will go on to have the biggest hit of their career at the end of the year with 'Lily The Pink'. The event organizers probably had trouble keeping up with Bowie's artistic endeavours, so his participation was announced under his name alone (and not Turquoise). The trio will also open for The Strawbs and Third Ear Band, two groups similarly hard to classify and with whom David will later again cross paths.

Ken Pitt is not too sure about Turquoise, but Tony Visconti agrees to produce two of their songs in October. That's when David Bowie discovers Trident Studios[26], a place where he will often record over the coming years. At the end of the month, Tony Hill leaves Turquoise and forms High Tide, a solid group whose first album, *Sea Shanties*, will come out in 1969. He is replaced by John Hutchinson, who has reconnected with David, and the trio becomes Feathers. They will give three performances, the last one in early December at Sussex University near Brighton. Bowie spends the Christmas holidays in Cornwall. On 24 December, a poster by the entrance to the Magician's Workshop in Falmouth advertises a free performance of 'Tibetan mime', which Bowie is putting on as the opening act for Steve Miller Delivery (a band from Canterbury with no relation to the American Steve Miller Band). Even if his intentions were sometimes lost on the audience, David Bowie's few appearances with Hermione Farthingale were far from irrelevant. Like his mime performances, they were indicative of his creative development, a bubbling river forever drawing energy and inspiration from its many tributaries.

In January 1969, David Bowie is at home at 22 Clareville Grove[27], where he's been sharing the top floor with Hermione Farthingale for six months. He is absentmindedly strumming chords on his 12-string guitar, chords he's been playing around with since the previous summer when they saw *2001: A Space Odyssey*[28], Stanley Kubrick's film, which he wrote with Arthur C. Clarke[29]. But, as explained in the exhibition *David Bowie Is*, which Bowie himself will approve in 2013, the real inspiration behind this song is a photograph, *Earthrise*, published two days before his twenty-second birthday in a special edition of *The Times* dedicated to the space mission Apollo 8. Slowly but surely, long before the days of the internet, this photograph will travel around the entire world, inspiring awe in all who see it. While the future looked bright, the fragility of the blue planet (and the Earthlings on it) became blatantly clear. Humans had not yet set foot on the moon when, on a cold winter day in London, the legend of Major Tom was born.

Mike Vernon   John Hutchinson
Gus Dudgeon   Hermione Farthingale
Roger McGough
Craig San Roque
Alan Mair
Lou Reed
Tony Visconti
Dana Gillespie
Billy Ritchie
Edward Sanders

MIKE VERNON

I didn't know David Bowie's music very well before I produced his first album. I knew about a single he'd made with The Lower Third, but I'd never listened to it. To be honest, I'd never even heard of him before Hugh Mendl phoned me and arranged a meeting about him. If I remember correctly, David wasn't there that day. It was just Ken Pitt, his manager, and Mendl, who was my immediate boss at Decca. I've read, several times, that I produced *David Bowie* because I'd been Anthony Newley's recording engineer. That's not true at all! It's rubbish! I've never met Newley, and I wasn't even an engineer when he became famous. Hugh Mendl was involved with him, and I think that's what brought Ken Pitt to Decca. Pitt had talked about this artist he was managing, who was at once a poet, a mime artist, a singer, a composer... And so, when Hugh heard some of the demos Bowie had just recorded, songs that hadn't come out yet, he must have thought they'd be right for me. And yes, I noticed straight away that Bowie was a young version of Anthony Newley. But crazy as it sounds, when we first met, and even later, I never mentioned it. I honestly think that when I met him, he was trying to distance himself from Newley's influence, especially because the similarity wasn't ideal for a young artist trying to assert his own style.

Hugh Mendl could easily have forced me to produce the album, but he gave me a choice. Meeting Ken Pitt wasn't enough to convince me. Hugh said to me, 'If you like this artist, and I think you will, the job is yours.' To be completely honest, I'm not sure I really understood what that young Bowie was trying to do. At our first meeting, he told me where he was from and what he liked – the blues, soul music – and that of course triggered my interest. I've covered many genres in my career, but that's the type of music I like best. I had a passion for the blues, so it didn't take me long to see that Bowie was anything but a blues musician. Working with him, I'd be out of my safe area. But Hugh kept encouraging me, if only to help bring out in Bowie things he didn't even see in himself. I don't know if I succeeded, but I thought to myself at the time that it couldn't hurt to branch out a bit into unfamiliar territory. I wanted to stretch my horizons.

During the sessions for *David Bowie*, the orchestra musicians weren't very forgiving of Dek Fearnley, who was able to do some arrangements and write chord charts. They happily threw them back in his face, saying they weren't right. It was a real baptism by fire for him. It was obvious that it would have been easier to record the album with drums, a bass and a guitar. The fact that David wanted most of the songs to feature an orchestra definitely made everything more complicated. I don't think Dek wrote the string parts, but he certainly contributed to the brass arrangements. He did a good job and he is credited for it, as he should be.

After the album's commercial failure, David definitely wanted to end his time with Decca and leave Dek behind[30]. That's when he started doing mime, to break with all that. I have to admit he had a lot of guts to do that in smoky clubs, opening for bands like Fleetwood Mac or Chicken Shack! David knew what he wanted, but it was really bizarre. I can't remember Ken Pitt spending a lot of time with him in the studio but, you know, when it came to his music, Bowie was pretty much in charge. Usually, during recording, there's always a manager present, a publisher or some useless guy from the record label, but he stays back, like a fly on the wall – the type of guy who lets you know what he thinks of the bass sound, and you just want to tell him to get lost. However, I remember that Hugh Mendl did stop by to hear how our work was going and I regularly went to Decca to keep him up to date. Hugh was very supportive and encouraged us to follow the artist's direction.

But then again, David and Dek had a true musical relationship. David thought it was great to have Dek on board because he understood the songs. He was the conduit between Bowie, the musicians and me. Gus and I helped David to find the true picture of the stories he wanted to tell. But saying that I knew exactly what I was doing or where I was going with that record would be a lie. No one did actually, except – possibly – Bowie! In the back of his mind, I'm sure he knew how he would perform the songs; I guess he had some kind of concept. We went along with that, although not always. But most of the time I had the feeling he was creating the record rather than me. I was in charge of the sessions, making sure we were getting a good result and not spending more money than we were allowed. Gus and I did have a few ideas, but David was the creative force. It was a record that was fun to make but, to be honest, I still don't know how we made it. For example, Gus got really involved in 'The Laughing Gnome', which took forever to record and contains loads of sound effects. He even sings on it! When the single came out, it got some good reviews but it still wasn't a success. Decca had been happy to release 'The Laughing Gnome', thinking they couldn't go wrong with a song for children. I've always thought that some of the songs on that album felt like nursery rhymes and were too gimmicky. But more to the point, I had the feeling that Bowie was seeing the world through the eyes of a kid who was in no hurry to grow up. He told me he loved 'The Inch Worm', which he must have heard from Danny Kaye in *Hans Christian Andersen*.

When the orchestral version of 'Love You Till Tuesday' failed as a single,

David and the label started to become disillusioned. I was so sure this version would be a hit, but it didn't even make the Top 40. Bowie's time with Decca wasn't successful. In the end, the record did sell a fair few copies each time it was reissued. It's crazy to think that this record came out in the summer of 1967, the famous year when pop and rock really took off. But David Bowie had no rock edge and I had to admit, listening to the final album, that we were a strange fit. That record is still pretty incongruous and, you know, David never asked me to come and see him in concert...

With him, I kinda felt like a fish out of water. The songs we recorded together were pretty poetic, but he used his lyrics to tackle some serious subjects, sometimes set against a backdrop of war. But as I said, I did the best I could, despite feeling quite uncomfortable most of the time. And I still wonder if I was the right person for the job. However, like all of Deram's albums, *David Bowie* doesn't sound dated even now. You can think what you like, musically, about these records, but their sound quality is undeniable – they still sound big even though the studios had pretty primitive technology. The stereophonic image benefited what David Bowie was doing at the time, just like it benefited the Ten Years After's albums. The most complex songs on *David Bowie* were recorded on two 4-track tape recorders. From a purely technical standpoint, what surprised me most about Bowie at the time was how fast he did his vocal takes. He was really quick. Usually, he just needed one take, which he would listen to carefully. Only when he thought he could do better, he'd do a second take and that would be the one! I don't remember him struggling with any song and we didn't have much to do in terms of fixing.

I rarely listen to the records I produced, but whenever I happen upon that first Bowie album, hearing the quality of his voice, I can see him again in the studio – so focused, so determined. He was on his job and knew exactly how he wanted to perform. When he felt it was time to record his vocal, Gus was happy just to set up a mic in front of him, probably a Neumann U87, and off he went. Gus always had good ideas, and he and David got along very well during the sessions. I was not surprised they ended up working together again. Gus was a real character, hilarious. He used to wear the tightest trousers in rock business, very short, so everyone could see his pink socks! More seriously, I was so happy for him when 'Space Oddity', with his name on it, made the charts. There are some epic songs on *David Bowie* – 'There Is A Happy Land' and 'When I Live My Dream' – but I think it was a good record at the wrong time. It's good, but it missed the mark. There was a crack between pop music and rock back then, and it fell through it. Had it come out six months later, it could have been a hit. (2016)

GUS DUDGEON[31]

David's first album? I have wonderful memories of it! First of all, I often wondered if that funny little song, 'Please Mr Gravedigger', was about me! After all, I'm Mr GD. The subject wasn't very cheerful though, but we laughed a lot during the recording. We really made the most of Decca's sound library – there are sound effects everywhere on that record. (1990)

JOHN HUTCHINSON

I left The Buzz as I was going to leave Feathers some time later: on friendly terms, and because I had to earn some money to provide for my family. Concerts with The Buzz were increasingly few and far between... I didn't have a choice. David understood and he told me he'd offer me work again if he could. Which he did... In September 1968, I was able to commit to music full time again. I wanted to play acoustic guitar and I'd got better at singing and doing vocal harmonies. I gave him a call and he invited me to his house on Clareville Grove, and took me on the Feathers adventure. As always with him, it happened naturally. The David Bowie I knew in 1968 wasn't all that different from the one I'd known two years before, but he was a lot more relaxed. (2016)

HERMIONE FARTHINGALE

From the age of 12, I'd been going to dance school and I grew up surrounded by music. I listened to it with my body, because I had to move to it. I played a bit of piano and, like everyone my age, I started to sing along to a few guitar chords. But I was by no means a musician. At the end of January 1968, I was hired to dance a minuet in *The Pistol Shot*, an episode from the television series *Theatre 665* on BBC2[32]. There were a few ballet dancers there that day, most of them way overqualified... You had to make a living somehow! Lindsay Kemp, who was always broke, brought David to the set, but I'm not sure if he choreographed the sequence or not. At first, David didn't seem to belong there. He wasn't a dancer.

David and I finally came face to face when we started rehearsing. Honestly, I didn't know his music and I hadn't listened to his first album, which had come out the year before. He was very disappointed by his lack of success, but he didn't talk about it much when we first started seeing each other. In those days, he wanted to become a mime. He was very talented and he had the body for it. But he never went to mime school and only took a few lessons from Lindsay. Lindsay loved David's songs, which he used in his shows. During the *Pierrot In Turquoise* performances, David would sit on the edge of the stage and sing. He was the perfect narrator, like a sort of bard, a travelling gypsy who performed wherever he could. Of course, he had an incredibly beautiful voice.

We fell in love instantly. We met on a Wednesday and by Friday we were completely in love. I kept the Valentine's Day card he sent me a few days later. In those days, he was playing hide-and-seek with his manager, Ken Pitt, who never knew where to find him – of course he was with me. Before that, he was either with Ken, or with his parents in Bromley. Everyone thought he'd disappeared, except for me. A lot of people wanted to know where he was... There was something about him that made you want to protect him. Ken was instrumental and played an undeniable and really positive role in his cultural education, but he had trouble keeping up with David. Everything interested him, he wanted to absorb as much as he could, try lots of different things. Whenever we went out, we'd go to the theatre or to the cinema – I have a diary from that year. I wish it was more full... Some days I wrote at length, others not so much[33]...

We lived in a pretty Georgian-style house in South Kensington, not in a small studio as I've seen written. At the time, you could rent that sort of place for a reasonable price... In fact, we were sub-letting a room in the house. Breege Collins, who was just a bit older than me, was renting the whole house, which I think had six bedrooms. Breege had a bit of a mind for business and had placed an ad to find renters. Also living in the house with us were two models, a girl who was doing an internship at a radio station, a writer named Tom, someone called Ray[34], and photographer Vernon Dewhurst. My bedroom was on the top floor, and from the window I could see a beautiful tree. It was a very nice room with a fireplace. That was where David worked on his songs and practised with John Hutchinson when he came to visit. They were more relaxed up there than in the living room downstairs, where there was always someone coming or going.

At first, I was just David's girlfriend and there was no reason for us to make music together. I was a dancer who wanted to join a ballet troupe and there were very few of them at the time – I didn't want a career in music. But then I started singing with David because when he was writing, he sometimes needed an extra voice. He would ask me, 'Can you sing this verse?' and then he'd harmonize over it. The funniest thing was that my voice, although not great, blended perfectly with his.

It would have been impossible to have three David Bowies singing together, but my voice and Hutch's complemented his really well. But I wasn't planning to go down that path; I was just a friend who was helping out.

Before Feathers, I found myself on stage performing with Turquoise, the short-lived trio that we formed with guitarist Tony Hill. It turned out that Tony was not at all the man for the job, so Hutch, who'd played in The Buzz, joined us. David's voice was so compelling. Which made it even harder to sing alongside him. And it had nothing to do with any technique. The quality of his vocals, that sort of magic, came from his intelligence, which powered his lyrics. He believed in the strength of words.

The time I spent with David, he was a sort of unemployed songwriter with all these people flashing around and trying hard to make him big... His father thought it was about time he earned some money with his music. Ken Pitt thought David should turn toward cabaret... He'd hired Hutch because he was a good musician and David himself wasn't yet – Feathers couldn't work unless we had a really solid player. And our trio looked pretty good. We didn't wear anything special, but our stage clothes were usually black to make our silhouettes stand out clearly. Feathers was based on the songs of Jacques Brel[35]. Especially 'Amsterdam', which I thought tackled a particularly grim subject, with its references to night life, ports and prostitutes... I'm not sure the audience was ready for that. We also covered 'Next' and 'My Death'. Looking back, I'm surprised that David was interested in such serious subjects. He was just a kid. It took him a while to become a man – he didn't need to shave very often! Singing 'My Death' at 21 years old! It's such a sad song, about the great beyond on a spiritual level... But we also covered 'Life Is A Circus' by English folk group Djinn and 'Love Song'[36] by Lesley Duncan, who was one of his good friends. Hutch and I really liked that part of the set, those really beautiful melodies and vocal harmonies...

David used to perform a brave mime act, *Jetsun And The Eagle*, to the song 'Silly Boy Blue'... We also did a mime together, something called *The Seagull*. Hutch started the tape recorder and made scratchy noises and percussive sounds with his guitar, and David and I did this mime that we had worked out, like interpretative movements really. Hutch recited a poem by Roger McGough, *Love On A Bus*[37], and of course David mimed *The Mask*. You know, our trio was more remarkable for its nature – a mix of song, mime and poetry – than for its repertoire. David was experimenting, trying things. We were friends and he felt safe with us. These were the things he enjoyed and he wanted to know whether this type of performance would work. The audience was never big and people sometimes scratched their heads, wondering what they were looking at. When you think about David's career, you can see how those few months were seminal for him.

Sometimes he also played 'When I'm Five', a song of his that I thought was rather strange. Because of its similar chord progression, it turned into a cover of Carole King's 'Going Back'. One night, David wrote 'Ching-a-Ling' and we played it to Tony Visconti the next day. He loved it because it had a bit of Marc Bolan in it and they were working together at the time. David had the idea for the bit at the end while listening to the tape played backwards[38]. Musicians used to do that in the studio back then, especially The Beatles, whether they were stoned or not. That technique contributed to the mythology around them. David wanted to give the impression that a crowd of people was singing along with him in the chorus. But the verses are complete gibberish, utter nonsense! You can't find any meaning in them, but it's still funny to see people trying. Anyway, it wasn't an easy song to perform and I don't think I ever sang it very well. After Tony Hill left, Hutch recorded his voice onto the song, but he and Tony Visconti didn't get along very well. Their personalities were too different, and Tony had him sing in a key that was too high for him... (2016)

ROGER MCGOUGH

I met David Bowie twice, the first time at the Roundhouse at the end of the 1960s. We were at the bar and he came up to me and introduced himself by saying, 'Do you know that we recite one of your poems?' At the time he wasn't famous, but you could tell that he wasn't like the other musicians either. He really did stand out from the others. The fact that he chose mime as a mode of expression said a lot about his desire to be unique. His eyes were also unique! So I said that was fine by me. The funny thing was that Bowie wasn't the only one to use that poem. Bernard Wrigley, a singer-comedian known as The Bolton Bullfrog, also recited it. He told me about it one day, and I asked him if he told his audience that I had written it. He said, 'Only when it's a flop!'

The Mersey Sound was a hit when it came out, and it still sells today. We've sold more than a million copies. People liked it so much because we proved that poetry could come from places other than London. We were from Liverpool, a popular place in the 60s. We were working class. Our poetry was new and came from real life. It was well received by the general public and by people like Bowie, who were curious by nature.

The second time I saw him was in February 1972 when The Scaffold opened for him at Sheffield University. After our set, John Gorman accidentally walked into one of the big speakers next to him and it fell over at the back of the stage. Well, I understand that didn't make Bowie laugh! I remember that we slunk away as quickly as possible after that... You're the first to tell me that what I wrote might have inspired 'Five Years'. Honestly, that makes me happy. It was a dystopic era... All the musicians borrowed heavily from literature, and apparently Bowie was no different. (2019)

CRAIG SAN ROQUE

First, let me say the only reason I'm talking to you today is because your book is about David Bowie as a musician, and that you are giving a voice to those who worked with him. Personally, I think that's the best angle to approach him. I could talk about other parts of his life, but I don't want to do that. You see a man and, through him, you see yourself, from the age of 20 to the twilight of existence – there's a whole lifespan there. You're in your role as biographer and I'm the psychoanalyst. You write about lives and I listen to people tell me about theirs, so I'm used to becoming involved in people's biographies. I don't approach them in the same way you do. I focus on themes. In this case, the music theme, the creative theme, the psychological theme... And of course I'm interested in the themes that I have glimpsed in David's life.

I first want to mention silence. France. Silence. Jean-Louis Barrault. Marcel Marceau. The contribution to theatre, how mime heightens silence. We can't forget the context in which *Les Enfants Du Paradis* was shot. Under German occupation. When I saw the film in Australia in the mid-60s, for people my age, the country was synonymous with psychological depression and stagnation. Everyone I knew left for Europe because they didn't feel like killing themselves. So I went with my then wife. My generation never imagined that silence, in theatre, could be so moving and eloquent. We owe that to the French.

I spent some time in Italy, in Spain, and of course in France before finally finding myself broke in London. I'd tried to get into a mime school in Paris, but that was in May 1968. The Théâtre de l'Odéon, managed by Jean-Louis Barrault, was occupied by students so of course I couldn't make any connection. One day, as I was walking in the street in Soho, I noticed a poster saying, 'Mime lessons, Lindsay Kemp'... There was a telephone number. I called him and started lessons with Lindsay at the same time as Jack Birkett. I had the desire to pursue the art of silence as performance. I quickly noticed that Lindsay – and I mean no disrespect by this – was happy to just copy Marcel Marceau. Short performances, beautifully done, repertoire pieces. We started wondering how to perform a whole event, not just a performance piece.

In the summer of 1968, theatre was really blossoming, with pop and rock music involved. Lindsay wanted to know how he could bring contemporary music into traditional mime. One afternoon, I went to see him and he said, 'You have to listen to this voice, it's the one we need for our performance.' And he played 'Sell Me A Coat', a song from David's first album. His voice immediately spoke to me. It was a sort of working-class/cockney kind of English at that time. That was the first thing that struck a chord with Lindsay; he wasn't really a refined kind of artist. I'm not talking about sexual relations, but an artistic connection between two Englishmen, each aware of their own working-class background. David wasn't singing rock'n'roll at the time. He was nothing like The Rolling Stones or Small Faces. If Lindsay were standing in front of me today, I would ask him how David's music touched his heart to the point that it became a source of artistic inspiration. In those days, all he wanted to do was improve as a performer and he wanted to do it through theatre. David's voice matched what Lindsay, the artist of silence, was after. The two of them together stimulated a direction for them both, that each of them then developed in their own way. At that moment, the combination of their abilities really helped to generate the next development for David. And David kept doing this throughout his career – his growth as an artist was down to his continual meetings with other minds.

David was very stiff when he met Lindsay, who pushed him, as a teacher, to relax on stage. After that, through various performances, you could see it happening. David became looser, less shy, less narcissistic; he made mistakes, like everyone else, which is necessary. He got a lot out of those lessons. On the other hand, I was lucky enough to watch one of David's recording sessions at the time, and he was simply masterful as a musician. He managed the situation, the musos around him, with confidence and ease. He was completely in his element.

You can't talk about David without mentioning Tibet – what he learned on the subject, how intensely he dedicated himself to it, and the aborted film project on the life of Jetsun Miralepa[39]. Like many of us at the time, Pete Townshend for instance, David really connected with traditional Tibetan Buddhism and he was supposed to play Miralepa in the film. But I think his appetite for this form of spirituality had everything to do with the compassion that David developed, which was already part of his character. In ways that we can't really know, Miralepa, as a Tibetan who went through transformations, who was also a musician and a singer, planted a kind of seed in David's mind that we must take into consideration. Much of Bowie's mystique, a big part of his enigma, comes from this already active, compassionate attentiveness to learn, to be a student, to be a disciple. These notions were completely unheard of in the entertainment industry and probably made it harder for him to find his place; they were unique to him. David's meeting with Chime [Rinpoche] was crucial in the sense that, psychologically and spiritually speaking, it helped him focus during a turning point in his journey, through all these complications and this confusion. At his age, his connection with Tibetan culture, which matched his music and the complexity of his potential, gave him something he probably couldn't have found in English culture. Tibet was like a jewel in David Bowie's story. (2017)

ALAN MAIR

In the 1960s, I played bass with The Beatstalkers and we had the same manager as David Bowie. We sometimes shared the bill with The Lower Third but, at that time, David was as much trying to write songs for other people as he was trying to make a career with his band or under his own name. He'd started composing very young and, at that stage in his artistic journey, Ken Pitt was a bit baffled and wondered if David was really made for the spotlight. He was only 20 when he wrote 'Silver Treetop School For Boys' – it's crazy that he came up with a song like that at such a young age. He had a very elaborate way of writing and singing songs: his phrasing was typically English, and our Scottish singer really struggled to get it right. I've always considered 'Silver Treetop School For Boys' a superb song that would have sounded good in any style.

Every time we recorded one of David's songs, back when sessions, including the mix, only lasted about three hours, he would be there in the studio with us. He played some acoustic guitar and put a lot of effort into the backing vocals. Being a bit older than him, I was already a father when he was writing songs for his first album, but we spent quite a lot of time together. Sometimes I'd go to Ken Pitt's house with Frankie, my three-year-old son. David got on well with him. 'Little Bombardier' was originally like a folk song, then David changed it and also changed the lyrics. But initially it was inspired by Frankie, Little Frankie Mair[40]! (2018)

LOU REED

When I found out that David Bowie had a thing for The Velvet Underground, I wasn't surprised. He'd always been drawn to what was different from him, even things that frightened him a bit. He felt the same kind of attraction to Iggy And The Stooges, Mott The Hoople and others like that... Also, he was intrigued by Andy Warhol... (2003)

TONY VISCONTI[41]

One day in the autumn of 1967 David Platz called me into his office: 'You seem to have a talent for working with weird acts. I'd like to play something for you to consider,' is the condescending way he framed it. After six months working in London, Platz seemed to be irritated by my very presence. 'This is an album made by a writer I've been working with for some time,' he went on. 'We were hoping he'd be right for the musical theatre, but he's become something quite different since he's made this record.' From the speakers came an amazingly mature voice, the phrasing and subtlety was something you'd expect from a seasoned stage or even a cabaret singer. The songs were humorous and dark; the backing was imaginative. But Platz was right – what was this? I listened to half the album and remarked that although it was all over the place, I liked it. 'His name is David Bowie and he's 19. Would you like to meet him?'

Behind David Platz's office was a small room with a piano; it harked back to the days, not that long before, when a publisher actually had a member of staff sit at the piano and play a song to a prospective singer, or a songwriter would play their latest compositions to the publisher. Platz led me into this inner sanctum and there was David Bowie – nervous and shy. I realized then that this casual encounter was a set up. As I shook Bowie's hand I realized that he had two different-coloured eyes. The only other person I ever met with two different-coloured eyes was Jerry Leiber, of Leiber and Stoller. After a brief introduction, Platz wisely left us alone. I liked David Bowie immediately.

We talked for ages about anything and everything, like two people getting on really well at a party. David seemed obsessed with American music in the same way I was with British music. He told me he bought as many American records as he could. He adored Little Richard. He also liked American jazz – sax player Gerry Mulligan in particular. He said he also played baritone sax. He loved underground music, like Frank Zappa and The Fugs; I had the same records in my collection. Another album that we shared a mutual love for was Ken Nordine's *Word Jazz*. He was a radio announcer from the American Midwest with a very deep voice. He made a spoken-word album with jazz music and some sound effects for accompaniment. It was another album I had bought back in the States and David had it too; we must have been one of a dozen people who had bought it.

We decided to leave the stuffy office and take a walk and eventually found ourselves on King's Road. We came across a small cinema showing Roman Polanski's *A Knife In The Water*; we watched it and discovered another shared interest – foreign art films. If it was in black and white, made anywhere but the USA or UK, and it was scratchy and had subtitles, we loved it. I left David around 6pm and went back home to Elgin Avenue and told Siegrid about my new friend. [...]

David and Turquoise were very enthusiastic about one song they had written and were anxious for me to record it with them. It was called 'Ching-a-Ling' and, after I'd heard it, I begged Denny and David Platz to let me record it. But Denny was explicitly anti-Bowie: 'You know I've never "got" him,' was Denny's take on things. 'I'm not about to finance another of Bowie's follies,' was how a slightly less than generous Platz put it. I was slightly baffled because it was he who had initially wanted me to work with Bowie. Once again, I did my 'embezzling' gambit and booked Trident Studios in St Anne's Court in late October to record 'Ching-a-Ling' and a second song written by Hill, which was called 'Back To Where You've Never Been'. Unfortunately within a few days Hill was out of the band and David's friend John 'Hutch' Hutchinson was in. I needed another day in the studio to take Hill's voice off and put Hutch's voice on. I thought Platz would be over the moon with the results of this session.

'What's this? Who's Feathers? I didn't know we had a group called Feathers on the label?'

I thought that Denny recorded so much bullshit stuff, wasting so much time and money in the studio I could just slip this session through. I wasn't a great 'embezzler', because I didn't think of writing 'Joe Cocker' on the work sheet. Yet again I was severely reprimanded and almost fired. The Beatles' 'Hey Jude' had been recorded at Trident a few months earlier, but none of their magic rubbed off on us[42]. (2007)

DANA GILLESPIE

A lot of people have talked about Anthony Newley's influence on David Bowie, which of course wasn't just musical. David undeniably cultivated vocal similarities, but what also impressed him at the time was Newley's fame. He was blown away by his weekly television show, his references to aliens... We watched it with our noses glued to the screen. From then on, David was intrigued by anything that seemed weird. He was fascinated by things other people hardly even noticed. Later, after seeing photos of a kabuki theatre in a magazine, he'll become passionate about all things Japanese. Being unique himself, he was attracted to whatever was unique.

In those days, we hung out on Carnaby Street, which was quite trendy. It wasn't yet the horrible trap for Japanese tourists it is today! I remember the time he bought the military jacket with epaulettes he's wearing on the cover of his first album. I also saw the London premiere of *Pierrot In Turquoise* at the Mercury Theatre[43], a tiny place that I'm sure no longer exists. There weren't a lot of people there... David was dressed in a sort of Pierrot costume and was very keen on his mime, which of course he'd learnt from Kemp. Lindsay later said that he used to do all his shows on acid, himself, but I'm sure David wouldn't. Lindsay also had his wonderful friend Jack in the production and one could see that David was seriously influenced by these two great men. David was a born actor, both on and off the stage, so this was a great learning experience for him.

As for his Buddhism leanings, I really can't say, except he never shaved his head! He never told me about that, but he changed his mind and his roles pretty regularly and, if I didn't see him for a few days, I risked missing something! It was the era for all of us to be experimental and he could easily have been studying Aleister Crowley one week and Buddhism the next! It's what we all did then, only he sometimes took things a little further than most... (2017)

BILLY RITCHIE

1-2-3 played the Saville Theatre with Jimi Hendrix and we shared a dressing room[44]. David came with us and, at one point, was carrying Jimi's guitar like a roadie. Later, in the dressing room, I introduced him to Jimi. Of course, at that time, David was completely unknown. The irony of their meeting didn't become apparent until much later, when David was a star and Jimi was dead. But at the time, David felt a bit offended by Jimi; he thought he was being aloof and not taking him seriously. But he was wrong. Jimi was just very shy. (2017)

EDWARD SANDERS

I don't know much about David Bowie, but I'm honoured that he liked the music of The Fugs. And that my book, *Tales Of Beatnik Glory*, was in his list of favourite works[45]. I had no idea he'd covered our songs with The Riot Squad. Like Frank Zappa and Leonard Cohen, Bowie made a big impression on a whole lot of people. That much was clear when we saw the tsunami of grief and sadness that came with his sudden death. (2017)

1. Ironically, 'Join My Gang', the A-side of Oscar's previous single in 1966, was written by Pete Townshend. On David Bowie's first album we find... 'Join The Gang'. In 1970, Paul Nicholas will perform in *Jesus Christ Superstar* with Dana Gillespie.

2. In 1965, the idea for a musical project, in partnership with Tony Hatch, started forming in David Bowie's mind.

3. A sample record made for professional and promotional use.

4. An anagram of the word 'dream'.

5. We now know that recording engineer/producer Mike Smith was the one who chose Brian Poole And The Tremeloes over The Fab Four. Dick Rowe had asked him to choose between the two bands recording that day. But the controversy over this decision continues to rage among Beatles fans. However, the fact that Hugh Mendl insisted that Decca take on The Beatles before they became famous surely motivated its directors to let him manage Deram. Around the same time, Decca also turned down The Who, Manfred Mann and Georgie Fame; they will sell millions of records.

6. Released in 2013 on the independent label Acid Jazz Records, *The Toy Soldier* EP is a 4-track vinyl record by The Riot Squad with David Bowie. It features 'Waiting For My Man' (instead of 'I'm Waiting For The Man') and three songs David penned: 'Toy Soldier', 'Silly Boy Blue' and 'Silver Treetop School For Boys' (already covered by The Beatstalkers). On these recordings, The Riot Squad musicians were Bob Evans on tenor sax, Rod Davies on guitar, Brian 'Croak' Prebble on bass, Butch Davis on organ and Del Roll on drums. During his short time with The Riot Squad, Bowie sometimes used the pseudonym Toy Soldier.

7. Many bands of the time made reference to Tolkien's world and the creatures that inhabit it, including Led Zeppelin, Camel, Rush, Uriah Heep, Black Sabbath, Genesis, Tomorrow and Pink Floyd. Many people have said that 'The Laughing Gnome' was inspired by 'Three Jolly Dwarves' by Tomorrow and 'The Gnome' by Pink Floyd, but the albums on which they appear came out after *David Bowie*.

8. A French singer who went by the name Caroline covered 'The Laughing Gnome' in 1967. Her version, called 'Mister A Gogo', appears on a Polydor single which, with its original sleeve, is worth more than its weight in gold.

9. For more than half a century, many people have believed that The Beatles' top album was released on Thursday 1 June 1967. However, EMI knew it was about to drop a bomb and decided to send it out to British record stores on 26 May, a Friday, because that was usually the day the label released records. The other reason for getting it out early was that on 22 May, The Beatles had caused a stir by announcing that they would be representing the BBC and the nation by performing the following month on the show *Our World*, the first programme in the history of television to be broadcast by satellite. EMI took advantage of the publicity and released the album six days earlier.

10. From now on, the author will refer to the album as *Sgt. Pepper* rather than *Sgt. Pepper's Lonely Hearts Club Band*.

11. Later on, in some interviews, Bowie will 'add' details to his childhood, which will include a long stay in the countryside.

12. The Moors Murderers is also the name of a band Steve Strange will form in 1977, in which Chrissie Hynde, leader of The Pretenders, made a brief appearance. These heinous crimes will also inspire Morrissey to write 'Suffer The Little Children' for The Smiths' first album in 1984.

13. In 2010, the year EMI will reissue *Station To Station* in a box set, Deram will release a double-CD edition of *David Bowie*, the most complete to date. It includes the mono and stereo versions of the album, as well as many bonus tracks.

14. In late summer 1967, Arthur Greenslade and Ivor Raymonde will both work on *New Masters*, Cat Stevens' second album. Herbie Flowers, who will soon play with David Bowie, is the bassist on this record.

15. According to Lindsay Kemp, an employee of NEMS (North East Music Store), Brian Epstein's management company, gave him a copy of *David Bowie*. The song that first moved him, and the one he reportedly used to open his show with, was 'When I Live My Dream'. It's not entirely clear exactly when Kemp played Bowie's songs – some say it was before the show, others say it was during the show itself, or in the intermission. Even Bowie has contradicted himself on the matter.

16. The use of the word 'turquoise' in the name of the show (and for the name of the folk trio he will form a few months later), was probably Bowie's suggestion. For Tibetans and Buddhists, turquoise is a spiritual stone with many beneficial qualities.

17. Jack Birkett was Lindsay Kemp's travelling and stage partner until the end of the 1980s. He was a particularly expressive British dancer, mime and actor. From 1965, he will gradually lose his eyesight, but this will not stop him from continuing to perform. Birkett will be on stage with David Bowie and The Spiders From Mars at the Rainbow in August 1972 and will appear in Derek Jarman's extravagant *Jubilee* six years later alongside Toyah Wilcox, Jayne County and Adam Ant.

18. In 1991, while in Paris, Bowie found out his taxi was passing by the building on Boulevard Montparnasse where Eugène Ionesco lived. He started speaking passionately about the dramatist and his plays – so convincingly and knowledgeably that he would put experts in the shade.

19. In 1967, Advision Studios are still located at 83 New Bond Street. The Who, The Yardbirds and The Move also recorded there. Two years later, Advision will move to 23 Gosfield Street, in Marylebone, and became the 'house of progressive rock'. Emerson, Lake & Palmer, Gentle Giant and Yes will make many of their albums there. *The Hoople* by Mott The Hoople and 'Fire' by The Crazy World Of Arthur Brown were also recorded at Advision.

20. This is the drummer who, on 11 September 1962, replaced Ringo Starr during the recording of the famous 'Love Me Do', the A-side of The Beatles' first single. George Martin's assistant Ron Richards – not The Beatles' producer, who wasn't there at the start of the session – made the request for the replacement.

21. Some of them having been recorded in a rudimentary way, it's not easy to know precisely how many songs David Bowie taped at the end of the 60s. 'April's Tooth Of Gold', 'Angel Angel Grubby Face', 'Goodbye 3d (Three Penny) Joe', 'The Reverend Raymond Brown (Attends The Garden Fete On Thatchwick

Green)', 'Now That You Want Me', 'Silver Sunday', 'A Social Kind Of Girl', 'Lincoln House' and 'Home By Six' are among those known to exist. Kevin Cann mentioned the last three in *Any Day Now: David Bowie The London Years (1947–1974)*. Many of them had probably been destined for Bowie's second album for Deram, which he didn't end up recording, not because Tony Visconti was too busy with Tyrannosaurus Rex, but because the label wanted to let Bowie go. In 2019, *Spying Through A Keyhole*, the first box set of singles Parlophone released to celebrate the half century of *Space Oddity*, gathered together some of the aforementioned demos as well as 'Love All Around', which contains particularly elaborate chord progressions and a line that is used as the title of the box set. The most remarkable song, which says a lot about how David Bowie worked and about his ability to sit on a good idea for many years, is 'Mother Grey'. It contains practically the whole melody of the chorus of 'Changes' (which Bowie would go on to release in 1971), as well as the harmonic sequence he would use again in the second part of 'Memory Of A Free Festival'.

22. Mick Wayne from London, who was in The Outsiders with Jimmy Page, also played on *Space Oddity*. Through the book, the author has used this title to refer to David Bowie's second album, which was originally also called *David Bowie*, so as not to confuse the two. RCA renamed it when they reissued it in 1972.

23. In order to make a little money, despite help from his parents, David Bowie will work part-time at Legastat for a few months that year. It was a print shop that specialized in confidential documents.

24. This anecdote comes from the author's book *David Bowie Ouvre Le Chien* (La Table Ronde, 2015).

25. Built a century before David Bowie's birth, in the Chalk Farm area of London, the Roundhouse (which is round in shape) was originally the turning plate in a railway engine shed. It became a concert venue in the mid-1960s and Jim Morrison and The Doors played their only gig in England there on 7 September 1968. David Bowie will play there four times in 1970 (two with Hype and two as David Bowie). The Roundhouse is still an important concert venue and cultural centre.

26. Located at 17 St Anne's Court in Soho (near the Marquee), Trident Studios was owned by the Sheffield brothers and Bowie will record there regularly until 1974. According to Tony Visconti and the recording engineers who worked there, it was 'the most rock'n'roll studio in London'.

27. In 2019, to commemorate the 50th anniversary of David Bowie's second album, Parlophone will release several products, including the *Clareville Grove Demos*, a set of three singles recorded in early 1969 with John Hutchinson. Two of the six songs will officially be released for the first time on this occasion: 'Lover To The Dawn' (which became 'Cygnet Committee' on *Space Oddity*) and 'Life Is A Circus'. Hermione Farthingale owns an acetate of these songs; she will not part with it.

28. David Bowie will claim he saw the film while under the influence of drugs, which further inspired him to turn it into a song. He will sometimes add he tried heroin in 1968. However, his friends of the time said that Bowie liked wine, but didn't even smoke hash. Bowie was probably 'enhancing' this story as he often did in interviews. He told *Rock&Folk* in 2004 that 'telling everything and its opposite' to journalists kept him from getting bored.

29. The years it took to make the film (and book) are an odyssey in themselves, and most of the books written about Stanley Kubrick only scratch the surface of the complex nature of his collaboration with Clarke. Suffice to say, in terms of the film script, *2001: A Space Odyssey* was a team effort, but disagreements between the two strong personalities gave rise to the disparities between the film and the book, which was published afterwards. Each work reflects the person who created it.

30. Dek Fearnley died of cancer on 1 November 2008, at 69 years old. David Bowie paid tribute to him on BowieNet. Mark Adams, editor of the website, said that after he was diagnosed, Dek had given each of his children a copy of *David Bowie*, saying, 'That's my legacy'.

31. Gus Dudgeon will talk to the author in the summer of 1990, at Master Rock Studios in London. At the time, he was recording in one of the studios while Dudgeon was producing an album by French singer Elsa in the other. The keyboardist and saxophonist Richard Cottle, and bass player Paul Westwood, were also working on Elsa's record. In the 1980s, they will both play with David Bowie. Cottle and Westwood have been interviewed by the author for *Rainbowman*.

32. It aired in May 1968.

33. In her diary, Hermione Farthingale mentioned several of the films and shows she and David saw together: the musical *Sweet Charity*; the films *Closely Observed Trains* by

Jiří Menzel, *Only When I Larf* by Basil Dearden and *Herostratus* by Don Levy; and the plays *The Barrow Poets* with Gerard Benson and *Time Present* by John Osborne at the Duke of York's Theatre. Osborne also wrote the famous *Look Back In Anger*, a play that would give Bowie inspiration for the title of a song on *Lodger* in 1979.

34. Ray Stevenson, who was also a photographer, took the photos of David Bowie as a mime and playing with Feathers at Middle Earth.

35. David Bowie discovered Jacques Brel's work through Scott Walker, who'd covered three of his songs on *Scott*, his first album, released in 1967. David heard it at the home of Lesley Duncan, a singer-songwriter and renowned backing vocalist who sang with The Walker Brothers and co-wrote some of their songs. Later Bowie will cover two of Brel's songs: 'Amsterdam' and 'My Death', which featured on *Scott*. But it was only after seeing *Jacques Brel Is Alive And Well And Living In Paris* the following year in London with Hermione Farthingale, that he will fall in love with Brel's work. The musical showed about 40 times at the Duchess Theatre (and almost 2,000 times at the Village Gate theatre in New York, starting in 1966). Bowie reportedly held on to his copy (a double vinyl) of the show's soundtrack all his life. Lesley Duncan's name is largely unknown, though many rock fans own a recording of her voice without knowing it – she will be a backing vocalist on *The Dark Side Of The Moon*, released by Pink Floyd in 1973.

36. 'Love Song', covered by Elton John in 1970, will launch Lesley Duncan's solo career. She will record half a dozen beautiful folk-rock albums before retiring from music in the mid-80s. She will marry producer Tony Cox and will spend

her final days on the Isle of Mull in Scotland. She passed away in March 2010, to the sound of 'Love Song'.

37. This poem is actually called 'At Lunchtime – A Story Of Love', and it comes from a 1967 collection called *The Mersey Sound*, also containing poems by Brian Patten and Adrian Henri. This collection was influenced by beat poetry.

38. This technique probably gave rise to several of David Bowie's songs. In the late 1970s, he will say he found the melody for 'Move On' on *Lodger* by playing 'All The Young Dudes' backwards.

39. Aside from David Bowie's fascination with this figure in Tibetan Buddhism, it's interesting to note that he seemed uninterested in the events that shook Europe in 1968. *Jetsun And The Eagle*, a brave mime piece he performed, was based on Miralepa's vengeance for the humiliation of his mother and sister, and the consequences for his own destiny. As it has been impossible since the 1950s to portray Tibet without reflecting back on the Chinese genocide there, the English Maoists who saw the show made a point of voicing their disapproval, some even waving copies of *The Little Red Book*.

40. The spelling of the name varies according to the transcription of the song's lyrics, but on the original sheet music and in the official songbooks, it's 'Mere'.

41. In this book, and with his permission, some contributions from Tony Visconti (dated 2007) are taken from his autobiography, *Bowie, Bolan and the Brooklyn Boy*, which was translated into French by the author and published that year

by éditions de Tournon, under the title *Bowie, Bolan et le Gamin de Brooklyn*. That edition is now out of print.

42. The Feathers single never came out, but 'Ching-a-Ling' will appear on the compilation *Love You Till Tuesday*, whose first edition came out in 1984 on CD and vinyl.

43. Located at 2 Ladbroke Road, the site is now a private residence. It was turned into a theatre in the early 1930s by author Ashley Dukes (dancer Marie Rambert's husband). A former school, then a parish hall, it is known to Beatles fans as one of the five locations used in a photo shoot on Sunday 28 July 1968. That day, war photographer Don McCullin, who'd been chosen for the quality of his work, shot The Beatles in several places around London, including this empty theatre. They were recording *The White Album* at the time. Oddly, McCullin doesn't mention the Mercury Theatre in *A Day In The Life Of The Beatles*, a book containing his best photographs from that crazy day.

44. From the mid-60s, Brian Epstein regularly produced concerts at this famous London theatre on Shaftsbury Avenue. In 1967, The Beatles shot the video for 'Hello, Goodbye' there. The concert Billy Ritchie is referring to took place on 7 May 1967.

45. This list of books, from which the literary quotation at the beginning of each chapter here is taken, will be made public in 2013.

DAVID BOWIE
(SPACE ODDITY)
PHILIPS – 14 NOVEMBER 1969

'What has happened to me is exactly what I willed to happen.
I am my own draughtsman.'
(JOHN BRAINE, *ROOM AT THE TOP*, 1957)

'Of all the characters I'm supposed to have created, probably because he's the one I'm asked about least, I have a soft spot for Major Tom. It may also be because he wasn't a conscious invention. He was more of an emanation of the times, a sort of phantom. And also, it's ironic that this song, "Space Oddity" which has a rather tragic end, was used as a soundtrack for the wanderings of real astronauts. When I wrote it, it was fashionable to be sceptical about the relentless thrust of progress, which was perfectly embodied by the conquest of space. In any case, in my mind, it was never a case of cashing in on mankind's first steps on the moon. [...]

When my father died, I remember vividly that at that moment, I couldn't believe that he was never coming back. Somewhere at the back of my mind, for many years, I always had this feeling he'd come back, that he'd only gone on a very long trip. That's how "Everyone Says 'Hi'" came to me, thinking about my dad and how much I miss him. Our physical relationship no longer exists, there's no longer that bridge.'

DB (1992/2002)

In late January 1969, David Bowie, Hermione Farthingale and John Hutchinson are shooting scenes in London for *Love You Till Tuesday* – a sort of compilation of Scopitone-style music video clips directed by Malcolm J. Thompson, an ex-assistant of Ken Pitt who is working in the film industry. Bowie is wearing a wig because he had his hair cut short a few weeks before for a bit part in *The Virgin Soldiers*, John Dexter's first film. None of the three musicians is particularly thrilled by this project. David met television producer Günther Schneider the previous September while shooting a show in Hamburg. Schneider hinted that the German network ZDF might be interested in such a programme. Well aware that the career of his protégé is at an impasse, and wanting to show his talents to the widest audience, Pitt decided to fund the project himself. But despite his good intentions, *Love You Till Tuesday* will end up widening the gap between them. Similar in style to Bowie's first album – four of the eight filmed songs come from it – released more than a year and a half before, it has little to do with Feathers and even less with what is currently going on in Bowie's head. *Love You Till Tuesday* isn't the only cloud on the horizon because around this time David and Hermione break up, which will have a terrible and long-lasting effect on David.

The silver lining is his new song 'Space Oddity'. At the request of his manager, who wanted at least one new song for *Love You Till Tuesday*, Bowie came up with the tale of Major Tom. It is a serious composition, a sort of prog rock[1] hallucinogenic ballad preceded by a dialogue with 'ground control' and a countdown. He and Hutch recorded it at Clareville Grove as a demo – David acquired a Revox reel-to-reel tape machine in 1968 – with two voices. As well as the influences discussed in the previous chapter, a feeling of isolation pervades the lyrics and will also be felt in some of the other songs on his next album after Hermione broke his heart. The first studio recording of 'Space Oddity' is produced by Jonathan Weston, the music supervisor for *Love You Till Tuesday*. The session takes place at Morgan Studios[2] in early February with Colin Wood on keyboards and flute, Dave Clague on bass and Tat Meager on drums. The recording is later used in the promotional film, which also features a version, with added sound effects, of Bowie's mime act known as *The Mask*, in which his character ends up being unable to remove 'the mask' from his face. In the end, no television network – German or British – will agree to air *Love You Till Tuesday* and it will remain officially unreleased until 1984 when Polygram Video puts it out on VHS. A digitally remastered version (sound and image), with *The Looking Glass Murders*[3] as a bonus, will be available on DVD in 2005 from Universal[4].

Tyrannosaurus Rex's brief tour, which David Bowie opens with a mime act, ends in March. That is also the month when Calvin Mark Lee, a Chinese-American working for Mercury Records, takes it upon himself to convince Lou Reizner to sign David Bowie. Reizner is his boss and doesn't particularly like Bowie's songs so Lee, hoping to make a direct appeal to the label in the US, asks Bowie to record a few demos. Bowie and Hutch tape some Feathers songs, which they are still playing together on stage, along with some new compositions, including breakup tracks 'Letter to Hermione' and 'I'm Not Quite' (which will later become 'An Occasional Dream')[5].

In April, David moves in with Mary Finnigan at 24 Foxgrove Road in Beckenham. She is a journalist and single mother of two children. She and David, with the help of a couple of mutual friends who are renting the upstairs flat, will open an arts lab of the type common in the UK at the time[6]. He wants to perform there himself, but he is also looking to create a buzz by inviting artists he and Finnigan think have potential. The Three Tuns pub on Beckenham High Street provides David and Mary with a room of modest capacity. From May, this place – soon to be named Growth, but better known as the Beckenham Arts Lab – will be central to David Bowie's artistic endeavours. Many bands, musicians and singers, some famous, others less so, will perform at the Three Tuns, including Tim Hollier, Marc Bolan, Steve Harley, Comus, The Strawbs, Keith Christmas, Rick Wakeman, Tucker Zimmermand, Ron Geesin and Peter Frampton[7]. In the mixed-media spirit of Feathers, it will also be open to other forms of expression and host marionette shows, the stand-up comedy of singer-songwriter Lionel Bart (*Oliver!*) and lectures by lama Chime Youngdong Rinpoche.

That spring, the ebullience will be heightened by the sudden arrival of Angela Barnett in Bowie's life. She is a young American student from a well-to-do family, born in Cyprus, educated in Switzerland, and a friend of Calvin Mark Lee and

Lou Reizner. They'd briefly met the year before after a Turquoise performance at the Roundhouse, but they will get to know each other better in early April at the Speakeasy[8], during the first concert by prog rock band King Crimson, with support from Donovan. For a while they will be inseparable and, according to many trustworthy people, Angie[9] will be one of the driving forces behind David's success. They will get married a year later.

Love You Till Tuesday wasn't the waste of time it might appear. It led to the creation of 'Space Oddity', which finally convinced Mercury (under pressure from Calvin Mark Lee) to sign David Bowie. On 20 June, he records the song at Trident Studios with new musicians (Mick Wayne on guitar, Herbie Flowers on bass, Rick Wakeman on the Mellotron and Terry Cox on drums) and also with cellist and string arranger Paul Buckmaster. The same day he signs with his new label, in the presence of Ken Pitt who has negotiated the deal. Tony Visconti wasn't thrilled about the song and chose not to be part of it, but Mercury is very happy with Gus Dudgeon's production and insists that the single is released to coincide with the launch of Apollo 11. 'Space Oddity', with an acoustic version (guitar, vocal, cello) of 'Wild Eyed Boy From Freecloud' on the B-side (this song, like others on the upcoming album, was written at Mary Finnigan's place) comes out on 11 July, five days before the Saturn V rocket launch.

But on the night of 20 July, when Neil Armstrong is stepping onto the moon, the ballad of Major Tom in distress is not aired on the radio. Not wanting to bring bad luck to the astronauts, BBC programmers decided, at the last moment, to pull the song from the playlist. They will only add it back when the mission returns safely. But in their haste, they forgot to warn their television colleagues and 'Space Oddity' will be broadcast alongside the lunar walk. The repercussions are minimal and success is not immediate, but the single receives some good reviews and many radio presenters, especially the inimitable John Peel, are thrilled that Bowie is focusing on his music (Peel is not fond of his mime work) and will play the song on their shows.

David Bowie also starts recording his second album in the summer of 1969, at Trident, with Tony Visconti back at the wheel. Malcolm Toft[10], Barry Sheffield and Ken Scott[11] are the recording engineers. Tony suggests that a London band, called Junior's Eyes, should accompany David. Mick Wayne is their lead guitarist and the other musicians are John 'Honk' Lodge on bass, John Cambridge on drums and Tim Renwick on second guitar. David had met a few of them at a Turquoise show at the Roundhouse the year before, and Visconti had just produced their first (and only) album, *Battersea Power Station*.

At the end of July, Ken Pitt accompanies his artist to Malta, then to Italy, where he takes part in international song festivals[12], but their return to London is overshadowed by the news that David's father is seriously ill. He dies of pneumonia at home in Bromley a few days later.

On 16 August, at a free festival organized by Growth in Beckenham, David Bowie manages to look happy on stage, but is in a dark mood as soon as he comes off. A lot of his musician friends perform that day, including Bridget St John, Amory Kane, Keith Christmas, The Strawbs and Comus. Almost 3,000 people reportedly attended the festival (although Angie Bowie happily doubled this figure in her autobiography) and the event makes a pretty penny, mostly thanks to the food stall that Angie runs for most of the day (Calvin Mark Lee was in charge of poster sales). The money is intended to better equip Growth, but David reproaches his friends for having turned his 'free' festival into a commercial event. Later, when he retells the event in idyllic and bitter-sweet terms in the lyrics of 'Memory Of A Free Festival', some of those close to him will think he has dissociated himself from it.

Around the same time, Angie spots an imposing red-brick Victorian mansion called Haddon Hall at 42 Southend Road in Beckenham. She convinces the owner to rent her the ground floor for a modest price (£7 a week) and she and David move in with Tony Visconti and his girlfriend Liz Hartley. Ken Pitt and Peggy Jones aren't too happy about the arrangement, but until Bowiemania drives them away, Angie will do all she can to turn the place into a perfect, cosy base for David and his musicians. It is at Haddon Hall that he will write most of the songs that will mark the last few miles of his path to fame.

Recording for the album is carried out over several blocks of days, and will last until the autumn. The tenacity of Dick Leahy[13] finally got 'Space Oddity' into the charts in early September. It will stay there for 15 weeks, getting to Number 5 by the end of the following month. Six years later, in 1975, its reissue will get David Bowie to Number 1 in the British charts for the first time. The song will make the charts again, reaching Number 24, just after his death[14].

In October, Bowie makes his first appearance on *Top Of The Pops*, performing 'Space Oddity' with the BBC orchestra conducted by Gus Dudgeon, and takes part in a ten-date tour of the United Kingdom with the band Humble Pie, who had just released their first album, *As Safe As Yesterday Is*. While he had initially planned to perform a mime act, David is opening as a singer-songwriter. Since the audience has not come for him, he receives a lukewarm reception, but he gets along well with members of the band, including his long-term friends

Steve Marriott and Peter Frampton. He then tapes a handful of songs for the *Dave Lee Travis Show* on Radio 1, and Ken Pitt accompanies him on television appearances in Germany and Switzerland. Backed by Junior's Eyes (who sometimes open for him), Bowie headlines a series of concerts in Scotland in early November. They are poorly organized and don't do well, but David notices that people recognize 'Space Oddity' and, even though he only plays his 12-string guitar[15], he feels like he's gaining more and more confidence on stage.

The new LP, called *David Bowie* in the United Kingdom and *Man Of Words/ Man Of Music* in the USA, comes out on 14 November on Philips Records, which distributes Mercury in England. Although Tony Visconti modestly believes the record could have been better if he himself had been better, it is a true reflection of the past year. While in 1967 Derek Fearnley and David Bowie took care of most of the basic arrangements themselves, Bowie contented himself, this time, with giving indications to the musicians suggested by Visconti. He will adopt this method – of giving those he decided to work with the freedom to express themselves in order to get more from them than if they'd just been following orders – right up until his last studio album. For the instrumental part of 'Space Oddity', David urged Mick Wayne to play in octaves in the style of American guitarist Wes Montgomery (a technique borrowed from gypsy jazz), but he appreciated Wayne's input when, to wrap it up and not knowing what else to do, he loosened his low E string and let it vibrate. Similarly, he accepted John Cambridge's suggestion to allow Benny Marshall, The Rats' lead singer, to pepper 'Unwashed And Somewhat Slightly Dazed' with blues harmonica parts. Marshall was with Cambridge the day they recorded that song, one of the two on the album whose vocals were recorded live as the musicians played.

The dominant acoustic guitars have led many to call *Space Oddity* David Bowie's folk-rock album, but the chord progression of 'Unwashed And Somewhat Slightly Dazed' is not typical of that genre. Battered by the year's events, especially those in his private life (his breakup with Hermione Farthingale and the death of his father), Bowie pours everything he has into this song (there's even a nod to Marc Bolan just over halfway through) and takes his time doing it: 'Unwashed And Somewhat Slightly Dazed' is almost seven minutes long. As for his musicians, joined by a brass section, they keep a beat à la Bo Diddley and a jam spirit[16] in the vein of The Band or Neil Young, whose first albums had just come out. Of the two songs David Bowie wrote for the one who left him, 'Letter to Hermione' is the simplest (played on acoustic guitars) and is exactly what the title suggests. The lyrics have a dream-like quality, accentuated by the open chords played by David on his Gibson 12-string guitar that Keith Christmas, called in as backup[17], is content to embellish sensitively.

Following on from his scepticism about the London music scene two years earlier, David casts a wider net and reports, in 'Cygnet Committee'[18], his disillusionment with the hippie movement. As well as being the longest track on the album (almost ten minutes), this prog rock song is an assembly of disparate parts, without verses or chorus, and Tony Visconti ramps it up, conjuring the rhythm of Maurice Ravel's classic *Boléro*.

'Janine' was named after George Underwood's girlfriend of the time, though nobody, least of all George Underwood, could understand why. In 1968, he'd illustrated Tyrannosaurus Rex's first album and he also does the artwork for the back cover of Bowie's second album. 'Janine' is one of the most conventional songs of the record, although, again, the chord progression of the verse is not. David draws some notes from a kalimba (an instrument with metal tines that he found in the studio), while Mick Wayne sparkles on the electric guitar.

'An Occasional Dream', the charming and discreet masterpiece of the album, is another excuse for David to sing about his life with Hermione, with guitar chords that flowed best when he played them. From the delicate bars at the start of the track to the dramatic tones at the end – which, in terms of chord progression, heralds *The Man Who Sold The World* – the song is sublimely orchestrated by Visconti, who turns it into a tribute to the happy couple he watched unravel.

The epic 'Wild Eyed Boy From Freecloud' has a more solemn register – Wagnerian, as Visconti conceded. Tony shows off his talents as an arranger in this song, which was miraculously taped with an orchestra of fifty classical musicians crammed into Trident. On the day of the recording, the studio's brand new 16-track tape machine played up and was only working properly on the last take. Background hiss (the bane of all recording engineers in the days of tape recorders) will remain audible on the track until Rykodisc's reissues. Like more and more of Bowie's lyrics in the late 60s, his inspiration for 'Wild Eyed Boy From Freecloud' came from a number of sources, including Miralepa and Buddhism, as well as Victor de l'Aveyron, a feral child who was discovered living wild in France at the end of the 18th century. French doctor Jean-Marc Gaspard Itard took an interest in the boy and 170 years later, so did filmmaker François Truffaut with *L'Enfant Sauvage*, released in the UK as *The Wild Child*. Aside from being feral, Victor wasn't stupid but suffered from autism, which Bowie couldn't ignore. The grandiloquence of the chorus is mainly due to a descending chord movement, a classic pop trick that David Bowie will go on to use twice on the album *Hunky Dory* ('Changes' and 'Oh! You Pretty Things') and famously in 'All The Young Dudes'. Live with The Spiders From Mars, he will often merge 'Dudes', written for Mott The Hoople, and 'Wild Eyed Boy from Freecloud'.

Many have compared *Space Oddity* with Bob Dylan's music but, when listening to the album closely, it's clear that 'God Knows I'm Good' is the only song that shows any similarity. The lyrics are based on a true story Bowie heard, an elderly person caught red-handed as she was shop-lifting. For the second time on the album, David dispenses with the drums and lets the acoustic guitars ring out (including his 12-string). Needless to say, his nod to Robert Zimmerman will be much stronger in 'Song For Bob Dylan', on *Hunky Dory*.

Space Oddity ends on a high; what continues to amaze to this day is that, in 'Memory Of A Free Festival', for the whole part before the famous 'Hey Jude'-style finale (Marc Bolan is one of the backing vocalists), David Bowie laid down his vocal in one take, accompanying himself on a Rosedale organ. The Rosedale was almost a toy, with ready-made chords on the left of the keyboard and, again, what David got, harmonically, from this instrument barely more sophisticated than a Stylophone, is astounding. Of course, the lyrics are a tribute to the festival held in August in Beckenham, not as David experienced it, but as he wanted to remember it a few days after. For their fans, the breakup of The Beatles marked the end of the 1960s. For Bowie's disciples, it's this song.

On the front of the original (British) album cover, there's a full-face photograph of David taken by Vernon Dewhurst. He appears to be emerging from a geometric image by visual artist Victor Vasarely[19]. In the United States, Philips will be satisfied with a simple blue background. It's a gatefold sleeve (it can be opened, like those for *Aladdin Sane, Diamond Dogs* and *Lodger*), and symbolically illustrates David's kaleidoscopic and tormented mind – having gathered as many elements as he could, hoping to become a catalyst himself, he is starting to extract some of them from his system. But at the end of 1969, the world is not yet ready for this David Bowie. 'Space Oddity' is losing steam in the charts and the new album won't get in at all (*Abbey Road* by The Beatles is dominating). David's second LP is getting mixed reviews from the music press and isn't able to win over an audience, who don't know what to make of him and his ever-changing repertoire (and look – for several months, David's been sporting a curly Syd Barrett hair cut). However, his concert at the Purcell Room on 20 November, entitled *An Evening With David Bowie*, with Comus and Junior's Eyes, turns out to be a relative success (there are just under 300 people in the audience, and the venue could accommodate only about 50 more). But the invitations to music journalists were not properly sent out and, that evening, there are only a few of them.

By December, as he starts to doubt Ken Pitt's ability as a manager, David Bowie agrees to record an Italian version of 'Space Oddity' ('Ragazzo Solo, Ragazza Sola', whose words were written by Milanese lyricist Mogol) at Morgan Studios. Then he hides out at Haddon Hall, appears at the Beckenham Arts Lab and, on Christmas Day, he phones Angie, who's gone to see her parents in Cyprus. He plays her a song he's written for her, 'The Prettiest Star'. At the other end of the line, she is crying. Bowie records it at Trident in January 1970, along with a new version of 'London Bye Ta-Ta'[20]. Tony Visconti, who produces the session, invites Marc Bolan to play some electric guitar, but his heart isn't in it. He is grumpy and, in the end, the charm of the song relies more on its catchy melody and on the groove of Godfrey McLean, the drummer of the soul band Gass (Visconti had just produced a couple of their songs, but not their album *Juju*, released that same year, which was produced by saxophone player Mel Collins), than on Marc's scratched licks[21].

On the night of his birthday, David Bowie is on stage at the Speakeasy with Tony Visconti on bass, Tim Renwick and John Cambridge. He doesn't know what his future will hold, but he has an inkling things are about to change for the better. Later that month, he appears for the first time on the cover of a magazine (*Mirabelle*, for teenagers) and, on 3 February, after a concert with Junior's Eyes at the Marquee, a crucial meeting place for Bowie, John Cambridge introduces him to a friend of his who was in the audience. It is a blond guitarist named Mick Ronson.

Keith Christmas	Jonathan Weston
Tim Renwick	Hermione Farthingale
Paul Buckmaster	Dana Gillespie
Ralph Mace	Mike Vernon
Terry Cox	Mary Finnigan
John Cambridge	Tim Hollier
Tony Visconti	Mark Pritchett
Gus Dudgeon	Bridget St John
	Alan Mair
	Bobbie Seagroatt
	Glenn Goring
	Roger Wootton
	Chris Simpson
	Billy Ritchie
	Steve Harley
	Vernon Dewhurst
	Phil Manzanera

KEITH CHRISTMAS

I'd be lying if I said David Bowie made a strong impression on me when I met him at the Beckenham Arts Lab, but it was obvious that he already had a tremendous following of people interested in him and what he was doing. And also, at that time, 'Space Oddity' hadn't come out yet! I was regularly booked at the Arts Lab, but I can't remember who phoned me to come play on the album – maybe David or someone from his label – but whatever the case, even though I didn't know him very well, it was like a friendly favour. Actually, I had never been on anyone's record before and I didn't get paid for this. I didn't ask for money and they didn't offer me any. So I can't blame them for that. Anyway, I went to this studio near Marble Arch. It was a huge place with a cavernous sound, ideal for recording orchestras[22]. The control room overlooked the studio and we communicated with the recording engineer through an intercom. I don't remember meeting Tony Visconti. The assistant gave us two wooden chairs, one for David and one for me. He set up a mic for him and two more for our acoustic guitars. He had his 12-string guitar and I had my acoustic Fender Palomino. We were facing each other, and of course I didn't know the songs. No one had written any chord chart, so I learned them as David played. I was trying to follow him as best I could, and I remember thinking that being a studio musician might not be that cool! I felt a bit under pressure because there were people around, and his songs were far from simple.

We started with 'Letter To Hermione', and because I liked running riffs, I took a chance and played the one you hear at the start, that David picked up on vocals. I noticed he had a rather instinctive way of playing the guitar. For example, he was the one who thought of these harmonic notes[23]. It could have sounded messy, but it really did work. I enjoyed playing on 'An Occasional Dream', because I heard that it was also about his ex-girlfriend, Hermione, and he sang it really poignantly. We recorded both songs and he did the vocals at the same time. Tony Visconti might have been there, but David was the one explaining what he wanted. As for me, I'm quite a solitary person, so I was listening and watching in that studio, but I didn't really talk to anyone. I honestly think I was there because David wanted me to be – I was pretty much ignored and didn't interact with the others. It was obvious that David's label wanted the sessions to be as cheap as possible. So they didn't hire five different guitar players to see who was the best! Anyway, at the time, I wasn't blown away by the quality of his songs; but of course he became one of the most talented songwriters of his generation. I never had that gift of writing unforgettable pop songs. (2017)

TIM RENWICK

I didn't know much about David Bowie before the sessions for *Space Oddity*. I'd seen him on television with his band, The Manish Boys, which quite impressed me. I was also aware of his Anthony Newleyesque 'The Laughing Gnome', which, I think, confused many people! When I met David at Trident Studios, he'd already recorded 'Space Oddity' with Mick Wayne, of Junior's Eyes, on electric guitar. I also played guitar in the band, which is why they called me in. I found David's songs very interesting right from the start – they were very personal, about girlfriends, his folk club... I wasn't quite sure what to make of him really. We had the feeling he was about to take off as a musician, and maybe even as an actor. Being both at the same time seemed a bit complicated. Of course, you also had the Lindsay Kemp mime training to throw in the pot – that made things very confusing indeed! Perhaps this was why his first hit took more than three months to rise in the Top 20. The public at large didn't really know who he was. Things went quiet after the big hit. There was no successful follow-up to 'Space Oddity', which was, itself, rather a one-off event.

Tony Visconti was very easy to get along with. I was pleasantly surprised to learn that he played the recorder. In school, I'd started a recorder group, so right away we had something in common! We both played it on 'An Occasional Dream'. Tony was a fairly quietly spoken chap from New York. He played bass very well and knew his musical stuff.

At the time, David hired Junior's Eyes to back him up on a series of live shows. The Scottish concerts were a bit odd; the crowds didn't really know what to make of us and most of the songs must have been unfamiliar to them. I seem to remember we had a lukewarm reception! At one of the shows, there was a length of wire netting fixed across the stage. They told us that if the crowd liked us, they might throw things at us... This was way before punk! We wondered what might happen if they didn't like us, but we never had to find out, because they did.

I ran into David again when my band Quiver played at the Roundhouse in 1970. He was headlining that day. Funnily enough, even though I played on his folk-rock recordings, I personally liked his Thin White Duke phase. (2017)

PAUL BUCKMASTER

I met David at the very start of my career, in the office of Gus Dudgeon at Essex Music, David Platz's music publishing company. I'd been writing arrangements for less than a year and he came off as a very nice person, and funny too. That day, my manager Tony Hall was also there and David and I soon got chatting about our favourite sci-fi authors. He played 'Space Oddity' for us on his guitar in Gus's office[24]. I was given total freedom to write what I pleased, and they didn't change a single note of my arrangements. I wrote the sheet music for all the instruments, wrote down the chords for the guitarist and orchestrated the flutes, as well as a small string section. The session at Trident took place in the morning, from 10am to 1pm. I think we recorded on one of the first 8-tracks in London[25] but, in order to get everything on tape, many elements had to be bounced[26]. Rick Wakeman was asked to play that cheesy Mellotron 'string' part, and David recorded his 12-string guitar at the same time as the group. Then he played the Stylophone. As far as I recall, the strings and flutes were done as a stereo overdub. 'Space Oddity', including vocals, was taped within the three-hour union session. 'Wild Eyed Boy From Freecloud' took even less time. David's voice, his acoustic guitar and my cello, which I improvised, were recorded together in one take. (2017)[27]

RALPH MACE

When I met David Bowie, I was running the pop department at Philips Records. My job was to promote the label's artists in Europe. The first thing that struck me was that he seemed really young. He looked more like a student than a musician! I had almost no knowledge of his music, but I noticed that he had a little team around him. Many people have said that Bowie was obsessed with success, but when I met him, he was more worried about his next song, his next gig. He was always wondering whether he should use a band or sing alone, accompanying himself on guitar. He was worried that his upcoming concerts weren't being properly advertised. 'Space Oddity' changed David's life, but the song wasn't an immediate hit and the people who worked in promotion – except for Dick Leahy, who insisted we backed it – wanted to pull it from our list. Obviously, man's first steps on the moon encouraged the general public to buy the single. But what if one of the astronauts had been stranded out there, like Major Tom? (2016)

TERRY COX

My involvement with David Bowie was sadly very brief. When I was asked to play drums on 'Space Oddity', I was in the band Pentangle. Just before, we'd been on television with The Strawbs and David had performed a mime act. I think it was Gus Dudgeon who suggested me and he got Herbie Flowers on bass for what I think was his first studio session[28]. At this point, I'm bound to tell you that much of my musical life came about by luck, an important part of my life in the deep end. What I also remember is that Gus covered my drums with a blanket to get the sound he wanted on 'Space Oddity'. All went very well and this trick, like the final cut, passed into history. (2017)

JOHN CAMBRIDGE

I met David at Haddon Hall and I actually remember he was late as he was already very busy. He seemed quite normal to me, compared with the Junior's Eyes members – who were more the beatnik hippie type, with long hair and everything... When we were recording the album, he wasn't bossy at all. At the start of the session, he would play a song for us once or twice, so we could pick up the structure and chords. Then we'd play the track for a while, and he'd suggest doing a take. We'd usually do one or two and that was it – he and Tony had what they wanted. The style was very different from that of Junior's Eyes. In our music, there were quite a few guitar solos, but David's songs centred more on the melody, and were definitely more 'poppy'. (2016)

TONY VISCONTI

In the spirit of 'let's have an artist's commune and all live together,' Angela and David proposed that we join them in sharing a place in Beckenham, Kent. They had found a huge flat in Haddon Hall, a large Victorian mansion on Southend Road; it was about a ten-minute walk to the train station and from there it was a forty-five minute journey to London. The front door of the beautiful old building opened directly into a vast hall; at the far end was a staircase leading to a wrap-around 'gallery'. In the gallery were sealed up doorways, which once led to the bedrooms of the family who had originally lived there when it was first built; these had been converted into seven separate flats. To the right of the entrance was a small kitchen and bathroom. Just beyond that was David and Angela's bedroom; Liz and I took the back bedroom. On the left was our sparsely furnished communal living room; we were always short of furniture. Soon after we moved in, Angela flew to Cyprus to spend the holidays with her parents. It was quite cold; there was no central heating and we would huddle round the big fireplace in the hallway. Our landlord, Mr Hoy, a charming septuagenarian, allowed us to create a rehearsal space in the basement. While it was a splendid setting for a commune, we all had the distinct feeling that it was haunted. And it was.

David and I were both Beatles fans. Most musicians our age were at the time. We lived in their shadow and were always in awe of them. A topic of discussion would be: 'How did they make that sound?' Their song-writing influenced all of us, especially coming up with 'Beatlesque' chord changes. I know my favourite Beatle was John, and perhaps he was David's too. After all, he eventually recorded 'Fame' and 'Across The Universe' with him years later. I don't recall, however, that David ever said he had a favourite Beatle.

After David was dropped from Deram, he didn't stay disappointed for long. He had other things in his life that he was pursuing, like his mime performances with Lindsay Kemp, his Feathers group with Hermione and Hutch, and his romance with Hermione took up much of his time. I found him very optimistic actually, despite being dropped from the label. He had also begun his Arts Lab in Beckenham at the Three Tuns pub and that afforded him a lot of time to be the curator and the performer, trying new songs on the audience. I used to sit in on bass with him. I was also very close to Marc Bolan; he and David were both ambitious, but I would say that David was less obvious about it and Marc was more overtly ruthless about his ambitions. It was clear that they admired each other, yet they understood they were in competition. I know that David always liked Marc as a friend and they knew each other before they met me. I have the feeling that David always wished Marc well, but that didn't necessarily go both ways...

I didn't produce the 1969 version of 'Space Oddity', but I did work on the much more minimalist one that came out on the B-side of 'Alabama Song' in 1980. I don't want to rehash this old chestnut, but I do love the song and I have re-recorded it and remixed several versions of it over the past decades for various purposes. I even performed it live on many occasions and wrote and conducted a string arrangement when David performed it with Philip Glass for one of the Tibet House charity concerts in Carnegie Hall. I'd just like to say that my original objection to 'Space Oddity' was that it was inappropriate at that stage of my young folk-rock artiste's career. I told him it could be a hit, but he would find it hard to follow up with a second hit single. As it happened, it did take several re-releases to become a hit and our follow up, 'The Prettiest Star', was a massive flop. It would take the invention of Ziggy Stardust to come back to the style of that 'Oddity'[29], maybe two years after it was a hit... Anyway, there was never a grudge. We are okay with how history played out. 'Space Oddity' is almost the definitive David Bowie song, the one the public probably recognizes the most.

Trident has become a mythical place for anyone who loves David Bowie's music. It was an amazing place, created by the Sheffield brothers, yet full of quirks and inconsistencies. It was the first really great indie studio and they ran it in an unorthodox way at the time. Unlike EMI, there were no senior engineers there, they were all young and hip! Marc, David and I loved the place. It was in fashionable Soho and conveniently very near cool food places, pubs and public transport. Sometimes the equipment didn't work too well in the first year or so because the tape machines came from America and needed a 60 Hz current to operate at the right speed. I was the first to use their new 16-track on 'Wild Eyed Boy From Freecloud' and they took that machine out of the box the night before. It was a nightmare! But soon The Beatles used it and the floodgates opened. It was hard to get into after a while, which led me to build my own professional 16-track studio in my home, where I lived with my wife, Mary Hopkin, and our young son, Morgan. My console of choice was, of course, a Trident! It was designed and built by Trident house engineer Malcom Toft.

They might all seem like bridges to *Ziggy Stardust*[30], but the albums David recorded before it are very important. He was simultaneously learning new writing and recording techniques at a very rapid rate. He was forming his very complex style, which encompasses many genres. Eventually he would feel comfortable throwing himself into great albums that were extremely diverse, like *Young Americans* and *Heathen*. If you were to represent David Bowie as a tree trunk, you would need to have many limbs and branches growing out of him to symbolize all the styles he has not only mastered, but also created, spawning new genres of pop music.

When we remixed 'Space Oddity' for its 50th-anniversary edition, a lot of memories came back. For example, the recording of 'Wild Eyed Boy From Freecloud'. The orchestra musicians were packed into the studio like sardines, in a long rectangular room, and David, who was playing his 12-string alongside them, was sitting in the middle. When I remixed the track, I noticed there was quite a bit of 'leakage'[31] on the microphones, but the sound was glorious. David didn't sing live thankfully. It took me five days to write the orchestra arrangements and I did it with my classical guitar! For 'An Occasional Dream', Tim Renwick was playing a clarinet and a flute and I played two recorders. David's 12-string was impeccable, as it was on the rest of the album. His timing was even better than the drummer's... As for 'Memory Of A Free Festival', it was the only song where I was bold enough to change the ending. Obviously I didn't add anything, but there was some material on the tape that hadn't been used. In any case, I was delighted to have been able to remix *Space Oddity*. I've been waiting 50 years for that. (2007/2015/2019)

GUS DUDGEON

I could never thank Tony Visconti enough for dumping the 'Space Oddity' session on me! Thing is, I never understood what his problem was with the song – personally, I never thought it was too commercial or opportunistic. It was David's label who thought releasing the single at the same time as the Apollo mission was a good idea... Ken Pitt was getting nowhere with him, and when Mercury signed him, our own personal mission was to record him as cheaply as possible. Before the session, I spent quite a bit of time listening to the demos to avoid wasting too much time in the studio... Tony thought the song would only be a B-side... When you think about it, he was lucky that David didn't hold a grudge, and that he still let him do the rest of the album! I would have liked to produce that too, but I was warned: I was only going to be working on 'Space Oddity'. But that's okay, because its success boosted my career. I was asked to produce Elton John because he and Bernie Taupin loved the song, especially its arrangements, and they decided to bring in Paul Buckmaster. He recommended me to produce Elton's second album. Their first choice had been George Martin[32], but George refused because he also wanted to do the arrangements, and that's how I got the job! Since then, hardly a week goes by without someone telling me they love the sound and atmosphere of 'Space Oddity'. The musicians played to perfection and I think I even managed to make the sound of the Stylophone tolerable! Mick Ronson is one of the reasons I would have liked to continue to produce David, but Tony, and later Ken Scott, did an excellent job with him. And I had Elton anyway, just like Tony had Bolan. With those two, we had a lot on our plate. (1990)

JONATHAN WESTON

I was at the Royal College of Art in London, and I had my own band in which I played saxophone. In 1965, I met Denny Cordell who worked for Essex Music and became my mentor. He was a flamboyant guy who travelled a lot and, in addition to being a producer, he was an A&R executive. That's around the time I met David. He had a very good sense of humour and as a singer-songwriter he was already a free spirit. I think I remember that he painted too, and he sometimes gave the impression that music wasn't his priority. But he 'played guitar'! We bumped into each other a lot and I saw him even more when Ken Pitt was managing him.

I was also friends with Malcolm Thomson, which is how I ended up working on *Love You Till Tuesday*. It was pretty ambitious – the first pop videos in a way. Hermione and Hutch, David's musician friends, were in it as well as Suzy Mercer, one of the two girls you see in the 'Space Oddity' sequence, who was my girlfriend back then. While we were working on *Love You Till Tuesday*, we thought the songs from David's first album were okay, but we needed a stronger one. I pointed that out to him and he laughed and said, 'Okay, I'll write something tonight.' So we ended up with 'Space Oddity', which he played for us at his place, or maybe it was Malcolm's... Either way, Malcolm came up with the title of the song, which was about an astronaut in his 'tin can'...

We did it in two night sessions at Morgan Studios. We didn't waste any time: the main track one evening, the rest the following day, just before mixing. A band came and recorded at the same time as David sang and played the Stylophone. It wasn't any more complicated than that. I would have liked it to become a single, but David was tied up with Essex Music, and other people including Tony Visconti, and he re-recorded the song later. Of course, that is the version people know. I never really compared the two, but I'm sure there are many similarities between them. Honestly, it didn't take us more than one or two takes to tape 'Space Oddity'. In those days, musicians really recorded together, and you can tell!

Later on, I'd occasionally run into David, in airports, and he even came to my wedding in 1982, when I married actress Leslie Ash. Actually I have a little story from 1975: in those days, he was working on the music for *The Man Who Fell To Earth* with Paul Buckmaster in Los Angeles and I happened to be living there too. One day, his driver came over in a limousine and gave me a drawing by David with writing underneath that said, 'You know that without the song we recorded for *Love You Till Tuesday*, I wouldn't be where I am today...' I thought that was really nice of him. (2016)

HERMIONE FARTHINGALE

The sad thing is that what remains of Feathers is the film *Love You Till Tuesday*; it is absolutely not representative of us. Feathers was brief but what we were doing was quite dark, it was mixed media. When you watch it, you can see how Hutch and I were just slotted on the side, without any real artistic justification. We were incredibly uncomfortable and looked a bit like a poor version of Peter, Paul And Mary. Hutch and I didn't make a single penny from our appearance in *Love You Till Tuesday* and, in late 1968, I had to look for work. After I'd auditioned for *Song Of Norway*, I dreaded being chosen for the role but, when I was picked, my financial situation meant I had no other choice but to take it. While we were doing *Love You Till Tuesday*, I'd already started rehearsing for *Song Of Norway*. I knew that it would complicate things for David and me because shooting began in February and I was going to be stuck in Lillehammer, Norway, for several months. But I've always followed my instinct. I continued to dance, I even went to the United States for a bit... Maybe things didn't turn out exactly the way I'd imagined. Since then, people joke that I left David Bowie just before his rise to stardom, to focus on my career, and that no one knows who I am now. But I wasn't trying to be famous, it wasn't my intention at all, I just wanted to work... It's both moving and difficult for me to listen to 'Letter To Hermione' and 'An Occasional Dream' because they are heartfelt songs and I understand every line of both. We didn't burn 'one hundred days', as he sings, but we did have blue sheets... (2016)

DANA GILLESPIE

Once David phoned me and said, 'I've just written a song I think might be something special. I wrote it half an hour ago.' Ten minutes later he was at the door and came in to play 'Space Oddity' on the guitar. That's the kind of relationship we had. He was desperate to play it for me and I knew right away that it was going to lead to great things. He was so determined, so ambitious, that his success seemed certain. Long before he was giving press interviews and frequenting radio or television studios, he hung out at places where other musicians were. For example, if he heard about a record launch party, he'd go to it. He was slowly building a network of contacts. When I was invited on *Ready Steady Go!*, he helped me choose the songs. When his career was taking off and he could have just focused on himself, he continued to give me advice and to support me in his own way. That evening, he suggested I sing 'Love Is Strange'[33]. I remember that in order to convince me, he hummed the bass line to me, which he knew by heart. (2016)

MIKE VERNON

After Gus had the chance to make his mark with 'Space Oddity', he continued with Elton John and achieved the success we all know him for. In those days, I had my own label and I lost touch with Gus a bit, but I knew things were going well for him as a producer. We remained close until the end[34] and today, of all my friends who have passed away, he's one of the ones I miss the most. (2016)

MARY FINNIGAN[35]

David's professional expertise in the music department is impressive from the start. His gear is battle-scarred by many gigs and clumsy roadies. But he decides on what he needs, tests it and assembles it in a manner that does not create an obstacle course for my children. Naturally they are intrigued by the activity, especially Caroline, who has learned to play the Stylophone and is hoping to be invited on stage. And she was, a couple of weeks later. I was misty-eyed as I watched her, so pretty and self-assured, perched on a stool behind a microphone in a red velvet trouser suit playing the Stylophone part in 'Space Oddity'.

It turns out that David is well integrated into a network of folk musicians in London and has no trouble finding a headline act for our first night. He chooses Tim Hollier, who agrees to play for a measly fee – which is generous on his part. We have no idea if any, or how many, paying customers will turn up and, as a result, no idea if we will be able to pay him anything.

While David takes care of the music, I get to grips with the décor. On the basis of my experience at London's psychedelic clubs, I commandeer all our Indian bedspreads, every cushion in the flat and as many San Francisco and Indian posters as I can muster. I buy candles and incense and liberate cups and saucers from the kitchen to hold them. My big hit is an early version of a light projector, lent to me by Barry Lowe, a London friend and psychedelic lightshow artist. I find plain white sheets to hang on the wall behind the stage so I can project a show onto them. Barry has given me a brief tutorial on how to operate his contraption, and now I am on my own. (2016)

TIM HOLLIER

I met David Bowie in the autumn of 1968. I was with my wife Wendy and my first album, *Message To A Harlequin*, had just been released on United Artists. He was really nice and humble. We were not well known at the time, but I think we understood what each other was about. I'd just spent five years at art college, art being, of course, David's other love, so that brought us together. In terms of our wardrobe, we were pretty similar because we both got some inspiration from The Fool[36] and we liked what they sold at the Apple boutique. To be honest, I didn't know much about David's music, but I immediately noticed his stuff was very different. It was the way he 'acted' through his songs and poems, instead of simply singing or reciting them. I'd never seen anyone able to sing an a capella song about eating a fly at the age of five without being sick!

I was really glad David invited me to the opening of the Beckenham Arts Lab and surprised to see that I was the only one on the bill that evening, in addition to him... If I remember correctly, I must have performed there four or five times altogether. David was starting to break into the folk scene, but even though he looked different, he wasn't as well-known as Nick Drake, Peter Sarstedt[37], Roy Harper or Al Stewart... At the end of May 1969, I performed at the venerable Wigmore Hall, a major classical music venue in London, with American singer-songwriter Amory Kane. Guitarist Rick Cuff was also there, a Canadian with whom I wrote most of my songs. It was a pretty ambitious performance with a light show and sound effects. David, who at the time was working with Lindsay Kemp, offered to do a mime show on the side of the stage during our last song, 'Evolution'. When he came on, he was wearing a sort of astronaut suit and over the course of the song he stripped down until he was practically naked. Needless to say, the folk audience was pretty stunned!

I wasn't surprised to see him make it big a few years later. He had something not seen in many of us: presence. Whenever he walked into a room, you felt it immediately, even if you had your back to the door. But I never really understood why he dressed the way he did! He really was a special artist. The last time I saw him, he was on the steps of Ken Pitt's flat – he was wearing a tweed suit. We hugged and that was the last I ever saw of him. I never went to any of David's concerts when he was Ziggy Stardust, but Ziggy was wonderful. Of course I carried on following his career and I think 'Ashes To Ashes' has never been bettered in the field of pop music as an art form. (2016)

MARK PRITCHETT

In the spring of 1969, I was walking around Beckenham when I noticed a flyer pinned to a tree. It was announcing the first get-together at the Three Tuns pub with singers, musicians, performance artists... People of all artistic persuasions were welcome. The following Sunday I went along and, over the next few weeks, read some of my poetry and played guitar. David and I got on well. Come the day of his free festival in August, he was super-animated, but it turned out we were short of mics. I told David I had some at my flat. We jumped into his Fiat 500 and went to my place. As we pulled up, David said, 'Amazing! I've just leased the ground-floor flat in that big old place opposite!' The big old place opposite was Haddon Hall.

Until I first heard David at the Three Tuns I had no idea of him or his music. Within a few minutes of first seeing him before me, perched on a stool, 12-string in hand, I knew I was in front of a talent that connected to me, especially lyrically. He was charming on that stool – funny, disarming and forthright. In those days between 50 and 70 people were enthusiastic about his songs...

But, more than this, I found David very supportive of my poetry and the songs I was writing for my college band Rungk. He attended some rehearsals from time to time and I can assure you that his advice didn't fall on deaf ears! His look was pretty standard late hippie – coloured jeans, t-shirt, Afghan coat, long, blond, tousled hair... Maybe not every mother's dream son-in-law, but certainly less stressful than bringing home a Rolling Stone! (2019)

BRIDGET ST JOHN

I don't remember everything that happened in the 60s in London, but I do remember David Bowie in Beckenham, especially the famous free festival he sings about in his song. That day, in a house near where the concerts were taking place, he played the acetate of 'Space Oddity' for us on a little record player. I was young and very impressed by this song, which he played several times. It was my first contact with his music and what struck me right away was that it didn't sound like anything I'd heard before. I came to the Three Tuns at the very start of my career, which was incredibly intimidating because everything was new to me. I was naive, very shy. I didn't have a driving licence, so I had to take a train to get there, and even that was overwhelming! What I remember of Bowie was that he was very down-to-earth, likeable and approachable... He did everything to make the artists feel welcome. We didn't talk a lot, and I was very surprised to have been invited as I had only started to play gigs less than six months before... I always wondered how he'd heard about me. It was proof that he already had his ear to the ground, listening to everything that was going on. But I felt comfortable playing there and, as I said, it was like a whole new world for me really. There was such a good energy around. (2018)

ALAN MAIR

Towards the end of The Beatstalkers, I started making a few clothes, initially because it was hard to find cool stuff in Scotland. After the band broke up in 1969, I needed to travel to London more often, so Ken Pitt offered to have me to stay at his place on Manchester Street. I lived there for about a year. David would still go there fairly often. That's where we really became mates. We'd go to concerts and, since he didn't have a driving licence, he'd sometimes ask me to drive him to the Three Tuns. There was just a handful of people, but there was a nice bustle and David took the Arts Lab very seriously. I remember that when we got home, Ken would scratch his head, wondering what he was going to do with David. The late-60s trippy-hippie vibe wasn't exactly his thing... Once, Ken asked me if I wanted to be David's tour manager but, having been a musician, I thought it was the worst job in the world, so I turned him down. To be honest, at the time, I never thought that David Bowie would become a huge star. However, I did understand his ability to make his songs appetizing, just by the way he would perform them. Watching him sing in a room, sitting on a chair or cross-legged on the bed, you couldn't help but be impressed by his confidence. (2018)

BOBBIE SEAGROATT

The first time I saw David Bowie was at the Beckenham Arts Lab, but nobody introduced us. I was 16 years old, I'd just joined Comus and I was just starting out with this prog rock band, which David really liked. Actually, that was my first gig. David was very nice, very friendly, very pleasant to be around. So, at the time, I was singing harmonies on songs that already existed before my arrival, I played a bit of tambourine... I listened to The Beatles, like everyone, but I didn't know much about what was happening in the charts. I don't think I even heard 'Space Oddity' when it came out as a single, so I wouldn't have made the connection to David when I met him. Bands like Comus were in their own little bubble, the blasé kind, and they weren't really impressed by anybody. I belonged to that universe and had the tendency to act the same way.

Of course, I remember the festival David organized, the one that inspired the song. Comus was one of the main attractions that day, and it must have been the first time I heard him sing 'Space Oddity'. You know, I've never been awestruck by anything, so I wasn't particularly impressed by Bowie. To be honest, I used to get dreadfully nervous of doing anything in public so, before getting on stage, I was trying to concentrate, and maybe subconsciously I was trying not to let myself be distracted or intimidated by anything or anyone else... The funny thing is, we always talk about this festival because of the song, even though he organized another one a year later that was really nice and just as important for us.

I also clearly remember the time we opened for David Bowie at the Purcell Room. I thought he was really good that night.

In 2013, my husband and I were on stage with David Tibet at the Meltdown festival. We'd known him for a while and were members of his band, Current 93. That day, he was performing with Myrninerest, another band he'd asked us to join. The concert was at Queen Elizabeth Hall and I found a moment to go and poke my head into the Purcell Room, which was in the same building and wasn't locked up. I hadn't been there since November 1969. (2016)

GLENN GORING

I first met David Bowie in the spring of 1969 when Comus, the band in which I played guitar, performed at the Three Tuns pub in Beckenham. The Arts Lab – founded there by David Bowie and Mary Finnigan – held its weekly events in the spacious back room of the pub. David was really enthusiastic about Comus and we were the nominated resident band. The first time we played there, I remember David sitting cross-legged on the floor, just a few feet away from the bar-stool on which I was sitting. He was rocking backwards and forwards, a big grin on his face, enthralled. This impressed me, as he had already made a name for himself as a singer-songwriter and here he was, revelling in Comus' music.

David regularly headlined at the Arts Lab (Comus and David shared the residency). I was really struck when, sitting on the same bar-stool I'd just vacated, David produced the famous Stylophone and performed 'Major Tom'. The Stylophone was seen at the time as a kind of toy, made famous by Rolf Harris. It was not generally taken seriously as a musical instrument in its own right. It looked so insignificant resting on David's knees as he began to slide the small plastic stylus across the metallic 'keyboard'. I had to ask myself what the hell he was doing. But suddenly, hearing those warbling notes booming out of the PA, this 'toy' was transformed into something totally unique. It had, for me, a strange mixture of the cheap-and-nasty and, at the same time, something much more haunting and profound. David would also play along to a tape machine set up behind him on the small, cluttered dais and sync his performances with pre-recorded tracks. I don't remember seeing anything like it before. It was typically David. He was constantly surprising, original and eminently entertaining.

The Beckenham Arts Lab, as it was officially called, was always busy with musicians, artists, poets. Being young at the time, I saw it as a real community of like-minded folk in the midst of a very creative enterprise and environment. People wanted to be part of it and learn about it. And, as far as I recall, no particular trend or social group was excluded. You'd meet all kinds of people who'd drifted over from the other bars to see what all the fuss was about and got drawn in. Maybe I'm idealizing it, but I can't remember there being any fights or trouble there. Everyone seemed to get on well. As David once commented, it was no pseud's corner. I guess that was the biggest crime: pretending to be something you were not.

Shortly after I moved to Beckenham, I bumped into David one afternoon while travelling on a bus. I hadn't known him long. He was older than me by several years and much more confident and self-assured. In fact, being a bit shy, I sometimes found him a little intimidating. He wasn't one to mince his words, as they say. The bus was a 194, heading in the direction of West Wickham. I got on and saw David sitting toward the back, on the left. He was alone, staring out of the window. I caught his eye and we exchanged nods, but he didn't smile, as he normally would have. He turned back to his window, apparently distracted by the passing world. I sat down next to him. He didn't look up or turn my way. It was obvious he wasn't in the mood for conversation. Eventually I broke the silence and asked him how he was. Then, with a hint of anger and bitterness in his voice, he came straight out with it: 'My father's just died.' And that was that. I was stunned. I sat there, immobilized, unable to comment. I couldn't even utter a cliché like, 'I'm very sorry to hear that, David', because, as this phrase formed in my head, it sounded like some crass, throwaway remark from a bad film. But, a second passed, and those very words just tumbled out of my mouth. It was as if they had a will of their own – anything to fill the gaping vacuum that had opened up. The bus rumbled on, and David and I sat in complete silence. I had no idea where he was going and I had missed my stop. (2016)

ROGER WOOTTON

We first met David at the Three Tuns pub, where the Arts Lab was to be held. He and Mary Finnigan, with whom he had shared a flat, explained that they wanted to start this weekly, mainly folk-orientated venue and needed a resident band. Comus had just formed and were also based in Beckenham. It was the launching pad for both David and ourselves. Most of the time David performed on his own, on a 12-string guitar. He used a tape recorder for the backing guitar part of 'Space Oddity' and played the Stylophone live, which was very innovative. He used to play most of the material that ended up on the *Space Oddity* album, including the Jacques Brel songs. He was quite extrovert on stage, but fairly quiet otherwise. I think we were all focused on our art.

A few days after his father died, we played with him at the famous free festival in Beckenham, but I did not notice any particular melancholy. His performance was as it had been at the Beckenham Arts Lab with the same material. It's important to remember that Angie was much more outgoing and vivacious. She was very much the drive behind him and helped promote him. She was wild and exciting and a very good cook.

Comus' first major gig was An Evening With David Bowie at the Purcell Room. It went well for all and I remember there were a lot of fans from Beckenham in the audience. We shared this one enormous dressing room, where we watched David put on make-up and display an ambiguous image for the first time. This would have been around the time of the release of *The Man Who Sold The World*. He played most of the tracks and was with a band similar to The Spiders From Mars. I once had dinner with them at Haddon Hall, in 1972, where he played me the *Ziggy Stardust* album on tape before it was released. Honestly, I didn't see the impact of glam rock coming. Few people did. (2016)

CHRIS SIMPSON

We had made the first Magna Carta album[38] using my self-penned songs in Phonogram's London studios. There were three of us – and we were not at all sure where it would lead. If it would, in fact, lead anywhere! We set off across England, playing in the folk clubs that had sprung up like mushrooms in every town and village. We found a ready audience who, much to my relief, loved what we did. In fact, the very first gig was in the Coalhole Folk Club in Cambridge – we went in with ten songs, mostly off the album, and we played them all. And then, believe it or not, we played them again. Nobody minded and off we went back to London five pounds richer and full of the fact that what we had seemed to work.

London then was a stimulating scene, vibrating to the sound of rhythm'n'blues, folk, rock'n'roll and what came to be known as 'progressive' rock. But 'the times they were a-changin''. Bob Dylan and Joan Baez arrived in London and added to the whole cavalcade, kicking over the traces and heralding the dawn of a new era in both music and fashion. Then the vast, rolling gravy train was ignited by the unforeseen explosion of four lads from a one-time jazz cellar on Mathew Street in Liverpool, which after some 200 gigs had turned into a rock'n'roll Valhalla. No one in their wildest dreams would have imagined that a musical Armageddon would come out of this cold, grimy backwater in the north-west, from a stark and forbidding city, resplendent only in past glory. They were, of course, The Beatles.

This whole scene was a fertile bed that spawned, among so many, The Rolling Stones, The Kinks, Free, Small Faces, The Who. And, folk-wise, The Pentangle, who based their sound on the brilliant twin acoustic guitar sound of Bert Jansch and John Renbourn and the brilliant string bass of Danny Thomson. He played on our first album and wrote the sleeve notes. It meant that we were able to play support to The Pentangle, emphasizing the point that, as is so often the case, to get the breaks it is not what you know, but who you know. We were very lucky.

One night, on returning from Manchester down the freezing motorways to London, I decided to break the rules and write a concept album. By dawn I had finished it, written on cornflakes packets and containing soliloquys – spoken word. Things ran on ahead from there. Gus Dudgeon heard it and wanted to produce it. He saw us live with The Pentangle at the Lyceum and, having sold a creditable number of copies of the first album, we were off, so to speak. Gus had learned production the only way, starting off as a tape operator at Decca Studios. He was just brilliant and became a good friend. The production on the first album was a very unskilled business. Gus was the opposite – great intuition and a studio craftsman. He was also beginning to record songs written by an office boy from DJM Records called Reg Dwight, who played in a band called Bluesology. At one point Gus said to me, 'Oh, I wish he and his writing partner, Bernie, could come up with a hit!' Much later, Reg changed his name to Elton John, and the rest is history.

Around this time Gus had, I sense, some animosity towards an anglicized New York producer – Tony Visconti – over just who did what in a hit recording by a Beckenham Arts Lab folkie with a pseudo-Afro haircut. The artist called himself

David Bowie. When we discussed the production of *Seasons* with Gus, he said we should have Tony Visconti as an arranger. I'd noticed that, for Elton's arrangements, Gus always used Paul Buckmaster from Third Ear Band. We met Tony and I was so impressed by his grasp of everything musical. He was lovely. And incredible. Then, aware that we were now walking in the corridors of musical greats, we were suddenly in Tony's house in South London. Tony was so hospitable. He lived in a lovely, fragile Edwardian house, sleeping on the edge of rolling lawns. Tony pointed out that the ghost of a young girl often strolled through the grounds beneath a parasol. We sat there with our acoustic guitars to run through *Seasons* with him. 'Do you mind if a friend drops in?' Tony asked. 'He lives upstairs.'

We were fine with that, and a young guy came on down with his wife, Angie, and introduced himself. Slim, curly hair, sparkling eyes and, I noted, long fingers. And a dichotomy in his eyes. The man was David Robert Jones... He introduced himself as David Bowie. I thought, 'Oh wow, this is a man with a hit record.' Gulp. We played, on two acoustic guitars, the whole 21 minutes of *Seasons*. When it ended, David sat on the floor, silent, staring a hole in the trendy, elegant, sanded floorboards, next to Angie... A warm summer breeze ruffled the trees in the garden beyond the French windows, half open to allow the voices of the summer to seep through. Oh, that the vignette with the parasol would silently parade like gossamer across the summer lawn beyond David's head... Silence. As if in silent contemplation of the floorboards, hands crossed over his knees, he said, 'That is one of the most beautiful things I ever heard.' And that is the sheer, inescapable, fragile beauty of music – ineffable, indestructible, emotive, evocative – and alternately heartbreaking or uplifting. The triumph of creation. There will always be music.

Roll forwards to the next year. Along with Dusty Springfield and an all-star cast, we were on stage at the London Palladium for a royal charity show. I was delighted to meet David again. We rehearsed our set and played the show. David went out with curls akimbo and sang 'Space Oddity' and an assorted – I thought, privately, innocuous – collection of tunes. Afterwards, so sadly, I tried to sober up a broken Dusty Springfield. Back in David's dressing room, we nattered on about rock'n'roll destruction and then he put his hand on my arm and said, 'Chris, my dread in this world we are in? I don't want to be just another one-hit wonder...'

'Don't worry', I said, 'That won't happen to you.' But such is the way of things in our nefarious world, I was not so sure. Lady Public is a fickle mistress.

The last time I saw him, I was going up one side of Wardour Street, he up the other. We met and hugged each other in the middle of the road. 'Hey man,' he said, 'weren't you always into that Elvis/Sun thing?' For sure. I followed him up into Trident Studios and hooked up with Marc Bolan on an acoustic outfit called Tyrannosaurus Rex. On a borrowed Les Paul, we cooked our way through an afternoon of Memphis music riffs. For some reason, I thought the song was called 'The Prettiest Star'... I will never know but, some years later, in conversation with Scotty Moore, Elvis's guitar player, I asked about Memphis riffs. 'You were born to it,' he said. So was my friend for a short while – David Bowie. (2016)

BILLY RITCHIE

There wasn't such a thing as prog rock when David and I were friends. The only version of what it would become around that time was us – 1-2-3. David loved what we did and, even in recent times[39] he has commented about that. He would always support experimentation and creativity, he was that kind of person. That's why I found it difficult to understand why he often did 'safe' stuff, though I now realize it was probably because of the pressures of the record business and money issues. We were close, up until 'Space Oddity' was a hit. He had played me that song ages before, and my comment was that it sounded like The Bee Gees – and it did! David's approach was always to hear a voice in his head that wasn't his – like an actor – and use that as a vehicle for his song or comment. Just before 'Space Oddity' hit the charts, he came with me to a concert we did at the Royal Albert Hall. He was in the dressing room with me, Jethro Tull and Ten Years After. I recently told Ian Anderson that, and Ian was really surprised. 'I don't remember that!' he said. But of course, David was just a bloke then, not the famous Thin White Duke.

I didn't see him for a while after that – I suppose the hit song took over for a time – then we played together at the Brighton Dome[40]. David's first quarter of an hour on stage went really badly. He only played a few songs, then got loudly booed and had to leave the stage. He came off pretty upset and we walked up to him to say hello. Harry and Ian reached him first; I was some way behind. As they approached, it seemed that David was 'blanking' Ian and Harry, acting like he didn't know them. He actually said, 'Do I know you?' and he wasn't joking. I felt the hairs on the back of my neck stand up and I quickened my steps. David looked up and saw me striding purposely towards him; our eyes met and he even looked a bit scared. I pointed at him aggressively and said, 'Why don't you go fuck yourself?', then turned and walked away. He had a girl on his arm, and I only found out when I did a recent Sky show called *Trailblazers* that the girl was Annie Nightingale, the famous BBC DJ.

She told the TV producers that she took David to the pub afterwards because he was upset about the audience's reaction, but also because a friend had sworn at him – me! After the Brighton Dome, David tried to get in touch with me several times, but I avoided him. I was really annoyed with him and the way he had behaved though, in hindsight, I realize he was probably suffering from the experience on stage, so it wasn't a great moment for either of us. Ian and Harry always said afterwards that I was unreasonable and that David was OK with them after the initial misunderstanding. I wasn't convinced. (2017)

STEVE HARLEY

I first saw David at the Beckenham Arts Lab, sitting on his stool with his blond, curly hair and his cheap 12-string guitar. He was already pretty glamorous and the girls couldn't help but gaze at him. But he had these wonky teeth, that he fixed later, and a strange-coloured eye and I don't really know what they saw in him… You know, he was skinny, not exactly James Bond, but he sang these beautiful songs. Well, I'm not a fan as such, but if you're talking to me about Bowie in terms of music, I'm gonna say to you that the greatest album he ever released was *Hunky Dory*. I never really moved on from there…

So, at the Arts Lab, the audience was completely spellbound. And I performed there too, and Mary Finnigan actually paid my first fee! When success took David away from Beckenham, I continued to perform regularly at the Three Tuns. That's where Cockney Rebel was born. There were a lot of hippie bands there, somewhere between folk and prog rock, like Comus and later Spirogyra[41]. I even went to Haddon Hall when Tony Visconti lived there. I'm sure he doesn't remember… My friends and I gatecrashed a party there. We just went through the gate and went up to the front door. We could smell the dope! They didn't kick us out, and we stayed until three in the morning.

At the Arts Lab, I sometimes dealt with Angie, who was a bit mad, a pretty boisterous American, not exactly in her element in middle-class Beckenham! But I performed there a few times with a friend who played bongos. I used to sing songs that ended up on *The Human Menagerie*. Needless to say, I was pretty left-field with my musical fairy tales… That didn't stop Mary from inviting me to host a few Sundays. I remember nobody came on the first, but I got paid 15 pounds! A bit later, I shared a flat with some friends from Bromley and Beckenham, and they built what they called a shrine to David Bowie in the kitchen! I was writing my own new songs – 'Muriel The Actor', 'Sebastian', 'Loretta's Tale' and all that – but whenever I played one, someone would always say something like, 'Yes, it's great. But have you heard 'Kooks'?' I can't really blame them; those were good times. I also remember Peter Frampton coming to the Arts Lab. And the time David sang 'Life On Mars?' at Wembley[42] in 1999 is forever etched in my memory. Those were four magical minutes in my life. You had to be there. Mike Garson played in a phenomenally imaginative and sensitive way. Mike is entirely simpatico – he played a lot of notes, but he never got in the way of David's singing[43]. (2017)

VERNON DEWHURST

Well, I only knew David Bowie for a couple of years – 1968 and 1969 – and he was a young, unknown guy, not yet painted by the brush of fame. He lived in the room above mine before I split for Paris at the end of 1969. My memories of him are of a talented guy with a great sense of humour and burning ambition. We would often meet up in his top-floor flat in Clareville Grove for a smoke and a chat and to listen to music, and it was here that he first played me 'Space Oddity' on the Stylophone he had just got. I thought it was a bit of a gimmick at the time, but it proved its unique and effective sound in the track.

David liked my photos of him at the Arts Lab and asked me to show them to this A&R guy at Mercury Records – Calvin Mark Lee, with whom I became close friends. Calvin had a collection of Vasarely prints on the walls of his office at Mercury. When David asked me to make the cover of his LP, he wondered if I could shoot him with a Vasarely print in the background. I saw no problem, but thought that, instead of just using it as a background, it would be better to have David's face appearing to emerge from the print. These days that would be so easy in Photoshop, but then it was quite a complicated process involving masks and dupes. But after a couple of tries we arrived at an acceptable result. The photos were shot at my studio on St Michael Street in London. I used a Hasselblad camera with a Distagon lens and Ektachrome 64 film.

There are many other memories of that time; 1969 was an epic year signalling the end of the 60s and the emergence of a new culture that David did so much to instigate and influence. I want to say that Calvin Mark Lee was influential on David at that time and played a huge part in his breakthrough. Also, it's good you are getting all this stuff down before we guys who lived through it forget or disappear into space... (2019)

PHIL MANZANERA

My father died in Venezuela in 1965 and I moved to Clapham, London, with my mother. I went to Dulwich College, in the south of the city, and most of the students who got in for free, after having passed an exam, were from Bromley. At the time, I'd started a band with Bill MacCormick and everyone was talking about a certain David Bowie, who'd started the Beckenham Arts Lab in the neighbourhood. Some of the kids had gone there and even played with him. Shortly after, I noticed that this guy who had made a hit with his song 'Space Oddity' was the David of the Arts Lab. It was the year of man's first steps on the moon, and people were talking about that. From then on, my friends and I followed his career. (2016)

1. In 1969, David Bowie is going to indulge his passion for this musical genre and the British psychedelic scene by hosting some prog rock bands at the Three Tuns, by hanging out with Chris Simpson of Magna Carta and The Strawbs (in mid-June, he will open their show at the Marquee as a mime), and by going to see emerging bands like The Deviants. In 1970, three of The Deviants' members will form the Pink Fairies, a punk band far ahead of its time (with Twink on drums). After his ousting from Tyrannosaurus Rex, Steve 'Peregrin' Took will make a brief appearance on drums. *Kings Of Oblivion*, the Pink Fairies' third album, released in 1973, will owe its title to a line from 'The Bewlay Brothers', the last song on *Hunky Dory*.

2. Located in Willesden, London, the studio belonged to Barry Morgan, Blue Mink's drummer. Their bass player Herbie Flowers and guitarist Alan Parker will soon work with David Bowie. After several changes in name and ownership, the studios no longer exist, but between the 1960s and 1980s they hosted rock performers of all types (Jethro Tull, Paul McCartney, Rod Stewart, Ten Years After, The Cure). Lou Reed will record his first solo album at Morgan as well as his third, *Berlin*. Rick Wakeman will also work there several times, Alice Cooper will record bits of *Billion Dollar Babies* there in late 1972, and Bridget St John her *Jumble Queen* album two years later.

3. *Pierrot In Turquoise Or The Looking Glass Murders* is an adaptation made by Brian Mahoney in early 1970 for Scottish Television of Lindsay Kemp and David Bowie's show from three years before. Bowie reprises the role of Cloud and performs two new songs ('Columbine' and 'The Mirror'), as well as 'Threepenny Pierrot', a version of 'London Bye Ta-Ta' with different lyrics, all to a minimalist orchestration (12-string guitar or keyboards played by Michael Garrett).

4. Although there are photos of the filming of *Love You Till Tuesday*, Universal, who also holds the rights to the compilation of the same name, used photos from 1966 for the DVD cover.

5. For the 50th anniversary of *Space Oddity* in 2019, Parlophone will release *The 'Mercury' Demos*, a vinyl album in a tape box simply credited to David Bowie. Its ten songs (including 'Janine', 'Conversation Piece' and 'Ching-a-Ling') were recorded (very likely at Mercury in London) at the request of Calvin Mark Lee, and constitute the embryonic version of the album.

6. Founded by Jim Haynes, the most famous arts lab was at 182 Drury Lane, near Covent Garden. It was a cinema, theatre and art gallery. David Bowie performed there in late 1968. He enjoyed several works he saw there, including *Chelsea Girls*, a film by Andy Warhol and Paul Morrissey.

7. David Bowie has known him since childhood – he's the son of his art teacher at Bromley Tech.

8. Located a stone's throw from Oxford Circus, the 'Speak' was the place to be seen in the music industry for 20 years. Many major bands from the 1960s and 1970s performed at the Speakeasy, and it was there that some played for the first time. That was the case for King Crimson and Deep Purple (Mark II, with Ian Gillan on vocals).

9. Angela Barnett is not the Angie of The Rolling Stones song.

10. Malcolm Toft, who joined Trident as a sound engineer, will become studio manager in 1971. He said that, to improve the famous in-house consoles, the engineers would change the components themselves.

11. Ken Scott, a former recording engineer for The Beatles, will co-produce four of David Bowie's albums between 1971 and 1973.

12. He will win Best Produced Song at the Monsummano Terme festival for 'When I Live My Dream'.

13. Employed by Philips in the 1960s, first in the publicity department and then as artistic director, Dick Leahy will manage Bell Records and GTO during the glam period. Later, he will found a publishing company with Bryan Morrison and will sign, among others, Wham!. Those who worked with him still admire his dynamism and tenacity in fighting for the artists he believed in. Leahy died in 2020.

14. The dates and positions of David Bowie's songs in the charts vary according to different sources. In this book, when he hasn't used his own press archive, the author referred to officialcharts.com in the UK and billboard.com in the US.

15. There are very few photos of David Bowie in the studio, so it's nearly impossible to know exactly which guitars he used on his albums. However, he did own several 12-string guitars made by Framus, Gibson (B-45), Hagstrom, España, Guild, Harptone, Egmond and Takamine (electro-acoustic).

16. On the original British version of the album, 'Unwashed And Somewhat Slightly Dazed' continues for about 40 seconds after the main

track. This hidden piece (not mentioned on the jacket) is called 'Don't Sit Down'. The jam will be withdrawn from the album for its RCA release in 1972. It will reappear in 1990 for Rykodisc's reissue campaign and its title will appear on the jacket. 'Don't Sit Down' will be dropped for good on subsequent re-releases.

17. In 1969, this guitarist and singer-songwriter released a very good first album of folk-rock, called *Stimulus*. 'Bedsit Two-Step', the second song on the A-side, contains an introduction like the one Bowie will conceive for 'Andy Warhol' on *Hunky Dory* two years later. Still recording, Christmas will release *Crazy Dancing Days* in 2016 and *Life, Life* three years later.

18. Inside the album's original jacket where the lyrics appear, 'Cygnet Committee' is called 'The Cygnet Committee'.

19. From the series *Folklore Planétaire*. The original jacket misspells the artist's name as Vasarelli.

20. In March 1970, Decca and Ken Pitt agree to release *The World Of David Bowie*, a compilation of songs from his first album, complete with unreleased tracks such as 'Karma Man' and 'In The Heat Of The Morning'. They'd also wanted to add 'London Bye Ta-Ta', recorded in the spring of 1968, but Decca couldn't find the tapes. In 1973, Deram will release a more complete double album: *Images 1966–1967*. The cartoonish design of the jacket is the work of American artist Neon Park, who also illustrated albums by Little Feat, Frank Zappa and The Beach Boys.

21. Rick Wakeman is very likely the keyboardist on this session, with Lesley Duncan one of the backing vocalists. On 'The Prettiest Star',

a Lowrey organ, named after the American who designed it, can be clearly heard. The instrument was very much in style at the time, and had an 'automatic accompaniment' function. The Band often used Lowrey organs, as did The Beatles, The Who and Soft Machine.

22. In the timeline he wrote for the booklet accompanying the EMI double-CD reissue of *Space Oddity* in 2009 (it includes the remastered original record plus a collection of B-sides, different mixes and live songs recorded for the BBC), Kevin Cann points out that, on 11 September 1969, a session for the album took place somewhere other than at Trident, possibly at Pye Studios, near Marble Arch. According to Keith Christmas, that was the day he played his guitar parts. The problem is that his description of the place doesn't sound like Pye. Tony Visconti doesn't remember that day, but he told the author that what Christmas described might be Lansdowne Studios, in Bayswater.

23. On a guitar, you can get a harmonic by touching a string over a fret and removing the finger right after playing the note.

24. In the bonus material of the 2016 re-release of *The Man Who Fell To Earth*, Paul Buckmaster will say that, that day, he had in fact heard the demo for 'Space Oddity'.

25. Six months after officially opening in 1967, Trident had an 8-track tape recorder (Ampex AG 440). A 16-track one (3M M56) was installed in late 1969. Trident was the first British studio to make one available to its clients. David Bowie recorded his albums, from *Hunky Dory* to *Aladdin Sane*, on this 16-track recorder. *Pin Ups* was mixed at Trident too, but partially recorded at the Château d'Hérouville.

26. A technique that consisted of pre-mixing what had already been recorded and 'reducing' it onto a single track (or two to keep the stereo). This was done to free up tracks at a time when the number was limited.

27. Paul Buckmaster will die on 7 November 2017. He was very wary of talking about David Bowie, thinking, like a lot of his colleagues, that his words would be twisted by the press again. The interview in this book is one of the last he gave. You can see Buckmaster talk about Bowie and *The Man Who Fell To Earth* in the bonus material of the 2016 40th-anniversary edition.

28. Herbie Flowers played on *Tomorrow Today*, the first album by Hardin & York, two former members of The Spencer Davis Group, which was released in 1969. The title song, which opens the album, starts off exactly like 'Janine' on *Space Oddity* (with the same three repeated chords).

29. 'Oddity' is a play on words from the title of *2001: A Space Odyssey*.

30. To make this book easier to read, the title *Ziggy Stardust* will be used instead of *The Rise And Fall Of Ziggy Stardust And The Spiders From Mars* after its first mention.

31. In a studio, when the sound of an instrument is poorly isolated, it is likely to be picked up by other mics. When tracks are cluttered with extraneous sounds coming from other instruments, mixing becomes more complicated.

32. Also a possible choice for 'Space Oddity', but The Beatles' producer turned down the invitation.

33. 'Love Is Strange', a future hit for the Everly Brothers, was co-written by Bo Diddley and performed by Mickey & Sylvia, an American duo. It was one of three covers The Manish Boys recorded in October 1964 that Decca turned down. Mike Smith reportedly ran this session.

34. Gus Dudgeon and his wife Sheila will die in a car crash in England on 21 July 2002. BowieNet relayed the news and revealed that the doctored voice in 'The Laughing Gnome' was actually Gus.

35. With her consent, Mary Finnigan's contribution here comes from her superb 2016 book *Psychedelic Suburbia* (Jorvik Press). Since she'd already written all she had to say there, she and her publisher gave the author permission to use a few lines here.

36. A Dutch artistic collective that was very active in the 1960s and regularly worked for The Beatles, The Fool decorated their vehicles and instruments, designed costumes and painted the famous mural on the Apple shop (the whole building actually) on Baker Street.

37. The least-known of the four folkers mentioned, Peter Sarstedt was English, of Indian origin. He will have a hit in 1969 with 'Where Do You Go To (My Lovely)'. He will die on 8 January 2017, David Bowie's birthday.

38. Released in 2007 on Repertoire, the double-CD *Tomorrow Never Comes / The Anthology 1969–2006* is one of the best introductions to the music of Magna Carta, who are still around today.

39. In November 1994, in a brief article about 1-2-3 in *Mojo*, David Bowie will answer a few questions from James Alexander. He will say he

did like the band, but was pretty harsh about them too, blaming their failure on a provincial naiveté and lack of a distinct image.

40. Billy Ritchie is talking about a concert on 19 November 1969 (the night before An Evening with David Bowie at the Purcell Room) where several bands with a more rock style than David's performed. They included Edgar Broughton Band and The Strawbs.

41. Spirogyra (a duo at the start) from Canterbury will release three albums in the early 1970s. The third one, *Bells, Boots And Shambles*, includes a few tracks whose vocals (by Martin Cockerham) and arrangements sound a lot like Marc Bolan and/or David Bowie, especially 'The Sergeant Says', which is very *Hunky Dory*.

42. On 9 October 1999, at NetAid – a charity concert for the Jubilee 2000 campaign, which aimed to reduce Third World debt – David Bowie will sing 'Life On Mars?' accompanied only by Mike Garson, and 'Survive' with his whole band.

43. In late November 2017, Steve Harley will sing a few David Bowie songs on stage in England with Mike Garson and Kevin Armstrong as part of a tribute to *Aladdin Sane*.

David Bowie
The man who sold the world

Cane Hill Hospital

THE MAN W
THE MO

ROBERT A. HEINLE

THE MAN WHO SOLD THE WORLD

MERCURY – 10 APRIL 1971

'We suffer because we overlook the fact that, at heart, we are all right.'
(DOUGLAS HARDING, *ON HAVING NO HEAD*, 1961)

'Tony Visconti sometimes criticized me for not putting enough into *The Man Who Sold The World*. He said the songs I brought were just skeletons, but I think he's exaggerating. I was much more present in the studio than he thinks – appearances can be deceiving. Look at this book: the pages that take you from one passage to another, I haven't read them yet. That doesn't mean I'm not interested in them. Maybe I know exactly what the author wrote there. Not knowing doesn't mean ignoring. Not being present isn't always the same as being absent. [...]

"Zane, Zane, Zane, ouvre le chien" in "All The Madmen" is a tip of the hat to *Un Chien Andalou* by Luis Buñuel. My brother had visions, so I felt some distant relationship between the film and my brother's state of mind.'

DB (1996/2014)

Even Mick Ronson wasn't sure and could no longer recall it clearly. As Tony Visconti intimated[1], Ronson probably came to Trident during the recording of *Space Oddity*, but it's possible he just turned up with Benny Marshall the day John Cambridge invited him to the studio to play some harmonica on 'Unwashed And Somewhat Slightly Dazed'. Or maybe Ronson recorded a guitar part on 'Wild Eyed Boy From Freecloud'. And on that famous 3 February 1970, was Mick really at the Marquee, or was he first introduced to David Bowie at La Chasse[2]? Or later that evening, at Haddon Hall? Or even the next day? Those who are still with us each have their own version of this event, and Mick Ronson can no longer shed light on it. What we know for sure is that he owed a great debt to the drummer of Junior's Eyes.

Like John Cambridge and the other future Spiders From Mars (Woody Woodmansey and Trevor Bolder), Mick Ronson comes from Hull in Yorkshire, where Davie Jones played with The Manish Boys in late 1964. As a child, he received a classical music education (he knew solfège – the essentials of music theory, took flute, piano and violin lessons, and played drums), but chooses to play guitar after discovering Duane Eddy and The Yardbirds. He listens to Jimi Hendrix, Keith Richards and George Harrison, but his guitar hero is Jeff Beck. Like him, Ronson loves the sound of his instrument put through a big amp, as much as the sublime arrangements of The Beatles songs. He knows how to play heavy, but admires the work of the best pop orchestrators.

In 1966, after playing in several bands, Ronson joins The Rats, who are getting noticed in Hull. Their accomplishments, however – live or in the studio – will remain modest[3]. After a residency at Golf Drouot in Paris, and two concerts in Rouen and Dieppe, John Cambridge becomes The Rats' drummer. The band records briefly at Fairview Studios in Hull, then decides to set out and conquer London. They will return a week later, without having stepped on a single stage. But on their way back to Hull, during a stopover in Grantham, they are given the opportunity to open for Jeff Beck, and they take it. After briefly changing their name to Treacle in 1968, the quartet will return to Fairview the following year, but John Cambridge accepts an invitation from Mick Wayne to join his band, Junior's Eyes. Woody Woodmansey then replaces Cambridge in The Rats and they carry on, until Mick Ronson – even though he is happy with his job working for the parks department, looking after the green spaces of his town – agrees to return to London[4] to meet a singer-songwriter that Cambridge keeps harping on about.

If there's one thing everyone agrees on, it's how quickly Mick Ronson, David Bowie and Tony Visconti got along – on a personal level certainly, but especially on a musical one. After two brief rehearsals, Ronson is catapulted into the BBC Studios on 5 February 1970 to play on one of John Peel's famous radio shows and tackle a few songs that are much harder to play than it seems. In front of an audience, Mick Ronson does his best to follow the chords by never taking his eyes off the hands of David Bowie and Tony Visconti. Ronson's ability to decipher the songs arouses the admiration of their creator. Some *Space Oddity* tracks are on the set list, as well as a few covers, including two penned by Biff Rose, an American actor and stand-up comedian turned singer. Bowie has discovered his music through Tiny Tim[5]. He's been listening to *The Thorn In Mrs Rose's Side* a lot since its release in 1968, and he regularly sings two tracks from this LP: 'Buzz The Fuzz' and 'Fill Your Heart'. 'The Prettiest Star' and a short version of 'The Width Of A Circle' – which Mick Ronson and Tony Visconti will further develop during the recording of *The Man Who Sold The World* – are on the set list of this programme broadcast the following Sunday (*The Sunday Show*). A few days later, Bowie receives the Brightest Hope Award at a ceremony at the Café Royal on Regent Street (where the famous 'Last Supper' will take place after the farewell concert of Ziggy and his Spiders From Mars). The award is bestowed by readers of *Disc And Music Echo*, the weekly paper that called him a 'human oddity' when he made the front page in October 1969.

But by the end of February, David Bowie's career and that of his musicians will take a pivotal turn. On 22 February, they share the bill at the Roundhouse with a few others including the prog rock band Caravan. The week before at Haddon Hall, perhaps encouraged by photographer Ray Stevenson who loved comic superheroes[6], Angie and Liz Hartley suggested that the musicians dress up to perform. This is how

Bowie – who wears the costume from the 'Space Oddity' video filmed for *Love You Till Tuesday* – becomes Rainbowman. Tony Visconti, with an H on his chest and a Superman cape, is Hype Man. From then on, even if it doesn't appear on the promotional posters for this show, the name Hype (or The Hype) is used for Bowie's band. The week before, David had asked his manager to help find a name for his new band 'about to cause some hype' and Pitt suggested using that word.

David will work with the same group of musicians until the end of March. They perform at the Beckenham Arts Lab (it's the last time Bowie will play there), then in Hull, the stomping ground of John Cambridge and Mick Ronson, whose friends are surprised by their eccentric outfits. Their gig on 11 March at the Roundhouse is memorable for two reasons: firstly because they play 'Instant Karma!' by John Lennon (David will be a huge fan of his first solo album, released at the end of that year); and secondly because their street clothes are stolen from their dressing rooms! The previous week, 'The Prettiest Star' had been released as a single that will disappear without trace – the media won't be able to resist poking fun at this possible one-hit wonder. 'Conversation Piece', a beautiful song that was recorded during the sessions for *Space Oddity,* and that was supposed to appear on it, is hidden on the B-side of 'The Prettiest Star'. Influenced by American folk music, David Bowie references a Biff Rose song in the second line and describes one of the many internal 'conversations' he has when he feels sorry for himself. David will always remain very attached to this song. It will be part of a batch of old titles he will revisit at the dawn of the 2000s, for the 'lost' album *Toy* (finally released on Iso/Parlophone at the end of 2021).

David Bowie and Angela Barnett are married on 20 March at Bromley Registry Office. Tony Visconti, stuck in a studio with The Strawbs, can't be there for the ceremony. But when John Cambridge, replacing Tony, is about to sign the register, Peggy Jones bursts in, picks up the pen and writes her name.

At the end of the month, Cambridge performs his last concert with Bowie in Croydon, Surrey. A few days before, he'd struggled through sessions to re-record 'Memory Of A Free Festival' (suggested by Ken Pitt) at Trident (and later Advision) for a new single, and through takes for a new song called 'The Supermen'. He will be replaced by Woody Woodmansey, The Rats' s drummer Mick Ronson couldn't wait to bring to London. David Bowie gave the call in person to offer him the job. Right up until the end of his life (and his career), Bowie will almost always call the musicians he wanted to work with personally – much to their surprise, as many recount in this book. In his autobiography[7], Woodmansey will explain how he weighed up the pros and cons for a day or two before accepting the job.

In early April, the efforts of Ralph Mace, stimulated by Angie Bowie, for Hype to sign as a group in their own right, pay off and Olav Wyper, the general manager of Philips Records, gives the musicians a much welcome, substantial advance. Hype will record a few tracks with Benny Marshall on vocals, including Tucker Zimmerman's '4th Hour Of My Sleep'[8] and 'Power Of Darkness', written by Marshall and Visconti.

That month, as the recording of his new album begins (sessions with Woodmansey on drums and Mace on synthesizer will take place at Advision and Trident), David Bowie hints to Ken Pitt that he no longer needs his services and intends to take charge of his own career. Because of the friendly relationship between Bowie and his manager, the decision had certainly not been easy to make. Surprised at first, Pitt is going to suspect, on receiving a letter confirming this desire to separate, that someone else is behind the breakup. David was unhappy with the way his career was going and confided in Wyper, explaining that he was worried about being contractually bound to Pitt for years to come. Olav Wyper gave him the name of several legal experts, with Tony Defries at the top of the list. Since the start of the 60s, Defries has been like a fish in the murky waters of English show business, biding his time. When Bowie comes knocking, he sends him directly to Laurence Myers, an accountant who specializes in managing artists' finances. Myers and Defries have been waiting for an opportunity to move into management. Despite Bowie's chaotic course, they see him as a potential goose that will lay a golden egg.

In the first week of May, Tony Defries and David Bowie go to see Ken Pitt for a courteous but somewhat tragi-comic meeting – Bowie will not say a word, letting his 'adviser' explain that his client wants to regain his freedom. Pitt will recount this strange encounter in *Bowie: The Pitt Report* (Omnibus Press, 1985), his book about their relationship, professional and otherwise. In four years, Ken Pitt had not succeeded in making Bowie a star but, although sometimes unsuitable, his methods at least attested to his laudable intention of nurturing all of Bowie's artistic talents at the same time. Pitt also participated greatly in Bowie's emancipation and was among the precious few who enriched a creative process of an intensity and influence no one, except perhaps he himself, realized.

David Bowie cut ties with his manager abruptly and of his own free will, but his relationship with his producer will unravel gradually. Mick Ronson and Woody Woodmansey are now living at Haddon Hall, so Tony Visconti and his girlfriend move to Penge, not far from Beckenham, where they can maintain contact with

David without being 'on top of each other'. But Bowie keeps failing to turn up at recording sessions for his third album, which annoys Visconti and he ends up losing his patience. Some have said (and even Bowie himself will) that his marriage to Angie was purely a convenience that allowed her to work and live in England, but still she and David spend a lot of time together that spring. While they hang around at Haddon Hall or browse junk shops to furnish their home, the three Hype musicians (who continue to back Bowie in concert when he asks) are left on their own. This doesn't affect Ronson who, for five weeks up to the end of May, will be involved a lot in the record, but Visconti, who manages schedules and budgets, is sometimes tearing his hair out. He is on the point of exploding when, on the last day booked in the studio (initially set aside for mixing), David Bowie turns up at Advision with a light step and a few lines jotted in a notebook. After finalizing and polishing his lyrics 'at the mic', he records the lead vocal on 'The Man Who Sold The World' in one take. This last-minute writing method will almost become the norm.

Two weeks before, Bowie had received a prize, a special Ivor Novello Award for originality (!) for 'Space Oddity'', but this recognition doesn't seem to make him happy. In June, the new version of 'Memory Of A Free Festival' is released on both sides of a single. It is no better than the first and, like its predecessor, will only sell a few hundred copies in the UK. The excitement over recording the new album is fading and Tony Visconti has returned to Trident to produce T. Rex's first LP (Marc Bolan will become famous under this name, a contraction of Tyrannosaurus Rex suggested by Tony). In the middle of summer, Visconti tells David Bowie that he wishes to end their collaboration. Since then, he has commented on his decision extensively. First, he claims that he saw through Tony Defries' game early on, took a dislike to him and tried to warn Bowie. Also, at the start of the new decade, Marc Bolan seems more motivated, less unstable and, according to Visconti, more likely to make it big. The future will prove him right, since between late 1970 and mid-1973, T. Rex will have ten singles in the British Top 5 (four of which will get to Number 1) and four of their albums will be Top 10 bestsellers, including *Electric Warrior* at Number 1.

Bad things never happen in isolation. Mick Ronson and Woody Woodmansey will also jump ship, in a pretty spectacular way. They were disappointed by the decline in the number of concerts and as a result, they were always broke. They were also confused by the constantly changing line up on stage – sometimes only two or three of them performed, with Woodmansey on percussion, Tyrannosaurus Rex style. In early August, they are on their way to a gig up north, with Bowie in one car and his two musicians in another. Without warning, the musicians turn off at a fork in the road and head for Hull. That night, Bowie is alone on stage without a backing band.

More problems arise in late 1970, some more damaging than others. First of all, it is becoming apparent that the delay in the album's release (it won't appear on the shelves until April 1971 in the UK), is down to the record label's lack of enthusiasm for it, and for David Bowie's music in general. Also, the cover and the choice of title for the record cause a few difficulties. During his last meetings with Ken Pitt, David rejected several artists put forward to create the visuals (including Andy Warhol). He decided to commission Mike Weller, a regular at the Beckenham Arts Lab, who'd made a few posters. Weller came up with a pop art-style illustration of a cowboy (modelled on John Wayne), in front of Cane Hill, the mental hospital where one of his friends was staying. He didn't know that Terry Burns was also being treated there[10]. Initially excited, David approved this draft after requesting a few changes – he asked for some words to be put in the speech bubble by his face. In reference to the film *Metropolis* by Fritz Lang, Weller called his work *Metrobolist*. David hadn't seen it yet, but decided to use this name.

But after the tapes and artwork for the record, complete with instructions, have been sent to the Americans, Bowie changes his mind. He asks Philips to organize a photo shoot with Keith 'Keef' MacMillan[11]. In September, MacMillan immortalizes David dressed in one of his now-famous men's dresses (by designer Mr Fish), lying in a sensual pose on a sofa at Haddon Hall. The atmosphere of the shot is reminiscent of the work of pre-Raphaelite painter Dante Gabriel Rossetti. The British label will agree to take a risk on this androgynous image that Bowie and his people are demanding. To generate publicity, Defries – and, according to him, Angie – start to put about rumours about Bowie's sexuality, revealing rather a lot about himself and his methods in the process.

But Mercury in the US refuse the new jacket artwork and stick with Weller's. In November, the album comes out in America as *The Man Who Sold The World* (considered too abstruse, *Metrobolist* has been rejected) – the title is a simple and direct reference to the most commercial song on the album, according to the record company. When he finds out that Weller's artwork has been used and altered (the words in the speech bubble have been removed), David Bowie has a fit. The deteriorating relationship between the artist and his label will lead to even more delay in the release of the album in the UK. However, the incident will work in

Tony Defries' favour. He is determined to break the contract with Mercury and take his client elsewhere.

In November, frustrated by the way things are going (or, rather, not going), Bowie will suggest that the British album is named after 'Holy Holy', a song he's just recorded at Island Studios[12] under the guidance of Herbie Flowers, which contains references to Aleister Crowley. Philips will balk, but agree to finance David's first promotional trip to the United States. At the end of January 1971, just before leaving, Bowie finds out that 'Oh! You Pretty Things', a song he'd written the summer before, has been proposed to Peter Noone (and his producer Mickey Most), former frontman of Herman's Hermits. Bob Grace of Chrysalis Music, David Bowie's new publisher, gives him the happy news.

Because he doesn't have a work permit, Bowie will not be able to perform on this first trip to America. But he will make some important contacts and get to experience the land of dreams, fantasized about by all young people in Britain and Europe during the 60s and 70s. Direct exposure to American culture, which he'd embraced wholeheartedly since childhood, will stimulate his senses and his imagination. David is travelling alone, so Ron Oberman, head of publicity for Mercury, meets him in Washington and takes him from city to city – New York, Los Angeles, Philadelphia, Detroit, Chicago and Houston. He will be interviewed on many radio stations and by music magazines including *Circus*, *Creem* and *Rolling Stone*. Bowie will also do the rounds of record stores, museums and second-hand shops. In New York, he sees Tim Hardin and The Velvet Underground (without Lou Reed[13]) on stage, and talks to Moondog, who is performing on the street. With his long hair in the style of Greta Garbo, his Mr Fish dresses and a bag over his shoulder, David Bowie does not go unnoticed and sometimes even elicits a hostile reaction. His aim is to showcase his difference, but he soon develops a talent for provocation.

Local celebrity Rodney Bingenheimer[14], a radio presenter at KRQQ who works as an intern at Mercury Records on the West Coast, shows Bowie around Los Angeles and is much impressed by him. Bowie also meets Tom Ayres, a producer for the RCA music label, who reportedly introduces him to Gene Vincent. According to Ayres, and as legend – even more 'urban' in Los Angeles – would have it, David recorded demos of new songs at Ayres's place, some inspired by his trip and one of which, 'Hang On To Yourself', was for Vincent. Unfortunately, Vincent died that October before he was able to sing it.

On Valentine's Day, David Bowie party-hops around Los Angeles and plays a few tracks at Paul Fegen's home – Fegen is a lawyer and party animal who is friends with Bingenheimer and lives behind the Whisky A Go Go. Before flying back to London in mid-February, his luggage bursting with new records, David watches a performance by little-known singer-songwriter Biff Rose, whose influence on him is growing.

On his return to London, Bowie can't wait to get back into the studio, but doesn't want to give Mercury even one new song, so he will record secretly with different groups of musicians[15]. At the end of the month, he is at Trident Studios with members of Rungk, a trio whose guitarist is his neighbour and friend Mark Pritchett, who sometimes played with Hype. Under the name Arnold Corns (sometimes The Arnold Corns), they record 'Moonage Daydream' and 'Hang On To Yourself'. To cover his tracks even more, David will put about a rumour that the singer of this fake group is Freddie Burretti (born Frederick Burrett), a young aspiring fashion designer who works in a boutique on the King's Road. Bowie has taken a liking to Burretti after he and Angie met him at the Sombrero, a popular gay club in London where he and his friends have become regulars[16]. This Arnold Corns single, with Pete De Somogyl on bass and Tim Broadbent on drums, will be released on B&C Records in early May, to general indifference.

On 10 April 1971, a year after its recording has started, *The Man Who Sold The World* finally comes out in the UK. By the time of release, its music and lyrics are in stark contrast to the artist David Bowie has become. The famous 'drag cover', with an androgynous Bowie striking a dramatic pose, may look stylish but it is deceptive. The beige and faded blue cover image is far less dark than the songs inside. Even though the influence of certain authors can be found in the lyrics of *The Man Who Sold The World*, it would be an exaggeration to say that Friedrick Nietzsche, Khalil Gibran or Aleister Crowley really shaped David Bowie's writing as he was moving on to the next decade.

'The Width Of A Circle', crawling between prog rock and heavy rock (with a boogie part and another purely incantatory one), is the first track on the album. Bowie has been playing it live since the beginning of the year. In the studio, this song, whose 'on the edge of the abyss' lyrics reference the aforementioned authors, was a field of experimentation for Mick Ronson (often close to Jeff Beck in how he approached playing his Gibson Les Paul). Inspired also by the audacity of Led Zeppelin, Black Sabbath and Deep Purple, competitors who keep raising the bar higher in terms of construction/deconstruction, Ronson and Visconti made many changes to the track. On stage with The Spiders From Mars, 'The Width Of A Circle' will exceed the eight minutes of its studio version and, with bass player Trevor Bolder, will look like a man-to-man fight.

Did David Bowie see his half-brother's mental health problems as a manifestation of evil (or even devilry)? We don't know, but it's clear that Terry's condition inspired 'All The Madmen', one of the most pivotal songs on the album. Tony braces David's 12-string guitar with a solid rhythm section (his bass is the most melodic element), in which children's flutes (an allusion to Hungarian composer Béla Bartók, as Visconti will explain in 2015) create fine cracks that Ronson opens up with some wicked licks. The chorus, jolted by Woodmansey's drum fills, the quiet middle part and the instrumental part that, again, recalls Ravel, are the pieces of a puzzle assembled gradually right through to an opaque conclusion (despite David's explanation at the beginning of this chapter), which clouds even more this first example of a recurring theme in Bowie's work: mental alienation seen as the worst constraint or the ultimate refuge.

Another song with overlaid Les Paul riffs, 'Black Country Rock' offers a rare chance to take a breath in *The Man Who Sold The World*. Despite its vocal reference to Marc Bolan in the last chorus, the apparent similarity to T. Rex's simple songs is deceptive. The chord progressions on the whole album (notably the chorus of this song) are much more convoluted and mainly owe their power of seduction to the spiralling melodies created by the singer to adorn them.

'After All' is a twilight ballad recorded by Bowie on acoustic guitar, then 'dressed' by Tony Visconti and Mick Ronson. It's a sort of farewell to the hippie movement, like 'Rebel Rebel' will be to glam rock four years later. The use of the Stylophone, Ronson's mandolin playing and the instrumental section's ternary rhythm show that nostalgia is no longer what it was, but the references in the lyrics to Aleister Crowley and the repetition, like a mantra, of the expression 'by Jingo[17]', herald the storm gathering in David Bowie's head.

Like others in the know, Chris O'Leary writes in his book *Rebel Rebel* (Zero Books, 2015) that the soldier mentioned in 'Running Gun Blues', the first song on the B-side of *The Man Who Sold The World*, who continues to kill everyone around him after returning from the front, was a reference to the situation in Vietnam. A few years before, the Vietman war, so emblematic of its time, drove hordes of young people (especially hippies) onto the streets in protest. Echoing 'We Are Hungry Men' on the album *David Bowie*, the singer fools everyone by evolving his melody in a fairly clear musical atmosphere on a distinctly rock chord progression, paving the way for similar pieces on *Ziggy Stardust*.

We'll never know what a Feathers album produced by Tony Visconti would have sounded like, but since Hermione Farthingale called the trio 'very experimental and much darker', we can assume that 'Saviour Machine' fits her description. Coincidentally, it also recycles (through Mick Ronson's guitar) the melodic line of the coda of 'Ching-a-Ling'. The band vigorously tackles (again) a beat of three-time (6/8 actually), quite rapid here – like a jazz waltz, a nod to Dave Brubeck – and pairs it with synthetic brass on the Moog, causing the song to shake up the traditional structure (where's the chorus?), juxtapose different atmospheres and attempt to channel opposing winds. Nietzschean philosophy thickens the lyrics: the man of tomorrow is controlled by the machine, and the people submit to a totalitarian regime. The tormented tormentor, or the disillusioned illusionist, declaims from the top of a cliff of doubt.

More reserved in the liner notes for the album (reissued and included in the *Five Years (1969–1973)* box set in 2015) than in some recent comments to the press, Tony Visconti has sometimes implied that Mick Ronson composed 'She Shook Me Cold', the heaviest rock track on the album (and in Bowie's discography), and that David just wrote the lyrics. It seems more likely that Bowie also composed the melody that took shape, like others at the time, in the basement of Haddon Hall where many songs were roughed out. If Ronson provided the chord chart, he should have been credited as co-composer. This is what his fans assert. From the end of 1973 when Bowie breaks with his guitarist, they will lament that Tony Defries' company only paid him a modest weekly wage despite the sheer quality of his work. Here, while Mick Ronson's style borrows from Jeff Beck and Jimi Hendrix, the power trio mostly emulate Cream, Black Sabbath and Led Zeppelin (the song was Ronson's response to the first two albums by Jimmy Page's band[18]).

After agreeing to work on *Lazarus* in 2014, theatre director Ivo van Hove will ask David Bowie for a special meeting: he'll ask him to explain, line by line, the meaning of the 20 or so songs selected for the musical. Van Hove, to honour the trust Bowie placed in him, will choose not to divulge what he learned that day. He is probably one of the only people on the planet who knows what/who 'The Man Who Sold The World' is actually about. At the end of the meeting, Corinne Schwab, David's friend and assistant, also there that day, will tell the director that, to her knowledge, David has never provided such an in-depth explanation of his lyrics before. Therefore, us ordinary mortals can only speculate, but as 'All The Madmen' demonstrates, the internal upheaval caused by Terry's mental state bore heavily on Bowie's psyche as he created *The Man Who Sold The World*. Terry is half his blood, and he doesn't know to what extent his loss, though he might dread it, could be liberating. Terry's shadow will sometimes obscure the more or less faithful pictures that David will paint in the moment, before hanging them on the walls of his labyrinthine life. In 'The Man Who Sold The World', the undeniable pop masterpiece of the album, David Bowie uses his brazen talent to conjure this brother out of nowhere and bring him to life. But he is nothing more than a subconscious reflection, a doppelgänger with a roughly sketched outline, which allows the artist to confront himself (when he was younger, Bowie read *The Man Who Sold The Moon*, by Robert A. Heinlein[19]). And, as if by chance, for this song, the only one on the album recorded with an 8-track machine (at Advision – all the other songs were recorded on 16-track), David's voice is double-tracked on the choruses and modified by a phasing effect[20] achieved through a complicated process (two 8-tracks were actually needed). 'The Man Who Sold The World' wouldn't be what it is without the (Oriental? Celtic?) theme rehashed by Mick Ronson. Just as later with the 'Rebel Rebel' riff, very few subsequent guitarists will be able to play this haunting melody as well as Ronson on the original version. As for the harmonized vocals in the final part of the song, they didn't rise from Hell but from Tibet.

The track listing of *The Man Who Sold The World* was carefully put together at a time when albums were considered a cohesive whole. It reveals that David Bowie did not want to end on the (relatively) optimistic note of the title song, preferring instead a new version of 'The Supermen'. Subject to much analysis, and therefore of their literary, cinematographic and television references, the lyrics of this song, re-recorded with Woody Woodmansey on drums and tuned timpani, seem to be a mixture of personal references and reflections. At the end of the 60s, the concept of a superior man – the superman – was explored in all creative domains, from the trivial to the philosophical. David Bowie would incorporate it into his work by adding religious, sexual or violent elements, and more generally, by injecting dystopian imagery into his lyrics. This could first be heard in 'We Are Hungry Men' but, by 1969, the tone was no longer comedic. Bowie and Visconti use backing vocals, very elaborate throughout the whole album, to dramatize the tone and the subject of 'The Supermen'. It's hardly surprising that, 46 years later, they will arrange vocals on 'Blackstar' in a similar way.

The Man Who Sold The World solemnly blends a number of serious themes that will recur in the work of its author. He uses them as subterfuges to tackle some of the personal issues that will fuel his entire discography (this will be particularly obvious in *Diamond Dogs, Station To Station, Outside* and *Heathen*). An entanglement of traumas and aspirations, more or less significant, more or less obvious, infuses every inch of this material. David Bowie, like a human note pad, has stored strings of words and phrases, before rearranging them according to the awakening of his senses. Then, creating a false reflection, more in order to leave it to interpretation than to make textual analysis impossible, he regurgitated them with confidence and sometimes haste. In this album (which will only reach the bottom of the charts on both sides of the Atlantic), Bowie has found a way to draw energy from his melancholy and give shape (and soon the face of a character) to the confusion that is rumbling louder and louder inside him. As Nietzsche put it, 'One must still have chaos in oneself to be able to give birth to a dancing star'. He will be at the same time the prime agent and prime disruptor of an artistic spirit that will propel him to success a year and a half later. And it doesn't really matter that, at this moment in his story, David's instincts threaten to turn him into collateral damage. And it's not important that his quest for total emancipation, to explode heads like those of the characters on Mike Weller's Beckenham Arts Lab posters, is always being crushed by a God with a cruel finger pressing on the spot where David Bowie is suffering the most. In the spring of 1971, to end his era of doubt and obscurity, he convinces himself that if he doesn't find buyers for his world soon, selling off his soul to the highest bidder is the price he will pay, so that his path to coveted glory will transform into an avenue teeming with teasing billboards. If the avenue has to pass through Hell, so be it.

Mick Ronson	John Cambridge
Tony Visconti	Mark Pritchett
Woody Woodmansey	Phill Brown
Ralph Mace	Michael Chapman
Gerald Chevin	Glenn Goring
	Russell Mael

MICK RONSON

I never found out whether the radio show where I played with David for the first time was an audition or not. In any case I didn't think of it as one, although over the past 20 years, some journalists have said it was. When we started recording *The Man Who Sold The World*, I tried to learn as much as I could by watching Tony Visconti. We wrote most of the record's arrangements together, and no one said anything about the sound of my guitar, which was a bit, um, unorthodox[21]! I haven't seen Tony in a long time, or John Cambridge for that matter. As well as the fun of touring with David, I loved that he let me do my thing in the studio. During the recording of *The Man Who Sold The World*, sometimes he wouldn't turn up during the day, but he'd stop by at the end of a session, usually to approve what we'd done and sing a few lines he'd just jotted down. His confidence was disarming. Some bits on the album sound like The Rats... Maybe he let me do what I wanted so I wouldn't regret leaving Hull! (1990)

TONY VISCONTI

When David and I heard Mick Ronson play, we looked at each other as if to say, 'We have to hang on to him at all costs!' John Cambridge, our drummer, had tried to convince him to join us, telling him that playing with David was a good gig. But Mick wasn't interested, he loved his work as a gardener, and he was reluctant to come to London to audition. Two days later, we had a very important radio show with John Peel – I've still got the tapes... It was the first time Mick played live with us and since he didn't know the songs very well, he sat where he could see David's hand on the neck of his 12-string guitar. That's how he played the whole set, but he was already great. We loved him.

There were only two bedrooms at Haddon Hall, one for David and Angie, and the other for my partner and me. During sessions for *The Man Who Sold The World*, Mick Ronson and the others slept on the floor on mattresses! I think I taught Mick quite a few things, like arranging strings, for example, but I also learned a lot from him: he was more than a friend to me. I saw him at a party six months before he died and we got along like before. He came over to my place in New York the following week, then asked me to meet him in London to help him finish his album. I agreed, but his health deteriorated and I never saw him again. Mick Ronson is one of the best musicians I've ever had the privilege of working with.

In the studio, David is mercurial, totally innovative and enormously talented, when inspired. Marc Bolan was always 'on', quite manipulative and ingeniously simple. Both loved to have a good time in the studio, and they didn't take the recording process too seriously. They both had a sense of making history during sessions, and were aware of the effect of their music on the listening public and critics alike. Well, Marc was very impatient in the studio. As for David, he is not that comfortable spending a lot of time there, but he is patient. If I tell him that a certain concept will require a lengthy set up, he will find something to do, like writing lyrics, reading a book or watching television. I know that he is not wasting his time. And whatever he reads or sees often ends up in his lyrics! Neither David nor Marc were perfectionists, in the sense that their records didn't have to be flawless. Both loved spontaneity and if something was recorded with too much distortion, they'd both love it rather than 'correct' it.

To be honest, *The Man Who Sold The World* wouldn't be the great 'dark horse' it is without Mick Ronson. He inspired the rest of us to rock out like we'd never done before! I think both David and I knew that, after *Space Oddity*, we had to do something more dramatic and more powerful for the next album, and being introduced to Mick was our good fortune. He also introduced us to Woody Woodmansey. We quickly evolved into a power trio with the best lead vocalist in the UK. I know not many fans agreed with us at the time, but that was how we felt. During *The Man Who Sold The World* we were all getting along fine. For us, it was just a one-off, a one-album situation. That's why Mick and Woody were happy enough to sleep temporarily on the floor of the gallery at Haddon Hall. No one was being paid anything, including myself! We just wanted to make the best kick-ass album possible. We rehearsed in the wine cellar of the apartment for weeks before we went into the studio and we all hung out in the evenings, watching television, sometimes jamming on acoustic guitars, cooking dinner. I don't remember going to the pub since we couldn't afford to spend a lot of money on entertainment, but that was okay since we were living for the album 24/7. I think it was during this period, just before we recorded, that we sanded down Mick's black Les Paul to its natural finish. Just something to do in the evenings...

Before *The Man Who Sold The World*, I played bass on hundreds of songs in New York and London. I started playing acoustic bass in my high school symphony orchestra, then with local jazz groups. In early discussions with Mick and David, Mick made me listen to Jack Bruce, whom he idolized, and told me I'd have to play like that. He didn't ask me, he told me! I was also a guitarist – I'd had three years of weekly lessons from the age of eleven – so I put two and two together and, voilà, I realized that Mick wanted me to play 'lead bass'[22]. So I did just that, combining bass and guitar technique. After a few days of rehearsals in my new role, I was almost giddy with power, but I was always looking towards Mick for approval. Mick had quite a stony face in those days; he rarely smiled. He kept his cool at all times. He did have a very droll sense of humour and dropped some very funny comments when we'd least expect it. But, at rehearsals, I learned that a slight uplift at the sides of his mouth, the very hint of a smile, meant I was doing all right. As for David, he was very impressed with the power-trio energy we were creating.

I think my music producer skills were very good for the *Space Oddity* album, although my skills as a mixing engineer were nascent. I had a lot to learn. I think I did a great job on the orchestral version of 'Wild Eyed Boy From Freecloud', but the folk-rock songs with the band were just too lightweight sounding. I chose not to mix *The Man Who Sold The World* – it was too risky. Of course, I was present for the balance of the instruments but I stayed away from the equalization and compression – I left all those decisions to our engineers. With my hand on my heart I have to tell you that it was Mick Ronson who kept insisting that my bass should be louder in the mix. On a few songs I played more than one bass. On 'After All', I played a Gibson EB3, a Fender Precision and an Ampeg Baby Bass. The bass part was very 'phasy' as a result – no special effects, just three bass guitars playing at once. On the title track I played two basses – the Gibson EB3 and I bowed the Ampeg Baby Bass on the choruses. I arranged a lot of the backing vocals, which at times were a little operatic and classical, like in 'The Supermen' and 'The Man Who Sold The World'. We got Ralph Mace from Philips to come in and play the huge Moog we hired, with Chris Thomas getting the sounds for us.

Mick Ronson and I also wrote the arrangements for 'Saviour Machine', 'Running Gun Blues' and 'All The Madmen'. It certainly had more synthesizer parts than most other albums during that period. The Moog synthesizer was a very expensive instrument in those days, but George Harrison and maybe three other people had one. It was also expensive to hire one and it had to come with an operator. The word 'preset' didn't exist with regards to early synthesizers; only instruments like the electronic organ and piano had that.

The Man Who Sold The World was not entirely piano free. There is a Jerry Lee Lewis-style piano in the outro of 'Black Country Rock'. I think Mick and I played it together, one of us playing the chords and the other the glissandos. Even though there are mixed musical genres on the album, it has the right amount of each.

There is the predominant rock genre, but with a couple of diversions. That's a good formula. Too many different musical genres on one album sound like confusion. It is a lot harder to skip a song on a vinyl disc, so LPs had to be conceptualized for an audience who expected one song to flow easily into the next. I don't know if today's albums have that attention to detail – some do, some don't. Also, we got Woody to play two instruments he'd never played before – timpani and guiro[23]. Today he still talks about his guiro debut when we play *The Man Who Sold The World* live.

The total recording time was a little more than a month – not every day of the week though. We had time to listen to rough mixes and plan overdubs. We rehearsed a lot before recording, although some of the songs were conceived in the studio, like 'Black Country Rock', the second half of 'The Width Of A Circle' and 'The Supermen'. Some of the rehearsal arrangements were altered in the studio, like the addition of the jazz *Boléro* rhythm in the middle of 'All The Madmen'. We weren't so rushed. Getting David to write lyrics was another matter though. He put himself into a rush to get them finished on time. I would guess that half the songs were recorded without lyrics. David wrote the lyrics, melody and sang the lead vocal for 'The Man Who Sold The World' on the final day of the recording! We then mixed that track late into the evening. We ran out of money – that was it! I guess the title track could have been the album's single and David proved it to be a hit when he got Lulu to cover the song in 1973[24]. But at that time, 'The Man Who Sold The World' didn't feel like single material. It just didn't fit with what was considered a hit.

David, Woody, Mick and I had parted company well before the album was released. Indirectly this was due to conflicts with David's new manager, Tony Defries. As I was no longer part of the team, I don't have any knowledge of how they intended to market it. Because we broke up as a band, David never performed the album live on tour. I think David and Tony Defries might have considered *The Man Who Sold The World* too much of an anomaly, something unmarketable, so they moved on to preparing the way for David's next LP, *Hunky Dory*.

During recording, David was spending a lot of time with Angie, but this didn't really interfere with the schedule. We worked fast and kept up the pace. David was always quick to sing his vocals within three to four takes, maximum. There were many single takes in his recording career too. As we were working on both 8- and 16-track tape, we didn't leave many tracks open for lead vocals. 'The Man Who Sold The World' was recorded on 8-track and, when the time came to do the vocals, we had only one track left (we had a similar situation for the vocals on "Heroes"). In those days, you couldn't keep a vocal in a folder the way you can with digital recording. If you thought the artist could sing it better, you would have to erase the previous vocal forever! David was used to this method and he was a great singer, due to this technical discipline. He knew the consequences. He sang so well that it would be a difficult decision to make. 'Could he sing it even better or will it be worse? Shall we stop here and say, yes, this is the best vocal?' This was always a nerve-wracking, butterflies-in-the-stomach experience. This element of tension and expectation is missing entirely from today's digital recording. Back then, it was taken for granted that an artist had to be a great singer to get a recording contract. Don't get me started on that...

I thought many times, 'If only David, Woody and I had played *The Man Who Sold The World* live back in the day...' And this is what we've been doing since 2014 with Holy Holy, the band I've formed with Woody Woodmansey. Actually we are not playing the album exactly the way it was recorded, note for note. Even in rehearsals, each song evolved into something at least 10 per cent different from the original. When The Spiders played 'The Width Of A Circle' years later, they changed the song considerably too. Glenn Gregory of Heaven 17, our vocalist of choice, puts a lot of swagger into these songs – more weight as a mature baritone, unlike the clear sharp tenor of a 23-year-old David Bowie. I'm really pleased with that – we never tried to come up with a Bowie clone. We play the songs even harder than when they were recorded. In my case, I improvised a lot of my parts on the album. If I had been given the opportunity to play it live in those days, I'm sure I would have continued to refine my parts, standardize them or play some parts even more wildly. I think Mick, David and Woody would have done the same. Holy Holy is very faithful to the original, but we can't hold back from evolving the songs further. To the credit of our guitarists, James Stevenson and Paul Cuddeford, they are both Ronson experts and they have learned most of the solos exactly as Ronson played them on the record. I am so happy to be doing this, because it is not just a tribute to a past album, it has been made fresh for the present time! We have played to thousands of Bowie fans who shout in delight after each song – we have their approval. This was a worry before we played our first show, but with Woody and I in the band – the original drummer and bassist – I think we were expecting a lot of positivity from the audience anyway. For me, I just wanted to know if I still had it in me. I answered that question myself – I do! (1994/2001/2015)

WOODY WOODMANSEY

At the end of the 60s, I had been in a band in the north of England with Mick Ronson, called The Rats. We played early blues stuff and Yardbirds and Hendrix covers, some progressive rock. I had replaced the drummer in the band, John Cambridge, a couple of years earlier. John had moved down to London and joined the band Junior's Eyes. They were kind of American country, but were also working as David Bowie's backing group. Apparently the guitarist was not working out, and John Cambridge suggested Mick to David. So Mick left The Rats and moved to London. That band was David Bowie's Hype. Several months later, David called me and asked me to join.

I knew that Bowie had released some singles and albums, but I didn't know his music. I had not heard of him. My first impression was... this guy really means it. He looks the part and has the attitude. He was wearing red trousers, a rainbow t-shirt and red shoes with a blue star he had painted on each one... I was all in denim with desert boots! The songs at that time were okay; I thought them a bit lightweight, but I could see potential. And David could write and sing – a good start! On *The Man Who Sold The World* we did all the backing tracks without him. I think he had discussed it with Tony Visconti, who was the producer, so he had some input. Later, as if he sensed that his dreams were about to come true, Bowie took control of things... (2015)

RALPH MACE

I had a very good relationship with Angie Bowie, who advised David, but I never dealt with Tony Defries. On the day of their wedding, which I didn't know about, they stormed into my office in Stanhope Place with a crate of beer and a large cake. We partied until late and it was a little wild. Later, I saw David on Wardour Street and asked him what he was doing there. He said he'd started recording a new album and invited me to stop by some time. I was working for Famous Music, Paramount Pictures' music publishing wing, just round the corner from Trident Studios. One evening, after work, I went over there. David and Tony Visconti were both very busy with a Moog synthesizer, which was placed on the control desk. They were working on a tricky part that had a number of chromatic runs and neither of them had the keyboard technique to play it properly. They tried several times but it was getting no better. At that time, I still had a pretty good piano technique, so I said, 'If you want to get home before breakfast, why don't you let me try?' It worked and, in a comparatively short time, we had put down the Moog part for 'Saviour Machine' and some other tracks. So I discovered the songs on *The Man Who Sold The World* by playing on them! Of course, I had to wait for the album to be released to hear the final result. During those sessions, I was also very impressed by Mick Ronson, who was a sort of catalyst and seemed to make things happen even when David was not around. And, of course, Mick added a touch of rock[25]. (2016)

GERALD CHEVIN

I first met David Bowie almost 50 years ago and I can't remember what he or I looked like at the time! As I recall, he was driven and very enthusiastic. Like me, he was as naive as he was young... I'd only been at Advision for two or three years and I'd hardly heard David's music when I started working on his songs. That must have been between his first two albums[26]. But I already knew Tony Visconti, from sessions with producer Denny Cordell, for whom he wrote arrangements. Tony was all excited about recording *The Man Who Sold The World* with David, who was still pretty intimidated by technology. Between 1967 and 1970, the British music scene was literally exploding! Studios were like beehives, operating day and night. Several recording engineers worked on *The Man Who Sold The World*: Eddy Offord and me at Advision, and Ken Scott at Trident. As for the division of labour between Eddy and me, it was simple: we based our tasks on who was the least tired, as we worked every day, 18 or 20 hours per day, including weekends. It didn't take long to see that David Bowie had a unique talent and was a gifted all-round musician. And unlike many others at the time, he was well educated and very respectful. He should also be remembered for that. (2016)

JOHN CAMBRIDGE

When I introduced Mick Ronson to David Bowie in February 1970, I'd already been playing with him for six months. During that time, David and I became very close. He even lived with us for a week in Hull! I was with him when his father died, at his wedding, when he got his driving licence and his first car. Most biographers say that Mick Ronson started the Spiders and all that, but I was the one who got him to come to London, so I made the connection with David. I lived at Haddon Hall for a few months, but I didn't sleep on the floor on a mattress like Mick, Woody and Trevor later on. David gave me a room, which I shared with our roadie, Roger The Lodger. But, honestly, Mick was crucial in helping David craft his songs. I don't know whether David would have got so big without Mick, and whether Mick would have got so big without David – all I know is they were a perfect match. And I don't think things happen by chance – we were at the right place, at the right time, and maybe it was my fate to introduce them.

Angie Bowie and Liz Hartley were largely responsible for our appearance during Hype concerts, which Tony Visconti always called pre-glam rock. They suggested we dress up and gave us nicknames. I had a cowboy hat, so I was Cowboy Man! Mick's sequined outfit belonged to David, who wore it at the *Disc And Music Echo* awards ceremony. They were sometimes chaotic, but I loved Hype's shows. I had two big bass drums and the drums weren't miked with a bunch of microphones like they are today. Mick's guitar was really loud, to the point where, except in the quieter passages like the intro of 'Space Oddity', David struggled to hear his own 12-string acoustic guitar.

One time, in the front room at Haddon Hall, I heard David and Mick rehearsing a new song, 'The Supermen', which appeared on *The Man Who Sold The World*. I wanted to stay with them to think about what I could add, but they kept me at arm's length and ended up telling me to piss off. In the studio, when it was time to record this track, I had trouble playing the instrumental bit. Mick kept saying, 'Come on, it's easy', which made it even harder. We decided to take a break and went for a drink with David and Angie at La Chasse on Wardour Street. Tony and Mick stayed. When we got back to the studio, I played my part – one take, done! A few days later, I was at Haddon Hall painting the ceiling and David came over to me. That's when he told me he was going to find another drummer. David insisted it was nothing personal. I had no money and asked him for five pounds so I could go home. To this day, I still don't know why I got kicked out of Hype. (2016)

MARK PRITCHETT

At the Three Tuns on Sunday afternoons, before the Arts Lab gathered, Hype was pretty good in rehearsals. But live, at cavernous venues like the Roundhouse, the sound was poor. The audience near the stage were sporadically impressed but, further back, they were generally lethargic! David was understandably depressed about this, but had faith in the venture... *The Man Who Sold The World* didn't do much and, during the difficult months of late 1970 and early 1971, David, fed up with his label and management, started to write new material, songs that would fuel *Hunky Dory* and even *Ziggy Stardust*. Trouble was, he had no route to market. So, David set out to write and record under the radar of his existing, but failing, contracts. He dreamed of touring as David Bowie And Friends, with Dana Gillespie, George Underwood, Geoff MacCormack and me, as a stable of artists who could hold their own individually but with David at the hub. Arnold Corns was the first of these ventures. To be honest, I was surprised that David wanted Freddie Burretti to front the enterprise. Freddie was well known to me by then but, great dancer that he was, he had no real singing voice, being beset by nerves when asked to sing. David, Svengali-like, was trying to create a star but, from the first vocal session, it was not to be. (2019)

PHILL BROWN

I only worked with David Bowie once. In November 1970, I was the recording engineer on 'Holy Holy'. Bass player Herbie Flowers was the producer and he'd brought the musicians from his band at the time, Blue Mink – Alan Parker on guitar and Barry Morgan on drums. I think it was a decision by his record company to try and make a commercial single, and Blue Mink were very successful at the time. They were union sessions, with a strict schedule: laying down the tracks in the morning, overdubs and vocals in the afternoon, and mixing in the evening. I remember Bowie as a clever and handsome guy with long blond hair and a silk shirt. He already had a reputation for 'borrowing ideas' and would soon become a real chameleon. I knew Angie better through Dana Gillespie, who I used to work with. I wasn't too thrilled with 'Holy Holy', and David came off as a quiet guy, a bit too reserved. I was pretty surprised when a year later things really took off for him. I did love *Hunky Dory*, and later, *Let's Dance*, but I was not interested at all in the Thin White Duke. (2016)

MICHAEL CHAPMAN

I met Elton John and David Bowie when they were starting out, mostly because we had the same publisher, but we never hung out together. Sometimes we ran into each other when I came to London, but that was it. You know, because I always refused to live there, I wasn't part of the guitar mafia of the day. I was always a northerner, and that's fine by me. Right before recording my second album, *Fully Qualified Survivor*, the folks from Harvest, my label, told me they were going to hire some great musicians, London hot shots, to play on it. I said, 'Get rid of them!' because I knew this gardener from Hull, Mick Ronson, a hell of a guitarist who was much better than this lot! It took me a long time to convince them, but as soon as they heard him play, they got it. So I introduced Mick to Gus Dudgeon, the producer of my record, who then introduced Mick to David. When the album came out, I put a band together to go on the road. I asked Mick to be in it, but he refused. He said he'd only accept if I also took Trevor Bolder on bass and Woody Woodmansey on drums. I didn't really like the way they played, so that didn't happen. But when David turned up and took all of them, Mick was happy to go. Ronson was a really honest, decent, normal guy. He said, 'No, I'm not leaving without my friends', and I always admired him for that. God knows what would have happened if he had been in my band. (2017)

GLENN GORING

Haddon Hall was pretty much open house, if I remember. You didn't have to make an appointment or anything formal like that to visit, which I often did. At that time, Zowie Bowie was an infant. So you would have this very interesting, nappy-changing, toy-rattling, baby-crying, family environment woven into this Bohemian, very creative, but slightly crazy atmosphere.

I remember David and Angie were having new tiles laid in the entrance hall. They were a particular interlocking design, in simple buff-coloured clay. I'd never seen anything quite like them before – Angie said they were especially imported from Spain. It was another indication to me that whichever way you turned in this environment you landed in an original or arresting moment.

I think it was in a conversation at the Arts Lab one evening that David invited me round to Haddon Hall, to show me an 'interesting' object he had recently acquired. He knew I was an artist as well as a musician and, I presumed, valued my opinion. It was on this occasion that I discovered that David was an avid collector of Victoriana[27]. Well, I believe it was his 'current' passion, as he had a keen eye for anything he considered original, beautiful and, ultimately, inspiring. To say he was glowing with enthusiasm when he produced this object would be overstating it, but he marvelled at it and wanted me to share the moment. This recent discovery was the reason he had invited me over that day and, in all honesty, I did share that moment of marvel with him, as he presented me with a perplexing and curious ceramic bowl. It was the size of a fruit bowl, maybe ten or twelve inches in diameter and roughly six or seven inches deep, an unusual, washed-out viridian and pale cream in colour. The most striking feature, and obviously the reason David had acquired it, was the ghostly arrangement of nymph-like heads modelled in low relief that 'swam' all the way around the outside of the bowl. These heads were raised, as if out of water, under which, like reeds swaying in a clear stream, you could make out the vague outline of their submerged bodies. This image really stuck in my mind. It was captivating; a real one-off, like David himself.

Time and distance play tricks with the memory, but I believe that it was after he showed me the 'spirit' bowl that David asked me if I would like to hear his latest album, *The Man Who Sold The World*. I don't think the album had actually been released yet. So, I thought, as you would, 'Great! What a treat! He's going to give me a pre-release playing of the record.' I was flattered. I followed David into another room. It was a smallish space with a fireplace. There was a kilim or some other Indian-type rug on the floor. Then, to my astonishment, David picked up his guitar and sat down, cross-legged, on the floor. He invited me to do the same. I sat opposite him, with the rug, like a sort of dormant magic carpet, between us. Then he said, 'This is called "The Supermen"', and he started to play and sing. I sat there while he performed the entire album for me. Every now and again, he would ask me what I thought of this or that song. And I had to ask myself, what the hell was my opinion worth at that moment? Some pieces were certainly more melodic than others and I hoped my muttered approval was understood for what it was. In all honesty, I was not a huge fan of David's music in that particular period of his career. I preferred the later stuff. Amusingly, I remember thinking, as I watched his chord positions played close up and his right hand churning over the strings, that he wasn't a great guitarist. But what the hell did that matter? He didn't have to be a virtuoso, did he? He was David Bowie. (2016)

RUSSELL MAEL[28]

In early 1975, still living our Anglophile dream, we arrived at Tony Visconti's west London home studio to continue work on our Indiscreet album. That morning we were greeted by an all-too-familiar, iconic bass melody emanating from our producer's hands: C-D-E-F-G-A-Bb-C-F-G-A-Bb-C-D-E-F. 'My God! Act cool! Don't become a babbling idiot! Don't acknowledge outwardly how significant those ascending bass lines were to my musical upbringing!' Okay, so it wasn't David Bowie himself, but it was the guy who produced and played bass on *The Man Who*

Sold The World, giving Ron and me our own personal performance of this song that was among the defining moments of my early years growing up 5,000 miles from London, in sunny Los Angeles. 'The Man Who Sold The World'. C-D-E-F-G-A-Bb-C-F-G-A-Bb-C-D-E-F. To this day, I have never let on to Tony how cool that moment was. (2016)

1. Not in his autobiography, but in *The Spider With The Platinum Hair*, Weird & Gilly's biography of Mick Ronson (Independent Music Press, 2003). Tony Visconti will tell the author in 2019 that Ronson was at Trident during the 'all hands on deck' mix of 'Wild Eyed Boy From Freecloud'.

2. A private club in Soho upstairs at 100 Wardour Street (the Marquee was at Number 90), managed by Jack Barrie and frequented by established musicians or ones who were on their way up. At the time, The Ship pub on the corner of Wardour Street and Flaxman Court was the other popular place for thirsty Trident Studios clients.

3. Released in 1995 on Tenth Planet (and reissued in 1998), *The Rise And Fall Of Bernie Gripplestone And The Rats From Hull* is a compilation of a few original recordings of The Rats and three songs the band will play (with Tony Visconti on guitar), at the tribute concert for Mick Ronson at the former Hammersmith Odeon on 29 April 1994.

4. In 1969, Mick Ronson played on *Fully Qualified Survivor*, the second album of Michael Chapman, a singer-songwriter from Leeds. It was his first session in London (at Regent Sound Studios) as a backing musician. Rick Kemp (bass) and Barry Morgan (congas) also played on this LP produced by Gus Dudgeon. According to John Cambridge – in his 2021 book *Bowie, Cambo & All The Hype* (McNidder & Grace) – it appears that Mick Ronson was asked to come to London because Tim Renwick, David Bowie's first choice as a guitarist, was not available (he was playing live with Fantasia, Terry Reid's band at the time).

5. Herbert Buckingham Khaury, better known under his misleading pseudonym Tiny Tim (he was a tall and stout man), was an eccentric American singer whose voice, from high pitch to baritone, was as crazy as he was. Popular in the 1960s and 1970s, he had a special way of covering songs (mainly by accompanying himself on the ukulele) from any genre or era. On *God Bless Tiny Tim*, his first (and best-known) album, released in 1968, he covered 'I Got You Babe' by Sonny Bono, and 'Fill Your Heart', which is sometimes attributed only to Biff Rose; in fact, Paul Williams, composer of *Phantom Of The Paradise*, co-wrote it. In 'There Is A Happy Land' in 1966, David Bowie made reference to a certain Tiny Tim, but since this song was about happy childhoods, he was probably referring to the Dickens character.

6. From the Fantastic Four to Daredevil, not to mention the Hulk, X-Men, Spider-Man and Iron Man, all of Stan Lee and Jack Kirby's characters first appeared in the 1960s.

7. *Spider from Mars: My Life with Bowie* (Sidgwick & Jackson, 2016).

8. In 1969, Tony Visconti produced *Ten Songs By Tucker Zimmerman*, the first album by this unique American singer-songwriter.

9. When Peter Sarstedt died in early 2017, many books and online articles claimed that David Bowie had 'shared the award' with the creator of 'Where Do You Go To (My Lovely)'. This is not true, because they did not win in the same category. Sarstedt won the award for Best Song, in terms of music and lyrics, for his one and only hit.

10. Later in life, David Bowie will say that he regretted not having spent more time with his family, but his success didn't keep him from visiting Terry at Cane Hill. Terry also stayed with David when he wasn't at the institution (especially in early 1971). In 1966, George Underwood also received care at this hospital, and told his friend about it. His story may also have inspired 'All The Madmen'.

11. This English photographer is known for his beautiful album covers for prog rock groups Affinity and Colosseum, hard rock band Black Sabbath and just plain rock Rod Stewart.

12. Located in the same building as the label (Island Records) at 8–10 Basing Street, Island Studios was founded by Chris Blackwell, a British producer and talent scout as legendary as the artists he worked with and discovered. A great number of major albums were recorded there, and continued to be after ZTT (producer, Trevor Horn's label) bought it in the 1980s.

13. This story is well known: After a concert at the Electric Circus in Manhattan (The Velvet Underground played there on 29 and 30 January), David Bowie went to talk to the singer, thinking it was Lou Reed. In fact, Reed had already left the band and had been replaced by Doug Yule, who pointed out David's mistake after a ten-minute chat.

14. After living in England for a brief spell as the glam wave was taking shape, Bingenheimer will return to Los Angeles to open the legendary English Disco club at 7561 Sunset Boulevard. An outstanding publicist, he was instrumental in David Bowie's career in the US. Later, he also championed a lot of punk, new wave and Britpop bands. Bowie will appear in *Mayor Of The Sunset Strip*, the marvellous documentary about Bingenheimer, directed by George Hickenlooper in 2004.

15. One of the places he frequents the most, thanks to his publisher Bob Grace who got a very good price, is the Radio Luxembourg Studio at 38 Hertford Street in London. It's not exactly a commercial studio, but its equipment is good enough to record some perfectly decent demos.

16. Located on Kensington High Street, the Sombrero (the actual name of the club, downstairs, was Yours Or Mine) became an inspirational place for Bowie and Burretti. That's where they met the emerging fashion designers of the day, like Anthony Price, and discovered looks they used for Ziggy Stardust. Daniella Parmar, Burretti's best friend, sported an androgynous look for some time and had an ultra-short (bleached) haircut like Ziggy's first. David Bowie and his friends also frequented the Masquerade, a gay club on Earl's Court Road.

17. Jingoism means extreme patriotism. The term was used in the Boer War, and to refer to the large part of the population in favour of massive rearmament after World War I. The term originates from a popular song of the 1870s, during the war between Russia and Turkey, which Britain considered joining. The song contained the very old exclamation, 'By Jingo' as a euphemism for 'By Jesus'. 'Oh, By Jingo' was the title of a love song which first appeared in 1919, but was featured in well-known films and shows in the 1940s and 1950s. It was also known as 'Oh By Jingo! Oh By Gee! You're The Only Girl For Me'.

18. It seems that the sexually explicit lyrics (and title) of 'She Shook Me Cold' reference 'You Shook Me', a blues song by Willie Dixon and

J.B. Lenoir covered by Led Zeppelin and Jeff Beck on their respective first albums (released while David Bowie was writing the songs for *The Man Who Sold The World*). However, 'She Shook Me Cold' is far from being blues and the song's lyrics are much more explicit than those of 'You Shook Me'. As for Mick Ronson's slick performance on the song, it's closer to that of Jeff Beck than Jimmy Page.

19. None of the works by this American sci-fi writer will appear in the list of 100 books recommended by Bowie in 2013 (Isaac Asimov, Arthur C. Clarke and Walter Tevis won't be mentioned either), but some of these stories will inspire him. In July 2020, MainMan will start uploading a series of podcasts on their new website. In these half-hour episodes, the staff of the management company, some artists they took care of and, of course, founder and president Tony Defries, will tell their own side of the story of a time when the 'main man' was David Bowie. In one of the episodes about *The Man Who Sold The World*, Defries doesn't fail to recall that 'Antigonish', written in 1899 by the American poet Hughes Mearns, influenced Bowie in the lyrics of his third LP's title song.

20. The superimposing, real or artificial, of two identical sounds can create a phasing effect. The sound distorts, changes in unusual ways and can even seem to disappear. Usually controlled by a pedal (and now a plug-in), phasing effects were used a lot by guitarists and keyboardists.

21. Analysed by many rock guitarists – whether aspiring or established, whether fans of David Bowie or not – for over half a century, Mick Ronson's sound was first and foremost due to the way he played, as is the case with other great musicians. The author once heard Ronson play a few chords on a Telecaster plugged into a little

Mesa Boogie amp in his room at the Novotel next to the Palais Omnisport de Paris-Bercy (now AccorHotels Arena), where he and Ian Hunter were staying during their last concert together in Paris at the Élysée Montmartre in February 1990. Sitting on his bed, Ronson recreated his signature sound, but not as loud. On stage and in the studio, when he played with Bowie, he created this sound by plugging his 1968 Custom Les Paul into a 100-watt Marshall amp. Compared with modern guitarists, who have a Boeing instrument panel at their feet and create a much less personal sound, Mick Ronson played it simple with one or two pedals. For the distortion, he usually used a Sola Sound or Vox Tone Bender and then inserted a wah-wah pedal between the guitar and the amp: the Dunlop Cry Baby. His defining move was to engage it and then use it as an equalizer (to favour a frequency, usually medium), although he reserved it only for the most crazy parts of his solos (for example in 'The Width Of A Circle' or 'Moonage Daydream').

22. Paul McCartney is one of the greatest lead bass players in the history of rock. He originally played guitar in The Beatles, and didn't start playing bass until Stuart Sutcliffe left. McCartney developed a technique based on his knowledge of the two instruments and created a melodic style that later inspired many important bass players, including Nicolas Godin of French band Air. In 2015, in the song 'Lazarus' on *Blackstar*, Tim Lefebvre will also play his bass as if it were a guitar.

23. A percussion instrument from the idiophone family made from a hollow gourd with notches cut into it. A stick is drawn across the notches to make a sound.

24. Recorded at the Château d'Hérouville during sessions for *Pin Ups*, this version produced by David Bowie and Mick Ronson will be released in 1974 on the A-side of a (Polydor) single, with 'Watch That Man' on the other side.

25. This recent account comes straight from the lips of Ralph Mace, who, when this book was written, lived in a retirement home in Portland in the US. There is confusion between the events described in books and what Mace said in interviews back in the day. Though Mace probably did play the Moog on the second studio version of 'Memory Of A Free Festival', which was recorded at Trident and Advision in March and April 1970, the chromatic runs he describes, which were fast and therefore difficult to perform, relate to 'Saviour Machine'.

26. Gerald Chevin probably worked on the 'Let Me Sleep Beside You' and 'Karma Man' sessions, David Bowie's first with Tony Visconti, in September 1967.

27. Objects from Victorian times.

28. Russell Mael and his brother Ron make up the American duo Sparks.

HUNKY DORY

RCA – 17 DECEMBER 1971

'Necessity compels her to be swift, so fast do men come to their turns.
This is she who is much reviled even by those who ought to praise her,
but do wrongfully blame her and defame her.'
(DANTE ALIGHIERI, *THE DIVINE COMEDY, INFERNO*, 1303–4)

'I think having gone to the USA before recording *Hunky Dory* really kick-started me. The space and size and excitement of it just gave me the motivation that anything was possible. Some people say this album is rather conventional but still, they think it's a crucial one. I guess it's because of a combination of the fairly unusual subject matter treated in a 'pop' context more than anything. I also think the song structures are pretty nice. You know, I never considered *Hunky Dory* a draft of *Ziggy Stardust*. It opened up a lot of writing channels. Thanks to this record, I became more international, less parochial. Although it might look like it, it wasn't a naive album, the pressure at the *Hunky Dory* stage was very intense but of a different nature. Ken Scott's role, more than anything, was to give us as pure and good a sound technically as was possible. He was also a great moral booster and had no problem telling us when something was as good or not so good as our average.

At the writing stage, I very much knew how I wanted the songs to sound, and arrangement-wise, Mick Ronson's major contributions were his guitar parts, of course, and the string writing that he did after I hummed a few melodies.

When I talked to George Underwood about the sleeve, I was very insistent on having a photograph that dealt as much with ambiguities as the content of the album. I wasn't looking to be provocative, least of all on a sexual level. I only understood the impact of this sleeve later.

While I was recording with Ken, Tony Visconti was producing T. Rex, but I never envied Marc Bolan. I value the work that I did with Tony in the same way as I do with Ken. Equal but different, in my mind. You know, these sessions at Trident didn't leave much room for experimentation. They were lots of really hard and straightforward work. I had everything on demo so it was just a case of getting it all to sound like a more professional version of my tapes. But at the time, I was still writing lyrics right before going to the studio! Except for "The Bewlay Brothers" – I only had the lyrics for that one and the melody came to me just before recording. I have very often thought of doing that song live. It is still a big fave of mine.

As for why I chose to cover "Fill Your Heart" or "It Ain't Easy" on *Ziggy Stardust*, there's no logical reason at all. I just loved these songs. And you know, I'm still very happy to have my music heard anyway I can, especially now with the state of radio formats, the way they are. In 2001, it's not even ironic anymore that "Starman" and "Life On Mars?" pop up in ads for devices that help people communicate.'

DB (2001)

Our destiny is shaped by chance encounters and our passions, which together lead us on a winding path. David Bowie's destiny, perhaps more than anyone's, is the perfect example. Jovial, relaxed and happy with his life – funny but not cynical – he often described himself as a fan while he was still talking to the press in the early 2000s. And he was. But since blissful ignorance and passivity weren't his style, he was constantly returning the favour. He was a fan of Lou Reed, Iggy Pop and Mott The Hoople, but it wasn't enough for him just to listen to them. By producing their music, giving them his time and talent (and that of Mick Ronson), he could actively support his idols. It was just the way he was, although some people have called it manipulative. They were wrong. To describe Bowie's altruism in a world motivated by money, Iggy Pop speaks of an outstretched hand – and we wouldn't dare argue with him.

In the 60s, Bowie felt that being a fan meant not just listening to records and going to concerts, but also hanging out where the musicians he liked would gather. Approaching them. Trying to connect with them, so he might learn something – anything – from them. Phil May described him as a pupil eager to learn from his elders. Billy Ritchie from 1-2-3/Clouds points out that so he could understand everything about them, David Bowie observed his idols wherever they went: in clubs, backstage, at parties. (The two other members of Clouds helped record demos for *Hunky Dory* and *Ziggy Stardust* at the Radio Luxembourg Studios, but not Ritchie, even though he was close to Bowie for a while.) All these scheduled or chance meetings, fleeting infatuations or lasting passions, fits of productivity or stalled momentum, help forge David Bowie's destiny, shaping his career. For example, if American composer/pianist Annette Peacock had wanted to play with him, she never would have mentioned Mike Garson's name. If Carlos Alomar hadn't been asked to work with Lulu at RCA Studios in New York, he probably never would have met Bowie. If Reeves Gabrels's wife hadn't given David a tape of her guitarist husband's playing at the end of the Glass Spider tour, Tin Machine and *Earthling* never would have happened. And if Billy Ritchie hadn't got angry with Bowie, he probably would have played on 'Life On Mars?'.

David Bowie's interest in prog rock, and the musicians who invented and developed it, will fade with time. What he really dislikes is the musicians' lack of stage presence: sure they play well, but they are hunched over their instruments, curled up into themselves. While there is plenty to hear at a Soft Machine or King Crimson concert, there is not much to see. And members of these bands aren't that great at communicating with their audience (or even with each other). Usually, people clap politely at the end of a piece as it is being drawn out into a long solo, and the musicians barely lift their heads before moving on to the next song. David Bowie wants his music to be taken seriously and played by the best musicians, but he also wants to feel a sense of complicity with his audience, like Elvis Presley or The Beatles. In the 1960s, when a starstruck David went to see The Pretty Things, The Yardbirds, The Who or The Rolling Stones, he could feel the electric relationship they had with their fans. Towards the end of the decade, tired of sitting cross-legged at the edge of the stage and singing mostly to unresponsive hippies, Marc Bolan took to his feet to try to elicit a reaction from his audience. Like Bob Dylan before him, he picked up an electric guitar and summoned the youth – they fell in love with his music just as much as they did with his dark eyes. Bolan's meteoric rise to fame happened with him at the helm of a real rock band. He didn't lose his shine until the summer of 1972, when he was overshadowed by a certain Ziggy Stardust. For now, David Bowie knows how important it is to surround himself with excellent musicians, but he has no intention of neglecting the visual side of things. Bolan took in every detail from the shows by Hype that he went to, and Bowie also found that performing with Hype opened his eyes to the need to cultivate a look, to wear make-up[1] and to bring more theatre into his shows. And he thinks the best way to do this is to find a guitarist, a partner who can serve as a foil on stage. So he decides to ask for help from the one person he is missing: Mick Ronson.

Late spring 1971 was an emotional time for Bowie. Again, not everyone's memories of the time agree on the details and David's were sometimes hazy. One thing's for sure though: Angie Bowie gave birth to Duncan Zowie Haywood Jones on 30 May. According to her husband, he was listening to a Neil Young album when it happened. Overcome with emotion, he quickly wrote 'Kooks'[2] (which would appear on *Hunky*

Dory). It's probable that the song, which is addressed to his only son (and, indirectly, to his wife), was already partly written, along with some others he'd been working on – the good news just helped him finish it. Any similarity to Neil Young and the more upbeat songs from his album *After The Gold Rush* are mostly in the style of production. Composition-wise, 'Kooks' is relatively sophisticated, and described wrongly as a minor work. It includes a Bolan-like descending chord progression in the middle of the chorus and the album version will owe a lot to the high quality of both the musical arrangement and the mix. Throughout this time, Bowie was drawn to America and, like Bryan Ferry[3], he was impressed by the music of Neil Young. In 2001, he will cover 'I've Been Waiting For You' on *Heathen*.

Two weeks before, after recording some songs with the musicians from Clouds and trying to form a band with some old acquaintances (Terry Cox, Tim Renwick and Tony Hill), David Bowie phoned Mick Ronson. Ronno, the band that he and Woody Woodmansey had been trying to set up since returning to Hull, had already hit a brick wall. A single from the sessions with Hype the year before (with '4th Hour Of My Sleep' on the A-side) came out in late January on Vertigo Records, but it was notable only for its lukewarm reception. In addition, Tony Visconti had been kept busy by T. Rex in London and was no longer in the band. Ronson doesn't hesitate long before joining Bowie again.

The first musicians Bowie approaches for the rhythm section of the group are not the future Spiders From Mars. Mick (or maybe someone else) suggests that drummer Ritchie Dharma and bass player Rick Kemp audition, but they do so without success. Of Indian origin and very active in the early 1970s, Dharma will move in Bowie's circles for a while, most notably by playing on *Transformer*, the Lou Reed album David Bowie and Mick Ronson will produce the following year. He will also play on Ronson's first two solo albums. Rick Kemp, the bass player for singer-songwriter Michael Chapman, will do a stint with King Crimson but refuses to become a permanent member. Then he will join the folk-rock group Steeleye Span.

Once back at Haddon Hall, Mick Ronson and Woody Woodmansey urge Bowie to call bass player Trevor Bolder, a solid musician from the Hull music scene who has performed with Ronno. In June, sessions for a new album start at Trident, although some of the recorded songs will appear on the album after that. The musicians work with Ken Scott, who David Bowie soon starts calling 'my George Martin'. After his disappointment with *The Man Who Sold The World*, things are looking better for Bowie. Tony Defries has freed him from his contract with Mercury, and

Peter Noone is making it big in the charts with his version of 'Oh! You Pretty Things' (on which Bowie plays piano). The song will climb to Number 12, and stay in the charts for a good ten weeks.

The same month, always seeming to be everywhere at once, and in spite of the total failure of the previous single released a few weeks before, David Bowie records two new tracks at Trident with Ronson, Bolder and Woodmansey, under the name Arnold Corns. The voice of the official singer, Freddie Burretti, is absent from 'Man In The Middle' and 'Looking For A Friend' – or it is drowned out by the vocals of Bowie and Mark Pritchett (who also wrote the first song). Micky King[4], whom Bowie had met at the Sombrero, briefly enters Bowie's world and stands in front of a mic to participate in the sessions, but he doesn't leave much of a mark. The instrumental part of 'Man In The Middle' heralds some of *Ziggy Stardust*'s most upbeat songs, while 'Looking For A Friend' emulates the style of The Rolling Stones. Bowie takes to the stage for the first time that year on 23 June, for the second Glastonbury festival, which draws a few thousand people (Keith Christmas had performed at the previous one). Due to the incompetency of the organizers, Bowie doesn't come on stage until just before dawn[5], but many in the audience call his performance magical, including future director Julien Temple, and Mick Farren who was just then starting to dedicate himself to writing[6].

In July, work continues at Trident. Some songs, including the cover of 'It Ain't Easy' with Dana Gillespie on backing vocals, are scrapped during the final selection, or will be released later on *Ziggy Stardust*. The proliferation of recordings from that year means that the track lists for these two albums, which were practically recorded at the same time, will change a lot before the final cut. Many of them were composed on the piano at Haddon Hall and David thinks some of them would be improved by an experienced keyboardist. With Billy Ritchie out of the loop, he contacts Rick Wakeman[7], whose contribution to *Hunky Dory*, especially 'Life On Mars?', 'Quicksand' and 'Fill Your Heart', is crucial[8]. But Wakeman, who according to Ken Scott was directed in his playing by Mick Ronson, isn't there for all the songs on the album – for example, it is Bowie playing on 'Oh! You Pretty Things'. In the end, he's so happy with Wakeman's work[9] that he will ask him to join Mick Ronson and the others. Wakeman will refuse and will find success with Yes and, later, as a solo artist. We also know that Dudley Moore was considered to play on *Hunky Dory*. He's remembered best as an actor and as the comedy partner of Peter Cook, but Moore, who died in 2002, was also a talented pianist. Influenced by Oscar Peterson and Erroll Garner, he composed many original film scores.

In August, as recording for the new album is coming to an end ('Life On Mars?' is one of the last songs recorded[10]), Bowie signs with Gem, the company Tony Defries and Laurence Myers have started. They promise to support his interests better. The following summer, with MainMan, his new company, Defries will officially become Bowie's manager. An altruist who realizes increasingly that this is what he is, David will immediately insist that Defries find a label for his friend George Underwood. While Bowie and Mick Ronson play two gigs as a duo to small audiences, one of them at the Marquee, Tony Defries flies to the United States with a promotional record in his hands. On the A-side are several of the new songs Bowie recorded that summer[11], on the other are some tracks by Dana Gillespie. During his trip, Defries will contact most of the major labels (there were more in those days than there are today) and set up meetings, then end up accepting RCA's offer made through head of A&R, Dennis Katz.

At the time, RCA, Elvis Presley's label, is losing steam, partly because sales of its main star are falling fast. RCA is trying to modernize its dated and somewhat macho image. Katz believes, quite rightly, that salvation could come from this strange and trendy Englishman who wears dresses and who is receiving more and more positive reviews in the music press (especially from Lisa Robinson[12], one of Katz's friends). So in early September, Bowie joins Tony Defries in New York to sign the contract with RCA (Angie Bowie and Mick Ronson were also there), and also to make one of his dreams come true: to meet two of his idols, Lou Reed and Iggy Pop, who are both going through a bad patch in their careers. In true Bowie fashion, he does everything he can to make the most of those ten days. The day after meeting Iggy Pop, singer with The Stooges, at Max's Kansas City, Bowie suggests he sign with Gem. He asks Tony Defries to find a label for the follow up to the remarkable *Fun House*, The Stooges' second album, which came out more than a year before and whose failure has been crushing.

Since he is in New York, Bowie catches up with some of the cast of *Pork*, Andy Warhol's play directed by Tony Ingrassia, whom he was in contact with after having seen the show at the Roundhouse in London, before he left for the States. The script comes from recordings of conversations Andy Warhol had with Brigid Berlin[13]. It caused a great scandal in London – there was even more nudity in it than in *Hair* or *Oh! Calcutta!*, which had come out a few seasons before – so it caught Bowie's attention. While in New York, David also seeks the company of famous 'superstars', androgynous beings, who are even more provocative and unsettling than the London drag queens at the Sombrero. He makes a connection with Leee Black Childers, Tony Zanetta, Cherry Vanilla and Wayne County. He also has an audience with Andy Warhol, the king of pop art, but the meeting is a fiasco. After exchanging a few embarrassed glances and very few words[14], Bowie leaves Warhol's studio, the Factory, but not before giving him a test pressing of the song he's written for him. Andy always claimed he hated it.

On 25 September 1971, just after returning from the States, David Bowie performs at the Friars Borough Assembly Hall in Aylesbury, an hour and a half drive north-west of London. The club will become legendary as the place where Ziggy Stardust And The Spiders From Mars will play live for the first time four months later. But that September it is the place where Mick Ronson, Trevor Bolder and Woody Woodmansey accompany David Bowie for the first time in front of an audience. First planned for 11 September, but postponed because of the trip to the States, the concert is more of a showcase (with a 50p entry fee), during which Bowie plays 7 songs (of a set list of 14) from his upcoming album. At the start, David is on 12-string guitar with only Mick Ronson on bass. He talks a lot between songs, starts off the set with two Biff Rose numbers ('Fill Your Heart' and 'Buzz The Fuzz'), and invites the other musicians to join him on stage throughout the evening. The band still hasn't mastered all the songs very well – some chords are badly played, even by Bowie himself. From 'Changes' they are joined by Tom Parker[15], the first of a long line of pianists who will perform live with David until, in September 1972, he settles on Mike Garson.

That night they were due to be supported by a trio called America, three Englishmen who, like Bowie, dreamed of the promised continent[16]. But ironically (with David just returned from America), the trio isn't able to open for him as planned. Among other covers, Bowie also performs the Arnold Corns song, 'Looking For A Friend', this time as a Stones pastiche and now openly sung by the song's writer. As the encore, they play 'I'm Waiting For The Man', which is the second reference that evening to Lou Reed, as earlier they had done 'Queen Bitch', which David claimed was a tribute to the former frontman of The Velvet Underground. He doesn't know it yet, but the following summer, Bowie will produce Lou Reed's second solo album.

Soon after getting back from the United States, David Bowie found out that 'Right On Mother', a song he'd written for Peter Noone, was coming out as a single. Even though it was written around the same time as 'Oh! You Pretty Things', it won't appear on *Hunky Dory*. With its Gilbert O'Sullivan-style verses and its piano in the style of 'Velvet Goldmine', 'Right On Mother' wouldn't have felt out of place on the album. In October, even though his new record isn't out yet, Bowie surprises everyone by announcing he and his band will start rehearsing new songs he's just written for the following one[17]. It is clear to those around him that David Bowie is getting ahead of himself, moving even faster than his music.

On 7 November, he and his band go to an Alice Cooper concert at the Rainbow in London, but not just for the fun of it. Bowie wants to see, first-hand, someone he already considers to be a rival. In 1971, Alice Cooper is still a band and the epitome of American shock-rock[18]. Their provocative style is pretty trashy, but an Alice Cooper performance is a real show, which is what appeals to David Bowie. Despite what Alice did or didn't say (music journalists were already very good at putting words into rock stars' mouths), Bowie didn't take much inspiration from him when creating the Ziggy Stardust concept. His influences clearly came from elsewhere. However, it is true that long before the appearance of those from Mars, Alice Cooper's band was called The Spiders[19], then The Nazz. But after listening to 'Ziggy Stardust', even the most die-hard Alice Cooper fans can't claim that the words, 'The kid was just crass, he was the nazz', were a reference to their hero[20]. Bowie wants to see what others are up to so he can try something different. Like Marc Bolan and Alice Cooper, he relies heavily on his outfits and he'll soon be wearing satin, quilted and glittery suits, but long hair is no longer his thing. On 17 December 1971, when *Hunky Dory* comes out (its title was long thought to have been suggested by Bob Grace), David Bowie no longer has the androgynous look inspired by a photo of Greta Garbo, which he sports on the album cover. He doesn't yet have the Ziggy crop, but his hair is only long down the back of his neck. On the sides and top of his head, it is short. His changes are rapidly spinning now, into a permanent revolution.

And indeed it is a redemptive impermanence which David Bowie sings of in 'Changes', the song which opens side A of Hunky Dory, with its themes of serious-minded rebellion[21], introducing more and more iridescent and shimmering colours. 'Changes', the perfect introduction to his work, is a magical piece, its verses wrapped in his silky voice and a chorus that rushes like a torrent. A hymn to glory, full of an impertinence which he felt more than ever, the song was created in the image of the rest of the album, which the media see as a change of direction for Bowie: more pop than rock. Dotted with esoteric and Nietzschean references, the upbeat 'Oh! You Pretty Things' (which also alludes to *The Coming Race*, a sci-fi novel by

Edward Bulwer-Lytton, written in 1871) clearly needs to be taken with a pinch of salt. Juggling with different concepts (including that of the superior man he had already touched on in 'The Supermen') has become Bowie's main intellectual pastime, but while appreciating the beauty of a gesture as much as its consequences, the form as much as the content.

'Eight Line Poem' is often dismissed as an interlude on *Hunky Dory* but this calm song, which comes before the storm that is 'Life On Mars?', is perhaps more significant than it may seem. Boldly conceived, the chord progression David Bowie plays on piano is the only harmonic component of that song. Mick Ronson starts and ends with a simple light strum on his Les Paul plugged directly into an amp. Unless the cactus is an allusion to the 'beautiful tree' he and Hermione Farthingale could see from the window of their room on Clareville Grove, the lyrics are incomprehensible.

'Life On Mars?' is the main course of *Hunky Dory*, for those who don't prefer 'Quicksand'. Of course it's a musical response to 'My Way' (the Frankie mentioned on the back of the jacket is Sinatra, who contributed greatly to making that song famous). It's the story of a girl disappointed with reality, who takes refuge in fiction. The song is one of the most direct reactions to Bowie's trip to the United States, which he said was the catalyst for the album. Thanks to Rick Wakeman's delicate piano and the powerful build-up towards a chorus which is swollen with skillfully orchestrated strings, a perfect frame for one of the most acrobatic vocals in Bowie's entire repertoire (on stage, from the following year, he would perform it a tone lower than on the record – from F, the verse will start in E flat), 'Life On Mars?' could, if needed, sum up Bowie in 1971 in less than four minutes.

To be approached with caution, the lyrics of 'Quicksand' contain an overwhelming flood of literary influences scattered from all kinds of sources, Crowley first and foremost among them. In the chorus, Bowie turns hope into resignation and describes death as the second-to-last stop on an exalting inner journey. Musically, that song is as majestic as its Martian sister, but perhaps more restrained. It's like a crystal staircase, a spiral towards the light of a chorus whose harmonies owe their charm to two diminished chords that Mick Ronson extracted from the jumble of 12-string guitars in the original demo (a bonus track on Rykodisk's 1990 re-release of *Hunky Dory*[22]).

The original version of 'Fill Your Heart' (on Biff Rose's first album) leaves something to be desired in comparison with David Bowie's, which is more slender. The drums can barely be heard – they were surely played with brushes. This first cover on a Bowie album has a strong brass intro (as on 'Changes', he plays saxophone, his childhood instrument, which he didn't use on the two previous albums) and features Rick Wakeman's skipping piano and string arrangements so similar to those which Tony Visconti was then weaving for T. Rex – especially on 'Beltane Walk', a song from the first album T. Rex released under their shortened name, recorded at Trident and released in 1970 – that it couldn't be a coincidence. In the handwritten notes on the back of the sleeve, David ironically thanks Arthur G. Wright for his work on the 'prototype' of 'Fill Your Heart'. A rhythm'n'blues guitarist who worked on many soul recordings in the 60s, Wright arranged some songs on *The Thorn In Mrs Rose's Side*. By implying that his version is the finished one, Bowie confirms that *Hunky Dory* is the album of a singer-songwriter who is asserting himself and, at the same time, plotting to take America by storm.

The tracks 'Andy Warhol', 'Song For Bob Dylan' and 'Queen Bitch' are obvious tributes to David's idols. But their sound has been anglicized by Ken Scott, a former builder of the Beatles house, who knows a lot of their secrets. Bowie sings all three tracks openly, like a 'London boy' pawing at the barricade of his illusions on the other side of the Atlantic, without stealing the accents of the singers he loved[23].

Long before technology made it easy, Bowie was a human sampler. He sampled authentic American records, not just those he could find at Tower Records, but others he sought out in collectors' shops[24]. Music by deviants. In addition to Lou Reed, Iggy Pop and Biff Rose, who in the very early 1970s weren't popular even in their own country, Bowie became passionate about Ron Davies. He was a Los Angeles-based, edge-of-the-blues-scene folk-rocker, another unknown talent. David brought his album, *Silent Song Through The Land*, back from the United States. One of the songs is called 'Change' and it's obvious Bowie robbed two chords from the four intro bars (including the acoustic guitar riff) of the title song for 'Andy Warhol'. In 'Song For Bob Dylan', David settles for copying the great Bob by proxy, drawing heavily on the voice and essence of 'Lover And The Loved', which Ron Davies clearly wrote and sang with Zimmerman in mind.

'Queen Bitch', Bowie's nod to The Velvet Underground, doesn't have much to do with Lou Reed in terms of composition, but it contains a lot of Eddie Cochran and his brother, who wrote 'Three Steps To Heaven'. David and Mick copied its intro (and verse) chord progression, with just a slight rhythm variation, without any qualms or royalty payments. When some of the more astute music journalists listen to the album, they will note the similarities and rebuke Bowie. In 1971, a big lawsuit was launched by the publisher of Ronnie Mack, the singer-songwriter of

'He's So Fine', a song made popular eight years before by New York girl band The Chiffons. George Harrison's 'My Sweet Lord' sounded a bit too much like it. But David Bowie doesn't commit grand larceny, even unintentionally. While he pilfers a few things here and there, he does so consciously, and then, covering his tracks, he lets his natural grace, his tangled lyrics and his sophisticated way of composing give his music its own colour. Because with *Hunky Dory*, the obvious is only on the surface – don't be fooled by appearances.

Like the previous album, *Hunky Dory* ends with a lurch in the form of 'The Bewlay Brothers', a wild-goose chase of a song carried along by verbose mumbling. David confirmed that the title (and probably the chorus) is a reference to him and Terry – Bewlay was the brand of pipe they stole puffs from while hiding from their parents – but he would never shed light on all the mysteries in those verses. After 'Eight Line Poem', 'The Bewlay Brothers' is the second song on the album, and the last in his discography, to be recorded with only Mick Ronson. His contribution, especially his acoustic guitar supporting Bowie's majestic 12-string, is breathtaking. The intriguing character of the final part is accentuated by Ronson strumming the chords as close as possible to the bridge, in a way acoustic guitars aren't usually played.

What David Bowie started with *The Man Who Sold The World*, he finished with *Hunky Dory*. The two albums were released the same year in the United Kingdom, yet they were so different. On the two records, David Bowie asserted himself as an outrageously literary singer-songwriter, drawn to the road less travelled and not inclined to explain his work. *Hunky Dory* is the first album that seems truly his. In late 1971, even though the charts, once again, are impervious to his music (like *Space Oddity* and *The Man Who Sold The World*, *Hunky Dory* would have to wait for its re-release on RCA to get into the hit parade), he feels like he is doing something right. He doesn't intend to deliver any future songs to the public (the very people who will soon love him and follow him by the hundreds of thousands) until he is totally happy with them. Deliberately failing to dot all the i's, stirring up trouble, Bowie starts seeing himself as an actor (he wrote it on the back of the album cover[25]), evolving in a changing setting. A stowaway on an artistic adventure without a compass in his hand, he is only taking care to check, from time to time, that the silent shadow clinging to his feet is picking up the pebbles as quickly as he lays the trail.

Mick Ronson	Alan Mair
Trevor Bolder	Robin Mayhew
Ken Scott	Nicky Graham
Dennis 'Blackeye' MacKay	Billy Ritchie
	Harry Hughes
	Tony Visconti
	Mike Garson
	Iggy Pop
	Mick Rock
	Hermione Farthingale
	George Underwood
	Dennis Katz
	Dana Gillespie
	Glenn Goring
	Bobbie Seagroatt
	Michael Chapman
	Marc Exiga
	Richard Strange
	Pete Keppler
	Lenny Kravitz
	Chris Martin
	Giles Martin

MICK RONSON

When David said I was his Jeff Beck, I have to say I was quite embarrassed. However, I was happy people were saying nice things about my string arrangements for *Hunky Dory* and *Ziggy Stardust*. But let me tell you, I didn't have much time to write them. Sometimes I started on them the night before recording and did the final touches at the last minute, right before the orchestra musicians arrived. It was better to be ready because those people weren't the type to try too hard to understand what you wanted, and even less to hang around the studio. I think that one of the first songs I orchestrated with real strings was 'Life On Mars?'.

David gave me a lot of freedom from the start, because he was still finding himself and he didn't know exactly what kind of artist or musician he wanted to be. By letting us do our thing, he was presented with a number of directions and could eventually choose which one to take. He had no problem making himself understood, except maybe by the other Spiders! Sometimes he asked me to talk to them for him. We were on the same wavelength and I was kind of his translator. (1990)

TREVOR BOLDER

I remember this festival in Hull where The Rats were playing, and I was in a blues group. Throughout our set, there was a guy next to my amp who wouldn't stop looking at me. I only found out later that night that it was Mick Ronson – we didn't talk that time. Later, The Rats invited me to one of their gigs and, weirdly, their bass player refused to get on stage because he was afraid of being electrocuted! So Mick asked me to replace him and I didn't wait for him to ask twice! We were always together after that. He and Woody Woodmansey asked me to play in Ronno with them, then Mick went to audition for Bowie before sending for us – that's when we became The Spiders From Mars. The same thing that happened to Mick kind of happened to me. As soon as I arrived from Hull, I had to learn all of David's repertoire because there was a radio programme coming up. Herbie Flowers was supposed to play bass, but he couldn't make it...

It's not easy to distinguish between the Bowie albums I played on, especially the first two, which were recorded one after the other. Okay, *Hunky Dory* is the one I played the trumpet on[26]! In the studio it looked like David was in a mad rush. For *Ziggy Stardust*, we had some time to rehearse, but when we were making *Hunky*

Dory, all he did was show us the chords and ten minutes later, he was asking Ken Scott to press the record button! I wasn't there for *The Man Who Sold The World*, but Woody always said that David really started to write songs with *Hunky Dory*. They were pouring out of him like he was a tap. He mainly wrote songs on guitar but, for this album, a lot of them were written on the piano. I heard him play some at Haddon Hall. In the mornings he'd be trying chords but, by evening, he usually had a song! By the way, this might interest you: we almost played in France in the summer of 1971. We had a few concerts scheduled, as well as in Belgium and Holland I think, but it all fell through – of course we never knew why. (1994)

KEN SCOTT

The first time I saw David Bowie, for the recording of *Space Oddity*, he didn't make much of an impression on me. I thought he was a very nice guy. He obviously had a certain amount of talent, but I didn't have the feeling he would become that big. I think what caused that is the fact he was not controlling what was going on – it was Tony Visconti. So David's vocal talent was allowed to come out and so was his songwriting talent, but none of the other ideas. At first, I didn't get the full scale of what he was all about. I have the firm belief now that the reason why David moved from Tony to me was because Tony, as a musician, had so much control over the arrangements and how everything sounded. Especially for *The Man Who Sold The World*, on which he even played bass. I think David needed to find his own voice and get confident putting out what he heard in his head. I'm not as musical as Tony, so David knew I wasn't going to control things as strongly. So I think working with me allowed him to find himself. Then he could go back to Tony and, if he didn't agree with him, he would be able to argue with him.

You know, I obviously learned a lot from working with George Martin. And there is that saying: 'Give someone enough rope to hang themselves' – it's kind of what happens in the studio. You help the artists to find their own way but, if they go off track too much, you can always sort of pull them back in. And that's how I have been working. During sessions for Arnold Corns I agreed to work on *Hunky Dory*, which was the first album I produced. I thought it would be a good idea to get my hands on a record that probably wouldn't make much of an impact. If I bungled it, no one would know. To be honest, I finally noticed David's talent the day Bob Grace, his publisher, came over with Angie to play the *Hunky Dory* demos for me. That's when I had the feeling that this could be huge.

Most of what happened in the studio with David was done for a specific reason. I remember him coming in right towards the end of the sessions for *Hunky Dory* and saying, 'Okay, we've got one more song to record.' I thought he was joking and he said, 'No, it's called "The Bewlay Brothers" and the lyrics won't make any sense to you whatsoever.' Aside from the fact that it may contain a reference to his half-brother Terry, the song was specifically written for the American market, so they could read lots of things into it. This was very shortly after the 'Paul is dead' rumour and, at the time, Americans were reading things into lyrics, finding anything they could to come up with stories. The whole thing affected him and he wrote that song with strange lyrics for that reason. So that shows how much he wanted to break into the American market.

From *Hunky Dory* onwards, I could see that David's partnership with Mick Ronson was incredible. It was one of his gifts: knowing how to surround himself with competent musicians who would help him craft whatever was going through his brain at any given time. The band and I were very close and went along with David's music. The albums we recorded between 1971 and 1973 wouldn't have turned out the way they did if it hadn't been for Mick, Trevor, Woody, David and me being together. We were all equally important in terms of what we brought to the records. It didn't mean much to me at the time but, in hindsight, it still amazes me to think that I usually found myself alone for the final mix. David left it all in my hands. Mick Ronson sometimes came, but I had to make decisions on my own that helped shape songs that have become classics. If I remember correctly, 'Lady Grinning Soul', on *Aladdin Sane*, was the first mix David attended. (2016)

DENNIS 'BLACKEYE' MACKAY

I started out as a tea boy at Trident when I was 16 years old, before becoming an assistant engineer. I was fortunate to gravitate towards Ken Scott, whose work ethic I admired, and who himself was learning how to produce records. Like in other studios, most of the recording engineers at Trident didn't play any instruments, and the choices they made – to put a delay on some vocals, for example – were actually rather like production. Ken and I got along like a house on fire and I learned a lot from him. He started to work with David Bowie as an engineer, then David asked him to co-produce.

From our first meeting, I knew immediately that David was extremely gifted. All his ideas were great, original and new. A lot of solo artists of his generation were kind of undecided in the studio and needed someone to guide them. Not him: everything he did was exciting. I often read that Mick Ronson was the one to talk to the band members, with the excuse that he knew how to handle the other musicians from Hull. But David, whom they obviously thought was a bit strange, was just as good at rallying his troops when necessary. For example, he inspired the musicians to do more – he would say to Woody Woodmansey, 'Come on man, just roll those toms!' He was the one who got the band excited.

I was also amazed by how easy it was for him to record vocals. After putting up his microphone, usually a Neumann U67, it was no good asking him to do a run-through so we could get a level. We quickly learned that, with him, the first take was usually the one. We had to record it with care because it would probably end up on the record! It was unreal, and honestly, I've never seen that since – it was kind of magical. But that's not all – here's the freaky part! When it was time to double-track, to sing the same part again to get a bigger sound, David could do it perfectly. In 'Changes', at one point, he triggered that famous effect called phasing. He immediately made us stop the tape recorder to remove the effect. Of course, we hadn't added any. We explained that what he was hearing was just phasing, due to the fact that he was too precise! It was unbelievable! As for the vocal harmonies, even the most tricky ones, he recorded them just as quickly. First takes only!

Every time a Bowie track I've worked on comes on the radio, I can see him singing in the studio again. I remember his determination, his sense of humour, even the make-up and the glam outfits he wore! I'm so thankful I was around; I only wish I had my name on the cover of *Hunky Dory*. Talking of which, you know David gave me my nickname – 'Blackeye' – because every time we saw each other, the first thing we'd do was shadow boxing. It stuck and, later, it even became the name of my company. (2016)

ALAN MAIR

David Bowie would catch anything flying past and put it to good use! When he was spending time with The Beatstalkers in the studio, he noticed that one of my favourite expressions, originally Scottish, was to say that everything was hunky dory. The first time he heard it, he asked me what it meant and I told him that I always used that expression without realizing it. I was surprised he didn't know it. Hunky dory means 'everything is going to be fine!' He told me he loved the expression and that he wanted to use it... (2018)

ROBIN MAYHEW

In 1971, my wife Mardy and I had returned from a failed venture in Ibiza and I had no job. I went to visit my old school chum and producer friend Glyn Johns, who had recorded my 60s band The Presidents and was now living in the house the late Ian Stewart, the 'fifth Stone', had rented in Epsom, Surrey. Nicky Graham was also staying there. He had a new band called Tucky Buzzard who were about to record an album. I explained my position and he said that they needed someone to help with equipment and, most of all, their new sound system, which was ready to collect. I went and met Mike Turner, who had designed and made this new concept PA system. He explained the workings and set-up procedure and eventually I set off back to Epsom for rehearsals. Having recorded the album, Tucky Buzzard and I did two tours, then it was decided that we needed stronger management if we were going to get anywhere. That's when we found Tony Defries, who had just signed David Bowie, who I knew because of his hit 'Space Oddity'.

Defries had organized a semi-private concert[27] at the Haverstock Hill Country Club, in North London, for record company executives to hear some of David's new material and suggested that it would be good for Tucky Buzzard to do a short opening set. We did our performance, which was as loud as ever, but clear and clean, and then I had to remove all the equipment as David was using his own set-up. We had to remain for David's set, which was plagued by feedback howl and though only three musicians, including David, were playing[28], the entire show was a disaster. When they had finished, we got the okay to take our gear out and I felt a tap on my shoulder. It turned out to be Angie Bowie, who said David wanted to talk to me. I went and sat with them and David asked me, 'How was I able to hear everything your singer sang with all the rest of the mix so clear?' I told him about the unique Turner PA system and how I had got the band to keep their stage volume down and allow me to mix. He asked me if I would bring the system to a rehearsal to see what I could do with the band he had put together for the promotional tour of his upcoming album *Hunky Dory*. The venue was Beckenham Rugby Club – when I had set the PA system up, David and the band arrived. I asked their technician, Peter Hunsley (who'd been the roadie for The Rats), not to stack the guitar speaker cabinets as I had learned how this can destroy the front-of-house mix for the audience. The band was very well rehearsed and, after just two songs, there were smiles all round. David came off stage beaming and put an arm around me and said something like, 'This is it!' (2016)

NICKY GRAHAM

I first met David when I was in a band called Tucky Buzzard who were being managed by Tony Defries and produced by Bill Wyman of The Rolling Stones. We had been booked to open for David Bowie at the Haverstock Hill Country Club in the summer of 1971. It was an odd pairing as he was a solo artist playing an acoustic guitar and we were a heavy rock band. We had a big sound and David didn't! My girlfriend at the time, Diana Mackie, was personal assistant to Tony Defries and his partner Laurence Myers, so I found myself in the office pretty much every day. Of course, David knew I was a pianist and he invited me to play on stage when he needed one. When I met him, David had the most beautiful long hair and wore a dress. This would have been around 1971 and *The Man Who Sold The World* was out and creating a few waves. Things really changed with *Hunky Dory*. It was a wonderful album and one couldn't fail to see that 'Changes' was a pop hit waiting to happen. As was 'Oh! You Pretty Things' and the seminal 'Life On Mars?'. David's voice and range were pretty impressive, rather like Elvis Presley, who was a baritone, with a richness to his vocals. His guitar playing was rudimentary and more of an aid to his songwriting. The foil of Mick Ronson was an ideal addition to the excitement level each time it came to recording and on the tours that came afterwards. Mick was like the cherry on top of an already mouth-watering cake. (2017)

BILLY RITCHIE

I recommended David Bowie to Terry Ellis. He was our manager and founded the label Chrysalis with Chris Wright. In the spring of 1971, David was doing some demos for his forthcoming album, *Hunky Dory*. He sent a message asking the three of us to play with him on the sessions, but I refused to do it, though Harry and Ian did play. I think many of these songs were used on both *Hunky Dory* and *Ziggy Stardust*. Ian and Harry said he was fine and that the sessions were good, though they noted it was a bit awkward and embarrassing that I wasn't there. David had been hoping I would change my mind and turn up. Shortly after that, through Bob Grace, our publisher, David asked me to play on 'Life On Mars?', but I again refused. I wish now I had, for I think that was his best recording. Rick Wakeman was my replacement and he did a great job, but no better than I would have done. So many regrets... (2017)

HARRY HUGHES

We met David Bowie when we were playing a lot at the Marquee; he and Billy quickly became close friends. David used to carry my drums into the club so he could get in for free. He did that on several gigs. The recording session came about because David asked the three of us to help him with some demos, but Billy had fallen out with him and refused to do it, which was quite embarrassing for me and Ian, and also David. He seemed a really nice person, perhaps a bit anxious to please or be liked. Actually, he looked up to Billy a lot at that time. I didn't pay that much attention to the songs we did, though I gather they ended up on his future albums. There were a lot of guys like David around then, all trying to get a foothold in the music business. He didn't stand out, though Billy always told us that David had a lot of quality; he wasn't just a frontman according to him. He thought he would make it big sooner or later. (2017)

TONY VISCONTI

Hunky Dory is one of my favourite Bowie albums, even though I didn't produce it. It took David a long time to discover his strengths and this album became a reality nearly two years after we parted. *Hunky Dory* was a consistent work, full of glorious melodies and lyrics. David seemed to just wander through *The Man Who Sold The World*, because his lifestyle was more of a priority to him than his music at that time. *Ziggy Stardust* and *Aladdin Sane* were masterpieces too. By then I was very proud of him from afar and reasoned that it had to take all this time for him to learn how to create his alternate universe – that's what it is with Bowie! His world is uniquely his; he creates fashion in music and genres. I regret I didn't have the faith after *The Man Who Sold The World* to stick it out with him.

Albums like *Hunky Dory* and *Electric Warrior* were conceived as they are. You really had to listen to them from beginning to end several times before you got them. Nowadays, an album seems to be composed of three hit singles, usually produced by the flavour-of-the-month producer, and the rest of the songs are bland fillers, hastily recorded with what's left of the budget.

I can't say which songs I like best on *Hunky Dory* or *Electric Warrior*. Of the albums I worked on, I love *The Man Who Sold The World*, *Low*, *"Heroes"*, *Lodger* and *Scary Monsters*[29].

I think studios are just places where very talented people do their thing.

If a studio has a cool vibe but mediocre equipment, you can make a good record there. There was nothing spectacular about Trident's equipment. By today's standards, they hardly had any outboard equipment to speak of. But the consoles sounded really good, we can all agree on that. I remember at the time of the heyday of Trident, I would go to Paris and record. The average French studio had about four times more equipment than Trident. Actually, even smaller studios had more equipment! The sound of David's music at Trident had more to do with Ken Scott's style of engineering. Ken brings his 'sound' with him everywhere he goes. I do that too. (2001/2003/2015)

MIKE GARSON

You often hear about Rick Wakeman's piano on 'Life On Mars?', which I agree is absolutely fabulous. But he only played that song once – I had the chance to play it loads of times with David, always in a different way. (2016)

IGGY POP

I think the first David Bowie song I heard that impressed me was 'Black Country Rock', on *The Man Who Sold The World*. I remember very well that Tony Defries played the whole of *Hunky Dory* for me in New York, in a suite at the Warwick Hotel. I also remember the sleeve, with that Katherine Hepburn look. David and I met for the first time in the back room at Max's Kansas City. Journalist Lisa Robinson was there too and had given Danny Fields[30] a ring, who called to tell me that David wanted to meet me. I was at home, watching *Mr Smith Goes To Washington* on TV, and I was really enjoying it! I was pretty shy and I didn't agree to go until they called me back two or three times. Danny got fed up, and said, 'You know what? If these people can give you a hand, go and meet them!' I thought that David was extremely confident, very 'artistic', the complete opposite of a philistine, the type of person to be the leader of a band. (2016)

MICK ROCK

Hunky Dory was decisive, and remains a seminal album. David Bowie looked like a glam musician, but his music wasn't really like that. He was more like one of the singer-songwriters that we listened to religiously. I was fascinated by 'Life On Mars?', and got the chance to direct the video for it later. RCA gave me my first copy of *Hunky Dory*, but I had to buy another one later because I'd listened to it so much! (2016)

HERMIONE FARTHINGALE

I very much doubt that the lyrics of 'Life On Mars?' have anything to do with me, as I've read so often. The confusion came because, at one concert, David apparently said, 'I was in love once, this is a love song…' and then he did 'Life On Mars?' People assumed it was me, but I don't think so, especially because I never had mousy hair. My hair is red, which I actually think David has been referencing all his life, starting with Ziggy Stardust. But, you know, David's mother was an usherette in a cinema, she lived at home with her parents… Anyway, after a few lines 'Life On Mars?' goes off into such obscure stuff that nobody can understand it. I mean academics can analyze it forever; they'll come up with 40 different interpretations. (2016)

GEORGE UNDERWOOD

In late 1969, David had got me at Trident to record 'Hole In The Ground', which was going to be released as a single, but never was. Two years later, Tony Defries sent Mickie Most a few song demos that David had written for me, including 'Song For Bob Dylan'. Mickie had already produced 'Some Things You Never Get Used To', which I'd released under the name Calvin James in 1965. After that single came out, David and I didn't see much of each other. He was very jealous of my connection with Mickie. Then Defries tried to get me a recording contract, but David was his absolute priority. No one knows how David's career would have turned out without Tony Defries but, at the very least, he was largely responsible for David's success in America. (2016)

DENNIS KATZ

I signed David Bowie after hearing an early mix of half of *Hunky Dory*. I was a bit reluctant because I didn't really know how to handle the theatrical aspect of his music, but Angie and Tony Defries were very persuasive, and my wife convinced me that David had something special. She's partially responsible for us signing him! I also brought Lou Reed onto the RCA team. I introduced him to David Bowie and I worked hard to get them to collaborate on *Transformer*. (2000)

DANA GILLESPIE

David, Angie and I went to Glastonbury by train, all three of us in one compartment. When we got off, no one was there to take us to the site, so we had to walk quite far. David and Angie were both wearing Oxford bag trousers and looked like brother and sister. He had super-long hair and hers was extra short. There was loads of sitting around as the whole festival was chaotically organized and the timings of artists on stage went completely out of the window. Lots of workers in the Pyramid[31] were on acid and it was all peace and love. As the timings got later and later, David's slot to play kept being pushed back. At one point they didn't even know if he'd get on stage. In the end, he performed at about 5am, so that when the sleepy, muddy festival-goers slowly woke up with the morning sun, they were serenaded by David singing – 'The sun machine is coming down and we're gonna have a party...' People started coming out of their tents to greet the new day with David singing solo, just with his guitar[32]. I can't remember how we all got home, so I guess it was a good party!

As he was breaking onto the international scene, David put aside some time to help me with my first album, *Weren't Born A Man*. He was supposed to produce the whole thing, but couldn't in the end because of other commitments. But he did write 'Andy Warhol' for me, which I thought was a really nice gift. He was there for that session, but Mick Ronson finished the album in his place. I remember that David was very bossy, very focused, as if he was recording one of his own songs. For example, he was the one who insisted I sing the first verse without any emotion. That's absolutely not my style, but I went along with it, thinking it would be good for the song. (2016/2017)

GLENN GORING

David made a couple of trips to the United States. He was spending more and more time there and coming into contact with new influences and musicians such as Lou Reed. The States was really impacting his ideas about style, especially where music and fashion were heading. In one of our conversations, he was excited to tell me that the days of long hair and flower power were over. The new 'look', as he had seen it emerging from the USA, was much more masculine: short hair, sharp suits and glamorous styling. He was acutely aware of trends and the way fashion and music were constantly changing and he wanted to play a major role in directing and influencing those changes. (2016)

BOBBIE SEAGROATT

When I was going out with Glenn Goring, David invited us over to his house on Southend Road. I remember sitting in some sort of back room and he played 'Queen Bitch' for us and we thought it was an amazing song. We loved what it turned into, a little later, on *Hunky Dory*. The production on that is fantastic. Of course, I have a sentimental attachment to this song, because he played it for us, but it's a bloody good track with such a crisp sound. When I was really young, I didn't know what 'production' meant, but I realize now that the songs that affect me are the ones that also sound good. And the ones on *Hunky Dory* really do. (2016)

MICHAEL CHAPMAN

Strangely enough, I've heard and read this ever since it came out: *Hunky Dory* is David Bowie's version of *Fully Qualified Survivor*. I've been told that all these years. But, you know, I'd never heard it. A month ago I went out and bought a copy and I don't agree. *Hunky Dory* doesn't sound like my record – that's David Bowie you know[33]! (2017)

MARC EXIGA

I worked for RCA on two separate occasions. First, between 1966 and 1968, then from 1970 to 1980. I was international director. I got the chance to release *Hunky Dory* and, when I did, everyone thought I was crazy. Well, perhaps not the staff at *Rock&Folk* magazine – in the 1970s I was good friends with the two Philippes[34], and they knew perfectly well who David Bowie was. There was no obligation to release the album in France, I'm the one who decided to do it. Often, after three or six months, the Brits would ask us to release certain albums in France to help develop an artist or band's international reputation, but in this case, that's not what happened.

Hunky Dory wasn't exactly incomprehensible, but let's say that even at RCA, most people thought it was weird. I think there were many reasons for that. First, Bowie's music didn't really fit any genre. But what some people thought was really strange, was that RCA in America decided to sign an artist like that. In a way, it was going against the grain, the opposite of what the label normally stood for. I released *Hunky Dory* out of professional conviction. Knowing full well that David Bowie was ahead of his time, I knew it was going to be a bit of an adventure... To be honest,

I'm not sure we even sold 1,500 copies that first year. Music lovers who were really into the British underground scene probably bought the album, but everyone else was completely oblivious to it. A similar thing happened with Lou Reed. You might think 'Walk On The Wild Side' was a huge hit everywhere, but in France, people who knew his music wanted to buy the album instead of the single. (2018)

RICHARD STRANGE[35]

I saw David Bowie for the first time in April 1968 at the Purcell Room in London. He was opening for Tyrannosaurus Rex, my favourite band at the time. If I remember correctly, he was performing a mime act about the Dalai Lama and Chinese Buddhism. I thought he was brave and provocative. 'Space Oddity' had a big impact on me the following year, but it was mostly *Hunky Dory* that got me hooked. Even though 'Changes' and 'Life On Mars?' are the most well-known songs on the album today, it was two of the more intimate tracks – 'Quicksand' and 'The Bewlay Brothers' – that made me want to learn more about the guy. I was 20 years old and this album wasn't just speaking to me, it was screaming in my ear! Bowie's references were my references, both literary and musical: The Velvets, Brel, Burroughs, Nietzsche, Crowley ... what was there not to like? (2017)

PETE KEPPLER[36]

I remember the first time I saw the cover of *Hunky Dory*. I noticed David Bowie's dilated pupil and I realized that because of this guy – who didn't appear to be from the same planet as the rest of us – things were going to be different from that moment on. It's an understatement to say that he was really special. (2016)

LENNY KRAVITZ

As a kid, I only listened to black music. When I first heard 'Fame', like my friends I thought that this Bowie must be black too. The song tore a hole in me and I went out and bought everything he had done. David Bowie really blew my mind with *Hunky Dory*, which shows his enormous talent – 'Kooks', 'Life On Mars?', 'Changes'... (2000)

CHRIS MARTIN

Oh, the one thing I love more than anything right now is David Bowie and Mick Ronson's work on *Hunky Dory* – especially 'Life On Mars?'! That's quite a production, it kills me... And it's real team work – Mick Ronson, Ken Scott... I could record ten solo records, but they'd be better albums with input from the other members of Coldplay. Likewise, David Bowie is a genius, but he's really transcendent with a partner like Mick Ronson. He died, didn't he? (2001)

GILES MARTIN

Hunky Dory is one of my favourite albums of all time, along with *Transformer*, both of which were coproduced by Ken Scott, who worked with my father on Beatles' albums. At home, growing up, we had this compilation, *ChangesOneBowie*, and I danced to it without even knowing who David Bowie was! But then when I started out in music, I was a sort of promotions assistant and I spent a day or two with him to manage his interviews, I don't recall for which album. But I remember that, during a break, he asked me to go get him some Marlboros! I bought fags for David Bowie! Of course, I didn't tell him I was George Martin's son, but he was incredibly elegant, kind and generous. People who say that you should never meet your heroes don't know what they're talking about! You had to meet David Bowie, no matter what. (2018)

1. The texts for the *David Bowie Is* exhibition will point out that, 'Bowie brought make-up back with a vengeance in the 1970s', as it was commonly used by rock 'n' rollers two decades before.

2. David Bowie will mention this before performing the song for the first time on John Peel's show *In Concert* on 3 June. This was also the first time that Bowie played with Mick Ronson, Trevor Bolder and Woody Woodmansey.

3. From the early 80s, Bryan Ferry will sing Neil Young's 'Like A Hurricane' live.

4. In April 1971, David Bowie and some members of Blue Mink had Micky King record 'Rupert The Riley' (Bowie owned two old Riley cars). This song, which was similar to the 'comedy pop' spirit of The Scaffold, never officially came out, nor did 'How Lucky You Are', recorded during the same session. Also known as 'Miss Peculiar', this song (also on a ternary rhythm) is a rather indigestible combination of parts influenced by The Beatles, Jacques Brel and certain Slavic tunes.

5. David Bowie had been scheduled for the day before, in the early evening, right before Gong, but because of the delay he ended up playing on the 23rd.

6. Mick Farren was the frontman of The Deviants between 1967 and 1969. He then produced Twink's first album, but didn't join the Pink Fairies, who were also at the festival that year. The talent of Paul Buckmaster and Twink can be appreciated on *Mona – The Carnivorous Circus*, Farren's first album, released in 1970.

7. After the death of David Bowie, Rick Wakeman will talk a lot about his contribution to *Hunky Dory*, especially on British television. He will say that Bowie played the songs for him at Haddon Hall, on his acoustic guitar, then asked him to adapt them for the piano. Let's not forget that David Bowie himself composed a lot on the piano (there was one at his parents' house and one at his). And as the demos show, a lot of the chord inversions that make *Hunky Dory* and *Ziggy Stardust* so unique came from him. However, Wakeman is a distinguished keyboardist and undeniably played much better than Bowie (or Mick Ronson) could have done.

8. Like all pianists passing through Trident Studios, Rick Wakeman played the famous C. Bechstein grand piano, made in the late 19th century, which had been used by The Beatles, Elton John, Carly Simon, Queen and Supertramp. Norman Sheffield, who launched Trident with his brother Barry, rented it from Jaques Samuel Pianos and Mike Garson also used it on *Aladdin Sane*. Trident will end up buying the piano in 1986. The last time it was heard about was in 2011, when it was put up for auction. The piano was estimated to reach about £500,000, but the final price and the identity of the buyer were kept secret.

9. Mick Ronson was a really talented pianist, as his contribution to 'Perfect Day' by Lou Reed demonstrates. Neither Ken Scott nor Woody Woodmansey could confirm it, but it's also highly likely that Ronson played on 'Lady Stardust'.

10. Just like 'Space Oddity', 'Life On Mars?' is one of Bowie's most iconic songs. As an orchestrator, Mick Ronson worked miracles with it. Just as Abbey Road's heating system can be heard starting up at the very end of 'A Day

Lady Stardust
Hang On To Yourself
Ziggy Stardust
Life On Mars
Supermen
* Changes
* Five Years
Space Oddity
Andy Warhol
My Death
Width of Circle
John I'm Only Dancing
* Starman
* Moonage Daydream
* Queen Bitch
* Suffragette
* White Light
* Waiting For The Man

The set list for the gig at the Rainbow Theatre, London,
on 30 August 1972, written by David Bowie for pianist
Robin Lumley.

David Bowie noticed that girls, especially the pretty foreign girls
in the London nightclubs, liked the haircut of Keith Relf (singer,
harmonicist and founding member of The Yardbirds), so he
imitated it for a while.

Since childhood, David Jones had been open to anything and everything. He had an insatiable curiosity. He was a voracious reader, more than most boys his age...

In mid-December 1967, the BBC invites David Bowie to play three songs from his album and a new track on the radio show *Top Gear*, accompanied by The Arthur Greenslade Orchestra. This is the first in a long series of sessions he will record up until 2002.

A feeling of isolation pervades the lyrics of 'Space Oddity' and will also be felt in some of the other songs on his next album after Hermione Farthingale broke his heart.

'Space Oddity' is a serious composition, a sort of prog rock
hallucinogenic ballad... David and Hutch recorded it at
Clareville Grove as a demo with two voices.

David Bowie was always wondering whether he should use a band
or sing alone, accompanying himself on guitar.

With his long hair in the style of Greta Garbo, his Mr Fish dresses
and a bag over his shoulder, David Bowie does not go unnoticed
and sometimes even elicits a hostile reaction.

The internal upheaval caused by the mental state of his half-brother
Terry bore heavily on Bowie's psyche as he created
The Man Who Sold The World.

Adding intrigue and a touch of scandal to his character and that of
Ziggy Stardust, could only get people talking and hopefully speed
up his rise to fame.

The person on stage on 29 January 1972 in Aylesbury is a skilled
and confident performer, no longer an awkward singer-songwriter.

In The Life' by The Beatles, a similar accidental noise was kept on the recording of 'Life On Mars?'. It was the studio's public phone, located in the toilet, which started ringing as Rick Wakeman rattled off his final notes!

11. To celebrate Record Store Day in April 2017, Warner will release a vinyl box set called *Bowpromo* featuring rough mixes of the seven Bowie songs that appeared on this promo record.

12. Lisa Robinson wrote for the best music magazines, including *Creem* and *New Musical Express*. She was also married to RCA's in-house producer Richard Robinson. In 1971, her husband produced Lou Reed's first solo album in London. Rick Wakeman played piano on it. Reed had just been signed by Dennis Katz.

13. Known under the pseudonym Brigid Polk, she was one of Andy Warhol's favourite actresses in the 1960s. She starred in *Chelsea Girls*, co-directed by Paul Morrissey in 1966, with Nico and Gerard Malanga. Polk always had a cassette recorder with her and that's how, in August 1970, she recorded a Velvet Underground concert at Max's Kansas City, which became a live album two years later.

14. The 'non-meeting' was filmed and it was shown as part of the exhibition *David Bowie Is*. Bowie will specify in 1997, in an interview on the BBC, that Andy Warhol had simply photographed his shoes, a pair of yellow Mary Janes Marc Bolan had given him.

15. This talented British multi-instrumentalist was best known for his short stint on keyboards with The Animals in the mid-1960s. He became a sought-after studio musician and

a particularly creative arranger. He did the arrangements for Mac And Katie Kissoon's pop version of 'Chirpy Chirpy Cheep Cheep' written by Lally Stott. It's not as famous as the cover by Middle Of The Road, but is much better. Tom Parker will die in 2013.

16. Among other American references, some songs on *Hunky Dory* mention the silver screen, on which films were projected. Photos of glamorous Hollywood actresses inspired at least three of David Bowie's album covers: *The Man Who Sold The World*, *Hunky Dory* and *Young Americans*.

17. These preparatory sessions will take place at Underhill, a rehearsal studio on Blackheath Hill in Greenwich, halfway between Haddon Hall and central London. Underhill, in the basement of a car parts dealership (it's now a pharmacy), was managed by Will Palin. This music enthusiast got along so well with The Spiders From Mars that he became the road manager for the Ziggy Stardust/Aladdin Sane tours. Like his sound engineer friend Robin Mayhew, Palin will later work with Lou Reed, Mick Ronson, Brian Eno and Mott The Hoople. At the start of the 1970s, Iggy And The Stooges and Lou Reed will also rehearse at Underhill. In 1973, Will Palin will ask his friend Chris Difford, a David Bowie fan and future founding member of the band Squeeze, to help him paint lightning flashes on the two enormous discs hanging at the back of the stage, for The Spiders' last tour. Palin will die in 2013.

18. In 1972 and 1973, with the albums *School's Out* and *Billion Dollar Babies*, Alice Cooper will sow panic in the charts on both sides of the Atlantic. After *Muscle Of Love* in 1974, the band will break up. Singer Vincent Furnier will keep the name for his solo career, which he continues successfully to this day. Right after the death of David Bowie, Alice, one of the most endearing and least ridiculous classic rockers still standing, will post a touching message on social media that ends with these simple words, 'The man that fell to Earth has gone back to the planet that he came from.'

19. When he was 16 years old, David Jones was constantly listening to *Blues, Rags And Hollers*, the first album by Koerner, Ray & Glover, a blues-folk trio from Minneapolis. John Koerner, who was born in 1938, was the frontman and had been going by the nickname Spider. John Lennon admired him and Bob Dylan, in his autobiography, recognized his influence on his music. His first solo album, released in 1965, was called *Spider Blues*. David mentioned *Blues, Rags And Hollers* in his list of favourite LPs. The acoustic 12-string guitar on this record appealed to him and it became his favourite instrument along with the saxophone (and the Stylophone).

20. And it certainly wasn't a reference to Todd Rundgren's 1960s band either. He was also quite a character, but his Nazz didn't have 'The' in front of it. In the lyrics of 'Ziggy Stardust' the word 'nazz' is in lower case, which suggests that David Bowie –probably inspired by The Nazz, a piece by American actor/stand-up comedian Lord Buckley, who was popular in the 1940s and 1950s – simply invented the expression. In fact, in Lord Buckley's sketch, which is an exploration of Jesus' life, The Nazz is the quintessential cool being.

21. The word 'impermanence' is associated with the writings of Miralepa, from his *Songs About Impermanence*. David Bowie had already used the word in the lyrics of 'After All'. Other Buddhist words (also associated with Miralepa) appear in the lyrics to some of the other *Hunky Dory* songs – for example 'bardo', which refers to an intermediate state between death and rebirth, appears in 'Quicksand'.

22. The re-release will also include a different mix of 'The Bewlay Brothers', and 'Bombers', which only ever came out as a demo or live recording. Although 'Bombers' isn't well regarded in terms of composition and is rather controversial (Bowie called it a parody of Neil Young and in it he mocks the antimilitarist movement of the late 60s), it does have good orchestration and arrangements that bear the mark of Mick Ronson. The version of 'The Supermen' released in 1990 is a re-recording made during sessions for *Hunky Dory/Ziggy Stardust*, first released in 1972 on *Revelations – A Musical Anthology For Glastonbury Fayre*. Apparently, David Bowie didn't want a song from his Glastonbury performance the year before to feature on this compilation, which was a motley combination of live (or not) songs by artists who were there (or not).

23. Ian Anderson of Jethro Tull makes this point in the *Aladdin Sane* chapter.

24. David Bowie often went to Bleecker Bob's Records, Robert Plotnik's record store in New York. Frank Zappa, Robert Plant and Joey Ramone were clients. Located between Greenwich and the East Village in Manhattan, the store moved three times but never left the neighbourhood until it closed in 2013. When he spoke to the author in the 90s, Plotnik told him that Bowie sometimes bought his records there and that the jazz section was his favourite. Plotnik died in 2018. In the 1970s, stores like that popped up in many capitals and big cities around the world. They were genuine hubs

where aspiring musicians often met for the first time. Without them, many rock groups never would have existed.

25. Taken by Brian Ward, an acquaintance of Bob Grace, an androgynous photo of David Bowie was used on the cover of *Hunky Dory*. George Underwood received it as a sepia print and Bowie wanted him to colourize it by hand, to make it look like an old portrait. Underwood called Terry Pastor, a master of airbrushing, and worked under his direction. The pair will also create the *Ziggy Stardust* cover.

26. In April 1978 in Le Havre, the author will speak to Trevor Bolder before a Uriah Heep concert. Bolder will play bass for this British hard rock band after The Spiders From Mars. He will tell the author he never touched a trumpet after *Hunky Dory*.

27. The cast who were performing *Pork* at the Roundhouse that summer (who Tony Defries hired to work for his company MainMan) were also at that concert. David Bowie saw the play on 12 August.

28. During the summer of 1971, David Bowie played at the Haverstock Hill Country Club twice – on 21 July, with several musicians, including Woody Woodmansey and probably Rick Wakeman on the piano (he was recording with Bowie at Trident) and again on 11 August. This was the concert (with Tucky Buzzard as the opening act), that Robin Mayhew and Nicky Graham refer to in their interviews. They mention the sound problems that led MainMan to hire Robin Mayhew as sound technician, but their statements don't match up regarding the number of accompanying musicians. Graham remembers that it was just Mick Ronson (on bass for certain songs)

and David Bowie, while Mayhew adds a third musician, Woody Woodmansey. Robin Mayhew's version seems more credible, since technical sound problems are more likely to occur when you have to deal with the sound of drums as well as vocals and guitars.

29. To make this book easier to read, the title *Scary Monsters* will be used instead of *Scary Monsters (And Super Creeps)*.

30. Danny Fields was a dominant force and big personality in the music (and punk!) scene for three decades. He managed acts like Iggy And The Stooges as well as The Ramones.

31. David Bowie performed on the Pyramid Stage, a one-tenth scale replica of the pyramid of Giza, designed by Bill Harkin and built for the second festival. It was a sort of triangular-shaped scaffolding covered by a tent and open at the front. Bowie only sang seven songs that morning, including 'Changes' for the first time in public. To his surprise, a drunk woman joined him on stage for a few vocal harmonies. In 2000, during his second appearance at Glastonbury, as a headliner this time, David Bowie will inaugurate the more recent version of the Pyramid Stage. Between two songs, he will mention that 'backing vocalist'.

32. Mick Ronson wasn't on stage with David Bowie at Glastonbury, as is often said.

33. Actually, the most electric songs on *Fully Qualified Survivor* are more reminiscent of some on *The Man Who Sold The World* than those on *Hunky Dory*. Mick Ronson is largely responsible for that, especially in the improvised parts, punctuated by some of his famous riffs. The similarity is also due to the fact that Steeleye Span's bassist, Rick Kemp, who also plays on *Fully Qualified Survivor*, does so in a similar way to Jack Bruce, who Tony Visconti was kind of emulating on *The Man Who Sold The World*.

34. Koechlin and Paringaux. Both were editors-in-chief of the magazine in the 70s.

35. Frontman of the British post-glam group Doctors Of Madness.

36. Recording engineer for the album *Toy*, discussed in the second volume of *David Bowie : Rainbowman*.

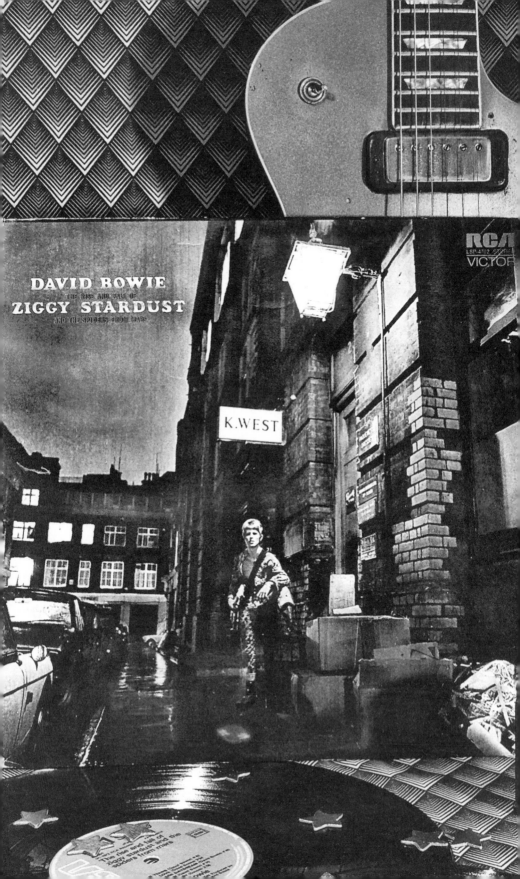

THE RISE AND FALL OF ZIGGY STARDUST AND THE SPIDERS FROM MARS

RCA – 6 JUNE 1972

'Mystification is simple; clarity is the hardest thing of all.'
(JULIAN BARNES, *FLAUBERT'S PARROT*, 1984)

'I didn't want my songs to be used in *Velvet Goldmine*' because two months before I was approached for the film, my people had got in touch with American agents to explore the possibility of doing a project based on *Ziggy Stardust*. For now, I don't want to say any more about its exact nature, as it could very well be more complicated than a simple film or musical. What I do know, is that I'm very excited by the idea of presenting my vision of the Ziggy years. It's going to be amazing, and in all likelihood, it'll come out in 2002[...]

'I'm working on a big project based on *Ziggy Stardust*. It will come out in three forms at the same time: an online version, a musical and a film. The result might just be – and for once it's me who's using this cliché – very post-modern! The Ziggy story will be narrated in different ways, each depending on its format. I have three teams of extremely talented people working on this simultaneously.

It's really ambitious but I think it'll be worth the effort[...]

I'd mention a film or a musical and then, after a while, I'd realize it was all useless. When I re-read what I said about it in the 70s, my blood runs cold! I have absolutely no idea how I could follow up *Ziggy Stardust* without diminishing what it already is. Impossible! It would set off a chain reaction. I'd always wanted to do something else with him, but as I was thinking about it, I found the idea less and less appealing. Ziggy is already huge in a lot of people's minds – why should I diminish that? So there you go, there won't be a Ziggy doll² [Author: Nor a Ziggy opera on Broadway?] No, nor a Ziggy appearance on *Oprah*![...]

The glam years, 1972 and 1973, marked the arrival of sexuality in rock music, which became a more and more powerful medium – until it became completely banal, and started to lose its power... I reckon that sexuality was always there, under the surface, with artists like Little Richard, Elvis Presley or Mick Jagger, but suddenly it was being articulated explicitly for the first time. And above all, it was no longer left unsaid. I never claimed that my famous "I'm gay" declaration was the most intelligent thing I'd ever said, as I've read from the pens of revisionists, but it did effectively show that rock could convey messages, whether good or bad, loud and clear. I remember all the episodes of my life with emotion but, to tell you the truth, I have no particular affection for the Ziggy period. I know it was a turning point though, because for the first time, I had a real audience. But I feel that I worked really hard to get there.'

DB (1998/1999/2003/1998)

Maybe it was a final wink. Or perhaps it was a snub? David Bowie probably didn't spend his life (his 'pre-death') calculating like a machine, pushing cryptic clues and subliminal messages into bottles thrown into the ocean for common mortals to discover and decipher. Hermeneutics was not his primary, or at least conscious, objective. But all the same, this absence, which cannot be an oversight, is remarkable. While Bowie mentioned, since the early 1970s, the possibility of turning *Ziggy Stardust* into a musical, he will not include a single song from this pivotal album in *Lazarus*, conceived during his final struggle. Not even 'Rock'n'roll Suicide', not even 'Starman', whose connection with the disillusioned extraterrestrial Thomas Jerome Newton might have seemed too obvious. Damn him.

David Bowie's ability to surprise the world over and over again has often been put down to an irresistible – and supposedly stronger than him – urge to stick his nose into other people's artistic affairs, to tear off a few ideas as if they were shreds of fabric, elements of sewing patterns for future reinventions that, after each moult, he will wear with pride. His pattern of trial and error was sometimes mistaken for hesitation, his outbursts for a symptom of excess and his most generous acts as a sign of a guilty mind. Some people found explanations where he offered none, put words in his mouth, analysed all his actions and failed to understand that they were part of a larger, slower process, similar to the revolving of the earth around the sun. Bowie's cycle was that of an extraordinary existence spent, for the most part, in the clothes of others. The most important of these alter egos, but not the first, would follow him like a shadow until the end.

Looking too closely at Bowie, marvelling over the delicacy of his craft or rolling our eyes, sometimes, at his predictability, we can miss the point. Suppositions can blind us to the evidence even when it's as visible as a lightning bolt on a face. While other people's opinions did matter to him[3], he didn't create

Lazarus in a rush, just so it couldn't be said, after his death, that he never made 'his famous musical'. So the absence of *Ziggy Stardust* songs has to be seen as a knowing smile at destiny, perhaps a way of sticking two fingers up to his illness. A way of screaming, through clenched teeth, that he was no fool and that he was not giving up. A twist of humour, even though death is no laughing matter, from an Englishman, a fan of Monty Python and Ricky Gervais, in New York. Will we ever know what leaving for good meant to the person who killed off Ziggy Stardust, the only Bowie character to have had a proper funeral? Hadn't Bowie already emerged from those ashes? Since the death of his creator, Ziggy 'Dust of Stars' belongs to eternity. Like a benevolent drone, he hovers above his creator's work and permeates *Lazarus*, though not a single song from the ultimate album of the 70s can be heard in it.

'Changes' is released on 7 January 1972, the day before David Bowie's birthday, but despite the support of radio presenter Tony Blackburn, who makes it single of the week on Radio 1, the song barely makes a ripple in the British charts. It did only slightly better in the United States, where it came out the month before. But it doesn't really matter – the wheels are starting to turn. Bowie is no longer alone on board and nothing will stop him now. Sessions for the follow-up album to *Hunky Dory* show that the musicians, until then mostly there as backup for Bowie, have come together as a genuine band. David warns Ken Scott that his new record will be more rock. Later on, the co-producer will say that *Hunky Dory* and *Ziggy Stardust*, recorded almost consecutively, were not dissimilar, but he is willing to listen to Woody Woodmansey, who asks him to make his drums more prominent as he feels they were previously undermixed and sounded 'like cornflake boxes'.

In the end, Woodmansey will be the one to kick things off: 'Five Years', the first song on the future LP, will start with a fade-in of his instrument alone[4]. The recording sessions are going well (in addition to the songs that will appear on the album, others were taped in late 1971 or will be drafted in the first weeks of 1972[5]) and when Bowie isn't at Trident, he is working in his 'lab' at Haddon Hall, formulating the development of his career like a chemist. He is reassured by the good reviews he's got for *Hunky Dory* and is certain that Tony Defries wants him to succeed as much as he does himself. He also gets a lot of support from his wife, who encourages him, reassures him and offers practical support and advice. A team is starting to form around him, a little disorderly but full of goodwill. David is starting to align the stars passing in his field of vision with those he has previously harvested.

As a teenager, David Bowie fantasized about joining a gang, like the Teddy Boys who were regulars of the Orpington clubs in Bromley. (He sang the aptly named 'Join The Gang' on his first album). Now with Mick Ronson, Trevor Bolder and Woody Woodmansey, he is starting to see himself as the leader of a pack that has everything but a look, a strong and playful image. While *2001: A Space Odyssey* didn't immediately motivate Bowie to write 'Space Oddity', he will decide, barely out of the cinema having watched *A Clockwork Orange* (also directed by Stanley Kubrick) in January 1972, to draw inspiration from the look of the Droogs, the main protagonists. Soon after, during Brian Ward's photo shoot in the alley of his studio in Heddon Street, near Piccadilly Circus, Bowie wears a quilted suit with geometrical patterns he's designed with his friend Freddie Burretti and Kansai Yamamoto platform boots bought from Boston 151 on Fulham Road. The photos for the cover of his next album will come from this shoot[6]. That same evening, Ward also takes studio shots of the faces of the four musicians, lit from above, like the image of Alex DeLarge (Malcolm McDowell) on the poster for *A Clockwork Orange*. In the film, DeLarge and his cronies can be seen with their famous lace-up high-tops, also worn by David and The Spiders From Mars on tour.

In 1967, Paul McCartney had wanted to inject some new energy into The Beatles so he suggested they reinvent themselves as a fictional group (Sgt. Pepper's Lonely Hearts Club Band). Similarly, Bowie makes the choice, not to change his name again but, at the risk of alienating his musicians who he often leaves out of the loop, to create a new persona, an aggregate of meticulously chosen influences, a 'plastic rock'n'roller' as he will call it. He'd written 'Ziggy Stardust' – the song that brings his character to life – the year before, but Bowie waited patiently before revealing it.

In January, while the final rehearsals for the tour – preceded by another concert in Aylesbury – are taking place[7] at the Theatre Royal in East London, David Bowie introduces Ziggy Stardust to the media. The origins of the name are relatively simple. Ziggy comes from Iggy (Pop)[8] and Stardust from the Legendary Stardust Cowboy. Nowadays, Google can tell you in a couple of seconds who these people are, but in 1972 London, the search engine was called David Bowie. Iggy Pop, whose lyrics leave David speechless, also impresses him with the sheer physicality of his performances or, more precisely, the way he teases the audience. When Bowie chooses the name Ziggy, he hasn't seen Iggy perform live, but he's seen photos of him with his body covered in silver paint or crowd surfing in the audience. It looks like he is walking on them and Bowie thinks this is amazing.

At least once during the following tour[9], he will try the same move, but with less success and panache.

As for the Legendary Stardust Cowboy, no-one knows who he is in early-70s Britain. Originally from Texas, Norman Carl Odam (his real name) is an otherworldly country musician who's been fascinated by the cosmos since early childhood. When David Bowie was with Mercury, 'The Ledge' released two singles on the same label[10]. He was initially mocked by almost everybody but, proving that ridicule doesn't kill, the Legendary Stardust Cowboy, alive and well, will accept David Bowie's invitation to perform at Meltdown, the London festival he will curate in 2002.

The other musician who strongly influenced Ziggy Stardust's character is Vince Taylor, a British rock'n'roll singer with a bad reputation who made it quite big in France. His music didn't interest David Bowie all that much, but his personality and chaotic lifestyle fascinated him – at various points Taylor succumbed to drugs, alcohol and religion. Bowie reportedly met him at La Gioconda in the mid-1960s and supposedly got to know him better when, seemingly possessed by demons, Taylor would climb on stage in a white toga and sandals and pretend to be Christ, or to have fallen from the stars. David Bowie was also interested in space (Major Tom's surroundings, Mars as a shelter...), so he puts some of Vince Taylor's confusion into his made-up rock star. References to Taylor's career (or Bowie's idea of it) will be found in the lyrics of 'Ziggy Stardust'.

Bowie may also have fleshed out his alter ego, who he had been sketching out in his mind as far back as *The Man Who Sold The World*, by taking inspiration from Jimi Hendrix – Ziggy's left-handed guitar playing, mentioned in the first verse, is probably a reference to him. Through Mick Ronson's guitar, Bowie had already made a musical allusion to the guitarist in 'She Shook Me Cold'. The ghosts of the first great victims of rock (Brian Jones, Jim Morrison, Janis Joplin) will also haunt some of the verses of 'Ziggy Stardust' and anyone who can feel the influence of Marc Bolan isn't wrong. 'Lady Stardust', which will open the B-side of the LP, will be presented as a tribute to the T. Rex frontman[11].

Ziggy Stardust is a rocker on the fringes like those who inspired him, under the influence of 'ultra-violence in Liberty fabrics,' as David Bowie will say in reference to the famous London department store where he and Burretti source their printed textiles for the stage outfits. As if his end had been planned before he was even born, Ziggy's creator sings about him in the past tense from the first verse. And it seems like he really did fall to Earth. With journalists, Bowie will deny this interpretation with varying degrees of insistence, but many fans maintain that Ziggy and The Spiders did come from the red planet and that the telephone box on Heddon Street is the portal they used to get here. People can believe what they want. Bowie is morphing into a master illusionist, part pastiche of his favourite inspirations and sources, part opportunist who waves his sequins around like Marc Bolan and the other glam rockers who have started to invade the charts – Gary Glitter, Slade, Sweet, Suzi Quatro... But he is going to give Ziggy Stardust a gravitas that will make him stand out from the rest.

In 1971, while he was writing songs for *Hunky Dory* and its successor, David Bowie couldn't help but notice his half-brother's deteriorating mental health. According to his family, he didn't know how to handle the situation. The musicians passing through Haddon Hall, though hardly psychologists, often attributed David's feigned indifference to Terry to his apparent difficulty in communicating with him. As his illness sowed confusion in his mind, Terry, whom David had once worshipped, could no longer be his spiritual guide. It makes one wonder whether there's a little or even a lot of Terry, his former idol in decline, in Ziggy Stardust. According to those who saw him on the 1972 and 1973 tours, the fictional rock star gave extraordinary performances on stage, but even so, he barely concealed David Bowie's true self, which was cracking under the strain of his brother's illness. Like a coin balancing on its edge, Bowie doesn't hide either side (he will reveal both in 'Rock'n'roll Suicide'), but he knows that the audience, swept up in and addicted to his whirlwind of doubts, aren't paying much attention to the meaning behind his lyrics. Perhaps he even hopes that those who actually listen to his words don't take them all literally. David naturally compared Terry Burns' madness – 'a family illness', as he sometimes called it – to that, fake or real, of the crazy 1950s and 1960s rockers from whom Ziggy evolved. Bowie transforms his compassion and feelings for his brother into a spiritual energy that animates his creation, perhaps because he doesn't know any caring gestures. Far from turning his back on his half-brother, David is going to take him along on his journey the only way he can, even as he leaves him behind. To extrapolate, one could say that by offering his time, resources and sometimes money to his heroes when they are down (Mott The Hoople, Lou Reed, Iggy Pop), as he will in 1972, Bowie will spur himself along too. By revving up their engines, he will also rev up his.

While Ziggy Stardust is impatient to exist somewhere other than in the brain of his designer, the latter is going to wait for the perfect moment to launch a torpedo at the media. He wants his unveiling to stun the media. In the 22 January issue of *Melody Maker* – with David Bowie on the front page in his Ziggy outfit, photographed by Barrie Wentzell – David tells Michael Watts that he is gay and always has been, even when he was David Jones. Whether it is true or not, this revelation is like pouring petrol on a fire. For the last 50 years, people have speculated over whose idea it was – it certainly caused a stir. Many have long thought that Tony Defries made Bowie say it, partly because it became apparent later that his influence was so strong at the time. But actually, during the years he 'managed' him, it looks like Defries didn't call all the shots (not even the bigger ones). He didn't make even a hint of an artistic decision, nor did he ever make Bowie participate in any radio or television programmes[12]. To say that Defries conned Bowie is perhaps unfair, because even though their relationship eventually turned toxic, Tony Defries never held a gun to his artist's head. There's no denying that Bowie strongly resented Defries' methods, but the clauses in the contract that were supposed to have trapped him – and which took David years to escape – were not added later, they were in plain sight on the document he signed. So the shocking revelation that he was gay probably came not from Tony Defries but from David Bowie himself. He probably thought, and rightly so, that adding intrigue and a touch of scandal to his personality and that of Ziggy Stardust, could only get people talking and hopefully speed up his rise to fame. A decade later, they would call this marketing.

Some people claim, like Tony Defries, that Angie Bowie is behind David's announcement but, whatever the case, RCA aren't happy with it. The label can't see how a self-proclaimed gay singer could make it in the United States, even though he is already a father at the time and probably meant to say he was bisexual. Even Marc Bolan, who wasn't gay at all but who was known for his delicate features and curly hair, would never really find success beyond the Atlantic, and RCA thinks its new recruit is playing a dangerous game. But David Bowie knows what he is doing and remembers what he's read and experienced. As a teenager he devoured *City Of Night*[13] by John Rechy, the American odyssey of a young prostitute living in urban decay – he may have read extracts in the irrepressible *London Magazine*. Whether discreet (Ken Pitt), staged (Lindsay Kemp), trendy (the Sombrero and Freddie Burretti) or exuberant and out there (the cast of *Pork*), homosexuality has long been a part of Bowie's life. Whatever his own preferences[14], it's obvious that David appreciated the edgy side of homosexuality – he saw it as dangerous and flamboyant, qualities that would stimulate his art, magnify his physical uniqueness and make people talk about him.

That summer, during a press conference at The Dorchester Hotel with Lou Reed and Iggy Pop (an event photographed by Mick Rock), Bowie will try even harder to assert his individuality. He will appear as a dolled-up prophet and reveal himself to be a subtle manipulator of the media, both British and American. They will lap up his flashy statements, including his famous quote: 'Any society that allows people like Lou and me to become rampant is pretty well lost. We're both pretty mixed-up, paranoid people – absolute walking messes. If we're the spearhead of anything, we're not necessarily the spearhead of anything good.'

On 29 January, David Bowie returns to the Friars Borough Assembly Hall in Aylesbury to unveil Ziggy Stardust, in person, to the public and to the media. The creation's name doesn't appear on the concert poster, nor does that of The Spiders From Mars, but the person on stage that night is a skilled and confident performer, no longer an awkward singer-songwriter. The set list includes songs from *Hunky Dory* and the new album – among them 'Suffragette City', which Bowie wrote for his beloved Mott The Hoople, and 'Starman', written in haste after Dennis Katz asked for a more radio-friendly song than the ones he's heard on the first test pressing.

David Bowie's first British tour as Ziggy Stardust begins at the Toby Jug in Tolworth in the second week of February with the Pink Fairies as an opening act. A few days before, David Bowie and his band (in their Spiders outfits) were filmed for the music show *The Old Grey Whistle Test* on BBC2. David played piano on 'Oh! You Pretty Things' and Mick Ronson on 'Five Years'. They will do it again for the first few performances of the tour, before Nicky Graham, ex-member of Tucky Buzzard, takes over.

In late winter, the media frenzy David Bowie and his band have created is not being felt on the ground, and the concerts aren't drawing large crowds. This doesn't put him off, however, and he takes advantage of it to perfect his show which, while not exactly theatrical, incorporates routines and costume changes. As he will often do right through to the end of his career, Bowie (or his management) invites bands and artists to open for him who have been recommended to him or that he likes. Bridget St John opens for him at South Parade Pier in Southsea on 4 March and hardly recognizes the artist she knew at the Beckenham Arts Lab[15]. A few days later, in Birmingham, David Bowie meets Mick Rock, who will become his official photographer for the Ziggy years.

On 24 March in Newcastle, Bowie takes to the stage with freshly dyed red hair and a new cut. The style was inspired by Daniella Parmar's haircut changes and by photos of model Marie Helvin he'd seen in *Harpers & Queen*. Helvin was wearing a creation by Japanese stylist Kansai Yamamoto and had a sort of bright red lion mane inspired by kabuki theatre. Bowie asked Suzi Fussey[16], his mother's hairdresser, to ruffle his hair on top while keeping some length in the back. It isn't quite a mullet yet, but it is certainly an early version of this haircut, which fans of both sexes will try to emulate with varying success. Since 1969, Bowie has had curly hair, long hair, short hair and now red hair. Right up until the early 2000s, these changes will mark the steps of his career and help in dating photos of him with some accuracy.

Through spring 1972, the rate of concerts increases and David Bowie attracts more and more people. Even so, he finds time to help other musicians he deeply respects, first and foremost Mott The Hoople. Up to that point, they have released four studio albums on Island but, after learning that the band had technically broken up after returning from a disastrous tour (in Switzerland), Bowie asks Tony Defries to find them a new label. In May and June, after writing 'All The Young Dudes' for Mott – a song he could very well have kept for his own LP – Bowie (assisted by Mick Ronson) will produce the band's fifth album at Olympic[17] and Trident Studios. Recorded in two nights, this excellent song whose chorus is based, again, on a descending chord movement, will be released as a single by CBS at the end of July.

In early September, when the album of the same name comes out, 'All The Young Dudes' will be in the British Top 10, alongside 'Starman'. It will be the first time in David Bowie's career that two of his songs have made the charts at the same time. Bowie will continue to play 'All The Young Dudes' until his last tour as a performer and it will also be included in his musical *Lazarus*. More importantly, the song will revive Mott The Hoople's career and several hits will follow. 'All The Young Dudes' will become a kind of hymn for Bowie, in part because in the early 1990s, it will be performed at tribute concerts for both Freddie Mercury and Mick Ronson. It is the only song in the 70s that David Bowie wrote for another artist he also produced. The year the generous donor died, Ian Hunter (Mott's singer and songwriter) will write the moving 'Dandy', a tribute to David Bowie's transformation into Ziggy Stardust (see pages 4–5). As well as Ronson, Bowie wanted other members of his team to be a part of *All The Young Dudes*. Mick Rock conceived the cover and George Underwood colourized it. Bowie also suggested that Mott The Hoople record 'Sweet Jane', a song written by Lou Reed for *Loaded*, his last album with The Velvet Underground, which came out in late 1970 (Reed taped a guide vocal to show Hunter the correct phrasing).

In August, while David Bowie and his band spend their evenings rehearsing for the important upcoming concerts at the Rainbow, he and Mick Ronson will produce Lou Reed's second solo album, *Transformer*, at Trident. These sessions, engineered by Ken Scott, will really demonstrate their talent as arrangers, especially in the now-classic 'Perfect Day', 'Satellite Of Love' and 'Walk On The Wild Side'. Trevor Bolder will play trumpet (as he did on 'Kooks'), while Klaus Voorman (The Beatles' German friend) and Herbie Flowers will share bass duties. While recording 'Walk On The Wild Side'[18], Flowers will suggest adding a double bass to his electric bass but, since 1972, he's been claiming he only made the suggestion so he'd get double the money[19]. As for the *'do-do-doos'* sung by The Thunderthighs (three backing vocalists who will also sing on *Mott*, the successor to *All The Young Dudes* in 1973), their progressive volume in the song is only due to the fact that Ken Scott, who mixed 'Walk On The Wild Side' alone, was tired of hearing them come in loud every time. The following month, David Bowie will not actually attend the sessions for Iggy And The Stooges' new album at CBS Studios, but since Iggy and his band have arrived in London, they have benefitted from his help. Tony Defries has landed them a recording contract.

From 1972 onwards, everything David Bowie does, however insignificant, is going to be analysed and scrutinized by those who doubt his altruistic behaviour. But there is really nothing to discuss. Before having been influenced by Mott The Hoople, Lou Reed and Iggy Pop, he had been impressed by them. Unlike most other artists in this dog-eat-dog profession, Bowie felt like giving something back to those he felt indebted to. We don't know the details of his contracts as a producer, arranger and mixer (in the case of Iggy And The Stooges' *Raw Power*), but they probably weren't very lucrative for him. A better way for David Bowie to take advantage would have been to get these artists to sing his own material and hope it did well. No one ever forced Mott The Hoople to record and perform 'All The Young Dudes' and they never regretted doing it. And by allying himself with '1960s underground refugees', as Mick Farren called them, David was taking a risk – if they had sunk, he'd have gone down with them. We now know this wasn't a worry for him and he was prepared to take any risk to help them.

After *Transformer*, Bowie will never again produce an album for another artist, except those he made with Iggy Pop. A few planned collaborations – especially during the late 70s, with Kraftwerk, Devo and Talking Heads[20] – will never occur. Over the following decades, he will refuse many requests (The Red Hot Chili Peppers, Coldplay...), sometimes taking offence at being asked.

Brian Eno, the untouchable genius of ambient music whose superhuman hearing skills cannot be denied, proved long ago that he knew the limits of his artistic integrity. And much to the delight of his bank manager, he will find that production can be lucrative.

That summer, David Bowie and his band make two appearances on British television that will accelerate Ziggy's rise to stardom and forever change the game. On 6 July, they appear on prime time television on *Top Of The Pops* on BBC1, watched by an audience of almost 20 million. They perform 'Starman' dressed in all their glam, displaying to the world the sexual ambiguity they'd been cultivating (albeit less and less) in the shadows. In just under four minutes, Ziggy scandalizes narrow-minded Britain, at the same time enchanting a whole generation of young people, left wide-eyed and speechless in front of the family television set. The bedrock of Britain shakes when David, in a quilted Burretti suit, puts his arm around the neck of Mick Ronson, golden from his hair to the trousers tucked into his high-tops. And when, during the chorus, Ronson shares the mic with Bowie instead of singing into his own, rock's macho foundations tremble and the tremor can be measured on the Richter scale. T. Rex were on the same show more than a year earlier and Marc Bolan caused a stir performing 'Hot Love' dressed in a silver outfit. But although his performance was significant for glam rock, compared with Ziggy's it was fairly tame.

Glued to their screens, most of the future British punk and new wave musicians understand that their lives have just changed. And the people who aren't planning on making music are happy to simply become Bowie fans. At that moment, and in his own way, Bowie is also offering a hand to those who are uncomfortable in their own skins, to encourage them to come out of their shells and be proud of their differences, especially homosexuals who have chosen to ignore or suppress their true selves. Any young Brits who were unlucky enough to miss the show that evening might instead have seen Bowie and his band singing the same song, in the same costumes, on 21 June in *Lift Off With Ayshea* on ITV, which had only slightly fewer viewers. That same day, the concert poster up at the Civic Hall in Dunstable would feature the name of The Spiders From Mars for the first time.

Ziggy Stardust came out on 6 June 1972 and was selling relatively well, but the day after Bowie's appearance on *Top Of The Pops*, sales of the album will skyrocket. This isn't a concept album. It's a tormented piece of work, from the birth of an idea (which germinated during David Bowie's first trip to America) to its final unravelling, a year later at the Hammersmith Odeon. Between abreaction and jubilant release. Like the songs on *Sgt. Pepper*, another album of its decade, those on *Ziggy Stardust* don't have a particular narrative thread, but the fact that the word 'star' appears in the title of four of the eleven tracks on the album shows that Bowie sings of courted success. His elevation towards the heat of the spotlight ('The rise...') is now irreversible, even if it means he might burn himself. 'Rock'n'roll Suicide', which closes the B-side, shows that fiction was a year ahead of reality. Because if the idea of reinventing himself at the end of this cycle was already in Bowie's mind when he created the record, it's obvious that the decline ('... and fall') of Ziggy was already planned. But in the notes scribbled on his pad, the fall of his creation didn't have to mean his own demise...

'Five Years' opens the A-side of the album and, long before the invention of the 'Overshoot Day' neologism, Bowie announces that humanity will end after using up all its resources or beliefs (he will specifically worry about this in the decade leading up to his death). In the lyrics, he draws on a wide set of references – mostly American – including *At Lunchtime – A Story Of Love*, a poem by Roger McGough, and sci-fi literature that will later inspire the directors of *Melancholia*, *Seeking A Friend For The End Of The World* and *Interstellar*[21]. Bowie begins by holding back the melody, controlling it for two minutes and fifty seconds with a slow rising pressure, but only so he can scream these 'five years' at the end of the song. Since this was a planned apocalypse, the 'five years' he refers to are not those between his first album and *Ziggy Stardust*. But listeners had the right to believe they were, and David Bowie didn't mind at all. For more than half a century, he delivered material which those who love his work are entitled to knead in their own way. In interviews, he even interpreted his own lyrics in different ways at different times. There's something primal about this song – Bowie seems to hold out his lyrics to adversity, like a backstage pass. It's almost as if he's saying that despite disaster, not all hope is lost. And as Mick Ronson's strings rise (generally eight violins, four violas and two cellos), the prophetic psalm splits in two and lets the light in. At a conference after the release of his book in 2012[22], Ken Scott will reveal that at the end of his first (and last) vocal take for 'Five Years', David was crying.

In 'Soul Love', Bowie brightens the mood with lively strumming of his 12-string guitar (he plays it on every song of the album with the exception of 'Star') and added saxophone embellishments. However, the harmonic complexity of the chorus (and pre-chorus) make it impossible to call this piece 'light'. While he is singing about love, Bowie does also include the kind of love which ravages, or creates dependency.

Written for Freddie Burretti (the fake singer of Arnold Corns) the year before, but improved with a new arrangement and more biting lyrics, 'Moonage Daydream' is the first explosive moment on the album. As he does in 'Five Years', but with a more vindictive tone, David Bowie brandishes the Americanisms he picked up during his recent trip. He makes reference to *Freak Out!*, the first LP by The Mothers Of Invention, released in 1966 and more of a concept album than *Ziggy Stardust*, according to him. He also includes references to space, notably to the invader he's pretending to be. The instrumental part, where he plays saxophone and flute[23], is built on a descending chord movement identical to the one in 'If There Is Something' by Roxy Music (which he will later cover with Tin Machine), whose first album came out that same month. The lead up to the climax is impressive: the last chorus is repeated and followed by the best guitar solo in David Bowie's entire discography – Mick Ronson, coming in quietly, throws a few darts before plunging, with intoxicating melodies, into a bottomless pit of high-pitched notes, themselves trapped by reverb and echo. His Les Paul, with strings stretched thin, ends up screaming in pain, but it comes across as ecstasy. Then Ronson rises to the surface again, calming his playing, simply toying with medium notes as he holds them and annihilating the future efforts of string-pluckers that rock history will wrongly remember in his place. For some, David Bowie's entire body of work is encapsulated in these 75 seconds. And he can take partial credit, because Mick followed some indications that David had drawn.

Although it starts with a jangly chord, 'Starman', whose verses' nursery rhyme accents are reminiscent of Paul McCartney's work, is one of the most catchy pop songs on *Ziggy Stardust*. The chorus, a nod to 'Over The Rainbow' sung by Judy Garland in *The Wizard Of Oz* – as the verse of 'Life on Mars?' was to 'My Way' – starts off with a major chord, which contrasts with the minor one at the beginning of the first verse. The song, with its strongly mixed orchestrations, owes a lot to this juxtaposition. And the T. Rex-style boogie passages, far from sounding out of place, actually tie-in perfectly.

It has been suggested, but also refuted by specialists of David Bowie's work[24], that inspiration for some passages in the lyrics of 'Moonage Daydream', 'Starman' and *Ziggy Stardust* in general, could have come from the writings of Robert A. Heinlein, and more specifically from *Starman Jones*, one of his young adult novels, published in 1953. Since the book is about a young boy who wants to travel to the stars (and not a person who comes from them), it's doubtful that it was a direct source of inspiration, but there are riveting similarities. Among them is the fact that Ziggy appears as an alligator in 'Moonage Daydream' and Heinlein used the term 'astrogator' to describe his fictional space traveller in *Starman Jones*. And in the book, the astrogator's name is Hendrix!

Although many people think 'It Ain't Easy'[25] (the only cover) feels out of place on the album, it makes more sense if you take the title of the song at face value. Throughout his career, David Bowie will often say he worked really hard to give birth to Ziggy. Perhaps that's what his voice, much more trenchant than Ron Davies', is trying to state here.

The B-side of *Ziggy Stardust* starts with one of his masterpieces, composed on the piano and played impeccably by Mick Ronson. He signs his name on the track with his superb arpeggios – those between the first two lines in each verse are the most remarkable. 'Lady Stardust', decidedly British, since David Bowie sings it with phrasing slightly like Elton John's, is one of the songs that, according to Ken Scott, could also have featured on the previous album. He is totally right, as this is one of the first written for *Ziggy Stardust*. It is a tribute to Marc Bolan (the 'song that went on forever' is probably 'Hot Love' and its several minutes of coda) but also contains a nod to The Velvet Underground ('femme fatales emerged from shadows').

Throughout his career, before starting on a new record, Bowie often looked back at his old demos, half-written songs, snippets and ideas he'd recorded to see whether he could uncover a forgotten pearl and make it shine. For *Ziggy Stardust*, he reworked 'Star', which his publisher Bob Grace had given to the band Chameleon, who'd recorded it but never released it[26]. Like Lou Reed in 'Walk On The Wild Side', but at a much more rapid pace, David lists the names of the fictional or real characters in his world – it's easy to get lost in them, but 'Rudi' is Rudi Valentino, Freddie Burretti's stage name as the Arnold Corns frontman. The use of the conditional (he says he *could* make a transformation as a rock'n'roll star) implies that while stardom has never been so attainable, it still depends on one thing: the public's full support. As on most of David Bowie's albums, especially those he produced with Ken Scott, the backing vocals on 'Star' are playful and inventive. Holding an F sharp over an E minor chord could even be considered an act of bravery.

If there's a song that really showcases the agility of the rhythm section of The Spiders From Mars, it's 'Hang On To Yourself'. It had already been recorded by Arnold Corns[27], but on *Ziggy Stardust* its 175bpm tempo, even faster than 'Star' at 143bpm, makes it flow swiftly. Woody Woodmansey firmly holds the beat (which he punctuates with expert snare drum fills), while Trevor Bolder bursts into the arrangement with a merciless bass line. An impeccable rhythm guitarist,

Mick Ronson chops the chords forcefully as if he wants to get rid of them, anticipating the work of Wilko Johnson, the king of machine-gun guitarists[28]. Who is David Bowie, the impending star, addressing in 'Hang On To Yourself'? Angie Bowie has never been cited as a likely candidate, but some of the lyrics suggest that it's not impossible, especially 'praying to the light machine'. During her husband's concerts at the time, Angie was often in charge of stage lighting. Like the PA, the lighting wasn't always great and once the musicians had to keep their fingers crossed that it would keep working to the end of the gig. The Spiders From Mars are mentioned for the first time in the lyrics of 'Hang On To Yourself', and also in the next track on the album, 'Ziggy Stardust'.

Of course Mick Ronson's contribution to those Bowie records on which he played was invaluable, but that doesn't mean he should be credited for arrangements he didn't write. Whatever his fans think, listening carefully to the 'Ziggy Stardust' demo (which will appear as a bonus track on the Rykodisc re-release of 1990[29]), will reveal that Bowie came up with the riff, primarily based on the coming and going of a high G (fourth) when passing into D major. It's also interesting that, in this demo (as also on the LP version of the song), in the second half of the verse, an A major chord comes after the E minor, instead of the bland A minor that the musicians on the Heathen and A Reality tours (who were largely the same people) will insist on playing.

As it says on the cover, *Ziggy Stardust* must be 'played at maximum volume' and 'Suffragette City' perhaps benefits most. With Mick Ronson's guitar tracks, Ken Scott erected a genuine wall of sound in the stereo (Mick's solo, a model of its kind, is double-tracked) and the song allows Trevor Bolder to display his talent on bass. He shows off some amazing finger work because this upbeat song accelerates as it progresses and ends on a tempo 5bpm faster than the start. This was common when rock bands didn't play to a click track[30]. From the first chorus, the eighth note beat of the piano, dear to rock'n'roll pioneers like Jerry Lee Lewis and Little Richard (and also heard on 'Star'[31]), adds a distinctive touch to 'Suffragette City'. And so does the fake brass part played by Mick Ronson on the ARP 2500 synth at Trident[32], which sends the listener swirling through a maelstrom of sound. With a voice sharp as glass and perfectly double tracked, David Bowie screeches lyrics infused with sexual connotations. He refers to a girl as a 'total blam-blam', later used by Mark Adams as a pseudonym on BowieNet. Right after the song's false ending, Ziggy launches into his famous 'Ooh, wham bam thank you ma'am'. David will admit later that he borrowed the line from jazzman Charlie Mingus – 'Wham

Bam Thank You Ma'am' is a track on his solo album *Oh Yeah,* from 1962 – but could he be unaware that there was a song called 'Wham Bam Thank You Ma'am' on the B-side of 'Afterglow Of Your Love', a single released by his friends Small Faces[33] in 1969, just before they broke up?

Many people listened to what David Bowie had to say, but he in turn listened to a lot of other people's opinions. His childhood friend Geoff MacCormack was the one who introduced him to soul music and James Brown, but it wasn't until the mid-6os that Bowie first became aware how sophisticated Brown's music was. On stage with The Spiders, he covers songs by many different artists, including Lou Reed ('I'm Waiting For The Man', 'White Light/White Heat'), Jacques Brel ('Amsterdam', 'My Death'), The Who ('I Can't Explain', which will appear on *Pin Ups*), The Beatles ('This Boy' and 'Love Me Do', soon incorporated into 'The Jean Genie'), The Rolling Stones ('Let's Spend The Night Together'), Cream ('I Feel Free') and Chuck Berry ('Round And Round'[34]). Now he adds two James Brown songs, often combined into a medley, to the set list: 'Hot Pants', released in 1971, and 'Gotta Get A Job' – its real title is 'You Got To Have A Job (If You Don't Work, You Can't Eat)' – which Marva Whitney sang with Brown in 1969. But in the studio in February 1972, during the last sessions for *Ziggy Stardust*, the funk dimension of James Brown's music wasn't what Bowie wanted to emulate. In 2003 (a decade before revealing the list of his 100 favourite books), Bowie will give *Vanity Fair* a small selection of his favourite records – '25 albums that could change your reputation'. In the article, Bowie will explain that ballads like 'Try Me' and especially 'Lost Someone', which he first encountered listening to *The Apollo Theatre Presents – In Person! The James Brown Show*, his first live album, released in 1963, partly influenced 'Rock'n'roll Suicide' and inspired the dramatic way he performs the second part of the song.

As proof, if proof is needed, that David Bowie noticed everything (and could usually recycle it), it is undeniable that at least one song from *Jacques Brel Is Alive And Well And Living In Paris*[35] is referenced in 'Rock'n'roll Suicide'. When he sings, 'Oh no love, you're not alone', it's with the exact same tone and phrasing as the musical actress Elly Stone in her performance of Brel's 'You're Not Alone'. Although David Bowie often purloined components from other artists for his songs, sometimes subconsciously but often shamelessly, what's really important is how well he integrated them into his own orbit. 'Rock'n'roll Suicide' is a dazzling example.

Like 'Five Years', but in little more than three minutes, the track, with no chorus, picks up pace when bass and drums come in and, even more, when Bowie raises his voice. The most spellbinding part of the song is the vocal melody and the chord progression in the dramatic passage 1 minute and 45 seconds in, which David Bowie tackles like a *chanteur réaliste*. Whether he found it on the guitar (more likely) or the piano, the chord progression in this part of the song is an almost demonic weaving, heated by emphatic string and brass arrangements that only an artist convinced of the importance of his work would have the audacity to create. It's a piece that only a vocalist as agile as he could sing – his voice is on the verge of breaking, but he's in total control – and again, according to Ken Scott, a single take was all he needed. Despite its alarmist title, the finale of 'Rock'n'roll Suicide' is less tragic than feared. As the dialogue between the lead vocal and the backing vocals fades out ('Give me your hands ... Cause you're wonderful'), Mick Ronson wraps up a final solo over two bars and four chords which are full of hope, including the last, a major! The complicit and incandescent silence that comes in after a final burst of strings is still David Bowie and The Spiders From Mars.

At the end of June 1972[36], when Tony Defries officially launches MainMan, his biggest star is recording 'John, I'm Only Dancing', a new song with explicit lyrics, at Trident and Olympic Studios. Several versions of this song will be taped, including one with violinist Lindsay Scott, then playing with JSD Band, a Celtic rock band that opened for Bowie many times that year.

On 8 July, when the album hits Number 5 in the British charts (it won't reach Number 75 on the *Billboard* charts before 1973), Ziggy and The Spiders perform at the Royal Festival Hall in London for Friends Of The Earth, a charity started in the late 60s for the conservation of the environment. The proceeds from the show will help finance a campaign to save the whales (that same year, Lesley Duncan dedicates 'Earth Mother', the title song on her second album, to Friends Of The Earth). That night, Lou Reed climbs onto a British stage for the first time. Extremely drunk, he has been asked to sing three Velvet Underground songs as the encore – the two that David Bowie is covering, and one he suggested for the Mott The Hoople LP. Japanese photographer Masayoshi Sukita is also in the room that night. A real friendship will blossom between him and Bowie, leading Sukita to photograph David regularly, right up until March 2004 and the Japanese leg of A Reality tour[37].

A week later, before taking a few days off, and because he feels that the place brings him good luck, David returns to Aylesbury for the last performance of this tour that started in February. Tony Defries has invited several American journalists along, including Lenny Kaye, to come and see his wild performer in action. Upon their return, they will speak about what they saw and create a buzz.

In August, as 'Starman' finally breaks into the British Top 10 (the single, with 'Suffragette City' on the B-side, comes in a proper sleeve with a photograph on it[38]), David Bowie and his musicians rehearse at the Theatre Royal in Stratford, northeast London, for their concerts at the Rainbow[39] on 19 and 20 August. They will sell so many tickets for these theatrically enhanced shows that another will be added on 30 August. Bowie refers to them as 'spectacular and multimedia' (which Feathers was meant to be, but with far more limited means) and takes inspiration from the sets made with platforms, scaffolding and ladders that New York company the Living Theatre are using at the time. They have been influenced by the ideas of Antonin Artaud, who believed that the visual aspect of a performance could be more eloquent than its script. The platforms are like mini-stages where several parts of the show will take place at the same time. The choreography of the various elements (mime, dance, Andy Warhol-like projections and rock concert) is entrusted to Lindsay Kemp – David asked Angie Bowie to hire him – and the costumes are the work of Natasha Korniloff[30], another of his old acquaintances. She creates the famous crochet spider web outfits, which look like the ones worn by the Ballet Rambert dancers in *Pierrot Lunaire* and *Ziggurat*, two shows she worked on that were directed by American choreographer Glen Tetley in 1967. In both, the action took place on a stage with metal structures...

David Bowie and Mick Ronson spend time in the studio with Lou Reed that summer, but they are with their band for the final rehearsals before the Rainbow concerts. Performances of the special multimedia show from the Rainbow will be planned for the United States but the idea will be dropped because of the cost. The Spiders have recruited Procol Harum organist Matthew Fisher, and The Astronettes, dancers from Lindsay Kemp's troupe, including Jack Birkett and Annie Stainer, who were in the television adaptation of *Pierrot In Turquoise* (though not in the stage show), will also perform. George Underwood illustrated the concert programme, on which Ziggy and The Spiders appear as comic book characters. Blues-rock guitarist Lloyd Watson opens the show, followed by Roxy Music. The set list, identical on all three evenings, is about twenty songs long, around one-third of them from *Ziggy Stardust*. 'Lady Stardust' is played for the first and last time during these three shows, and 'My Death' enters Bowie's repertoire.

Although they were supposed to be the last concerts of the Ziggy Stardust tour before leaving for the United States, MainMan is going to strike while the iron is hot and add a handful of extra shows in the first week of September. Robin Lumley replaces Matthew Fisher on the piano and David Bowie adds 'John, I'm Only Dancing' to the set list. The song was released as a single on 1 September in the UK, but not in the United States, as RCA thought the lyrics were too suggestive. A few days earlier, as the scene was being set at the Rainbow, Mick Rock shot a video for 'John, I'm Only Dancing' in which The Astronettes can be seen.

History, which sometimes has a 'memory that fails', has forgotten whether Mike Garson was on the session on that day in September 1971, when David Bowie tried to introduce himself to Annette Peacock, an avant-garde jazz musician and synthesizer player he had heard about (they were signed to the same label), and who was recording at RCA Studios on 6th Avenue in New York[41] (he had just signed with the label). With the excuse that she only allowed her own musicians in the studio (Garson was one of them at the time and is on two tracks of *I'm The One*, the album she was working on then), Peacock refused to let David in. But the Englishman was determined, especially when he'd spotted a phenomenon. A year later, just after arriving back in New York and a few days before launching the American leg of the Ziggy Stardust and The Spiders From Mars tour, David Bowie asks Annette Peacock to come to the Plaza hotel. He has listened to *I'm The One* and has been blown away by it. He would like her to tour with him and maybe play keyboards on the new album he plans to record as soon as possible. But she turns him down once again. Of course, Bowie has spotted the pianist on *I'm The One* and he agrees with Annette when she says that this other phenomenon would be a good fit (funnily enough David confesses to Annette that he has previously tried to get in touch with the pianist, without success). David Bowie doesn't know it yet, but this exchange with Annette Peacock will lead to a meeting that will forever change his music and, at the same time, the life of Mike Garson.

Mick Ronson	Lloyd Watson
Trevor Bolder	Norma Palmer
Woody Woodmansey	Bridget St John
Dana Gillespie	Mick Rock
Ken Scott	Masayoshi Sukita
John 'Twink' Alder	Billy Ritchie
Nicky Graham	Steve Harley
Matthew Fisher	Phil May
Robin Lumley	Alan Mair
Robin Mayhew	Brian May
Gail Davies	Hermione Farthingale
Ian Hunter	Patti Brett
Lou Reed	Brian Molko
Klaus Voorman	Courtney Taylor-Taylor
Iggy Pop	Marc Exiga
James Williamson	Mark Pritchett
Phil Manzanera	Chris Frantz

MICK RONSON

I never had a problem with the stage costumes David chose – after all, he was the one wearing the craziest outfits! We were happy to go along with it because that was his vision, but he never forced us to do anything. I wasn't too happy about cutting my hair, so I kept it long. Things were more complicated after he announced he was gay to *Melody Maker*. I think he'd have liked The Spiders to say it too, but that was the one thing that was out of the question... David was interested in the idea of turning people into stars, an idea he pinched from Andy Warhol. Ziggy Stardust certainly came out of that idea, and so did his tendency to want to help his idols. (1990)

TREVOR BOLDER

What I've said about my time with David Bowie has often been twisted, so I have to be careful... But actually, I enjoyed those years and I'm sure he did too. I don't regret what I've said and I don't think he does either. From *Ziggy Stardust*, The Spiders played a really important role in his music and so were largely responsible for his success. Because he let us do our own thing, we arranged songs, we didn't just play them. 'Moonage Daydream', which is one of my favourites, was really the product of a team effort, and everyone present in the recording room would confirm that. Except for David, maybe... (1978)

WOODY WOODMANSEY

On *Ziggy Stardust* and *Aladdin Sane*, David was totally involved all the time. To be honest, we played what he asked us to play. Mick Ronson was the link musically between David and Trevor and me. David didn't really know how to communicate in musical terms. On the tracks where Mick had written string parts, we talked over what they were doing rhythmically, so it didn't clash. Mick would often have ideas on the approach in a section, so we worked it out. On all the albums, we never did more than three recordings of a song. Often we got it in the first; David would just say, 'That's it!'

Ziggy Stardust only took two weeks from start to finished mixes. Ken Scott's input helped to capture the sound we made; he is fantastic at getting sounds that fit together and his mixing is outstanding. I think his sound production contributed to the album never sounding dated, especially when you hear a track on the radio alongside modern bands. It doesn't sound like it was done in the 70s. Mick, Trevor and I knew each other's playing so well from doing so many gigs; we had a lot of telepathy. At the time of recording, we were just doing the best we could for each song, the best feel to get the message of the song across, to make it live, if that makes sense. Yes, I think we were maybe the best band around!

Mick also took David's acoustic chords and turned them into rock'n'roll chords. He was an incredible guitarist, he had feel – not 50 notes a second, although he could do that. When we recorded *Ziggy Stardust*, we didn't really feel like we were creating something special, but we knew it was good, it felt different to other music. It was part of the gamble really – we liked it, but would anyone else get it? Now I'm very proud of that album; it follows you through your life and doesn't sound dated. I guess the test of an artist is what you leave behind. Did it do what it was supposed to do? Yes? Good. (2012)

DANA GILLESPIE

I didn't see as many of David Bowie's concerts as Ziggy Stardust as I would have liked. At that time, I was playing Mary Magdalene in the musical *Jesus Christ Superstar*. I had to earn a living! When I think that just before that, he and I were running around between casting calls... We both auditioned, unsuccessfully, for *Hair*, which really makes me laugh... A little later, before leaving for the United States, David and Angie came to see a performance of *Jesus Christ Superstar*, but to my great disappointment they left during the interval. I wasn't offended, because I knew they hated that kind of music.

In 1972–1973, David was really busy professionally, but was still messing around in London with his new friends. That was when he really started to think about how he was presenting himself. At home, he usually wore jeans and a t-shirt, but when he went out, he dressed up like a prince! The day David introduced me to Lou Reed, what struck me most was that he was wearing black nail polish. I was also at Trident when David was recording *Ziggy Stardust*. We'd run into each other and that's how I ended up doing backing vocals on 'It Ain't Easy'. Mick Ronson, who I got along with really well, was a gentleman and really helped create a great vibe in the studio. He really was the type of guy everyone loved. By the way, I can tell you that to start with, Ronno[42] wasn't thrilled about wearing skin-tight sequined trousers and shoes with heels, and finding David kneeling in front of his guitar giving him a fake blowjob. None of The Spiders From Mars were particularly happy with that... (2016)

KEN SCOTT

Ziggy Stardust was the result of real teamwork and, when a team works together, it's impossible to say, especially later, who was responsible for what. We were all going along with the songs, the music. The album only took two weeks to record. It was forty years ago, so no one remembers the details! But one thing's for sure: we had an incredible time and we worked really hard. I watched David's metamorphosis, from folk singer to long-haired guy to androgynous rock star from space – with short hair, then red hair – but to tell you the truth, things happened at just the right pace.

Some people claimed he'd changed a lot, musically, between *Hunky Dory* and *Ziggy Stardust*. But I don't agree with that because it's obvious that a song like 'Queen Bitch' could have easily featured on *Ziggy*. Thing is, David was always at least one step ahead, and at the time of *Hunky Dory*, he was already thinking about the follow up. That's also why he worked so fast in the studio – he was on a mission, the technical side of it wasn't going to hold him back. In any case – and this was great – the record company people never came to his sessions; they left us in peace! The only time they stepped in was when they asked for a commercial song for *Ziggy Stardust* and we recorded 'Starman' in a rush! There were only a few weeks between recordings for the two albums – it's almost a double album.

I enjoyed the company of 95 per cent of the musicians I've worked with. Being in the studio with them was always enjoyable, but I have some really excellent memories of making music with David Bowie and Mick Ronson. And it's the same with John Lennon and Paul McCartney. For *Ziggy Stardust*, Mick arranged the strings and played the keyboards with David. On one of the songs, the piano was recorded in two takes: one for the left hand, one for the right... David always had a special relationship with the instrument. On *Hunky Dory*, Rick Wakeman was rather classical. On *Ziggy Stardust*, the piano was very basic. And then on *Aladdin Sane* and the three following albums, David preferred the very avant-garde style of Mike Garson... In a way, the piano defined Bowie's evolution in the 1970s.

In the studio, my job and that of the assistant was to facilitate David and Mick's work. David made the artistic decisions. He knew what he wanted to the point where he would tell Woody when to hit toms or do a drum roll! But during the mix, I made the decisions on my own. I also set the order of the songs on *Ziggy*. We had the vinyl cutting in mind and we needed to balance the sides...

The success of *Ziggy Stardust* changed everything, and hardly a day goes by when someone doesn't mention it to me. And it surprises me every time! I knew it was a good album – I still love it – but I don't know why people were so impressed… In those days, Bowie, like other musicians, made a new album every six months, and the best we could hope was that people would still be talking about the previous one when the next one was released! There are as many songs I love on *Ziggy Stardust* as there are on *Hunky Dory* and *Aladdin Sane*, but *Ziggy* is definitely the more consistent of the three, the one that works better from start to finish.

Since then, the role of the rock producer has changed, but what has changed most is that a lot of people now succeed in music without having any talent. To get there they work with producers who hide their shortcomings. My role was to allow David Bowie to record his songs in the best possible conditions, but I was dealing with a serious player: most vocals on *Ziggy Stardust* were recorded in one take. No Auto-Tune, no computer, everything you hear is authentic. What's happening in studios these days is ridiculous. If the musicians are good, the job in the control room is really easy – you'd have to be really bad to screw it up.

To be honest, I don't have much to say about *Transformer* except that Lou Reed was at Trident without really being there… I put as much into that record as I did into David's, but I was only credited as the recording engineer. Go figure! (2012/2016)

JOHN 'TWINK' ALDER

David and I bumped into each other regularly so, when he was looking for musicians for Iggy Pop, he suggested I phone him. So I called Iggy, who was staying at the Royal Garden Hotel, and we chatted for a while. He thought I could do the job, and we talked about bringing in John 'Honk' Lodge on bass, but then he told me that he wasn't sure that playing with British musicians was the best idea. He was planning on going back to the United States to form a band there… After that, I phoned David again to tell him it wasn't happening. I remember we had a long chat, because we were both really interested in mime. We even thought about doing something together, but sadly we never did. (2018)

NICKY GRAHAM

Throughout 1972, the tour was a rollercoaster ride, with 'Starman' riding high in the charts, followed by the release of the album. David was a very bright man and he knew his market and crafted his songs to appeal to that market. Students loved his attitude and his showmanship was part of his glam rock world, hanging out with Marc Bolan and dressing to kill. His attitude to his art was very impressive. His songs and production ideas were all linked to a plan that included film and live performance. Our stage outfits during the Ziggy days were borrowed from *A Clockwork Orange*, which represented a rebellion of youth and a statement of freedom, post-Swinging Sixties.

With The Spiders, I was often playing with my back to the audience but, on 27 May 1972, in a small club with a capacity of 300 people – Ebbisham Hall in Epsom – we watched the birth of the Ziggy Stardust phenomenon. That afternoon, to promote the show, myself and sound engineer Robin Mayhew went around Epsom pinning photocopied posters of an A4 drawing depicting Ziggy onto trees and in the local newsagent's window. We did a sound check at 5pm and then went off to eat something. To our utter surprise, when we came back at 7.30, there were about 400 kids queuing around the block waiting to get in. The gig was amazing and was a definite sign that Ziggy and David were going to be huge.

We'd been doing gigs before that, as David Bowie, but these had been booked by an agent and Tony Defries had asked me to book a whole tour during my time hanging around the office. Wherever we played there were Ziggy lookalikes in the audience and it felt as if we were in the groundswell of a huge movement.

By now, Tony had split from his partner, Laurence Myers, and formed MainMan, which managed David, but also Mott The Hoople and Iggy Pop. I went with MainMan and my then wife Diana stayed on with Myers, who was managing Gary Glitter. Most of my time was spent working at the MainMan office in Chelsea, looking after all the bands, while still playing piano on stage with The Spiders From Mars. Finally I think I must have upset Angie Bowie – something to do with money, I guess – and Tony fired me. That meant I no longer played piano in The Spiders. (2017)

MATTHEW FISHER

In August 1972, I received a phone call from someone claiming to be David Bowie. Strangely, the voice sounded familiar, but at the same time, I thought it was a friend playing a trick. It took him a good five minutes to convince me it was really him! Then I told him how much I loved, not his songs, but the one he'd just written for Mott The Hoople, 'All The Young Dudes'. I didn't really think about who'd recommended me to him, but I think it was Ken Scott[43]. Anyway, I'll never thank him enough because he could have given him Gary Brooker's name instead, the pianist from Procol Harum!

I have this memory of listening to Radio Luxembourg, like so many Brits of my generation, hiding under my sheets one night. That was when I first heard 'Can't Help Thinking About Me', which I loved. I thought that as well as being a talented musician, Bowie was a remarkable songwriter, on a par with Bob Dylan. He tackled subjects that were uncommon in your usual pop songs. I remember one of his appearances on television, which I'd seen advertised not long before. I was really excited to see what he looked like and I don't know why, but I pictured him wearing denim from head to toe, with a black jacket, like a rocker. Needless to say, when I saw him on screen in a white outfit, I was pretty disappointed. But from that moment on, I realized that this guy definitely didn't do anything like anyone else, was never where you expected him to be, and I bet that was the effect he was trying to create. Oddly enough, I'd never seen him play live before I got on stage with him for the concerts at the Rainbow.

I saw him again the following year, when I was invited to the Hammersmith Odeon because I also happened to be an RCA artist in 1973. The thing is, because I only played a few songs, I had time to watch him, and also when he was rehearsing for these parts of the show Lindsay Kemp had choreographed. Of course his voice was amazing and powerful. You know, he was able to control his pitch and I realized that any odd effects or things that seemed out of place, were actually very deliberate.

I played 'Starman' at the Rainbow, and because David was really approachable, I asked him about that funny chord at the beginning of the song. I was really struggling to reproduce it on the piano. He showed it to me on his guitar. It was a B flat with an A fingering – the E strings, low and high, were open. No normal guitarist would have come up with that. Sometimes Bowie used some very elaborate chord progressions, which set him apart from most composers of his generation. Marc Bolan's, for example, were much more basic.

I only did those two concerts with Bowie and The Spiders From Mars, and only played on some of the songs, including 'Lady Stardust', 'Suffragette City' and, of course, 'I'm Waiting For The Man'. I was the one who asked to play on 'Starman'. And to everyone's surprise, during the song, because we were at the Rainbow, he started singing, 'There's a starman, over the Rainbow...' Of course, it wasn't too hard to follow him! I never played with Bowie again after that, but during recordings for *Aladdin Sane*, Ken Scott invited me along to a session and they were overdubbing some brass. There was this strange thing... When Bowie was talking to musicians, he never used musical terms. He preferred more artistic terms and used words like 'baroque' or 'renaissance', or even colours to describe what he wanted!

That made me think of John Lennon: instead of counting in '1, 2, 3...', he would go 'sugar, plum, fairy, sugar...'. Really off the wall, you know... I really loved some of David's later albums, *"Heroes"* especially. Although I was never really a fan of *Let's Dance.* (2017)

ROBIN LUMLEY

During one of my first sessions as a pianist, I met Ritchie Dharma, a drummer who'd just played on Lou Reed's 'Walk On The Wild Side'. David Bowie was at a loss as to how to replace Matthew Fisher, who had been taken ill and had had to leave the tour a few days earlier. So he phoned Ritchie to get some suggestions and he recommended me. I apparently did all right on those sessions and I lived round the corner from David in Beckenham.

At that time, I was driving a bread delivery van to support my life as a trainee pianist, learning and practising. When the phone rang, the voice at the other end said it was David Bowie. I didn't believe him; I thought it was a hoax from some of my friends... and hung up. While musing on which friend it was and planning my revenge, the phone rang once again and a voice said, 'No, it really is David Bowie here!' So, I believed him, but not without coming within a hair's breadth of fainting. He told me about the pianist problem and asked very politely if I could 'help him out' for a few concerts and one at the Rainbow on 30 August[44]. I arranged to meet him at the rehearsals and duly showed up, full of trepidation.

My worries were completely unfounded as David was polite and welcoming. He gave me two albums to rehearse with and the chords/artwork that he'd just written out on exercise-book paper. As for Mick Ronson, he wrote some chords on proper music paper. I took them home and learned the songs. Don't forget that summer, London and all of England were riding the David Bowie train. I had watched 'Starman' on *Top Of The Pops* and now I was going to be part of it! I couldn't sleep for excitement...

David was a true gentleman in the widest sense. He was always extremely friendly, as if we'd known each other forever. I also got along well with Woody Woodmansey, Trevor Bolder and, of course, Mick Ronson. They accepted me straight off and I remained friends with them, especially Mick when he moved to Woodstock and I was producing albums there.

There were a lot of rumours going round about David's lifestyle and eccentricities, and the team at MainMan, but all that mostly came out later around the time of the American leg of the Ziggy Stardust tour. I remember that David's favourite tipple was Campari and soda! I also noticed that Angie and David wore each other's clothes on alternate days, which nobody took the slightest notice of! My contact with his people was limited to the musicians. I didn't mix with Angie or Tony Defries, who we nicknamed Tony Deep-Freeze, as he was so cold, at least superficially.

Early September, the end of the UK leg of the Ziggy Stardust tour was also the end of my collaboration with The Spiders From Mars. I joined Brand X a bit later... I ran into David in the 80s. Terry Glinwood, who passed away very recently, had worked as executive producer on the movie *Merry Christmas Mr Lawrence*, which David was in. Terry was a friend of mine and I reacquainted myself with Mr B. at Terry's house. Of course, I continued to follow David's career. I became a lifelong fan! (2017)

ROBIN MAYHEW

I started working with David Bowie as a front-of-house engineer in February 1972. All of us – from the band members to the technical team – were living the dream. We felt the Ziggy Stardust phenomenon happening from the very first concerts, even though there weren't more than 50 people at the Toby Jug, a pub in southwest London, or at Bristol University. But little by little, the rooms filled up and it was obvious that something was happening. Enthusiasm was the driving force behind all of us and we knew that sooner or later, we'd hit the jackpot. Angie Bowie was brilliant at resolving problems, and nothing escaped her. Given how fast things were moving, I don't think David always realized what was going on. But he was very professional and present during sound checks.

Everyone loved the shows but they didn't get hysterical, the crowd behaved. This was probably because David's performances were very theatrical and the audience was literally spellbound. Most of the time they stayed seated, taking it all in with their eyes and their ears. There were a few times when one or two excited fans broke onto the stage, but it was nothing compared to the assaults from raving lunatics that other rock stars had to put up with. Mick Ronson was also a real pro and every night, he asked me to record the show so he could listen to it again later. He wanted to make sure there were no slips or unusual events! The band was so tight that mistakes were extremely rare. The sad thing was that I was using the same tape, recording each concert over the previous one, so only Ziggy's last show survived.

Angie Bowie didn't just provide moral support for David, she was also a big help on the logistical front. She could work miracles. For the Ziggy Stardust tour, she hired a lighting crew – Heavy Light, run by Nigel Olaf. He was working for T. Rex but Angie was very persuasive and she convinced him to join us! (2016/2017)

GAIL DAVIES

It's a pleasure to talk about my brother in a book about David Bowie's music. He was very proud that 'It Ain't Easy' was the only cover on *Ziggy Stardust*. But he was disappointed when he saw the song was credited to 'R. Davies' on the jacket. Many people thought it was Ray Davies of the Kinks! Actually, 'It Ain't Easy' had already been covered the year before by Long John Baldry, and the year before that by Three Dog Night[45]. Their version was a big hit, and both of them used the song title, 'It Ain't Easy', as the name of their album. So when Ron's publisher told him a British singer he'd never heard of had also covered his song, he wasn't all that impressed. However, he was furious when he found out that David Bowie had changed the words. It was really important to my brother that people respect his lyrics and the blues side of his music. The verse Bowie changed is the one that refers to a blowjob, though he didn't seem to be very prudish at the time[46]!

When Bowie toured in America with The Spiders From Mars, my brother and I were living in Los Angeles, but we didn't see him in concert and he and Ron never met. A few years ago, I started working on a compilation of covers of Ron's songs by musicians who loved his music. Shelby Lynne[47] did a great version of 'It Ain't Easy'. I'd initially thought of Jack White, so I went to see him in concert and gave him a CD of the song. He must have liked it because he played it live with The Raconteurs, but I would have preferred to have him record it for the tribute album[48]. Of course, their version was the one with Bowie's lyrics... (2017)

IAN HUNTER

We knew David Bowie before he was famous. He played at universities, in venues that could accommodate no more than 500. I'd seen him mime in 1968, but that was about it. I thought, 'Who is this faggot?' But I also noticed the line of girls waiting outside his dressing room to get an autograph! He wore dresses, had a bit of a perm in his hair, but was far from being an idiot. Mott The Hoople was in a rut at the time and Pete[49], who'd heard that David Bowie needed a bass player, went to see him. Bowie, who'd loved *Brain Capers*[50] asked, 'Why do you need a job? You have a band, don't you?' Pete told him about our situation and David officially became a Mott The Hoople superfan. I'd already refused to sing 'Suffragette City', which he'd written for us. The afternoon he met with Pete, at his manager's office on Regent Street, he played him 'All The Young Dudes', which he'd just finished writing. We listened to it the next day. I still can't understand why he didn't keep the song for himself. I immediately knew it was going to be a hit, and David did too! It was an incredible feeling I'd never felt before, and have only experienced a few times since. Mott was trapped – we needed the radio and a future classic song to be played on it. I couldn't believe he was giving us this song! Much later, Mick Ronson told me they'd tried playing it themselves, but weren't thrilled with the result.

David found Mott fascinating. He liked our rough edges – the fact we were a gang. When we played, it was total chaos, a ruckus. He'd never seen that before. His audience was taken aback, their eyes were glued to him, they were unable to move. He was lucky to have Mick Ronson, who brought a human touch to the show. For six months Bowie was Mott The Hoople's number one groupie, and Tony Defries took us on, but only because of David – he wouldn't have done it otherwise. Wayne County and Dana Gillespie, the other MainMan artists, weren't going to overshadow his cash cow, but Mott The Hoople might. Also, we were a very democratic group. Decisions were made when the five of us agreed, which Defries couldn't stand. Mott was a nightmare for everyone we worked with! We weren't egocentric about our music, but we were about the band. David Bowie and Mick Ronson, who learned everything they knew about recording from Tony Visconti, were truly gifted. They didn't spend long in the studio but they achieved amazing things.

We all thought 'All The Young Dudes' sounded a bit too commercial, too tame for us. We even had a fight about it, but we were incredibly grateful at the same time. When David came during rehearsals, we had a bet that he was going to try to give us more tracks of his, but he didn't. He loved our songs and encouraged us to record them. He never tried to tell us what to do. But the cover of 'Sweet Jane' was his idea: he was crazy about Lou Reed and thought it was a good idea, which was fine by us. David would come to the studio with Angie and we listened to what he had to say. In those days, he copied her. Short hair? Short hair. Orange? Orange. Wherever we played, he had flowers delivered to us, mountains of flowers with a little note or a telegram. Island had never done that for us! But there was a down side... At first, our audience numbers dwindled because they didn't recognize us anymore, decked out like glam queers. Some people started to think we were nothing without David. But the thing is, he really taught us a lot about studios and writing. In the end, our morale improved, as did our playing and our shows. And suddenly, we found ourselves in the charts and America was calling.

Luckily, we never signed anything with Tony Defries. But he was pretty brilliant. His idea of getting together a team of outrageous wannabe-actors, weirdos and professional groupies was really clever. Those people really made you cry laughing, they were totally useless! Defries' idea was to give jobs to everyone who surrounded the artist to create a kind of elaborate myth around him. He reasoned that if the roadies were bizarre and interesting, people would think the artist was too. On paper, MainMan was divided in two: one part of the team took care of David, and the other was for everyone else. But of course, David's success mattered more to Defries than ours did, and that didn't work because at one point, the whole of MainMan was focused on Bowie. We'd be twiddling our thumbs in London waiting for some attention. Defries was a hustler – Bowie knows about that. He was planning to buy out RCA, which he deceived to the point that, at the time, some of the label's bigwigs seriously considered letting him do it. We would have all been managers! Hilarious, isn't it? (1998)

LOU REED

Mick Ronson's arrangements on *Transformer*, particularly the strings, are astounding. Not bad for a guy from Hull! Ronno was extremely talented. The funny thing was that I didn't understand a thing he said, but he was a sweetheart. David was great too. Honestly, his backing vocals on the album add a lot to the unique sound of the songs. Those voices at the end of 'Satellite Of Love' are miraculous – really brave and not the slightest bit banal. Anyway, I only believe in details, not in technical skill.

Unlike Bowie or Alice Cooper, I never felt the need to create an alter ego. I was already double, triple, quadruple – however many you want! And all those versions of myself were just as real. I wasn't David Bowie though: what I was doing scared people stiff. But I write from the heart, speaking directly to those who listen to me. Bowie and Ronson helped me do that on *Transformer*. You just have to listen to the end of 'Perfect Day', the solemnity of the strings arranged by Mick, with his little melody on the piano, to see that they more than succeeded.

I really love sound, beautiful sound! If I was in love with diamonds, I would look for some. In my line of work, sounds matter, so I try to make good ones. If I bought my records, I'd want them to sound good, so yeah, I care about that kind of quality. I can't see the benefit of having a bad guitar sound. Of course, all this only matters if you know how to listen... I think most people are deaf. They're not good at discerning sounds. They don't really know the difference between good, really good or mediocre. They're interested in other stuff; sound is not at the top of their list. Real music lovers – people who truly love music, who collect – know what I'm talking about, but the average guy couldn't care less. If it really mattered to him, most rock concerts wouldn't take place. The sound at most shows is appalling, but people don't realize. They think it's normal that it sounds like they're in an underwater cave. They can barely make out the words but they're happy with that. (2003)

KLAUS VOORMAN

I played bass on *Transformer*, but the album was nearly finished when I entered the scene and I think I was only on the sessions for two days. A few things were apparent, though: David Bowie and Lou Reed got on like a house on fire[51]! There was a lot of wit in the room, a lot of 'campness' too – like in the lyrics of 'Vicious': 'I'll hit you with a flower...' I remember Lou had the nail of his right hand little finger painted black, which was quite unusual at the time. And David was so thin; I didn't think anybody could be that thin. When you looked in his face, the two different coloured eyes really got you. I remember Lou was an outstanding guitarist, which I didn't expect. There was a great atmosphere at Trident. One story, one pun, was followed by another; we were all on the floor with laughter. We actually spent more time talking and joking in the control room than working in the studio. I had a great time there and wish I could have stayed longer with that bunch. (2017)

IGGY POP

I saw David Bowie live for the first time during his first tour with The Spiders From Mars, somewhere on the outskirts of London. The venue was an old wooden theatre, and it was more of a warm-up concert to see what worked and what didn't, in terms of staging and set list. There must have been 150 people in the audience at the most and a third of them were guests. I quickly realized, especially when I recognized a lot of myself in Ziggy, that I was part of a deal, and I was right. I don't have much to say about it except that it was a good deal for me. David could be impressed by other artists, sometimes by the way they looked... Like all of us, he tried different things, and that first time, he thought he was a bit like Iggy Pop!

David didn't produce *Raw Power*, he just mixed it. But there was something deeper, which makes people think he did. Honestly, if you listen to the music I wrote between *Fun House* and *Raw Power* just before leaving Detroit[52] – on my own or with James Williamson – you can hear that even if it was unfinished and all over the place, what came next was already there. London really allowed us to grow as artists, but the three other Stooges didn't agree. They hated that time[53]. They thought people weren't taking them seriously enough. I want to make it clear that nobody forced us to do anything, certainly not something we didn't want to do.

David and MainMan put us up in a nice neighbourhood, filled our bellies and gave us free rein on a musical level, as well as access to a rehearsal room – a bit of a seedy one perhaps, but that was fine. We had everything we needed to make music. Marc Bolan was rehearsing nearby and so was Led Zeppelin... When the Ziggy phenomenon started to take off, David still came by to see us and listen to what we were doing... He and I went to local cafés – that environment was good for our creativity. The Stooges, at that time, reached their peak...

But Defries never had control over us. He never even came to see us rehearse. In New York, he'd suggested I record a solo album with a different band, but I wasn't ready for that. I wanted to continue along the ultra-aggressive path we'd chosen and that appealed to David. They came up with the idea of making me work with the rhythm section of the Pink Fairies or bands like Third World War, or Edgar Broughton Band[54]... But whatever anyone else says, we never auditioned any of those musicians. I'd listened to all those bands carefully and they were already fully formed entities and I didn't see any reason to change them. I thought the Pink Fairies were like MC5 and there was no way I wanted to be like them. Same thing for Third World War and Edgar Broughton Band. They rocked hard, their music was powerful, but I had no desire to take anything from them... no desire to be Nico! I wanted to do my own thing, in my own way, which is why Defries reluctantly agreed to let James join me. When the other Stooges arrived, he suggested Ron Asheton play bass.

I clearly remember a conversation with David in a café near my hotel on Kensington High Street. We were both pretty skinny and he was munching on sugar cubes while I drank honey from a jar left on the table. He looked me straight in the eye and asked me, 'Do you want me to produce your album?' I said no and explained I had my own vision of what my music should be. I wasn't exactly 100 per cent sure, but I was well on my way to figuring it out. And he got it. He didn't try to change my mind... We got along well and spent a lot of time together. I went to see him at Haddon Hall and, once, he even drew a sketch of me. We know about his paintings, but he was also good at drawing. He seemed fascinated by the fact that I couldn't sit up straight! And he started to sketch me, a bit in the style of Cocteau; he made me a sort of reclining rock star!

David Bowie was an amazing singer. I remember he told me in the early 1970s that he knew his limits. He had no illusions of being Aretha Franklin, but he knew he had an impressive vocal range. Listening back to 'Space Oddity', or to his albums from *The Man Who Sold The World* to *Ziggy Stardust*, you can see why, at the time, no singer under the age of 40 would have dared hit such high notes. He built up a very solid vocal and melodic background and he was able to adapt to different styles while still keeping the feeling in his voice. He didn't have to worry about technique – he already had it. We sang 'Real Wild Child' together at the same mic, face to face, while recording *Blah-Blah-Blah* in Montreux, and it was really badass: he had some fierce energy! I was amazed! The only other person I've met like that is Grace Jones. When I sang with her, she nearly knocked me over! I'm not talking about volume, but inner power. I was asked to talk about David on the radio recently, and I played 'Black Country Rock' – his vocals on that prick like a needle.

You know, The Stooges, and a lot of rock fans from small-town America, had heard of Bowie, but they didn't like the few songs they knew. I liked them from the very start. In school, I played in several orchestras and I listened to music as diverse as Sinatra, Ravel and The Ronettes. I didn't necessarily want to make music like them, but I knew they were the real thing. Looking back, I think that the music David recorded before *Ziggy Stardust* came too soon, it was too daring for rock audiences. With *Ziggy*, he put a bit of water in his wine, or guitar in his rock, if you like. Thanks to Mick Ronson, who I loved, his carefully crafted songs started to appeal to a wider audience. (2016)

JAMES WILLIAMSON

It's no secret that David Bowie was fascinated by Iggy. He'd met him in New York, got The Stooges to come to London and convinced Tony Defries to manage us. Bowie was very good at connecting people and also artists. He wanted to be connected to Andy Warhol, Lou Reed – the list is long. So seeing a good opportunity, we went to London, Iggy and I, hoping to find a rhythm section and record an album. But things didn't really go as planned and we were swept up in this glam rock whirlwind that was completely alien to us. Bowie was in the centre of it all and musicians like

Marc Bolan revolved around him... Glam, such a British thing, was at its peak. We had perfectly good lodgings near the King's Road. Bowie and MainMan introduced us to quite a few musicians, but none of them was what we were looking for. One day, Iggy and I were watching television and I said, 'You know what? Let's stop arguing about this: we already know a rhythm section that would work.' I was of course thinking of the Asheton brothers. Ron had already played bass, most notably for The Prime Movers and The Chosen Few, so we invited them over. It was basically The Stooges again, but the line-up was different.

Artistically, David Bowie's input was minimal then, but he and MainMan really helped us out logistically. Let's not forget one thing about The Stooges: we might have been wrong, but we weren't crazy. No one could force us to do anything! Initially, Bowie's idea was to produce a single a bit like he'd just done with Mott The Hoople. But even though he was great at it, we decided it wasn't for us. So we recorded a few demos ourselves – CBS turned them down and later they ended up being pirated. To tell you the truth, I never knew whether Bowie, Defries or our label[55] were responsible for that. Maybe it was a combination of all three! Or maybe it was because Defries tried to find in our music, but never succeeded, that pop touch that he liked in Bowie's. David was starting to make hits, maybe more in the US than in the UK, and all of MainMan's attention was focused on him. So we were left to ourselves. We gave a concert in London, then we went to the studio with no one there to help us or even advise us. We made *Raw Power* as best we could, any old how, but I think that contributes a lot to its singularity. Since it came out, we've never heard another album like it! And that's not so much because of the mix, but because of the way we played and recorded. And because *Raw Power* was my first record, while Iggy had already made two with the other Stooges, I trusted him. That was a mistake, but we tried our best to do what Don Gallucci had done on *Fun House*. (2017)

PHIL MANZANERA

When I joined Roxy Music, my ex-wife's parents ran a pub in Bromley. We were opening for David Bowie nearby, at the Greyhound in Croydon[56]. I arrived before the others because I lived with my in-laws. I climbed the stairs to the small venue, which could accommodate about two hundred people. David was there with The Spiders From Mars, in his stage outfit, all rhinestones and sequins. I introduced myself saying that I was playing guitar in the support band and I have to say that

I was impressed, by them of course, but also because they had this entire lighting system on some sort of scaffolding, even though the place was pretty tiny. It was an amazing show and it stuck with me! The room was packed and they'd had to turn a lot of people away. Every time I saw David after that, he'd joke, 'Phil, if everyone who claims they were in Croydon that night gave me ten quid, I'd be a millionaire.' I'd usually joke that he was anyway, which made us laugh even more.

In fact, David had read an article on Roxy Music in *Melody Maker* and he was really interested, even intrigued, by our music. David Bowie always supported us... For years he'd been struggling to make it, but that summer he really took off. If I remember correctly, Bryan Ferry and Andy Mackay, our sax player, had also seen him in concert, elsewhere, and had been completely stunned by his performance. A few weeks later, we opened for him again, at the Rainbow this time.

Roxy never copied David Bowie, but he undeniably influenced us and taught us things about how to present ourselves on stage. The similarity between him and us was that we both had a lot of substance. Our music was anything but superficial. And we all had very strong personalities. Of course, Roxy Music was more of a band, but let's not forget that his was fantastic. After seeing The Spiders From Mars on stage, a great many British youths thought, 'I want to do that too!' And above all, what they had more than others was a very professional side. The rhythm section was impeccable and Mick Ronson was an astounding guitar player. It was a classic rock band that worked beautifully. Roxy Music was impressed by all of that. David loved Andy's look, as did *Rock&Folk* magazine, who featured him on the cover[57]. (2016)

LLOYD WATSON

In 1972, I entered a competition in *Melody Maker* to find the best band and best solo artist in the UK. My band had just broken up... but I went anyway and I asked if I could compete as a solo artist. Until then, I'd only ever played alone at home, but I still won! I signed with Chrysalis, who booked me some concerts, including one opening for David Bowie and The Spiders From Mars at the Rainbow. I'd heard that David was a fan of the blues and rhythm'n'blues – any serious musician knows that that's where it all started.

Those two nights, my performance, right before Roxy Music, lasted half an hour. I played blues on an electric slide guitar in the style of Robert Johnson and Elmore James. It was old African-American music and to that audience, I must have looked almost as extra-terrestrial as Ziggy Stardust! But people seemed to like me.

I met David before the first concert and I saw him again backstage. That night, someone stole my guitar from my dressing room. The following day, Bowie lent me one of his so I could play. I thought that was cool of him.

I watched his show both nights. On a technical, visual and musical level, it was incredible. Mick Ronson has always been underrated as a guitar player but he was the ideal foil for Bowie. He could go from hard rock to lyrical pop in the strum of a pick. The following year, I opened for David again, this time in Bournemouth[58]. That *Melody Maker* competition opened a lot of doors for me, including an appearance on *The Old Grey Whistle Test* the week after I won. Meeting Roxy Music allowed me to tour with the band and also with King Crimson. I opened for many artists, including John Lee Hooker, Jethro Tull and Robert Palmer, and I contributed to the albums *Here Come The Warm Jets* by Brian Eno and *In Search Of Eddie Riff* by Andy Mackay. I was also a member of the supergroup 801, who released a great live album in 1976. (2016)

NORMA PALMER

My family and I were invited to accompany my brother Lloyd Watson to the party after the second concert of David Bowie and The Spiders From Mars at the Rainbow. My mum couldn't take her eyes off Elton John, who had green streaks in his hair. When Elton came over to talk to her, she was speechless. Even more so after he went to get her a gin and tonic! David was surrounded by a crowd of people, but he found the time to come say hi to my parents and he hugged my sister and me. He asked me what kind of mascara I wore. My mum had a problem with Bowie's make-up, but even though she found him 'a bit strange', she had to admit that he was 'extremely polite'! (2016)

BRIDGET ST JOHN

I saw David again when I opened for Ziggy and The Spiders in Portsmouth in 1972. To be honest, he'd changed so much I hardly recognized him! Unfortunately, we weren't able to talk that day because there was a bit of a drama. There'd been a big storm on the afternoon of the concert and a Hovercraft had capsized. No one was talking about anything else in town and that night, the room was far from full. That didn't stop Bowie playing his best. Last time I'd seen him he was a very laid-back guy at the Arts Lab, but now I found myself in the presence of a born performer who was really professional and had a great band. I'm not someone who follows people's careers and I didn't really know what was happening with him – needless to say, I was shocked at his transformation. (2018)

MICK ROCK

I met David Bowie at Birmingham Town Hall[59], where, officially, I went as a journalist. Some magazines were sending photographers to concerts and would also ask them to interview the musicians. That way they wouldn't have to pay two people! So I watched the show in a half-empty room. The circumstances weren't ideal because the audience didn't know his songs, but still he didn't hold back. We saw each other backstage after the concert and he was very happy with his performance.

In fact, two of my closest friends in music were Lou Reed and David Bowie. And I often had the feeling that they were two sides of the same coin. David was on fire, he was always on high alert, very London. Lou could be very sullen, difficult with the media, not exactly friendly, even though he was charming with the people he liked. I took quite a few photos of David that night, on stage and backstage, and he let me because in those days, photographers weren't chasing him down. Not long before, Syd Barrett had given me his last interview and that interested David. I think those two had a lot in common, including choosing not to sing with an American accent for the sake of it. They didn't pretend to be someone else. They were both deeply English and David, even when he was living in New York, remained so until the end of his life. Of course, he was greatly influenced by American artists like Lou and Iggy Pop, but he still kept his own identity.

I remember that after that first concert, David joked about my surname and I pointed out that at least I didn't have to adopt a pseudonym! He thought it was mad that my surname was really Rock! In the end, I don't think I actually interviewed him that night. Birmingham was the last city on that leg of the tour, so he wanted us to meet the following day instead, at Haddon Hall. That first real conversation lasted for hours and a big part of it was about Syd who, I'd realized the night before, really fascinated him. It didn't take long to fill my cassette tape! David didn't know Lou and Iggy like I knew Syd, but we talked a lot about the three musicians we both loved. He also told me he'd just signed with RCA Records in New York and he was really proud of it, because *The Man Who Sold The World* had been a huge flop. Now *Hunky Dory* had just come out and the media loved it. I was also impressed by how interested he was in Lou and Iggy – no one really talked about them and they weren't selling any records. Very few people understood that *The Velvet Underground & Nico* and the first Stooges were crucial albums. But David knew right away...

I never shot Bolan. Some people dismissed him, thinking he only made singles for teenagers. Bowie was really for people of my generation and, aside from his look, we truly connected with his music. And then, while doing his thing at full bore, David was about to save Lou[60] and Iggy's careers. Okay, so maybe it was a bit more complicated with Iggy... In those years, Bowie was a kind of coach, an 'enabler' who got the best out of his musicians and even his idols! I recently found the recording of another interview he'd given me after 'Starman'[61] came out, and he talked about all that. You can hear excerpts of it in the documentary[62] about me and my work. There are also a few minutes of David and The Spiders, filmed backstage before going on stage. I wonder why I kept that tape and not the others. However, in that interview, David warned me that he didn't plan always to tell the truth! Okay, he was joking, but maybe not that much. That year, he created his own legend. Instead of the naked truth, he favoured his own.

What was so striking about him in the early 1970s was his ambition, his ability to see himself as a star in the future. He was far from being one in those days, but he knew it would happen. And he managed to convince everyone in his way. People thought he must be important because he had an official photographer, which I became soon after meeting him. From then on, I was allowed to shoot anything I wanted. David never directed me or stopped me shooting anything. I saw him in his underwear, sleeping, eating, putting on his make-up and I photographed him as I wished, from every angle. Don't forget that in those days, the hippie movement still had some influence and having ambition was frowned upon, especially when it was displayed openly. Before him, I'd never met anyone so focused on his future. One day, he even said, 'You know, if someone told me my best friend had died, I'd be like, "Ah well, what a shame!" before going back to work.' It was strange to hear that from a 25-year-old man, and it said a lot about his determination. At the same time, Buddhism had an important place in his spiritual life and his beliefs went hand in hand with his aspirations. Lou and David both had Buddhist funerals.

The guitar fellatio? It was just before *Ziggy Stardust* came out. It's really interesting and I only realized it recently when David and I were working on the book *Moonage Daydream*[63], but you can clearly see that he started by biting on the strings on the guitar Mick Ronson was handing to him. And when Mick ended up lowering his arm because of the weight of the instrument, David saw an opportunity and continued to munch while kneeling and holding on to Ronson's ass. He immediately knew something special had happened and as soon as he got off the stage he asked me if I'd got the shot. I wasn't sure, but I hoped so. I only had a small flash, but it was enough given how small the stage was. (2016/2006)

MASAYOSHI SUKITA

I'd never heard of David Bowie when I came to London in 1972, but I knew a little about Marc Bolan, whom I'd met and photographed. Soon after I arrived, Bowie performed at the Royal Festival Hall and I went with some friends, but without my camera. I'd been intrigued by a poster for the concert, showing Bowie with his leg raised... I thought it was great. Lou Reed was also playing and the show was a revelation. I was surprised to see that the performance continued into the audience: most of the crowd were wearing make-up – I'd never seen that before!

I soon got an opportunity to photograph David Bowie in the London studio of one of my Japanese colleagues, and I owe that to Mick Rock, because when I showed Tony Defries my portfolio of fashion shots, Mick was there and told him my work was good. What struck me most when I met David was his kindness and elegance. His physical appearance and clothing made him a photographer's dream, but he was also very polite and very considerate. During our sessions, he drew a lot from his experience as a mime. He would see a lens and suddenly become a sort of actor who posed without anyone having to give him direction. He asked me to photograph him at the Rainbow, where he was planning a particularly ambitious show... (2015)

BILLY RITCHIE

David Bowie played me his songs often; as a songwriter myself I appreciated them, but I never thought of him as a great songwriter. He was very creative and intelligent, but I always felt that his real forte was acting. He was great at playing roles and using other people's voices and ideas, adapting them for his own purpose. I think that was the whole basis for his subsequent career. In the end, he played the part of David Bowie brilliantly on stage and on camera and in interviews. I thought his best record was 'Life On Mars?', and his best songs were things like 'Oh! You Pretty Things' and 'All The Young Dudes' – I actually think those, and some he wrote for other people, were often better songs than the ones he used himself, much stronger than the ones on *Ziggy Stardust*. Bowie was more creative as an artist than as a songwriter. (2017)

STEVE HARLEY

I saw Ziggy Stardust And The Spiders From Mars in 1972. My friends and I went to a concert at the Rainbow where Matthew Fisher played the piano, and we were literally stunned. I was working at Abbey Road at the time; I'd been recording *The Human Menagerie*, and I was really focused on what I was doing. But that night, he completely floored us. I'd seen David and his band play a few months before, but there were barely three hundred people in the audience. We had managed to sneak into the room while they were starting the sound check. We sat at the back and no one chucked us out. I can tell you, there's no way I'd let anyone watch my sound checks! I remember that David had two microphones in front of him, each on a stand, and he was going from one to the other, probably choosing which was best. He was such a perfectionist... The Spiders From Mars were a great band but today, apart from Woody, they're all gone... It's terrible.

And how could I not fall madly, madly, madly, madly in love with the *Ziggy Stardust* album? Of course, I did. Because Mick Ronson was all over it. He was everywhere. Mick was really gifted. When David was writing and planning the production, guitar parts and so on in the studio, he must have thought he had got Stravinsky in his band. Mick was that special. He was a great talent; close to genius. You know, a song is a song, but once it's produced, it's a record. A different thing. And Mick was excellent at making records. (2017)

PHIL MAY

David Bowie focused so much on the visual side of his shows in the 70s that we sometimes forget that his music was amazing. But he spent so much time on his image that it was obvious that sooner or later there'd be a sort of backlash. Yet anything went in those days and there was nothing wrong with trying to establish yourself as a visual artist and also a good musician. And he brought others along with him. The Spiders From Mars were his first real band – some great blokes who agreed to dress up! And with Mick Ronson as a bonus: he was a hell of a right-hand man who got it all on the guitar. (2017)

ALAN MAIR

In the late 60s, I managed a clothes shop in Kensington Market[64]. I'd turned my back on the music scene and it was going well for me. I was very creative – I made clothes, shoes, purses. I was good at my job. I didn't watch *Top Of The Pops* and I didn't read *Melody Maker*... On 6 May 1972, some friends came to see me at the market and asked me if I wanted to go with them to a David Bowie concert. I don't remember clearly, but I was like, 'How do you know David Bowie?' I was moving in different circles, but apparently people were talking about him more and more. My mates couldn't believe I didn't know about this guy. They told me he was playing at Kingston Polytechnic[65], which wasn't a small venue, so I wondered how in the world he was going to fill it. My mates laughed at me and said I was square! In the end, I went with them.

About ten of us got to the concert thinking we'd buy tickets at the door. I was amazed to see hundreds of people queuing up outside! I realized David would be playing to a sold-out venue that night. At the entrance, there was a guy with a top hat, and after quietly explaining that I was friends with the star, I asked if it would be possible to tell him his friend Alan Mair was there. I think at that moment my mates were starting to see me differently. The bloke walked off and came back ten minutes later. He told us we could all go to the artist's entrance – my mates couldn't believe it! We were shown into a room for journalists. When we walked past the dressing room door, I heard David warming up. I knocked, he opened the door and he was dressed as Ziggy Stardust from head to toe. I was shocked! Even though we hadn't seen each other in ages, he screamed my name and hugged me. My friends nearly fainted!

I know the expression 'a star is born' is a cliché, but that night it was all I could think about. The concert was fantastic. And the band were spectacular. I wondered what had happened to the young man living in Ken Pitt's spare room, the ex-mod, the folk singer with long hair who didn't seem to know which way he was going. David came with us to the press area, we had a drink and he signed some autographs for my friends. At one point, I couldn't help but whisper in his ear, 'Hey, this is incredible!' It must have been the biggest transformation of a rock star in the history of music.

We stayed in touch after that. My wife was a model and since Angie wanted to model too, she often came to her for advice. The funniest thing was that the pianist that night was Nicky Graham, who later became the A&R guy for The Only Ones, the band I've played with since the 1970s. I don't think David ever saw me in concert with them, which is a shame. (2018)

BRIAN MAY

Most of the members of Queen saw David Bowie on stage during the Ziggy Stardust tour, but I have to say that being a guitar player, it was Mick Ronson who impressed me the most. I always wanted to know how he managed to get that sound out of his Les Paul with just a simple pedal! It was incredible. He's one of the guitarists who inspired me, and I'll never forget him being on stage with us at the Freddie Mercury Tribute Concert – it'll always be etched in my memory[66]. (1998)

HERMIONE FARTHINGALE

When I was going out with David, I don't remember him reading sci-fi books or anything by Robert A. Heinlein, but I certainly can't swear that he didn't. To be honest, we did not have time to read a lot then. We were constantly on the go, or talking, and our relationship was too new to behave like an old couple, and be comfortable enough to read. We did not read much in that year. I think he read a lot when his career took off, and he had time travelling on tour. And before, when he lived at home and was bored. But when people described him as a big reader, it surprised me at first, because around me he didn't read at all. But I knew he loved books... (2018)

PATTI BRETT[67]

I'd already heard 'Space Oddity' and 'Changes', but they hadn't really done anything for me... Then one day in June 1972, I was coming back from school with some friends and someone in the car asked for the windows to be rolled up: 'Memory Of A Free Festival' was on the radio and they didn't want to miss a single note! I thought the song was okay and after finding out that it was David Bowie, I wanted to know more. Ziggy Stardust had just come out so I bought the album and fell completely in love with it. When David performed at the Tower Theater in Philadelphia[68] at the end of the year, I was there. As soon as he came on stage, I just stared at him, speechless. I'm pretty sure I spent the whole show in that state. That was it – I was hooked, I was addicted. That day, my life changed forever. I was 17 years old and I'd been going to concerts for some time by then, but I'd never seen anything like that. (2016)

BRIAN MOLKO

There are worse things than being associated with the glam rock hero. Placebo is a quintessential glamorous band, with all that implies in terms of heritage. We never denied our influences! I also never hid the fact that I was a dedicated fan of David Bowie, particularly his *Hunky Dory/Ziggy Stardust* period, which was the richest in my opinion.

It all started when I was 11 years old. I asked one of my schoolteachers, who was into music, if he had any Bowie records. A few days later, he gave me a cassette of his favourite album. So I spent my pre-teen years listening to *Ziggy Stardust* and that's the one I've listened to the most, from beginning to end. To me it is utter perfection, as it creates its own universe, one that is so finely crafted that it enables you to surrender and inhabit it cinematically, in 5D. I only had a cassette copy, with no artwork, so I created my own inner universe while listening to it – full of romance and abandon, sex and longing, self-destruction and the inevitability of it all. Listening to *Ziggy Stardust* was a transcendental experience and, though I wasn't aware of it at the time, it was an experience that I would continue to seek out in all music I bought afterwards. (1998/2016)

COURTNEY TAYLOR-TAYLOR[69]

Ziggy Stardust is a perfect equation: Bowie at the top, inventing a magical character, and Ronson, better than ever... It's such a clean record. I don't think it's the same kind of record as *Abbey Road*. *Ziggy Stardust* is closer to a musical. With that bubble-gum side the Beatles lost in 1964. (2012)

MARC EXIGA

David Bowie really did shine with a different light. When you look at the RCA catalogue from the 1970s, he and Lou Reed are the two that stand out. Before that the label had been completely dominated by Elvis Presley. Aside from the Nashville imprint, in the days of Chet Atkins or Owen Bradley, most of the artists on the label didn't leave a mark. RCA in Los Angeles felt like a graveyard... the carpet was thick – it was a big company, without any atmosphere. Which was why it seemed strange that they signed David Bowie[70]. It would have made more sense for him to go with Warner or Elektra. Then everyone would have thought, 'Ah, they found another weird guy.' For Bowie, at RCA, things really took off after *Ziggy Stardust*, but especially after *Aladdin Sane*. Those two albums brought back the crowds of people who'd been fascinated, but a bit overwhelmed, by him when *Hunky Dory* came out. (2018)

MARK PRITCHETT

The guitar in the photograph on the *Ziggy Stardust* cover was my number one instrument when I played with Rungk. One night, David arrived at my flat and asked to borrow it for a photo session. I sold it a couple of months later to help fund the purchase of a new Gibson SG Custom, the one I played on *The 1980 Floor Show*. When the album came out, I ruefully realized that I had let go of Ziggy's borrowed guitar; it was not stolen! (2019)

CHRIS FRANTZ

Long before I became Talking Heads' drummer, the first David Bowie song I heard was 'Space Oddity', which was played a lot on the radio in America at the end of the 60s. It might not surprise you, that was also when we started smoking quite a bit of weed... while driving! After that, we didn't hear about him much until *Hunky Dory* and *Ziggy Stardust*. Tina Weymouth, David Byrne and I were going to the Rhode Island School Of Design and we had another friend called Charles Rocket. He's not around anymore because he committed suicide, but in 1972, he was the lead singer of The Fabulous Motels. One morning, I was sitting on the steps out the front of my building in Providence, when Charlie came by and said, 'Chris, you'll never guess who I saw last night: I went to Boston[71] and I saw David Bowie and The Spiders From Mars.' I really wanted to know what it had been like, and he said, 'Well, my friend, it changed my life!'

That morning, I ran to the nearest record store and I bought *Ziggy Stardust*. For a while, it was all I listened to. I couldn't get enough – I felt like it was taking me to a parallel world, another planet altogether. I don't know where my copy is now, but I'm pretty sure I wore out the grooves.

Before Talking Heads, David Byrne and I had started The Artistics, and we had no greater ambition than playing at school parties or making the neighbourhood kids dance. Our biggest concert was on Valentine's Day! Talking to you now, I realize we never covered any Bowie songs, probably because, at first, we just didn't know how to play them. But we felt his influence on a higher level. His story impressed us. It amazed us that a guy from suburban London could become such a huge star. He had a big impact on us emotionally and intellectually.

The funny thing is that Lou Reed also influenced Talking Heads a great deal, and the record that had the biggest impact on us was *Transformer*. And that's the one David Bowie, as if by chance, put so much of himself into. I think I can speak for all four of us when I say he really inspired us to make music. We felt like he was speaking directly to us. And he wasn't just talking to our brains, but also to our hearts. (2018)

1. This 1998 film directed by Todd Haynes is discussed in the *Heathen* chapter in the second volume of *David Bowie : Rainbowman*.

2. Ironically, in early summer 2019, Mattel, the American toy company that manufactures Barbie, will announce the release of a Bowie/Ziggy Stardust doll.

3. '…Even though it's for informational purposes only,' he will confide to *Rock&Folk* in 1999.

4. A gradual increase in sound from silence to the level of the rest of the track.

5. 'Velvet Goldmine', 'Sweet Head', 'It's Gonna Rain Again', 'Shadow Man', 'Bombers', 'Holy Holy', 'Amsterdam', 'Round And Round', 'The Supermen', 'Only One Paper Left', 'Black Hole Kids'… These are original songs that will appear on B-sides, some will be recorded with the future Spiders From Mars, and a couple of covers. Many of them will be released on various reissues.

6. These photographs will undergo a similar colourization process to the one on the cover of *Hunky Dory*.

7. It's difficult to list which producers or musicians almost worked with Bowie, because of course they never did. But it's quite possible that, in the early 70s, Tony Defries and Bowie discussed working with producer Christos Demetriou. Born in Cyprus, this keyboardist was best known for having co-written 'He's Gonna Step On You Again' with John Kongos, his hit from May 1971, which was produced by Gus Dudgeon. A Gem employee, Demetriou rubbed shoulders with Bowie during promotions and in the studio. Around the same time, he worked with Mike D'Abo, Manfred Mann's second lead vocalist, on his excellent album *Down At Rachel's Place*, with Ken Scott as the recording engineer. Demetriou also worked with the British pop group Milkwood, under contract to Gem and formed by three ex-members of The New Seekers. According to Kevin Cann, Laurie Heath (the group's guitarist) was approached to join The Spiders From Mars in early 1972. A former actor, Heath will give his song 'This Is For You' to Mick Ronson, who will record it for *Play Don't Worry*, his second solo album. Ronson beautifully arranged 'Watching You Go', the A-side of Milkwood's first single. Don Hunter, also represented by Gem, produced it. For this book, the author reached out to Laurie Heath, but he declined to be interviewed.

8. He wouldn't bet his life on it, but that's what Iggy thinks. Another theory is that the name Ziggy came from a tailor's shop that Bowie saw from the window of a bus or train.

9. This will happen on 12 February at Imperial College London, during the encore. Part of the concert will be filmed by French TV channel Antenne 2 and a clip will be aired on 3 April on the show *Pop 2* (probably the first appearance of David Bowie on French television).

10. 'Paralyzed', his 'hit', and 'I Took A Trip On A Gemini Spaceship', which David Bowie will cover on *Heathen* in 2002.

11. At the Rainbow concerts later that year, Marc Bolan's face will be projected onto the stage during this song.

12. During a week-long break in mid-January, David Bowie and his band performed on *Sounds Of The 70s* twice, first with John Peel,

then with Bob Harris. They played songs from the upcoming album as well as 'I'm Waiting For The Man'. The shows aired on 28 January and 7 February.

13. It will be on David Bowie's 2013 list of 100 favourite books.

14. Since this book is about David Bowie's music, the author doesn't delve into his private life, but it does seem that, throughout his career, Bowie had intimate relationships with many people of both sexes from his entourage, as well as others he met along the way.

15. This British folk singer-songwriter recorded a handful of excellent albums in the early 70s. They were funded by John Peel, who founded the label Dandelion for her. In terms of writing, she was on a par with Nick Drake, and on 'Ask Me No Questions' and 'Songs For The Gentle Man', her voice sounds rather like Nico's.

16. Suzi Fussey will follow David Bowie on the road and become his stylist. After The Spiders From Mars split, she will work exclusively with Mick Ronson, whom she will end up marrying. They will have a daughter, Lisa Ronson. Lisa is a musician and sometimes sang in the band Holy Holy.

17. On this occasion, David Bowie will collaborate with recording engineer Keith Harwood, whom he will work with again in late 1973 on *Diamond Dogs*, also at Olympic.

18. Like a lot of other Lou Reed songs of that era, 'Walk On The Wild Side' wasn't a new one. He'd written it a few years before and had intended to use it on his previous album. The inspiration was of course *A Walk On The Wild*

Side, Nelson Algren's novel. Edward Dmytryk made a brilliant film adaptation of the book in the early 60s.

19. Herbie Flowers explains this in the documentary about the making of *Transformer*, from the *Classic Albums* series, which Eagle will produce and release in 2001.

20. In early June 1972, David Bowie, Tony Defries and Mick Ronson went to New York for three days of intense promotion ahead of their American tour. They saw Elvis Presley in concert at Madison Square Garden, but the two RCA stars (the established one and the rising one) never met. However, rumours of collaboration and/or production weren't completely unfounded since Presley and his management did get in touch with David Bowie. The fax Presley sent him in 1976 will be on display at the *David Bowie Is* exhibition. David Bowie might not have written 'Golden Years' (on *Station To Station*) with Elvis in mind, but he often said he would have loved Elvis to cover it. Like many aspiring stars of his generation, Bowie grew up wanting to be like Presley, even though he sometimes said the person who made him embark on a career in music was Lonnie Donegan, the Scottish musician who started the skiffle craze. As a child, David had a key ring shaped like a fan that contained photos of Elvis Presley, Guy Mitchell and British stars like Tommy Steele, Frankie Vaughan and David Whitfield.

21. While 'Life On Mars?' and 'Ashes To Ashes' (released in 1971 and 1980 respectively) will be used in 2006 and 2008 as the titles of a British crime television series created by Matthew Graham (their common point is time travel), 'Five Years' will lend its theme to *Hard Sun*. In this British series, created by Neil Cross and released in 2018, two police officers investigate the impending extinction of the human race.

22. *Abbey Road To Ziggy Stardust* (Alfred Music Publishing, 2012).

23. This combination of instruments was used regularly in the 1960s, especially in film scores. Ken Scott believes that, for the instrumental part of 'Moonage Daydream', David Bowie took direct inspiration from the arrangement in 'Sho' Know A Lot About Love' by The Hollywood Argyles. This song was on the B-side of the first single by this American music ensemble founded by Kim Fowley and Gary S. Paxton, with the hit 'Alley Oop' by Dallas Frazier on the A-side. Bowie recycled '*Well look at that caveman go*' from the lyrics in that song (which was also covered by The Beach Boys) for the chorus of 'Life On Mars?' ('*Look at those cavemen go*').

24. These include Kevin Cann, Nicholas Pegg, David Buckley, Mark Paytress, Peter Doggett, Chris O'Leary, Peter and Leni Gillman and Paul Trynka, whose writings stand out among the vast body of work about Bowie. Other books are not so reliable, but are even less so now since David Bowie's death led to a proliferation of mediocre journalism.

25. This is a Ron Davies song, which opens his album *Silent Song Through The Land*. Rick Wakeman plays the harpsichord on David Bowie's version of this song, which was also reportedly recorded by Arnold Corns.

26. Actually, Chameleon wanted David Bowie to produce the song, but Bob Grace suggested someone else.

27. This version came out as a single in August 1972, with 'Man In The Middle' on the B-side.

28. To illustrate the fact that David Bowie's songs sometimes included melodic or harmonic references to other pieces of music, here's an anecdote related by pianist Sean Mayes in the early 80s. During rehearsals for the Isolar 2 tour in Dallas in 1978, while Adrian Belew was practising the guitar solo on 'Hang On To Yourself', violinist Simon House said that, when Mick Ronson played it, it always reminded him of the theme tune for *Hancock's Half Hour*, a BBC show from the 1950s and 1960s. Bowie burst out laughing and confirmed that that was in fact where the melody had come from. Ronson's guitar playing, especially on 'Hang On To Yourself', inspired many punk bands, including The Vibrators. This influence can particularly be heard on 'Wrecked On You', which will appear on their first album *Pure Mania*, produced by Robin Mayhew.

29. A piano/vocal demo of 'Lady Stardust' will also surface on this disc, along with a different mix of 'John, I'm Only Dancing' and two other beautiful songs, 'Sweet Head' and 'Velvet Goldmine'. The first, a pop track despite its explicit lyrics, is imbued with melancholy. The second is a pastiche of a Russian song that foreshadows 'Time' on *Aladdin Sane*. 'Velvet Goldmine', released for the first time in 1975 (without Bowie's knowledge) on the B-side of the reissue of 'Space Oddity', will lend its title to Todd Haynes' film in the late 90s. On 'Sweet Head', The Spiders From Mars sound like they are Chuck Berry's group or Free (Bowie was blown away by the voice of Paul Rodgers, the band's frontman). It would have remained officially unreleased if David hadn't dug out the track himself – several Rykodisc bonus tracks will come from his personal vaults.

Ziggy Stardust will also be reissued (and remastered by Peter Mew) for its 30th anniversary. This double CD will add to the 'rarities' of 1990: the 1971 re-recording of 'Holy Holy', 'Amsterdam', 'Round And Round', a new mix of 'Moonage Daydream' (used for a television ad), the version of 'The Supermen' from the compilation *Revelations*, as well as 'Moonage Daydream' and 'Hang On To Yourself' by Arnold Corns. Ken Scott will remix *Ziggy Stardust* in 5.1 in 2003 and Ray Staff (who was in charge of remastering at Trident), will do it again in 2012 for its 40th anniversary. These different mixes and masterings will be available in the box set *Five Years (1969–1973)* in 2015. *Hunky Dory*, on the other hand, apart from its Rykodisc reissue and a 2021 picture disc on Parlophone, hasn't received any special treatment – it's simply outrageous.

30. To help a drummer keep a consistent tempo throughout a live take, he's sent a simple beat, through headphones, from a drum machine or computer to act as a metronome.

31. This simple way of playing the rhythm piano was used a lot in rock and pop. Later, David Bowie will often recycle the eighth note beat of 'I'm Waiting For The Man' by The Velvet Underground – for example in "Heroes", 'Blackout', 'DJ', and 'Boys Keep Swinging'.

32. In the late 60s and early 70s, it was very expensive to rent a synthesizer, and the cost of a technician who could extract sounds from it had to be added. This is why Barry Sheffield, co-owner of Trident Studios, decided to buy one in 1971. He went to ARP in Boston (Moog's rival company), with David Hentschel, the most musical of the assistants at Trident, to buy a modular 2500 model. That's how Hentschel

ended up playing on *Honky Château* by Elton John, which was partially recorded in France but completed and mixed in London. Like The Beatles, David Bowie became really interested in the instrument and will play it live in 1978. While Elvis Presley, before going on stage, had his musicians perform 'Sunrise', the introduction to *Also Sprach Zarathustra* (the Richard Strauss tone poem inspired by Friedrich Nietzsche's book), which can be heard in the film *2001: A Space Odyssey*, David Bowie chose an excerpt from the fourth and final movement of Beethoven's *Ninth Symphony* (widely referred to as 'Ode To Joy' or 'Hymn To Joy', which, incidentally, became the official anthem of the Council of Europe in 1972 and of the EU in 1985). This piece was interpreted on synthesizer by the American musician Walter Carlos (and used in *A Clockwork Orange* under the name 'March From A Clockwork Orange'). Towards the end of the Ziggy Stardust/Aladdin Sane tour, as can be heard on some bootleg recordings, Mick Ronson and the band will sometimes play the final notes of 'Ode To Joy' arriving on stage. In 1978, Walter Carlos changed gender and became Wendy Carlos. During the recording of *The Man Who Sold The World*, Tony Visconti and David Bowie asked Ralph Mace to play the synth like Carlos did on *Switched-On Bach*, an album paying homage to Bach that they'd loved since it came out in 1968. David Hentschel worked with Bowie in 1972 as a recording engineer during sessions for *All The Young Dudes* at Olympic.

33. Steve Marriott, the singer and guitarist of Small Faces, later started Humble Pie with Peter Frampton. In October 1969, David Bowie performed in England with them on a joint tour.

34. This 1957 song, the B-side of the single 'Johnny B. Goode', was originally called 'Around And Around'. David Bowie and the future Spiders From Mars recorded a version in 1971 with Ken Scott which was meant for *Ziggy Stardust*, but 'Starman' was chosen instead. David started playing 'Around And Around' when he was with The King Bees.

35. Performed by Elly Stone, Shawn Elliott, Alice Whitfield and Mort Shuman (who also helped adapt the songs with Eric Blau).

36. A few days before, during a performance on 17 June at the Town Hall in Oxford, David Bowie gave Mick Ronson (and his guitar) the famous blowjob simulation that Mick Rock captured on camera. Bowie was thrilled with the shot, Ronson less so. Whatever MainMan may have claimed at the time, David Bowie was not the first famous singer to kneel in such a suggestive way in front of his guitarist. During the famous Doors concert at the Dinner Key Auditorium in Miami on 1 March 1969, a very drunk Jim Morrison also behaved in a way that the media and FBI deemed obscene. As the photos from that night confirm, he basically pretended to perform fellatio on his guitarist, Robby Krieger. However, none of the photos showed him with his penis out, which was the main reason for the indignation and possible charge. The Doors and their management always denied that Morrison had gone to such... extremes. Interviewed for this book, The Doors' manager Bill Siddons debunked the rumour, put about by Bowie at the time, that he might have met Jim Morrison at the Roundhouse in September 1968. According to Siddons, who was always with The Doors, it's highly unlikely they even crossed paths.

37. In 2012, Masayoshi Sukita will bring together his David Bowie photographs in *Speed Of Life*, a magnificent book published by Genesis. Bowie will contribute to the work by adding a few relevant notes.

38. Up until then, David Bowie's British singles had been sold in plain paper sleeves just featuring the name of the label. During the RCA years, a few singles will appear in proper covers with tailored visuals, but not all. Some of Bowie's singles will be marketed with designed jackets in several countries from 1967. In *David Bowie: World 7" Records Discography 1964–1981* (B&B Press Limited, 1994), Marshall Jarman will identify all the singles Bowie released around the world during that period.

39. Known in the 1960s as (the) Astoria (The Beatles gave some Christmas shows there, and it was also where Jimi Hendrix fired up his Stratocaster for the first time), this concert venue in Finsbury Park with a capacity of 3,000 people will become, in the following decade, an important spot for live music in London. Many big pop and rock acts will perform, record albums and even be filmed there (including Yes, Gary Glitter and Bob Marley). Several videos will be shot at the Rainbow, also used as a projection room. It will close its doors at the very start of the 1980s and it is now a church.

40. Natasha Korniloff will also make David Bowie's outfits for the Isolar tour in 1978, as well as, two years later, his famous clown costume for the cover of *Scary Monsters*, also worn in the video for 'Ashes To Ashes'.

41. People have said that David Bowie, who will record there soon, was delighted to work where Elvis Presley had recorded his first albums for RCA back in late 1955. But actually, the studios were in a different place then – they were located on 24th Street, north of Gramercy Park. At the start of the 1970s, RCA Studios migrated up to 1133 6th Avenue.

42. Mick Ronson's friends sometimes called him by the name of the band he tried to form in the early 1970s.

43. This was the case.

44. Robin Lumley, the cousin of actress Joanna Lumley, was the last in a line of British pianists who joined The Spiders From Mars before they left for the US and recruited Mike Garson in September 1972. Through the words of these three musicians (Nicky Graham, Matthew Fisher and Robin Lumley), it's obvious that things were not simple when it came to the piano, and that clear and precise communication was not always the forte of Bowie's management. Lumley was told he was replacing Fisher (for a few concerts and the added one at the Rainbow on 30 August), who was ill, but he didn't seem to be. As for Graham, he never really knew why Angie Bowie had him fired. He thinks it had something to do with money, but there's also the theory that Nicky, also working for MainMan at the time, may have forgotten to put some of her friends on the guest list for one of the first two Rainbow concerts, which would have made her very angry. Lastly, the theory that David Bowie already had Annette Peacock in mind to replace Lumley in the US is greatly undermined by the fact that, before he left, several British keyboardists auditioned for the job, unsuccessfully.

45. In early 1971, as well as the rumour that Gene Vincent had taped 'Hang On To Yourself', people were saying that Three Dog Night wanted to record three David Bowie songs on their upcoming album; David Bowie himself mentioned it to the press. However, *Harmony*, the fifth album by this Los Angeles band, came out in late September 1971 and didn't feature a single note of his music.

46. Or indeed afterwards! David Bowie will describe an act of fellatio in the first verse of 'Reality', three decades later.

47. Shelby Lynne, who in 2017 will release *Not Dark Yet*, an album with her sister Allison Moorer, is a big fan of David Bowie's music. During the writing of this book, she told Mike Garson that she loved Bowie's saxophone playing and that he'd inspired her to try her hand at it. According to Garson, Lynne particularly likes 'the most esoteric songs' on *Hunky Dory*.

48. *Unsung Hero: A Tribute To The Music Of Ron Davies*, released in 2013.

49. A founding member of Mott The Hoople, Peter 'Pete' Overend Watts was the bass player. He took part in the band's reunion concerts in 2009 at the Hammersmith Apollo (former Odeon). He died in January 2017.

50. Mott The Hoople's fourth album, released in 1969.

51. Klaus Voorman's word can certainly be trusted, but sessions for *Transformer* were not all known for their good cheer. Ken Scott doesn't have great memories of them and, even though he didn't speak openly to the author about David Bowie and Lou Reed's difficulties working together, they were real. The clash of those two very different egos in a confined space made that first collaboration the last major project they did together. Reed, who was quite sarcastic at the time, took a vicious pleasure in persecuting the idealistic Bowie and the two men won't work together again until *The Raven*, in 2003. The substances that troubled Reed's mind sometimes caused him to have angry outbursts, and Bowie would hide in the Trident toilets to wait out the storm. In the decades that followed, Reed will never dispute the fact that 'Walk On The Wild Side' had turned him into a rock star, but he will express all sorts of opinions about *Transformer*, sometimes calling it his best record and sometimes saying the exact opposite. Like Scott, Lou Reed will claim that Mick Ronson played a major role in the making of *Transformer*, sometimes acting as a buffer between him and Bowie. In April 1979, diners at a chic restaurant in Knightsbridge will watch David and Lou come to blows, an event the British press will eagerly report.

52. This timeframe corresponds to the four-disc live box set of *You Don't Want My Name, You Want My Action* released by Easy Action in 2009.

53. Iggy Pop initially arrived in London with James Williamson in the spring of 1972. Scott and Ron Asheton joined them a few weeks later.

54. When mentioning this period, Iggy Pop will sometimes confuse Third World War (often wrongly called World War 3), the British proto-punk band produced by John Fenton in the early 1970s, with Edgar Broughton Band, a psychedelic combo, equally rough around the edges, that hit the London scene in 1968. This confusion is probably due to the fact that David Bowie, who had his finger on the pulse of the times, brought many musicians into the rehearsal room where Iggy and James Williamson were working on the follow up

to *Fun House*, before the rest of The Stooges arrived.

55. It's not clear what happened with the contract. Clive Davis, who ran CBS, reportedly showed an interest in Iggy Pop, but it's likely that the management deal with MainMan included control of the recordings. The contract may have been signed by Defries, who would have then 'managed' the advance money in his own way: meaning he probably syphoned off a good part of it. What's certain, is that the deal was with Iggy Pop and not The Stooges, whom neither Defries nor Davis wanted anything to do with.

56. This concert took place on 25 June 1972.

57. The cover for Issue 72, from January 1973.

58. On 31 August at the Royal Ballrooms in Boscombe.

59. David Bowie and The Spiders From Mars performed there on 17 March 1972.

60. David Bowie and Mick Rock went to see Lou Reed together at his first concert in England on 14 July 1972, at the King's Cross Cinema in London. The next day, at the same venue, they watched the only Iggy And The Stooges gig in the United Kingdom before they reunited in 2003. Two of the most iconic album covers (*Transformer* and *Raw Power*) were made from the photos Mick Rock took those two nights.

61. 'Rock'n'roll Suicide', the second single from *Ziggy Stardust*, released in April 1974, much later than it should have been, as Bowie had by then moved on to his soul period, will remain just out of the UK Top 20.

62. *Shot! The Psycho-Spiritual Mantra Of Rock*, directed by Barney Clay in 2016.

63. *Moonage Daydream: The Life And Times Of Ziggy Stardust* (Genesis, 2002). Mick Rock died in 2021.

64. That was around the time Alan Mair was hanging out with a certain Freddie (whose real name was Farrokh Bulsara), who had a shop opposite his in the market. Freddie's business was failing so Mair offered him a job, although Freddie did warn him that sooner or later he'd leave because he was in a band. One day in 1969, David Bowie stopped by the shop and Freddie asked him if he wanted to buy a pair of boots. Bowie said he couldn't afford them so Alan Mair decided to give them to him. Now, Mair regrets that no photo was taken of the future Freddie Mercury helping David Bowie try on a pair of boots.

65. This concert was one of the few that were recorded for a live album of the 1972 tour. However, it never officially came out. In this chapter, Nicky Graham relates events that are also mentioned in Kevin Cann's book (about the London years of David Bowie). He refers here to a concert on 27 May 1972 and, in Cann's book, it seems to be the one on 6 May (that Alan Mair attended). Anyway, the date is not that important and it is more than probable that Nicky Graham and Robin Mayhew 'pinned posters onto trees' in several towns during the tour.

66. In late 1973, David Bowie will arrange for Queen to open for Mott The Hoople during a British tour. That same year, he'll be too busy to produce Queen's first album. In 1973, Iggy And The Stooges, New York Dolls, Peter Frampton's Camel and Aerosmith will be among the bands that will play at least once before Mott in the US.

67. Patty Brett is one of the two 'Sigma kids' interviewed for this book. They talk about meeting David Bowie in Philadelphia in 1974 in the chapter on *Young Americans*.

68. On 1 and 2 December 1972.

69. Courtney Taylor-Taylor is the singer-songwriter of the American band Dandy Warhols.

70. David Bowie's signing with RCA caused quite a stir in the press, and an outpouring of bile from homophobes all over the US. They apparently disapproved of his nice figure, his feminine side and his sequined outfits. The author can't help but remind them that even Elvis Presley who, among other things, was a heterosexual idol for macho Americans, spent his last years as an entertainer (in the 1970s) wearing satin, short capes and rhinestones. In his choice of clothes, the King of Las Vegas was undeniably glam, though perhaps more like Sweet, Slade or Gary Glitter than Bowie.

71. They performed at the Music Hall in Boston on 1 October 1972.

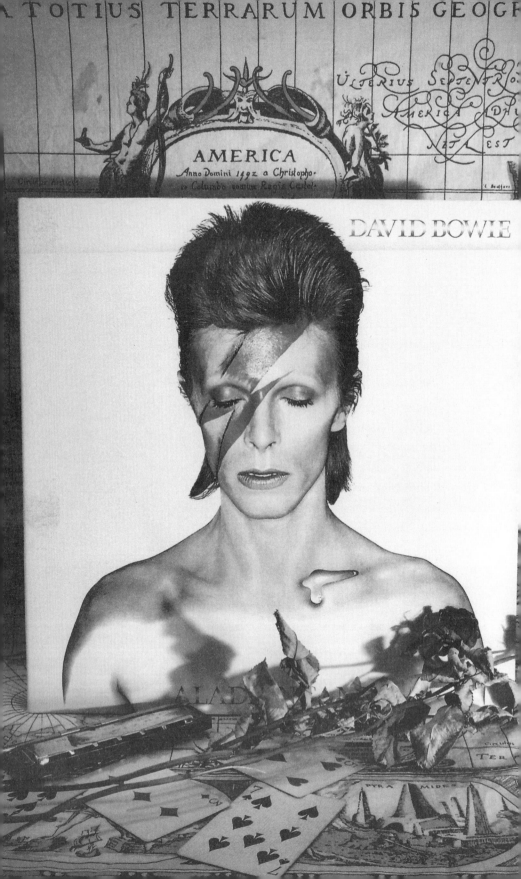

ALADDIN SANE

RCA – 13 APRIL 1973

'I received life like a wound and I have forbidden suicide to heal the scar.'
(COMTE DE LAUTRÉAMONT, *LES CHANTS DE MALDOROR*, 1869)

'The Ziggy Stardust and Aladdin Sane tours wore me down. Mostly, the routine bored me and since I've never been very artistically stable... As soon as I have created something, the only thought I have in mind is to move on to something else. Looking back on that period, I think it's important to distinguish between two types of glam rock. What Roxy Music and I were trying to do was to enrich the rock vocabulary. We tried to include in our music a range of strong visual inputs from the so-called fine arts, references to theatre and cinema. In short, everything but rock. Personally, I liked to bring in Dadaist elements and a lot of material borrowed from Japanese culture. I believe we saw ourselves as avant-garde explorers, representatives of a kind of embryonic form of post-modernism. The other bands came directly from a rock tradition – the strange clothes, the make-up, all that. Actually, we were highly elitist. I can't speak for Roxy Music, but I was a damn snob. More than The Spiders were, anyway! I think there were two levels of glam rock, a higher level and a lower level. We were the top level! We saw things on a much broader scale than other bands I won't name. Marc Bolan was a key figure, but I'm not sure he really liked being associated with glam rock. In his head he was Bolan first, T. Rex, not the leader of some trend. I saw him as a transitional figure somewhere between hippie culture and something much more flamboyant, embodied by what he would become, and wear: satin jackets and coloured velvet trousers. He borrowed the look from The Rolling Stones, but added glitter around his eyes. Marc launched the era, but I don't think he was glam enough to wear high-heeled boots. He was very happy with his little hippie shoes from Anello & Davide, where I bought my ballet shoes. But his position was very interesting. He was a bit like Johnny Ray, somewhere between crooners like Frank Sinatra and Elvis Presley. Ray knew he was there, in the middle, not exactly a crooner any more, but not a rock star yet... Yes, Marc was a bridge. We had the chance to talk about this when we became good friends again. As you know, we became friends two or three times during our careers! Marc was fine with the idea of being a bridge or a missing link – that's exactly how he felt. [...]

Ah, Le Havre! *Le France* departed from there, didn't she? I spent quite a lot of time on ocean liners. It wasn't the fastest way to travel, but it allowed me to read, to work. Ships, trains... I wrote a lot moving around... During the crossings, I usually went to the restaurant on the first evening, but the other passengers would gawp at me as I walked by, so I ended up taking my meals in my cabin. Sometimes I'd find sailors in the canteen and I'd play songs for them on the guitar. It was my way of partying on board. Knowing me, I must have sung "Amsterdam" for them. [...]

The Beatles' *Anthology* impressed me a lot and I plan to do something like that some day. For example, I've got this old demo of "Aladdin Sane" [he sings]: "Da-da-da-da, da-da-da..." It's a piano/voice version called "Ali Baba". I thought it sounded like flying carpet music! I must have kept the multitrack tape: if I want, I can remix everything! [...]

[Seeing himself in an asymmetrical Yamamoto outfit on the cover of *Rock&Folk* from July 1973] That's the kind of photo I showed my son when he was a teenager so he'd understand what his dad had to do to earn a living! I'd love to know what happened to the other leg of that outfit... And that one [the April 1975 cover of *Rock&Folk*] was taken by Mick Rock in 1973, the day we shot the video for "Life On Mars?". I seem to remember that that outfit was stolen... I was not robbed of much though, I kept pretty much everything else. Oh wait, I'm an idiot: Kate Moss recently did a photo shoot with Nick Knight for British *Vogue* and she's wearing several of my outfits from the Ziggy years, including that one! She even called me afterwards to tell me I must have been really skinny at the time! When Kate Moss phones to tell you she can't get into your old clothes, you know you can't have weighed very much.'

DB (1998/1996/1999/2003)

It's funny to think that when, in September 1972, David Bowie and the MainMan circus arrived in Cleveland, Ohio, only a few rock fans were 'waiting for the man'. That year, the British press was more and more adoring, but Bowie was only 'almost famous' in the US. The first of these two allusions to *Almost Famous*, the semi-autobiographical film directed by Cameron Crowe about a young music-loving journalist eager to see his byline in *Rolling Stone* magazine[1], is all the more ironic because, from the beginning of the 1970s, Bowie proclaimed his dislike for drugs of all kinds. That will not stop this paradox of a man from developing a cocaine habit and covering 'I'm Waiting For The Man' by Lou Reed a considerable number of times throughout his career. Bowie definitely considered Reed a master until the end of his life[2]. In this song, an addict despairs of seeing his drug dealer arrive on a street corner in New York. Cameron Crowe is a bit of an expert on rock history and, in his film, the fictional band Stillwater is a combination of the groups he wrote about when he was a rock critic – Led Zeppelin, The Eagles, Lynyrd Skynyrd, The Allman Brothers. Crowe will use Bowie's version of 'I'm Waiting For The Man' as the soundtrack for the sequence where William Miller (played by Patrick Fugit) arrives in Cleveland and at the legendary Swingos Hotel.

For a whole decade, this seething microcosm of a building opened its doors day and night to a rock'n'roll clientele prone to excesses and deviancy of all kinds. Rock was no longer the music of the devil, but it still undermined the prevailing puritanism, especially when played – in New York, Los Angeles and elsewhere – by boys wearing make-up and satin.

Jim Swingos opened a restaurant in 1971 before purchasing the hotel. He was no lover of rock to begin with but, at a time when his business was struggling, Elvis Presley showed up and asked to turn the place into a base for his tour of the Midwest. Presley booked about a hundred rooms over three floors for several weeks.

So Swingos decided to tap into this opportunity and build up a reputation as a hotelier who would welcome travelling rock stars. Keith Moon, drummer of The Who, threw some memorable parties there, at one point dressing up as a police officer and handcuffing a radio host to a young blonde girl before doing a runner. The actor Yul Brynner came to blows with guitarist Ritchie Blackmore at Swingos because his band Deep Purple were making too much noise; and whenever Led Zeppelin passed through, the hotel had to carry out repair works (which never bothered the owner because the band paid him in cash for everything they destroyed). Ian Hunter said about the place[3], 'I only remember checking in and checking out, nothing in between.'

And again 'almost famous', because the only real instruction Tony Defries gave his employees (in London to perform in a scandalous play the year before, the cast of *Pork* had left town recruited to MainMan and decked out with titles – and roles – as puffed up as the company name itself) was to act as if David Bowie was already a star. Which was still far from the truth. But no matter. Inspired by Presley's manager, Colonel Parker, right down to the cigar, Defries will shamelessly use a sort of autosuggestion tactic, on steroids. The scene from *Almost Famous* where a Bowie character is hustled into a lift in the hotel foyer, making it look like he is being chased by a horde of assailants, is a reference to the MainMan method. In reality, there's no danger of that happening to David Bowie in the USA in 1972. Cameron Crowe also shows fans with lightning bolts painted over their faces, yet *Aladdin Sane* won't be released until seven months after Ziggy Stardust's Cleveland stop, so this reference, as well as the copy of the album in their hands, is completely anachronistic. However, even if the director took a few liberties, his overall portrayal of the American scene in the early 70s is pretty accurate, especially the bits he shot at Swingos. It was in rock'n'roll hotels[4] like this that the MainMan entourage felt comfortable. In fact, Bowie's band will stay at Swingos during the Isolar 2 tour. In September 1972, they didn't.

David Bowie and his musicians will come across a good many record company people and journalists in hotels like Swingos, as well as clubs and concert halls, and they will help to build up a sort of myth around him. These people could create a buzz and spread rumours and propaganda. Far from being absurd, Tony Defries' choice to launch Ziggy Stardust And The Spiders From Mars' American journey at the Cleveland Music Hall made perfect sense.

In 1972, thanks to rock music, Cleveland was enjoying a revival. A decade earlier it had been stagnating, with no prestigious sports teams, a failing economy and a polluted river whose water could have been used as lighter fluid – the surface of the river Cuyahoga was covered with flammable materials and had caught fire a few years earlier. The WMMS radio station, the only one with a hint of rebel spirit, was helping to define the zeitgeist. At the suggestion of radio director Billy Bass and his programmer Denny Sanders, the station's DJs were rolling out the red carpet to David Bowie, Roxy Music, Mott The Hoople, New York Dolls and Bruce Springsteen by playing their songs. WMMS even sponsored The Spiders From Mars' historic first American concert. Most of the people who will attend that night (and even those who won't) will be talking about it many years later with a tear in their eye[5]. But those who claim that Ziggy Stardust won over America on that one night are exaggerating.

After the show on 22 September, David Bowie knew he had Cleveland in the bag, but at the after-party at the Hollenden House Hotel, he must have been thinking about the rest of that huge country he still had to seduce. When he found out that Tony Defries had threatened to cancel the show because of the size of the piano provided (the spec sheet clearly stipulated that it had to be the largest model – not a baby grand and definitely not an upright piano) and demanded it be replaced with the required instrument, Bowie realized how seriously his manager was taking this American campaign. Mike Garson doesn't remember the change of piano but that concert in Cleveland was the first time he brought a baroque touch to David Bowie's repertoire, although the pirate recordings show that his parts were still limited then. According to Garson in January 2018, the day after the first Celebrating Bowie tribute concert in Paris, 'It wasn't the type of thing MainMan talked about, but it's possible. It was a really beautiful piano, not like anything you'd usually find in that type of venue, and it sounded brilliant!'

In mid-September 1972, David Bowie arrives in New York from the UK with his wife, child, entourage (or part of it) and friends, including George Underwood and his wife Birgit. After a bumpy flight when he was returning from holiday in Cyprus the month before, Bowie has decided not to fly any more, and makes the trip from Southampton on the *Queen Elizabeth II*, Cunard's flagship vessel. The Spiders From Mars, Mick Rock and the rest of the clique fly to New York and everyone stays at the Plaza Hotel on 5th Avenue, where The Beatles stayed on their first trip to the US in February 1964. They spend enough time in Manhattan to audition pianist Mike Garson – who easily lands the job – and watch New York Dolls at the Mercer Arts Center[6]. After seeing this wild rock band with singer David Johansen and guitarists Johnny Thunders and

Sylvain Sylvain dressed up as women on and off stage, The Spiders will overcome their reluctance to wear make-up. They will also see how the queue of groupies at the dressing room door gets longer and longer as the tour progresses.

The night of the Dolls concert – they are the band that fascinate him the most, apart from The Velvet Underground and The Stooges – David Bowie meets a young actress with the stage name Cyrinda Foxe[7]. Andy Warhol adores her (she was in the American version of *Pork*), she looks eerily like Marilyn Monroe and she knew Marcel Duchamp – those are reasons enough to prompt Bowie to introduce himself to her. Foxe will go on to work for MainMan for a while and appear in the video for 'The Jean Genie', which Mick Rock will direct in late October.

A week after they arrived in New York, David Bowie and his team charter a Greyhound to Cleveland. That first concert, in a venue with just over 3,000 seats, is sold out, but not all of the shows will go as planned, especially on a logistical level. David is now firmly against flying and intends to travel by coach and train during the whole 30-date tour (through to December). The distances in the United States are so great that they will have to leave travelling days between concerts, and the cost of transport, food and lodgings for the 50-odd people in the entourage, who have a soft spot for expensive hotels like the Plaza in New York or the Beverly Hills Hotel in Los Angeles, will add significantly to the bill Tony Defries intends to present to RCA.

Some cities won't be as welcoming as Cleveland. Leee Black Childers and Cherry Vanilla, who are working for MainMan[8], go on ahead to each stop to prepare the ground for the new rock Messiah. But despite their efforts, they won't always be able to convince the media and local radio hosts to roll out the red carpet for David Bowie. Some venues will only be half-full and others three-quarters empty. On 11 October in Saint Louis, Bowie will have to invite the audience dotted around the Kiel Auditorium (much too large) to come closer for a more intimate performance. David won't always take it well, and sometimes he will perform while drunk.

On the upside, he uses the endless journeys to write. He finds inspiration looking out of the windows of buses and trains, and from America in general, which excites his senses. Likewise, some of the scenes he sees at parties and the conversations he has with friends will make their way into frantically written lyrics. Having devoured Jack Kerouac's most famous novel – a portrayal of the nomadic lifestyle that became the manifesto of the beat generation[9] – as a teenager, David Bowie is himself now 'on the road' and living it to its fullest. And whenever he feels the urge to record, he does it. He finds a studio wherever he is. Sessions will therefore be held in New York, Chicago[10], Nashville and New Orleans. Ken Scott can't be in the States in October and November, so Mike Moran usually replaces him as recording engineer. He is well-liked and discreet, and will later work on a few Elvis Presley records. Although he didn't know him at the time, Moran was at Madison Square Garden as a substitute recording engineer when David went to see the King; he didn't mix the concert though, only the press conference that preceded it[11].

During the ten long weeks of this first American tour, weighed down by fatigue and the stress of last-minute scheduling, David Bowie will sometimes crack. It happens in Phoenix on 4 November where, after a few days of sitting around and a show with a disappointingly small audience, he shaves his eyebrows off in his hotel room. In 1999, on the show *Storytellers*, he will claim that he was driven to do it after Mott The Hoople's refusal to sing 'Drive-In Saturday', which he'd written for them. This is unlikely, because Ian Hunter didn't hear about the song until a month after the incident. Ian believes Tony Defries wanted Bowie to keep the song for himself, so he made up a story about the band refusing it. Mott did go on to record a version of it, but it was never released.

While Bowie's relationship with Mott The Hoople is still good when they run into each other that autumn[12], it is less friendly with Lou Reed and Marc Bolan, who make snide remarks about him every time they talk to a journalist. Iggy Pop doesn't give in to jealousy and he and James Williamson readily accept David's help in mid-October, during a long stay in Los Angeles, when they mix *Raw Power*.

Bowie is happiest on stage when the venues are full. That was certainly the case on the third date of the tour at Carnegie Hall in New York, where he performed on 28 September in front of an audience made up of fans, hordes of journalists rounded up by MainMan and a handful of VIPs – these included Andy Warhol, whose very presence turned the show into a social event. Despite having a bad cold, Bowie made a great impression by delivering an impeccable show, unleashing a media storm the following morning in the press and on the radio.

The welcome was no less enthusiastic on 20 and 21 October at his two performances in Los Angeles. RCA was planning to make a live album of the first one[13], so it seems quite strange that local radio station KMET FM was allowed to air it (it was David Bowie's first show to be broadcast live on the radio). Just a few weeks after Ziggy and his Spiders performed at the Civic Auditorium in Santa Monica, a bootleg double album started to sell under the counter (in the best record stores). It is often considered by fans of his glam era as the best live album of Bowie's discography and EMI will finally release it officially in 2008, 36 years after the show, with the title *Live Santa Monica '72*. Mike Moran is credited as the recording engineer in the sleeve notes, but it is Grover Hesley who actually took care of the mix. In the 70s, the bootleg recording was called *In Person, In America* (sometimes the other way round!) or just *David Bowie*. KMET, which specialized in progressive rock, will close down in 1987.

Things won't go so well in San Francisco, at the famous Winterland, managed by promoter Bill Graham. Four years later, Robbie Robertson of The Band will ask Martin Scorsese to shoot *The Last Waltz* there, a seminal concert film. But on 27 and 28 October 1972, David Bowie will play to a sparse audience, which many observers find strange given that the city is known for its significant gay population. One of the opening acts will be the androgynous Sylvester, a future star of disco, and the other is Flo & Eddie[14]. They'll be performing as The Phlorescent Leech & Eddie with a band featuring Aynsley Dunbar, one of the best freelance British drummers of his generation who, at the time, had already worked with John Mayall, Jeff Beck and Frank Zappa. Mick Ronson will be impressed by his playing and will mention it to David Bowie. Later on, Dunbar will play with Lou Reed, on both Ronson's RCA albums and, obviously, on *Pin Ups* and *Diamond Dogs*.

In early October, Bowie and his band recorded 'The Jean Genie' in New York. It's a simple, straightforward rock song reminiscent of The Yardbirds (particularly their cover of Bo Diddley's 'I'm A Man', faster than his version) and American rock band The Shadows Of Knight (who found success speeding up 'Oh Yeah', also by Bo Diddley). According to George Underwood, 'The Jean Genie' was written on a coach. George was playing around with a blues riff on his guitar, and Bowie asked him to pass him the instrument. He played the riff, then drafted a melody, which he later finished off in New York. In his colourful memoirs[15], Mick Farren claims that 'The Jean Genie' might have been inspired by 'I'm Coming Home' from *Ptooff!*, the first album by The Deviants, whom David had known in the late 60s. The same riff was also used in 'Blockbuster!', a hit by glam band The Sweet, which came out after 'The Jean Genie' (and was also released by RCA).

'The Jean Genie' is definitely not a tribute to Jean Genet[16]. The lyrics refer in part to Iggy Pop, but the track, mixed a little later in Nashville, was reportedly finalized to 'amuse' Cyrinda Foxe. She appears (in scenes filmed in the street near the famous Mars Hotel in San Francisco) in the video that Mick Rock will make for the song, also using footage from the Winterland. Trevor Bolder makes at least two mistakes in the recording – for example, he plays the note of the first chord of the first chorus a bar too soon. Oddly enough, it would have been easy to record another take with the whole band or have him replay those notes alone, but the mistakes were kept. Later, David Bowie will develop a habit of keeping certain imperfections, in the name of art.

'The Jean Genie' is released as a single in late November, the day before Bowie and The Spiders return to Cleveland for two more concerts. As in September – and because it might have been considered good luck – British folk-rock band Lindisfarne are the opening act. But this time, David Bowie is playing at the Public Auditorium, a venue hosting a crowd of 10,000. It is packed to full capacity on both nights. Tony Defries had hoped his artist would receive a hero's welcome when they returned to the city where the tour had begun, and he wasn't disappointed.

Before leaving the United States, with Ken Scott who just arrived from London, Bowie puts aside a week to record some new songs and asks Mike Garson to join The Spiders From Mars in the studio. A few days before leaving, he invites his friend Ian Hunter to his suite at the Warwick Hotel to play him some of the songs he's finished. Hunter recognizes Dylan's influence in 'Drive-In Saturday', which Bowie plans to release as a single, but he is less thrilled with his version of 'All The Young Dudes'. However, he likes the half-finished track that doesn't have a name yet, but will be the title song of the next album. Bowie says there will be a lot of saxophone on the record and that a brass section will soon reinforce his live band. When Ian spots a synthesizer on the floor, David tells him he plans to play it on stage. The singer of Mott The Hoople is hugely impressed, and amazed by David's confidence and his ability to project himself into the future. Yet he is not surprised to hear that Ziggy Stardust intends to be back in the US very soon – this first tour has just been a warm-up for him and MainMan.

David Bowie returns to London just before Christmas but he isn't interested in having any time off. 'The Jean Genie' is climbing the charts and will do way better than any of his previous records – while in the United States the single will only get to Number 71, only Chuck Berry's 'My Ding-A-Ling' keeps him off the Number 1 spot in the UK. *Ziggy Stardust* had sold about 100,000 copies, and the media plans to celebrate the patiently awaited return of their native son, who now only grants them limited access. On 23 and 24 December, Bowie and The Spiders (with Mike Garson on piano) perform again at the Rainbow. On the first night, Bowie asks the audience to return the following day with toys for the orphans at Dr Barnardo's. On Christmas Eve, he gathers enough toys to fill a truck. The set list is shorter than before and starts off with a cover of 'Let's Spend The Night Together' by The Rolling Stones, which David begins alone by fiddling with his Minimoog.

The tour continues into January, with Fumble and Stealers Wheel opening the show. Bowie had spotted Fumble, led by singer-guitarist Des Henly, on *The Old Grey Whistle Test*, while Stealers Wheel, with Joe Egan and Gerry Rafferty, will go on to release 'Stuck In The Middle With You', one of the biggest hits of 1973. The audience are enjoying his concerts, but David is showing signs of exhaustion. At Green's Playhouse in Glasgow, three days before his 26th birthday (and two days after receiving his first gold record for *Ziggy Stardust*), he forgets to sing part of the second verse of 'Starman'. Eager to complete his new album before returning to the US, Bowie goes back to Trident.

He isn't talking much to the media at the time, but David gives a remarkable interview on *Russell Harty Plus*, his first on British television. He reveals the name of his next persona: Aladdin Sane. In the studio, the atmosphere is productive even though the warmth isn't quite there – success is actually widening the gap between Bowie and his musicians. Ken Scott might not have been aware at the time but, before the recordings, Tony Defries asked Phil Spector to replace him. Luckily, these tensions are going to inject energy into the new LP rather than damaging it.

On 13 January, David goes to Swiss Cottage to meet with photographer Brian Duffy, who takes a series of pictures for the album cover. Mick Rock may have been the official photographer at the time, but Defries hadn't given him exclusivity – the previous summer, he allowed Masayoshi Sukita to shoot Bowie in a studio and at the Rainbow, guessing that sooner or later Bowie could benefit from being introduced to several of the photographer's contacts in Japan. Brian Duffy, who belonged to an agency created by Tony Defries, was asked to take some shots of David Bowie in 1972 as Ziggy Stardust – they were never used. Bowie's manager gives Duffy Design Concepts, whose graphic art/concept director was Celia Philo, a single instruction: the cover should cost as much as possible. He believes that a common four-colour printing job won't be good enough for a rising star like Bowie. Also, if the packaging costs a fortune to create, the LP will stand out from the other RCA releases, and the label executives will move heaven and earth to sell as many copies as possible to recoup their investment. Duffy knows how to make the process expensive and will use seven colours with a metallic silver effect.

For the inside of the gatefold sleeve, the initial idea is to emulate the Pirelli calendar that Duffy Design Concepts had made a few weeks before. In *Duffy Bowie – Five Sessions* (ACC, 2014), a book by Kevin Cann and Duffy's son Chris about the photographer's work with Bowie, Celia Philo explains that the titles 'The Jean Genie' and *Aladdin Sane* made her come up with the idea of a genie jumping out of the sleeve as you opened it. If Celia Philo knew the title of the album then, it must have been decided by January, three months before it came out, which contradicts some other accounts.

The origin of the lightning bolt on David Bowie's face in the photograph, also used in the background on stage, is uncertain, or rather has two possible explanations. In *Moonage Daydream*, Mick Rock's book of photos, David Bowie noted that the idea for this 'flash' was inspired by a very mundane sight: one of the many electrical junction boxes around the UK. But the small lightning bolt which Bowie asked make-up artist Pierre Laroche[17] to paint on his cheek was copied from two logos on the front of the 'National' rice cooker (made by Panasonic) which Duffy had in his studio. Duffy thought it wasn't quite right, so he drew a larger one with lipstick covering the whole of David's face – the outline of the one in the photograph. Then he asked Laroche to colour it in. These photos of David Bowie were taken in black and white with a Hasselblad camera, then colourized and airbrushed by Philip Castle, who illustrated the iconic poster for *A Clockwork Orange*, among other things. The liquid in Bowie's collarbone, which could be mercury or something else, would make the imagination of his fans run wild. From 2013 to 2018 (five years!), one of the photos from this session will feature on the poster for the travelling exhibition *David Bowie Is*. It is certainly the best known and most definitive image of the musician.

David Bowie returns to New York in late January 1973. Rebuked by RCA, Tony Defries said he'd try to stem the haemorrhaging 'operating expenses' of his artist, who crossed the Atlantic on the *SS Canberra* with a smaller entourage. Geoff MacCormack, recruited as a backup singer and percussionist, was on the trip. Bowie takes advantage of the two weeks before the first concert of this new American tour (mainly a series of short residencies, with twenty shows in six major cities) to attend some gigs himself, including Biff Rose at Max's Kansas City with Bruce Springsteen opening – David prefers the second half of his performance, the one with the band[18]. He also attends a performance by The Rockettes at Radio City Music Hall and, that night, he is much impressed by a silvery gyroscope one of the dancers uses as she is lowered onto the stage. He will ask if he can use it himself. The second leg of the Ziggy Stardust and The Spiders From Mars tour begins at this Art Deco venue within the Rockefeller Center. MacCormack is not the only additional musician who has been familiarising himself with Bowie's songs during rehearsals at RCA Studios. John Hutchinson, from The Buzz and Feathers, is back on acoustic guitar (a Harptone 12-string Bowie lent him) and electric (his own Telecaster). A brass section, made up of Ken Fordham and Brian Wilshaw, who played in recent sessions at Trident, also came from England with Hutch.

During the first of two concerts at Radio City Music Hall, Bowie notices that the seeds he sowed the year before have borne fruit. His arrival is all over the local press and all of New York is there, including Andy Warhol, Bette Midler, Allen Ginsberg, Salvador Dalí, Todd Rundgren, Johnny Winter and Truman Capote. Supported by the new recruits, the band is more impressive than ever. David plays a bit of synthesizer and Mike Garson switches to the Mellotron on some of the songs (including a new arrangement of 'Space Oddity'). Most of the set list comes from the upcoming album and Aladdin Sane, an extremely sensual 'rock'n'roll animal', reveals himself to be even more extroverted than Ziggy Stardust.

On the afternoon before the first show, Kansai Yamamoto brought David Bowie several stage costumes, each more extravagant than the last. Visually as well, David is evolving into another dimension and, at Radio City Music Hall, Masayoshi Sukita is the first to photograph him in outfits designed by his compatriot.

With Fumble as the opening act, the tour will pass through Philadelphia, Nashville, Memphis, Detroit and Los Angeles and most of the venues will be packed. On stage, The Spiders From Mars show no sign of weakness but, behind the scenes, the grains of sand that for some time have been grinding the gears of the MainMan machine have turned into gravel. After they find out that they are being paid less than Mike Garson, The Spiders will demand a pay rise, which Tony Defries will have to give them. However, he is going to torpedo the group's plans to work on a Spiders From Mars album (without Bowie), by dangling a solo career in front of Mick Ronson.

The tour had barely started up again when David began looking more and more exhausted; he passed out during the first concert – some people thought it was part of the performance, but that's not very likely – and he will catch flu during the Japanese leg of the tour. In addition, he received serious threats in some of the more homophobic American cities. But, on the positive side, he is happy to make some new acquaintances, including Mick Jagger and Ava Cherry, an aspiring singer he hopes to work with someday.

After performing his last show in the US as Ziggy/Aladdin at the Hollywood Palladium on Sunset Boulevard on 12 March, David Bowie travels to Japan for the first time, accompanied by Geoff MacCormack. They set sail from San Francisco on the more modest SS Oronsay, chartered by P&O. After a stopover in Hawaii, the ship berths at Yokohama the day before the British release of the 'Drive-In Saturday' single (with 'Round And Around' on the B-side[19]).

In America, Bowie and his musicians were changing set lists almost every night, looking for the best combination of songs from the previous album and the one to come (they played most of it, except for 'Lady Grinning Soul' – quite risky live). In Japan, with less songs from *Aladdin Sane*, the set list will stabilize. When David Bowie arrived, Kansai Yamamoto gave him a pile of new outfits, which were increasingly inspired by kabuki theatre and samurai costumes. The shocking nature of some of them will bother him less than the practicality of wearing hot and heavy garments under the spotlights (he will change costumes up to seven times a show). Loving the attention he is attracting, he also performs a few songs in nothing but a tiny red loincloth like a sumo wrestler.

Bowie will also use his time in Japan to immerse himself in the local culture, going to the theatre, visiting famous Zen gardens and acquiring new make-up techniques from onnagata Bandō Tamasaburō V, a kabuki theatre actor who specializes in playing female roles. He will also learn more about the life and work of Yukio Mishima, the writer who performed hara-kiri in late 1970 and whose novel, *The Sailor Who Fell From Grace With The Sea*[20], made an impression on David at a younger age. After passing through Nagoya, Hiroshima, Kobe and Osaka, the tour culminates with a final show in Tokyo, where it started twelve days before. David Bowie's popularity is enormous in Japan, particularly in its capital but, even so, he will have to wait another five years before performing there again. That April, he reads in the Japanese press that he is the 'most remarkable [pop artist] since The Beatles.'

Back in the UK, the British media are hailing the commercial success of *Aladdin Sane*, released on 13 April. British record shops pre-ordered more than 100,000 copies, so the album is certified gold on that Friday 13th.

No one can deny that Mike Garson's piano defines *Aladdin Sane*. The monumental musician will play on eight other David Bowie studio albums up until 2003 (three fewer than Carlos Alomar), but he will never be better than on this one. And not just because Ken Scott brought out his instrument during the mix (the last step in making a record, before cutting, which Bowie himself was involved in for the first time). The supreme quality of his performance and his incredible technique launch the album into another galaxy. On the three tracks he entirely takes over (the title song, 'Time' and 'Lady Grinning Soul'), Garson, the supplemental spider, doesn't really blend in with the music of David Bowie and his band. He acknowledges the musical information they offer him, but doesn't use it to shape his playing. Bowie's intricate chord progressions, the arrangements he devises with Mick Ronson and the few instructions they issue are like cues for Mike to dive into his performance; he gets going at the slightest sound in his headphones and the sound engineer should always record the first take.

To draw out Mike Garson's genius, you have to set him free. No one could instruct him how to play the kind of magic he unleashes on *Aladdin Sane*. His arpeggios, his soaring flights of romanticism, his avant-garde bursts of fury, his borrowing from jazz and classical music, his syncopated melodies and his hails of notes do not stand alone: they orbit around the songs like UFOs around an alien planet. And you don't hear Garson coming; he appears from nowhere with no regard for etiquette or rules. Under his silver-tipped fingers, the ebony and the ivory – water and fire – acknowledge that he is more volatile than them and succumb, allowing him to caress or manhandle them as he wishes. Of all the pianists who sat at the famous C. Bechstein at Trident, Mike Garson is the only one who played it like it was his own. All the pianos in the world are equal before him and the sound that comes out of them has little to do with the instrument itself. Whatever his technique, Garson, like Miles Davis, embodies his own voice.

And not even he, whose mind wasn't fogged by alcohol or drugs at the time, can remember precisely where he recorded his piano for the album. The first *Aladdin Sane* sessions took place at RCA Studios in New York and other cities along the US tour, so it can be reasonably assumed that what Mike recorded in America were essentially rhythm parts. This means that no *Aladdin Sane* song was completed in the US, with the notable exception of 'The Jean Genie', released as a single six months before the LP and on which Garson did not play. There's still doubt over where the other takes were taped but Mike Garson will give some clues in 2018, confirming that his contributions to 'Aladdin Sane', 'Lady Grinning Soul' and 'Time' were recorded at Trident in London. As for the ubiquitous Mick Ronson, he also played rhythm piano on at least two songs: 'Drive-In Saturday' and 'The Prettiest Star'.

Mike Garson's contribution to *Aladdin Sane* is also remarkable because he was reacting to David Bowie's music – his melodies, his impeccable vocal inflections, his gift of the gab, his attitude – rather than to his words. By his own admission, the meaning and subtleties of Bowie's lyrics often escaped him. Mike is the instrumentalist who played with David the longest – 34 years of loyal service (with a major break), compared with 28 for Alomar – and he was in awe of the musician within. And likewise, Bowie was fully aware of the effect Garson had on his records, to the point that he will later choose not to include him when he wants to explore other directions. In particular, Mike's absence is notable on *Station To Station* and *The Next Day*. He will feel bad each time, but he also knew that nothing mattered more to Bowie than his art. Like Mick Ronson and Carlos Alomar, Ken Scott and Tony Visconti, and to some extent Brian Eno and Reeves Gabrels – Mike Garson made an enormous contribution to David Bowie's work. He will ignore the fact for many years, but Garson undeniably modified the path of the English musician whose name will forever be associated with his. If *Aladdin Sane*, between *Ziggy Stardust* and *Pin Ups*, was part of a series of albums that ended up making a logical sequence, Garson's extraordinary piano is what allowed Bowie to take his first decisive step in a new direction.

Aladdin Sane is not only a record. It's a rock powerhouse. A huge transformer. Twice here, Bowie and The Spiders, at their peak that winter, show who they are without make-up: vocals (and harmonica), guitar, bass and drums. During the three minutes of 'Cracked Actor', David Bowie delivers his own version of *Hollywood Babylon*[21], while 'The Jean Genie', undeniably, is turbo-driven. In both songs, Bolder and Woodmansey play hard. Ronson is everywhere in the stereo panning; after passing through the Marshall amp, his notes and licks, stained blue, are filtered by the Cry Baby and the Tone Bender pedals. They come out gleaming, piercing, fraught, reduced to their divine essentials. As for the man at the mic, he sings about a fading star in 'Cracked Actor', and about one he would like to see rise in 'The Jean Genie'.

In the middle of the second side, David Bowie confirms what 'Watch That Man' implied from the beginning of the album: right then, and for a few months after, The Rolling Stones are his thing. Mike Garson is the only additional player to the four from Mars on the cover of 'Let's Spend The Night Together', which they speed up and embellish with synth spasms. David Bowie shows his canines throughout and barks just like Iggy Pop at the end of an interlude added to the original – quite quirky – before the storm of the last chorus. Garson always said he played a lot of jazz and very little rock'n'roll before working with David Bowie, but it's hard to believe listening to him running up and down his keyboard like Jerry Lee Lewis, and proudly replying to Mick Ronson, Chuck Berry's rightful heir on this track. Like the title song of *Diamond Dogs* in 1974 and 'Rebel Rebel', its heralding single, 'Watch That Man' is almost a tribute to Mick Jagger's band. Bowie didn't cover any of their songs on *Pin Ups*, but he certainly wrote in the style of the Stones[22] here. Ken Scott went with the flow by burying Bowie's voice in the mix, a bit like

Jagger's in the rockier parts of *Exile On Main Street*, which had been released the year before.

David had warned: he wanted wind in his sails – brass and saxophone – something he will repeat in 1974 and again in 2015. Ken Fordham, Brian Wilshaw and sometimes Bowie himself add brass (and a bit of flute) to five of the album's songs. They support Ronson's chords on 'Watch That Man', duel with Garson on 'Aladdin Sane' and swing about madly on the lavishly arranged new rendering of 'The Prettiest Star'. Forget the wishy-washy version of the song released in 1970, which Marc Bolan Bolan streaked with his guitar solo. On this LP, 'The Prettiest Star' can hold its head up high, supported by doo-wop backing vocals – an allusion to the 1950s, also found in 'Drive-In Saturday'. And if Mick Ronson does play the solo better than Bolan, it's because in January 1973 at Trident, he was quite simply the best guitarist in the world.

Mick confidently proves this again in 'Time', which a year and a half earlier was called 'We Should Be On By Now'. At the time (!), David Bowie thought the song would go to George Underwood, whose musical career was still current. For Ronson, the second half of the song – a nod to Kurt Weill and Jacques Brel[23] with allusions to the toxicity of success in a *Back To The Future* way – is an excuse to show off his talent as a rock guitarist with an appreciation for the lyricism of classical music. After a squawking and minimalist four-bar part in sustained notes, Mick from Hull interacts with the majestic melody by launching into a meticulously arranged solo until his boss adds his voice to the haunting, Russian-sounding backing vocals. This series of heartfelt themes propels the listener into a parallel universe and makes them forget that the chord progression, used as a springboard, is repeated six times.

Mick Ronson is no less transcendent in 'Lady Grinning Soul'. While Mike Garson tries to channel the Niagara of notes falling from the C. Bechstein half way through the crystalline ballad, Ronson, with a simple acoustic guitar, calmly replies with a Spanish touch which almost comes out of nowhere. Defeated by such grace, Garson surrenders to the concluding motifs which they play together in unison.

In the total absence of strings, the backing vocals play a major part on *Aladdin Sane*. In true fashion, David Bowie and Mick Ronson harmonize beautifully throughout the album, while Juanita Franklin and Linda Lewis spice it up. In the rather tribal 'Panic In Detroit' (a nod to Iggy Pop's mention of the racial protests of 1967, and in which Geoff MacCormack plays a set of congas), they add heat to the chorus and accentuate the ferocity of the ending, which Ronson heavily sprinkles with napalm. For the backing vocals of 'Watch That Man', Franklin and Lewis take advantage of the chaos (Woodmansey's drum fills, Garson's assaults), while Bowie disappears in body and voice, leaving the others to liven up the end of the song as if it were the last gospel before the apocalypse.

That imminent collapse, flirting with chaos, rapidly spiralling success and its perils, a debauched society and utopia trampled underfoot are all themes covered by the lyrics of *Aladdin Sane*. There was at one time an unsuccessful plan to create a book about the 1972 American tour, but this album will prove to be a suitable substitute. It can be seen as a log book and might just as well have been called *The Adventures Of Ziggy Stardust In America*. *Aladdin Sane* is more of a concept album than its predecessor. Even from the eye of the MainMan hurricane, David Bowie was always watching and taking notes, and never claimed to be anything other than an observer (two decades later, he will use the word 'voyeur'), whether he was seeing the country go by from the windows of his imagination, playing concerts and accumulating sleepless nights, or spending his days catching up on sleep in besieged hotel rooms. In the first half of 1973, Bowie is in the thick of it and splits himself in two[24]. Aladdin Sane is happy to go through the mirror, but David Jones stays on the other side watching, being content with himself, or lamenting some of his actions without regretting any.

The album is full of references to places and people. It's his only one that provides GPS coordinates for where he was when he wrote the songs: New York, Seattle-Phoenix, Detroit. These location notes even specify the ocean liner (RHMS *Ellinis*) and for 'The Prettiest Star' there's a mysterious mention of Gloucester Road – David Bowie was a long way from there when he lived at Haddon Hall where the song was almost certainly written, but close by when he was with Hermione Farthingale. The 1960s model-muse Twiggy is 'the wonder kid' in 'Drive-In Saturday', which is a fond look back at days gone by. Cyrinda Foxe is Lorraine in 'Watch That Man', and Billy Murcia (the first drummer of New York Dolls, who died of an overdose in November 1972) features in 'Time' as 'Billy Dolls'. The man who 'looked a lot like Che Guevara' in 'Panic In Detroit' is an old school mate of David's who became a drug dealer and followed him to New York in September on the trail of cash. From the early 70s onwards, more and more merchants of death will begin to circle around Bowie, infiltrating the MainMain entourage, who didn't mind succumbing to vice.

In their great book *Bowie: An Illustrated Record* (Eel Pie, 1981), Roy Carr and Charles Shaar Murray claim that Claudia Lennear[25] was the 'Lady Grinning Soul' but the timing doesn't seem quite right. While David Bowie might have met this

American backing singer (who inspired The Rolling Stones' 'Brown Sugar') before January 1973 when he wrote the song, it's more likely that he met her a few months later, or even a year later. Lennear will speak about this at length in 2016, when she says she first met David at the home of Michael Lippman, the Los Angeles lawyer who later helped Bowie extricate himself from the clutches of MainMan. Although he was in Los Angeles in October 1972, it's probable he didn't meet Lippman until later on. If the character in 'Lady Grinning Soul' was, in fact, flesh and blood, it's more likely that she was Cyrinda Foxe, which is what Woody Woodmansey believes. The other theory – that she could be Amanda Lear – is rather unlikely. David Bowie did meet this future singer in 1973, but it was definitely not before he wrote the lyrics to the song. (Lear is the sublime creature who appears with a panther on a lead on the cover of *For Your Pleasure*, Roxy Music's second album, released later that winter.)

What Carr and Shaar Murray probably didn't know when they wrote their book, was that there are references to *Vile Bodies*, the satirical Evelyn Waugh novel, in the lyrics of 'Aladdin Sane'. In the song, Bowie mentions 'bright young things', which was the name the British media used to describe young hedonistic aristocrats between the two world wars, who were indifferent to the economic difficulties of the times and the threat of war hanging over society. Instead they turned to decadence, dancing to jazz and enjoying large quantities of alcohol and drugs. The young women generally wore their hair short, in a boyish manner. Once Bowie's interest in Waugh's work has been established (*Vile Bodies* was among his favourite books), other references to his work become clear in 'Watch That Man' and 'Drive-In Saturday'. Apparently, Waugh got the idea for *Vile Bodies* in 1929 on a cruise ship in the Mediterranean, and started writing as soon as he returned to England. At the beginning of the novel, Adam Symes, the main character, is also on a boat returning home.

Pushing the envelope even further, some people saw in Aladdin Sane a sort of 'Evelyn Sane'. The track on the original vinyl album was listed as 'Aladdin Sane (1913-1938-197?)' – the first two years are clearly those that precede the two great wars, but the third, which ends in a question mark, continues to fuel a range of different theories. Did Bowie think that a third world war would come before the end of the decade? Maybe, but it's clear that *Aladdin Sane*, in its entirety and through his prism, was his interpretation of *Vile Bodies*.

In the 1970s, David Bowie is the ultimate object of desire and fuel for his own myth, but the culture of excess at MainMan would also make him a kind of collateral victim of conscious decadence. This is admirably symbolized in the title song by Mike Garson's deranged and gushing solo. Feeling the noose starting to tighten around his neck, though still perhaps believing the worst couldn't happen, Bowie was probably already planning to scamper off, maybe even in his Yamamoto rabbit costume, which he didn't like as much as the other ones. He just wasn't sure when he'd pluck up the courage to do it. Ian Hunter did say, in late 1972, that you could already see in David's eyes what would happen six months later.

The 2-week journey of nearly 1,000 miles that David Bowie and Geoff MacCormack (with Leee Black Childers) took in returning to the UK from Japan is described in detail in *From Station To Station – Travels With Bowie 1973–1976*, the gorgeous book MacCormack published with Genesis in 2007. First they sailed on the *Félix Dzerjinsky* from Yokohama to the Russian port of Nakhodka. Then they took what they thought was the Trans-Siberian railway and arrived in Khabarovsk, six hundred miles north. There, they finally got on the Tsar's train and, a week later, stopped in Moscow. They stayed long enough to watch the International Worker's Day celebrations on 1 May, then they left for Paris, where they arrived three days later. After meeting up with Angie, giving a boring press conference at the George V[26] and missing a meeting with Jacques Brel[27] who was stuck on a film set (and possibly another meeting with Michel Polnareff), Bowie and friends took a train to Boulogne, then crossed the Channel in a hovercraft.

The long journeys David Bowie took during the 1970s, from the Ziggy Stardust/Aladdin Sane tour to the Isolar 2 tour (also referred to as the Stage tour, a nod to the live album that will come out in 1978), had a decisive impact on his writing. Without an e-reader, a portable media player or a smartphone, Bowie went from one place to another with several trunks, one of them containing books, records and tapes for his amusement. Even time on his longest ocean voyages wasn't wasted; he spent it catching up on his work. Whether he was flicking through their pages over a coffee on the deck of an ocean liner, or devouring them at night in his cabin, the books he carried with him gave him ideas. He took notes from them and they permeated his lyrics.

Just as the books David Bowie read before he was 25 years old flavoured his first six LPs, those he discovered later would infuse his later albums. As the America he witnessed during his trips in 1972 is reflected in the lyrics of *Aladdin Sane* (and sometimes in the mood of the music), so his rail crossing of the red continent – then Soviet Russia – would permeate *Diamond Dogs*. Any Bowie fan knows that an obstacle to adapting *1984* to his style will be the impetus behind his 1974 studio album (and the American tour that will follow). Many earlier books had also been inspired by totalitarianism and utopian aspirations. Often in literature, despots who threaten basic liberties are portrayed as beings or entities from another place, or machines that have started thinking for themselves. The portrayal in literature of dystopia, a place where society has fallen into chaos and despair because of an ideology that has been followed blindly or under duress, is usually the result of an author's observation of political upheaval, brutal conflict or the Cold War and, by extension, atomic threat. Along with *1984*, Anthony Burgess' *A Clockwork Orange* is the only one on Bowie's list of 100 favourite books that can be called dystopian, although he will mention that he'd also read the major works of Aldous Huxley, Eugène Zamiatine, René Barjavel and Ray Bradbury.

After David Bowie's arrival at Charing Cross station, made eventful by the fans who are waiting for him there, he has a free week before embarking on a series of new shows. That gives him the opportunity to catch up with Tony Defries and reconnect with Tony Visconti, whom he invites, along with his wife Mary Hopkin, to a party at Haddon Hall[28]. But his home on Southend Road is by now besieged by admirers, and it becomes obvious, for the sake of both the star and his family, that he will have to leave Beckenham for good. Although he had nothing but contempt for the London suburbs as a boy, Bowie has still spent 26 years of his life there (and it's where he will live the longest). He and his family temporarily move into a chic hotel in central London.

Like a bad omen, the first date of the new leg of the tour in mid-May at Earl's Court is a fiasco. In the borough of Kensington and Chelsea, this impressive 1930s building is used for conferences and exhibitions, but it is the first time a rock group performs there. The 18,000 tickets sell out in a few hours, but Tony Defries is increasingly under pressure from RCA and doesn't rent adequate sound equipment for the venue. The dissatisfied audience starts fighting, girls take off their clothes in the aisles and, at the back of the hall, couples can be seen having sex.

The day after the show, his first in London for almost six months, David Bowie knows it's out of the question, but he would like the tour to end. However, he still has sixty concerts to go. Meanwhile, Defries is planning to milk Bowie for as long as he can and is starting to organise a future series of shows, at least one hundred, that will begin as soon as the next album is finished. He is planning for Bowie and The Spiders From Mars to perform in Europe, then the USA, before travelling to Australia and maybe even China.

Over the next two months, rioting will get worse and worse inside and outside the venues, near stations and around the hotels where the musicians are staying – in fact, everywhere they go. Fights between fans and police will become legendary. The audience are loving this more substantial show, punctuated with costume changes and a bit of mime, but practically every night (and even during the matinee performances), Bowiemania leads to chaotic scenes, reported and denounced by the media.

At each venue, Barry Bethell, a press officer from RCA, 'warms up' the audience before The Spiders From Mars take the stage. The truth is that the label sent Bethell to watch over expenses. The situation gets more complicated every day for MainMan, despite the fact that Tony Defries is getting the attention he wanted for his artist and *Aladdin Sane*[29] is Number 1 in the album charts (it will stay there for five weeks, while 'Drive-In Saturday' reaches Number 3 in the singles charts – in the US, the album will make the Top 20 on the *Billboard* charts). With very little in the way of strong foundations, and with only one lucrative artist – who is being shamelessly exploited and is technically in debt – Defries' so-called empire is starting to show signs of weakness. Its other artists turn away from the company without a shadow of regret –including Mott The Hoople, Iggy Pop (whose album *Raw Power* comes out on 1 June), Lou Reed (his single 'Walk On The Wild Side' makes the Top 10 on 2 June) and Annette Peacock, who had been courted by MainMan. In June, Tony Defries is still at the helm, but the ship is going slowly under. And the decision David is about to make official will soon ruin all his plans.

RCA Records president Rocco Laginestra hinted that the label will not participate in financing another tour as expensive as the current one, so Defries is going to turn Bowie's decision to his advantage. David hoped to stage the last two Ziggy Stardust and The Spiders From Mars concerts at Aylesbury, although at one point they'd been planned for the Roundhouse or even Earl's Court. In the end, they will take place at the Hammersmith Odeon, in west London. This is another 1930s building, decked out in sumptuous Art Deco, but it is genuinely made for music. In the following decades, an impressive number of rock bands and musicians will perform and record live albums there[30]. Many shows will also be filmed there.

RCA commissioned Donn Alan 'D.A.' Pennebaker to shoot the concert on 3 July, the last date of the tour David Bowie had started eighteen months before. Initially, the American director of *Don't Look Back*, *Monterey Pop* and *Sweet Toronto* was supposed to film a few songs for an experimental video disc – Laginestra was convinced that records should be visual as well as audio. But this new format will be dropped and RCA will never release the footage. Pennebaker, arriving in London in time to see the concert the night before, ends up shooting the entire show on

3 July. His film (made with basic equipment compared with today's standards), called *Ziggy Stardust And The Spiders From Mars* on its first release on VHS in the early 1980s, is not perfect, but it remains the only official video documentation of this tour, and therefore of Bowie's glam period.

Who knew? Who didn't? Who suspected? At first glance, it looks like Tony Defries, Mick Ronson, Geoff MacCormack and D.A. Pennebaker[31] were in the know. The film director has sometimes denied it, but in the liner notes he wrote for the film's reissue on DVD in 2003, he says that when they arrived at the Hammersmith Odeon, Defries warned him and his team and made them swear not to tell anyone. As for the tour's devoted technicians, recording engineer Robin Mayhew confirmed that Suzi Fussey knew and that she probably told the stage manager, Peter Hunsley – he's the one who warned Mayhew halfway through the set. And since they worked for MainMan, it's unlikely that Defries would have been able to hide the truth from key collaborators like Tony Zanetta, Jamie Andrews or Cherry Vanilla. But for the other Spiders From Mars, Trevor Bolder and Woody Woodmansey, Bowie's momentous announcement on stage on 3 July – that this concert would be their last ever – felt like a punch in the guts. A really nasty one.

The musicians, technicians, and anyone along the path to success who noticed the glass bridge starting to crack, should have seen the signs – on the set list for the gigs at the Hammersmith Odeon (identical for each of the two nights), David Bowie re-introduced a song he hadn't sung for several weeks: 'My Death'. He may not have written the lyrics, but just before Ziggy Stardust committed suicide, he symbolically used this song of 'death' to cast off the mantle of Aladdin Sane. 'My Death', which ended the first half of the set on a particularly dramatic note (while of course 'Rock'n'roll Suicide' would end the second) had all the trappings of a eulogy. The occasion was made even more solemn by a solo set from Mike Garson[32] at the start of the 19-song show. Bowie's set-list those two nights included a medley of 'Wild Eyed Boy From Freecloud', 'All The Young Dudes' and 'Oh! You Pretty Things'.

Bowie and his band were splendid that night. Exhaustion and tension did not overshadow the brilliance of their set. Jeff Beck, one of Mick Ronson's heroes, was invited to play and, during the encore, he let loose some riffs and crazy notes on 'The Jean Genie' and 'Round And Round', two songs that unfortunately did not make the cut for D.A. Pennebaker's film and do not feature in the soundtrack[33]. That night, because he was in London, England, Bowie made a point of quoting The Rolling Stones ('Let's Spend The Night Together') and The Beatles (a few bars of 'Love Me Do' spiced up 'The Jean Genie').

And yet, at certain moments in the concert – which because of the circumstances and the power of art will be remembered as the most famous of his career – David Bowie seemed already to be elsewhere. The look in his eyes, while not exactly suffering, was one of disenchantment. It is the same look Mick Rock has captured in the video for 'Life On Mars?', hastily shot in a studio on Ladbroke Grove, at RCA's request, to promote the June release of the single (which David thought was completely anachronistic[34]). During the show, he was well aware he had to escape the trap, but he made a terrible mistake in not telling two of The Spiders From Mars that he'd come to the end of his journey with them. For David Bowie, art prevailed over everything else, including basic human consideration. Nothing could shake his deep conviction that creation, as pure and harsh as it could be, was his special ticket to the future. This very rock'n'roll suicide was announced in a breathless voice and resigned tone after thanking the band and technicians – 'Not only is it the last show of the tour, but it's the last show that we'll ever do.'

The audience had witnessed an inevitable, spectacular and admirably staged transformation of a chameleon who was incapable of staying the same colour. Who would spend the rest of his career trying on different genres and ideas, discarding anything which no longer excited him. At the slightest change in mood, Bowie would start again from nothing except a few essential principles etched in his genes. Build, destroy, build, destroy, but always from a solid foundation, as strong as the pedestal supporting the Statue of Liberty with its poem by Emma Lazarus.

Those who, on 10 January 2016, will claim that David Bowie managed to make his death a work of art, will fail to mention that history, in a much more tragic way, was merely repeating itself. Forty-three years earlier, by killing his 'plastic rock'n'roller' under the spotlights of the Hammersmith Odeon, he had already spilled his blood and also the blood of 3,500 disciples who, that night, 'gave him their hands'. A few days later, Tony Defries will try to have the last word by cancelling the future tour, but his announcement won't make much of a tremor in the face of Bowie's earthquake.

By unplugging Ziggy Stardust, David Bowie proved to himself that he was still alive and that the defiant artist in him wasn't anybody's puppet.

After the concert, he spends the rest of the night[35] partying with his friends and most of the London in-crowd[36] at the Café Royal on Regent Street, a five-minute walk from where Brian Ward had photographed him for the *Ziggy Stardust* sleeve. And, despite all the drama, the next morning in the first light of dawn, David Bowie knows that the best is yet to come. This is the first day of the rest of his life on Earth. Mars will have to wait.

Mick Ronson	John Cambridge
Trevor Bolder	John Hutchinson
Woody Woodmansey	Robin Mayhew
Mike Garson	Ian Hunter
Ken Fordham	James Williamson
Linda Lewis	Jeff Beck
Geoff MacCormack	Rod Clements
Ken Scott	Bryan Ferry
Mike Moran	Dana Gillespie
	Leee Black Childers
	Steven Tyler
	Des Henly
	Eddie Clarke
	Claude Gassian
	Norma Palmer
	Billy Ritchie
	Marla Feldstein
	George Underwood
	Tony Visconti
	Phil Manzanera
	Mary Finnigan

MICK RONSON

I didn't see the film of The Spiders From Mars until the early 1980s. I have to say, I thought we were really good. There were a lot of good shows during those tours. Funnily, I remember the big ones, but also the smaller ones in pubs. I knew the concert at the Hammersmith Odeon would be our last. David had mentioned it to me and made me realize we couldn't go on like that forever. He wanted to move on to something new, but it was more than that... (1990)

TREVOR BOLDER

I didn't take the farewell concert well. Especially after things had started to flare up in the spring when we found out that Mike Garson was making ten times what we were! We became a bit paranoid during that tour. We felt like we were going to be ejected – even Mick Ronson was feeling the pressure; he was always saying Bowie would have loved to replace him with Jeff Beck. Tony Defries was constantly talking to him about a solo career – that's how he did it... What can I say about it now? Those years, the best of my career, went by like lightning. They were just three years. But they were huge – at one point, all of Bowie's albums were in the Top 20! It was mad! And three singles in the Top 10 – crazy! The famous *Live in Santa Monica in 1972* is about to come out again? Everybody's had the bootleg for ages, no? I hope they will remix it properly! Good thing the labels have a few odds and ends they can bring out again to keep the money coming in. I don't expect we'll get anything from that. Also, I haven't heard from David for a long time, not even a phone call. I even stopped going to his shows: 'Yoohoo, it's me! Let me in, I was The Spiders From Mars' bass player!' I'd get my face smashed in by security. But if he invited me, I'd go. (1994)

WOODY WOODMANSEY

People who think that Bowie ruled over us with an iron fist in the studio couldn't be more wrong. One of the rare times he asked me to play a specific rhythm, it was for 'Panic In Detroit'. He wanted a Bo Diddley-style groove, which I have to say, I had doubts about. But I agreed, of course, because he'd asked, but also because I soon saw how well it went with the song.

We were there when David conquered the world. It was huge! I'll never forget the audience's hysteria when we performed. Touring the US for the first time was awesome; we were probably the first band to do it in style! Tony Defries wanted people to think we were big stars – it was a brilliant idea. We had it all – the best hotels, the best food. We worked hard, but played hard too. We were a bit like Queen, a real band. We travelled together... Things only started to change in 1973 on the last tour we did, travelling separately. Mike Garson was always a bit on the outside, as an American, and not being from rock'n'roll. Great pianist though.

Ziggy's 'suicide' shocked the audience, but I wasn't all that surprised. We had talked about future music, 'plastic soul', I was not so sure... I think 'When the kids had killed the man, I had to break up the band' was a perfect ending. It was tough at first when it finished, but if we had not done our job as a band, he wouldn't have had the opportunity to go on to do other music. I think Ziggy was a fantastic idea: brilliant songs, great musicians, arrangements, mixing... It ticked all the boxes really. Seeing the effect on audiences when we played live is what I enjoyed most. It seemed to pull out the creative side in people. We saw David again on A Reality tour in Dublin. I was in the audience with Trevor. He waved to us. (2015/2012)

MIKE GARSON

Before September 1972, I didn't know anything about David Bowie or his music. But I had a sort of intuition, a strange feeling – I knew that audition was going to be special. I was mostly playing jazz at the time, but I'd replaced Dr John in a band called Brethren[37] and accompanied Martha Reeves, from Martha And The Vandellas, at Madison Square Garden. David would have loved working with Annette Peacock, the coolest keyboard player at the time, but she turned him down and recommended me instead.

I never knew how MainMan got my phone number, probably from one of my students – Tony Defries called me while I was teaching! I was candid enough to tell him I'd never heard of this Bowie, but after thinking about it for a minute, I jumped at the opportunity! To be honest, I accepted mainly for the money, because I was playing at small clubs in New York and had trouble making ends meet. My first daughter had just been born, my wife and I were struggling financially... So when I heard about these British pop-rock artists turning up over here in need of musicians, I thought it would probably pay better than jazz.

I rushed from Brooklyn to Manhattan like a madman to get to the audition at RCA Studios. I remember it was so dark in there I couldn't see anyone very well. But the people I did see seemed to be wearing brightly coloured clothes and platform shoes! One of them stood up – it was Mick Ronson. He handed me the music for 'Changes'. I sat down at the piano and banged out the chords written on the sheet... The one with the orange hair quickly got up and put his hand on mine, saying, 'That's good. You got the job.' I barely had the time to realize what had just happened before he was gone.

So I became a Spider From Mars[38] and Mick pointed to Tony Defries, who was the money guy. In those days, I barely made $30 a week playing jazz and I guessed that the rock guys must make $2,000. So when he asked me how much I wanted, I shyly said that $800 would do and Defries agreed. The following year, I realized how naive I'd been! On the bus, Trevor and Woody asked me how much I was making and, thinking I was underpaid compared to them, I didn't want to answer. In the end, I told them and suddenly they looked really pissed off; I realized they were only making $30 a week, like jazz musicians.

The first time I got on stage with Bowie and The Spiders was in Cleveland. Before that, we'd had a few rehearsal days with David. I remember this studio with a grand piano and I noticed, right next to my stool, these enormous speakers pointing at me that went almost up to the ceiling. I said to Ronson, 'Mick, it might be best not to point the whole sound system at me, because it might knock me flying.' He said, 'No Mike, those are just yours!' That's when I realized I was no longer in the jazz world! Once, there was a technical issue with the PA system we were using. David was furious. He wanted to get rid of all the equipment and the following morning, a truck brought in new stuff. He also took that opportunity to change part of the technical team! That was MainMan – money never seemed to be a problem.

At the beginning of the first American tour, we found the audience was a bit dubious about us, but usually two or three songs were enough to convince them. With all that charisma, David had no problem making an impression. I should know, because at the beginning, I wasn't playing all the time, so sometimes I'd go into the audience so I could watch people's reactions.

I should also say that, in terms of the media, Tony Defries' non-communication policy paid off. The less people knew about David, the more they wanted to know. The mystique kept growing, as did the number of records he sold and the size of the audience. Everyone wanted to know how this Brit, totally unknown a year before, could turn up with such a big entourage at places like the Beverly Hills Hotel. Defries was ruthless when it came to business, but like Angie, he did everything he could, in his own way, to make David a star. And it happened, before our eyes, in less than a year. David was determined, intrepid, sometimes reckless. I can still see him climbing up the walls of speakers at the side of the stage. He'd size up the crowd and then, like he thought he could could fly, he'd jump off. Once or twice he hurt himself and I even saw him finish one of the shows sitting in a chair[39].

On the night of 3 July 1973, we suspected something was going to happen because the performance was being filmed, but we didn't know what. Bowie surprised us too! In fact, some of us didn't really understand what he was saying – it was the audience's reaction that told us. Personally, I was relieved. Without him actually saying anything, I knew David had come to the end of that part of his life, and deep down, I was happy for him.

Working with Bowie showed me how insatiably curious he was: when I travelled with him in his limousine, he'd ask me things about jazz, and especially about the musicians who approached the genre in unusual ways. I told him about pianists who seemed to play any which way, using their elbows or even their feet. He was hanging on my every word!

What few people know or realized, was that the relationship between Mick Ronson and David Bowie was based on trust. Their bond was so strong that nothing could stop them, and Mick got so much from David that he wanted to give him his best in return. Like him, each time I played with Bowie, I gave it my all. And it's just as well that he liked it because when I get started, I just can't play the same thing twice in a row! In the studio for example, if I was asked to do a second take because of a single bad chord, I'd always play something completely different, sometimes forgetting what chord it was! That rarely happened to me on stage with David, but with The Smashing Pumpkins, I sometimes played completely different parts from one night to the next, and Billy Corgan would look at me like I was crazy! In concert – and I'm not proud of this – I react to my environment, either positively or negatively.

My solo on 'Aladdin Sane' is so much bigger than me. It's the pinnacle of my collaboration with Bowie: I was able to create a solo like that for a number of reasons, including the freedom David gave me, Mick Ronson's attitude, the quality of the rhythm section The Spiders From Mars had pre-recorded, the general mood of the time, and Ken Scott's talent as a recording engineer. Bowie started by asking me to play in different styles, but nothing was working. In the end, he told me just to let myself go in the free-jazz style of pianists like Cecil Taylor[40]. So that's what I did!

The craziest thing is that since then, I've played hundreds of thousands of solos, but that's the one people always ask me about. It's undeniable that that recording had something magical about it – something happened. And it will forever be part of the history of Bowie's music and the history of rock music. You know, the music I was playing at the time helped me find myself. I realized that just over twenty years ago. And since the Internet, not a day goes by when I don't receive a message about 'Time', 'Lady Grinning Soul' and especially 'Aladdin Sane'. I was supposed to play with Bowie for eight weeks but, in the end, with a few breaks in between, it lasted for more than three decades. (1991/2016/2017/2018)

KEN FORDHAM

I'd been away from England for almost a year. I was playing saxophone at casinos in the Bahamas and then I did some sessions in Miami. When I got home, I'd just started doing the rounds of the music scene, looking for gigs, and I received a phone call from David Bowie's management. To be honest, having been out of the country when he became famous, I had no idea what kind of music he was doing! They asked me to come to the MainMan office in London and, on the day of the meeting, David was waiting for me. I talked about my experience, but the mood was a bit strange. I had nothing to do with his universe, so it was a bit of a clash of cultures. When you're a musician, you're used to meeting all sorts of people, but to be honest, with his orange hair, I thought he was weird. But also very nice. I later found out he'd studied saxophone with Ronnie Ross. He said he'd just phoned him up when he was a kid – it was a bit forward of him, but it apparently worked![41]

Soon after, I was called in for sessions at Trident Studios and that's where I met Mick Ronson. He wasn't officially running things, but he was heavily involved and he was often the one briefing the musicians. He and David gave me some pointers, but that was all. They let me do my thing, which was kind of what people did back then, and I played a lot more than what you can hear on the record! I really liked that kind of original rock, and Mike Garson added a crazy vibe – honestly, that was more my thing. Bowie was both very relaxed and very focused. He didn't miss a thing, but he didn't pressure anyone either. At the start of the 1973 tour, he asked me if I felt comfortable with the repertoire. I told him it was a piece of cake, and from then on, he called me Mr Kipling[42].

MainMan's organization was a bit rubbish, but that was not a major problem, except in Japan, where people wanted things to be very organized. Aside from that, we were staying at the best hotels and the dressing rooms were well stocked! I got along really well with Mick and with Trevor Bolder, who was happy just to do his job as well as he could. Woody Woodmansey was having a harder time dealing with

The Spiders' fame… At the time I didn't realize everything that was going on, but the band was good. When I come across photos of us at that time, online for example, I'm often pleasantly surprised. Of course we knew nothing of David's decision to 'kill' Ziggy Stardust and, to be honest, I was really disappointed because I was excited by the idea of going back to the US. I was young and loved to travel. (2016)

LINDA LEWIS

David Bowie and I hung out with the same crowd. After I left school in 1967, I lived in a community house with other artists – Cat Stevens, Elton John and Marc Bolan. David would come round sometimes and we'd jam. The famous DJ Jeff Dexter and producer Ian Samwell lived there too. I didn't have any idea how special David was, because I thought everybody was! I was a starry-eyed hippie writing songs and developing my music while gathering admirers.

David and I were at Glastonbury together in 1971. I posted a piece on my Facebook page from a gig he did in New York in 2000, where he recalls the stoned night he had with me before that festival gig. In 1973, he asked for me to come and sing at Trident Studios. I had a reputation as a unique backing vocalist by then, as well as a solo artist. I sang on lots of people's stuff. You know, that session was just another paying job to me. I remember David came in all made-up from a photo shoot and I had a laugh with him. He said I could sing whatever I felt was right on the tracks. I don't remember Mick Ronson being at Trident. After that, we were both pursuing our own careers but, when we did cross paths, like at after-show parties, he was always sweet and normal. He always gave me a cuddle, no matter how famous he was! (2016)

GEOFF MACCORMACK[43]

Throughout the train journey we had been lucky enough to have with us a very amicable middle-aged American gentleman named Bob Musel. Bob was the Moscow correspondent for the UPI news agency so, naturally, knew Moscow very well and offered to show us around. When we met him for a stroll, we quickly realized we were every inch the freakiest show in town. Presumably in an attempt to tone down the impact of his bright red hair, David wore a blindingly luminous yellow zip-up jacket, a bright yellow scarf, orange trousers, three-inch heels and a camp, floppy hat. I was his poor understudy in a dark-blue version of his jacket and a mere two inches of heel – though my boots were bright red. Bob looked like any smart businessman in any big city in the world, which made our trio seem even more surreal. Everywhere we went, people stared in amazement but few had the courage to approach us. Those who did were kids. They asked for chewing gum and gave us badges with patriotic designs on. (2007)

KEN SCOTT

I wasn't with David Bowie and Mick Ronson when they recorded 'The Jean Genie', but RCA was rushing them to come up with a new song and I think they did a good job. Their version, in mono, became the single and I only did the stereo mix for the album. Working in New York was special. Because of the rules imposed by the American technician's union, I wasn't allowed to touch the mixing desk. The only time I did, all hell broke loose! Also, like David and The Spiders, I thought Mike Garson really added something to what we were doing. He was a quiet bloke who expressed himself with his piano. He wasn't talkative, except when he was trying to persuade Trevor Bolder and Woody Woodmansey that scientology was amazing...

The Spiders' farewell? Let's just say that David finally realized something we'd all known for a while: his manager was ripping him off. But he was young and wanted fame at any cost. On the other hand, he never used his music to achieve his goal, in the sense that he always refused to give in to what was easy: he made music for himself before he made it for others. Although, of course, he hoped people would like it. (2016)

MIKE MORAN

Bowie and his music were not known in the US when I first met him and worked with him at RCA Studios in New York in October 1972. He was there to rehearse and record some new songs. At first, we did not understand each other, because he used English terms for technical jargon, like 'earth' for 'ground'. Eventually we would figure it out and laugh about it. We had a lot of fun in the studio, he was a funny guy... One of the American practices that surprised him was that the tape recorder was always on. I would tape everything and he would constantly say, 'Mike, you are not recording this, are you?' He was used to not putting much down on tape because of the expense in England; however, since RCA was paying, I recorded everything! He would say he was just rehearsing new tracks, but I recorded them. Amazingly, although every take sounded perfect the next one would be even better.

While in Los Angeles, I took them to the RCA Hollywood Studios to record and got in trouble because I did not get the clearances in advance from the senior A&R executive, Don Burkheimer. Previously, during a couple of days off between two concerts, we'd mixed some songs in Nashville, including 'The Jean Genie', which became the next single. Bowie, as you know, was afraid to fly, so my bosses at RCA had asked me to go to Saint Louis to pick up David and Mick, then drive them to Nashville. I was busy at the time and told my bosses that I was not a chauffeur and I would meet them there.

In Nashville, Bowie and Ronson insisted on going out for lunch as they had heard about a local place called Lum's that made hot dogs cooked in beer. Although I was hesitant about being seen in Nashville, which was still considered a redneck town at that time, with a skinny dude with an orange 'rooster do' and Mick with his long platinum blonde hair, sights that had never been seen in the city before, I agreed. As I was driving them out of the studio parking lot, Jim Foglesong, a conservative A&R guy who had transferred from New York to the Nashville operation, almost crashed his car after he waved to me and then saw Bowie and Ronson! Once we got to the restaurant though, to the locals' credit, no one stared too obviously and the boys enjoyed their frankfurters, beers and other local food.

After we got back from Nashville, David started appearing in the studio in much more fashionable clothes. Also it was quite interesting at times with Angie, Cherry Vanilla and some other MainMan people who would attend the sessions. I remember their son was also with them in the US and David was delighted he was there.

While I was working with David and Mick Ronson, I had the opportunity to see David perform at Radio City Music Hall. He astounded the audience by coming down from the ceiling in a spacesuit during his opening number.[44] The Americans had never seen anything like that before! He blew everyone away with his performance. He was the consummate performer on stage and the consummate musician, singer, songwriter in the studio. Of all the artists I have ever worked with, he was the greatest visionary in the studio and on stage. He and Mick Ronson formed a duo a bit like Mick Jagger and Keith Richards, and they loved the sound of The Rolling Stones.

We worked on some of the songs that ended up on *Aladdin Sane* and, even though some of them seemed pretty straightforward, 'The Jean Genie' for example, David paid a huge amount of attention to the smallest detail. He was always very serious in the studio and would always say he could do the track better and, unbelievably, he would. Mick would say the take was good, but David would insist on doing his vocal over again.

At the time, I was given all of my recording assignments by the head of the RCA Studios operation, and when David Bowie requested me, I had to be pulled off other projects. It happened when I was asked to mix *Ziggy Stardust And The Spiders From Mars – The Motion Picture Soundtrack* with the film's director, D.A. Pennebaker. It was meant to be released on RCA's new laser-disc configuration SelectaVision, which ultimately failed and which RCA quickly abandoned[45]. The quality of the recording of the concert was not good and it had to be re-synced with the film, which took hours and hours to complete. (2016)

JOHN CAMBRIDGE

In early 1973, I read in an interview that David wanted new musicians to flesh out The Spiders From Mars. In particular, they were looking for a guitarist to play the 12-string. It so happened that I'd just received a call from John Hutchinson so I gave him David's number, which I'd kept. That's how he got the job. After Mick Ronson, Hutch was the second guitarist I got to play with Bowie! (2016)

JOHN HUTCHINSON

I was pleased to join The Spiders in 1973, but I think Trevor Bolder would have liked David Bowie and Mick Ronson to choose his younger brother, who was also a musician, instead of me. As the tour dragged on, David distanced himself from the band, but earlier, in New York, I spent a lot of time with him. We went to see The Rockettes and also Charlie Mingus. He even took me to Max's Kansas City, where he was in his element...

The night of 3 July, during the 15-minute interval, David asked me to wait for his signal before I started to play 'Rock'n'roll Suicide', which was going to be the last song of the set. Naively, I thought that because it was the end of this tour, and that we had a break coming up before a new series of concerts, he was going to make a thank you speech. I had no idea that he was going to fire us instead! I was only an interim Spider From Mars, but it still felt like he'd thrown a bucket of cold water over me. Later, I understood what really happened, that MainMan had wanted to outsmart RCA. Whatever the case, I got to experience all that first hand and I have no regrets, except maybe not spending all that much time with David. Sometimes I think that maybe I should have been more forward, but forcing people to hang out with me has never been my thing. In fact, I think that deep down – and Geoff MacCormack, one of the people who knew him best, would agree with me here – David's always been the same. You know, I prefer to play music than to talk about it and I never thought of myself as a star musician who was going to profit from Bowie's success. I was happy to play with him when he asked me to and I loved every minute of it. Mick Ronson had a different experience, but he realized he wasn't meant to be a star either. (2016)

ROBIN MAYHEW

MainMan allowed us to work with the best possible setup. When Peter Hunsley and I said to Defries that we needed more microphones and a lorry to transport all the equipment, he would just say, 'Go and get what you need,' giving us a blank signed cheque. That attitude prevailed throughout the whole Ziggy period wherever we were and whatever was needed. We just had to ask, and bingo!

Overall, as FOH engineer, I have great memories of that adventure. But the whole experience was a rollercoaster ride and now, every show is a bit of a blur! I have to admit though, that the Earl's Court show, in May 1973, was a disaster and, although the fans loved it, from a technical point of view it was hopeless. The sound was appalling, due mainly to the low stage and the breakdown of the house PA system, which I had linked to for extra power. People crowded in front of the stage, stopping those who were behind from seeing the show.

I had a lot of great times during those shows and on the road. I got to know Mick Ronson really well. He was a very humble man and his on-stage persona was not much like his real self. With his guitar and dressed in his stage gear, he radiated a fair bit of tough sex appeal. He was certainly the musical director and leader of the band. When Mike Garson joined the entourage, and with *Aladdin Sane* now released, the sound did change and I was able to do justice to his excellent work, confident that it would embellish the overall mix. I know that Garson was the source of some sort of uprising that may have led to the end of The Spiders From Mars, but I wasn't on the bus at the time and didn't hear those conversations. Before the Hammersmith Odeon, I didn't even know that was going to be the last Ziggy Stardust concert, but I have to say I couldn't see where else things would go. I learned of the break up about halfway through the second half of the concert, when Peter Hunsley spoke to me over the intercom and said, 'I think David is going to break up the band tonight.'

It was certainly the right choice as there was nowhere and nothing we could do to make it any different. Ziggy would have died a sad death if it continued... After the show, my wife Mardy and I went to the Café Royal and had a wonderful time. I have to say that, when we left, I went to say goodbye to David, who was talking to Mick Jagger and Lou Reed. David said, 'See you soon!' and Jagger was a little rude, making sort of pussy cat noises. I've written in my book that I wish I had told him that it was me who got The Rolling Stones their first gig, when Ian Stewart asked if they could play at my band's – The Presidents – club at the Red Lion pub in Sutton, Surrey[46]. It might have made him think!

Towards the end of the tour, in 1973, David was a little bewildered I think. Everything happened so quickly. Still, he was always calm and focused and enjoyed a laugh with all of us. Having mixed so many of his concerts, I can say that he was one of the most inventive musicians I've ever had the opportunity to work with. His songs never ceased to amaze me: when you thought you knew what the following chord would be, another more unexpected one would come along and make the song instantly haunting. I worked one last time with David on the set of *The 1980 Floor Show* and, since I'd started my PA rental company, Ground Control, I took on Mick Ronson's tour. That was another adventure, but I don't think he really liked being the frontman. (2016)

IAN HUNTER

David Bowie never really had a rock'n'roll spirit, but what an animal! When he and The Spiders From Mars were on stage, I only really saw Mick, even though I always admired David, who was dangerously charming.

During the MainMan years, no one, other than Tony Defries, had any money – everything stayed in his pocket. David had agreed. He had no idea he would get screwed like that. It's true that Tony Defries could do the impossible – you could ask him for an elephant at 6pm, and it would be on your doorstep the next morning. And those were the things David would demand. No one paid for their hotel, everyone went around in limousines, all the bills were sent to RCA. It was madness. Either we got our way, or we'd all end up in prison! And David found fame... We were in this surreal bubble, and miraculously, it never popped. In any case, MainMan and Bowie couldn't quit – they were in danger of being in debt to RCA for the rest of their lives. At the end of the day, they played their cards admirably well and I can assure you that even in the upper echelons of the label, there are still some people who don't understand what really happened, and others who continue to fawn over Defries and his genius. He knew how to use the idiots who were polluting the business. (1998/1994)

JAMES WILLIAMSON

When David came to mix *Raw Power* in Los Angeles, he only had a few options. We'd already done quite a few overdubs and his first job was to make the bass and the drums very low! We had to admit that our initial mix was not very good. Iggy had his ideas about how the record was supposed to sound, I had mine, and the result was terrible. So we decided to get the 'golden boy', David, to come save the album that we, primitive people from Detroit, were ruining! We'd left London for Los Angeles and because he was coming back to the US, David came round during a break between two concerts and mixed it. We did it in three days, at Western Sounds⁴⁷.

The thing is, it being what it is, I don't think you can mess *Raw Power* up. It will come through no matter what. When I look back on it, I really disapproved of the mix when David first did it, even though I really have nothing to disapprove of, because I was sitting right there, in the room. If I'd wanted to object or something, I should have done it then. But yeah, I thought it was too Bowie! Now, as I've lived with this mix for all these years, I've come to appreciate it and understand what David was up against. I think he did a fantastic job mixing the album considering he had very little to work with and because of how we had recorded it. I think it remains the quality mix, the one everyone goes to and loves. The later mixes, especially Iggy's, can't compete with David's. Listening to the original vinyl from 1973 is still the best way to appreciate *Raw Power*. I often thought of remixing it myself, but I don't think I'll ever get round to it, and what's the point anyway? *Raw Power* is good the way it is and that's how it should remain.

I wasn't surprised when MainMan lost interest in The Stooges. Actually they never got us. To be honest, it was impossible to control or manage The Stooges and the drugs didn't make it any easier. At least, after MainMan, we were able to play live more often. You know, Tony Defries had the Colonel Parker complex – he needed to control everything... The Stooges only played two shows the entire time we were with MainMan, and fifty after that! We carried on until we realized the band had run its course. The Stooges were not a viable commercial entity. Iggy and I later recorded the demos that ended up on *Kill City*⁴⁸ but it wasn't a Stooges album. Had we been successful at finding a record company, it could have become one. But nobody liked us and, when we got rejected that final time, it was more than any of us could take. (2017)

JEFF BECK

You know, sometimes I wonder what the hell I was doing on stage at the Hammersmith Odeon on 3 July 1973, when David Bowie killed off Ziggy Stardust! He was huge, mysterious, mythical. I'd initially turned down his invitation to play because I didn't feel comfortable in front of all those Bowie freaks. In the end, out of curiosity, and because I knew it was only rock'n'roll, I went along. Also, my girlfriend was totally into the whole androgynous thing and told me Mick Ronson was one of my biggest fans... I was even told I was his birthday present that night[49]! I wasn't in the film, or on its soundtrack for that matter, because of my bell bottoms! I said to David, 'Show them my trousers and I'll cut your head off.'

Not long ago, I found out that before recruiting Mick Ronson, David had thought about asking me. He came to see me at the Iridium in New York when I paid tribute to Les Paul[50]. He was in the audience and I invited him onto the bus after the show. We talked. His death is all the more terrible because now we won't be able to do any of the stuff we talked about... (1999/2016)

ROD CLEMENTS

Yes, I do remember Lindisfarne, the band I was playing bass in, opening for David Bowie in Cleveland. I think it was 1972. I only recall one show though... If there were two, they conflate in my memory.

Two things struck me: the first is that everyone other than the Bowie team were required to leave the theatre during The Spiders From Mars' sound check. That seemed strange to us. The second is that, during their set, which we watched from the back of the hall, under the balcony, the sound was very powerful and very, very loud. Simon Cowe, our guitar player, and I had to put our hands over our ears to keep them from falling off! So... it sounded great! I didn't have the chance to talk to David Bowie in Cleveland but, even though I wouldn't say I was a fan in the deepest sense, I had a very high opinion of him as an artist. I loved *Hunky Dory* when it came out and I used to listen to it over and over again. (2018)

BRYAN FERRY

David Bowie makes a distinction between high glam and low glam? I think he's right. Roxy Music sounded more like a crazy Pink Floyd than Chicory Tip[51]. (1999)

DANA GILLESPIE

Everyone at MainMan was partying like there was no tomorrow, because Defries liked crazy, unusual people around him. It was all showing off and posing, and the people at RCA in New York were mesmerized by this court of employees who, more often than not, knew nothing about the job they were supposed to be doing, but who kept the party going. It was obvious that Cherry Vanilla had no idea how to be a publicist, but she had these tattooed cherries on her chest, just here, and everyone listened to her when she said, 'There's this new singer called David Bowie...' (2016)

LEEE BLACK CHILDERS

What? No way! Cherry Vanilla didn't need to show the photo of David kneeling in front of Mick Ronson to the DJs to let them know how far she was willing to go if they played his records! Let's be honest, she was a really nice girl who never thought she had to demean herself to get what she wanted. My dear, don't believe what you've read about MainMan and the madness on the Ziggy Stardust tour – it was much crazier than that! Defries' only instruction was to spend as much money as possible and he didn't have to force any of us to do that... (2004)

STEVEN TYLER

When we started Aerosmith, the media saw me and Joe Perry as a sort of Keith Richards/Mick Jagger duo, but to be honest, we were just as impressed by Mick Ronson and David Bowie's look on stage in the days of Aladdin Sane. Bowie always knew how to put on a show... (2007)

DES HENLY

David Bowie? I can't really tell you any more than I told the local paper the day after his death – cool, kind, intelligent! Our band, Fumble, opened for him[52] because he liked us! We played a sort of revival rock'n'roll, but not totally retro, and for some reason he liked it! I always thought it was our innocence that attracted him. In late 1972, he was on the English circuit, but wasn't that impressed with some of the bands opening for him. We were asked too late to be there in London, but we did the last concerts for that leg of the tour, and then he invited us to the US. Fumble had some concerts planned in England, but we couldn't miss that opportunity. What he did wasn't exactly my kind of music, I thought he was a bit weird. But I had nothing against him, quite the contrary, and besides, he really liked us! I didn't know his songs very well – he was not an icon yet – but on stage, The Spiders From Mars rocked!

We spent more time with Bowie in the US and he regularly invited us to lunch at his hotel. He would stay at the Holiday Inn and we'd be at some Travelodge-type place, a cheaper chain! On the other hand, he travelled by bus, and we had a Chevy Impala! Thanks to Bowie, unlike bands like Wishbone Ash or Status Quo who we knew well, we really got to see the US. If we'd travelled by air, we wouldn't have seen anything of the country. He really understood that. We saw the Grand Canyon; we drove Route 66, which was fantastic!

America in the 1970s wasn't the same as it is today. In Nashville, for example, David got death threats. I remember the security was huge backstage, but he never let it get him down. Not once did he let himself be unsettled by people calling him a faggot. Anyway, those Americans didn't like black people either! There are things that small-town America could never stand. When Queen's video for 'I Want To Break Free' came out there in the 1980s – the one where Freddie Mercury appears as a woman with a moustache – that didn't go down very well either! We're talking about a country where people burned Beatles records! Okay, so we can't lump together all Americans, but let's just say they can be an odd lot. They're afraid of God, who's obviously white, and definitely not homosexual!

After our set, we watched his, and it was really good! With his mix of rock and theatre, his crazy outfits, Bowie had his audience in the bag from the very first song and he wasn't the type to hold back. Something about him seemed other-worldly, even though, in everyday life, he could pass for a regular bloke. After the shows, we hung out at bars with his musicians. David usually wasn't there, but he did occasionally have a drink or two with us. As the others have probably said, we got along really well with Mick Ronson, who really was a great guy. He almost produced our second album, *Poetry in Lotion*, but that didn't happen in the end... We sometimes ran into David later and, in 1978, he borrowed Sean Mayes, our keyboardist. Some memories are better than others when you're a musician, but I'll always cherish the time we spent with David Bowie. (2018)

EDDIE CLARKE

Three years before joining Motörhead as their guitarist, I saw the Ziggy Stardust farewell concert at the Hammersmith Odeon. It was really mad – I'd never seen anything like it. Bowie was like a cat: he was strutting about, he was being provocative, he was grinning... He was everything and everywhere. As for Ronson, he was and always will be one of the wildest guitarists. He's with Ian Hunter now I think... Bowie's parting from Mick was one of the biggest outrages in the history of rock! (1979)

CLAUDE GASSIAN

I took photos at the press conference at the George V hotel in Paris, which was really cheaply organized – an armchair, a table, a curtain behind David Bowie. He was very polite, but I can't remember the questions being particularly interesting! No one gave me a specific time slot, so I was able to shoot the whole thing. A few days later, I saw Bowie live for the first time. None of the French music magazines wanted to send me to London, so I'd paid for it myself and I bought a ticket from a tout outside Earl's Court. As soon as I stepped into that horrible building, I dashed to the edge of the stage and I stayed there for the whole set. There I could shoot what I wanted and one of my photos appeared on the cover of *Rock&Folk* soon after[53]. That night was a disaster. A fight broke out behind me and I think a lot of people didn't hear most of the concert because there was something wrong with the PA. (2018)

NORMA PALMER

I worked at the BBC and I saw Bowie and The Spiders at Television Centre once or twice. In 1973, while I was queuing at the radio cafeteria, the guy next to me turned around too quickly and almost spilled his drink all over me. He apologized profusely and offered to pay for mine. It was Mick Ronson. I told him that actually I was buying drinks for several colleagues and he insisted on paying for them all. We talked for a bit and I told him I was Lloyd Watson's sister. He'd opened for Bowie and The Spiders at the Rainbow the previous year. Before leaving, Mick asked me to say hi to Lloyd and waved goodbye. I bumped into him again on the street outside the BBC a few weeks later, and the person I was with couldn't believe he was coming to say hi. It was the last time I saw him. I'll never forget what a nice, easygoing guy he was. (2016)

BILLY RITCHIE

I always get linked with David, which is something of a double-edged sword. People tend to think how lucky I was to know him but, actually, it was the other way round. At the time, I was the relative big shot, and he wanted to know me. So of course, I followed his career. I thought he was wise to get out of the Ziggy persona. It was a lucky break for him, that *Top Of The Pops* had made him a star, but he was definitely in danger on several levels – most of all, his sanity. He escaped and survived by realizing eventually that he was David Jones, not David Bowie. He was able to separate the two, and the actor in him saved him until the end. (2017)

MARLA FELDSTEIN[54]

I first became a fan of David's at the age of 13, in late 1972. I was over at a friend's house and she was adamant about me hearing an album that she had recently discovered. She said something along the lines of, 'Marla, you have to listen to this album!' She proceeded to play *Ziggy Stardust* for me. I went home that night... a transformed person.

The first time I saw David in concert was at the Tower Theater in Upper Darby, west of Philadelphia, in 1973. I had just missed the chance to see him the year before at the same venue[55]... It truly was a dream-like experience. I remember being fairly far back in the theatre. At one point I was thinking, 'I have to get closer! I need to be closer!' I jumped out of my seat and made my way to the front of the theatre. I ended up against the railing of the pit area. Dead centre, just a few feet from David, the most captivating human I had ever seen. Human, yes, of course... but, at the time, and sometimes still, I cannot help but think there was something otherworldly about him. Peculiar, I know... but I am certain there are many who agree. I really thought we – David and I – had locked eyes. Well, I believe that we did... just like a thousand other people felt. Real or not... for me it happened. Feelings of astonishment and wonder soared through me. His voice, the music, the sights and sounds... all of it went straight to my heart.

Shortly after that show at the Tower, I had written David a pretty elaborate fan letter. I had traced various pictures of him from different sources, coloured them in and glued the tracing paper onto coloured paper. There were about four or five pages! I used this as the stationery for my sweet and candid letter, which I sent off to MainMan in New York. A few weeks after mailing the letter, I heard back from someone at MainMan, telling me that David was extremely touched by my letter and that it meant a lot to him! I was in utter disbelief and so elated that he had actually read it. (2016)

GEORGE UNDERWOOD

Because he'd asked me to go with him and I couldn't exactly turn him down, I was there for David's American tour in 1972. He was extremely brave to do what he did. He faced the adventure with a lot of passion and courage. It was stressful, but he coped well. At the time, we talked about the possibility of me drawing something for the sleeve of the upcoming album or for a live recording of The Spiders, but nothing ever came of that[56]. David also invited my wife Birgit and me to Japan the following year, but we'd just got married and needed to settle in, so we said no. I think I made the right choice and we remained friends. (2016)

TONY VISCONTI

As I was finishing their [Carmen's] first album, *Fandangos In Space*, in the summer, Bowie and I had just got back on speaking terms; David had rung me, and we talked over the phone a bit before agreeing to meet one evening to see Peter Cook and Dudley Moore live. I invited David to meet Carmen when I was mixing their album at Air Studios, in Oxford Circus and I was thrilled when David invited them to appear with him at the Marquee Club as part of a TV project. (2007)

PHIL MANZANERA

At the beginning of the 70s, rock and pop were very black and white, and to my mind, that had a lot to do with the fact that quite a few musicians did a lot of hard drugs. What David Bowie, T. Rex and Roxy Music embodied was a sort of multi-coloured new wave. It was about the music first, but it also included the album covers and the way we performed live. We woke everyone up! We were musicians with enquiring minds in close contact with fashion designers, photographers. All these people were barely 25 years old – we were the new generation, in the right place at the right time. We were the product of many influences from the past, but we made a point to make them contemporary. The funny thing with Roxy Music, is that you always hear about our look from the days of our first album – the sequins, the wedges, Brian Eno's famous feathers – but that didn't last for much more than a year. From the beginning of 1973, Bryan Ferry wore a smoking jacket on stage and we wore well-cut suits. We were part of the glam rock scene for a while, but we knew we had to move on quickly. (2018)

MARY FINNIGAN

The curtain comes down on the Beckenham era when David and Angie invite all of us involved in it to a Ziggy performance at the Earl's Court Arena in London.

We have guest seats in a prime location and are swept along by the magic of the performance, along with a capacity audience that erupts with enthusiasm after each song and screams for more at the end. It is loud, brash, theatrical and sensual.

David and Ronno, dressed in gaudy satins and silks, swoop and gyrate around and against each other in blatantly sexual manoeuvres. It has absolutely nothing in common with the t-shirt and jeans Three Tuns uniform. David has finally become a rock star. It is an electrifying, emotional experience for all of us who appreciated his talent before he entered the hall of fame.

Afterwards David and Angie throw a party at Haddon Hall. Daughter Caroline comes with me, by this time a precocious 13-year-old with an interest in boys.

Alongside the Beckenham contingent there is an assortment of London music biz people – performers, DJs and hangers-on – some of whom I recognize from my Fleet Street days. Chelita Secunda for example, a woman with a finely tuned instinct for the latest Big Thing. It is an excellent party with gourmet food and lots of champagne. David is in his Ziggy outfit and Angie wears Chanel – or a Freddie clone thereof.

When Caroline and I get up to leave, David puts an arm round my shoulders and escorts us to the door.

'Goodbye Mary,' he says. 'You are a wonderful woman and I will never forget you.'

I never see him in person or speak to him again. (2016)

1. The magazine, founded in 1967 by Jann Wenner and Ralph J. Gleason, was the giant of the US rock media, but it also covered politics and society.

2. 'He was a master', Bowie will say on his website, on 27 October 2013, when Lou Reed dies.

3. As portrayed in *Almost Famous*, Swingos was also popular with famous groupies, especially those who wanted to do more than just sleep with musicians. Some protected them, usually from dealers and minors (or from their mothers), and sometimes from themselves. Corinne Schwab, who met David Bowie in 1974, would have nothing to do with these alluring creatures, but she took care of Bowie better than anyone else in his entourage. She inspired a generation of rock stars' assistants – the stars owe them a lot and, most probably in Bowie's case, even their lives.

4. The Hyatt, on Sunset Boulevard in Los Angeles, was also known for the excesses of its guests.

5. In *Reckless (My Life)* (Ebury Press, 2015), Chrissie Hynde will reveal she went to this concert (she'd just turned 21 years old). She ended up in David Bowie's hotel suite and then took him out to dinner in her parents' car!

6. The Mercer Arts Center was a cultural complex founded in the early 1970s by Steina and Woody Vasulka. It was located in the Broadway Central Hotel building (on Mercer Street, on the other side of Broadway from Lafayette Street, where David Bowie will live at the end of his life). The centre had a small concert hall for 200 people, called the Oscar Wilde Room, and a larger one called O'Casey.

New York Dolls performed in these two rooms regularly at the start of their career. It's likely that Bowie saw the Dolls on 19 September, but it's possible it was 26 September. It must have been in O'Casey because, by September 1972, the Oscar Wilde Room was too small for their audience. Bands that Bowie liked often played in the neighbourhood at the time (theatres gave them residencies, especially because it brought in money at the bar). Among them were The Fugs at the Players Theatre on MacDougal Street, and Frank Zappa And The Mothers Of Invention at the Garrick on Bleecker Street. When David Bowie went to the Mercer Arts Center, there was a residency by a theatre troupe led by Rip Torn who, like him, will perform in *The Man Who Fell To Earth* three years later. Torn was also a member of the complex's management. A New York Dolls show at the Mercer Arts Center, on the evening of the collapse of the building, is a crucial scene in the first episode of the 2016 television series *Vinyl*, by Mick Jagger and Martin Scorsese. In reality, the century-old hotel, weakened by the destruction of its load-bearing walls, will fully collapse on 3 July 1973 (the same day as Ziggy's farewell gig), when there is no one in the Oscar Wilde Room or in O'Casey. London's Café Royal also has an Oscar Wilde room (known as the Oscar Wilde Bar and also as The Grill Room, and once a favourite haunt of Wilde himself). In an extraordinary coincidence, this Oscar Wilde Bar in London was the venue for the party after that final Ziggy gig.

7. David Johansen's wife at the time, Cyrinda Foxe will later marry Steven Tyler of Aerosmith. Her behind-the-scenes memoir, called *Dream On* (Dove Books, 1997) and co-written by Danny Fields, is one of the funniest and most relevant books on US rock music in the 1970s.

After suffering a stroke in the early 2000s, she will receive support from friends like Myra Friedman (author of *Buried Alive*, the definitive biography of Janis Joplin), Steven Tyler and David Bowie. Foxe will pass away in 2002 after suffering from a brain tumour.

8. MainMan's operational and organizational structure was pretty fanciful, especially after they opened an office in New York in late August 1972. On paper, Tony Zanetta (Andy Warhol in *Pork*) was the president and tour coordinator, while photographer Leee Black Childers became vice-president and the following year opened a MainMan office in Los Angeles. Known for being a force of nature, Cherry Vanilla (real name Kathleen Dorritie), who also starred in *Pork*, was MainMan's very persuasive press liaison/publicist for some time. She will later make a few records, including two very respectable albums released on RCA in the late 70s. In 2010, Vanilla will publish *Lick Me* (Chicago Review Press), an autobiography prefaced by Rufus Wainwright, son of American folk singer-songwriter Loudon Wainwright III, and a big fan of David Bowie. In the book she'll refute certain 'promotional' tactics attributed to her. Meanwhile, Tony Zanetta will publish *Stardust: The Life And Times Of David Bowie* (Michael Joseph) in 1986, a biography co-written with Henry Edwards. On Bowie's death, Zanetta will pay tribute to Coco Schwab on his Facebook page. After working for David Bowie, Leee Black Childers will lend his tour-managing services – a very multifaceted role in rock'n'roll – to Iggy Pop and to Johnny Thunders' Heartbreakers. He will photograph all the crazy characters in 70s rock and in punk, and his best images can be seen in *Drag Queens, Rent Boys, Pick Pockets, Junkies, Rockstars And Punks*, an exhibition catalogue released in 2012.

Leee Black Childers will die in Los Angeles two years later.

9. American author Herbert Huncke might just be the father of the term 'beat generation', which was reportedly one of the working titles for *On The Road*. In the novel, the character of Elmer Hassel is based on Huncke, while Sal Paradise, Dean Moriarty and Carlo Marx are based on Jack Kerouac, Neal Cassady and Allen Ginsberg respectively.

10. A session took place in early October at the local RCA Studios. Lou Reed was also there and they apparently recorded the basic tracks for some of his songs (at least for 'Vicious', the opening song on his upcoming *Transformer*).

11. This is an important distinction because it has sometimes been said that Bowie chose Moran because he'd worked with Elvis Presley. Despite the mistake being made in several 'serious' books, this American Mike Moran should not be confused with the English Mike Moran, a reputable studio keyboardist who has worked with the second iteration of Blue Mink. He's also known for having co-written 'Rock Bottom' with Linsey De Paul in 1977. That same year, Moran and De Paul represented England at Eurovision with the song (which was originally written for Blue Mink) – it did well but did not win. This book's Mike Moran is the first American recording engineer to have worked with David Bowie and probably the last with Elvis Presley.

12. On 29 November, just before a three-day residency at the Tower Theater in Philadelphia (where he arrived by taxi after missing the train from Pittsburgh), David Bowie introduced Mott The Hoople on stage, then performed as a backing vocalist on 'All The Young Dudes'.

However, according to Ian Hunter, he didn't play saxophone on 'Honky Tonk Women' (the cover of The Rolling Stones song that wrapped up the set) as often claimed.

13. Other shows will be recorded for a planned live album, up until July 1973, including those at Radio City Music Hall in New York on 14 and 15 February. Those nights, 'Soul Love' will make a rare appearance on the set list with David Bowie on saxophone.

14. Mark Volman and Howard Kaylan, formerly of The Turtles from Los Angeles, did backing vocals for Frank Zappa and, a bit more glam, T. Rex. They can be heard on 'Get It On', a track on the excellent 1971 album *Electric Warrior* (Rick Wakeman is on piano). In 1968, George Underwood designed the cover of *My People Were Fair And Had Sky In Their Hair... But Now They're Content To Wear Stars On Their Brows*, Tyrannosaurus Rex's first album, produced by Tony Visconti. In the mid-1970s, David Bowie will ask Volman and Kaylan to act in a film he was planning to direct.

15. *Give The Anarchist A Cigarette* (Pimlico, 2002).

16. David Bowie was introduced to the work of the French writer and poet by Lindsay Kemp. According to publisher Paule Thévenin, Bowie's meeting with Genet did indeed take place in a restaurant, in the early 1970s. Genet wanted the musician to play the character of Divine in a film adaptation of *Notre-Dame-Des-Fleurs*. In 1970, Kemp adapted this book to create his most famous show, *Flowers: A Pantomime For Jean Genet*, in Edinburgh. David and Angie Bowie saw it during their visit to Scotland in the spring.

17. David Bowie met him during the photo shoot for the cover of *Aladdin Sane*. Born in Algiers, Pierre Laroche was the main make-up artist for Elizabeth Arden and, after this session, he'll became Bowie's. Until then, Bowie liked putting on his own make-up, using those moments in front of the mirror to get into character. From February 1973, Bowie will be increasingly made-up, Laroche adding even more. He will sometimes trace a gold circle on his forehead, inspired by kabuki theatre make-up and by the one Calvin Mark Lee had a few years before. Bowie never performed a concert with the Aladdin Sane bolt/flash on his face, probably because it was too difficult to draw on before getting on stage. However, hundreds of fans on both sides of the Atlantic had one on their faces. Pierre Laroche will later do the make-up for the actors in the film version of *The Rocky Horror Picture Show* by Jim Sharman. He will also work with Mick Jagger and give Daryl Hall and John Oates their androgynous look on the cover of their self-titled 1975 album, made controversial because of their appearance. Laroche died of AIDS in New York in 1991 (which Mick Rock will confirm to the author in 2018).

18. After the concert, Bowie introduced himself to Biff Rose, who thanked him for covering 'Fill Your Heart' on *Hunky Dory*, but pointed out that, in terms of arrangement, he could have done a version that wasn't so similar to his. That was the only time the two musicians met. David Bowie and Bruce Springsteen were also introduced that night. *Greetings From Asbury Park, NJ*, Springsteen's first album, had come out at the start of the month. A year and a half later, after seeing him live at the Harvard Square Theatre in Cambridge (Massachusetts), Jon Landau will write in a Boston paper the famous (but often misquoted) line: 'I saw rock and roll

future and its name is Bruce Springsteen.' He will go on to become Springsteen's manager.

19. In the United States, the new single is 'Time'/'The Prettiest Star'.

20. This book will also be on the list of works David Bowie will recommend in 2013.

21. See the chapter on *Station To Station*.

22. According to David Bowie himself, 'Queen Bitch' and 'Song For Bob Dylan' on *Hunky Dory* were also written in the style of The Velvet Underground and Bob Dylan respectively.

23. David Bowie enjoyed combining influences, which he called 'European', from French *chanson réaliste* and the music Kurt Weill had composed for Bertolt Brecht's plays and texts.

24. The album was going to be called *Love Aladdin Vein*, *Aladdin Vein* or *A Lad Insane* before David Bowie finally settled on *Aladdin Sane*. This title, which can be compared with that of 'The Jean Genie', reflects the ethereal side of Bowie's new character, which for him was less defined than Ziggy Stardust. The play on words (a lad insane) perhaps referred to Terry, whom David continued to bring into his work, maybe subconsciously.

25. Claudia Lennear, whom David Bowie hadn't seen since the mid-1970s, will say she was in touch with him not long before his death and that they were planning to write some songs together.

26. This press conference run by Cherry Vanilla was reported in France's two main rock magazines of the time, *Best* and *Rock&Folk*. According to the journalists who were there,

most of the questions were exceptionally stupid, like the first one: 'When we talk about David Bowie, should we say he or she?'

27. *L'Emmerdeur (A Pain In The A...)* by Édouard Molinaro, filmed in Montpellier between 19 March and 25 May 1973. This non-meeting caused a press sensation and, a decade later, some theatre people who knew Jacques Brel revealed that he hadn't wanted to meet David Bowie. According to them, Brel was rather homophobic, which might not be true and is impossible to verify.

28. That spring, David Bowie also made a surprise visit to see his old manager Ken Pitt.

29. The *Aladdin Sane* reissue of 1990 will be the only David Bowie studio album in Rykodisc's catalogue without a single bonus track. Jeff Rougvie, of the label, will say the only songs that could have been added already featured in the Sound+Vision box set, released the previous year and mentioned in the second volume of *Rainbowman*. In 2003, EMI will reissue *Aladdin Sane* for its 30th anniversary, adding a full CD of goodies, including a brass version of 'John, I'm Only Dancing' (it should have been the last track on the LP but, just before cutting it, they replaced it with 'Lady Grinning Soul'), 'All The Young Dudes' (mono, recorded with The Spiders From Mars in New York in 1972) and some live tracks from the American leg of the tour, including a remarkable acoustic version of 'Drive-In Saturday', performed for the first time in concert on 17 November 1972 at Pirate's World in Fort Lauderdale. To celebrate the album's 45th anniversary, Parlophone/Warner will release a silver vinyl edition in 2018.

30. Mick Ronson will perform at the Hammersmith Odeon during his 1974 solo tour, and Mott The Hoople will give their reunion concerts there in 2009. Lou Reed will also play there. As of 2023, the venue still stands, but is now called the Eventim Apollo.

31. The filmmaker will die at the age of 94, in 2019.

32. He plays a jazz medley lasting just under seven minutes, which includes 'Space Oddity', 'Ziggy Stardust', 'John, I'm Only Dancing' and 'Life On Mars?'.

33. Jeff Beck's absence from the film and its soundtrack is often attributed either to the clothes he wore (which he didn't like the look of) or to him playing not at his best that night. But Tony Visconti recalls that when Beck said he wasn't pleased with his playing, hoping that would get him excluded, he was invited to re-record his part, and did so. Still, it looks like he finally declined to appear in the film (and so also the soundtrack album).

34. But as proof that RCA wasn't wrong, the single, released in a sleeve with a photo, got to Number 3 in the British charts. Between 1972 and 1973, Bowie & Co often played a short version of the song (about a minute and a half) in the middle of a strange medley with a strong jazz feel (Mike Garson...) that started with a minute and a half of 'Quicksand' and ended with almost four minutes of 'Memory Of A Free Festival'. The idea was to have the audience sing the chorus in the final section ('*The sun machine is coming down*'). This medley was rehearsed for the Hammersmith Odeon, but was not played (at least not on the second night), so it's not in D.A. Pennebaker's film. In 1972 and 1973, in the midst of Bowiemania,

the labels that held the rights to his previously recorded songs re-released some of them, including 'The Laughing Gnome'.

35. According to some guests, the 'last supper' took place the day after the last concert with The Spiders From Mars, rather than immediately after it. For this book, Cherry Vanilla confirmed the party was on the night of the show. During the dinner, musical entertainment was reportedly provided by New Orleans pianist and singer-songwriter Dr John. Asked about this in Paris in 1990, he told the author he didn't remember the evening at all. He will not mention the party in his autobiography *Under A Hoodoo Moon* (St Martin's Griffin, 1994) either. Dr John died in June 2019.

36. Paul and Linda McCartney, Keith Moon, Lulu, Tony Curtis, Peter Cook and Dudley Moore, Cat Stevens, Ringo and Maureen Starr, Mick and Bianca Jagger, Jeff Beck, Aynsley Dunbar, The Spiders From Mars, John Hutchinson, Lou Reed, Barbra Streisand, Ryan O'Neal, Sonny Bono, Elliott Gould, Britt Ekland, D.A. Pennebaker and Edgar Broughton were among the guests.

37. Mike Garson didn't know it, but Lindisfarne, who opened for David Bowie in Cleveland, were first called Brethren. The band became Lindisfarne to avoid confusion with the American band with the same name.

38. Right up until his last interviews, even though he showered Mike Garson with compliments, David Bowie never considered the instrumentalists that boosted his band in 1972 and 1973 as members of The Spiders From Mars. For him, The Spiders were Mick Ronson, Trevor Bolder and Woody Woodmansey.

39. Mike Garson is referring to the 14 June 1973 concert at City Hall in Salisbury. David Bowie did a swan dive at the end of the show and, after telling the audience he was injured, he sang 'Round And Round' during the encore sitting in a chair. It was one of the only times on the Ziggy Stardust/Aladdin Sane tour that he talked to the audience. Usually, he only spoke when there was a problem.

40. Mike Garson told the author he was absolutely not familiar with King Crimson's music when he recorded *Aladdin Sane*. David Bowie, however, had always been a big fan of the band, but it's unlikely that he asked Garson to play in the unrestrained way of jazz pianist Keith Tippett on 'Cat Food', a track on the B-side of *In The Wake Of Poseidon*, King Crimson's second album. But he may have wanted to recreate its spirit, even if subconsciously. In the 'Aladdin Sane' solo, Mike references 'Rhapsody In Blue', 'Tequila' and 'On Broadway'. This was a common practice when music was played by real human beings (not computers) who liked paying tribute to other musicians. On *Pin Ups*, the strings on 'See Emily Play' will also reference classical pieces.

41. At the age of 15, David Bowie did give this saxophone player, who was a local celebrity (he lived in Orpington), a ring. He'd found his contact information in the phone book. In 1972, still inclined to call on people from his past he felt were important, Bowie asked Ross to play the tenor sax solo at the end of 'Walk On The Wild Side'. Ross died in the early 1990s. He was one of the few musicians to have worked with both David Bowie and The Beatles – he can be heard on 'Savoy Truffle', a song on the *White Album*, released in 1968.

42. Mr Kipling cakes were first made in the 1960s.

43. With his consent, these few lines come from the book by Geoff MacCormack mentioned in this chapter.

44. David Bowie will use this famous stage entrance – descending from above – again fourteen years later during the Glass Spider tour. In 1973, he wasn't actually wearing an astronaut costume at the start of the show, but images of space were shown on a screen behind the musicians.

45. Like *Live Santa Monica '72*, *Ziggy Stardust And The Spiders From Mars – The Motion Picture Soundtrack* will be available in several formats before settling on its current form. The soundtrack to the 'retirement gig' of Ziggy and his Spiders will be officially released for the first time in 1983, a decade after the concert. RCA tried to ride the wave of *Let's Dance*, Bowie's first album on EMI, which no one had predicted would be so successful. Available on vinyl and cassette at the time – the film will appear on VHS in 1982 – the soundtrack, originally produced by Bowie and Mike Moran, will be remixed by Bowie, Tony Visconti and Bruce Tergesen. Not all fans will like this version (with enhanced backing vocals, brass and keyboards) and many still prefer the pirate record: *Bowie And The Spiders From Mars' Last Stand – His Master's Voice*. Even though it was missing a good chunk of the original set, it was one of the most popular unofficial Bowie LPs of the 1970s. Tony Visconti will say that the quality of the sound on the night of 3 July 1973, done by Ken Scott (recording engineer) and Robin Mayhew (FOH engineer), left a bit to be desired. So, two decades later, Visconti will remix the soundtrack of the film in stereo and 5.1.

The DVD and soundtrack will come out in 2003. In 1992, the recording of the concert will be released for the first time on CD at the end of Toby Mountain and Jonathan Wyner's remastering process of David Bowie's RCA and EMI catalogues (those famous Rykodisc CDs and LPs with unreleased songs, which are no longer available). Lastly, in order to add to the confusion and pander to obsessive fans, Robin Mayhew will sell, via his website, a soundboard recording (the console was a 24-channel Turner) of the farewell gig. The two cassette tapes, which he'd kept since 1973, will be digitized in 2008. This CD is called *The Fall Of Ziggy Stardust – Live At Hammersmith July 1973*. Robin Mayhew will self-publish his memoir (*Ambition*) in 2016. He passed away in 2021.

46. In 1962, before The Rolling Stones completed their classic line up (Bill Wyman and Charlie Watts weren't official members yet), they opened for The Presidents, a band in which Robin Mayhew played guitar. A year and a half later, The Stones had made it big and returned the favour to The Presidents by inviting the band to open for them. It was at this concert, at the Red Lion pub in Sutton, Surrey, that Giorgio Gomelsky and Glyn Johns, key players in the future career of The Rolling Stones, saw them live for the first time. The Red Lion pub is still standing; it's now listed and is called the Winning Post. David Bowie never played there.

47. More precisely Western Recorders, one of the best and most legendary studios in Beverly Hills, where Frank Sinatra, The Beach Boys, Elvis Presley and Marvin Gaye recorded. Iggy Pop will return in 1990 as a solo artist to the same location (Studio 2), by then renamed Ocean Way Recording, to work on *Brick By Brick*.

48. For a fistful of dollars, James Williamson will do his best to mix the demos that the American label Bomp! will cleverly release in late 1977, the year of RCA's much-publicized release of *The Idiot* and *Lust For Life*.

49. It's unlikely, because Mick Ronson was born on 26 May.

50. This concert on 9 June 2010 will be released on DVD and Blu-ray (through Eagle) the following year. Coco Schwab and David Bowie, on very good form, will attend this show, despite the wild rumours about his health at the time.

51. Ironically, when he said this, Bryan Ferry didn't know that, in the mid-60s, the band Chicory Tip, from Maidstone in Kent, had performed with The Manish Boys who were also from Maidstone. At the time, their frontman was a certain David Jones. Chicory Tip rode the glam wave long enough to get a Number 1 hit, 'Son Of My Father', which was released as a single in February 1972. Fans call it a 'guilty pleasure'. The song is accentuated with a synthesizer and was co-written with Giorgio Moroder, who will work with David Bowie in the 1980s.

52. About 15 times in all, in the UK and US.

53. It's one of the photos David Bowie comments on at the start of this chapter.

54. Marla Feldstein is one of the two 'Sigma kids' interviewed for this book. They talk about meeting David Bowie in Philadelphia in 1974, in the chapter on *Young Americans*.

55. David Bowie and The Spiders From Mars performed at the Tower Theater in early

December 1972 and in mid-February the
following year for a mini-residency (seven
concerts in four days!).

56. Even a title – *Ziggy Stardust In America* –
was suggested. George Underwood was also
supposed to illustrate RCA's November 1972
reissues of the two Mercury albums, *Space
Oddity* and *The Man Who Sold The World*
but, due to a lack of time, photos by Mick Rock
and Brian Ward (for the second) were used on
the covers. In mid-December, the day he left for
England, David Bowie filmed an unadorned
video for 'Space Oddity' at RCA Studios in
New York, under Rock's direction. It was made
to boost sales of the two repackaged albums
on both sides of the Atlantic. They will join the
others in the charts.

PIN UPS

RCA – 3 NOVEMBER 1973[1]

'Each life is a game of chess that went to hell on the seventh move,
and now the flukey play is cramped and slow.'
(MARTIN AMIS, *MONEY*, 1984)

'It's completely wrong to think, for a single second, that Bryan Ferry and I were in competition with each other when *Pin Ups* came out. It was something the media engineered. While I was recording my album, a friend told me Bryan was working on his record of covers[2], and the two came out at the same time. Honestly, I've always loved Roxy Music – they opened for our shows on the Ziggy Stardust tour in 1972. Besides, I did a cover of "If There Is Something", didn't I? Okay, so it was with Tin Machine, but it counts! Not long ago, I saw Roxy Music on stage again and I thought they were fantastic. Superb. I go out quite a lot and see a lot of young people, but none of them come close to Roxy. They're modern, timeless and talented. I thought, "Shit, they're really excellent!" Okay, we miss Eno a bit, but they're great anyway!'

DB (2002)

On a promotional tour in France in 1991, David Bowie and his band Tin Machine appeared on a TV show, where he lip-synced 'You Belong In Rock N' Roll' (*Pin Ups* would show how wrong it was not to take that song title literally). As he sang, some girls in the audience started dancing in the style of Swinging London. Bowie said, right after, that he didn't need anyone to remind him of the 60s because he'd been there. He loved to tell everyone that he'd only chosen rock'n'roll as a means to achieve his goal, and that if another art form had allowed him to succeed sooner, he would have changed direction in a heartbeat. But despite this claim, David Bowie wasn't someone to simply scratch the surface of a subject, and he knew his rock through and through. Especially the music of the 1960s.

That day, while talking to the author, he realized his memories of France were a little hazy, even though he'd spent holidays there as a teenager and played Parisian clubs in late 1965 with his band The Lower Third. However, French culture was no mystery to him and throughout the conversation, he referred to Albert Camus, Eugène Ionesco, Gilles Deleuze, the Comte de Lautréamont, Jean Cocteau and Édith Piaf. That afternoon, he asked about Françoise Hardy and if jazz bands still played in the cellars of Saint-Germain-des-Prés. He'd just got married to Iman, and was planning to take her there.

Given he was in France, the conversation soon moved on to the recording of *Pins Ups* at the Château d'Hérouville. He had pretty good memories of his stays there, even though he never once expressed a desire to return to Auvers-sur-Oise (over the course of his career, Bowie returned to several studios he'd worked at, as a visitor, including Trident, Hansa and Sigma Sound) – Tony Visconti won't either, 20 years later. Jokingly, he remembered that at night, in their rooms in the *château*, he and the other musicians thought they saw or heard things, felt a presence. People said it was ghosts. The source of these visions may have been the drugs and alcohol they were consuming, but other visitors who were healthy in body and mind (as much as was possible in the 1970s), not only confirmed these accounts, but added to the mystery of the place. Ken Scott went to the Château d'Hérouville with Elton John in 1972[3], and Tony Visconti worked there as T. Rex's producer that same year[4], and both of them would also report strange happenings.

Discussing *Pin Ups* at the end of the afternoon in his suite at the Warwick in Paris, David Bowie mentioned Syd Barrett and recalled that his cover of 'See Emily Play' by Pink Floyd must have improved Syd's lot in the mid-70s[5]. He also mentioned Pete Townshend, whose confidence and talent fascinated him, and Pierre Laroche, who'd just succumbed to AIDS. Above all, Bowie made it clear that the British rock classics on *Pin Ups* (not necessarily well-known songs) were, above all, classic for him. Some tracks seemed obvious and others were suggested to him.

In early July 1973, while the public and the British music press are still reeling over David Bowie and The Spiders From Mars' farewell concert (David had confirmed to a journalist that he wasn't planning to play any more live shows in the near future), he arrives at the Château d'Hérouville with his entourage, including his wife, son, musicians, friends, a chef and a bodyguard. Ken Scott is travelling with them – he doesn't know it yet, but he is about to co-produce a Bowie album for the last time. Most of *Pin Ups* will be recorded in France (even the string section) but, like the previous three LPs, it will be completed and mixed at Trident, in August.

At the time, financial considerations were forcing a good many British musicians to record abroad – most of *The Slider* was taped at Hérouville, but sessions for that T. Rex album began in Denmark the year before. In the 1970s, English music stars used to pay a lot less tax in the UK on income from records that had been mostly (or partly) made elsewhere (some French pressings of *Honky Château* in 1972 had a sticker that said 'Enregistré en Europe'). Since then, the law has changed. Ken Scott, who has worked with Elton John and David Bowie, was adamant that it was the main reason they both went to record in France. All these musicians knew each other, so it seems likely that John advised Bolan to go to the Château d'Hérouville, and that he in turn recommended it to Bowie.

The Château d'Hérouville was an old coaching inn that reportedly witnessed the secret affair between Frédéric Chopin and George Sand. The film score composer Michel Magne purchased the place in the early 1960s and built a studio, the Strawberry, there. In 1973, there are two rooms: the Chopin and the better-equipped George-Sand, where *Pin Ups* will be recorded. Better known, even at the time, under its generic name the Château d'Hérouville[6], the Strawberry is one of the first so-called residential studios. Musicians can stay and eat there, and therefore can dedicate as much time as possible to their art.

Strawberry's brochure boasts of its technical excellence, but several artists and their technicians have reported faulty equipment or complained about the mediocre maintenance of tape recorders and consoles. In the booklet for the 2014 reissue of Jethro Tull's sixth album, *A Passion Play: An Extended Performance* (which was first published as an article by Martin Webb in *Record Collector*), Martin Barre will pull no punches when talking about the Château d'Hérouville. While he was there in 1972, recording the follow up to *Thick As A Brick*, the guitarist complained about the poor state of the equipment, especially that the tape machines were not properly wired up. Because of technical issues, Jethro Tull and their engineer Robin Black struggled to record anything good during these French sessions.

Like David Bowie and Tony Visconti each time they work there, members of Jethro Tull will also express serious reservations about the quality of the accommodation and food. The music the band recorded at Hérouville will never become an official record even though some songs will be reworked for *A Passion Play* and *War Child*. The Bee Gees will also come to the *château* in early 1976[7] to mix their live album *Here At Last...The Bee Gees.* According to Blue Weaver, their keyboardist during their rhythm'n'blues/disco years, the band will end up writing some new songs there because of technical issues. To kill time while waiting for repairs (and for equipment to be shipped from America), the three brothers will write and record early versions of songs that will appear in the film *Saturday Night Fever* and on its hugely successful original soundtrack.

When Ken Scott arrives at the *château* with Bowie, he complains about the absence of a drum booth, for avoiding sound 'spilling' when recording drums. Woody Woodmansey won't be bothered. Not long after the 'retirement gig', on the day of his wedding – which neither Mick Ronson nor David Bowie attended – Woodmansey received a phone call from Tony Defries to tell him he would not be travelling to France. While they were touring, Mike Garson had lured him into the sticky web of Scientology, and Woody had become a sort of spokesperson for the disgruntled Spiders From Mars who were annoyed that Garson and other musicians who joined them in early 1973 were paid better than the original members. Now Woodmansey was paying for his insolence[8].

Ronson and Bowie had spotted drummer Aynsley Dunbar less than a year earlier at the Winterland and he seemed to be a natural and capable successor to Woodmansey. In spite of tensions due to the recent events, Mick Ronson (he is already planning his solo career), Trevor Bolder (the most upset by Woody's eviction) and Ken Scott (he is bickering with MainMan over unpaid royalties from previous records) all commit fully.

Despite the notes' David Bowie hand-wrote on the back cover, the origins of *Pin Ups* and the reasons for making it have been the subject of much dispute over the years. One theory holds that he recorded *Pin Ups* just to give The Spiders something to do after they were left to their sad fate on 3 July. But this is very doubtful, even though Bowie publicly confirmed it. It is also unlikely that MainMan and he thought that releasing a collection of songs he didn't write, but that the American audience wouldn't know, could help him conquer the US market. There are no songs by The Beatles or The Rolling Stones on *Pin Ups*, but on the other side of the Atlantic, Pink Floyd, The Who, The Yardbirds, The Kinks and The Pretty Things weren't exactly unknown. Another explanation, and not the least probable, is that David Bowie was under pressure from MainMan and RCA to follow up *Aladdin Sane*, but he didn't have enough material in progress to fill an album. He probably thought, rightly so, that a covers album would allow him to stall them while he took a breath. Last but not least, one can't help thinking that, after helping out Mott The Hoople, Lou Reed and Iggy And The Stooges, the music lover in him wanted to reach out to other musicians, the ones he'd listened to when he was young. As if, before making his leap to the US, the next step in his career, he felt like thanking them.

In 1973, David Bowie claims he is looking to the future, and is therefore not inclined to nostalgia. Four decades later it will be clear that this was not the least of his untruths. As the exhibition *David Bowie Is* will reveal, he was a relentless 'collector' of things from his life. It's clear that the past, in its many forms, will haunt him until the end and will be, perhaps unconsciously, his main source of inspiration. The video of 'Where Are We Now?' (the song which will herald *The Next Day*) and the show, *Lazarus* will make this even more obvious.

In April 1974, a few months after moving into a new house at 89 Oakley Street in Chelsea (after a semester-long spell in actress Diana Rigg's posh apartment), Bowie will leave England, in body if not in mind, never to return except as a visitor. *Pin Ups* is clearly a parting tribute to London. David had known its wounded suburbs and then its beating heart; it was the source of fantasies which, since his childhood, had aroused his curiosity, and it fuelled his ambitions as a young man.

As a matter of fact, while choosing songs for *Pin Ups* with Mick Ronson and Scott Richardson (the ex-frontman of SRC[10], whom he'd met on the American leg of the Ziggy Stardust tour), David Bowie seriously considered including a new version of 'The London Boys' (he once described the track as the precursor to 'All The Young Dudes'), which he had penned seven years before, when the 'swinging' capital seemed inaccessible to him. Back when he was desperately hoping for his lucky break, he drew enough from the musicians who wrote (and played on) the original versions of the songs on *Pin Ups* to build himself up and wait. Bowie never just settled for listening to their records or going to see them live; he made damn sure he rubbed shoulders with them and learned as much as he could. *Pin Ups* is dedicated to these great artists, and that's how several of them took it.

The atmosphere at Hérouville is industrious. The backing tracks will be quickly recorded, and Trevor Bolder and Mike Garson will leave after just a few days. Aynsley Dunbar, who loves the Paris nightlife, will stay on a bit longer. Once again, Mick Ronson proves himself useful to have around. He plays several instruments, arranges most of the backing vocals and only leaves the studio to go to the dining room, with (string) scores under his arm. When they aren't working, David Bowie and his team enjoy merry meals together, and Ken Scott organizes table football matches. After everyone goes to bed, David sits down at the piano and composes new songs. It isn't unusual for the others to find him still there the next morning with bags under his eyes. Sessions mostly go smoothly, but sometimes the atmosphere at the *château* is fraught.

While David is giving interviews and friends drop by to see him, back in England, Tony Defries is juggling the fortune that RCA is continuing to dole out to finance his main artist's lifestyle and the many excesses of the MainMan teams in London, New York and Los Angeles. At the same time, he is syphoning off a big chunk of it. But the label will soon call MainMan to account and the foundations of the company are starting to crumble.

Before going to France, Ken Scott was told that they would have to put aside some time for mixing a live album of the Spiders' farewell concert – *Bowie-ing Out* is the proposed title. He didn't know, however, that Lulu was coming over to record a single. The Scottish singer was experiencing a dry spell and she and David had become friends during the tour – he'd met her at a hotel in June and she was at the party at the Café Royal. When Lulu walks into the studio, Scott gives up his seat at the console to an in-house recording engineer. Bowie's musicians play with her on covers of 'Watch That Man' and 'The Man Who Sold The World' (to which Bowie adds a Roxy Music vibe with his alto saxophone[11] while Ken Fordham plays the baritone). Mike Garson, who will later accompany Lulu live, lays down some electric piano tracks on both songs. These sessions are co-produced by Mick Ronson – 'The Man Who Sold The World' (with 'Watch That Man' on the B-side) will come out as a single in mid-January 1974 and will get to Number 3 in the British charts. Although she reached retirement age long ago, Lulu still sings today and, since 2016, 'The Man Who Sold The World' has been a staple in her live repertoire.

During those three weeks in July, David Bowie drafts another project, a sort of musical, with the working title *Tragic Moments*. A semi-instrumental piece called 'Zion' (in fact a succession of themes and variations fuelled by Ronson and Garson, on which Bowie, who doesn't have any lyrics yet, simply hums 'la-la-las') is the first brick of a building that will crumble shortly after, when *Diamond Dogs*' Hunger City springs up in his mind. As David may have already been thinking of a *Pin Ups II* when he was making the first one, they also record backing tracks for at least two additional songs: 'White Light/White Heat' by The Velvet Underground and The Beach Boys' 'God Only Knows'. As for Bowie's cover of 'Growin' Up' by Bruce Springsteen, featuring future Rolling Stone Ronnie Wood on guitar, it was not recorded at Hérouville but at Olympic Studios a little later (Bruce Springsteen's first album, *Greetings From Asbury Park, NJ*, had caught Bowie's ear earlier that year). And likewise, David's version of Jacques Brel's 'Amsterdam'[12] (available on the B-side of the 'Sorrow'[13] single in October) was not taped in France. It was immortalised at Trident two years earlier, during the first sessions for *Ziggy Stardust*.

Pin Ups is one of the few Bowie albums of whose production we have a visual record, in this case thanks to Mick Rock, Bowie's then official photographer. In July, David went to Paris for a photoshoot with Twiggy for the album cover. Justin De Villeneuve, the model's ex-boyfriend and then manager, took care of the shoot with the help of make-up artist Pierre Laroche. Born Nigel John Davies, De Villeneuve (who is not French) will later co-manage, with Bryan Morrison, the amazing Doctors of Madness. *Vogue* will turn down Tony Defries' offer to put this photo of Bowie and Twiggy on the cover of their magazine. In *Moonage Daydream: The Life And Times Of Ziggy Stardust*, David will explain that they refused because Twiggy (he thought of her because, in addition to being a 60s icon, her name rhymed with Ziggy) was already a bit passé in 1973 and also because *Vogue* was afraid of putting a man (!) on the cover.

Opinions differ regarding who was behind this photoshoot in the first place, but De Villeneuve always said that he and *Vogue* had come up with the idea.

Mick Rock shot the images of David Bowie, with his Paul Beuscher alto saxophone, used on the back of the cover (which he also designed) and on the inner sleeve. According to the panels at *David Bowie Is*, David's outfit was chosen as a nod to the style of Little Richard – he wanted a rock'n'roll touch to reflect the content of *Pin Ups*. It's very likely that this suit was purchased at City Lights Studio, stylist Tommy Roberts' London boutique. Freddie Burretti will later use it as inspiration for the Diamond Dogs tour's outfits.

Pin Ups is David Bowie's only album of covers (with *Toy* he will revisit his own songs and it won't be officially released during his life time). The LP divided opinion among critics when it came out on 19 October 1973, and continues to do so today. Faced with albums like this, music journalists tend to write that they prefer the original songs, but Bowie's versions of the ones he chose to sing (all excellent and beautifully performed by his musicians) are of a very high standard. Some were simply dusted off for *Pin Ups* ('Don't Bring Me Down' by The Pretty Things), some were revitalized ('Friday On My Mind' by The Easybeats[14]) and others were given a 70s touch ('Anyway, Anyhow, Anywhere' by The Who). But they all allowed multiple generations to discover their creators, members of bands they'd sometimes never heard of before, such as The Mojos and The Merseys. David Bowie, who shone his spotlight on The Velvet Underground in the 1960s and on Arcade Fire much later, was always happy to share his discoveries.

But that year, most Bowie fans swiftly decide that they prefer, not the originals, but these versions by the ex-Ziggy and his survivors from Mars, versions of songs like 'I Can't Explain'[15] by The Who (played at a slower tempo, from 140 down to 109bpm), 'See Emily Play' (with its cleverly planned chaos in the coda), The Yardbirds' 'I Wish You Would' (whipped up by an electric violin) and the cheeky 'Rosalyn', A-side of The Pretty Things' first single in 1964. The main thing for the fans is to prolong the thrill created by *Aladdin Sane*. And *Pin Ups* does just that, with cover songs no less thunderous than 'Let's Spend The Night Together' on the previous album. Overall, the public, especially the British, will show their approval by sending the album up the charts to the same spot occupied by *Aladdin Sane* seven months earlier – Number 1[16].

Only once will David Bowie play multiple songs from *Pin Ups* live[17] and that will be while filming *The 1980 Floor Show,* an episode of NBC's *The Midnight Special* shot at the Marquee[18]. The American public will miss out on the planned autumn tour, so Tony Defries and Burt Sugarman, the executive producer of the show, came up with the plan of dedicating an entire episode to Bowie. Under the direction of Stan Harris, filming lasts for three days from 18 to 20 October. *The 1980 Floor Show* marks the moment when Bowie says goodbye to glam forever. He is accompanied by Mick Ronson and Trevor Bolder (this will be their last appearance on stage with him), Mike Garson, Aynsley Dunbar, Mark Pritchett on additional guitar, and three backing vocalists known as The Astronettes – Ava Cherry, Jason Guess and Geoff MacCormack (this was also the name of the dancers at the Rainbow the year before). Matt Mattox helps to choreograph this farewell to glam and the musicians perform before an audience made up of members of Bowie's fan club and some other guests. David wears extravagant outfits for the last time, bringing back to life a still-warm Ziggy Stardust. Wanting to make a party out of it, he also invites The Troggs[19] to play, as well as Carmen and Marianne Faithfull (she and Bowie duet on 'I Got You Babe' by Sonny And Cher, and she performs Noël Coward's '20th Century Blues' on her own but surrounded by dancers).

At the exhibition *David Bowie Is*, the cobweb costume worn by Bowie during his performance of 'The Jean Genie' at the Marquee (the dancers at the Rainbow in 1972 sported similar ones) will be displayed and credited to Natasha Korniloff. However, when *The 1980 Floor Show* is aired in the US on 16 November[20], the closing credits, compiled by MainMan, will only list Korniloff as Amanda Lear's costume designer. During the show, Lear also duets with David (in a Freddie Burretti outfit) on 'Sorrow'.

Like Mike Garson, the brass section can hardly be seen on the programme, but they can be heard, especially on 'The Jean Genie' and '1984'/'Dodo', the devilishly funky-glam medley that shaped things to come. Actually they were on the far right of the stage, with no lights on them, almost hidden by white partitions, a bit like pianist Matthew Fisher when he played behind a hanging sheet at the Rainbow. As for Nicky Graham and Robin Lumley, who played before and after Fisher, they were usually relegated to the far left.

By not listing the names of the musicians (except The Astronettes) in the show's credits (which was, after all, quite heartbreaking for them), did David Bowie want to send a message that it was time to close Pandora's Box? The final track on *Pin Ups* is 'Where Have All The Good Times Gone'. On the back of the album cover, Bowie added an exclamation mark to the title of this Kinks song. But in late 1973, for Mick Ronson and The Spiders From Mars, a question mark would have seemed more fitting.

Mick Ronson	David Gilmour
Trevor Bolder	Roger Daltrey
Aynsley Dunbar	Jim McCarty
Mike Garson	Phil May
Ken Fordham	John 'Twink' Alder
Michel Ripoche	Amanda Lear
Ken Scott	Dana Gillespie
Dennis 'BlackEye' MacKay	James Williamson
	Mark Pritchett
	Neil Tennant

MICK RONSON

The more I recorded with Bowie, the more I became interested in production. I remember working hard on *Aladdin Sane* and *Pin Ups*, but not more than David, who was always master of his art. It's funny to see photos from the Château d'Hérouville. I look very bossy in them, but in my mind, I wasn't bossy at all. David asked me what I thought of his song selection and I may have suggested one or two more to him.

Bowie and his management treated me very well. It just got more complicated when Tony Defries got it into his head to make me a star. Maybe he thought he could pit us against each other, make me into a victim, I don't know. The only thing I cared about was the music. I went along with his plan and even though my two albums didn't sell very well, they gave me a lot of satisfaction, especially recording them. As for David moving on and wanting to try other things, I don't really have much to say about that. That's his nature and The Spiders were recruited because he wanted to evolve. In the months before the farewell concert, David became one with Ziggy Stardust. The situation couldn't really have lasted much longer. (1990)

TREVOR BOLDER

At Haddon Hall, we all lived together. In late 1972, in the US, we were all travelling on the same bus. Four months later, David was travelling without us, in a limo. I agreed to go and record *Pin Ups* in France because Mick Ronson was still there, but it wasn't the same without Woody. Sometimes I feel like Bowie used us, but those years with The Spiders were the best of my career. (1994)

AYNSLEY DUNBAR

In early July 1973, I was in London at Morgan Studios, working on *Berlin* with Lou Reed, when David Bowie phoned me up. I was rather amazed to hear his voice. Jim Pons, the bass player with Flo & Eddie, was a Bowie super-fan and he'd loaned me cassettes of his albums. It wasn't exactly my type of music, but I got interested in 'The Bewlay Brothers' and all that.

I wasn't working on 3 July and David invited me to the last concert of his tour at the Hammersmith Odeon, then to a party at a restaurant on Regent Street... Apart from Bowie and a handful of others, nobody could have guessed it was going to be the famous 'retirement gig'. On the phone, I did a stupid thing – knowing they knew each other and had worked together, I asked David if I could invite Lou. And he went, 'If you want to'. So I called Lou up to ask him to come with me. Next thing I know, even though it was planned to be a day off, Lou calls a recording session! He was so pissed that David had called me, he'd quickly organized a session! At the time, Bob Ezrin and Lou Reed were both using a substance that didn't exactly fill them with joy... That's one reason why I think *Berlin* is so dark and depressing...

So we did some recording we didn't have to do while Bowie was doing his show, but I told Lou I was still going to the party and he came with me. When we got there, he and David had a weird little chat, then we all sat down with a drink. I'm in some photos Mick Rock took that night, with Mick Jagger... In the end, David and Lou left in a friendly mood and only later did I find out that Bowie had actually wanted me to come up on stage with Jeff Beck during the show. That taught me to shut up!

Before I left, David asked me if I'd like to record an album with him and I obviously said yes. I think he wanted to know if I was interested before he fired Woody Woodmansey. He was just testing the water... Actually, Lou wanted us to keep on working together, but I thought David was a much better singer, so I jumped at the chance. He'd also asked Jack Bruce to replace Trevor Bolder on bass, but that didn't happen. I was fine with that because I always thought Bruce played too many notes! Which was okay in the studio, but if a bassist plays a million notes live, the rest of the band looks weak.

The Château d'Hérouville seemed charming – it had a feeling of quaintness – until you turned the tap on to take a shower! The plumbing was in such a state of disrepair that there was only a pathetic trickle coming out of the shower head, and if you wanted a bath, forget it! It was the worst for hygiene. Apart from that, I loved the place and we worked well there, without wasting any time. I can't say the same about sessions for *Berlin*... David hired me a limousine every night so I could go to the clubs in Paris. But seriously, I got along really well with Mick Ronson, who was a true co-arranger with David. Later, I also played on Mick's first solo album, and some songs that ended up on his second one. As for Mike Garson, he was great at what he did: he hurtled down the keyboard with real passion!

On *Pin Ups*, I came up with my own ideas. I changed the drum parts to suit me, rather than copying note for note what the other drummers had done. In fact, because I moved in different musical circles, I was used to playing on hit songs and I wasn't familiar with most of the tracks David had chosen. When he realized he was one short, I suggested 'Everything's Alright' by The Mojos, a band from Liverpool, my hometown, which I'd joined in the autumn of 1964.

We all got along well during those sessions and I liked the MainMan crowd. They were a bit mad and what have you, but that didn't bother me. I take people as they are! They were all very nice, ready to assist, all kisses and hugs! I don't know what I thought of David Bowie as a performer because I'd never seen him in concert before playing with him, and when we were recording *The 1980 Floor Show*, as the drummer I could only see him from behind! We didn't practise much for that show, and I had my work cut out with a whole repertoire to learn. Bowie was in complete control. His routines with Mick Ronson, especially on 'The Jean Genie', were absolutely spot on. (2017)

MIKE GARSON

What struck me most about France when I arrived there for the first time, was how narrow some of the streets in Paris were! It was fine in the country, where the Château d'Hérouville was, but in the city – in a taxi for example – I used to squeeze my shoulders together when a car came the other way. At the studio, the others often complained about the food, but I actually liked it. As for the place's strange vibes, they were a source of inspiration! I remember one cool but very quick recording, again conducted by Mick Ronson, who did it with such skill. In hindsight, I felt like he knew it would be the last David Bowie album he'd ever work on, so he gave it his all.

A few years ago, I was asked about my solo on 'See Emily Play'. I have to admit that I'd never re-listened to it since it came out on *Pin Ups*. Playing it again, I was blown away by it – not by the quality of my playing, but by how the solo was improved by David and Mick's arrangements. Ronson wrote some beautiful string parts for that song. Their ideas were all over the place, and Bowie made a point of experimenting, suggesting for example that the piano on 'Sorrow' go through a Leslie.

In those days – and I'm not proud of this – I was a bit of a jazz snob; I liked to brag. To begin with, I kept telling myself that compared with my standards, these Brits weren't making real music. Sometimes I wondered when I would go back to playing in my little smoky clubs in New York, where they paid me $5 a night. I was behaving like a spoiled brat who'd been brainwashed – 'If it's not this chord progression, if it's not that tempo, if it's not avant-garde enough, then I'm not interested.' Luckily, I soon realized how wrong I was. (1991/2016)

KEN FORDHAM

After Ziggy's farewell concert, I thought I wouldn't have anything more to do with David Bowie, but then the phone rang again! They asked me if I could go to France. I had to bring all my saxophones – the tenor, the baritone, and so on. I crossed the Channel and went to Hérouville, near Paris. Stuey George, David's bodyguard, was waiting for me at the station and he drove me to the *château*. I didn't stay for more than three or four days and, because I wasn't working the whole time, I was able to wander around, see the nearby farms. I also played in sessions with Lulu, who'd come to record a single with David. Were there any tensions with Ken Scott? You know, in those days, we didn't stop to ask: we were in the studio, we played, and that was it. (2016)

MICHEL RIPOCHE

In the early 70s, there weren't a lot of electric violin players around. There was Jean-Luc Ponty, who was at the conservatory with me and played jazz, Stéphane Grappelli, and an American violinist who accompanied Frank Zappa, whose name I can't remember[21]. While Grappelli made it onto a Pink Floyd record[22], I got the chance to work on *Pin Ups*. It was Bowie at his best – he was creative, but not too affected by chemical substances. Iggy Pop wasn't around and David was living on Marlboros and red wine.

You know, they often used to call me for sessions at the *château*. I can't remember if I'd already signed with Warner then... I'd started the band Zoo, but I was mostly just trying to earn a living so it was fine by me. I worked on a lot of soundtracks with Michel Magne... So basically, I spent a lot of time there and sometimes I even slept at the *château*! That's how I met Ken Scott's team – he was looking for a string quartet[23]. I got along well with Mick Ronson, who could read and write music, and did some of the arrangements too. The scores were quickly written, I set up the quartet and we spent two or three days with them.

David was almost always there and I only have good memories of him. He listened, he approved, he discussed the music and asked us what we thought. We recorded a lot of stuff and Ken Scott cut a lot out. At the time, we recorded on tape and soon deleted what didn't work. Bowie and Ronson only kept what they really loved. But we all enjoyed the experience and we were thrilled to be able to jam with a drummer like Aynsley Dunbar. As long as I was playing my electric violin, I was happy! *Pin Ups* is what it is, but recording it with this bunch of people was amazing.

Around midday, it was always amusing to see David wander in all dressed up, with his orange hair and red boots... In the evenings, after sessions, he sometimes asked me, 'Michel, are you going back to Paris?' I lived near Boulevard Saint-Germain and I often drank at a bar right next to Castel, a private club. Huguette Le Sénéchal was on the door of this private club, but I used to get in without a problem. So we took Bowie there, because he didn't have a car. The first time, Huguette said, 'Wow! You know David Bowie? You should bring him every night!' Everyone at Castel was thrilled! I don't know how he got back to the studio afterwards, but he obviously managed, because he was always there the next day.

On 'See Emily Play', Bowie asked us to play something classical[24], which we did for fun... We played for at least 15 minutes, so they didn't keep all of it! *Pin Ups* reminded me of The Mothers Of Invention's music. It was a bit wild, like Zappa's Mothers, and we let ourselves go completely. The guys who played with Bowie were amazing and when we weren't recording, we'd be jamming, having fun. Magne, who'd made quite a bit of money with his soundtrack for Jean Yanne, had invested in some good equipment. It was cool... Afterwards, I was told some sordid stories about Hérouville, but you have to take things like that with a pinch of salt. We did some really cool things there. Magne had created it all with his money; he must have been a bit mad... He knew how to welcome artists though: there were families staying there, children. In Elton John's day, Bernie Taupin came too, and there was a good atmosphere.

People tell me I was lucky to have met Bowie at that time. He always tried to create a mystique about himself for his audience, but he was a nice guy. He was thoughtful and polite. I can't say that about all the people I've worked with! He was so curious. If he had known how to play the violin, he would have. And if I remember correctly, they even paid us! (2016)

KEN SCOTT

Pin Ups was the last album we did together and the atmosphere was different. Woody Woodmansey had been fired on the day of his wedding and when Jack Bruce refused to play bass, David had to call in Trevor... I'd pay a lot of money to know what he told him! After that, Bowie more or less turned his back on glam rock and *Diamond Dogs* paved the way for the next era. I love *Pin Ups*, but sadly the recording was marred by my problems with MainMan. The quality of the record wasn't affected, but my relationship with David did suffer a bit. And my wife gave birth that summer so I had to leave for a few days...

In October 1973, I mixed *The 1980 Floor Show* and did my last session with David at Trident. He was listening to the first Barry White[25] on repeat and we worked with Mick Ronson and Trevor Bolder on an early version of '1984'/'Dodo'...

I didn't see David Bowie again for a while, mainly because of the legal dispute he was having with Tony Defries, which also affected me. My royalty payments weren't coming through... When I produced *Thank You* by Duran Duran, Nick Rhodes, who knew David, told me he might be coming round to do some backing vocals on their version of 'Diamond Dogs'. I'd just got divorced, I was living in Hollywood and one day, when I got home, I found a message from David on my machine. He wanted to talk to me about this cover. We continued our correspondence by email. When I went to see George Harrison at Friar Park in the early 2000s to sort out his master tapes, David asked me to pass on his regards. I did so at a dinner with Eric Idle. Eric told me he'd been the best man at David's wedding with Iman, which I didn't know. During his last tour, he played in Los Angeles[26] and I went to see him backstage afterwards, but it was so chaotic we didn't get to talk. (2016)

DENNIS 'BLACKEYE' MACKAY

There was nothing glamorous about Trident Studios – it was a pretty funky place, some might say rudimentary. Its reputation comes mainly from the songs recorded by the artists who worked there: Elton John, Queen, The Beatles, Carly Simon and David Bowie. A dream list by today's standards! Not to mention Lou Reed, who was high as a kite when he worked there, but David and Mick Ronson were able to get the best out of him: *Transformer*. Let's not forget Bowie was producing and writing for others too, in those days, including Mick. I did his first album with him, *Slaughter On 10th Avenue*, at the Château d'Hérouville. David came over in September 1973 because Mick needed words on three songs. He wrote them there and then and recorded the lyrics in no time at all. Three takes, one per song. Impressive! I tried to keep them, but Mick erased David's vocals after memorizing his melodies and intonations. It's often been said Mick didn't want to be the star MainMan wanted him to be... I can assure you that at least at one point he believed in it, and took it very seriously. (2016)

DAVID GILMOUR

Syd Barrett's personality and songs had a big influence on David Bowie. I remember really liking his cover of 'See Emily Play' on *Pin Ups*, but to be honest, I haven't listened to that in ages. (2016)

ROGER DALTREY[27]

I thought it was great that someone wanted to cover some songs by The Who – that doesn't happen very often! David was a real artist. He was a lot more than a singer or a composer. For me, it also meant Pete's work was being recognized. It was a hell of a challenge to take on those songs, but he did a great job. (2018)

JIM MCCARTY

It was a real surprise that David Bowie covered two Yardbirds songs. But what also surprised us at the time was that he did it so well! I think that in his mind, it was a way to pay tribute to his formative years, but we were also very honoured. At the same time, I always thought the best compliment he gave us was not 'I Wish You Would' or 'Shapes Of Things', but 'The Jean Genie', one of his own songs – on that he sounds like Keith Relf, even when he plays harmonica.

As a drummer, I was always at the back of the stage, but I knew he often came to see us at the Marquee... And Mick Ronson was also a huge fan of Jeff Beck. David Bowie was riding the glam rock wave at the time, but the success of *Pin Ups* really surprised us, especially because it wasn't made up of hits, but of songs that really meant something to him. I know some Bowie fans who say it's their favourite album!

David took a lot of inspiration from the Soho scene, and a lot of musicians of his generation, who were four or five years younger than us, had Yardbirds songs on their set lists. Of all the covers of our songs, David's are the ones we're most proud of. Oddly enough, I never met him or saw him live, and I didn't really follow his career. But it was a good Bowie album, that's for sure, and I liked what he was doing in the 70s. (2017)

PHIL MAY

Let's be honest – it was a surprise, a nice one, that David covered a couple of tracks by The Pretty Things on *Pin Ups*! Somehow, it made sense. We knew he loved the band – he never made a secret of that – and all of a sudden he was thanking us, in his own way. Until the album came out, we didn't know just how important we were to him. And I think that goes for all the musicians whose songs he covered – Pink Floyd, The Who, The Yardbirds. We're in damn good company! As for The Pretty Things, the interest generated by *Pin Ups* allowed us to make a come back at a time when we'd sort of become the princes of the underground... (2017)

JOHN 'TWINK' ALDER

I thought *Pin Ups* was really interesting, especially because of the choice of songs. David picked the ones he listened to back when he was still learning the ropes, which is a really nice tribute. He had really good taste. The two songs by The Pretty Things that he covered are their best ones. (2018)

AMANDA LEAR

I've spoken about my relationship with David Bowie so much that I feel like I'm harping on about it in every interview. I've just given another one in London for a new book on *The 1980 Floor Show* with Terry O'Neill's photos. Unfortunately, I can't talk much about music in relation to Bowie, because what we experienced was a love affair, out in the open and with his wife's blessing! But to be honest, the only musical period of Bowie's that I liked was that one. Obviously, I appreciated him singing 'Sorrow' for me at the Marquee. I didn't keep up with him any more after *Ziggy Stardust*, *Aladdin Sane*, *Pin Ups* and *Diamond Dogs*. I hated his disco songs, like 'China Girl'. I don't know if my musical opinion will be very useful to you[28]... (2017)

DANA GILLESPIE

Having seen them work together, I know how important Mick Ronson was in making the songs and albums that led to David's success. But I'll never say David depended on him. In the studio and elsewhere, the ideas always came from David and Mick just executed them. Bowie was the one who wrote the songs, and the others kind of did what he told them to do. You know, he would have succeeded with any musicians at that time. But Mick Ronson and The Spiders were there, and you can't take that away from them. A lot of people think that Mick, more than anyone else, suffered when the band broke up, but if you think about it, why would David continue with a British band when he only had eyes for America? He felt he was going to bring the country to its knees and he knew it was now or never. He lived fast, too fast for most people. I also think it was nice of him to help Ronno become a star in his own right after The Spiders broke up. Mick played the game and David supported him, but he wasn't cut out for it. It just wasn't him. (2016)

JAMES WILLIAMSON

It's probably well known that, from a personality perspective, I was not a friend of David Bowie but, on the other hand, I thought very highly of him as a musician, and as a producer for that matter. In those days, I got along really well with Mick Ronson, who was a terrific guy, an incredible arranger who was always straight up, while Bowie was like a different person every day... It was never proposed, but yes, Mick Ronson could have produced *Raw Power*! I think David Bowie learned a lot from him. I was really surprised when the two of them split up because Mick was a big part of David Bowie's music. Maybe that was the real reason behind the break up. David wanted to change his style, maybe to something Mick didn't like, and the split became inevitable. (2017)

MARK PRITCHETT

Mick was a breath of fresh air for David. A fine guitarist, yes, but much more than that. He ran the band by means of musical respect, thanks to his guitar playing, but also his ability to arrange. He arrived at Haddon Hall as a fairly tough Yorkshireman who said what he thought, when he felt the need. That said, he was a calm, quiet, thoughtful soul most of the time.

I doubt David ever thought of Mick as a 50/50 partner, just as I am in no doubt that David valued Mick immensely – as long as Ziggy remained something David wanted to continue with. Of course, by mid-1973, David could not imagine writing further Ziggy-based albums into his thirties and beyond, giving fake fellatio to Ronno's guitar to an ever-aging audience! After eighteen months, rather than the predicted five years, that incarnation was over. I can only imagine the hurt this surprise ending inflicted on Mick.

As far as I was aware, *The 1980 Floor Show*, as shot for NBC, was very much a Tony Defries strategy to make the Americans aware of David's imminent return to the States. The fact that a troupe of Warhol's Factory faces was present at the Marquee did nothing but reinforce that notion. The show itself was torturous – the place was tiny, so a two-camera set-up was as good as it got (causing multiple retakes per track to get enough angles); the room was hot (Mick had a particularly hard time with string breaks and tuning); the days were long and surprisingly tiring. For *The Midnight Special*, David wanted me to play a couple of tracks on a 12-string guitar. I had a 6-string, as did Ronno, but no 12-string. At rehearsal, David brought along his old Haddon Hall Hagstrom, saying something like, 'You remember this old girl?' After the gig, I took it home; David had split with his Warhol chums. A few months later, with David preparing to leave the UK, I reminded him I still had the guitar. 'Keep it, mate,' he said. 'And you can have the MK2 Jaguar as well – look after them!' And he was gone. (2019)

NEIL TENNANT[29]

As a 19-year-old Bowie fan in 1973, I thought this album of covers was part of the *Aladdin Sane/Ziggy Stardust* project. In the eighteen months before its release, I'd seen five Ziggy and Aladdin shows, and covers were integral to them: Chuck Berry's 'Round And Round', The Rolling Stones' 'Let's Spend The Night Together', The Velvet Underground's 'White Light/White Heat', even The Beatles' 'This Boy'. The recent rock past was acknowledged and dragged into Bowie's vision of the future. For Aladdin/Bowie to record an album of his favourite mid-60s rock club hits made complete sense.

In the early 1970s, nostalgia was chic. On Saturday afternoons, my friends and I hung out in the Art Deco palace that was the short-lived Biba superstore. We were there, in the Rainbow Room, when the wildly camp but ferociously rocking New York Dolls played their first London show in the same month as both Bowie and Bryan Ferry released their albums of cool covers. (One couldn't help wondering whether Bowie, always a huge admirer of Bryan Ferry, hadn't copied Ferry's covers concept.)

Bryan's album was more eclectic and nostalgic and introduced me to many 1960s' classics ('Sympathy For The Devil' and 'Don't Worry Baby', amazingly) that weren't on the handful of records under the Stereogram at home. Likewise, many of the songs on the more focused *Pin Ups* were obscurities to me – covers of songs by The Pretty Things, The Yardbirds or The Kinks that I'd never heard on the radio. 'See Emily Play' and 'Here Comes The Night'[30] were big hits though, and much more familiar. Both albums were lessons in rock history for glam rock teenagers. At the same time, I had developed a fascination for the 1960s and read George Melly's *Revolt Into Style*, Mary Quant's *Quant By Quant*, Christopher Booker's *The Neophiliacs* and other studies of the recent pop culture past. *Pin Ups* was the perfect soundtrack, performing the 60s as if they'd been the 70s; Twiggy, posing cheek to cheek with David Bowie on the album cover, visualized this exquisitely.

It was a shock to discover that Woody Woodmansey had been replaced on drums by Aynsley Dunbar, but the presence of Mike Garson on piano gave the album *Aladdin* authenticity. And I think we knew that Mick Ronson was preparing his solo career and that this was to be the last flowering of his magical collaboration with Bowie before he moved on, in theory, to solo stardom.

I seem to remember that critics were lukewarm about the album, but we, 19-year-olds, thought *Pin Ups* was fabulous and chic and rocked enough to sit next to the New York Dolls' debut album. Bowie was looking back before he moved forward. That much was understood. (2016)

1. The author first wrote about the recording of *Pin Up*s in his book *David Bowie Ouvre Le Chien* in 2015. Some snippets of information and a few paragraphs in this chapter come from that book.

2. *These Foolish Things*, his first solo album.

3. After four albums made at Trident, Elton John taped three at Hérouville between 1972 and 1973, including *Honky Château*, a direct reference to the French studio. At the start of his career, John often worked with three members of David Bowie's team: Gus Dudgeon, Ken Scott and Paul Buckmaster.

4. Ken Scott and Tony Visconti are not David Bowie's first colleagues to have worked at the Château d'Hérouville. In 1971, Tucky Buzzard, with Nicky Graham on piano, recorded part of *Warm Slash*, their second album, there.

5. In addition, in late 1973, EMI reissued Pink Floyd's first two albums under the title *A Nice Pair*. As a result, Syd Barrett's income will increase significantly the following year and David Gilmour will make sure he never lacks for anything until the end of his life. Barrett will regularly ask his publisher for money to buy guitars, but they will stop after Syd has acquired 30! At the time, Barrett's label rented him a flat, but he preferred to stay at the expensive Penta Hotel, where he loved calling room service at all hours of the day or night. David Bowie and Brian Eno were among the British artists who fell in love with Syd Barrett's music and will regularly try to work with him (and maybe even produce a record for him).

6. The *château* is in Hérouville, a village in Val-d'Oise, about 10km north of Pontoise and some 40km northwest of Paris. Some people

have confused this Hérouville with Hérouville Saint-Clair, near Caen, probably because one of the churches in Hérouville (Val-d'Oise) is called Saint-Clair!

7. That was also the year David Bowie returned for *The Idiot* and *Low* with Iggy Pop.

8. Woody Woodmansey usually told the journalists who interviewed him between the mid-70s and 2014 (when he forms Holy Holy with Tony Visconti), that his ousting from Bowie's band was due to musical differences. But in his autobiography, he will clear things up – apparently, he wasn't always happy to go along with the rest of the band and, for example, refused to wear any stage outfits he thought were too extreme.

9. 'These songs are among my favourites from the '64–'67 period of London. Most of the groups were playing the Ricky-Tick scene club circuit. Some are still with us.' Ricky-Tick was originally a club in Windsor where all the greatest emerging bands of the 1960s performed. It then became a circuit of venues (mostly pubs) that American musicians also played.

10. In the 1960s in Detroit, Scott Richardson was the frontman of The Chosen Few, one of Ron Asheton's pre-Stooges bands. His group SRC (previously The Scot Richard Case) only lasted two years, but they released three psychedelic albums, the first of which was influenced by The Pretty Things. It's called *SRC* and is well worth a listen.

11. Lulu's sessions were completed in late 1973 and early 1974 at Morgan and Olympic Studios, so it's possible that David Bowie recorded his backing vocals and saxophone parts there rather than at Hérouville.

12. 'Growin' Up' and 'Amsterdam' will be included in the Rykodisc reissue of *Pin Ups* in 1990. On the cover, Jacques Brel's song will be listed as 'Port Of Amsterdam'.

13. The only song from *Pin Ups* released as a single, 'Sorrow' was made popular in England in 1965 by The Merseys, but their version was a cover of a song written by Feldman-Goldstein-Gottehrer that had been recorded by The McCoys. The McCoys were Rick Derringer's American band known for their very famous hit 'Hang On Sloopy' (also a cover, of 'My Girl Sloopy' by The Vibrations). The release of 'Sorrow' was thwarted – and delayed – by Deram's reissue of 'The Laughing Gnome'. Nevertheless, 'Sorrow' will reach Number 3 in the charts. After 'Life On Mars?' it will be David Bowie's best selling single in 1973.

14. The Easybeats were Australian. All other bands whose songs appear on *Pin Ups* were British.

15. In his book, The Lower Third's drummer Phil Lancaster will write that the instrumental part of 'I Can't Explain' by David Bowie was a tribute to 'Shakin' All Over', a classic by Johnny Kidd & The Pirates. It certainly is a tribute to 'Let's Stick Together', a hit single by the American rhythm'n'blues musician Wilbert Harrison in the 1960s. The song is quite unusual because it is a blues with a simple but persistent riff – the same note repeats while the chords change. 'Let's Stick Together' was covered many times, most notably by Bryan Ferry, who named his 1976 album after it.

16. In the US, *Aladdin Sane* didn't make the Billboard Top 20, and *These Foolish Things* by Bryan Ferry will only reach Number 5 in the British charts. David Bowie only twice released

two studio albums in the same year: in 1973 and in 1977 (*Low* and *"Heroes"*). By comparison, The Beatles released two albums each year in 1963, 1964, 1965, 1967 and 1969. They only released one in 1966, 1968 and 1970. They all reached Number 1 in the British charts except for *Yellow Submarine* (which got to Number 3). *Magical Mystery Tour* also got to Number 1, but only in its original form, which was an EP.

17. He performed 'Sorrow', 'Everything's Alright' and 'I Can't Explain'.

18. David Bowie wanted the show to be filmed at the Hammersmith Odeon, but the budget didn't allow it. It was the last time he performed at the Marquee.

19. The Troggs, led by Reg Presley, could have had a song on *Pin Ups*. David liked their cover of 'Wild Thing' (written by Chip Taylor), which had been a hit on both sides of the Atlantic in 1966. Iggy Pop will say the British band was one of his favourites and, in the 1960s, when asked which group Paul McCartney could have joined other than The Beatles, he immediately said, 'The Troggs!' At *The 1980 Floor Show*, The Troggs played 'Wild Thing', while Carmen sang 'Bulerias'. Both bands were filmed playing other songs, but only those two aired.

20. The programme was only broadcast in the US. A restored DVD/Blu-ray version of the show would be nice because the clips from the concert and rehearsals that can be watched on YouTube are of mediocre quality.

21. Michel Ripoche is referring to Don 'Sugarcane' Harris.

22. In 1975, Stéphane Grappelli will play violin on the title song of the band's ninth studio album, *Wish You Were Here*, in a session at Abbey Road Studios. It was long thought that his part, mixed at a very low volume (to the point where the band will choose not to credit him on the jacket), had been erased. As part of the 2011 reissue campaign of the band's back catalogue, named *Why Pink Floyd...?*, the *Experience* box set of *Wish You Were Here* will feature another version of the song, with Grappelli's part 'found' and mixed at the right volume. It's also during these sessions at Abbey Road that Syd Barrett will pay Pink Floyd a surprising and upsetting visit. Michel Ripoche could also have mentioned that Jean-Luc Ponty, who was at Hérouville in early 1972 when Elton John recorded there (for the first time), played electric violin on two songs on *Honky Château*.

23. Violinist Pierre Llinares played in this ensemble. But actually, as can be seen in a photograph in *Station To Station*, Geoff MacCormack's book, there were at least six instrumentalists in the string section for *Pin Ups*. Later, when he lives in Normandy, Llinares will tell a journalist that David Bowie's assistant had asked the musicians who were planning to go to bed after dinner at Hérouville to stay in their clothes, in case there was an urgent need to record strings in the middle of the night.

24. Michel Ripoche does not remember recording at the same time as Mike Garson during sessions for *Pin Ups*, so his part on 'See Emily Play', a highlight of the album, was probably recorded after Garson's, who referenced Strauss, Mozart and Bach. Even though overdubs were later done at Trident Studios before mixing, Mike did play his parts in France. He recently told the author, 'They had a piano that was good.'

25. 'I've Got So Much To Give', released in early 1973.

26. David Bowie played Los Angeles three times on A Reality tour in 2004: on 2, 3 and 7 February.

27. Roger Daltrey's words were collected by Jonathan Witt, a *Rock&Folk* journalist who interviewed Daltrey in 2018.

28. Amanda Lear's openness justifies her presence in this book. Like Ava Cherry and, of course, Angie Bowie, Lear had a personal relationship with David Bowie while they were 'working' together. Because his personal life is not the subject of this book, Ava and Angie were not interviewed. This obviously does not detract from the vocal talent of the former and the role the latter played in Bowie's rise to fame. They both were told of the existence of this book and its angle was explained to them. An exception was made for Hermione Farthingale, because she is the only one whose name appears in the title of a Bowie song. In her autobiography *My Life With Dalí* (Virgin Books, 1985), Lear mentions David Bowie's fascination with Dalí, for whom she was a muse, and says David was the one who urged her to pursue a singing career. However, the film adaptation of *Octobriana And The Russian Underground*, Petr Sadecký's book, which Bowie often mentioned (and for which Amanda was supposed to play the lead), never saw the light of day. But she did take part in *The Midnight Special* and Bowie invented a Russian-sounding nickname for her: Dooshenka. Terry O'Neill, the official photographer who arrived on the second day of filming, has published a book about the show – *When Ziggy Played The Marquee* (ACC Art Books, 2017).

29. The Pet Shop Boys frontman saw David
Bowie on stage for the first time on 2 June 1972
in Newcastle. The following year, after having
moved to London, Neil attended both July
concerts at the Hammersmith Odeon, as well
as the one at the Gaumont State Theatre in
Kilburn the month before. David introduced
Mick Ronson as Suzi Quatro at that show.

30. In early January 2016, Van Morrison, who is
a very reserved character, will post a message on
his website: 'I'm sorry to hear of the passing of
David Bowie. A genuinely original artist who
always had something to say.' Morrison sang
'Here Comes The Night' – covered by Bowie
on *Pin Ups* – with Them, and it was the A-side
of the band's third single in 1965. The song was
written by American songwriter and producer
Bert Berns, whose name is associated with other
hits like 'Twist And Shout', 'Baby Please Don't
Go' and 'Piece Of My Heart'.

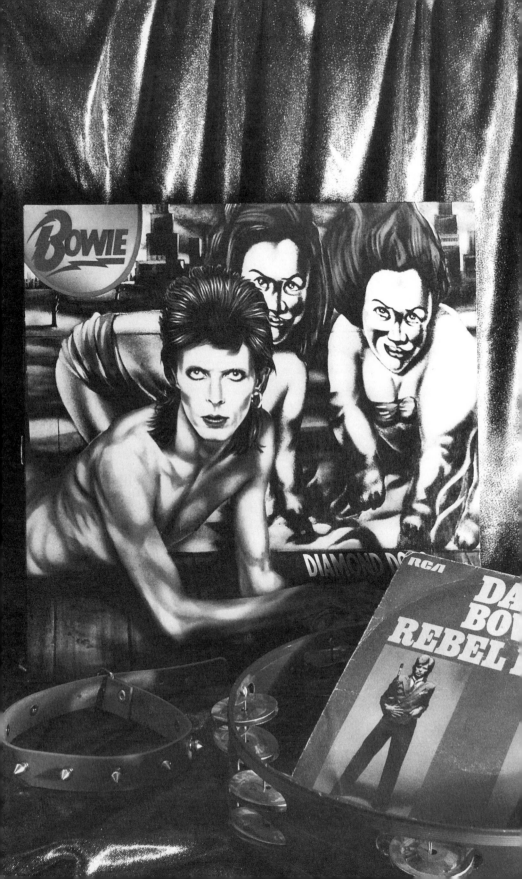

DIAMOND DOGS

RCA – 24 MAY 1974

DAVID LIVE (RCA – 29 OCTOBER 1974)

'I feel like a wet seed wild in the hot blind earth.'
(WILLIAM FAULKNER, *AS I LAY DYING*, 1930)

[Looking at himself dressed up as Halloween Jack on the April 1982 cover of *Rock&Folk*] 'Ah! The increasingly skeletal look. I don't look great, do I? It was a pretty rough time for me. I'm very glad I survived those years. Because that's exactly what it was. I have much worse photos than this from that tour. I look terminally ill', dreadful, it's horrible to see them. Maybe that was the price of artistic rebirth? I was free-wheeling and I still wonder... Would I have made a *cadavre exquis*? Ah, good one, I hadn't thought of that. Very good! Everything was going so fast. My every move was being analysed, dissected. The pirate look from the "Rebel Rebel" video wasn't supposed to be a pirate, you know. I had conjunctivitis that day and the only way to hide it was with an eye patch.

'*Diamond Dogs* was a transitional album and it's one of my favourites. It straddles two eras. Carrying the weight of a record on my frail shoulders, while the two previous ones had got me to the top of the charts, was very risky and my management tried to talk me out of it. And the theatrical tour was madness, really. Part of me was slowly dying while the other was picking up the pieces, one by one. It took me a decade to get myself back together. The only way forward was to hold on to the branches of my past. And this *A Clockwork Orange* t-shirt I was wearing in the photos with William Burroughs! It's funny to think that two or three years later I would be dressing like him...

'Let's talk about the cover of Peellaert's book, *Rock Dreams*. At least you can see me on the French cover! In some countries I was on the far right of the image and I was cut out. Guy should have drawn me in Dylan's place, right in the middle!'

DB (2003/1991)

David Bowie was moving fast. He wasn't hanging around. It was almost impossible to keep up with him – even his shadow was struggling. Bowie was aware of this, but he didn't feel like he was overdoing it. The momentum was stronger than him. In mid-November 1973, the new editor of *Rolling Stone* magazine, A. Craig Copetas, set up a joint interview with David Bowie and William Burroughs (the article would come out on 28 February 1974, in issue number 155). The musician must have been surprised when the writer mentioned 'Eight Line Poem', a short song (hence its title) on *Hunky Dory*. People rarely asked him about this one. And when Burroughs, the author of *Nova Trilogy* and *The Wild Boys,* compared the lyrics of 'Eight Line Poem' with *The Waste Land*, Bowie stepped back, declaring he'd never read T.S. Eliot's poetry.

Four decades later, Eliot's poem – a 433-line modernist epic from 1922, an extravagant tale of the fall of the West, the decay of classical culture, the loss of moral and aesthetic direction, and general disillusion – would be on Bowie's list of top reads. Conversely, while the panels of the exhibition *David Bowie Is* will mention his inspiration from Burroughs' work, none of the author's publications will feature in his list of favourite books. While David Bowie has implied that *The Wild Boys* helped to shape Ziggy Stardust, from the beginning of the 1970s he often said he was using the cut-up method of writing developed by Brion Gysin, which William Burroughs applied. Burroughs' sci-fi novel *Nova Express*, published in 1964 as a fold-in (juxtaposing two pages of text, folded vertically, to obtain a third one), had a big impact on Bowie's artistic methods, which he deployed to great effect on *Diamond Dogs*[2]. Bowie was not familiar with T.S. Eliot's work at the time of the Copetas interview, but it's safe to assume that he quickly got his hands on a copy of *The Waste Land*.

Faced with Eliot's unsettling telescoping of different fragments (ages, narrators, themes), which had exceptional evocative power, David Bowie will draw a huge amount of inspiration from it. George Orwell's novel *1984* will have the same effect on him and he will approach Orwell's widow for the rights to make a stage adaptation of the book. Upset and disappointed by Michael Anderson's cinematic adaptation in 1956, she will refuse.

The material on *Diamond Dogs*, the true successor to *Aladdin Sane* (*Pin Ups* was just a way to play for time), is so diverse because, in 1973, Bowie was pursuing more than one idea. Besides offering a new interpretation of Orwell's work, he wanted to see Ziggy Stardust expand within the framework of a theatrical performance, whose nature was yet to be defined – according to his creator, Ziggy's 'suicide' wasn't his end, it was the start of his journey into a new era: eternity. David Bowie was gathering together material for these two projects at the same time, but although they started out as separate entities, they would eventually merge into one.

Musically, *1984* led him towards a form of soul music which he would spend several months refining. This is clear from the trial and error in the making of the first versions of '1984', which was initially recorded during sessions for *Aladdin Sane*. Ken Scott also taped the song in October (the month of *The 1980 Floor Show*), with what remained of The Spiders From Mars, but they reportedly showed their inability to master the new musical genre Bowie wanted to explore. The same could be said about 'Dodo', previously promised to Lulu under the name 'You Didn't Hear It From Me'. David also had a couple of rock songs reminiscent of The Rolling Stones – 'Diamond Dogs' and 'Rebel Rebel' – meant for the Ziggy Stardust project. And because his words often flowed from his own experiences (good and bad), his feelings during the trip he'd taken with Geoff MacCormack earlier in the year, particularly the shock of what they'd seen behind The Iron Curtain and the hostility of certain travellers and authorities they'd met along the way, would reinforce the dystopian character of Bowie's work in progress, making it darker and more serious.

In October 1973, while Mick Ronson is at Trident Studios putting the final touches to his first album, David Bowie starts his next at Olympic Studios. Olympic is in Barnes, southwest London, an elegant suburb where many artists live. The studio is particularly well equipped at the time and has already hosted the very best of rock music: Jimi Hendrix, Led Zeppelin, Pink Floyd and The Beatles all worked at Olympic, and The Stones have made most of their records there since *Their Satanic Majesties Request* in 1967. Bowie was searching for a new sound, so he'd decided to leave Trident and Ken Scott behind. He is now handing his songs over to Keith

Harwood, the in-house recording engineer. Harwood is more rock'n'roll than Scott: he wears a leather jacket, drinks a lot and has nothing against drugs. This works out well for David, who is starting to use more and more himself, while drug references pervade his lyrics. In September, he went to see a Rolling Stones concert. He loves their sound and hits it off with Mick Jagger. Together, they will go to see Mott The Hoople live and Bowie will sing backing vocals on 'It's Only Rock'n'roll (But I Like It)' by The Stones[3].

For the rhythm section, Bowie called on Herbie Flowers and Aynsley Dunbar, who is replaced by Tony Newman after a few sessions. Newman isn't yet a British drum legend, but he's already worked with Gene Vincent, The Everly Brothers, Sounds Incorporated and, like Dunbar, The Jeff Beck Group. Already in high demand, he's on *Beck-Ola*, their second album. So is Ronnie Wood, who played bass on that record and probably advised Bowie to give Newman a try. Wood is the surprise guest at the Olympic sessions – he plays guitar on 'Growin' Up', a cover of a song on Bruce Springsteen's first album. They also record a draft of 'It's Hard To Be A Saint In The City' – another Springsteen song from the same LP – that will be taped again, the following year, at Sigma Sound Studios in Philadelphia (with strings arranged by Tony Visconti). Bowie was a big fan of Springsteen from the start – as he was of Biff Rose and Ron Davies – so he will help The Astronettes cover 'Spirit In The Night', a third song from *Greetings From Asbury Park, NJ*. They also record at Olympic this autumn, but the album will never officially be released[4].

Mike Garson, the only survivor of the *Pin Ups* sessions (Trevor Bolder was in a preliminary session for *Diamond Dogs*, but nothing came of it), is on piano, Mellotron, synthesizer and other keyboards. Alan Parker, the guitarist for Blue Mink, will join them for a few songs. As for David Bowie, he takes care of the vocals (no other backing vocalist will be mentioned in the credits), the saxophone parts and most of the guitars (mainly electric this time – his guitar playing is excellent on *Diamond Dogs*). After Garson leaves for the day, he usually adds more synth parts. Although Bowie is known for being swift in the studio, he will spend quite a lot of time on his new machines to extract the sounds he wants.

That autumn, while Tony Ingrassia is in London to help him with his projects, David Bowie gets the news that MainMan hasn't been able to secure the rights to *1984* from Sonia Orwell. Even though he knew she usually turned down all requests like his, Bowie will be angry with Tony Defries for not being persuasive enough or perhaps not offering enough money[5]. He will be disappointed, but he will do what he usually does when faced with an obstacle: he will find a way around it.

David is going to redouble his efforts to create his own dystopia. After agreeing to play a few notes of saxophone for British folk-rock band Steeleye Span, who were recording a Phil Spector song with Ian Anderson (the singer and flautist of Jethro Tull) at Morgan Studios, he goes straight back to his own songs. His Christmas break (which he spends with his family and friends at Oakley Street) is short. By the New Year, he's found a way to record his first version of 'Rebel Rebel' on his own.

Maybe David Bowie didn't always make his label happy in 1973, but at least he made them money – on 31 December, RCA presented him with an award for selling more than a million records since his signing, and having six albums in the British charts that year.

Things with Tony Defries aren't going so well. An unpaid bill is causing friction between Olympic and MainMan (the accountant at the Château d'Hérouville will have the same problem), so Bowie moves to Island Studios for a few days. That's probably also why he takes advantage of an opportunity in February 1974 to work at two Dutch studios while he's on a promotional trip to the Netherlands, doing interviews and singing his new single 'Rebel Rebel' on local television. He records at Soundpush in Blaricum, near Amsterdam, used by Shocking Blue, a famous local band; and Luc Ludolph's studio in Nederhorst den Berg, near Hilversum.

Not much is known about these sessions except that, not wanting to be disturbed and believing he no longer needed to answer to Defries, Bowie seems to have booked them on the quiet (with RCA's approval), then kept them secret. According to his schedule at the time, this clandestine trip only lasted for ten days or so, but he did work on some songs (among them was 'Diamond Dogs') at Ludolph's with the help of Jan Willem, a young recording engineer who was the son of the studio owner. Willem said Bowie primarily used these sessions to explore new sounds, reportedly trying out a 'white British synth-guitar'[6]. As for Dutch television producer Ad Visser's theory – that David came up with the name 'Diamond Dogs' after seeing the word 'diamonds' on the wall of a museum from the window of his hotel room in Amsterdam[7] – it doesn't seem likely. He had started to write this song a year earlier, and the word 'diamond' was already in its title.

In early March, unhappy with some of the mixes he's made with Keith Harwood, David Bowie decides to call Tony Visconti. Freddie Burretti took inspiration from Carmen, the band Visconti is working with at the time, when making the Hispanic outfit worn by Bowie in the Netherlands and on an upcoming photo shoot with Terry O'Neill. Bowie and Visconti haven't worked together since

The Man Who Sold The World, and the producer is still riding the wave of T. Rex's success, even though he's ended his collaboration with them. Marc Bolan's formula was no longer working its magic. A year before Bowie, Bolan had started to inject some soul music elements into his sound but, even so, *Zinc Alloy And The Hidden Riders Of Tomorrow – A Creamed Cage in August*, his last album with Tony, did not improve his ranking in the charts. Visconti was still making good money from T. Rex, however, so he took the decision to buy a house in Shepherd's Bush and set up a very good home studio there. Soundproofing the room had been more complicated than expected, but the equipment was of the highest quality – a 16-track MCI tape recorder, a Trident console made by Michael Toft, Klein & Hummel loudspeakers and several sound processors, including a brand new digital delay made by American company Eventide[8]. So when Bowie asked him if he knew a good studio where he could finish his record, Visconti suggested his own.

The first session is a bit rough and ready – there is no furniture, so they sit on sawhorses to mix 'Future Legend' together. In his autobiography, Tony says David called him the following morning at dawn to tell him he liked the sound of it and wanted to mix the rest of the record in his studio. That same day, MainMan delivered two armchairs to Visconti's house for the control room, a table, some chairs, cutlery and crockery. When he arrives, Bowie says it is a gift to celebrate their professional reunion. It will allow them to work more efficiently and take their meals there – food, washed down with excellent red wine, will be delivered by some of the best restaurants in London. Before leaving for the United States at the end of the month, David Bowie finalizes the mix of *Diamond Dogs* at Tony Visconti's.

The title of the album was revealed to Terry O'Neill and Belgian artist Guy Peellaert; he called both for its cover. Mick Jagger had sung the praises of Peellaert and Bowie met him when he came to London to launch *Bye Bye, Bye Baby, Bye Bye/ Rock Dreams*, his illustrated book of rock musicians from the 1950s to the 1970s with words by Nik Cohn. A picture of Josephine Baker lying on the ground inspired David Bowie's pose in O'Neill's photograph. Guy Peellaert will use it as a starting point to create the illustration – it evokes the atmosphere of an old-fashioned funfair or freak show[9]. The bright orange tones reference Ziggy Stardust's hair and Halloween Jack, a character Bowie is still developing. Peellaert has already used a similar theme, inspired by *Freaks*, the 1932 Tod Browning film, for 'The Greatest Show On Earth', a double-page spread in *Rock Dreams* which depicted musicians whose deaths, all at 27, were symbolic of the 1960s and 1970s (Jim Morrison, Brian Jones, Janis Joplin and Jimi Hendrix). Today, it seems clear that Bowie wanted the final depiction of Ziggy – sporting his iconic haircut – on a lavish album jacket, to be a tribute to his most famous character who had become... a freak[10].

Inside the jacket (a gatefold cover – the original British *Pin Ups* didn't open) is a Leee Black Childers' faded photomontage of a dystopian city, the infamous Hunger City. At the time, Childers was on MainMan's payroll, so rumour has it that Tony Defries didn't have to pay him an extra dollar. Meanwhile, on the other side of the Atlantic, blinded by his lust for success, the manager is starting to imagine himself as a film mogul and is seriously thinking of buying RCA...

Another sign that an era is coming to an end is that in March 1974, David Bowie sees two previously very close associates of his soar to a fleeting success of their own. Bowie remotely helped Mick Ronson with his first album, *Slaughter On 10th Avenue*, which is released at the beginning of the month. During his final tours with The Spiders From Mars, Bowie had sometimes talked to Ronson about his solo career[11]. It was he who advised his guitarist to cover 'Slaughter On Tenth Avenue' (he even gave him a copy of the record), which American musician Richard Rodgers had written for a George Balanchine-choreographed ballet piece in *On Your Toes*. Playing in theatres in 1936, *On Your Toes*, adapted from a Lorenz Hart libretto, was one of the first musicals on Broadway to mix jazz and classical music. Twelve years later the piece appeared in *Words And Music*, a fictionalized film based upon Rodgers and Hart's meeting and fruitful collaboration, and again, in 1957, in *Slaughter On 10th Avenue*, a film noir by Arnold Laven whose script had nothing to do with the ballet, but had retained the title and music. David Bowie thought the plot twists and theatrical approach summed up all there was in a Spiders From Mars show, and that Mick Ronson, therefore, would feel comfortable with it. David Bowie will also write 'Growing Up And I'm Fine' for Mick (the chorus from 'Changes' can be sung over its chorus), the lyrics to 'Hey Ma Get Papa' (making it the only song they penned together) and those to 'Music Is Lethal', the British version of 'Io Vorrei... Non Vorrei... Ma Se Vuoi' by Italian singer Lucio Battisti, which Ronson had heard while on holiday in Rome.

Also on the album are 'Love Me Tender', whose lyrics Elvis Presley reportedly co-wrote to music by George R. Poulton, and 'I'm The One' by Annette Peacock – both of these songs directly relate to what Bowie and Ronson experienced together. Mike Moran recorded 'Love Me Tender' at RCA Studios in New York, right after 'The Jean Genie'. Ex-Spiders Trevor Bolder and Mike Garson play on Mick Ronson's record, as does Aynsley Dunbar on drums. The release of *Slaughter On 10th Avenue* will be preceded by two concerts at the Rainbow (the first and last time David Bowie will see Mick Ronson live as a solo artist) and a brief British tour will follow. Bowie and Ronson's bond will weaken once they are separated by the Atlantic Ocean and, in 1975, David's sole contribution to *Play Don't Worry*, Mick's second LP, will be to grant him the right to use the playback of 'White Light/White Heat' from the *Pin Ups* sessions, as a backing track for his vocal. Some of Bowie's fans – heavy-hearted and somewhat short-sighted – will never forgive him for parting from Ronson.

Weren't Born A Man, Dana Gillespie's first album for RCA, is also released in March. Bowie and Ronson co-produced two of its tracks: her version of 'Andy Warhol' and 'Mother, Don't Be Frightened', which Dana wrote herself. Both songs were recorded at Trident in 1971. Rick Wakeman can be heard on the latter, which also features a superb string arrangement by Mick Ronson. The following year, Dana Gillespie will release a second blues-rock album for RCA with a rather misleading title (*I Ain't Gonna Play No Second Fiddle*). The MainMan logo on the cover will be its only link to David Bowie.

David's last studio session as a Londoner takes place a few days before he leaves for New York. With Lulu at Olympic, they record takes for 'Can You Hear Me' (initially called 'Take It In Right'), which he's written for her. After a quick stop in Paris, David Bowie and Geoff MacCormack take a train to Cannes and set off on the ocean liner *SS France*. Without knowing it, at 27 years old, Bowie is leaving England for good. He will return from time to time, usually for work, but only as a visitor. Despite his assertion that he was not interested in his own past, David Bowie will sometimes feel the need to revisit or to share the London he loved. In the early 1990s he will return to St Anne's Court to find that Trident is no longer there. In 2014, after he's been diagnosed with the illness that will claim his life, he will return one last time. With his wife and daughter, they will drive slowly past the places of his youth and, as a farewell gift, he will treat himself to one last view of his hometown, from the top of the London Eye.

No one saw her coming, let alone going, as she would end up staying until the end. As she explained in 2001 in a Q&A on BowieNet, Corinne 'Coco' Schwab started working for MainMan in the spring of 1973, after replying to an ad in the *Evening Standard*: 'Girl Friday for a busy office'. Born in New York to French parents (a photographer/war correspondent father and psychotherapist mother), Coco spent her childhood in India, Haiti and Mexico. That year, she'd been planning a road trip across the United States, by bus with a photographer friend; the editor-in-chief of a magazine had promised to publish an article about their trip. Their advance didn't completely cover the cost of the journey, so the two friends decided to work until they had earned enough to pay for it.

In May, a few weeks after Coco started at MainMan, she met David Bowie at a party at Haddon Hall to celebrate his return from Japan. She spent more time with him in early 1974 and she even went to some mixing sessions for *Diamond Dogs*. However, once she'd put aside enough money for her trip, she told David she was leaving MainMan. He asked her to forget her Greyhound trip and accompany him on his next tour of America instead. Coco would still be able to see the US, but with him, through the windows of his limousine. Although she wasn't really into rock music, she accepted. A few months later, much more than just a simple assistant, Coco will manage most of David Bowie's logistics and go out of her way to help the artist in him shine through. At the beginning, she will have a lot to do. Her first decade with Bowie will be the one he spends trying to extricate himself from the clutches of MainMan, a destructive addiction to cocaine and a meaningless marriage.

Criticized by those who pretend not to understand that she was only performing the (sometimes thankless) role which David Bowie assigned to her, Corinne Schwab will end up being, for nearly forty-five years, the key member of an entourage which, with time and the logical reaction to the MainMan years, will shrink to just a handful of people. Even though some of them didn't understand her, a lot of musicians, producers, record company people and journalists who worked directly with Coco all agree that, in addition to having saved the day for Bowie several times (not to mention his life), she was his best friend. She was dedicated to him and his art (one and the same thing), a sort of right-hand woman (even though David was left-handed) and, after having shown absolute discretion for almost half a century, she returned to the shadows with her memories after David died. Any editor would pay handsomely for her secrets, but a betrayal would simply be unimaginable. David Bowie shot back at anyone who expressed doubt about her, saying, many times, that aside from her talents as an organizer and protector, he enjoyed Coco's company and conversation. It seems likely that when he told his team what he had in mind for the show, *The Year Of The Diamond Dogs*, Coco – whose father was known for photographing the atrocities of the concentration camps at the end of World War II as the allies chased out the Germans – must have been attentive and receptive[12].

Bowie's fascination with the portrayal of dystopia in Fritz Lang's *Metropolis* (the 1926 film whose aesthetic was inspired by Manhattan's skyscrapers), Robert Wiene's *The Cabinet Of Dr Caligari*[13] and, more generally, German expressionist cinema, which was the product of the art and literature of the time, inspire the stage set of his next show. Likewise, as he read *1984*, Bowie's imagination was coloured by the idea of totalitarian domination as Lang interpreted it (Lang's wife and screenwriter Thea von Harbou had remained loyal to the Nazi party, which was fascinated by *Metropolis*, after its rise to power). Also shaping Bowie's thoughts will be comparisons between Wiene's film and the rise of Adolf Hitler, especially those expressed by author Siegfried Kracauer in *From Caligari to Hitler – A Psychological History of German Cinema*, which had been published in 1947. While there are no skyscrapers to speak of in *The Cabinet Of Dr Caligari*, aesthetically, the city created for the set of the Diamond Dogs tour (Hunger City), will pay homage to the work of Hermann Warm, Walter Reinmann and Walter Röhrig, the film's set designers. Warm was one of the first to suggest to German expressionist directors they replace painted canvas backdrops with wood and cardboard constructions to create a sense of depth. And instead of using horizontal and vertical lines and right angles, Warm preferred diagonals and vanishing points, which gave his sets a dreamlike and distorted appearance. Strangely enough, the Hunger City set will not make any reference to funfairs or freak shows.

David Bowie is back in New York in mid-April and moves into a luxury suite at the Sherry-Netherland Hotel[14], while his team takes up the rest of the floor. Soon after his arrival, he gets to know two people who will become very important to him: guitarist Carlos Alomar and composer and orchestral arranger Michael Kamen. Bowie meets Alomar at RCA Studios where he's booked time, initially so he and Geoff MacCormack can add percussion and backing vocals to the multi-track tape of 'Rebel Rebel'. This salsa-accented version will come out as a single in the US the following month (salsa was everywhere in New York clubs that year). During those same sessions, David Bowie, joined by Carlos Alomar, continues to work on *Can You Hear Me* – he is increasingly determined to turn Lulu into a soul singer. Like John Lennon, David's fallen in love with singer Ann Peebles, who's just released her album *I Can't Stand The Rain* at the same time as a single of the same name.

Alomar is 23 years old, born in Puerto Rico, and has played with Listen My Brother, a 15-member collective that performed regularly when Peter Long was producing shows at the Apollo Theater in Harlem. Long's wife Loretta was Susan on *Sesame Street*, a children's show that aired on PBS (with puppets made by Jim Henson) and Listen My Brother was the house band. Later, three other members of

Listen My Brother will work with David Bowie: singer Luther Vandross, drummer Fonzi Thornton and vocalist Robin Clark (whom Carlos Alomar had married in December 1970[15]).

David Bowie and Carlos Alomar hit it off immediately. As well as being a distinguished musician and arranger, Alomar knows all the young players on the New York music scene, some of whom will work on Bowie's next LP. David wants to record it that year in a city with a strong history of soul/rhythm'n'blues, so first he thinks of Memphis, where producer Willie Mitchell (who is working with Al Green, Ike And Tina, and Ann Peebles) runs the Royal Studios and the label Hi!. But he'll finally opt for Philadelphia and Sigma Sound.

In New York, David Bowie attends concerts (Todd Rundgren, Roxy Music and Television) and often goes to the Apollo. He and Carlos Alomar see B.B. King and Marvin Gaye there, as well as bands like The Temptations, The Spinners and The O'Jays. He's also invited to the premiere of a ballet documenting the life of sculptor Auguste Rodin at the Harkness Theatre. Michael Kamen, a New Yorker and Juilliard graduate who plays oboe and keyboards, has composed the music for it. Kamen is also a fabulous arranger who will go on to work with famous pop and rock musicians such as Pink Floyd, Queen, Eric Clapton, Kate Bush and, not long before his death, Coldplay. Bowie is impressed by his orchestral arrangements, so after the show, he asks Kamen to be the musical director for his upcoming tour. Michael Kamen agrees and will help David find the musicians he is missing. Mike Garson feels less lonely when he, Herbie Flowers and Tony Newman are joined by some other Americans: David Sanborn and Richard Grando on the saxophones, and Pablo Rosario (who's played with Celia Cruz and Mongo Santamaria) on percussion.

The guitarist proves more difficult to find, however. Unhappy with the money Tony Defries offered him, Carlos Alomar turned down the job and Keith Christmas, whom David Bowie invited to New York with that position in mind, didn't work out. So Kamen suggests Frank Madeloni, from Staten Island, who goes by the name Earl Slick[16]. Like Sanborn, he's played live with the New York Rock & Roll Ensemble, a fusion band (mixing rock and classical music) started by Michael Kamen and other Juilliard students. At 22 years old, talented and confident, Slick will be the perfect fit. Two vocalists and dancers (Geoff MacCormack and Gui Andrisano) will also join Bowie's team – Toni Basil, a choreographer from Philadelphia who worked on *American Graffiti*, George Lucas' second film, released in 1973[17], will have them dancing around Halloween Jack during the show.

As he prepares to launch *Diamond Dogs* and its tour, David Bowie has no illusions about his future with MainMan, but the company has convinced RCA to dedicate an enormous budget to a promotional campaign. This includes a television ad, a rarely used marketing tool at the time, shot at Olympic and featuring Cherry Vanilla's voice. MainMan still looks the part and, since David's main goal is to adapt the album, which is released on 24 May 1974, to the stage in the best possible way, he decides to put aside his differences with Tony Defries for the time being.

Diamond Dogs has its origins in disillusion, but this ultimate composite work couldn't have taken shape without the jumble of literary, cinematic and musical influences that were turning over in David Bowie's mind at the time. He himself adopted Ken Scott and Mick Ronson's roles and, driven by sheer determination, played a dangerous game (that would have scared off most of his supposed rivals), without knowing for sure whether anything would come of it. Bowie puts himself in a risky situation made even more precarious by the deterioration of his relationship with Tony Defries, but the imponderables were like spurs in his side. Up until and including *Scary Monsters*, his reaction to the hazards of his career or his private life, even those Coco Schwab was able to mitigate, will add spice to his art. Without them, his work would have been little more than an assortment of fragments pilfered from the spirit of the times.

Left to his own devices (without The Spiders), David Bowie set up a team. Sure, Mike Garson was still around but, by his own admission, he was barely more than a session musician on *Diamond Dogs*. He didn't particularly enjoy recording it and his playing is less notable than it was on *Aladdin Sane* or *Pin Ups*. As Brits who were used to the strange behaviour of other British rock stars, Herbie Flowers, Aynsley Dunbar and Tony Newman[18] were better at dealing with the stress and uncertainty. But although they tried, they never achieved the cohesion of the rhythm section of The Spiders From Mars since the time of *Hunky Dory*. During the tour, the Dogs will be played by two singer/dancers, but those on the album are multi-tasking Bowie clones.

David, now the eclectic electric guitarist, works hard to capture what he has in mind. Knowing he could never be better than Ronson, he put aside technique and focused on sound. It isn't a raw, authentic sound like Mick's, but one modified by effects like phasing and 'treated' like Robert Fripp's, the King Crimson guitarist, or like Phil Manzanera's when he was working his way through the various circuits of Brian Eno's VCS3 synthesizer. David Bowie is the entire brass section by himself: his baritone and tenor saxophones rise like a wave from the first chorus of the title song. He is also the tweaking keyboardist, who takes a devilish pleasure in inserting breaths, gasps and noises (sometimes white) into some of the tracks. David Bowie is the pack of dogs howling at the moon before the first note of the album, and barking at the end of 'Diamond Dogs', like John Lennon in the final bars of 'Hey Bulldog'.

The Astronettes were also working at Olympic, so it is likely that Geoff MacCormack and Ava Cherry contributed to the backing vocals, but David recorded most of his vocals alone in the studio. And what vocals! Cigarettes and fatigue (among other things) haven't caught up with him yet and he is able to vibrate his vocal cords on point. From one song to the next (or within the same one, as on 'Sweet Thing' and 'Rock'n'roll With Me'), he climbs a full octave and comes back down just as easily. His tone is so convincing that his lyrics – famously cryptic because of his writing techniques – almost become clear.

David Bowie, a demented narrator at first, throws the dice and starts off with 'Future Legend'. His deep, dark voice sets the nightmarish scene for Hunger City, a futuristic place haunted by gangs lurking on the tops of buildings[19] and packs of hungry dogs. The menacing musical backdrop is mostly synthetic until a guitar comes in with a snippet of the melody of 'Bewitched, Bothered And Bewildered' from *Pal Joey*, a 1940s' musical composed by Richard Rodgers, who also wrote 'Slaughter On Tenth Avenue'. This introductory minute closes with a crackle of applause from *Coast To Coast – Overture And Beginners*, Rod Stewart's live album with Faces, while Bowie, focused on his objective, declares, 'This ain't rock'n'roll, this is genocide!'

Like 'Rebel Rebel' and 'Rock'n'roll With Me', the title song of the album is probably a leftover from the Ziggy Stardust project. Similar to 'Watch That Man' and even more so to 'Telegram Sam' by T. Rex, 'Diamond Dogs' chews up The Rolling Stones and regurgitates them – traces of 'Honky Tonk Women', 'Brown Sugar' and, of course, 'It's Only Rock'n'roll (But I Like It)', which hasn't come out as a single at that point, can be detected. Guitar oriented, 'Diamond Dogs' is long, but it can afford to be because David Bowie uses it to unveil his new character: Halloween Jack, a hastily sketched alter ego, a dandy more frail than Ziggy, who will crumble even more during the tour.

Linked together, the next three tracks confirm two things: that *Diamond Dogs* is David Bowie's most conceptual album, and that he was able to draw not only on his passion for Lou Reed and Iggy Pop, but also on his penchant for a rock once called psychedelic, then progressive and, finally, when German musicians got involved, 'kraut'. The all-encompassing suite of 'Sweet Thing'/'Candidate'/'Sweet

Thing (Reprise)' vibrates as much with British art rock as with the experimentations of the foreign bands that he started listening to long before he considered a future in Munich or Berlin. This suite is also an opportunity to display his knowledge of the French revolution by referring to the '*tricoteuses*', the women who witnessed Convention debates and public executions while knitting. The noisy ending of 'Sweet Thing (Reprise)' pulses to a 'motorik' beat in the style of Neu! (especially 'Negativland', on the Düsseldorf duo's first album, which came out in 1972), and screeches like 'Venus In Furs' by The Velvet Underground.

Disdainful of verses and choruses, Bowie generates lyrics partly made up of random words, fruits of chance which, in Bowie, were never entirely arbitrary. Here they are coloured by confessions and messages reflecting his chronic uncertainties. He reveals all to us freely, without holding back. Everything is heightened and intensified by his use of cocaine, a drug he suspects to be less recreational than he has been told – he ignites the harmonies, floods the arrangements and, when he seems unstoppable, he gives himself a much-deserved break. Then the one-man orchestra sets off again, playing out the frustration, cutting and pasting everything that is going through his mind, finally offering a glimpse of a bleak future. He takes his Bowie knife, like the ones used by Burroughs' 'wild boys', and cuts out a path into a clearing created by the riff of 'Rebel Rebel'. Alan Parker manages to play it for four and a half minutes, without a hitch. Like the other musicians, Parker took on board Bowie's instruction to sound more Stones than The Stones and settles into 'repeat' mode on a steady beat and two major chords (separated by a tone). Meanwhile, Herbie Flowers at his best, grooves in the true Donald 'Duck' Dunn[20] manner.

In 1974, David Bowie knows full well that the writing is on the wall for glam rock. The genre will soon entice only that part of the audience unable to tell good from bad. Artistically, glam rock's glorification of hedonism and androgyny allows Bowie to fly much higher than the latecomers to the genre, who will finally sound its death knell that year. Nevertheless, 'Rebel Rebel' will only get to Number 5 in the British charts and Number 64 in the US, while Slade, Suzi Quatro, Alvin Stardust and Gary Glitter will all reach the top spot[21].

If there is a song on *Diamond Dogs* which makes clear why many of the best bands worked at Olympic in the 70s, it's 'Rock'n'roll With Me'. The natural sound of the instruments – the piano and organ, among others – highlights the acoustics of Studio 2 and the warmth of the Helios mixing desk (a 'wraparound' model designed to allow recording engineers to make adjustments without leaving their chair). Bowie pulls out all the stops on this ballad, which he wrote with Geoff

MacCormack at Oakley Street, one day (or night?) in October 1973. An ode to his audience or a cry for help, 'Rock'n'roll With Me' is a vocal tour de force. It anticipates the soul vibe of the upcoming tour, even though it also sounds a bit like The Band. MacCormack is credited as Warren Peace (a reference to Leo Tolstoy's book) because he, too, wanted an alter ego. On the cover of *Diamond Dogs*, David Bowie will drop his first name, using only 'Bowie'.

'We Are The Dead' and 'Big Brother', rather reminiscent of Roxy Music (especially 'Stranded', released in September 1973), point directly to their origin, with 'We Are The Dead' being words uttered by Winston Smith, the main character in *1984*, and 'Big Brother' being the name of the head of the political party he opposes. The cut-ups behind the lyrics of 'We Are The Dead' allow for a free interpretation of the song, but those of 'Big Brother' once again make direct reference to the concept of the 'superman' explored by Friedrich Nietzsche in *Also Sprach Zarathustra* (his 'book for everyone and no one', published in two parts in 1883 and 1885). Here the superman is portrayed as a leader or saviour. Like the German philosopher, David Bowie provides more of an assemblage of ideas still in the works than a prescribed system and, while he leaves some doors open, he is careful not to mention what's hiding behind the closed ones. Even though he spares no effort to stage a form of devotion and submission in his performance, the 'Pharisee' in him cannot hide. And he is even more visible when 'Big Brother' morphs into 'Chant Of The Ever Circling Skeletal Family', an unstable (with an impossible time signature) and incantatory piece set against a background of proto-punk guitars. The final minute is corrupted by a burst of sound from the Eventide delay (as if a helicopter were passing from one speaker to the other), stopped short when Bowie's voice gets stuck, in turn, in the device. And since the attempt to have it reproduce the word 'brother' in full fails, the stubborn machine repeatedly spits out the single syllable 'bro', mocking and terrifying, until the fade out. For David Bowie and Tony Visconti, mishaps like this often served to create a shift beyond their original intentions.

Last but not least, the version of '1984' on *Diamond Dogs* is probably the best, and this song is clearly one of the most representative of the album. This is more down to the richness of its composition than its soul and rhythm'n'blues vibes. The term 'disco' has sometimes been used to describe it, but it is far from that. The first minute, driven by Alan Parker's rhythm guitar, owes a lot to Charles 'Skip' Pitts' playing on *Shaft*'s original soundtrack, composed by Isaac Hayes. However, the 30-second bridges that twice lead back to the theme are marvels of Bowiesque music writing. The chord progression defies understanding, as does the melody that straddles it and takes the song to new levels. Of course, David Bowie owes a lot to Tony Visconti here. His string arrangement is excellent and could rival the work of the best in the genre, including Don Ronaldo and Gene Page.

Diamond Dogs, launched with a major fanfare of publicity, will be received to great critical acclaim and remains the favourite album of many Bowie fans to this day. Lester Bangs, who thought that David Bowie didn't invent anything and was happy to steal from others, arranging the pieces back together in a crude jigsaw, was one of the few discordant voices. Bangs' disdain for Bowie was only matched by the hate he felt for Roxy Music, especially Bryan Ferry. Like Roxy, David Bowie succeeded in making the experimental accessible to as many people as possible, mainly because the nightmarish impenetrability of some of his lyrics did not get in the way of the music. While he didn't see *Diamond Dogs* through to its completion, Keith Harwood[22], whose recording methods were less meticulous than Ken Scott's (Tony Visconti complained about this when he received the tapes before the mix), is largely responsible for the singular sound of the instruments and vocals on the LP. Bangs – he will later change his tune – was one of those people who chose to take to task its presentation, rather than appreciate the intentions of the artist. That was their right; but while they barked, the Bowie procession passed gently by, and David's diamantine dogs went to Number 1 in the British charts and Number 5 in the US.

Throughout his career, David Bowie always managed to surround himself with the best people – the best of their time, or the best for him. Before leaving London he met with John Dexter, director of *The Virgin Soldiers*, who, from 1974 to the early 1980s, was the production manager at the Metropolitan Opera in New York. A complex but passionate character, Dexter, like Ken Pitt and Lindsay Kemp, was one of a small circle of older gay men to whom Bowie turned for artistic advice in the 60s and early 70s. Knowing Bowie wanted to make his shows theatrical, John Dexter advised him to hire Jules Fisher, the American lighting designer who worked on *Jesus Christ Superstar* on Broadway, among other musicals.

Not surprisingly, when Fisher meets David Bowie, he is amazed by his well-considered artistic ideas and his open-mindedness regarding implementation. Bowie wants Hunger City to look more like the set of a musical, with the orchestra at the back, than a conventional rock concert. As production manager, Jules Fisher will set up the basic framework, then pass the design and construction of Hunger

City to Mark Ravitz. This American set designer will go on to work with Bowie twice again on the Serious Moonlight and Glass Spider tours. Chris Langhart is in charge of sound and Freddie Burretti is taking care of costumes. The role of each of these people is listed in the programme. Jules Fisher is also credited as lighting designer but, contrary to what has been widely reported over the past 45 years, Langhart wasn't involved in the set design and the sound company Showco didn't work on the tour at the beginning[23]. It is only due to problems after the first few dates that sound engineer, Buford Jones, also 'joined the gang'. Bowie was always a step ahead of his fans so it is interesting to note that many of the young Americans who'll come to see the show (fans in Europe and the rest of the world will never get the chance to see *The Year Of The Diamond Dogs*) will be dressed as Ziggy Stardust or Aladdin Sane, with a lightning bolt on their faces.

In early June, David Bowie and his musicians wrap up a month of rehearsals in New York with three days of run-throughs – of the full set and special effects – at the Capitol Theatre in Port Chester, northeast of New York City. They then embark on around forty performances, starting on 14 June in Montreal and ending in July with two shows at Madison Square Garden. Widely enjoyed by both the public and the media, the tour will have its difficulties, especially because of the nature of the performance and the complicated special effects. *The Year Of The Diamond Dogs*, more commonly known as the Diamond Dogs tour, is a sort of theatrical extravaganza. Its impressive stage set was shaped by the same influences that had led to the creation of the *Diamond Dogs* album. Only David Bowie/Halloween Jack, as he moves around Hunger City, is properly lit. Other than him, only the two vocalists/dancers are clearly visible among the ten other people on the stage. The musicians – who didn't find out until Port Chester[24] – are relegated to the back (and the right) of the stage, by the buildings. David Sanborn, Earl Slick and Mike Garson will have the opportunity to perform creatively, as can be heard on the upcoming live album (and the many pirate records that started circulating in the summer of 1974), but only within a well-defined, if not restrictive, framework, as the performance was carefully staged.

The audience were equally taken by surprise. Still reeling from the shock of the Ziggy Stardust tour (the last American performance had been on 12 March 1973), Bowie fans are taken aback by the simplicity of his new look, which contrasts with the outrageous set and special effects – he is decked out in a short jacket, pale blue pleated trousers and a more-or-less tidy haircut by Jac Colello[25]. Many of those who think David Bowie is a spectacle in himself will say that a normal concert would

This hairstyle was inspired by Daniella Parmar and model Marie Helvin. David had seen photos of Helvin in *Harpers & Queen*, in which she had a sort of bright red lion's mane created by Kansai Yamamoto.

The lyrics of *Aladdin Sane* are about immediacy, courted confusion, spiralling success and its dangers, deranged society and utopia trampled underfoot.

Visually, David is evolving into another dimension and,
at Radio City Music Hall in 1973, Masayoshi Sukita is the first
to photograph him in outfits designed by his compatriot
Kansai Yamamoto.

Rock was no longer the music of the devil, but it still undermined the prevailing puritanism, especially when played – in New York, Los Angeles and elsewhere – by boys wearing make-up and satin.

Aladdin Sane, an extremely sensual 'rock'n'roll animal', reveals himself to be even more extroverted than Ziggy Stardust.

In the set list for the gigs at the Hammersmith Odeon in July 1973,
David Bowie reintroduced a song he hadn't sung in a while:
'My Death' – it had all the trappings of a eulogy.

Pin Ups is clearly a parting tribute to London. Bowie knew its wounded suburbs, its beating heart; it was the source of fantasies which, since his childhood, had aroused his curiosity and fuelled his ambitions as a young man.

The recording of *Pin Ups* is one of the few that were documented, in this case by Mick Rock, Bowie's then official photographer.

While filming *The 1980 Floor Show*, before an audience made up of members of Bowie's fan club and some other guests, David Bowie says goodbye to glam forever.

David's outfit for the images on the back and inside album jacket of *Pin Ups* was chosen as a nod to the style of Little Richard – he wanted a rock'n'roll touch to reflect the content.

David Bowie's performance of 'Rebel Rebel' on Dutch television in early February 1974 will become the song's official video.

Freddi Burretti took inspiration from Carmen, the band Tony Visconti is working with at the time, when making the Hispanic outfit worn by Bowie in the *Diamond Dogs* photo shoot.

The show *The Year of The Diamond Dogs* allows David Bowie to unveil his new character: Halloween Jack, a hastily sketched alter ego, a dandy more frail than Ziggy, who will crumble even more during the tour.

have pleased them just as much. But that isn't all: the music has changed. On David Bowie's instruction, Michael Kamen gave existing songs[26] a more rhythm'n'blues flavour and even those from *Diamond Dogs*, which the audience have only just heard on the new album, are more soul-inflected live. The ubiquitous brass and percussion make 'Aladdin Sane' and 'Rebel Rebel' sound a bit Afro-Caribbean, and on 'All The Young Dudes' and 'Rock'n'roll Suicide', Bowie performs like Percy Sledge... in a cabaret! Although David's look is simple, he sometimes sings in a very overstated way, like an actor in a musical who overacts to make himself better understood.

All in all, the set, special effects and revamped music will be a big hit with the open-minded audience. David Bowie begins each show singing part of '1984' in the shadows. Then he performs 'Sweet Thing'/'Candidate' from a walkway reminiscent of the sky bridges in *Metropolis*, walks around with a mask on a stick during 'Aladdin Sane' and sings 'Cracked Actor' addressing the skull in his hand, à la Hamlet. But perhaps the best moments of the performance are when Bowie hovers over the audience in a chair mounted on a hydraulic arm singing 'Space Oddity' into a telephone, or when he appears in the middle of a giant illuminated hand during 'Time'. As the tour progresses, however, incidents will multiply and some of the special effects will have to go. Likewise, David's nightly destruction of part of the set (some torn paper buildings) during 'The Width Of A Circle' will be deemed too expensive and abandoned after a few shows.

However, the technical difficulties inherent in such an ambitious undertaking won't be the biggest risk. Although they may prefer not to dwell on it and just remember the good parts, most of the musicians on the Diamond Dogs tour did not appreciate being side-lined, nor did they like the fact that they had very little contact with Bowie. Focused on his artistic aim, David will not not let his worries show. Still, he becomes increasingly isolated as cocaine intensifies its grip on him; some performances are better than others and he starts to eat only sporadically. Still refusing to fly, Bowie travels from city to city in a limo and hardly speaks to anyone except Coco Schwab.

Although he usually loves performing there, tensions reach their peak in Philadelphia on 8 July. When they arrive at the Tower Theater in Upper Darby, west of the city, the band notice that mics have been added on stage and they realize that the show is going to be recorded. For a live album, musicians normally receive an additional fee, but MainMan has made no provisions in this regard, just as the company hadn't on 3 July 1973 at the Hammersmith Odeon. The band threaten to walk out if Tony Defries doesn't commit to paying them a much higher sum than the union rate and Herbie Flowers, a natural spokesperson as the oldest in the band, negotiates on their behalf. It may seem like a large amount, but $1,000 per musician was really not that much, because five of the six consecutive shows were recorded.

Financial disputes aside, *David Live*[27], Bowie's first live (double) album to be released (the 'farewell gig' didn't come out until the early 80s) brought together the best moments of this series of concerts. Ever since the record first came out on 29 October 1974, the sleeve notes have been somewhat unreliable. The original vinyl version said *David Live* was culled from shows on 14 and 15 July at the Tower Theater, but that has to be wrong – as many pirate recordings and a few film clips attest, David Bowie was performing in New Haven, then most likely in Waterbury, on those dates. The Rykodisc 1990 reissue will partially correct the problem (specifying 12, 13, 14 and 15 July) but that probably won't be entirely accurate either. The 2005 reissue, also included in the 2016 box set *Who Can I Be Now? (1974–1976)*, will come closest to the truth, stating that *David Live* was made by combining recordings from concerts on 8, 9, 10, 11 and 12 July, which seems more credible.

Similarly, since 1974, the album's tracklisting has been plagued by inaccuracies. The inside cover of the first pressings claimed the album featured a 'complete and exact' set list, but the addition of two other songs on the 1990 Rykodisc reissue – 'Time' and 'Here Today, Gone Tomorrow'[28] – proved that this can't have been the case. Two new songs will also be added to the 2005 reissue ('Space Oddity' and 'Panic In Detroit'[29]), which will make it the closest, in terms of content and order, to the set that was played in Philadelphia. The credits for the 1990 reissue will mistakenly attribute 'Here Today, Gone Tomorrow' to David Bowie, although it is a cover of an Ohio Players song, which opened *Observations In Time*, their first album in 1969. This error will be corrected on the next release. The last inaccuracy in the cover notes of *David Live* has to do with what was really recorded. While the liner notes from the original edition stated that aside from a few backing vocals[30], no overdubs were done, we now know that several brass, piano and guitar parts were replaced in New York.

The bad atmosphere backstage will not affect the quality of the performances at the end of the first leg of the Diamond Dogs tour, which will pass without major problem. The final two dates, on 19 and 20 July at Madison Square Garden, will be a sort of grand finale. New York's elite will be there, and while his musicians and the rest of the team will go clubbing after the last show[31], David Bowie and a few friends (including Mick Jagger and Bette Midler) will celebrate this break, in their own way, in his suite at the Plaza.

MainMan briefly considered bringing the tour to the United Kingdom and Europe, but eventually dropped the idea as too expensive. The concerts at Madison Square Garden were filmed, but the public never saw any of the footage. How much was shot? Was the material usable? These questions remain unanswered and these items only add to the body of Bowie's unreleased (and therefore fantasized) work. And, likewise, the feature film he planned to direct when he started working on *Diamond Dogs* would never come to fruition. In the winter of 1974, in his hotel suite in New York, he tinkered with a video camera, cardboard and clay to make a basic demo based upon an elaborate storyboard. Cyrinda Foxe, Lindsay Kemp, Iggy Pop and Bowie himself (as Harpie) were supposed to act in the film. Some of the visual elements that survived will be displayed at the *David Bowie Is* exhibition.

That summer, David Bowie is once again creating an artistic parallel universe by opening his mind to whatever influences come along and blending them into his daily life. By the time the tour resumes in September, he feels he doesn't belong any more in the extravagant, *trompe l'oeil* set, so he plans to get rid of Hunger City, piece by piece. He can also see that he is going to be the first victim of the coming financial and psychological debacle, so he will no longer content himself with turning the pages. He is going to burn some of them.

Alan Parker	Ian Anderson
Mike Garson	Ken Scott
Aynsley Dunbar	Dana Gillespie
Tony Newman	Geoff MacCormack
Tony Visconti	David Sanborn
Andrew Morris	Carlos Alomar
Jon Astley	Keith Christmas
	Mark Ravitz
	Chris Langhart
	Toni Basil
	Buford Jones
	Margo Sappington
	Terry O'Neill
	Guy Peellaert
	Laurent Thibault
	Gijsbert Hanekroot
	Marla Feldstein
	Patrick Boutoille

ALAN PARKER

One day, David Bowie rang up my home. My wife picked up and he asked if I could come and spend a few days at Olympic where he was recording *Diamond Dogs*. So I was booked by him directly; he always did this whenever he needed me or Herbie Flowers. We'd met four years earlier because, when we started Blue Mink, David was friends with Herbie as well and he often came to Morgan Studios when we were recording[32]. He'd sit in the control room with us and chat. We recorded a version of 'Holy Holy' with him back then. And now here he was, after all that time, a superstar, a monster!

I'm glad you're giving me the chance to talk because most people who write about Bowie only go looking for information online, regurgitating the same mistakes from the internet over and over again. On 'Rebel Rebel' for example, a lot of people think that David is playing the riff, but it's me! And he was the one who set the record straight! Also, the riff is only partly his, because I added some notes to it. Thing is, he wanted to give the song a Rolling Stones feel, hence the idea for this theme, which initially was only the first five notes. In the studio he asked me, 'Can we find a way to finish it?' We spent about half an hour messing around with the riff until I suggested the six following notes to make it work. David was great at getting what he wanted from his musicians, both in terms of sound and style, and he knew that different people were suited to different jobs!

Everything is overly complicated for guitarists today. Back then all we had was our instrument, a cable, an amp and maybe a pedal. On 'Rebel Rebel', I played a black Les Paul Standard plugged into a Fender amp. The aim was to make the sound yourself, without letting the technology replace the human. Some musicians today spend more time wondering what button to press than playing. Once we got the riff sorted out, we were ready to record 'Rebel Rebel' with Herbie and the drummer. Two or three takes, at the most. It was all finished in half an hour and David did his vocals right after. There was a really good atmosphere, a lot of his friends were there, including a black girl with white hair, Ava Cherry. It was very friendly, very easy going. David never acted like a star with us. It may seem strange, but he was just a regular bloke. A very talented one! He knew what he wanted, but was open to suggestion.

I added the guitar to '1984' later on; most of the other elements had already been recorded. We didn't do that at Olympic 2, but upstairs, in an overdub suite, a tiny room. It was just David, the recording engineer and me. He asked me what

I thought of the music and I suggested this sort of *Shaft* rhythm and off I went. It was as simple as that, off the cuff!

I didn't tour with David after that because I was first and foremost a studio musician and I didn't really want to be on the road. But, you know, Blue Mink's success really surprised us – Herbie Flowers, Barry Morgan and me. All of a sudden it was promotion, television appearances and all that... In 1969, our first single, 'Melting Pot', was so big we had to go on a tour, with Booker T. & The M.G.'s, whom we loved, opening for us[33]. After another couple of hits, we also played the Troubadour in Los Angeles for a week – this time Bill Withers and The Pointer Sisters were our opening acts. Those were crazy times...

I only saw David once more after *Diamond Dogs* – much later, at Island Studios... I don't remember when exactly. We recorded a few tracks. Herbie was there too. I don't remember the titles of the songs either – maybe they didn't have titles... That's the problem when you're a studio musician: you get there, you play, you go home and it's over! Just like that!

I continued to follow David's career, especially in the months that followed the release of *Diamond Dogs*. The album was a monster hit and songs like '1984' and 'Rebel Rebel' have become really iconic. When I hear these tracks, I can't help thinking, I'm on them! There are a lot of videos on YouTube of guys explaining how to play 'Rebel Rebel'. I watched a few of them at the beginning, then I stopped. You know why? No one can figure out how to play the bloody thing! (2017)

MIKE GARSON

David and I spent quite a bit of time together during the *Diamond Dogs* sessions, but the atmosphere was not the same as it was with The Spiders. He told me what he had in mind for this project and mentioned the cut-ups, William Burroughs, all that could modify the way he approached his lyrics. As for me, I didn't want to do what I'd done on *Aladdin Sane* again, to become a caricature of myself, and I think I managed that in 'Sweet Thing'/'Candidate'. Once again, this part worked because David let me express myself.

I hadn't listened to it in years, then Page Hamilton, the guitar player of Helmet who joined us in 1999, mentioned it to me with awe. Honestly, I barely remember those songs. We were on a plane, he put his iPod's headphones on my ears and I understood what he meant. I'm playing something very basic with my left hand, something I probably learned when I was about 12 years old and I played over and over again without anyone noticing. Only after David asked me to play those notes did people start crossing the Atlantic for piano lessons with me, asking me to show them how I did it. I recorded thousands of songs, most of which will probably never come out. They might contain elements that are just as strong as those I played on *Aladdin Sane* or *Diamond Dogs*, but without the context of David's encouragement, they're just plain piano parts.

On tour, before recording *Young Americans*, there was quite a bit of tension, especially because management wasn't all that efficient. On the first dates, there was a problem with the PA and David was furious. He got rid of it and the following morning a truck brought in new stuff. He replaced some of the technical team in the process! I remember that just before Madison Square Garden, where I was supposed to play a beautiful black Steinway piano, I said to my technician, 'You know what, I'd really like a white one!' It was a joke, but on the night of the concert, there it was on stage!

Once, Bowie confessed to me one of his greatest regrets: on the Diamond Dogs tour, he hadn't really managed to do what he had planned, or film it as well as he'd wanted[34]. You have to remember that it was a real show – like a Broadway show but with better music! We managed to go from one city to the next, even though we had to move the whole set. And it took a long time to build it at each venue. David realized, and I agreed, that it would have been better to play for a week in each of the five or six biggest American cities and then bring the whole show to London, Paris or Tokyo. He was frustrated that not everybody got the chance to see it. Like with most Broadway shows, the band was a bit apart, but Michael Kamen gave me a lot of latitude and I enjoyed it. Same for David Sanborn and Earl Slick.

I've said that if *David Live* had been recorded later in the tour, after we'd had a bit of practice, it would probably have been better, but I could be wrong[35]... These days I'm grateful for every note I play, live or in the studio. Before, I tended to play a zillion notes, I was a bit selfish, I mainly played for myself. During the Diamond Dogs tour, I was a bit of a mad dog, a bit naive, and I realized that David was not. (2016)

AYNSLEY DUNBAR

What I remember of the Olympic Studios is that it was very dark, but I worked on a few songs with David, for what would become the *Diamond Dogs* album. But then that's when I got the legal paper, handwritten... It was a piece of legal paper with six clauses, all for David, and I just look at it and I said, 'I'm not finding this very...' Well, it was over for me at that point. And I don't know if David and, whatever, the manager had anything going on there... But anyway, I was out and left. I came home to America and that was it. (2017)

TONY NEWMAN

In the winter of 1973, I got a call from bass player Herbie Flowers. I remember it well as I was recording with The Who at the time for the film *Tommy*. Herbie was with David Bowie and they needed a drummer, so they asked me to come as soon as possible. I got to Olympic pretty late that evening and that's where I met David for the first time. He was really nice and there was a great atmosphere in the studio, very relaxed. We first cut 'Diamond Dogs' and he was very happy when I suggested reversing the beat on the track. David had a very good sense of humour and we laughed a lot! There were instruments everywhere – a baritone saxophone, a synthesizer – but we were only three musicians: the pianist, the bassist and me. David made a lot of overdubs himself. Before we cut 'Sweet Thing', I asked him if he knew what kind of beat he wanted and he told me to put myself in the shoes of a French teenage drummer who was about to witness his first guillotining!

At the end of the sessions, David asked me to join him on a US tour, so I had to break off my Warner Bros. commitment with Three Man Army[36]. I met up with him in New York for some extensive rehearsals, where I had to learn a good chunk of his vast repertoire. To be honest, I had no idea of David's stardom... But I came to see it first hand on the road! The show was worthy of Broadway, very Kurt Weill – it was madness. Everything went well, except for a slight miff over the pay when we realized some concerts were being recorded for a live album. That was resolved with the threat of a strike and we ended up getting what we wanted.

David wanted to rearrange a lot of songs for the shows – the old ones and even the new ones! We slowed down 'Sweet Thing' and made it far more dramatic than the album cut. David was happy with the way I played, but everyone was great in that group. We all got on; there was no shit!

In July 1974, after the Madison Square Garden shows, Herbie left and, to be honest, my cocaine addiction got the better of me. I could no longer function, so I just didn't return to work! That drug was doing a lot of harm, it's sad to say, especially among musicians... Thank goodness I haven't touched the stuff in more than 30 years.

We spent a lot of time with David when we were recording *Diamond Dogs* and on the tour that followed. I remember that we talked about making something similar to rap, years before The Beastie Boys! But we never did, which is a shame. Of all the musicians I've worked with, David Bowie has a special place in my heart. I'll never forget him because he was a great artist and a visionary. (2016)

TONY VISCONTI

I was surprised when I listened to the tapes of *Diamond Dogs* because I didn't know what to expect. Actually, David always surprises me with his new directions. I thought the album was one of his darkest. The songs had been mixed many times in different studios all over London. David thought that the studios were at fault, so he called me out of the blue to ask my advice. I told him I had just finished building my own home studio and we mixed the album there.

Although *Diamond Dogs* was technically finished when I got it, David was impressed with my new digital gear and we added some special effects that were previously unheard, like the repetitive 'bro, bro, bro, bro, bro...' at the end of the album. I think he sang some extra parts but, by and large, it was mainly a mixing job for me. I had already contributed strings to '1984' but I hadn't heard the rest of the album.

I know David played more guitar and keyboards than on his previous records and he told me it was important that he did that, because he had a concept in his head that he didn't think session musicians could interpret. I thought his playing was excellent.

David can be brilliant with simple things that don't look or sound complicated, like 'Rebel Rebel' for instance. To me, he is Mr Concept and his ideas can sometimes be deceptively simple. But, of course, I love 'Sweet Thing' and its connected songs because this is an epic that came off well and is very compelling from beginning to end. It evokes imagery of a detective film noir.

The cover with the dog's genitals was a great idea. I think I have it in storage. Why it was censored is beyond me. By the way, David was born in the Chinese year of the dog, but I don't think they have 'diamond' years!

As an artist, David loves danger. Being without The Spiders was a situation that suited him. It is not like him to be dependent. He will be dependent on a musical association, up to a point but, if a situation compromises his creativity, he swiftly moves on.

I don't know if *Diamond Dogs* is a favourite album for his fans, but it has a timeless sound to it. It's the work of a visionary. David is obviously very good at changing his sound and style, yet remaining David Bowie at the core. Not many artists can do this; in fact, I can't think of one. Prince could, but he doesn't – he sticks to a formula...

David recorded his shows at the Philadelphia Tower Theater; I was not able to attend. It was reported at the time that my car broke down travelling from New York, but I don't recall that ever happening. David just took it upon himself to record the show for posterity, and then liked what he heard and decided to mix it into his first live album. There was one problem with this idea in that it was recorded poorly, not that the performances were anything less than excellent on most of the songs.

David and I went to Electric Lady[37] to mix the album, where the resident engineer, Eddie Kramer, intercepted us. 'I'm the only one who knows how to operate the complicated console in this studio.'

Having met Kramer when I first arrived in London, I was suspicious. He was an engineer that Denny Cordell never wanted to work with, so consequently I didn't either. Kramer's work with Jimi Hendrix was considered classic even by 1974, but having had the pleasure of hearing Hendrix live several times I never liked the way he had been recorded.

First we had to fix a few backing vocals and the backing singers were brought in to re-sing their parts; poor stage monitoring was the cause of this as the singers had a great deal of difficulty hearing themselves and the other performers. This took a day. Kramer proceeded to engineer the mixes the next day. This was a tough album to mix and Kramer's habit of throwing his head back as he 'played' the mixing console like a concert pianist was a little overdone.

I never liked the sound of *David Live* and was really gratified to get a chance to remix it in 2004 for a Surround Sound re-release. In all fairness to Eddie Kramer, the show was not recorded well and tools didn't exist in 1974 to fix some of the badly recorded tracks – there were big problems. In 2004, engineer Mario McNulty and I microscopically scanned through the sound files and corrected every abrupt change of volume and sound that the recording engineer made back in 1974. The new sonic quality makes it sound as if it was recorded today. (2004/2007)

ANDREW MORRIS

When I started working at Olympic, I was just a kid who made tea and helped the recording engineers. I met Chris Kimsey and Rod Thear and got on well with them. All the bands loved them. Rod worked regularly with The Rolling Stones and I worked on quite a few sessions with The Pretty Things and Badfinger. I was also there when the Stones recorded *It's Only Rock'n'Roll*. Mick Taylor was about to leave the band and Keith Richards was spending a lot of time with Ronnie Wood. Early one morning, I'd just finished a session when I saw the two of them on the other side of the glass door. I opened it and they asked me if they could quickly record something. The night before, they'd played a couple of tracks at a Kilburn & The High Roads concert – Ian Dury's band – so I couldn't say no! I set them up in an empty studio and two hours later they thanked me and left. I was about to leave when the phone rang. It was a Saturday and no one else was there to get it. I picked up, introduced myself and a voice said, 'Hello, it's David Bowie, I'm calling to see if you have any availability, by any chance.' He caught me off guard because I wasn't expecting a musician of his stature to make a request like that to me. I said that as far as I knew, Studio 1 was booked for the whole month, but Studio 2 might be free. The following Monday or Tuesday, the person who handled the bookings called me in: I was going to have to take over because David Bowie was coming to record in Studio 2 and Rod Thear, who should have been assisting on those sessions, had just been in a motorcycle accident. I had to stand in for him.

What struck me during *Diamond Dogs*, was that David Bowie was a perfectionist, but at the same time, he put a lot of trust in his people. He brought out the best in them without really asking anything in particular. Keith Harwood was a great recording engineer and I'm not surprised that he and David got on well. Most of the engineers who worked at Olympic became producers. At the beginning, I really had the feeling that Bowie wanted to start over and that being with other musicians felt liberating to him. The Spiders From Mars weren't there anymore, so Herbie Flowers was on bass... With Aynsley Dunbar, they were the cream of the crop... And in those days, people like them were far more than session musicians. They were free spirits who really put themselves at the service of others. David didn't really take many risks, but he looked like he wanted to break new ground.

Early one morning, while he was waiting for his driver, he started playing the chords of 'Rebel Rebel' on his Dan Armstrong guitar. He kept playing around with them until he came up with something. He wanted to record a demo right away, because he knew he was on to something good. He asked me to call Keith Harwood back in. He'd gone home more than an hour before, but he lived in Richmond, which wasn't very far. Next day we went to Trident to cut an acetate of the song.

David Bowie's curiosity seemed to know no bounds: he listened to the first

Bruce Springsteen album on a loop, even in the studio! He also played a lot of instruments. Everyone knew he played saxophone, but he was also very good on guitar and he experimented quite a bit on synths. He obviously expected something exciting from his musicians. As the songs took shape, we started to see the direction he was heading in. Listening to it again, you might think that *Diamond Dogs* is all over the place, but that's not the case at all. David was really excited when Lulu came to do backing vocals[38]. She was bursting with energy and sang like a goddess! At Olympic, I also worked on this record Bowie was planning to produce for The Astronettes, with Ava Cherry and his friend Geoff MacCormack, a hell of a character! Brian Eno came by to see us while Bowie was at Olympic and I helped out in sessions for *Here Come The Warm Jets*, his first solo album, which he was mixing there at the same time.

In December, after a night session, I was getting ready to ride my motorbike home, but I'd parked it some distance away. David told me to leave it where it was and he put me up with him and Angie in Chelsea. I stayed there two weeks and we went to work together every day in his limousine. I spent Christmas 1973 with them! Mick and Bianca Jagger were also there. It was a bit crazy, but they had a Christmas tree, like everyone else! All that definitely added to my happy memories of those recordings. I rubbed shoulders with David, but not just as a musician. He and Angie were wonderful to me. Even though I was only 16, I quickly realized that he was different. I've met other artists, but Bowie was a sort of musical Salvador Dalì. I also have good memories of Mike Garson, a real gentleman. And Herbie Flowers helped David a lot by giving him arrangement ideas.

I left for the US soon after the *Diamond Dogs* sessions and I bought the album the day it came out. I was devastated when I saw that I wasn't in the credits[39]. (2016)

JON ASTLEY

I first met David Bowie when I was still a student. I was working for a local radio station and I interviewed him when he came to play at Oxford Polytechnic[40]. Actually, I snuck backstage and even though he wasn't giving interviews, he agreed to talk to me. When I met him again at Olympic, I told him this story and he remembered me.

I worked on *Diamond Dogs* towards the end of the sessions at the request of Keith Harwood. That's when we recorded the vocals and quite a few overdubs. David played some guitar and replaced keyboard parts. Tony Newman re-recorded some drums... Bowie and I got along well and he trusted me. One day, he brought me all his albums and put together a list of songs he wanted to play on tour. He asked me to make some tapes for his musicians. When I tried to give him his records back, he told me to keep them.

The night Lulu came to sing 'You Didn't Hear It From Me', David had planned to go out with Keith Harwood so he asked me to record her vocals. I was just a tea boy and he gave me my first recording job! When he came back, he listened to it and liked the result. So when Keith Harwood wasn't at Olympic for whatever reason, I would replace him. I recorded parts of saxophone, Mellotron and, of course, some of David's vocals. He just needed one take! And, if some lyrics were missing, David would go into a corner for ten minutes and then come out and record it right away, in one go!

I remember a girl hanging around in the street outside the studio. One day, it was pouring with rain and David suggested we invite her in for a cup of tea. When he walked into the room where she was warming herself up, she almost fainted.

At one point some people from the label and from MainMan stopped by to listen to the record in progress and, when I pressed play on the tape recorder, the playback head took some time to start reading the tape. The sound was muffled, but it went back to normal after a few seconds. David asked me if I could reproduce that effect and you can hear it on *Diamond Dogs*. He loved that type of accident. It's a shame, but we were never able to work together again and I never even saw him again after those sessions. Later, I was asked to record Lou Reed, but I said no. I found him intimidating and his reputation made me think it would be a difficult project... (2016)

IAN ANDERSON

On what was otherwise a folk-rock album, Steeleye Span decided, I think unwisely, to include a 60s American pop song called 'To Know Him Is To Love Him'. They'd already recorded it, in fact, at the point where I became involved, but I didn't think it belonged on the album. Maddy Prior, the lead singer, asked me if I could get David Bowie to play saxophone on the song. I had no idea it was his main instrument, and honestly, I didn't know a whole lot about him except that he was a kind of theatrical pop singer of the time. I imagine that Steeleye Span must have assumed that, because I was in the music business, I knew everyone. But that really wasn't the case. You know, my world was, and still is, a very self-contained, small one. I don't go to parties,

I don't involve myself in the social scene, I don't do the drugs, I don't do the sex, I don't do the rock'n'roll. I'm a loner, I'm the cat who walks alone, I just don't know people in the music business. So I scratched my head and said, as a good producer should, 'Leave it with me, I'll see what I can do'.

So I asked around, probably through my record company, Chrysalis, and they managed to get me a contact number and I spoke to somebody who knew David Bowie and he agreed to do it. On the day he was due to arrive, he came on time to the studio[41]. He had an entourage of six or seven people who were obviously there to give him some kind of moral support or something. I was a bit uncomfortable about this, because they filled up the control room and the studio, extra bodies hanging around... But anyway, David introduced himself, I said hello, we had a microphone set up and we played him the track once so he could play along with it. Then he said, 'Right, let's do a take.' I don't think it took more than two to record his part. He got it straight away, he was great. He was quick and really organized. He was there for less than 30 minutes – it was extraordinary.

Many years later, when he was with Tin Machine, a band I rather liked that was more rock, more punchy – he wasn't being quite as theatrical – he and I were both invited to some big televised show in Germany. Millions of viewers! I saw he was also on the programme and I went to his dressing room. Two big thugs, two apes, stopped me from going in and I said, 'Why don't you tell your boss that Ian Anderson wants to say a quick hello?' So they went into the dressing room and the next moment the door was opened and it was David Bowie who let me in. We talked for a bit, then I told him, 'Some years ago, back in late 1973, you came and played on that track by Steeleye Span and I was so impressed by your professionalism and the fact that you didn't ask for money. There was no fee and that was a really nice thing to do and, since then, I took that lesson to heart. Every time I play on somebody's record, I never charge any money, I just do it as a gift and I try to do the best I can, just like you did. So I just wanted to say thank you for that little lesson in life, to be a generous musician.' Then he looked at me, with horror in his eyes, and said, 'You... you mean I didn't get paid? Is it too late to send an invoice now?' And I was a bit surprised by that, but then he laughed and I realized he was just teasing me. We actually laughed so hard I could see his new teeth, and I told him that his dentist had done a good job. Because he and I were quite famous in the 1970s for having pretty, umm, irregular teeth, that stuck out or that didn't quite match up. So I told him his new teeth were perfect and maybe I could have his old ones! (2017)

KEN SCOTT

I only worked on early sessions for *Diamond Dogs*. I didn't take it personally because David Bowie had something else in mind from mid-1973: his own vision of soul music. In the same way he got rid of The Spiders From Mars, he left me behind and turned to Keith Harwood for what came next. He knew how to form different teams, depending on the artistic goal he wanted to achieve. As proof that he'd moved on, he even left Trident for Olympic! I don't like that David's former musicians spread rumours about his drug habits. Personally, in all the time we spent together, I never saw him take anything. His addiction to cocaine started in the *Diamond Dog* days, and I think I know who gave it to him first... (2017)

DANA GILLESPIE

When David chose Tony Defries as his manager, he could have just thought of himself. But he wanted to introduce me to him too, and I must admit that I liked him right away. I know about all the controversy that marred the end of their relationship, but I've learned to remember just the good parts. It may not be the best way to analyse things, but that's how I am. Whatever Tony Defries' faults were, he allowed David to thrive and achieve the success he so wanted. Suddenly, his money problems disappeared. He could focus on his music and surround himself with musicians who were all properly paid. Defries also helped him make it in America. I've seen a lot of concerts in my life, but if I had to pick a top ten, I think I'd put one from the Diamond Dogs tour at the top of the list. Defries worked hard to finance David's dreams – including his futuristic cardboard metropolis. David used MainMan's technique of simulating success by spending lavishly and thereby attracting it – and applied it on stage by setting up an extravagant show that was more like a musical than a traditional rock concert.

I was with him and Angie at the Sherry-Netherland, which was one of the most expensive hotels in New York. All his new friends were staying in the same neighbourhood, including Mick Jagger, who was at the Plaza. Tony Defries gave David anything he wanted. One time, it was a grand piano, but it could easily have been an elephant! A lot of people have joked about Tony Defries being in love with David. I would say he probably did love him, and helping him make his dreams come true was his way of showing it. Defries, the quintessential Jewish manager, was the captain of HMS *MainMan*. He had an Afro, wore a fur coat in all weathers and smoked cigars! He didn't force David to wear a dress on the cover of *The Man Who Sold The World*, or make me pose in a corset and garter belt, but he loved all the fuss that came from it. All that madness was only going to last so long, and I knew that sooner or later, I'd be going back to Europe. That's where I really feel at home. Little by little, David became a master of manipulating things in his favour. Naturally, it was in the US that he really blossomed, that he became aware of who he was. Everyone knew he hardly slept at that time because he had better things to do...

After David moved to the United States, Tony Defries realized he had less and less control over him, and he even had a hard time getting in touch with him. Before leaving England, David had wanted to buy a house. He'd hardly ever owned anything before. It didn't take him long to realize he didn't have any money. It had never occurred to him for a single second that the whole of MainMan was living off the advances on his earnings and spending more than what was going in. The house of cards that was MainMan was about to collapse.

During the Diamond Dogs tour, because he still refused to fly, David travelled mostly by limo. We tried not to leave him on his own because he was as thin as a rake and we were worried about his health. Angie travelled with him sometimes, and I did too. But I don't remember him talking very much during those times. He listened to music, but it was usually stuff that made you drowsy. David was just skin and bones, but behind the make-up and despite his problems, he was still a fierce fighter who loved music. (2016)

GEOFF MACCORMACK

[In Philadelphia] there were talks with the management that were predictably inconclusive. When, just ten minutes before curtain-up, Herbie was still threatening not to play, David had to give the performers his personal guarantee that they would get paid. Personally, the situation was a pill I was prepared to swallow. I felt supremely lucky just to be there and for the chance to travel the world by land and sea. But the band was right and the management wrong and David never should have been put in that situation.

Everybody got paid eventually. But it left us all feeling shitty as we went on stage, so the gig was not a great one. In that sense, everything and everyone suffered. If there's a worse way of managing a great artist, I'd like to know. (2007)

DAVID SANBORN

Allowing musicians of David Bowie to give their side of the story makes you remember just how incredibly collaborative he was as an artist, and that he also had a unique way of tackling recordings and performances. What I'm saying here is just my point of view – I've been trying to think back to how it was at the time. It was a long time ago and those days are a bit hazy, especially with all the drugs. But I remember his determination and professionalism really well. Thanks to Michael Kamen, who I'd already worked with, I was invited to play on the American tour that followed the release of *Diamond Dogs*. I was impressed that David wanted to meet with me face-to-face to explain what he had in mind for the shows. He asked to meet at the Pierre Hotel in New York and spent quite a bit of time describing his vision. I thought he was a very interesting guy, more than most of the people I had been dealing with up to that point. He was in a state of transition and I noticed that he loved to be surprised, to have things happen spontaneously and that became even more apparent later.

His songs were really incredible. They were carefully crafted, but they also allowed for extension and different ways to approach them. David encouraged that: I never heard him tell a musician he was overdoing it. He was actually thrilled when stuff happened. During rehearsals, I realized how much he loved hearing us play. When I met Bowie, I was working with Gil Evans[42]. He was, of course, a great composer and arranger, but he was also very generous about how he would allow people to reinterpret his music. One of David's strengths was to incorporate things that we did into the direction of the music. He was a great listener and a voracious creator who was fuelled by curiosity and open mindedness. Nothing escaped him… It's mind-boggling to think about the way his music morphed between *Diamond Dogs* and *David Live*, which came out just a few months later. I'm so glad it got chronicled! It was such a huge transformation, not only in terms of sound, but in the content of the music, the character of the tunes – it's really obvious on 'Changes', for example. When we started to rehearse, all we had were some skeletal charts. But, you know, he used to tell me, 'Play a little more on this, I want you to play more!' It was always kind of outstanding to me that he not only didn't discourage me, but actually encouraged me to play freely. (2016)

CARLOS ALOMAR

I was a session musician at RCA Studios in New York and I got the chance to work for a long list of visiting artists. In the spring of 1974, I was asked to play on a song for Lulu, a British singer. I knew her because of 'To Sir, With Love', which she sang in the film with Sidney Poitier[43]. I immediately knew it was going to be an important recording. The last time I'd gone to the A was for a live session with Peter, Paul And Mary. I walked into the studio and David Bowie was there on his own. He'd written the song and was producing it too. That was the first time we met. He looked like he'd just emerged out of The Spiders From Mars, with his red hair, eccentric outfit and all. Suddenly, he was standing in front of the exact opposite of himself (at least in appearance) – a Puerto Rican with an Afro! What a culture shock! He immediately bombarded me with questions and I realized I'd just met one of the most enquiring people on Earth. To be honest, his thinness scared me a bit and my first thought was to invite him to dinner so my wife could feed him up. Later, I realized that some people are naturally thinner than others, but at the time I thought he looked completely drained, partly because he was so pale.

After the session, we went to my place in his limousine. We spent that first evening talking about music, laughing, getting to know each other. Like all the Brits I met at the time, he wanted to know everything about the rhythm'n'blues scene. He told me his story, about The Spiders From Mars, and I found it fascinating. Honestly, he was an angel. We became good friends on the spot and when we parted that night, he said we'd work together soon, but didn't say when.

Not long afterwards, I got a phone call from his manager. I was touring with a band called The Main Ingredient, whose co-founder, Tony Silvester, had recommended me for the sessions with Lulu. Tony Defries asked me if I could play with David Bowie on a series of concerts in the US. I was already married and wanted to know what the pay would be. Since I was making three times more with The Main Ingredient, I turned him down. (2016)

KEITH CHRISTMAS

David called me one evening, in April I think. He was in New York, he needed a guitar player for his tour and his office sent a plane ticket. I was singing in a prog rock band called Esperanto at the time and I also played a bit of electric guitar, even though I never mastered it, really. But anyway, David got wind of this and got me over.

So, being more of an acoustic guitarist, I was wondering if I would be right for the job, but he seemed to really want me there. And after all, you didn't turn down a trip to the States! As a matter of fact, I don't really remember auditioning; I just tried out. He had booked RCA Studios for the evening, but it didn't work out. I guess I wasn't good enough. I tried something on *Diamond Dogs* that I thought was quite good, but very quickly after that the session was over! David didn't say much actually; it was always difficult to know what he was thinking. And, at the time, he was not exactly taking care of himself properly. I mean, doing coke is one thing, but you can't spend your life smoking. After a certain age, you seriously put yourself at risk. But anyway, we went clubbing after that and it was fun.

You know, it was the MainMan circus and all that. But don't get me wrong – looking back, I wasn't given much time, but I could have been a lot more professional than I was. But, you know, I always had a strange attitude to life. I was a bit... I was very casual and I still am. I don't know if it has anything to do with being folky or an old druggy. I wouldn't bother learning anything or even changing my guitar strings. I didn't have the kind of attitude of a top session musician. I didn't do myself any favours, let me put it that way. If I had been asked to come along and just busk the song on stage, it could have worked, but I never had the head to get into complex arrangements.

I arrived with no money at all and they put me up in this fancy hotel. At the airport, I was met by this black guy. He had a sign with my name on it and he took me to this enormous limousine. I remember 'floating' to New York like that. I had holes in my jeans, long before it was trendy, and one pound in my pocket. Once at the hotel, I phoned this bloke at MainMan, it must have been Tony Defries, hoping I would be given a bit of cash. I went there and, oh my God, you would have thought that I had asked him for 5 per cent of Bowie's royalties... I remember him – hostile face, large desk – looking at me as if I'd crawled out from under a stone. He didn't want to part with anything. So I had to insist and he eventually gave me the smallest amount to stay alive in New York. Well, that was MainMan – a cheap, cocaine-fuelled circus. (2016)

MARK RAVITZ

In the spring of 1974, I got a phone call from Jules Fisher, who'd been contacted by MainMan. He was calling me in his role as production supervisor for *The Year Of The Diamond Dogs*. Fisher was my lighting design teacher in the theatre department at New York University. After graduation, he'd hired me as a set designer – my speciality – for the rock-opera *Tommy*. The Diamond Dogs tour programme credits Chris Langhart on sound design, but at that time, the concept of sound, for a show like that, wasn't as advanced as it is today. Because Chris had worked at Woodstock and the Fillmore East[44], Jules asked him to take care of the sound. In those days, we called in people we knew, whoever was on hand, depending on what jobs were available. When Jules called me, he gave me only three words of input: *Metropolis*, power and Nuremberg[45]. It's what David Bowie had asked him to tell me. So, from those references, I started to let my mind flow and made up a list of different ideas.

Then, one fine day – Easter Sunday I think – Bowie invited me to his hotel, the Sherry-Netherland, so he could hear my ideas. I was taken aback: he had orange hair, a whole entourage over there – a freak show actually, as you can imagine. There were no two people with the same hair colour! Everyone was wearing make-up... Cherry Vanilla was there, and Angie... I showed Bowie what I'd been working on. It was pretty funny because I'd listed my suggestions in columns, with numbers, and it looked like a Chinese restaurant menu! So I started reading it all out and he stopped me whenever he liked a suggestion. From there, I was able to figure out a direction. I went home and refined everything over the following days. We met up once or twice more and I was able to start building the first models for the stage. We quickly agreed on what the set would look like. At one point, there were so many models going around, and I didn't make them all. Jules Fisher wanted to build some of them based on my drawings, which he needed for the technicians.

Because there was also choreography involved, Bowie and the others rehearsed the show a lot. On the night of the premiere, suddenly faced with reality, I could see just how ambitious the tour was. Nothing of the sort had been done before. It was really very theatrical. It had stage movements, it had scenery, it had elaborate lighting, the kind of things nobody was doing at that point. The tour was groundbreaking in that it was more like a travelling Broadway show than a series of rock concerts. And it cost a fortune, because we had to transport everything by road and reassembling it all could take anything up to two whole days.

The set was mainly buildings, scaffolding and a walkway that went up and down. The towers, which were lit from behind to create depth, looked really good. There were a few technical problems, but that was mainly due to the fact that everything was still mechanical. For 'Big Brother', David made his entrance in that vehicle that, to me, was like a giant mirror ball. At Madison Square Garden, when the spotlight hit it, it glowed all over the arena. It was spectacular! I had a lot of fun designing it.

In those days, my speciality was an effect I created by dripping paint, and Bowie let me apply it to the buildings on stage. I'd never given such depth and scale to this effect before. David welcomed most of my suggestions and I tried to implement his – it was a true collaboration and the freedom of expression I had was terrific. It's a shame the show wasn't properly filmed in its entirety, but I suppose it was 1974 – music videos were still in their infancy and it was very expensive to film a two-hour performance. (2018)

CHRIS LANGHART

Before the Diamond Dogs tour, I was associated with site planning and the architecture of some buildings on the Woodstock festival site. During my time at New York University, I also did sound and rigging at the Fillmore East, which was in an adjacent building on Second Avenue. After this venue closed, I had three years at the Rainbow in London as technical director. Then it also closed, after Frank Zappa got pushed off the stage by an irate patron[46] and fell into the orchestra pit, breaking a few bones and being out of service for about three-quarters of a year after that.

I did sound design for the Diamond Dogs tour, which opened in Canada. For this, I had some brief conversations with David Bowie, but mostly with his scenic designer, Mark Ravitz. I knew him because he had been a student at NYU, where I had taught previously in the theatre department. Those shows were really something out of the ordinary. I remember this song – 'The Width Of A Circle' – with the paper bulletin boards for scenery, with imprints of city buildings on them, which David tore down while singing! The whole thing was built at a shop that I worked at – Design Associates Scenic Studios. On another song, we had a painter's bridge that was motorized and came down from the top of the set with David Bowie standing on it and singing. It was the width of the stage, maybe 40 feet or so. The significant story is that there were problems with the brake mechanism and, when it came down slowly, everything was fine, but when the brakes failed, the motor gearbox freewheeled backwards and it came down quite quickly. Okay, it didn't drop as if the cable had broken… One evening, it landed on the stage very suddenly and David asked us, after the show, 'Is that the fastest it can fall?' It wasn't so bad an experience and I think he was less concerned after that. (2016)

TONI BASIL

In the autumn of 1973, my agent asked me to go to London to meet David Bowie, who wanted me to work on a future project – I wasn't told much more about it. When I got there, I was introduced to this slightly strange man, who was also handsome and charming. We talked about art and had some good creative conversations, then he suggested I go see *The Rocky Horror Show*, Richard O'Brien's musical that had just premiered in the West End. I was wined and dined by David's management company who were spending a lot of money. So, after passing what I think might have been a sort of interview, I returned to Los Angeles. A few weeks later, my agent called to tell me that David was in New York working on a new show and he was hoping I would choreograph the opening song. I remembered our conversations and how we'd got along, so I told my agent that I would do it only if I could choreograph the whole show!

I met up with David in his hotel suite. I was wearing a sort of Zazou outfit, a jacket with pegged pants, and I'd brought along a drawing I'd done, inspired by a photo by Man Ray, of a huge woman lying across some buildings. It was my starting idea. He liked that, and I think that was when I landed the job! He also asked me where I'd got my pants and I told him my friend Richard Famiglietti had made them. He managed Jenny Waterbags, a men's shop in New York. We went there straight away and he asked for the same pants!

I think it's fair to say that he was in a state of metamorphosis, on several levels. During this second meeting, I realized I was not first in line – he had wanted Michael Bennett, who'd choreographed *A Chorus Line*[47]. During 'Diamond Dogs', David wanted his two singers/dancers to be on a leash, like dogs, but from what I gathered, Michael was very uncomfortable about that idea. Personally, it didn't make me think of bondage and I saw it as an opportunity to create geometric patterns with the chains – ropes actually. David already had a little mock-up of the set and there was a sort of bridge between the cardboard buildings that lowered and came up, where he could stand. I suggested that we use long-enough ropes to go from the bridge to the bottom, so the dancers could create these patterns while running. And when the bridge lowered, of course, the dogs 'bondaged' him and that was it. I remember his reaction distinctly – he called to his assistant, who was in the next room, 'Coco! The dogs are back in the show!'

But that wasn't all! During a rehearsal, while he was on his knees wrapped up in the ropes at the end of 'Diamond Dogs' and he had to go straight into 'Panic In

Detroit', he looked up at me and I saw a lightbulb appear above his head, like when someone has an idea in a cartoon! It was one of the most extraordinary experiences I ever had with an artist. I was lucky enough to see the moment of creation. Because David was always 'in the moment', like great artists should be. You make a plan? You throw it away. Another plan? Throw it away too. During the first notes of 'Panic In Detroit', he started to unwrap the ropes. He grabbed two chairs and he made a boxing ring with the ropes and the chairs. Actually he had been working out with his trainer, boxing, and maybe he thought that, at some point, this could be used in the show. So, anyway, he grabbed his boxing gloves, he sang 'Panic In Detroit' and, as the end of the number was coming, I said, 'Knock yourself out!' And he did, and that was it. It was instantaneous.

Then I realized that, if you're an artist and if you trust yourself and you trust the people around you, if you leave your mind open and if you have the brain that David Bowie had, you'll never stop creating. He did an enormous amount of research before starting on that project. And he was open, and spontaneous! It's a very brave place to be. You know, I have a background in the intensive training of street dance[48] and David sometimes reminded me of a street dancer. They'd get up there, facing each other, and they have no idea what music is gonna be played. So part of the battle and the judging is how they deal with the music. A bit like Miles Davis, who walked out on the stage without knowing what he was going to play. But he was so well prepared, he wasn't afraid of improvising. I never saw Bowie hesitate or panic. He trusted himself.

Obviously, it was a great experience for me, working with him in 1974, and it probably shaped my life as a creative artist. I'd studied a bit with Sam Blazer, a pioneer of experimental theatre, and I had a keen interest in the Living Theatre. So I had a lot of experience and knowledge by the time I came into Bowie's art, but he reaffirmed my boldest choices and he really set me on the right creative path. A lot of research, a lot of planning, a lot of being open to changes at any given moment. Besides, before I went to London, I looked him up and saw the Ziggy Stardust film by D.A. Pennebaker. That allowed me to get a better idea of how he looked, and to see what he was capable of live. I also remember thinking that, despite his androgynous look and the reputation he had, he was straight! And that first meeting! Well, he looked like a sex god to me! In those days, men, women, children – all living things – fell in love with him. He was quite alluring! When he was working with you, he spun his web around him, but in a good way! And yes, he stole a couple of moves from Elvis Presley, but he didn't really try to imitate him, he just took inspiration.

The Diamond Dogs tour was preceded by a lot of rehearsals. David prepared physically in the day and then he rehearsed at night with the band. He wasn't a slacker. You know, I saw him solve many different problems and, at some point, I thought he didn't need any of us. But he was the performer and couldn't do it alone. And, most of all, he loved to collaborate. (2016)

BUFORD JONES

In 1974, my boss at Showco phoned to tell me I was going on tour with David Bowie. I'd just done Lynyrd Skynyrd and ZZ Top, so I imagined this might be quite different! I didn't know his music very well and I had this image of him, with orange hair, the lightning bolt on his face... I wondered if I was the best choice for sound technician. I went to see the Diamond Dogs tour in Akron, Ohio, and I was really impressed by Bowie. After the show, I was pleasantly surprised by the warm welcome he gave me. He acted as if he'd known me forever and he won me over right away! I was asked to come because there'd been quite a few sound problems during the first performance. I don't remember what company they were working with, but I did notice that the sound system wasn't good enough for a show like that and wasn't at all suitable for the rather large venues they were using. So we brought in a whole new system that we tested the next morning in Pittsburgh[49]. That was the start of my collaboration with David Bowie.

I was his sound technician for three of the tours he did in the 1970s, and we worked together again in 1990 for the Sound+Vision Tour. I still have a notebook he gave me. It contained printed song lyrics with handwritten notes on the mixing he wanted for each piece. It's incredibly detailed. When he gave it to me, he told me he'd done it as a guide, and that I didn't have to follow it to the letter. Actually, he encouraged me to be creative. In the notebook, he'd marked down some specific things, like guitar solos, piano parts and passages where he wanted some pre-recorded effects. We had to use a tape machine and send them from the console! He'd made this notebook especially for me, because I had to familiarize myself with the music as quickly as possible because I'd joined mid-tour, after a dozen shows. Needless to say, the notebook is very dear to me, and one day I'll give it to my children.

The Diamond Dogs tour was both ambitious and complicated. It had a theatrical set and vocalists who danced... The band was towards the back of the stage, but it was really good rock'n'roll, which is what I love! You know, the job of a sound technician is very important. In the end, we're the last link between the artists' music and the audience, so we have a major responsibility. Personally, I was happy to be considered as part of a team, and not just as a simple employee. I have David to thank for that. It was necessary because we had quite a few problems, especially as many of the technicians were in a union and didn't seem to have much experience on the road! Also, a lot of the special effects regularly broke down... (2016)

MARGO SAPPINGTON

My husband, Gui Andrisano, joined the band of the Diamond Dogs tour thanks to Michael Kamen. Michael and I had just finished *Rodin, Mis En Vie*, a ballet I'd choreographed and that he'd composed. It premiered in April 1974 in New York. In those days, Michael, his wife Sandra, Gui and I went out a lot and even vacationed together. David came to one of the performances and that's when I met him. He was charming, and because I knew what Gui was capable of, I wanted them to work together. From the first rehearsals, we saw that Gui was a good match with Geoff MacCormack, both of them sort of dark and swarthy to David's pale look. Also, Gui loved David's music, as we all did, and had no trouble adapting his repertoire. You know, he did a little of everything. He had a good singing voice and was an adequate dancer – I think he was a better singer than dancer.

I was stuck in New York during the tour, so I didn't see a lot of shows, but I remember going to a run-through when they were still rehearsing. Gui managed very well on vocals, but I thought the choreography should have been more unusual.

We all went out with David. At the time I believe he was dating Ava Cherry and we all went salsa dancing at the Corso in New York, if you can imagine that! I remember it was fashionable for women to wear men's suits and we were all in pants and jackets. David's suit was, I believe, a pastel/mint green. A very handsome Latino man asked him to dance. When David said thanks, but no thanks, the guy realized he was a man and was more than a little shocked!

I loved David then and always. I loved him as a person and as an artist and I always took an interest in his work. He had a natural grace, strengthened by his training as a mime. He wasn't afraid of taking risks, of reinventing himself, whether his efforts were popular and a critical success or not. We stayed in touch for a while after the Diamond Dogs tour. When Geoff was in New York, he often stayed with us, and Michael Kamen and I continued to work together on ballets. And please give my love to Geoff! (2016)

TERRY O'NEILL

I never knew whether David Bowie was completely insane or just under the influence of a particularly nasty drug the day we did the photo shoot with the dog for what should have been the cover of *Diamond Dogs*. As soon as my flash went off, the animal would leap up on its hind legs like it was going to jump on me, but Bowie didn't bat an eyelid.

Yes, it's true that Guy Peellaert reworked my photos, the same thing was going to happen to Duffy a few years later. But that's to be expected with an artist like David Bowie. He always follows his instinct, which wins out over everything else. The funny thing was that he gave us no choice! Peellaert and I thought we met by chance, but David had planned it. (2013)

GUY PEELLAERT

David Bowie and I were having breakfast together in London and he told me he was just off to do a photo shoot with a dog for the cover of his next album. He asked me if I had time to go with him and I said yes. When we were there, he suggested I direct the shoot and create some illustrations based on the photos. I felt like I'd been tricked, but it was a nice trick! RCA of course turned down the cover with David's genitals as a dog, but I was told they used it for a reissue! In any case, I was thrilled that Bowie had sought me out during that phase of his career, because it's my favourite period[50]. (1999)

LAURENT THIBAULT

At the Château d'Hérouville, while we were recording *The Idiot*, the album he produced for Iggy Pop and for which I worked as recording engineer, David told me he was fully aware that he pinched ideas from others. He said those who knew him well knew that, so they could hardly complain. He told me the story of the *Diamond Dogs* cover: 'One day, Mick Jagger phoned me and told me about this great painter and illustrator – The Rolling Stones wanted him to work on the cover of their next album.' It was Guy Peellaert. He continued: 'As soon as I hung up I asked Coco to look up this Peellaert guy and he did my cover. Obviously, my record came out before theirs, so people were like, 'Oh yeah, the Stones got the guy who did the cover for Bowie's album!' But anyway, Mick couldn't blame me. He shouldn't have said anything'. (2016)

GIJSBERT HANEKROOT

I started photographing rock musicians at the end of the 1960s. In those days, in Holland, there weren't many of us doing that! I'd shot David Bowie at Earl's Court in 1973 and I remember it was an incredible concert, even though, at the time, I didn't really enjoy it. I'm a photographer, not a journalist, but *Muziekkrant OOR* magazine had asked me to write a few lines about the show. The sound was not great that night. The average age of the audience couldn't have been more than about fifteen and the crowd was hysterical. All I could think of was to stay as close as possible to the stage to get the best shots.

In February 1974, I got the chance to photograph David Bowie in Holland, in Amsterdam, and on the set of the television show *TopPop* in Hilversum. He sang 'Rebel Rebel' and, that time, I wasn't the only one trying to get a picture! During filming, he was wearing an eye patch that made him look like a pirate and the footage became the song's official video. Bowie was very friendly and helpful that day. He played the song several times for the sake of the guy who was doing the lighting and the cameramen... And he let me take as many photos as I wanted, which today, would be completely unthinkable with an artist of his stature. I also shot him when Ad Visser, the host of *TopPop*, presented him with an award for *Ziggy Stardust*, and during the press conference that followed. I also took some photos at the Amstel hotel, where he was staying with his wife and son. One of them is in the catalogue for the *David Bowie Is* exhibition. (2016)

MARLA FELDSTEIN

In late 1973, I learned that David would be on the road with the Diamond Dogs tour. I was ecstatic! In the meantime, I met some other Bowie fans and we formed a quick and lasting friendship. To this day, I have some of the most fabulous connections with people I would never have known had it not been for David. A couple of those marvellous people are Patti and Leslie. There are so many others, I could not begin to name them all, but they know who they are and they are awesome!

For weeks, Patti, Leslie and I, and many others prepared for David's week of shows at The Tower. We made our outfits and searched out places in the city, trying to figure out where he may be staying. Finally, the week came – David Bowie was in town!

I had talked to various people at MainMan and I had found out some of David's favourite things. I went searching the city for some of those items and the night before the show I had a package for David. It contained: a bird of paradise, his favourite flower, a bottle of Moët & Chandon, his favourite champagne, and a lobster tail dinner! I still don't quite know how I pulled that off, but I did, and the person at the backstage door assured me that my unusual gifts would be given to David. My friends and I had front row seats for every show. That night, during one of his songs, David walked towards me, leaned over, put his arms around me and, before I knew it, I was kissing David Bowie and saying in his ear, 'I'm Marla... your fan who wrote to you.'

Of course, I do wish I had better recollection and I do wish I could remember more clearly, but it has been a long time since the Diamond Dogs tour, more than four decades and unfortunately even such spectacular memories have faded. At the intermission, someone came over to me and told me that David was very grateful for my fan letter and thanked me for the goodies I had sent backstage. Each night, after the show, we would head to his hotel, the Bellevue Stratford on Broad Street. David would come outside and chat with us until after midnight, often into the early morning! It was during one of these amazing encounters that David told us to keep an eye out for him, for he would be returning to our city in the next couple of months to do some recording. So, in fact, it was him who told us he would be in Philadelphia to record in August of 1974.

The David Bowie I met was very charming... almost shy. Quite different from the persona he portrayed on stage, where he seemed... where he was... larger than life! In person, David definitely came across as a bit timid, as if he could not believe how much we admired him. He was humble and unassuming and seemed truly interested in our thoughts and opinions. It was an extraordinary time in David's career, and I was – and still am – so very, very thankful to have been there to experience it... (2016)

PATRICK BOUTOILLE

I was a bellboy on the *France* from 1972 to 1974 and what I remember most from the crossings was David Bowie with his red hair and his androgynous look. He'd booked the Île-de-France suite. I was shocked to see the cabin crew's lack of consideration for him. I was young and I wanted an autograph, so I went to the U Center and said to his cabin boy, 'I want to see David Bowie.' 'Who's that?' he asked. 'A singer,'

I answered. 'So knock on his door,' he said. He wouldn't have done that for anyone else. So I knocked and David Bowie opened it. He very kindly let me in and gave me his autograph[51]. (2013)

1. Strangely enough, in 2012, David Bowie will urge English designer Jonathan Barnbrook to use an upside down shot of him at Radio City Hall in New York during the 1974 American tour for the cover of *The Next Day*. In the end, it will be used for the 'Where Are We Now?' single.

2. While it was being made, like most of David Bowie's albums, it didn't have a title. When he talked about his as-yet unfinished records, he often gave them fanciful names, or used the name of the last song he'd recorded.

3. The title track of *It's Only Rock'n'roll* (a song actually called 'It's Only Rock'n'Roll (But I Like It)') came out of an informal session at Ronnie Wood's house (who played guitar with Faces at the time). On that December day in 1973, Mick Jagger was the only Rolling Stone in attendance – Kenney Jones (of Faces) played drums and Wood played bass and guitar. Most of the takes will be kept, but Willie Weeks will add the definitive bass part in early 1974 at Olympic. A few months later, David Bowie will ask him to play on *Young Americans*. That same year, Bowie's voice will also be heard in the backing vocals of 'I Can Feel The Fire', the opening track of *I've Got My Own Album To Do*, Wood's first album. When guitarist Mick Taylor leaves in 1975, Mick Jagger and Keith Richards will ask Ronnie to join The Rolling Stones. Jeff Beck had turned them down.

4. The Astronettes will record several songs before David Bowie leaves for the US, including 'Seven Days' by Annette Peacock, 'God Only Knows' by Brian Wilson and Tony Asher, and 'How Could I Be Such A Fool' by Frank Zappa. They will also record four of his songs – 'I Am Divine', 'I Am A Laser' (or 'Lazer'), 'People From Bad Homes' and 'Things To Do'; he'll rework the first two for his later albums. Geoff MacCormack will be invited to sing (and dance) on the Diamond Dogs tour, but Ava Cherry will have to wait for the recording of *Young Americans* to work with David Bowie in the studio. The Astronettes never released an official record but, in 1995, the semi-unofficial compilation *People From Bad Homes* came out through Deadquick Music/Golden Years.

5. Ironically, David Bowie's '1984' will be on *Songs Inspired By Literature (Chapter Two)*, a 2003 benefit CD by Artists For Literacy. In the early 1980s, after Sonia's death, the owners of the rights to Orwell's work will grant Michael Radford the right to make another film version of *1984*. The film's score will be composed by Dominic Muldowney, who'll arrange *Baal* for David Bowie in 1982. But to Radford's dismay, Virgin, the main producer of the film and label of Eurythmics, will impose many of their songs instead of Muldowney's score. Since then, the director has recommended that film fans get their hands on DVDs on which these songs have been replaced with Muldowney's music. The 'original' soundtrack was also released on CD in 1999.

6. The Hi-Fli, made by EMS, is the model that best fits Jan Willem Ludolph's brief description. Electronic Music Studios has been a British synthesizer maker since the end of the 1960s. They're responsible for the famous VCS 3 and Synthi. Pink Floyd, The Who, Roxy Music (and Brian Eno), Hawkwind and Kraftwerk are some of the famous bands that have used EMS instruments. David Bowie's visits to one or more Dutch studios in early 1974 have been mentioned by those who were there, but their stories are quite confused and unreliable. Likewise, usually the name Ludolph is scratched out as soon as it's written,

as for example on the 30th anniversary reissue of *Diamond Dogs*. It will add a second CD to the remastered album that will include '1984'/'Dodo', as recorded at Trident with Mick Ronson and Trevor Bolder (their last session with Bowie), a version of 'Rebel Rebel' for American audiences (completed at RCA studios in New York in April 1974), 'Dodo' ('You Didn't Hear It From Me'), as recorded for a possible duet with Lulu (without her vocals), 'Growin' Up' and 'Alternative Candidate' (a demo that, apart from a few words, has nothing in common with the 'Candidate' on which Mike Garson plays in the style of Roy Bittan, the pianist of Bruce Springsteen's E Street Band). 'Dodo' and 'Alternative Candidate' (under the title 'Candidate') will also be added to the Rykodisc reissue of *Diamond Dogs* in 1990.

7. The city has several diamond museums.

8. Not to be confused with the harmonizer, also made by Eventide, that Tony Visconti will later use during the sessions for *Low* and *"Heroes"*.

9. In 1988, French pop singer Étienne Daho will ask Guy Peellaert for an illustration based on a photo of James Dean in *Rock Dreams* for the cover of his fourth studio album, *Pour Nos Vies Martiennes*. Peellaert will develop the funfair concept again. As for Mick Jagger, we'll never know whether he kicked himself for telling David Bowie that The Rolling Stones had asked Peellaert to illustrate the cover of *It's Only Rock'n'roll* –*Diamond Dogs* came out six months before it.

10. As a teenager, David Bowie read *Strange People*, a collection of short stories about odd, misshapen and anomalous people (some with inexplicable powers), by American author Frank Edwards. It will be in his list of favourite books.

11. RCA wanted to turn Mick Ronson into the 'next David Cassidy'. Funnily enough, the two will work together two years later, with Ronson playing guitar on the title song of *Gettin' In The Street*, Cassidy's 1976 album.

12. In 1998, German periodical *Die Zeit* will ask David Bowie to choose the most representative photo of the 20th century. He will pick one called 'Dysenteric Dying', a photo of a prisoner at Buchenwald who died of dysentery a few hours after the liberation of the camp. Bowie will say, 'For me, this photo is an expression of the violence and destruction that shaped this century to a large extent. The horrific tragedy of the man who dies just after regaining his freedom breaks your heart.' The image was taken in 1945 by Éric Schwab. He will pass away in Paris in 1978.

13. This silent German horror film from 1920 takes place at a fun fair.

14. In New York, David Bowie will also stay at the Pierre and Plaza hotels. Like the Sherry-Netherland, they are located a few feet from one another on the southeast corner of Central Park.

15. Robin Clark and Carlos Alomar were the only married couple to accompany David Bowie on stage. They were both generous with their time during the writing of this book and provided a lot of information.

16. Earl Slick, influenced by The Beatles and The Rolling Stones, popped up around the New York bar circuit with various youth bands before his friend Hank DeVito, who played the pedal steel guitar, asked him to join the New York Rock & Roll Ensemble... as a roadie! He sometimes played with the band as they were

setting up shows and, one day, David Sanborn suggested to Michael Kamen that he take Slick on as a guitarist. Slick liked Mick Ronson's guitar playing. He wasn't a fan of the outfit David Bowie made him wear on the Diamond Dogs tour, though he kept it afterwards anyway.

17. In 2019, fans of Quentin Tarantino and David Bowie will be happily surprised to find her in the credits, as a choreographer, for the excellent *Once Upon A Time In Hollywood*.

18. It's impossible to know with any certainty which drummer is playing on which song of *Diamond Dogs*. Aynsley Dunbar played in sessions before Tony Newman, but David Bowie also had him play over and/or replace some of Dunbar's parts (and not always the whole track). Likewise, Bowie seems to have played a lot of percussion himself, usually attributed to drummers.

19. An image David Bowie got from his father's account of Anthony Ashley-Cooper, Seventh Earl of Shaftesbury and famous philanthropist who fought against the misery and exploitation of poor children in Victorian times. Bowie didn't talk much about his childhood to the press, but he sometimes mentioned gangs of youths. In truth, unlike some of his friends, he was far from being a thug and spent most of his time at home, not on the street.

20. The bass player of Booker T. & The M.G.'s.

21. Like 'Rebel Rebel', 'Diamond Dogs', the second UK single from the album, was released in June 1974 without a designed sleeve. 'Diamond Dogs' (with The Spiders From Mars version of 'Holy Holy' on the B-side) reached Number 21 in the charts, just above 'Rock'n'roll Suicide', released as a single in March. In the US,

'1984' and 'Rock'n'roll With Me' were chosen as the A-sides of two singles.

22. In 1974, Keith Harwood recorded the concerts from the Diamond Dogs tour that would appear on the double album *David Live*, produced by Tony Visconti. Harwood never worked with David Bowie again. He died in a car accident in September 1977 while returning from a mixing session at Olympic Studios for The Rolling Stones album *Love You Live*. He was only 27 years old. Marc Bolan died almost in the same place two weeks later.

23. The programme for the two July shows at Madison Square Garden will significantly alter the credits used earlier in the tour. The show will be called *Bowie And His Music* with Toni Basil as co-director. Chris Langhart's name will be replaced by Showco.

24. On 14 October 1997, in the middle of his Earthling tour, David Bowie will return to the Capitol Theatre for a live concert filmed by MTV. The Rolling Stones were supposed to perform, but Mick Jagger was ill, so Bowie replaced them at the last minute. This was the last time he played there.

25. Since 1974, David Bowie's look during the first leg of the Diamond Dogs tour has made a lot of people talk. While everyone has their own theory, one cannot help but notice that the jacket/trouser suit and especially the crewneck sweater worn by Halloween Jack are strongly reminiscent of the outfit of German actor Conrad Veidt in his role as Cesare the sleepwalker in *The Cabinet of Dr Caligari*. Likewise, the photo on the back cover of *David Live* shows Bowie in a pose very similar to the one Cesare adopts in the film, when Dr Caligari reveals him to the audience. It's also interesting

to note that this cover doesn't show any of the set, which was a huge part of the show, and that there is no sleeve designer or photographer credited on it. Those photos were taken by Dagmar Krajnc.

26. *Diamond Dogs* will be played in its entirety almost every night, as well as at least half of *Aladdin Sane*.

27. Some tape boxes confirm that the title *Wham Bam Thank You Ma'am* had been considered.

28. It's been reported that 'Here Today, Gone Tomorrow' was only played at the shows in Philadelphia, but no audience member would bet their life on it now. The theory that this cover, which David Bowie initially wanted on the live album, could have been recorded during a sound check, isn't completely far-fetched. What's certain is that to make time for 'Here Today, Gone Tomorrow', Bowie didn't play 'Drive-In Saturday' in Philadelphia.

29. 'Panic In Detroit' will be the B-side of a single released the month before *David Live*. 'Knock On Wood', on the A-side, is a cover of a song Eddie Floyd co-wrote with Steve Cropper.

30. In the mid-1970s, it was common practice to 're-do' live backing vocals. Those on *Live!*, Bob Marley And The Wailers' first concert album, recorded at the Lyceum (London) in July 1975, were largely re-recorded later. Not by the I-Threes (Marley's official backing vocalists), but by Sue And Sunny, a British duo made up of the two Wheatman sisters. They are best known for having sung with Brotherhood Of Man and accompanying Mott The Hoople and T. Rex. In January 1970, they sung in sessions for 'The Prettiest Star' and 'London Bye Ta-Ta'

with Lesley Duncan. Highly recognizable, the backing vocals for *Ziggy Stardust And The Spiders From Mars – The Motion Picture Soundtrack* were likewise redone by Tony Visconti and David Bowie.

31. From the beginning of the 80s, when the first serious books about David Bowie started coming out, it was reported that the musicians of the Diamond Dogs tour met up at the Ice Palace after the second concert at Madison Square Garden. It's possible, but this Long Island club was about 60 miles from New York, which seems a bit far for a few drinks after a show. There was an Ice Palace 57 (on 57th Street) in New York, but it didn't open until the disco boom in 1977. None of the interviewees in this chapter were able to shed light on this subject.

32. In the mid-1960s, Alan Parker auditioned for The Blue Dukes, one of Phil Lancaster's first bands (Phil was the second drummer of The Lower Third). Parker already played well and certainly would have fit the bill, but he was only 16 years old, too young at the time to join a group legally.

33. Recorded after this tour in 1970 and released in early 1971, the last album by the original Booker T. & The M.G.'s, probably their best, was called *Melting Pot*.

34. Except for *Cracked Actor*, Alan Yentob's documentary for British television, which hasn't been officially released since 1975 when it was first broadcast, there are very few usable clips of these concerts and even fewer of the Soul/Philly Dogs tour that followed the recording of *Young Americans*. Apparently, none of the shows from the Isolar and Isolar 2 tours in 1976 and 1978 was filmed well enough to be used commercially either. The best visual record of the Station To Station tour, available (to the public) online, was filmed during rehearsals in Canada.

35. In fact, as with most live records in rock history, some tracks of *David Live* were re-recorded afterwards in the studio. Mike Garson replaced his solo on 'Aladdin Sane'.

36. A British psychedelic group led by singer/ guitarist/keyboardist/songwriter Adrian Gurvitz. Tony Newman played on three of their albums.

37. Located on 52 West 8th Street, north of Washington Square in New York, the Electric Lady Studios were built in 1970 in a former night club by (and for) Jimi Hendrix, who wasn't happy with the places he'd recorded in until then. Hendrix died a few weeks after it opened. AC/DC, Frank Zappa, Blondie, The Cars, Chic, Led Zeppelin, Lou Reed, The Rolling Stones and many other major rock artists have recorded albums there. David Bowie will finish *Young Americans* at Electric Lady in 1974. *Blackstar* will be mixed there by Tom Elmhirst in 2015.

38. Lulu sang harmonies on 'Dodo', which ended up being withdrawn from *Diamond Dogs*, but it was included in the 1990 and 2004 reissues. David recorded a duet version with her, full of soul arrangements, but it was never officially released in that form. David Bowie's voice is the only one we can hear on any available version of the song.

39. The names of studios and less important contributors weren't always mentioned on album credits at the time. The booklet accompanying the box set *Who Can I Be Now?,*

which will be released in 2016 and includes the most recent reissue of *Diamond Dogs,* contains a photo of a man leaning over a console with Bowie. The caption says it's Andy Morris, but he told the author it was not him. According to Andy, it's Keith Harwood in the picture.

40. David Bowie and The Spiders From Mars performed there on 19 and 20 May 1972.

41. The session took place at Morgan Studios, where Jethro Tull regularly worked. In 1971, Rick Kemp, the bass player of Steeleye Span, was approached to join David Bowie's band, but it was Trevor Bolder who ultimately landed the job. Kemp also played with King Crimson and Michael Chapman.

42. A giant of jazz orchestration who famously worked with Miles Davis.

43. *To Sir, With Love* is a British film directed by James Clavell in 1967. It gave Lulu her first acting role.

44. New York's companion to San Francisco's Fillmore, one of the most popular concert venues on the West Coast. In the late 1960s, it was managed by Bill Graham.

45. Several painters (or their paintings) make discreet appearances in David Bowie's work, either by being mentioned in songs (Georges Braque in 'Unwashed And Somewhat Slightly Dazed' on *Space Oddity* in 1969) or as inspiration for record covers and videos. The work of German artist George Grosz, known for his damning portrayal of his country in the inter-war period, was one of Bowie's references for Hunger City, especially his paintings *Explosion* and *Metropolis*.

46. This incident took place on 10 December 1971. The week before, during a Frank Zappa concert at the casino in Montreux, a member of the audience had set fire to the place by setting off a flare over the stage. This incident inspired Deep Purple, whose members had been at the concert that night (they were due to start recording their next album at the casino, with a mobile studio, the next day), to write their most famous song, 'Smoke On The Water'. Aynsley Dunbar was the drummer at Zappa's concert at the Rainbow.

47. *A Chorus Line*, which showed off Broadway and then on Broadway in 1975 (a year after the Diamond Dogs tour), can't be the musical that made David Bowie want to work with Michael Bennett and Jules Fisher. But it is highly likely that he'd heard or read great things about Bennett's *Seesaw*, a musical Fisher also worked on, even if he probably didn't see it (Bowie didn't spend much time in New York between March and December 1973).

48. Toni Basil formed The Lockers with Don Campbell. They were a famous American street dance troupe in the 1970s.

49. There were actually two concerts in Pittsburgh during this tour: on 26 and 27 June 1974 at the Syria Mosque. The one at the Civic Theatre in Akron supposedly took place on 25 June but is actually missing from the official list of David Bowie shows that year. In all likelihood (and according to Buford Jones), it probably happened as a replacement for the concert at Cincinnati Gardens, cancelled, a few days before, due to poor ticket sales.

50. These words were taken from *David Bowie Ouvre Le Chien*.

51. This is an excerpt from *Les Mémoires du France* (Editions du Havre de Grâce), courtesy of the author, Béatrice Merdrignac.

AFL1-0998 STEREO
YOUNG AMERICANS
David Bowie
RCA VICTOR
10320
David Bowie
FAME

YOUNG AMERICANS

RCA – 7 MARCH 1975

CRACKED ACTOR (LIVE LOS ANGELES '74)
(PARLOPHONE – 22 APRIL 2017)

*'Because this man was a great artist, and art cannot tolerate chains
any more than science can.'*
(WILHELM REICH, *LISTEN, LITTLE MAN!* 1948)

'That thing about the fly in my milk, someone's always reminding me of that! Honestly, that's kind of how I was feeling and I'm not proud of it. I found the questions a bit boring, so of course, the answers were too. It wasn't long before I pulled the alarm! Well, at the same time, we were listening to some great tunes in the car, weren't we? Aretha Franklin, right? "(You Make Me Feel Like) A Natural Woman", was no small feat. Carole King, I'm sure you love her in France. You've always had better taste than the Americans. From jazz to Suicide, your country has always welcomed good music from the USA. [...]

'A journalist asked you to proofread my obituary? That's funny. Tell him you never met me, and that I died in 1974, when I was recording *Young Americans*! [...]

'Sometimes the presence of a person in the studio can have an effect on what you're trying to do there, even if their contribution isn't just musical. That's what happened with John on "Fame". He was there and if he hadn't been, the song probably never would have existed.'

DB (1991/2003/1991)

Whether you're a famous musician or just a music lover, what you listened to and loved when you were young propels you through life. The music we pretended to like or snubbed can matter a lot too. David Bowie must have been 16 or 17 years old when he experienced, or felt, what prompted him to write 'The London Boys', which is often correctly considered one of his first key songs. The chord progression in the verse was a precursor to those in other major songs he would later write.

In this serious ode placed in a very real setting (Soho, Wardour Street...), Bowie sings about leaving the family home, the suburbs, and meeting new people – friends, the gang. Those who knew, who understood and could show him the way. 'The London Boys' is about taking the first job that comes along, being initiated into the world of drugs (pills). If they made you sick, you couldn't show it. You could never lose face because appearances were too important. But at that age, even if he did sometimes tell a lie to get at the truth, or pretended to be a misunderstood artist because it was fashionable, Bowie didn't lie to himself or to his friends.

At the height of the mod period, he had already fallen for jazz, blues and rock'n'roll, and when Geoff MacCormack talked about James Brown, the name of the godfather of soul didn't mean much to him. Many people broaden their horizons according to their friends' tastes, but David Bowie sometimes resisted, sticking with what he knew until the moment he decided to let in a new influence. So he has Geoff MacCormack to thank for his discovery of Mr Dynamite and all he had to do was to keep pulling on that spool of wool to enjoy soul music to its fullest.

It was more usual for British teenagers to prefer literature or poetry, but at 16 years old, Geoff the mod enjoyed spending evenings at The Flamingo Club[1] and was into Purple Hearts[2]. With the exception of a few Mose Allisons and Georgie Fames, his record collection was almost exclusively by black musicians. By introducing his friend to the live album of James Brown at the Apollo, Geoff lit a spark in him that would smoulder for a decade before bursting into flames. In 1974, it will make just as much sense for Geoff MacCormack to be spending his nights in Harlem and ending up at Sigma Sound Studios as it will for David.

It's important to remember that Bowie is not the only British musician who's going to dabble in rhythm'n'blues, soul and disco music in the 1970s. In early 1976, at the Château d'Hérouville, the Gibb brothers from the Isle of Man will write a handful of hits forever associated with John Badham's film, *Saturday Night Fever*. In so doing, they'll vindicate their decision two years earlier to put their musical destiny in the hands of Arif Mardin[3], starting with *Mr Natural*. Robert Palmer, from Batley (southwest of Leeds), was more focused on the sound of New Orleans, but he will be a classy performer of the 'blue-eyed soul' scene and will release four high-quality albums with very pronounced rhythm'n'blues accents between 1974 and 1978. Likewise, Leo Sayer will contribute great vocals and melodies to a few pop hits with some very funky arrangements by Richard Perry (still enjoyable on the *Endless Flight*[4] and *Thunder In My Heart* albums). Also in the 70s, Average White Band and especially Kokomo – less well known but a much better band – will champion a sort of British soul. Steve Winwood's first solo album, which will come out in 1977 (with Willie Weeks on bass and Andy Newmark on drums) is a model of this musical genre.

Until the end of his career, several of David Bowie's albums will go through a difficult gestation – false starts, drastic changes, staff cuts, production adjustments or title modifications. These upheavals, whether amicable or not, will have consequences. *The Gouster*, which became *Young Americans* halfway through its production, perfectly illustrates these problems. The facts aren't easy to establish and Bowie's records haven't always come with reliable liner notes. Different people have interpreted them in different ways, some more accurately than others. And memories are not infallible, adding to the difficulty of telling the story correctly. Many aspects of the making of this album – which took eight months to record – are still up for debate. While some interviewees have agreed to talk about it here (Tony Visconti, Carlos Alomar), others (Harry Maslin, Jean Millington) decided against it. That's not a good sign. Among the most forthcoming interviewees were those working at the now-defunct Sigma Sound Studios, especially former-owner Joe Tarsia. They helped to reconstruct this puzzle, although the pieces were so widely scattered that it was sometimes hard to put them together.

Ava Cherry's session at Sigma – at 212 North 12th Street in Philadelphia – in July 1974 was probably not the only thing that prompted David Bowie to record there the following month. Bowie loved the songs and sound of Kenneth Gamble and Leon Huff (and their partner Thom Bell) who marketed their productions on their label PIR (Philadelphia International Records), and while he did consider alternative studios, since he'd returned to America, the 'Philly sound', as played by The O'Jays, The Delfonics, Teddy Pendergrass, Harold Melvin And The Blue Notes and Billy Paul, was all over the radio stations and dance clubs. Released in April, 'TSOP' (The Sound of Philadelphia) by MFSB[5] was Number 1 in the States that spring and it became the theme tune for *Soul Train*, an American television programme featuring mainly African-American soul and rhythm'n'blues artists. Most of Sigma's tapes are now stored at Drexel University in Philadelphia – Joe Tarsia donated them – but the one from Ava Cherry's session isn't among them. So it's impossible to know exactly who was in the studio with her and Bowie. Apparently, MainMan had booked the session, with Michael Kamen producing – 'Everything That Touches You', written by Kamen[6], was one of the songs Cherry recorded that day.

However, that session was probably when David Bowie met some of the musicians who worked regularly at Sigma Sound and would be likely to play on his future album. In order to make his music more black – which was the direction he was heading in – those he worked with also had to be black. It's also highly probable that Bowie didn't want to record with all or even part of the band from the Diamond Dogs tour. The mutiny that took place before the Tower Theater concerts left a bad taste in his mouth and didn't bode well for the musicians who might have wanted to continue the soul adventure in the studio. To get more money from Tony Defries, some had threatened not to play and the manager, who still held the purse strings at that point, probably considered that their fate – like Woody Woodmansey's in 1973 – was sealed. When Flowers and Newman said they wanted to return to the UK because the various excesses of the tour were harming their health, no one at MainMan asked them to stay. But on that July day at Sigma Sound Studios, as demonstrated by the slow-burner that production of *The Gouster/Young Americans* would be, it probably escaped the usually sharp Bowie that things would not be going his way.

In the interview section of this chapter, Tarsia, his son Mike, and Sigma recording engineer Peter Humphreys propose several theories to explain why the MFSB musicians would decline to work with this British 'white boy'. But

MainMan are not aware of this when they book some studio time for their prime artist. Bowie and Coco find out a few days before the first session that percussionist Larry Washington will be the only representative of the 'Philly sound' on the album – they realize they have to form a band, and quickly.

First they recruit Andy Newmark from Port Chester, a young drummer who made a name for himself the year before by playing on *Fresh*, Sly And The Family Stone's sixth LP. He is joined on bass by Willie Weeks[7], whose performance – the long solo on 'Voices Inside (Everything Is Everything)' – on Donny Hathaway's 1972 live album, still excites rhythm'n'blues lovers everywhere. And, not surprisingly, since he finally reaches a financial accord with Tony Defries, Carlos Alomar becomes Bowie's guitarist. Mike Garson, David Sanborn and Pablo Rosario, survivors from the first leg of the tour, complete the band.

Initially, Geoff MacCormack is the only backing vocalist. In addition to Washington and Rosario, a third percussionist will join the sessions. This is Ralph MacDonald, from Trinidad and Tobago, who grew up in Harlem and began his career by playing the steel drum in Harry Belafonte's orchestra. In the early 1970s, MacDonald also helped write timeless songs such as 'Where Is The Love', sung by Roberta Flack and Donny Hathaway, and 'Just The Two Of Us', most famously performed by singer Bill Withers and sax player Grover Washington.

David Bowie also chose Sigma Sound because of in-house engineer Carl Paruolo, but after two days of working with him, he realizes that his methods do not suit him and calls Tony Visconti to the rescue. For the first time since *The Man Who Sold The World*, he is back in the co-producer's seat for a Bowie album (for *Diamond Dogs* he was mostly in charge of the mixing).

At Sigma, Tony discovers David's new way of working. Before Visconti's arrival, Bowie has been showing his musicians some chord progressions on guitar or piano, then encouraging them to play them as they pleased. While waiting for Bowie to say something, Newmark and Weeks sometimes sent enquiring glances to the musicians more used to working with him. David could sit in the control room with his eyes half closed for a very long time without saying a word to his band, but he always let them know if he heard something he liked. This is how many songs of the future album were structured and some basic tracks were recorded. Within about a dozen days, they will tape 'John, I'm Only Dancing (Again)', 'Somebody Up There Likes Me', 'It's Gonna Be Me', 'Who Can I Be Now?', 'Can You Hear Me', 'Young Americans' and 'Right' – this will be the first track listing of the album. But Bowie's habit of not starting the sessions until the evening, coupled with the fact that the songs essentially come from informal jam sessions, tends to irritate Visconti. He takes care of many overdubs on his own before he knows what they are likely to keep and what David will approve.

To keep up with this challenging pace, Visconti starts using the same stimulant drug as Bowie, but to a lesser extent. Tensions in the studio are sometimes palpable. It doesn't affect their work, however, because they also manage to record 'Shilling The Rubes', 'I'm A Laser' and 'After Today', three songs which won't make the album. Despite his unconventional hours, Bowie is still prolific, partly because he wants to sing live while the band plays – Tony Visconti will confirm later that 90 per cent of the lead vocals were recorded this way. The backing vocals will be added later.

When Robin Clark visits her husband Carlos Alomar at Sigma, she is accompanied by Luther Vandross. That summer, Vandross, a 23-year-old music lover from New York who's founded the first fan club for singer Patti LaBelle, gets the chance to sing on a whole album and also leads his first backing-vocals sessions and even co-writes a song with Bowie. On some tracks, Clark and Vandross will be joined by Ava Cherry, Diane Sumler and Anthony Hinton. These last two are friends of Vandross and will go on to sing with him in Luther, a vocal group that will record two LPs before the end of the 70s (many musicians from the Bowie galaxy of the time – Carlos Alomar, Andy Newmark, Pablo Rosario, Dennis Davis, George Murray – will also play on these albums). This first phase wraps up in late August and David invites the fans who've been following him since he got to town (squatting in front of his hotel and Sigma Sound) to a special listening session of the record. Almost 50 years later, they're still talking about it.

By the end of the month, David Bowie is still plagued by his problems with MainMan and is now fully aware of the gravity of the situation. But he is excited about what he's just recorded. He hops on a train to Los Angeles with Geoff MacCormack and uses the time on the trip to think about the next leg of the tour, which is due to start up again in early September with a six-day residency at the Universal Amphitheatre in Hollywood. The location, where *Jesus Christ Superstar* was staged two years before, is ideal for Hunger City. But once again, Bowie has evolved so fast that his music, and even more so his show, can't keep up with him. Although he is still proud of *The Year Of The Diamond Dogs*, it no longer reflects his state of mind. The technical team builds the impressive set once again, but David tells Tony Defries that he is going to start getting rid of it afterwards.

David Bowie also makes changes to his band. Willie Weeks and Andy Newmark have left to play on *Dark Horse*, the album George Harrison will release later that year, so Doug Rauch and Greg Errico replace them. Six months before, Rauch quit Santana after replacing David Brown, the original bass player. As for Errico, he's also played with Santana, and with Sly And The Family Stone before Newmark's time with them. This rhythm section brings new blood into Bowie's increasingly funky band, which is also enhanced by the presence of seven (!) backing vocalists, Carlos Alomar on rhythm guitar[8] and Earl Slick on lead. This mutation in the sound can be heard on *Cracked Actor (Live Los Angeles '74)*, recorded at the Universal Amphitheatre[9] that month and released by Warner in April 2017. This live album produced by Tony Visconti and mixed at Human (his current studio in New York), will feature two songs – 'John, I'm Only Dancing (Again)' and 'It's Gonna Be Me' – whose studio versions were also recorded at Sigma in August 1974. Their inclusion shows David Bowie's eagerness to play his 'new music' to his audience. *Cracked Actor (Live Los Angeles '74)* will be released on (triple) vinyl for Record Store Day, then on CD a few weeks later.

Many people think David Bowie invited his 'devotees' in Philadelphia to listen to the results of his sessions at Sigma Sound out of pure kindness, but it was also because he wanted their honest opinion. For some music artists, what their fawning fans think doesn't hold much value. But those who've had the privilege of getting at all close to Bowie know that, until his withdrawal from public life, when he asks people for their opinion, it won't be to seek praise. He'll listen to their comments, especially technical ones, and more often than not, will take them on board.

Up until the last show of the tour, on 1 December in Georgia, David Bowie will add more and more songs from his upcoming record, replacing those from *Diamond Dogs*. He wants to see the reaction of the audience and make sure his new style doesn't disappoint people, even if it doesn't make up for the diminishing set[10]. Since its release (and since Bowie's death, which prompted many to re-evaluate his work or to suddenly appreciate it), it is fashionable to prefer *Cracked Actor (Live Los Angeles '74)* to *David Live*, which was recorded just two months before. The honest way to approach these albums is to think of them as two stages of a metamorphosis which was accelerated by playing live – the sound and look of the concerts would change again between the dates in Los Angeles and the end of the tour.

Like those in New York, the shows at the Universal Amphitheatre draw their fair share of VIPs, including Michael Jackson, who's just turned sixteen and doesn't miss a second of David Bowie's stage performance, especially the mime parts. Alan Yentob, a BBC producer who was granted permission by MainMan to direct a documentary on Bowie and the soon-to-be-over Diamond Dogs Tour, is filming live footage of the show. *Cracked Actor*[11], which will air for the first time on British television in late January 1975, is not perfect (except for 'Space Oddity' – the sound for which comes from the original record – none of the songs shot in Los Angeles and Philadelphia feature in full), but it is the only official (and therefore tolerated) record of this unusual tour. Unsurprisingly, although Hunger City is shown in the documentary, it is the less formal footage – scenes showing surreal interviews, Bowie backstage or snatched conversations in the back of his limo – that will please fans the most. David looks fragile in *Cracked Actor*, but stays sharp as soon as he speaks.

While he will be very good in Nicolas Roeg's *The Man Who Fell To Earth* the following year (his first feature film), the 'cracked actor' is perhaps at his zenith in the limousine scene of Alan Yentob's documentary. We see him sitting with Coco Schwab, wearing a Borsalino on his head, saying he feels like the fly floating in the milk that he's drinking straight from the carton. He's no less excellent in the opening sequence when he snaps 'Good!' back at *Eyewitness News* reporter Wayne Satz, after he admits being reluctant to judge what category Bowie fits in. Regularly removed from YouTube and Vimeo, but put back online just as quickly, *Cracked Actor* was never made into an offical video, and Bowie said he did not enjoy watching it.

David Bowie spends the last two weeks of September in Los Angeles. Other concerts were planned (even some performances in Brazil), but they were cancelled because of MainMan's rapaciousness – some organizers were put off when the company asked for 90 per cent of the proceeds. During his forced stay, he meets Liz Taylor and John Lennon, is photographed by Terry O'Neill, and rehearses with his group for the final leg of the tour.

The rhythm section changes again when bassist Emir Ksasan and drummer Dennis Davis join. Bowie appreciates Davis' playing and personality from the first day of rehearsals. A former student of Max Roach and Elvin Jones, he will contribute a lot to the quality of Bowie's music until *Scary Monsters* in 1980. When the tour starts up again in October in Minneapolis, Mike Garson is the new musical director instead of Michael Kamen. Eddie Jobson of Roxy Music was asked to play keyboards, but he declined. Actually, when Garson legitimately claimed a pay rise to match his new responsibilities, Tony Defries – cheaper than ever – fired him. Mike only kept his job at Bowie's request.

Bowie's entrance on stage is now preceded by an opening act playing for about 40 minutes, during which each backing vocalist sings a track accompanied by The Garson Band. The show now has a real soul review vibe to it[12]. The media was still excited about the September concerts in Los Angeles, but they are less complimentary about the October shows. Some journalists from Indianapolis, Milwaukee, Detroit and Chicago do not like the new direction the material is taking as much as the majority of the audience do. Other songs recorded in Philadelphia that summer ('Young Americans' and 'Can You Hear Me') make the set list, but those from *Diamond Dogs*, which RCA is still promoting, are progressively removed – on the last night, they'll make up less than a quarter of the material.

While Bowie goes to great lengths to make a good impression in his elegant, beautifully cut suits made, for the last time, by Freddie Burretti (he wears a tartan tie and his main accessory is a cane), his voice is letting him down. On the nights he isn't performing, he sometimes stays up at hotel bars until dawn and the alcohol, drugs, cigarettes and fatigue are significantly impairing his vocal abilities. He dealt with this problem at Sigma Sound Studios, but he is struggling live and sometimes lets the backing vocalists reach the high notes in his place. The raspy timbre of his voice lends itself well to his new genre, but David Bowie isn't Rod Stewart and, when he sounds like he is over-singing, it's actually his vocal cords giving out. In fact, his whole body is put to the test, and his stage performances take on an increasingly convulsive character, which worries his musicians.

Carlos Alomar and most of his band mates (more than two-thirds of whom are black), are in their element playing this 'plastic soul'[13], but Earl Slick, survivor (like Garson and Sanborn) of the original line-up, isn't too happy with the style of the new material, even though he is relieved not to be playing in the shadow of the cardboard buildings anymore. As the first album by The Earl Slick Band[14] will prove two years later, Slick is more of a rock guy.

David Bowie gives a series of concerts in New York straddling October and November[15], with MainMan adding the first two dates at the last minute. But on those nights, although the press has been invited to watch Bowie's latest iteration, the Radio City Music Hall, which can hold 6,000, isn't quite full.

When the tour stops by Philadelphia again in November, David Bowie, Tony Visconti and a few members of the band return to Sigma. In all likelihood, these sessions were initially intended for overdubs. In August, Tony Defries told Bowie he didn't approve of his new soul sound, arguing that he was confusing his audience and risking his commercial viability. RCA on the other hand, though concerned about Bowie's constant changes of direction, thinks the opposite. Bowie does not care about his manager's artistic preferences and, given the situation, he is even suspicious of his opinions.

Wanting his next record to sell well in the US, Bowie believes that fine-tuning the arrangements can only make it more attractive. He also decides to lay the foundations for two new songs that will be finalized in New York the following month: the ballad 'Win', and 'Fascination'. The latter is an adaptation of 'Funky Music (Is A Part Of Me)' by Luther Vandross, which he is singing as part of the opening act. David Bowie, who hears the song from his dressing room while getting ready and thinks it is simple but effective, asks Vandross if he can record a version with partially rewritten lyrics. The young singer, who will release his version two years later (on *Luther*, his first album), eagerly agrees.

David Bowie's return to Philadelphia doesn't help clear up any confusion over the recordings in progress, specifically regarding personnel. The 'Sigma Kids', who were back squatting outside the Barclay Hotel and the studios, saw many musicians coming and going who won't be credited on the cover. They definitely recorded two or three long jam sessions in November (from which Bowie probably extracted the best parts), but the accuracy of the liner notes was not among the strong points of his albums (see *David Live*), so it's impossible to know exactly who played what and where. As photographs attest (although even fewer were taken than in August), Mike Garson participated in these sessions, as did the backing vocalists and Carlos Alomar, whose role as sideman is reinforced in late 1974. Other musicians probably stopped by Sigma Sound, and Bruce Springsteen visited David Bowie there in November.

It is also during these sessions that the name of the album seems to have stabilized. Before then, its title changed every time a musician spoke about it – *Somebody Up There Likes Me, One Damn Song, Dancin', Shilling The Rubes* and *Fascination* were all considered. The origins of the title *The Gouster*, as written on some tape boxes, has been the subject of much debate, but it can reasonably be assumed that it refers to the look of black Chicago teenagers from the early 1960s. They wanted to look like bad boys, so the *gousters* borrowed fashion inspiration from the gangsters of previous decades (who sometimes called themselves that), like the ones in *Boardwalk Empire*, the 2010 television series directed by Martin Scorsese[16]. Also, we know that Bowie was fascinated by the French and Italian Renaissance, and that in his *Essays*, Michel de Montaigne talked about his taste for both travelling and writing as forms of human intellectual exploration. In his text (David Bowie preferred to read writings in the original language), the philosopher frequently used the word 'goût' (taste) and the verb 'goûter' (to taste or have a taste for), which was then spelled 'gouster'.

Before wrapping up the longest American tour of his career (it became the Soul Tour, then the Philly Dogs Tour, and comprised almost 80 concerts) with an excellent show in Atlanta[17], to an audience of 18,000 people, David Bowie booked some time at a studio in New York. In early December, he and Tony Visconti start new sessions at The Record Plant[18]. They make some overdubs, particularly on 'Fascination' and 'Win', two songs that are really starting to take shape.

One night, Bowie invites Visconti to the Sherry-Netherland, where he is staying. John Lennon will be there and David felt like Tony's presence would help to keep the conversation flowing. At the end of September, at a party held at the house of actor Dean Martin in Los Angeles, Liz Taylor had introduced John to David, but they didn't really get the chance to talk. The admiration being mutual, they were bound to meet again. However, since the ex-Beatle had completed his album two months before, it's unlikely that David Bowie, as has sometimes been said, happened to bump into John Lennon at The Record Plant while he was mixing *Rock'N'Roll*. So Tony meets John Lennon and his Lost Weekend girlfriend, May Pang[19]. In his autobiography, Tony recounts the evening (which ended at 10am) better than anyone else could. It was apparently a surreal meeting but, as Bowie had predicted, it was Visconti's curiosity – he had about '10,000 questions' for Lennon – that helped launch it.

In early December, Bowie makes his infamous television appearance on *The Dick Cavett Show*. In the live section of this performance, which had been filmed a few weeks before, he sings raspy versions of '1984' and 'Young Americans', and his interview is a disaster. Unable to keep still, he twitches his cane compulsively, is visibly craving something and his answers, much shorter than the questions, are gibberish. However, he maintains his sense of humour, admitting for example, that he 'nicked from Mick Jagger' the idea to use Guy Peellaert for the cover of *Diamond Dogs*. His sense of irony also allows him to tackle more serious subjects, including his relationship with his mother. And when Cavett asks what he thinks of the journalists who over-intellectualize his work in an attempt to analyse it, Bowie says that he only reads the good reviews and that in any case, there is nothing to understand in his art.

Since he liked the sound of *Diamond Dogs*, David Bowie asked Tony Visconti to mix the album in London, at Sound House[20]. So he will work on the seven songs which would later resurface on the 2016 version of *The Gouster*, as well as on 'Win' and 'Fascination'. During a quick session at AIR Studios[21], Tony adds strings to some of the tracks (including the two most recent ones) and, following David's detailed instructions, he mixes the record and sends the tapes to the US.

Scrapping the idea of going to England for the holidays, Bowie leaves the Sherry-Netherland for the Pierre Hotel just before Christmas. He will then live in a brownstone on West 20th Street until his departure for the west coast. Bowie was a master of cultivating paradoxes: while he spent the latter half of the year leaving *Diamond Dogs* behind, he devotes the last days of 1974 to working on a related project in his hotel suite. Video camera in hand, he shoots some short scenes in black and white. The rudimentary film takes place in a mock-up of Hunger City.

Many have written (and read) that David Bowie had hit rock bottom in Los Angeles in 1975. But he was already at the end of his tether, both physically and emotionally, the previous winter. Cocaine, which miraculously hasn't killed him (his use of the drug, witnessed by John Lennon or Mick Farren, drained 'abuse' of all its meaning), opened the floodgates and airlocks of his mind, leaving gaping wounds which he allowed, indiscriminately, to swallow up all that was dear to him, and anything which haunted or harmed him. Trapped in this restless brain, each emotion (admiration, happiness, worry and anger) took on a proportion that most artists couldn't have handled and, for a time, even Bowie seemed incapable of doing so. Perhaps that's what he wanted. Later, he will claim he lost his sanity towards the end of the Soul Tour, and that he only started putting himself back together again in Berlin.

But his excesses in 1974 and 1975 didn't completely destroy him. Despite appearances, David Bowie was still in control. His time as Ziggy Stardust had revealed his fascination with physical and emotional violence – Iggy Pop And The Stooges, the Droogs from *A Clockwork Orange*, Burroughs' wild boys. In 1974, Bowie was impressed by American artist Chris Burden, who crucified himself on the back of a Volkswagen Beetle. Three years before, in the name of art, Burden had had himself shot in the arm. Endangering oneself to enhance creativity? How could Bowie not have thought of that? A good many fans of his music have benefitted from the fruit of this temptation: *Young Americans* and *Station To Station*, its successor, are among the masterpieces (if not actually *the* masterpieces) of his discography. By violating his body and mind, weary of working in an environment defined by others (his management, the media), Bowie would become the context himself. The skin on his skeleton, his quivering nostrils, his brain taken over by bitter blades – he basically turned himself into his art. The height of the risks he took equalled that of his ambition. While he won't use this ploy systematically, with *Low* and *"Heroes"*, later with Tin Machine, then with *Outside, Heathen* and *Blackstar*, he will step into this breach which, for the confused but inquiring artist, comes down to becoming his own worst enemy.

In interviews from that year, it was obvious that David Bowie wasn't losing his marbles, but he wasn't all that sharp either. Instead of showing the world his insatiable curiosity, he spoke of flying saucers, black magic and fascism in random and tense ways, which made him look unhinged, consumed by anxiety. He was a weather vane in the wind. It's not surprising that those he worked with would be the first to bear the brunt of certain U-turns and decisions made all the more cruel by their suddenness and lack of explanation. Mike Garson was fired at Christmas, a gift he could have done without. Likewise, Tony Visconti wasn't thrilled to learn that, in early 1975, Bowie had taped two more songs, but without him. He'd recorded them with Harry Maslin and John Lennon.

Since the end of the tour, just as he had taken Mick Jagger's advice about grasping managers in late 1973, David Bowie has been listening to the opinion of his new 'best friend' on his situation with MainMan. The ex-Beatle is in the middle of a contractual dispute with Allen Klein (the American businessman who in the late 60s took advantage of disagreements among The Beatles to sink his claws into them), so he advises David to find a solicitor to extricate himself from Tony Defries.

In her book, May Pang tells a funny story about an evening she spent with John, along with Paul and Linda McCartney, in David's suite at the Pierre Hotel. All excited about having them listen to his latest album (which, at that point, after another change, was called *Fascination*), Bowie wanted to play it for them a second time. When he was about to start it again, Paul asked if he had any other records they could listen to instead. Bowie pretended not to hear him. Lennon, who'd already experienced a similar session, finally intervened on Paul's side. David seemed surprised and, after telling Pang to put on whatever she wanted (she chose Aretha Franklin), he disappeared into another room and never reappeared.

In mid-January, David Bowie invites John Lennon to Electric Lady Studios to play him his cover of the Beatles' 'Across The Universe' (written by Lennon). He has just recorded it, much to the surprise of his friends and, even more so, John, who will later say that he always wondered why David had chosen that song. Intrigued, Lennon agrees to play some acoustic guitar on Bowie's version and meets Earl Slick[22] who is on lead (the other musicians are Carlos Alomar, Emir Ksasan and Dennis Davis). Originally from Philadelphia (he was the sound technician at the Electric Factory Club in the 1960s), Harry Maslin, the recording engineer who worked with Tony Visconti in December at The Record Plant, has been promoted to co-producer. As a matter of fact, without telling Visconti, Bowie contacted Maslin in late December and together they made other overdubs on the album. Then they mixed it[23]!

Everybody knows what came out of these January sessions: 'Fame'. On 20 September and 4 October 1975 (John Denver's 'Sorry' slid in for the week between – you couldn't make it up!), a month after being released as a single, this unexpected hit song will get David Bowie to the top of the Billboard Hot 100 for the first time.

Was 'Fame' really just a stroke of luck? Or was it part of a set-up, Bowie's Machiavellian plan to secure RCA's support after telling Defries he wanted to end their association? Once again, this is open to interpretation. Also, isn't the Bowie-Alomar-Lennon writing credit a bit over the top (Lennon did not actually write any of the track and Alomar had contributed riffs to many other songs without credit)? And what to think of the fact that it was a simple song like 'Fame', instead of something more elaborate (like '1984'), that finally helped David Bowie achieve the cross-Atlantic success coveted by so many British artists of his generation?

The song is subject to much debate. Apparently, John Lennon had suggested they do 'something else' after they'd worked on 'Across The Universe'. This seems very likely, because after the wanderings of his Lost Weekend, and after finishing *Rock'N'Roll*, John had started to enjoy the studio again. So Bowie suggested trying 'Foot Stomping (Part 1)' by The Flares[24], a doo-wop band from Los Angeles. Frontman Aaron Collins had written this fairly minor song that became a hit in 1961. When the Diamond Dogs tour started up again in October, 'Foot Stomping (Part 1)' was on the set list and Bowie even played it on *The Dick Cavett Show*, paired with 'I Wish I Could Shimmy Like My Sister Kate', a Dixieland jazz standard. The Beatles had done their own doo-wop cover of it, like The Olympics before them. Bowie and his musicians also tried to record it at Sigma Sound and then at The Record Plant, but unsuccessfully.

The version they try to record at Electric Lady doesn't seem to be working either, until Carlos Alomar slows down the guitar riff he's been playing on their live version of 'Foot Stomping (Part 1)' – not 'the riff' from the original, which didn't have one – to match a beat that Emir Ksasan and Dennis Davis have spontaneously started. John Lennon grabs a guitar, then Bowie, who likes the funky groove he is hearing, starts to build up the song. Except for the introduction (repeated halfway through), 'Fame' is basically a blues track without the third chord.

In 2007, in the liner notes of the 5.1 reissue of *Young Americans*, David will contradict Carlos, who remembers having recorded more guitar takes than were actually taped. While Alomar is most certainly on the funkier guitars, Bowie and Lennon played the others. John did add a barely perceptible acoustic guitar (and supervised the backwards piano intro[25]), but it is definitely David who plays the electric riff, saturated and menacing, which seems to answer his vocal part[26].

John Lennon joined in the backing vocals, but David Bowie managed the more acrobatic ones on his own, including the descending line – the word 'Fame' repeated some 20 times, from high to low. Jean Fineberg and Jean Millington also provide backing vocals. Millington is a friend of Bowie and the bass player of Fanny, a female rock band he likes and supports[27]. For their fifth and final album (*Rock And Roll Survivors*, released in 1974), she wrote 'Butter Boy' as a tribute to David. Since he was always on the lookout and had a talent for spotting good ideas and keeping them in mind, it's interesting to note that 'Butter Boy' starts with finger snapping (as will be heard in 'Under Pressure') and the 'Wa-wa-oos' of the backing vocals are identical to the ones in 'Absolute Beginners', which will be written and released a decade later. Jean Millington will marry Earl Slick in 1978.

As for the subject of the lyrics to 'Fame' (most likely written in haste, the day of or the day after recording the playback), it was very topical because, at the time, most of David Bowie and John Lennon's conversations revolved around the price of fame, public recognition and whether or not it was all worth it. They also talked a lot about the role of managers and Bowie couldn't help but notice that Lennon didn't have one and wasn't any the worse off for it. After Tony Defries, David will hire two other managers for a while, but then he will decide to get rid of them, and just work with a small team. Coco Schwab will be his mainstay until the end.

In 1975, after having grown up in the public spotlight, David Bowie will take a step back. He will later state that, in the mid-70s, he came to understand that show business, the music industry, its ways and customs, were not for him. Over the decades, claiming that his art is the only part of him he wants to display, he will withdraw even further, eventually bordering on the reclusive. Bowie will spend his time in places where his anonymity is respected, keeping out of the spotlight except when his work demands otherwise. When he wins awards, he will prefer to be represented or will ask his friends to go in his place. He will generally eschew tributes, celebrations and honours – he won't be attending his induction into the Rock And Roll Hall Of Fame in 1996 and will refuse a CBE in 2000, then a knighthood three years later.

On 1 March 1975, at the 17th Grammy Awards, David Bowie presents Aretha Franklin with the award for Best Rhythm'n'blues Vocal Performance (for her version of Ashford-Simpson's 'Ain't Nothing Like The Real Thing'), but the stage at the Uris Theatre seems to burn his feet. However, he does take the opportunity to make a short but brilliant speech (starting with 'Ladies and gentlemen and others') and, later that night, he will meet up with John Lennon – who is also presenting an award – and with actress Ann-Margret, who will charm everyone, especially Geoff MacCormack.

You'll have to hear it to (not) believe it – David Bowie will later describe the songs on *Young Americans* as 'little', saying he wrote them in a hurry! Proud at last to be artistically free and without an agenda, he provides a checkerboard context to launch his ninth album. Echoes of black heat stand in sharp contrast to white powder. From the first notes of the title track, not only does he master the sound he was looking for, he has imbibed it to create another one. The rhythm section grooves with panache, David Sanborn blows his horn to get out of the fog, while Bowie portrays an American couple. But despite the tense flow of words sculpted by his throat and mouth, it's just a sketch. And he sings his heart out, using, at full throttle, the register of a voice that has not yet been overcome by excess. The 'breakdown' in the song, with the 'moan' of congas and a change of key (from C to D), announces a dazzling finale, in which David Bowie invents melodic pre-rap phrasing, cites John Lennon ('I read the news today, oh boy,' – an allusion to 'A Day In The Life') and, as a daysleeper, responds tit for tat to the backing vocals of his American nights.

'Win' is like a jewellery box with a slowly opening lid. The verses are as light as clouds, but The Beatles-inspired arpeggiated choruses, with their tail-spinning keyboard arrangements and that crooning voice on the side lines, are a call to disorder. The song ends up affecting the body like a demon. It raves on until a calm, naked drum beat emerges, close to the one that opened 'Five Years', but more syncopated.

Like 'Win', 'Fascination' was started in November 1974 at Sigma, but completed in New York. Bowie adapts Luther Vandross to his style as if 'Funky Music (Is A Part Of Me)' had been meant especially for that American *Pin Ups* that will never see the light of day (although Vandross hasn't recorded the song yet). Carlos Alomar on energetic guitar, and Mike Garson on percussive keyboards, make the arrangement vibrate and extend across a very basic chord progression shared by the verses and chorus (a simple rise in energy, fuelled by backing vocals which, as in The Beatles' 'Help!', precede the lead vocals, and allow the listener to distinguish one from the other). 'Fascination' is an ode to cocaine, but unlike

Lou Reed in 'I'm Waiting For The Man', Bowie is far from patient. The song was modified quite significantly and one of the instructions Bowie sent by telegraph to Visconti before the mix was to use a Mu-Tron pedal on the bass to create a 'wah-wah' effect.

The Mu-Tron pedal and Mike Garson's Clavinet also stir up the almost shamanic 'Right' (two chords only, but dangerously close to 'I Didn't Mean To' by Ann Odell). The backing vocals, which end up responding to themselves, play a huge part in making this song one of the highlights of the record. Since 1975, many gay men have interpreted 'Right' as a celebration of anal sex. While it's almost certain that Bowie was describing something else (a headlong escape from some demon), he was careful not to contradict them.

The corrupt media, misaligned planets, all-seeing television, extreme politics reflecting an underlying lack of ethics, religious devotion to cocaine – Bowie, like a bull in a china shop, turns these themes on their heads in 'Somebody Up There Likes Me'. Close to seven minutes long, the offshoot from 'I Am Divine' (recorded by The Astronettes and also known as 'So Divine') is a celestial amusement park for David Sanborn. He must have pursed his lips in ecstasy at the thought of having the freedom to send his instrument made of brass flying towards the stratosphere. Fevered preacher, calling all the shots, running the show with a gospel choir on his heels, David Bowie even dares to make a cheeky nod to glam rock, so recent but already from a past era – in the last two minutes of the song, he increases the volume of the backing vocals, reminiscent of 'Satellite Of Love' on *Transformer*.

No drummer has opened up his hi-hat on a Beatles ballad as much as Dennis Davis. He makes his first appearance on a Bowie album in the unlikely setting of 'Across The Universe'. Whether David had initially been using this song as bait to lure John Lennon into his net is irrelevant. What matters is that it showcases Alomar's talent and relegates Bowie's slightly excessive performance to the background (he still manages to spur on the funkster in Davis). 'Across The Universe' doesn't add much to this album, but it did lead to the creation of 'Fame', which closes it.

But sitting just before 'Fame': 'Can You Hear Me'. Andy Newmark's drum fills, the noble sophistication of Tony Visconti's strings at the end of the second line, Carlos Alomar's pure guitar weaves, Bowie's vocal that again defies reason in the second verse, and the salt and pepper plumes escaping David Sanborn's instrument, build up the emotion until the double chorus. According to its writer, this is a love tune, a song of perhaps not completely lost love, but at least a misplaced one. And these elements converge until it's clear that the answer to David's question in the title is a resounding 'Yes!'. 'Can You Hear Me' ends on an unexpected chord, taking the listener to a higher plateau. There, the dialogue between lead and backing vocals picks up where 'Right' left off.

David Bowie initially thought of Norman Rockwell to illustrate the cover of *Young Americans*. Rockwell was probably the most famous American illustrator at the time, having worked for the *Saturday Evening Post*, *Look* and *Life* magazine. He excelled at representing American urban life and emphasized the connection between the US and UK. So for Bowie, the 'limey' freshly landed on American soil, Norman Rockwell was the obvious choice. However, when David phoned him, Rockwell's wife warned him that it took her husband several months to complete a portrait. In the end, the young Eric Stephen Jacobs will shoot the photograph for the cover of *Young Americans*. Craig DeCamps will take care of the lettering. He was an RCA employee, which may be why he isn't credited on the original record or later editions. DeCamps also worked on the very 'Hollywood' cover of *Lost Generation*, Elliott Murphy's sublime album released in 1975. Murphy is a singer-songwriter from New York who's been living in Paris for more than three decades and was signed by RCA president Ken Glancy[28] in the 1970s. Glancy managed him, along with Lou Reed. As for Norman Rockwell, since he was wrongly considered to be too conservative he only illustrated one rock album cover before he died in 1978 – *The Live Adventures Of Mike Bloomfield And Al Kooper*, a live album released in 1968.

It was cheap marketing to call *The Gouster* an unreleased album, as Parlophone/Warner did when they released *Who Can I Be Now? (1974–1976)*, the second retrospective box set of David Bowie's discography, in September 2016. Of course, the press lapped it up. But *The Gouster* is nothing more, nothing less, than an interim version of *Young Americans* that David Bowie had decided not to release in its current state in early winter 1974. It features seven songs, four of which appear on the final album – 'Somebody Up There Likes Me', 'Can You Hear Me', 'Young Americans' and 'Right'. But three of these songs are significantly different – only 'Young Americans' was simply remastered. The version of 'Somebody Up There Likes Me' on *The Gouster* is just a rawer mix, but the lead vocals on 'Can You Hear Me' and 'Right' come from different takes. In the former, the differences in the melody showcase Bowie's ability to vary vocals depending on his mood (or the time of recording) and, by extension, prove that he improvised a lot. 'Right', rendered at a higher octave with a much less convincing result, demonstrates that Bowie was aware of his limits in any circumstance – he chose another vocal take for *Young Americans*.

Overseen by Tony Visconti, these 'naked' versions (without strings, and with fewer effects), a bit like the 2003 remix of The Beatles' 'Let It Be', highlight the rhythm section, the pianist and the backing vocalists.

Watered down and bearing little similarity to the original (it's not even in the same key, as some have said), 'John, I'm Only Dancing (Again)' sounds like a full-on jam session with new lyrics in the verses – only the intro and the chorus offer a nod to the 1972 song. David Bowie exhibits his talent as a soul vocalist, but the track loses most of its bite. And, of course, it's not right to call it a disco song, as RCA did on the cover and when promoting the single (and maxi single) in 1979. Andy Newmark plays a complicated snare drum pattern, going beyond simply hitting two and four, and his bass drum and hi-hat are significantly different from the 'four on the floor' and 'pea soup' techniques. As for Willie Weeks' bass part, a simple groove with an eighth note feel, that's not typical disco either. Four years later, the beat of 'Miss You' by The Rolling Stones and 'Do Ya Think I'm Sexy?' by Rod Stewart will be more accurately described as disco.

The epic 'It's Gonna Be Me' (formerly 'Come Back My Baby') isn't exclusive to *The Gouster*. This version, lasting more than six minutes, in which Bowie scrutinizes his relationships with women in an unflattering way, came out on the Rykodisc reissue of *Young Americans* in 1990. Also included were 'John, I'm Only Dancing (Again)' and 'Who Can I Be Now?'. At 61bpm, this song, removed from *The Gouster* along with 'It's Gonna Be Me', in favour of 'Win', 'Fascination', 'Across The Universe' and 'Fame', is one of the slowest of Bowie's repertoire (65bpm for 'It's Gonna Be Me'). As its title indicates, 'Who Can I Be Now?' tackles the matter of identity in a rather dramatic context[29]. The 2007 reissue of *Young Americans* (whose DVD includes David Bowie's appearance on *The Dick Cavett Show*) will add a version of 'It's Gonna Be Me' embellished with strings recorded in London in late 1974.

David Bowie always knew when it was time to slip away – to leave a place, to part from musicians or partners, or to get lost. In the first few weeks of 1975, although he will return regularly before moving there permanently in the early 90s, Bowie knows it is time to escape from New York. This is where Tony Defries, the man he wants to forget (Defries will reportedly try to block the new album's release, but RCA will side with their artist), has chosen to call home. New York is the city of MainMan, on the verge of collapse (Cherry Vanilla, with whom David will keep in touch for a while, jumped ship just before him) and, even though he enjoys the night life – he has recently seen Led Zeppelin, Roxy Music, Patti Smith (with Television opening) and Rod Stewart in concert – David Bowie has had enough of the whirlwind, of what drains him and messes with his head.

'Young Americans' comes out in February and makes it into the British Top 20. In the US, the single was released a few weeks before but only climbed to Number 28. On 7 March, the day the LP hits the stores, Tom Jones keeps Bowie off Number 1 in the UK with a greatest hits album. Back in the US, like *Diamond Dogs, Young Americans* takes its spot in the Top 10[30]. The reaction of the media is a little mixed but, overall, journalists laud Bowie's audacity and praise his stunning adaptability. Anyway, he knows he's right and will later say that after the *Diamond Dogs* experiment, *Young Americans*, one of his most personal records, gave him confidence and helped him find his voice and become a real musician.

The end of the winter is crucial, as David Bowie meets with director Nicolas Roeg, who's seen him in *Cracked Actor* and thinks he will be perfect to play Thomas Jerome Newton, the main character in *The Man Who Fell To Earth*. This is a film adaptation of Walter Tevis' science fiction novel that the director plans on shooting the following summer. Bowie is late for their meeting, but Roeg waits for him. It would be an understatement to say that those hours were not a waste of time. Roeg is going to offer David Bowie the role of his life, and without knowing it, of his death.

Carlos Alomar	Joe Tarsia
Mike Garson	Mike Tarsia
Emir Ksasan	Peter Humphreys
Andy Newmark	Eddie Jobson
David Sanborn	Eric Stephen Jacobs
Robin Clark	Elliott Murphy
Jean Fineberg	Donovan
Geoff MacCormack	Mick Rock
Tony Visconti	Cherie Currie
	Dave Stewart
	Patti Brett
	Marla Feldstein

CARLOS ALOMAR

During *Young Americans*, I got to understand how David Bowie worked in a studio. He often arrived with just a few ideas or a vague concept, and the musicians helped him develop it. The way I work is to first give them what they want. Once they get it, I can suggest something else, to make the music evolve. That's what I did with David: he'd show me a chord progression, I'd play it, then I'd suggest some variations that he usually found exciting. My thing is the rhythm guitar, harmony. I can play lead guitar, but I'm more interested in chords. I love their fluidity. With David, my basic concept was to develop what I call 'scale-wise progressions'. So if he asked me to play a G, I could do anything I wanted, meaning I could suggest a 7th, 6th, whatever, as long as I remained in the key of G! These different combinations built on what he'd asked for at the beginning.

When I met up with David for *Young Americans*, he already had a full band with him, a rhythm section, a saxophonist, and Mike Garson himself on the piano! I told him it would be impossible to play anything with all those people in one room at the same time. It would be better to work with a smaller band first, then the others could come in. We started off very simple, with some major and minor chords that helped him develop his melodies. Then it was easy to have people like David Sanborn, Luther Vandross and the backing vocalists join in. When Luther was in charge of vocal harmonies, he got what he needed in less than five minutes!

I told David not to worry when he found out that the musicians from MFSB didn't want to record with him. They didn't know who he was. I'd worked with Van McCoy[31], whose song 'The Hustle' would be a hit the following year, and I knew some cats that would fit the bill. They were really great studio musicians, just as good as the members of MFSB.

So we did what David called 'plastic soul'. That's when I realized what he was capable of vocally. I was very impressed by how high he could go, like a falsetto, and how low he could go to reach the baritone notes. Actually, I always thought 'plastic soul', which had negative connotations, wasn't quite the right word for what we did. Personally, I thought David, who looked far from ridiculous next to black musicians, did anything but plastic soul!

So he found out what it was like to record with studio musicians instead of a band. The Spiders From Mars played like The Spiders From Mars and were perfect for the albums that brought him fame in the UK, but I don't think they could play anything else. With us, he could do all the U-turns he wanted, go wherever his creative mind took him. Because he was drawn to our kind of music, we quickly saw where he wanted to go. During these sessions, none of the musicians tried to be prima donnas. They all carefully listened to the others and did what was best for each track. It never took us more than three or four takes for each song. First we did the backing tracks, then the overdubs and then the backing vocals. We worked so well with Bowie that we never needed a break until the end! Usually, if we started at 9pm, the song was recorded by midnight. After that, we'd sleep in the next room while Tony Visconti and David brainstormed ideas. Then they'd come wake us up at 2am to record something else.

At first, Robin and Luther only came to the studio to say hi. But then, even though they hadn't brought any clean clothes, they ended up staying for days! That shows how spontaneous and productive these sessions were. Some of the songs on what was supposed to be *The Gouster* are fantastic. Like 'It's Gonna Be Me', which unfortunately isn't on *Young Americans*. It shows David's ability to perform a perfect mix of soul and rhythm'n'blues. Like Tony Visconti, I was disappointed when some songs from *The Gouster* disappeared, but thankfully, some of them have finally been released. David was like that – unpredictable – and his meeting with John Lennon made the album take an unexpected turn. You know, the mid-70s was a time of musical openness – anything could happen!

When we heard The Bee Gees singing with their high-pitched voices, nobody wondered whether they were white or black. Personally, when a white singer manages to make me believe he's black, I think that's great! You have to understand that David appeared on *Soul Train*, which means the black community had accepted him. He'd scrapped the Diamond Dogs tour set because he'd started to evolve into a soul singer who no longer needed a mask to hide behind. Okay, so 'Fame' might have been stepping on James Brown's toes a bit, but the song is both mysterious and light, and has an irresistible groove. You know what I think – as long as it's funky! The first takes of 'Fame' were just the rhythm section, just bass and drums. Then I played the guitars and David added his, with more of a rock vibe.

The more I worked with Bowie, the more I felt the need to protect him from the dealers and parasites who hung around him. It's why I made a point to stay in control myself, so I could give him the support he needed. As a guitar player and friend, I gave him what he wanted at 300 per cent. Before me, he was definitely more rock; that was the sound of The Spiders From Mars. And after me, he formed Tin Machine. And when he tried to direct me towards styles other than soul or rhythm'n'blues, I remained faithful to my 'scale-wise progressions'.

In the 1970s, we were neighbours in New York. We went out a lot together, to the Apollo in Harlem, and later to the Pyramid Club[32]. There was so much to do! Later, we saw a lot of punk and new wave bands like The Cure and The Cars. This was before MTV – music was everywhere, you really lived it. No sooner had we finished absorbing punk than it was time for the New Romantic era! What could we do? That was New York! One night we'd get wasted at the Pyramid, and the next day we'd party even harder at Studio 54 and stay up all night. We took inspiration from everything we saw, everything we heard. And we used all these influences, no matter the genre. We only cared about the quality of the songs. (2016/2017)

MIKE GARSON

The musicians who played on *Young Americans* and the tour that followed its recording were amazing. David knew what he was doing when he picked them. Andy Newmark, for example, is an exceptional drummer and has been a dear friend since the 1960s. We played together at bar-mitzvahs in New York and later, he told me quite a few stories about Sly Stone, who often worked to a click, which explains why his songs were so tight!

One day, in Philly, David started writing a song on his acoustic guitar, right in the middle of a session. I can't remember which one it was, but he was very focused and had to move to another room. It was like an urgent call of nature! In the meantime, we kept jamming, waiting for him to run into the studio and say, 'Can you play that again? I love it and it's given me an idea...'

The session schedules for *Young Americans* were crazy. Sometimes we didn't even start before midnight and, when the musicians were awake, waiting for stimulants that were slow to arrive, all we had to do was jam. And David would snatch an idea, here and there[33]... At Sigma we were more like studio musicians and it was out of the question for me to do as much as on *Aladdin Sane*. The idea was to play more 'American style', to blend into a sort of big band that was both rhythm'n'blues and gospel. I always felt like *Diamond Dogs* was an intellectual effort, while *Young Americans* came more from David's heart. It was a charm offensive.

When Dennis Davis joined us on the Soul Tour in 1974, the music got even better, mostly thanks to him. Dennis is by far the best drummer I've ever played with. He was always in a good mood, and David loved him. I was very honoured to take Michael Kamen's place, but honestly, my job was made easier by the fact that I had such phenomenal players. And backing vocalists! As you can imagine, I more or less let Luther Vandross do what he wanted and direct the others. I remember that during sound checks, he'd sit at the piano, play one or two chords and say, 'You sing this, you sing that. That should work.' He'd add his voice over it and it was a feast for the ears. It's not surprising that he became such a big star. He was just a kid then, but when he sang on 'Young Americans' and 'Fascination', he was a giant. (2016)

EMIR KSASAN

Carlos Alomar and I played together in The Main Ingredient and I knew he'd started recording with this Brit who was interested in funk. They were looking for a rhythm section for the last sessions and I found myself working with them. I suggested they hire Dennis Davis on drums. We had both played with vibraphonist Roy Ayers. Dennis and I weren't that familiar with Bowie's music, but we were both RCA studio musicians and in the lobby there was a big poster of him with his saxophone. I can't remember if he had orange hair in it, but we knew his face! I'd seen him speeding down the corridors of the studio once or twice. I'd heard 'Changes' and 'Rebel Rebel' but they weren't my kind of music, so I didn't pay much attention to them.

Before we recorded 'Fame' and 'Across The Universe' in New York – the songs with our names on them – Dennis and I went to Philadelphia. I played on three or four other tracks, but I don't know what they kept. I also played bass at the end of the tour in 1974 and so I saw David live many times! You know, in hindsight, I don't think he went from rock to soul, because he had his own idea of the two musical genres and a unique way of approaching them. I think he was just doing David Bowie!

Before I met him, I'd never seen anyone work so hard. Even the way he sang was stunning. He was fast, very professional. He explained what he had in mind, but gave us free rein. He quickly learned that it was the best way to get the best out of people like us. I saw David as a sort of linguist whose talent was to talk directly to the spirit. He made music, but in his own way. He was a bit like that guy who thinks his friend looks awkward in his clothes, so he takes him shopping at budget stores just to find him something a little more casual. His blend of elegance and ease always worked. Okay, at the time, some people were running on special substances! Except for Mike Garson, who didn't touch anything. David Sanborn, on saxophone, was our King Curtis. In the 1960s, Curtis played with the best – Chuck Rainey on bass, Bernard Purdie on drums, a rhythm section that also accompanied Aretha Franklin... And it's no secret that David loved King Curtis[34].

I remember the 'Fame' session fairly clearly and I think I can say that Dennis Davis and I were at the origin of it, or at least of its groove. Between takes, while John Lennon, Carlos Alomar and David were in the control room, we started playing this beat from one of my songs. David joined us in the studio and asked us to go on because he loved what he was hearing. He gave us some suggestions, proposed some chord changes, and suddenly 'Fame' appeared! I had no idea that *The Gouster*, an early version of *Young Americans*, was supposed to come out instead. But we didn't always know what the other tracks were or who played on them. Some songs did take a while to come out... Whatever the case, even though it's not very clear when you read the liner notes, I'm pretty sure we also played on some versions of 'Win' and 'Fascination', a reinterpretation of a song by Luther Vandross, who was of course credited as the composer. He already had a good manager and a good publisher, and they weren't ready to let anything go!

I'd like to take this opportunity to pay homage to a musician who played with us in those days and who's never been mentioned anywhere as someone who accompanied David Bowie. I'm talking about Charlie Brown, who can be seen in the video for 'Right', made from the footage filmed at Sigma. Charlie, who also played with King Curtis and is unfortunately no longer with us, was an incredibly funny man. (2017)

ANDY NEWMARK

When the New York office of MainMan called to ask me if I was free to play some sessions with David Bowie, I wasn't familiar with his music. I knew he was doing well, but when I got to Sigma Sound Studios, I didn't know any of the musicians. I'd seen Tony Visconti once or twice in England, but that was all. What struck me right away was that Bowie was very clear, decisive and articulate about what he wanted from musicians around him. That made our job very easy. We had very strong direction from him. He was completely in charge, but very friendly, accessible, down-to-earth. He had a very clear vision of what his music should be and he was all business in the studio. I really enjoyed playing on these songs and I liked the musicians very much. I've got a lot of respect for them – Carlos Alomar, Mike Garson, David Sanborn, Willie Weeks...

I had no personal interaction with David Bowie that went beyond the music at hand. We recorded the tracks until he and Tony Visconti seemed happy with the result and that was it. David was at a turning point in his career and I was quite impressed with some of the tracks, and obviously the title song. That was really great Bowie, much more so, in my opinion, than 'Fame', which is a bit overrated. It may be good, but I'm not sure it reflects Bowie's talents as a songwriter. You know, he had a great ear, he never missed a thing. He spotted even the smallest pearl in what the musicians were playing and also the smallest piece of grit. I think David was the one who produced *Young Americans*. When sessions were over, I said goodbye and I left. As I already told you, if I had to name a Bowie song I really like, that would be 'Space Oddity': 'Ground control to Major Tom...' (2016/2017)

DAVID SANBORN

On *Young Americans*, David wanted to recreate the spirit of the tour he'd been doing just before. Initially, it was just Carlos Alomar, Andy Newmark, Willie Weeks and me. The percussionists and Mike Garson only came in later. When I asked David if he planned on bringing in a lead guitarist later on, he said I was his lead guitarist! Suddenly, you can hear me everywhere! Of course, I love the title song, as well as 'Fascination' and 'Fame', which I would have played on if I hadn't been on the road with Gil Evans. Actually, I also have a soft spot for 'Somebody Up There Likes Me', which is really epic.

I know that many of his former musicians say this, but he put so much trust in us that we just wanted to give him the best we could. We felt like we were creating something with him. He was so English, and yet he found himself teaming up with Americans. That didn't bother him in the least – he was just as at home with rhythm'n'blues as he was with glam rock! His courage was rewarded because *Young Americans* was the album that allowed him to make it in America.

I get that it's not the subject of your book, but let's not forget that this period in America was one of overindulgence of all kinds. And while he did take it too far, his creativity was never a victim of his addictions. Nothing could extinguish the flame burning inside him. In fact, I believe his excesses in part fuelled his creativity. He operated on different levels at the same time: he managed the music, the visuals, the tour, which combined rock and theatre, and the business side, as this was around the time he started having disagreements with Tony Defries. During the Diamond Dogs tour, it was obvious that each component stimulated the other: the songs showcased the staging, the staging highlighted the choreography, which in turn energized the songs...

When we took to the road again after recording *Young Americans*, there was even more jamming! David danced like a madman most of the time and sometimes he would just turn around and say, 'Play!' and I would play four, six, up to eight solos on a song. Some of the songs went on for twenty minutes! We jammed as if we were in a jazz club, with this great rhythm section, except that we were playing in front of thousands of people. It was extraordinary, we were really spoiled and we lived for the freedom that he gave us.

David allowed me to better understand what it means to be a musician and he raised the bar higher than anyone. Thanks to him, I learned what a concept is, the result of an overall vision. I blossomed while I was working with him and he encouraged me to start a solo career. He'd even said he'd like to produce my first album. It didn't happen in the end and I've often regretted it[35]. But, you know, working with David Bowie definitely changed the course of my life.

I lost touch with David after the 70s, but I remember once when I was giving a concert in London, suddenly, right next to the stage, there he was, watching me, with Mick Jagger. I felt pretty good then. I also saw him in Switzerland later, and we talked for a while, as if we were carrying on a conversation from the night before... (2016)

ROBIN CLARK

Carlos wanted me to come and see him at Sigma Sound, and I asked him if I could bring Luther Vandross, who was our best friend. It would be a fun trip! Carlos said it wouldn't be a problem, so we set off for Philadelphia. For us, hanging out in a studio was better than going to a party! Luther and I didn't know we were going to stay. We were just there to visit for the day...

Yet we found ourselves in Sigma listening to the tracks of *Young Americans*. When the chorus section of the title song approached, Luther leaned towards me and sang, 'Young Ame-Young Ame-Young Americans! Hey, what do you think of that?' We just started singing it in the chorus. Luther and I were always harmonizing so this was quite natural for us. We weren't doing it for David to hear us and hire us. That was the furthest thing from our minds. But David heard us and said, 'Can you sing that again?' So we sang it again and then he asked, 'Would you mind recording it?' So we taught the parts to Ava and that was that. The next thing we knew, David asked us to stay and record the entire album!

I knew David a little because Carlos had brought him home, but I didn't know how much he was at a turning point in his career, on several levels. I wasn't aware of his whole journey. I'd been working as a session singer for some years by then and

I was used to singing with different artists and producers. But that day at Sigma, I was enthusiastic about the music because I knew that we were making magic. Let's face it, I was recording with my best friends – my husband Carlos Alomar, Luther Vandross and Diane Sumler, who was a friend of ours from high school. What more could I want?

When the tour resumed, it was great to be with all those vocalists in The Mike Garson Band. For Luther and me it was a first, and we were excited and enthusiastic about touring the country doing what we loved most: performing and singing! Carlos and I actually already knew some of the band members from working with them in the past, so it was very much like travelling with one big family! David never sidelined us. We spent quite a bit of time with him actually. He usually turned to his musicians and other members of his team when he wanted to talk or ask for advice… That gave him the confidence to get close to the people around him. We weren't just working for David Bowie!

Can I choose a song from *Young Americans*? It's impossible, so I'll choose three: 'Win', 'Somebody Up There Likes Me' and of course 'Right', which David sings so beautifully and which I think has some really great backing vocals. But I think I probably prefer *Scary Monsters*, which is more rock'n'roll! (2016)

JEAN FINEBERG

In early 1975 I was hanging out with Jean Millington, and she was dating David or maybe they were just friends at that point. She had been invited to The Record Plant where David was recording, and I went with her. I brought my flute because I always bring an instrument to the studio, just in case! We walked in and David and John Lennon were in the control room, listening to playbacks of 'Fame'. We had a little chat and, when David found out I played the flute, he suggested I play on the record. He didn't give me any indication – they just put the track on and he told me to play whatever I wanted. So I did! I played a very long solo, but only pieces of it are on the recording I have. I have never heard the complete solo. David then asked Jean and me to sing some backups on 'Fame'. I wasn't really a singer, but I agreed. He told us exactly what to do and we made no suggestions. I think we also sang on a couple of other tracks.

It was an open secret that David Bowie did a lot of cocaine at that time. They had a cup filled with it – they were snorting it – and offered some to us. I have an image in my mind of one of them wearing camouflage pants, but that may just be a dream... At one point, the cup spilled, like in the Woody Allen movie *Annie Hall*, and we continued to snort the coke from their laps. Needless to say I had a blast recording the flute and singing!

After the session, Jean Millington and I went to the brownstone David was renting on West 20th Street. Lennon didn't come with us, but composer Philip Glass was there. We stayed up all night, doing cocaine and listening to the tracks. The night was a magical journey into music, philosophical discussion, joking and laughter. In the morning, Jean and I left, and I never saw him again personally. But like a lot of New Yorkers, I did see him later on in *The Elephant Man* on Broadway. His performance was amazing.

David was extremely animated, pleasant, welcoming and funny. He didn't know who I was – I had probably only recorded one or two albums by then – but he treated me with respect. I loved everything he did musically, and I was thrilled when he went in the soul/rhythm'n'blues direction as, in addition to jazz, that's my favourite genre of music. I love innovators when they cross genre lines à la Bob Dylan and Miles Davis. As for David crossing gender lines, I always saw that as a statement that humanity is beyond gender. (2016)

GEOFF MACCORMACK

After the rehearsals [in Los Angeles] the tour continued, now fully as the 'Soul' tour. Happily, Gui Andrisano's services had been retained as choreographer and master of ceremonies and this saved the touring experience for me. The changing line-up had made the band less cohesive, more fragmentary, but Gui and I remained a permanent team, always trying to make people laugh. Still, though we now travelled with Carlos and Robin – two of the nicest people on the whole tour – I missed the humour of Herbie Flowers, Tony Newman and Michael Kamen.

Perhaps it was the change in line-up, but the new shows lacked some of the precision of earlier dates and performances got a bit ragged at times. I'm not sure, for instance, if the audience in Boston appreciated Ava Cherry's loud, clear voice announcing, 'Good evening, Buffalo!' (2007)

TONY VISCONTI

[At Sigma] I instigated a visit of one of David's idols to the studio. One day before going to work I was listening to WMMR rock radio and the DJ, Ed Sciaky, announced that Bruce Springsteen had just visited his studio with a cassette of his latest songs. David loved Springsteen's music and played his first album to me. We had just recorded a cover of Springsteen's 'It's Hard To Be A Saint In The City'. I called the station and spoke to Sciaky off air and told him that he had to get Springsteen to our studio to meet David and hear the song.

'That's cool but the problem is Springsteen lives in a caravan, and he could be parked along the highway anywhere in the Tri-state area,' said Sciaky. Undaunted he went in search of him and brought him to the studio that evening. Springsteen was very shy and seemed to be bewildered as to why anyone would want to record one of his songs. After a while he warmed up to his surroundings and he and David ended up having a really long and in-depth conversation[36]. (2007)

JOE TARSIA

I landed in this business thanks to Dick Clark, whose music show, *American Bandstand*, was airing from Philadelphia. It was incredibly popular and caused quite a stir. It put Philly on the record industry's map. I opened Sigma Sound Studios in August 1968 and the one in New York, in the same building as the Ed Sullivan Theater, ten years later. David Bowie didn't come to Sigma by chance and his choice said a lot about his artistic aspirations at the time. But aside from that, it's obvious that the welcome from Philadelphia's young people really touched him. It was a special summer for all of them.

I want to be very clear about one thing: initially, David Bowie had planned on working at the studio with local musicians. He knew and liked a lot of the records that had been recorded at Sigma and wanted to play with the people who'd made them. He was one of those people who study album jackets. Before him, others had come to Sigma with what I jokingly called 'a shopping list'. Still, the guys from round here felt threatened by Bowie and were afraid he'd steal their sound. Only percussionist Larry Washington agreed to play with him, so he had to bring in musicians from elsewhere. Don't think for a minute that he only chose Philly because of Sigma; he wanted the whole package and, when he got in touch with us, he was very clear about that. No need to name names, but I know exactly who said, 'Why should we hand the secret of our sound over to this white boy?'

Back when David Bowie was working in the A, the studios were always full. It was extraordinary when he decided to invite all those kids to listen to his record. His presence here and in the city caused more commotion than any other artist, and he was also the sweetest and most generous with the fans. Sigma was so well known that when I had my car washed, the guys from the gas station would see the triple 'S' on my license plate and say, 'Ah, that's where the O'Jays and Teddy Pendergrass make their records!' But those were artists from an older generation. When this young Brit stormed in, everything changed. The studio took on a whole new dimension, and later, different types of clients came.

David loved Sigma because nobody bothered him there, but he still had a bodyguard who was built like a tank, and no one would have dared mess with him. One day, Bowie found out that Ahmet Ertegün was in the B and he asked me if he could go say hi. Ahmet was there to listen to a young guy that a local producer was trying to launch. Since there were a lot of us in the control room, I ended up being crushed up against David. He turned around and said, 'Would you mind not standing so close?' So I took a step back. No one had ever said anything like that to me in my own studio! That was the only time something not so nice happened.

Also, things weren't all rosy with Tony Visconti. If you want my opinion, he wasn't the one who thought of inviting those kids to listen to the finished record! When he got to Sigma, Visconti criticized our mixing console and some of us took that personally. The craziest thing was that that console still works and is still in use in a studio in Ohio. Actually, I'd like to have it back because there's a music museum project in Philadelphia and it would go well there.

I wasn't in charge of this back then, but it's quite possible that David Bowie himself called Sigma to book time. In 1974, the situation with his management looked complicated, and he seemed to be taking care of logistics on his own. Whatever the case, he loved working there. A documentary about the studio is currently being made and David features in it[37]. At one point, he says, 'The sound that came from Philadelphia was intoxicating.' He returned later for a concert that was broadcast on the radio. My son took care of that session and, to thank him, David signed the glass on the frame of the *Young Americans* gold record hanging on the wall. Now it's all dusty, but there's no way we're going to clean that!

In the end, the Philadelphia musicians who were sceptical about David Bowie's ability to make soul music all liked *Young Americans*. He had a perfect command of that music style. When I went to Europe in the late 60s, I realized that people there, especially the Brits, had a better understanding of black music than many Americans did. I visited many studios in London – Abbey Road for example – and I went clubbing. I realized that a lot of musicians and music lovers listened to some really obscure rhythm'n'blues records. Besides, let's not forget that The Beatles, with their covers and before all the others, did a lot to make this music popular.

Time passed, but the people of Philadelphia never forgot David Bowie's time there, especially because he often returned for concerts. We consider him a cultural icon, and not just because of Sigma Sound. (2018)

MIKE TARSIA

During the recording of the album that became *Young Americans*, I was only 18. I was a bit of a gofer in my dad's studio and one day I witnessed something extraordinary. My memory is a bit jumbled, but the recording engineer, producer and David Bowie were listening to a playback with some brass and strings. Bowie was sitting in the control room taking notes and his mind seemed to be elsewhere. And while everyone seemed happy with the result, he said, 'I want to listen to that again. I think there's a problem with one of the violins.' The recording engineer played the piece again without the other instruments and, in fact, he was absolutely right – there was a mistake! I have to admit that I was shocked that this skinny guy with orange hair, who didn't look like much, and didn't even seem to be listening, could notice such a small detail.

David felt at home right away at Sigma. However, at first, he wanted to work with local musicians, those who made the sound of Philly, like Ronnie Baker, The Trammps' bass player who was my friend. But they turned him down because they didn't want to give their sound away. As simple as that. The craziest thing is that later on, Ronnie's son listened to *Young Americans* and he said, 'Wow! That could have been my dad!' In the end, I think those guys should have played on the record. It would have opened their minds.

When Bowie returned in 1997 to perform an acoustic concert that was aired on the radio, I was completely stunned that he remembered everything. The names of the people who worked there back in the 70s, the equipment we used. People say that if you can remember the 70s, you didn't really live them, but I always thought that didn't apply to David Bowie. He didn't take note at the time, but he remembered everything! One of Sigma's employees was a crossword puzzle champion – I think he ended up publishing a dictionary. We used to say he had a photographic memory. It was the same for Bowie. He was much more than a sponge: he was a 'time printer'!

I've been hanging around studios since I was five years old and for me, nothing is more important than the music. I've had the pleasure of meeting everyone who's come by Sigma and I was lucky enough to work with Billy Paul until the end of his life. I think that for Bowie, music was just as important. For me, he *was* music and music was his life. And I'm not exaggerating, because I've been around many other artists. And during that whole time he spent with us, there was that bunch of kids who literally lived outside our door. You had to step over them to get in! He always had a kind word for them. Some 'Sigma Kids' made it onto Bowie's floor at his hotel and knocked on his door pretending to be room service. Instead of telling them to take a hike, he had a chat with them! Watching him at Sigma, I had the feeling that he was the ultimate rock star. His friends were with him, everyone tended to his every need and made sure he wanted for nothing. He opened his mouth and they listened religiously.

Sessions began without Tony Visconti, but David struggled with the fact that in the US, we recorded tracks without the effects then added them in during the mix. So the rough mixes sounded a bit flat, even more so when he listened to them in his hotel room. He may have been talented, but this album was taking him far out of his comfort zone and I think that, before Tony arrived, he was a little insecure.

But the atmosphere at Sigma was cool and David came back, so he must have thought so too. My father was easy-going and so were the musicians we worked with – everyone respected each other and there were no smart asses. There are very few photos of artists at Sigma because it wasn't our style. We didn't beg for autographs either and the only reason I asked David Bowie to sign the gold record of *Young Americans* in 1997 was because I was stunned that he remembered its recording so well. (2018)

PETER HUMPHREYS

David Bowie came to Sigma Sound Studios twice for two weeks with a two-month gap between, always in the A. The first time, he worked with Michael Hutchinson, the assistant, and Carl Paruolo, who was the chief engineer. David wanted to use Carl because he had done a lot of great stuff. He'd cut things like 'Disco Inferno' by The Trammps and *Be Thankful For What You Got* by William DeVaughn. So David wanted Sigma, he wanted Carl and he also wanted the MFSB rhythm section: Norman Harris, Ronnie Baker, Earl Young, Larry Washington, Vince Montana, Bobby Eli, all these different guys… There was a lot of controversy over why Bowie couldn't get them and I don't want to go down that road, but what I can tell you is this: those guys were very busy producing their own records. So one of the key reasons they couldn't do those sessions is because they would have conflicted with their very tight recording schedule. And David wanted to work all night and these guys had been at it all day! They absolutely could not afford to block time for anyone else. People have said that they didn't want to work with him, but actually, it was more a matter of scheduling. This forced Bowie to bring in his own musicians, which he hadn't planned on doing at the start. Because of Philadelphia's successful music scene, the instrumentalists who usually recorded at Sigma Sound were all stars in their field and were reluctant to play on records that weren't what they were used to. Percussionist Larry Washington was the only exception. He got on well with David from the start.

Personally, I think Bowie recorded the album in two blocks because this shift towards rhythm'n'blues was such a departure that he needed time to think about it and incorporate some rock and pop elements. In August, David and his musicians cut quite a large number of songs, rhythm tracks and vocals, and when they came back, they recorded some more songs and quite a few overdubs. These are the sessions that I worked on. Luther Vandross' vocal sessions were great moments. As I said, the sound changed over time and became more pop. Maybe that's not the right word, but knowing where he came from, that's the impression I got. Tony Visconti did an incredible job on this album, but let's not forget about Carl's input. At Sigma, we were all influenced by the greats who worked there: Gamble And Huff, Thom Bell and, of course, Joe Tarsia. Joe was fantastic and had a knack for finding great engineers and arrangers. He taught us everything! Before Sigma, he had worked for Cameo-Parkway Records. Think about this: he had been Chubby Checker's recording engineer!

One of the reasons Sigma's sound was so unique was that as well as having a talent for choosing his team, Joe had taken care to purchase state-of-the-art equipment. The console in Studio A was an Electrodyne, and Sigma was one of the first American studios to have a 24-track tape machine, and then to use automation. The sound of the records coming out of there wasn't as gritty as Tamla Motown's. Some people found it too sophisticated, but it was our identity.

Ironically, while Sigma Sound was known for its strings and the arrangers who wrote them, the ones on *Young Americans* weren't recorded there. Probably because of a scheduling problem… Yet we had a room for that – it could fit at least a dozen guys, who usually doubled their parts. The orchestra musicians had a secret agreement with the producers: they were willing to play twice without asking for a double fee, so long as it could be done within a certain amount of time. That wouldn't have worked in New York, because the musicians' union was already very strict.

At Sigma, I worked with the greatest, and I can assure you that when they were recording, these guys really got into it. But David Bowie could compare to them – I'd never seen anyone so focused, so intense, even though I think there was a falling-out with MainMan at the end… When I look back on those sessions, I don't even know what to think as they were so fantastic and different from anything I'd done before. David created a special atmosphere. It was unforgettable.

Not too long ago, I went to dinner with Carlos Alomar and Robin Clark, and of course we talked about the fact that *Young Americans* was a landmark of its time and still means a lot to many people. We remembered that, at the end, when we left the studio, some of the musicians and technicians were dragging their feet like they were afraid that it was all over and they'd never see David again. He was in total control, incredibly generous and open. He listened to suggestions and if he was stuck on a piece, he might say to a musician, 'You know, that part you found earlier, we should try that here.' We sometimes felt like his mind was elsewhere, but actually, in his head, he was looking at the bigger picture, and he was always thinking about what came next. All of his ideas were well thought out.

During that dinner, I reminded Robin and Carlos that David always had a legal pad filled with notes with him. He drafted lyrics and sketched drawings, all sorts of things, and the pages were blackened by the musical notation system he'd invented. For the backing vocals, he'd copied down the lyrics and underlined and put accents on the words. That's how he wrote music. It's been half a century and people still talk about how David Bowie was always moving forward, reinventing himself. But no one ever really mentions how he didn't forget his past either. I admired the fact that at Sigma, in a way, he was recreating some music he'd heard when he was young.

And he didn't think of himself as a star. He was always very humble. I remember when they came back, he played what has now become *The Gouster* album for Carl and me. He was like a kid – so happy and proud. And he wanted to know what we thought of the songs. I thought they were just rough mixes at the time, but now I know they were not! Well, he listened to people. Also, unlike many singers of his stature, he had no requirements for his microphone. He wanted it to be good, but not necessarily the best of the best. He sang divinely. At Sigma, he wanted to do his vocals with the band. For that, we came up with a mic technique. We stacked two, one on top of the other, and David would sing into one of them. Thanks to a phenomenon called phase cancellation[38], the other mic would cancel the spill in the room and there would be practically no leaking from the instruments.

The last sessions of *Young Americans* took place in New York, because Sigma wasn't available. Vivian, who was in charge of bookings had found a way to squeeze David Bowie into our schedule twice, but the third time, the producers were up in arms, so it didn't work. And David was a very impatient guy – not the kind to wait for a studio to be available! (2018)

EDDIE JOBSON

Yes, David Bowie did ask me to play keyboards on his Diamond Dogs tour. We met in New York the first time Roxy Music played there[39]. After the concert, David, Ava Cherry and I even went clubbing. The main reason I turned him down was because Roxy were doing well, especially in England, so leaving the band just to be an accompanying musician wasn't a great idea. The other reason was that I was well aware that if David poached the young, barely 20-year-old, keyboardist of Roxy Music, it would make his rivalry with Bryan Ferry worse. No one was talking about it, but even though it was amicable, it was real. I knew that David admired and was influenced by Roxy Music, and there was a bit of competition between the two sides. But on a more general level, I've always very much admired David Bowie's creativity and originality. He was an incredibly brave artist. The last time I saw him, it was in the 1990s. We lived in the same building in New York for a while. (2018)

ERIC STEPHEN JACOBS

The photo session for *Young Americans* put me on the map. I was only 23 years old, just starting out. Toni Basil, David's choreographer at the time, is responsible for all that. She's a really amazing woman and I'm still friends with her. She knew the editorial board at *Dance Magazine*. William Como, the editor-in-chief, also edited *After Dark*[40], a sort of semi-gay entertainment magazine. It so happened that I was one of the staff photographers. The editor-in-chief fell in love with Toni and he said he wanted to do a story about her in *After Dark*. He asked me to take the photos and loved the result so much he put her on the front page. David Bowie happened to see this magazine and said he wanted a photo like the one of Toni for his album.

One day, I was sitting in my studio in New York and the phone rang. I picked up. On the other end, the voice said, 'Hello, can I speak to Eric?' I said it was me and I heard, 'This is David Bowie.' Of course, I was surprised, so he quickly went on, 'I would like you to do my next album cover.' I was shocked, but managed to say that I'd be very honoured! We only had a brief conversation that day, and obviously I was surprised that he'd make that kind of call himself. At the time, David wasn't flying, so they got me come to Los Angeles. So there I was, at 23 years old, an inexperienced photographer, on a plane and then in Los Angeles with a limousine waiting for me.

The driver took me straight to a motion picture studio with these huge Klieg lights. David welcomed me and made me feel very comfortable. He told me he loved the retro look of Toni's photo and that that was the feel he was looking for. I noticed that he was already dressed for the shoot and realized that I wasn't going to get a moment's rest before starting. He suggested we get to work, so I took care of the lighting. To be honest, I was pretty nervous and not very confident. I kept thinking, 'Shit, it's David Bowie!' I was even more nervous because people from MainMan were there, but they really helped me feel at ease and I got friendly with some of them over the years.

I stayed in LA for a few days – I saw David in concert, which was just mind-blowing – then I went back to New York. I thought MainMan would ask me to send the contact sheets so David could choose the photo, but they told me to do it myself. And you know what? If I'd had more experience and more balls in those days, I would have said, 'David, you can't wear a shirt like that in a photo session!' I got that the checks, all that, made him look American, but still, he could have put a white one on. Or a black one! But I was young, a little insecure and didn't want to make waves. I then proceeded to hand-colour the black and white photo, and I also painted that smoke coming out of his cigarette.

At the end of 1974 and in 1975, David and I saw each other regularly – he came to my studio and I'd go see him on West 20th Street in Chelsea. And I got very friendly with Corinne, his secretary. When we did the photos with the American flag, pilot suit and handcuffs in New York, I spent lots of nights listening to him talk about art. I'd never met anyone so intelligent and so well educated. Some people can be jacks of all trades, masters of none, but he was a master of all! When he talked about architecture, it was like listening to a teacher. It was no accident that he was such a good artist – consistent – who stood the test of time.

During the shoot in New York, the conversation turned to the 1929 stock market crash, and that was why he suggested doing this shot, like a homeless man sleeping in the street: he used his shoes as a pillow and he made himself a sheet with newspaper. It became the cover photo for *The Gouster*. The only thing that bothered me then was how thin he was. When people take cocaine, they don't sleep and often forget to eat. Like many of the photographers who were lucky enough to shoot David Bowie, I can say two things: the first is that working with him was really insane because it was very difficult to mess up a photo of Bowie. The other is that I wish I'd had the chance to do something more with him before he died. (2017)

ELLIOTT MURPHY

In 1974, after spending many days listening to *Hunky Dory*, I had only one thing in mind: to get David Bowie to produce one of my albums. I met him one day at RCA in New York at a listening party for *David Live* I think. He told me he would love to work on my next record but he was about to go on tour. He was a true gentleman and he advised me to record with a very talented friend of his. But I was disappointed, so I refused. I later found out that the friend in question was Tony Visconti.

A year later, I met Mick Ronson, who offered to play on my album *Night Lights*. I was excited about that, but one morning he called to tell me that Bob Dylan had asked him to accompany him on his *Rolling Thunder Revue*, and that's the kind of thing you can't turn down. (1995)

DONOVAN

I have great respect for David. He did a phenomenal job bringing together his influences, and he's a hugely talented singer-songwriter. He's an extraordinary performer and a bit like a theatre director – he leads his career with style. And he loves to experiment... I recorded a version of 'Rock'n'roll With Me' in 1974, which came out as a single that same year, but some of my songs and some of my ideas had influenced him a bit in his early days. He returned the favour one day in Boston[41], during an American tour. That was back in 1974 and we didn't know it, but we were staying in the same hotel. In the corridor, I ran into one of his bodyguards who I knew quite well, and he told me that David was in town for a few shows. I decided to invite him to mine, which was called *7-Tease*, and was by far the most ambitious and most theatrical of my career. It was so freaking expensive and just being on the road with a whole troupe cost double what I made from it! David told me it would be cheaper to perform in theatres rather than in classic concert halls!

In Boston, the venue I was playing was also used for union meetings, and when they saw us all coming, the most powerful union in the city wouldn't let us in: and they didn't want to hear about a dance troupe either. So we ended up stuck backstage. The show was sold out, and some of the audience members, without tickets, were queuing up outside. So David took it upon himself to find a solution. After pacing back and forth in my dressing room for a while, he decided to go and negotiate with the union leaders. He came back half an hour later and said, 'Don, they don't want your show, not your band, nor your dancers, but remember where you started your career – alone with your acoustic guitar. That's what people came here to see and hear. You and your songs. So get out there.'

David handed me my guitar and got on stage. He walked up to the mic, but nobody recognized him. In his beautiful, calm voice, he went, 'Good evening ladies and gentlemen, please welcome Donovan.' I sang for two hours, sitting on my stool, and the evening was a great success. The next day, he left to go on with his own American tour and, after bumping into each other like two boats on this mad sea that was the 70s rock scene, we never saw each other again. (1996)

MICK ROCK

Yes, David once told me he sent his version of 'It's Hard To Be A Saint In The City' to Bruce Springsteen, but he didn't respond so David decided to forget about the song. (2018)

CHERIE CURRIE

David Bowie meant everything to me. And honestly, he changed the course of my life. I know that sounds a bit dramatic, but I'd never been so fascinated with a performer. That concert of the Diamond Dogs tour at the Universal Amphitheatre in Los Angeles was the first one I went to. When he got on stage, he was magical and I knew then what I was going to do with my life. I wanted to be up there too, and during my first year as lead singer of The Runaways, I basically pretended to be him! I was 15 and had no idea who I really was.

While Joan Jett acted a bit like Suzi Quatro, my thing was Bowie. He was just the best. He did a lot to help kids in the 70s find themselves. He gave us the courage to be ourselves; we were no longer ashamed of who we wanted to be. One day at school, I saw a kid being thrown in a trash can because he was wearing glasses and they called him a freak. And I said, 'You call him a freak? I'll show you a real freak.'

The next day, I went to school with red, white and blue hair and the Aladdin Sane lightning bolt across my face, and they understood what I meant!

Around the same time, for a school play, I sang '1984'. After that, a lot of teenagers who were quite nerdy started to loosen up. They'd come to school with a little silvery lightning bolt drawn on their cheek and it was really cool. My experience of school improved after that. Frankly, without David Bowie, I never would have sung in The Runaways. And to be honest, I still can't face the fact that he's gone, even today. It's too big a thing to take in.

I only met him once, at the Rathskeller in Boston. We played there in mid-March 1977, and he and Iggy Pop came to see us. He was wearing a hat, glasses and a scarf around his neck. I remember thinking he was smaller than I'd imagined. But I was wearing six-inch platforms! I'm grateful to Glenn Danzig[42] for letting me open his show at the Universal Amphitheatre because that venue obviously means a lot to me. David Bowie was Halloween Jack the first time I saw him and two years later, he'd become the Thin White Duke, who I loved just as much. I'm one of the people who truly believe that throughout his life, he was just better than everyone else. No one will ever come close. (2017)

DAVE STEWART

For the first time in a long time, I've been trying to be honest with myself, to go back to my roots. *Greetings From The Gutter* is my first solo record and I'd always wondered what it should sound like. So I launched into a genuine artistic introspection and a thorough study of my influences and came to the conclusion that for me, the David Bowie of *Hunky Dory* perhaps had the most influence. I also loved *Transformer* by Lou Reed, which David produced. But, at the same time, I was listening to some black music like The Staple Singers, which also had an effect on my musical development. So I was in a similar situation to David when he was about to record *Young Americans*. I also have a background in soul and rhythm'n'blues but, being European, that's not easy... I started by making demos on my own and, at one point, I found myself with a song that, incidentally, was very Staple Singers, and another that sounded like 'Heroes'! How was I going to get away with it? Then I realized that my thing was a blend of all that, and shit, a guitar only has six strings!

Later, at Electric Lady, I asked David Sanborn to play the saxophone because it perfectly matched the spirit of the album. He's a funky and voluble musician...

I haven't yet been able to give *Greetings From The Gutter* to David, but he came up to my apartment with Iman while I was writing some of the songs and I played them demos: 'Greetings From The Gutter' I think, 'Chelsea Lovers'... David really liked this one and he even took a tape to write some lyrics for it. But then I left London to record in New York and, a bit later, he started working on his new album with Eno. I haven't heard from him since. (1994)

PATTI BRETT

David Bowie came back to Philadelphia at the start of 1973. He played several concerts and I only missed one of them. We managed to find out which hotel he was staying at and, after the show, we went there. It was the first time in my life I was doing something like that, and the first time I met him.

During the 1974 tour, he came back to the same hotel and after each show he'd talk to us for a bit. He let us take photos, he signed autographs and, one night, he told us he was planning on recording an album in our town in August. That summer, knowing he travelled in a limousine with New York plates, we started to scour the city and we'd often drive past Sigma Sound to see if he was there! There was no internet in those days, no mobile phones... One night, my friend Marla called to tell me she'd just driven past the studio and had seen his limo. I alerted our little group and we went to hang around outside Sigma. It became our routine.

We ended up finding David's hotel, the Barclay, and we also spent a lot of time there, waiting for him to come out. He usually emerged around four or five in the afternoon and would spend a bit of time with us. We were everywhere: at the studio, at the hotel, and we'd follow him by car when he went from one to the other. Since we knew the city better than he did, we easily sped ahead, running the red lights, and we often got to Sigma Sound before he got there. That surprised him because he'd left us on the sidewalk by the hotel, and so we must have left after him!

Well, he was a massive star, but mostly in our eyes. In those days, David Bowie only played in mid-sized venues and he was a really friendly person. Let's not forget that this was before John Lennon's assassination, and he was probably not thinking that his fans could be any sort of threat. But we were seriously addicted to him, because when he'd leave, around four or five in the morning, we'd still be there, huddled together. We'd talk a bit more and we'd set off to the hotel behind him. Then, because we saw them every day, we became quite close with his musicians, especially Carlos Alomar and Robin Clark. Carlos usually took tapes of what they'd just recorded back to his hotel so he could listen to them before the next session. Sometimes we'd end up in his room, in the early hours of the morning, listening to the album as it came together.

Another funny thing was that there was a little window in the control room that looked out over the street. Carl, the recording engineer, sometimes left it open so we could hear what was going on. We were super-fans and were delighted with David's artistic transformation. It was mind-blowing to think that the year before, he'd been doing glam rock. We were very young and impressionable, but we are all ready to swear that that summer, something special happened.

David was incredibly nice to us, and he granted us his time, which must have been precious. We all fell in love with him! I don't think the listening session we were invited to was a spur-of-the-moment thing. Since we were there, he must have known that sooner or later, he'd play us his new songs. Because they were radically different from everything he'd done so far, he must have thought our opinion was important. One night, before going back into the studio, he said, 'If you're still here when I leave, I have a surprise for you!' So when he came out again, he said, 'You've been really nice to us since we got to Sigma. To thank you, I want to invite you to come and listen to the record.'

The next day, after making us promise not to tell anyone about this invitation, we went into the studio. There was a photographer there that he knew from the Diamond Dogs tour. David let us in before the listening session was due to start because it was raining that night and he didn't want us to get wet. An hour later, we went up to the studio and David was standing behind the glass in the control room. He leaned towards the talkback microphone and we heard his voice say, 'Here's what we've been recording since we arrived. I hope you like it. We can talk about it after.' Then, before the music started, he came over to where we were, but stayed at the back of the room. He couldn't stand still, he seemed nervous, and during the session, he watched our reaction carefully.

At the end, one of us said, 'Please, play it again!' That's when we saw a big smile creep across his face and he said, 'You're sure?' And then the party started. During that second listening he was much more relaxed. He started dancing with some of us, chatting with others. We really bonded. We were the 'Sigma Kids' and later, at each concert in Philadelphia or nearby, he'd look out for us until he found us. It never seemed like we were bothering him[43]. You know, I set a goal for myself: I wanted to see one hundred David Bowie shows. Except for the one I missed in February 1973, I saw all the shows he gave in Philadelphia and as many as I could elsewhere. The furthest one I went to was in England, and I reached my goal. I never missed any of his tours! (2016)

MARLA FELDSTEIN

When David and his entourage returned to Philadelphia in August 1974, it created a whirlwind of emotions, adventures and excitement. With a little luck and a lot of persistence, we were able to find out where he and the band were staying. We staked our place outside The Barclay Hotel, in beautiful Rittenhouse Square. Most days, round 5pm, David would emerge from the hotel and, on most occasions, he would graciously chat with us as he made his way to his waiting limousine. He would climb into the back of his car and we would run for Patti's. We would jump in our car and race – rather quickly – to Sigma. It was just over a mile from the hotel and we would arrive before or just as David's limo was pulling up to the front of the studio. Our car was often stopped in the middle of the street – we would just jump out and run to the entrance! We were ecstatic to have our idol in our city for two whole weeks!

That summer we were so fortunate to meet most of the remarkably talented people who contributed to the recording of *Young Americans*: the charming Coco Schwab, David's bodyguard Stu, his driver Jim James and even his hairdresser Jac Colello. There were times Jim would allow us to climb into the limo while David was recording. We would scour the seats for David's bright orange hairs and nick the Gitane butts from the ashtray. What a score! On several occasions Coco spent time with us outside and spoke with us. She was always caring and kind. I remember her telling us how she got her job with David by answering an ad in a music magazine. I recall Jac leaving the hotel – his hands bright, bright orange – having just hennaed David's hair! Carlos and his lovely wife, Robin, were particularly sweet to us. They truly appreciated our dedication and love for David. It was very evident that they were also having the time of their lives.

One night, David told us he had a special surprise for us. And it was a big one! We were invited into the studio on the last night of their visit. We were treated to a listening party of all the recordings that had been made. It was a magnificent evening... David sitting quietly, a distance from us, nervous about our reaction. We listened intently; for me, it was an extremely emotional experience. I knew we were all part of a unique event and I was in a bit of shock for much of the evening. The recording was played through a second time and everyone became more relaxed as we chatted, ate, drank, sang and danced... All this in the presence of David Bowie.

Thankfully the wonderful photographer Dagmar Krajnc was there and captured the evening on film with her numerous and, what some call, iconic photographs. Myself and the other fans who were there that night came to be known as the Sigma Kids. It still makes me laugh... me, today, still known as a Sigma Kid.(2016)

1. This nightclub in Soho, London, was a temple of British rhythm'n'blues and modern jazz. It was frequented, both on stage and off, by the best acts of the rock and pop scene of the time. It closed in 1967.

2. Nickname for Drinamyl, a mixture of amphetamines and barbiturates in pill form. It was very popular in the early 1960s and was the preferred drug of the mods.

3. An American producer and orchestrator of Turkish descent, whose name was associated with the prestigious Atlantic label for several decades, as well as with artists like Aretha Franklin, Dionne Warwick, Roberta Flack and Chaka Khan. Mardin will work with David Bowie on *Tonight* and *Labyrinth*.

4. Paul Buckmaster, Earl Slick and Willie Weeks also played on this record.

5. Mother Father Sister Brother, PIR's house band.

6. Michael Kamen has recorded the song under his own name in 1973, and Bonnie Raitt has covered it on *Streetlights*, her fourth album, released a year later.

7. Contrary to common wisdom, David Bowie did not meet Willie Weeks at Ronnie Wood's house during the recording of 'It's Only Rock'n'roll (But I Like It)', which he took part in. Weeks recorded his part later, at Olympic.

8. It's his first tour with David Bowie and he will go on to accompany him, with a few breaks in playing, until 1995. Nile Rodgers, a future founding member of Chic and Bowie collaborator, replaced Carlos Alomar in the Apollo's in-house orchestra.

9. David Bowie played there between 2 and 8 September 1974. The show from 5 September is the one on the live album.

10. Even though, by 1974, fans of David Bowie's music had realized that change would be constant with him, those who'd bought tickets in advance for *The Year Of The Diamond Dogs*, which MainMan had advertised as very theatrical, might have been disappointed when they saw that by autumn, Hunger City was gone. This situation put Tony Defries in a tight spot, with some organizers complaining that the show they got wasn't the one they'd paid for.

11. At one point, Alan Yentob considered the title *The Collector*.

12. Sometimes, some of the songs (mainly covers) were skipped, but those they played regularly included 'Baby, Baby', 'Funky Music (Is A Part Of Me)', 'You Keep Me Hangin' On', 'I'm In The Mood For Love', 'Deep In The Heart Of Me', 'Love Train' and 'Memory Of A Free Festival'.

13. Those who have criticized David Bowie for 'borrowing' from everyone will be happy to know that he didn't come up with the term 'plastic soul' either. African-American musicians had been using the term since the 1960s to describe the music played by British musicians, who were attempting rhythm'n'blues with varying degrees of success. More pejorative than 'blue-eyed soul', the term inspired the title of The Beatles' sixth album, *Rubber Soul*, released in 1965. Between the first two takes of Paul McCartney's song 'I'm Down', recorded in June that year and in which he sounds a lot like Little Richard, he can be heard using the expression jokingly. This detail in the history

of The Beatles will be revealed in 1996, in the second volume of their *Anthology*.

14. *The Earl Slick Band*, produced by Harry Maslin.

15. A veil of confusion hangs over these concerts: it seems they took place on 18 and 25 November (as David Bowie was playing in Pittsburgh on 19 November, and the sessions at Sigma Sounds reportedly took place between 20 and 25 November), but certainly not, as many have said, at the Spectrum Arena. Between 1967 and 2009, this venue in South Philadelphia could accommodate 15,000 to 20,000 spectators and was used for sporting events and large concerts. Its capacity could also be reduced by half using a curtain system, turning the place into the Spectrum Theater. It's likely that this was the configuration when David Bowie performed there – as it was for Frank Zappa, The Kinks, Bob Marley and Bruce Springsteen around the same time – as Bowie usually played in venues seating fewer than 10,000. However, during the Isolar tour two years later, and the Sound+Vision tour in 1990, Bowie will play at the Arena. The Spectrum will be demolished in 2011 and is now a parking lot.

16. In an interview in the 2000s, Ava Cherry will confirm the influence Chicago's fashions from the 1940s had on David Bowie (also mentioned by Margo Sappington and Toni Basil in the previous chapter). She will say she'd given him some outfits worn by her father, a musician and fan of baggy pants with braces. Kid Creole And The Coconuts and Morris Day from The Time (of Minneapolis) will also adopt this look. Lastly, 'The Gouster' was the dazzling A-side of a single released in 1964 by the Five Du-Tones, a little-known doo-wop band from Saint Louis.

17. Very few bootleg recordings are mentioned in this book (others are dedicated entirely to them), but those who seriously want to listen to the sound of David Bowie's North American tour of 1974 should know that the nine-disc box set released by Diamond Doghouse Recordings (!) in 2016 features shows and rehearsals from the entire tour.

18. Located in Manhattan at 321 West 44th Street, between Midtown and Hell's Kitchen, The Record Plant in New York was one of the most prestigious and popular studios in Manhattan from the late 60s to the early 80s. Some legendary albums were recorded there (at least in part), including Jimi Hendrix's *Electric Ladyland*, Aerosmith's *Toys In The Attic*, Alice Cooper's *School's Out* and John Lennon's *Imagine*. The soundtrack of the Woodstock festival film was mixed there and, in 1971, The Record Plant's 16-track mobile studio was used to record *The Concert For Bangladesh* with George Harrison and his friends. John Lennon will be killed outside his building on 8 December 1980 while returning home from a session (for the song 'Walking On Thin Ice') at The Record Plant.

19. The term is commonly used to describe the almost-two-year period (from late 1973 to early 1975) during which John Lennon and Yoko Ono put their relationship on hold. Lennon had an affair with May Pang, who talked about it in her book *Loving John – The Untold Story* (Warner Books, 1983). Pang will wed Tony Visconti in the late 80s. Their marriage will last a decade and they'll have two children.

20. Tony Visconti came up with this name after reading about a recording studio concept mentioned in the 17th century (!) in utopian novel *New Atlantis*, by British scientist and philosopher Sir Francis Bacon. David Bowie also read it in the 1970s. Visconti recorded most of Sparks' *Indiscreet* album at Sound House.

21. In 1965, unhappy with the negotiations with EMI to revalue his work for The Beatles, George Martin founded AIR, Associated Independent Recording, with some other producers. Then he continued to record at Abbey Road (which was then called EMI Studios), but on his own terms. At the very end of the 60s, Martin opened his first studio in Oxford Circus (at 214 Oxford Street), where Roxy Music taped most of their 1970s' albums. A decade later, he will open another studio on Montserrat, an island north of Guadeloupe, that will be severely damaged in 1989 by Hurricane Hugo. From 1992, AIR Studios will be located at Lyndhurst Hall (an old Victorian church) in Hampstead in London.

22. Earl Slick will play on *Double Fantasy*, John Lennon and Yoko Ono's last studio album, released in 1980, two weeks before his assassination.

23. According to the original sleeve notes, 'Young Americans' is the only song on the LP to be produced and mixed by Tony Visconti alone. 'Across The Universe', 'Can You Hear Me' and 'Fame' were produced by David Bowie and Harry Maslin. Visconti and Maslin are credited as co-producers and mixers on the four other songs.

24. As with the name of the band – sometimes spelled The Flairs – the name of the song had many variants, and was also sometimes spelled

'Foot Stompin' (Part A)' or written as all one word.

25. The tape was flipped and played backwards on the tape machine. This created a 'suction' effect that The Beatles had been using since the mid-60s.

26. Just over four decades later, David Bowie will also play the distorted chord progression on 'Lazarus', whose function is roughly the same as his guitar part on 'Fame'.

27. In the early 1970s, Fanny toured Europe, especially Germany, with Slade. The girl band met and hung out with David Bowie and The Spiders From Mars during their concerts in England.

28. In his book, John Hutchinson disputes the idea that Annette Peacock (or her music) was the link between Mike Garson and David Bowie. He wrote that Ken Glancy, a big jazz fan who knew Garson's work, suggested him to Tony Defries. Glancy's role was decisive for Bowie in the 1970s. While television ads were not commonly used for publicizing records, Glancy used them for Bowie's, starting with *Aladdin Sane*.

29. It's also the theme of 'After Today', which was recorded at Sigma in 1974. Oddly enough, the first appearance of this song in the box set *Sound+Vision*, released as a prelude to Rykodisc's reissue campaign, will also be the last. At least two versions of 'After Today' exist: a slow one and a fast one. It is the latter, on which David Bowie sings in falsetto, that was issued in 1989.

30. Would *The Gouster* have done better or worse than *Young Americans* had it come out earlier and in its place? No one can answer this question without making a fool of themselves. However, *Young Americans* – more pop and with a better balance – is overall the better album. In 2016, a few months after *Who Can I Be Now? (1974–1976)*, the second retrospective box set (available on CD, vinyl and digital), Parlophone will release part of the content separately. However, *The Gouster* is one of the David Bowie albums that, to this day, are exclusive to a box set and cannot be bought separately.

31. In the 1960s, Van McCoy wrote 'Some Things You Never Get Used To', which was covered by Cilla Black and appeared on the A-side of George Underwood's single under his pseudonym Calvin James.

32. Located at 101 Avenue A, this East Village club was, like the Limelight or Studio 54, a staple of New York nightlife in the late 70s and early 80s. Drag queens like RuPaul and Lypsinka went there. The Red Hot Chili Peppers and Nirvana gave their first concerts in New York at the Pyramid Club.

33. This was common practice at the time: in sessions, an artist sometimes let his musicians just improvise and, if he heard something he liked, he'd embellish it or use it as a starting point for a song he'd take full credit for, without any shame. Blue Weaver, for example, did much more than play keyboards with the Bee Gees during their partnership, especially when they were writing and recording the songs that will turn up on *Saturday Night Fever*. However, he was never credited as a writing partner. For more than two decades now, the musicians who participate in the composition are better protected (and defended). Some tracks on *Outside*, for example, which came

out of extended jam sessions, will be credited to the instrumentalists who recorded them at Mountain Studio.

34. As guest presenter on the show *Star Special* on BBC Radio 1 on 20 May 1979, David Bowie will play nearly 30 of his favourite pieces of music, including 'Something On Your Mind' by King Curtis. It's an instrumental cover of a blues song written by Big Jay McNeely, another African-American saxophonist. It was called 'There's Something On Your Mind' when Little Sonny Warner successfully recorded a vocal version of it at the end of the 1950s. During the same show, Bowie will also play tracks from *Lodger*, which he'd just recorded, two by Roxy Music and Ronnie Spector's version of 'Try Some, Buy Some'. Almost a quarter of a century later, he will record his own version of this George Harrison song.

35. Released in 1975, *Taking Off* is the first of some 30 albums David Sanborn recorded under his own name. It was produced by John Court with the notable contribution of Ralph MacDonald, one of the percussionists on *Young Americans*.

36. In truth, that day (or rather the night of 24 November), the two musicians didn't get on that well at all, partly because they were both shy and lived in different worlds. Bruce Springsteen wasn't too keen on the 'blue-eyed soul' Bowie was making at the time (he arrived while he was recording 'Win'), so David didn't play him the cover of 'It's Hard To Be A Saint In The City' he'd recorded at Sigma (the version that officially came out in 1989 in the *Sound+Vision* box set was supposedly taped during the *Diamond Dogs* sessions), arguing that it was not finished yet.

37. At the time of going to press, this film has not yet been released. However, *The Sigma Kids*, a documentary about the recording of *Young Americans*, featuring Patti Brett and Marla Feldstein, will be uploaded on YouTube in 2021.

38. In his book and in the liner notes for the 2007 reissue of *Young Americans*, Tony Visconti will take credit for this process.

39. The concert Eddie Jobson is talking about took place on 2 June 1974 at the Academy of Music. David Bowie had been to see *Rodin, Mis En Vie*, Margo Sappington's ballet on 17 April, and afterwards he met Michael Kamen. It can therefore be reasonably assumed that Bowie called Jobson to replace Kamen in October. Jobson refused and Mike Garson took over musical direction.

40. David Bowie appeared on the cover of *After Dark* in October 1972. Toni Basil made the front page of the September 1974 issue.

41. The Soul tour stopped in Boston in July, then again in mid-November. David Bowie played at the Music Hall on Tremont Street for three nights in a row. A year later, almost to the day, Bob Dylan will perform there as part of his *Rolling Thunder Revue*, with Mick Ronson on guitar. In 1976, Bowie will tell Cameron Crowe of *Creem* magazine that Ronson was the 'freshest thing' about Dylan's tour, which he called 'silly' and 'a parody of itself'.

42. Glenn Danzig is the frontman of American horror-punk band Misfits. In 2016, the consecutive deaths of David Bowie and Prince will prompt him to get back on stage with the original members of his band, which has been performing on and off since 1977.

43. On 22 September 1995, when the Outside tour stopped in Philadelphia, David Bowie spoke to the audience and did ask where the 'Sigma kids' were.

STATION TO STATION

RCA – 23 JANUARY 1976

LIVE NASSAU COLISEUM '76
(PARLOPHONE – 10 FEBRUARY 2017)

*'LA is the loneliest and most brutal of American cities; NY gets god-awful
cold in the winter but there's a feeling of wacky comradeship
somewhere in some streets. LA is a jungle.'*
(JACK KEROUAC, *ON THE ROAD*, 1957)

'Since Man, with the help of Nietzsche, Freud and Einstein, destroyed God to create a new god, in this case the atomic bomb, we are entitled to fear the worst. But Man must not come to believe that the internet can stand in for everything and control the world instead. He must evaluate his situation on the planet for himself, and do everything possible to keep technology from becoming the new god. If that were to happen, we'd really be in trouble. Man has wiped out his need for a spiritual life. He thought he had become big enough to fend for himself. But of course, he's shooting himself in the foot […]

'The real question is whether I was racist or not, not whether I once believed in nationalism. I can confirm that never in my life have I considered racism an option. In 1975 and 1976, I was very interested in the magical aspects of existence. In my readings, I obsessed over occultism. And I was really fascinated with the idea that at one point, the Third Reich went to England to look for the Holy Grail, so I added it to my negative paraphernalia. As for my country today, I'm proud to see that the music is again very exciting, that eccentricity is back. In fashion, this mixture of Dadaism and typically English self-destructive guilt is exploding through the work of designers like Alexander McQueen and John Galliano. Not to mention the particularly vibrant visual art and painting of today. So much so that it seems to me, without doubt, we can speak of a cultural renaissance [...]

'I'm not sure I was always the best friend to have, but I loved travelling with Geoff MacCormack and, later, Iggy. I was never afraid of being alone, but the company of friends was reassuring, some intelligent company, even if, to tell the truth, we messed around quite a bit!

'Many people have asked me what "Station To Station" was about. I have no problem with the fact that some of my fans thought I was talking about a train journey. And anyway, I was the one who caused the confusion by starting the song with the sound of a locomotive.'

DB (1999/1997[1]/1991)

Right from when music was first recorded, sold and performed in exchange for money, there have been unfair contracts between artists and their managers, between bands and their record labels, between writers and composers and their publishers, between performers and their concert promoters. Little Richard was well aware of it. He got practically nothing from 'Tutti Frutti', his most important song in the sense that, aside from being totally irresistible, it reminded the music industry, which was mainly white at the time, that black musicians were behind everything that sounded good. Elvis Presley, despite being The King, also knew a thing or two about being swindled. Up until his death, half his income (or more) went to Colonel Parker, his manager. Bob Dylan may have paid Albert Grossman less, but it was enough to make him angry. He expressed that anger in 1967 with 'Dear Landlord' (from his album *John Wesley Harding*) and refused to renew their contract three years later.

It was also common for managers to grant themselves the publishing rights to the songs, either openly or in the small print of a contract. Steve Leber and David Krebs made a fortune on the back of Aerosmith that way. Others, Allen Klein being the worst, managed to con a string of famous musicians, one after the other (or even at the same time). This American 'businessman' made a name for himself by first defrauding Sam Cooke, then The Rolling Stones and lastly (but not least), The Beatles. It could be even worse if family was involved – when his sons decided to part from him, the father of the Wilson brothers, key members of The Beach Boys, went behind their backs and gave away the rights to their songs for peanuts. Not even Nostradamus could imagine the fortune they would be worth...

And, even when they weren't lining their own pockets, when they were simply bad managers, the record labels could take advantage instead. Among those who paid a high price for their carelessness were Sam & Dave (Atlantic 'loaned' them to

Stax, then got them back and put an end to their career as a duo), The Jackson 5 (who were forced to leave behind their name when they moved from Tamla Motown to CBS) and John Fogerty (who was accused by Fantasy of plagiarizing his own band, Creedence Clearwater Revival, for whom he had written all the songs).

It was the same with David Bowie. No one forced him, least of all Tony Defries, to sign the tricky contract that bound them as he climbed the ladder of success. He might never have reached the top if it hadn't been for Defries. Or his fame might have been less durable if he hadn't caught the eye and attention of his fans at the beginning. We'll never know... The aim of this book isn't to unravel the financial aspects of Bowie's story – only those involved have the information needed to do that. And the main character is no longer here to fill us in on the details about that or anything else. Knowing now that David Bowie kept everything, we can deduce that his contract with MainMan is in his archives somewhere in or around New York. But its actual content is now far less important than the consequences it wrought. Bowie found himself in a state of moral and financial collapse after realizing, with bitterness, that the man who had made him had also – knowingly – unmade him.

As well as Bowie's appalling financial situation in the mid-1970s, this chapter also covers at least three other subjects outside the remit of *Rainbowman*: drugs, the occult (and its 'psycho-political' associations) and cinema. This explosive cocktail is what gave rise to David Bowie's tenth studio LP and, by extension, the three following albums, which were his last of the decade. Everything is inextricably linked.

While *Station To Station* is not the natural follow-up to *Young Americans*, it comes directly out of the extra-musical activities of the few months Bowie spent in 'Hollywood Babylon' (a term coined by American avant-garde writer and director Kenneth Anger to describe the sordid scandals in Hollywood in the first half of the 20th century, which he describes in his book of the same name). The places Bowie lived in Los Angeles in 1975 have often been wrongly reported. These mistakes were repeated again and again in books and articles, and have now multiplied across the enormous oil spill that is the World Wide Web.

While David Bowie seems to have lived in a house rented by Glenn Hughes, then the bass player and singer of Deep Purple (at the time, members of the British group were 'tax exiles' in California), it was probably not in Benedict Canyon, but in Los Feliz, on Sunset Boulevard². In the spring of 1975, after spending a few weeks in Hollywood with Michael Lippman – his lawyer turned manager – David Bowie lived at 637 North Doheny Drive, around the corner from the Troubadour. While recording *Station To Station,* up until he left for Europe, he lived at 1349 Stone Canyon Road in Bel Air.

In March, Hughes isn't in LA; he is in Europe with Deep Purple and guitarist Ritchie Blackmore is about to the leave the band. After watching the famous festival California Jam[3] on television the year before, during a party at the Beverly Wilshire Hotel, David Bowie decided he wanted to meet Glenn Hughes and find out how a 'soul guy' like him had ended up joining Deep Purple. Coincidentally, Hughes will also try cocaine for the first time in the summer of 1974, so the relationship between him and Bowie will be as unhealthy as it will be friendly. Glenn saw many concerts of the Diamond Dogs tour and David had stopped by the studio while Deep Purple were recording *Stormbringer* and the song 'Hold On'. Rumour has it that he joined in the backing vocals on this track, but this can't be verified – there are many voices on 'Hold On', but none of the backing vocalists are credited on the original album or its 2009 reissue. It's also possible that Bowie may have been thinking of covering it, as Hughes says. In 1975, David reportedly prevented Deep Purple from splitting up after Blackmore's departure had weakened the group. According to Hughes, he also offered to produce his first album[4].

In the spring days that preceded the delayed shooting of *The Man Who Fell To Earth*, David Bowie was hanging out with several musicians who, like him, were known for their substance abuse. He spent time with Ronnie Wood (an expatriate, like Glenn Hughes and him) and Iggy Pop. They met up at a demo studio north of Hollywood[5] in May and held a writing and recording session in which Bowie played almost all the instruments. One of the songs they drafted, 'Turn Blue', came out of some chords Geoff MacCormack had played on the piano and the song will be reworked for *Lust For Life*, Iggy's second album, released in 1977, a particularly prolific year for him and David Bowie. They scheduled another session at the same location the following day, but Iggy Pop forgot to show up[6].

In August, before the *Station To Station* sessions begin, Bowie will contribute backing vocals on 'Real Emotion', a song written by Steve Cropper, which Keith Moon will record at Clover Studios on Santa Monica Boulevard. It was meant for Moon's second solo album, never to be released, but it will appear as a bonus track on the 2008 reissue of *Two Sides Of The Moon,* his first LP.

In the half century since David Bowie's name has been selling paper, many articles and books have been written about his activities in 1975, which he spent mainly on the West Coast of the United States. To this day, people are still readily dissecting his foray into the occult and black magic, his sometimes questionable reading material and his vampiric lifestyle – all of it dusted with the pure and expensive cocaine that Freddie Sessler, Keith Richards' 'second father', kept in milk bottles. However, the actual source of these theories is nowadays more of a trickle than a geyser. Those who really knew Bowie during this time become fewer and further between, and their stories, over time, have passed from mouth to mouth and into often questionable pieces of journalism to become the stuff of urban legend. And it's true to say, without disrespect, that most of David Bowie's inner circle were in a similar condition to him at the time and therefore unable to recall the details with any certainty.

But there has to be some truth in all the legends about Bowie during this time. And you don't have to be a professional toxicologist to know that cocaine – his consumption will go from abusive to recreational, then it will disappear from his daily life and his body, 20 years after having been introduced – acted like a spark on an already highly combustible character. It's easy to blame Aleister Crowley's writings for encouraging Bowie to abuse cocaine. The father of modern Satanism has almost as many theorists as he has followers and critics, and those who, because of his *Diary Of A Drug Fiend*, only saw him as a common apologist for cocaine and heroin use, were probably wrong. In this 1922 novel, Crowley employed autobiographical elements (his childhood asthma was treated with a heroine-based substance, which caused him to become addicted) to tell the story of a couple who managed to kick their drug addiction. Their method was 'true will', which is also the foundation of Crowley's religious and philosophical system known as Thelema. He described this in 1901 in his famous *Book Of The Law*[7]. David Bowie's first identified allusion to Aleister Crowley was a line of his song 'After All', in 1970: 'Live till your rebirth and do what you will.'

But it is true to say that when it came to drugs, Crowley hardly preached abstinence. While he began advocating their use for ritual purposes or as fuel for creativity – leaving it up to the individual to decide how much to use – we know that the self-proclaimed Beast 666 and the members of his community in Cefalù, Sicily, took it to extreme, unhealthy ends. Bowie also mentioned Aleister Crowley in 1971 on *Hunky Dory*, at the start of the song 'Quicksand'. In the rest of the lyrics, he uses multiple references to subject matters that will pierce his work right through, up until *Blackstar* (and his music videos). The 'Golden Dawn' from the first line of 'Quicksand' (the chorus lyrics are a bit like a list of Bowie's commandments), is a reference to the Hermetic Order Of The Golden Dawn, an old British secret society devoted to the study and practice of paranormal activities through 'magick'. Later in the song, 'divine symmetry' is an allusion to numerology – the study of symbolism in numbers and their cosmic or supernatural influence – and according to believers of the Kabbalah, it also referred to the perfect organization of the universe as a manifestation of divine will and supreme intelligence. The song's lyrics, like others by David Bowie – an esoterist in his own right – also refer to the concepts of the Übermensch and the superior race developed by philologist Friedrich Nietzsche, Aleister Crowley and Edward Bulwer-Lytton.

At the end of the 1960s, David Bowie took an interest in rumours of secret organizations that may have altered the course of history, especially between the two world wars. One of these rumours had to do with the secret Vril Society, as described by Bulwer-Lytton in *The Coming Race*, which was supposedly taken over by the Nazis before they came to power. According to Bulwer-Lytton, 'subterranean people' (descendants of the Aryan race) knew how to use the power of Vril to take over the world and destroy an entire people. Allegedly, members of the 'real Vril' (whose existence was never proven) were in touch with obscure Tibetan lodges who'd discovered how to turn a man into a superman. Adolf Hitler, Hermann Göring and Heinrich Himmler, who was mentioned in 'Quicksand', reportedly belonged to Vril. To add to the confusion, many of Crowley's followers truly believe that he requested a meeting with Hitler during World War II, though no one can confirm whether it actually took place.

Bowie wasn't the only musician interested in Aleister Crowley, who had died the year David was born. British keyboardist Graham Bond, an orphan of Dr Barnardo's, was a committed occultist and was convinced he was Crowley's son. In 1978, Peter Perrett, the frontman of the magnificent band The Only Ones, will sing about Aleister Crowley in 'The Beast' and 'The Whole Of The Law' on their first album. He appears on the cover of *Sgt. Pepper*, and on the back of *13*, a 1970 compilation album by The Doors, in the form of an ugly statuette. Mick Jagger was also interested in Crowley, and Jimmy Page – guitarist in The Yardbirds and Led Zeppelin – has long been one of his most devoted disciples, even if he has tempered that passion in later years. For more than 20 years, Page will own Boleskine Manor, one of Aleister Crowley's former residences, north of Loch Ness in Scotland. After someone else buys the house in 2015, it will burn to the ground in, of course, mysterious circumstances.

In time, Bowie will learn to let go of the things that stirred him up and sometimes later he will downplay the role or influence of certain key figures in his life, whether they were collaborators or people he admired. According to some groupies at the time, Bowie and Jimmy Page met up again at Rodney Bingenheimer's place during David's first trip to the US. In February 1975, a month before he left for Los Angeles (and the day after a Led Zeppelin concert at Madison Square Garden in New York), David Bowie invited Page and Ronnie Wood to to his brownstone in Chelsea. That evening, instead of calmly discussing Aleister Crowley, they had an argument and Jimmy returned to his hotel earlier than expected. After that, Bowie thought the guitarist had cast a spell on him; in LA, he will later say he felt demonic presences (whether linked to their disagreement or not), which will affect, at least partially, the writing of the lyrics of *Station To Station*.

More than 20 years later, when Stephen Dalton from the *NME* asks him about Crowley, David Bowie will say he thought he was a charlatan and that believing in magick didn't have to imply the worship of any kind of devil. By minimizing Crowley's impact on his work and life, and by saying he'd been more impressed by the writings of Arthur Edward Waite and Dion Fortune[8], Bowie set himself apart from most occultists and dismissed his very real fear over Jimmy Page's behaviour.

So it's clear that, during this period, there was torment in both David Bowie's mind and his body. Wherever he was living in 1975, the curtains were often drawn. He spent hours sitting cross-legged, reading books by candlelight, carefully storing them away in their hundreds. He started writing screenplays and even some fragmented paragraphs for an autobiography, *The Return Of The Thin White Duke*. His desire to tell his story, whether through a character or not, would be with him his whole life, though it never seemed to obsess him. And yes, he drew pentagrams on sheets of paper scattered across the floor and maybe on the windows and walls. He thought he was being hunted, possessed. He feared he would be abducted, so he asked his friends for help and they came. They listened to him, and every three or four days, when he finally did fall asleep, they put a mirror under his nose to check he was still breathing. The few people who lived with him denied rumours that he stored bottles of his own urine (and something else...) in his fridge, fearing someone would use it for nefarious purposes. But if black magic were true, it would be a reasonable precaution, and certainly understandable considering the state he was in... When he saw the devil at the bottom of a swimming pool, 'white witch' Walli Elmlark advised him to exorcise it. After all, he was David Bowie, an idealist from England, who'd been sucked into a tornado and spat out the other side, wandering in a gigantic cloud of pessimism.

From 1972 onwards, as his popularity grew, Bowie sank into a deepening state of paranoia and depression from which he will only really begin to emerge when he moves to Berlin. For him, culture and knowledge seemed to be the spice of life. Actually they were his vital fuel, the blood in his veins. In cocaine he found a double-edged sword. From a physical point of view, it could have had dramatic repercussions for him even earlier – he could have suddenly collapsed, struck down by the powder, curled up in a dark room. Or he could have simply dropped dead on a sidewalk under the black sun of Los Angeles. But from a psychological point of view, the distortions of concepts and the drug-induced atrophied reality spurred the artist boiling within him. They offered breathing holes: he was feeling suffocated by rock and rhythm'n'blues, but sooner or later he would be done with these constraining musical genres. His management problems and his failing marriage, his whims turning into obsessions and his worries becoming terrors, that mishmash soaked in his pathological and insatiable curiosity will help fertilize his art up to *Scary Monsters* in 1980. He will create in pain, maybe, but without visible effort. Against all odds, despite the unfathomable pit widening beneath his feet, David Bowie will keep his head above water; he'll manage to stay on top.

Ultimately, Bowie's metamorphosis will just be a succession of anamorphoses. In the second half of the 1970s, he'll become his own field of investigation and play. He won't always feel like he is winning, but that will allow him to rise above the rest, annihilating the competition. Four decades before the prospect of death makes him hope – with his last bit of strength – that it was all just a bad dream, David Bowie allowed cocaine to put his health at risk, in order to discover what profit he could derive from his situation.

Still, he was a consummate refiner of the work of others, his soul crushed under the weight of books, which he swallowed up whole (the storm in his head showed no mercy). And there he was, issuing grandiose declarations, especially political ones, playing with fire and 'always crashing in the same body'. It was as if the future was attracted to him and he literally gathered his courage in both hands to face it. Since the dawn of time, the number of artists in any field capable of such audacity can be counted on the fingers of one atrophied hand.

With the help of Nicolas Roeg, David Bowie's multifaceted talents were to lead him through another slow mutation. Like a rubber ball, he will bounce back to Europe: Switzerland, then to Germany, in Berlin, after passing through France. In June 1975, in New Mexico, Bowie starts acting in *The Man Who Fell To Earth*, directed by Roeg, famous among cinephiles for *Performance*, *Walkabout* and *Don't Look Back*.

Whether he is at the Hilton Inn in Albuquerque where he is staying when filming begins, at the house he will later rent near Santa Fe, on set or in his trailer between scenes, David Bowie is in the throes of an anxiety and fragility that perfectly suit the role he is to play – an extra-terrestrial who's come to Earth to try to save his planet, which has run out of water.

David Bowie will be a magnificent Thomas Jerome Newton. While Nagisa Oshima will give him his other great film role in 1983, it is under Roeg's direction that Bowie will stand out. He is given free rein to move about in strange and unfettered ways, awakening the 'alien' that lies dormant within him. David is allowed to transpose his own reality into Walter Tevis' fiction, and the director encourages him to split his personality, to break down any differences between him and Newton. Schizophrenia and dissociative disorder are two very different conditions, but their origins (often a childhood trauma) and their symptoms are sometimes the same. Being *The Man Who Fell To Earth* perhaps gives Bowie the chance to feel what his half-brother is going through. He finds a kind of refuge, a controlled but validated area, in this mental illness – 'a family thing', as David Bowie will describe it – something his human condition alone can't offer him. Aware that the performance of his leading actor is enhanced by the freedom he is giving him, Nicolas Roeg allows him to choose his own wardrobe[10], use his limousine and driver and, importantly, asks him to write the film score. For Bowie, this is the light at the end of the tunnel.

In May, he gets down to writing an album, which he thinks will become the music for *The Man Who Fell To Earth*. He plans to record it once filming is over and sees this project as an opportunity to succeed where his peers have failed, particularly Mick Jagger and Jimmy Page. He knows that Donald Cammell and Nicolas Roeg wanted Mick Jagger and The Rolling Stones to get involved in the soundtrack of *Performance*, but Jagger didn't want the band to be associated with it. As for Keith Richards, he couldn't stand Cammell, thought the film was a waste of time and that, because of Jagger's involvement, The Stones would have to postpone their musical projects. In the end, Jack Nitzsche, Phil Spector's right-hand man, took care of the music and Mick Jagger's only contribution to the soundtrack of *Performance* was the song 'Memo From Turner'[11].

At the end of the 1960s, convinced that 'Sympathy For The Devil' was about him, Kenneth Anger circled The Rolling Stones like a shark, even asking Jagger to act in his short film, *Lucifer Rising*, and write its soundtrack. Mick suggested Anger hire his brother instead of him, but he did agree to record a few synth parts, maybe with a Moog Modular 3P, like the one Turner, his character, plays in

Performance. Ultimately, this contribution was not used in *Lucifer Rising*, but in *Invocation Of My Demon Brother*, an even shorter short (12 minutes) that Anger completed in 1969.

In those days, Kenneth Anger was also friends with Jimmy Page (legend has it that they met at an auction of Aleister Crowley's personal items), so he asked him to write the soundtrack for *Lucifer Rising*. During their brief friendship, Anger stayed with Page at Boleskine Manor. The musician recorded a few pieces for the film, in which he also appears, before Kenneth Anger fired him for being uninspired. After a bewildering series of changes of mind, which the filmmaker often had, it is Bobby Beausoleil who will finally write the music. Currently serving a life sentence in the USA (he is incarcerated in a Californian medical facility), Beausoleil was a musician and actor who featured in the previously mentioned Anger films. He is especially famous for having done the bidding of Charles Manson, who had ordered him to kill the American musician Gary Hinman with a knife. The murder was the first of three crimes perpetrated by the 'Manson family' in the summer of 1969.

After learning that Jimmy Page was out, Bobby Beausoleil – who'd been asked to do the soundtrack before Mick Jagger, but had been fired after Anger accused him of stealing film reels – offered his services again. They settled their differences and Beausoleil got hold of some instruments. Behind bars, he composed and recorded the music for *Lucifer Rising* with a group of other prisoners (The Freedom Orchestra). His and Kenneth Anger's names are the only ones to appear in the credits[12]. In 1975, on the set of *The Man Who Fell To Earth* in Los Angeles, David Bowie read everything he could get his hands on about Charles Manson's murderous summer[13]....

The month-long gap between the shooting of *The Man Who Fell To Earth* and the first sessions of *Station To Station* is another complicated time for David Bowie. The film role has affected him, and he spends most of his sleepless nights between four walls, thinking dark thoughts. And when he gets sucked into Los Angeles, it is to hang out at parties where he doesn't necessarily feel comfortable. That's how he ends up at Peter Sellers' place, on the actor's 50th birthday, and agrees to jam with Keith Moon, Ronnie Wood and Bill Wyman (according to Geoff MacCormack, the result was a cacophony).

The success of 'Fame' in the charts draws media attention to Bowie and, at RCA's request, he gives a few interviews – those to Cameron Crowe, published in *Rolling Stone, Creem* and *Playboy*, have gone down in history. He also appears on the *Cher Show* on CBS in November, dancing and behaving a little like Elvis Presley. He and Cher (who's just divorced Sonny Bono) sing a duet with a playback track of 'Can You Hear Me'. Then, accompanied by the show's orchestra, they perform a medley of classics that starts and ends with 'Young Americans'.

In late September, 'Space Oddity' lands David Bowie his first Number 1 song in the UK after RCA reissued it on an EP with two other tracks ('Changes' and 'Velvet Goldmine', a previously unreleased song from the *Ziggy Stardust* sessions).

At SIR (Studio Instrument Rentals), David and his musicians start to rehearse the songs he is planning to record at Cherokee Studios, which is actually the former MGM Studios at 751 North Fairfax Avenue, recently acquired by The Robb brothers. George Martin – he produced a part of Jeff Beck's *Blow By Blow* there – speaks highly of the studio, which is fitted out with high-tech equipment, including a Trident A Range console. Harry Maslin – whom Michael Lippman has hired as co-producer at Bowie's request – thought Cherokee would be ideal because it isn't yet well known and Lippman thought David Bowie could work there in relative anonymity.

Carlos Alomar, Earl Slick and Dennis Davis arrive from New York, along with bass player George Murray. Murray is then associated with Weldon Irvine but, in 1975, he hasn't yet done much recording with this unsung American genius of jazz and soul. Alomar[14] has recommended Murray to Bowie and, with Dennis Davis, they will be in his rhythm section until 1980 (many Bowie fans consider it the best he's had). The atmosphere at Cherokee is often upbeat and productive, but sometimes David's mood swings disrupt sessions – especially when he doesn't actually show up!

In the summer, all David Bowie could think about was the music for *The Man Who Fell To Earth*, but now he temporarily puts those instrumentals, written on the set and in Bel Air, aside. He focuses on more conventional, but relatively long, sung pieces – in their final versions, five of the six songs on his next album will exceed five minutes, and the opening track will be more than ten minutes long. The previous year at Sigma, Bowie was surrounded by lots of backing vocalists. Now, only one remains – the loyal Geoff MacCormack, who is homesick and will soon return to England.

Roy Bittan from the E Street Band is the pianist on *Station To Station*. He wasn't Bowie's first choice – he won't stay long at Cherokee – but he will play on all the songs except for the cover of 'Wild Is The Wind'. His main memory of these sessions is that for 'TVC 15', the first piece he worked on, David asked him to play à la Professor

Longhair, godfather of the New Orleans sound (a musical style as spicy as a gumbo).

Despite appearances and probably pressure from RCA to deliver the follow-up to *Young Americans* as quickly as possible, David Bowie, until recording sessions end in December, always had the music for *The Man Who Fell To Earth* in mind. Over the years, much has been written about the origins of this soundtrack, and ultimately its 'non-existence' (like *The Gouster*, it's sometimes called a 'lost album'). Books dedicated to the film[15] and notes in the booklet of the most recent Blu-ray edition barely scratch the surface. A good part of the five or six pieces (Bowie never mentioned more than that) that he wrote for the film seem to have been recorded in a rudimentary way at his home on Stone Canyon Road. But some music, with a little help from the *Station To Station* musicians, was definitely taped at Cherokee.

But for a whole host of different reasons, David Bowie's soundtrack for *The Man Who Fell To Earth* was ultimately rejected. The first one is that Nicolas Roeg wasn't thrilled with the little of it he heard – the bits and pieces crafted with Paul Buckmaster, the arranger of *Space Oddity* who had been recruited for the purpose. Roeg listened carefully, but the music was far from finished. Apparently it was the spirit of the material, despite its diversity of sound, that he didn't like. From the start of post-production, film editor Graeme Clifford had been using songs from *The Dark Side Of The Moon,* which clearly didn't bode well for what Bowie was delivering in small instalments. Released two years before, Pink Floyd's eighth album had gained worldwide success (only rarely has it left the *Billboard* Top 200 since it came out) and had started to permeate the collective unconscious. It's hardly surprising that Nicolas Roeg and his editor thought that scenes from the film would work well with this so-called 'trippy' rock.

Another problem was that Maggie Abbott, the agent who negotiated David Bowie's involvement in *The Man Who Fell To Earth,* reportedly neglected to have him sign a specific contract for the music. After listening to the few pieces that were (almost) ready and deciding he didn't like them, Michael Deeley – one of the two producers from British Lion, which funded the film – reportedly decided to cut Bowie's fee. It's also possible that they urged the musician to submit more material for approval and that he categorically refused. While his friends said his physical and psychological state, which worsened after shooting *The Man Who Fell To Earth*, didn't seem to have a negative impact on his performance (he will later play it down by saying he simply 'appeared' in the film), it undeniably affected his judgement regarding non-artistic decisions. Once again, David Bowie is in a terribly uncomfortable situation. Held responsible for the fiasco surrounding the soundtrack, Michael Lippman will be fired in early 1976.

There is one last argument that could possibly explain this failure and it is that Bowie's attention was elsewhere again. More than six months after being asked to write it, his engagement regarding the music of *The Man Who Fell To Earth* was perhaps just a hazy memory; a firm commitment when he made it, but one that couldn't stand the test of time. By late 1975 a lot of water has flowed under the bridge and too much cocaine is still flooding his nostrils. He skulks around at home, expecting the worst to happen at any given moment and continuing to feed himself badly (milk and peppers aren't enough to sustain any man, not even a thin one). He is also infected by the fear of 'family' madness. In other words, David Bowie is heading for trouble.

Against all odds, he will find the strength and resources to escape from this infernal trap and sever his ties with Los Angeles, a place which gives him palpitations and throbbing temples. By announcing another tour, he commits to do the very thing that he claimed a few months earlier he would never do again. First he needs to recover financially and touring will allow him to do just that. He also informs his band he will be parting from them after the last concert of the tour as he doesn't want to pay them all year round. But, above all, Bowie's decision to tour again is because he wants to return to Europe. Switzerland, the land of 'tax exiles', will be his base and Angie, keeping actively involved to delay the inevitable, has gone to find a place for them to stay – perhaps a nice house in a snow-globe, which she can shake to remind him that she still exists. Bowie also misses England – he hasn't seen his primary audience since July 1973, and the success of the reissue of 'Space Oddity' proved that, 5,000 miles away, they were still rooting for him, even more than before. At the beginning of the interview he gives to Russell Harty via satellite in November, David confirms he'll be performing in the UK the following spring. He lets Harty play cat and mouse with him and dodges tricky questions. Bowie finally offers to come on his show once he is back in London and, in a burst of generosity, he adds that he'll be happy to answer questions from the ITV audience.

'Golden Years', the first catchy and funky single from the *Station To Station* sessions (whose title was one of those considered for the album), is released in mid-November and will make it into the Top 10 on both sides of the Atlantic. Two weeks before, Bowie lip-synced the song, along with 'Fame', on *Soul Train*[16] but he looked slightly drunk, was not in time with the taped backup and in no state to answer Don Cornelius' questions.

Harry Maslin mixed 'Golden Years' (along with the rest of the album) in

New York, at The Hit Factory (237 West 54th Street). He was the house recording engineer there at the start of his career. While he'd played a significant role in the mix of *Young Americans* (sending a long telegram to Tony Visconti in London), David was not involved in *Station To Station*'s final stage. But when the record is remixed in 2010 (in 5.1 and stereo), he will approve these new versions.

In early January 1976, David Bowie and his band are in Jamaica[17] rehearsing for the tour, but Earl Slick isn't with them. Michael Lippman, whom Bowie has just fired, is now managing Slick and has advised him to focus on his solo career. Ironically, in 1983, when Stevie Ray Vaughan doesn't participate in the Serious Moonlight tour – for quite similar reasons – after having played on *Let's Dance*, Slick will be called to come to the rescue by Bowie. For now, he is replaced by Stacy Heydon, a young Canadian prodigy with guitar in hand. The other new recruit is keyboardist Tony Kaye, a former member of Yes (and Badger). He was stagnating in Los Angeles and Eric Barrett, Bowie's tour manager, didn't have much trouble convincing him to join the others[18].

David Bowie spends the week before the tour fine-tuning the set list at the Agrodome in Vancouver, and one of the run-throughs is filmed. On 2 February, Bowie and his band Raw Moon give the first of 60 concerts, at the Pacific National Exhibition Coliseum to an audience of 17,000, which bodes well. He will play there again twice in August 1983; it's also where David Mallet will shoot *Serious Moonlight*.

Station To Station has been the favourite album of many Bowie fans since it was released on 23 January 1976 in a matt cardboard jacket. A colour version of a photo taken by Steve Schapiro on the set of *The Man Who Fell To Earth* was supposed to appear on the cover, but in the end a black and white shot was chosen[19]. In 1975 (and not 1974 as reported in *Bowie*, his photography retrospective published in 2016 by powerHouse Books), Schapiro undertook a marathon photo shoot with the musician, which yielded the famous photos[20] used for that year's re-release of 'Space Oddity', and appeared on the covers of magazines like *Cash Box, Creem* and *Rolling Stone*. The notable photos of Bowie dressed in blue will be used on the back of the 1991 and 1999 reissues of *Station To Station*. He'd painted white stripes on his sweater and trousers, a style inspired by his Riot Squad days. He will recycle it for the Outside tour, then in the video for 'Lazarus', which will be revealed less than a month before his death. In some photos of David in this outfit, he was using chalk to draw the Kabbalah tree of life.

The song 'Station To Station' perfectly encapsulates the months that preceded the album's release, just as 'Changes' did on *Hunky Dory*. David Bowie uses it to announce, imperiously, the tone and direction of the album. Since he himself has dissected the song, we know that his over-three-minutes-long instrumental intro is a reference to the motorik beat, developed by the krautrock bands that provided background music to his spiritual wanderings in 1975. But there is more Neu!, Can and Faust in it than Kraftwerk, although he'd been listening to *Autobahn* on a loop since its release in 1974. Little known to the public (even among music fans), these bands best represent the genre. Still fearing planes, Bowie's repetitive beat is that of a train he is about to board without a return ticket – the following year, Kraftwerk will allude to the same mode of transport with *Trans Europa Express*. Clearly the stroke of genius was to get black musicians raised on rhythm'n'blues to play this slow, martial rhythm (66 bpm). Compelled, tied to a swelling guitar riff (Carlos Alomar) and another guitar, screeching with feedback (Earl Slick), George Murray and Dennis Davis are forced back to basics, and content themselves with emphasizing the dominant chord. They only relieve some of the pressure at three minutes in, allowing Bowie to introduce his new persona. Then the train sets off again and the only passenger on board is the Thin White Duke, with his haunting litanies. He has a big mouth and sings about magic, the bottom of dredged oceans and bewilderment, and he reveals the black and white tones of his upcoming tour. And, of course, he introduces his audience to Kether and Malkuth, the first and last of the ten Sefirot, the divine principles of Judaism represented in the Kabbalah by the tree of life.

Halfway through 'Station To Station', the Duke predicts his return to Europe, but before the train sets off again, he throws in one last reference to Crowley – the 'white stains' that allude to his book of sexual poetry, of the same name, published in 1898. As the train shakes and rattles (the piece ends at 125bpm), David Bowie's heady and redemptive voice offers love as the cure for cocaine, not the other way around. He confirms his final destination and detox, repeats that salvation is ahead, and with his thirties just around the corner, he sings that he doesn't have any more time to waste. In 'Station To Station', David Bowie really opens up, getting things off his chest and purging the American evil from his pores. Then he falls silent and Earl Slick takes the place of his vocal. On this drum-roll-induced mutant beat, to which Roy Bittan adds panic, the guitar player, instructed by Bowie, is confined to rock'n'roll. He dutifully whips around the riffs, like Mick Ronson in 'Round And Round'.

Released as a single several weeks before the album, 'Golden Years', in form and length, is its catchiest song. Earl Slick, supposedly inspired by 'Funky Broadway'[21] (popularized by Wilson Pickett in 1967), plays two major chords a full tone apart – a trick already used by Bowie in 'Maid Of Bond Street', 'The Supermen', 'Rebel Rebel' and the instrumental part of 'Aladdin Sane'. Alomar contrasts that with a counterpoint based on more elaborate inversions with a clear and slightly phased/ flanged guitar sound, bringing his own style to the piece. For many artists, that would have been enough to try and make a hit. But David Bowie was never one for simplicity and often chose to make things more elaborate. As a chorus, he extricates himself from a risky chord progression by using the higher range of his tessitura, then he inserts a sort of five-bar section to transition to the next verse.

Present for the last time on one of his friend's records, Geoff MacCormack contributes a large part of the vocal harmonies to this song – like the lead vocal, the backing vocals on the album were recorded with different microphones to enrich the sound. Geoff is the one who sings the high-pitched 'angel' in Bowie's place. Angie always thought David had written 'Golden Years' for her and, at that time, he still claimed he couldn't imagine life without her, which perhaps confirms it. It's also highly likely the song was offered to Elvis Presley. In the lyrics, addressing a loved one, Bowie implies that rebuilding his life, which won't be easy, is his only way forward.

In the 60s and 70s, with an anti-establishment vibe in the air, people were searching for a new moral and physical autonomy. In their quest, they turned Aleister Crowley and the like into cultural icons and saw dechristianization as a way to assert themselves and live freely. We don't know to what extent Bowie followed this trend but, in 1975, after adapting his idea of gnosis to the mood of the times, he felt trapped in his own depths. On the set of *The Man Who Fell To Earth*, some noticed his latent state of panic – it will be a long and slow process to leave this behind him. That's why he clung to symbolic objects like his mezuzah, which he was given by Michael Lippman and his wife while staying with them.

Both a ballad and a hymn, 'Word On A Wing' isn't a confession to God (whoever that may be), but a great show of passion. While the three chords of the verse point to a traditional ending, the composition develops around daring harmonic twists that go against pop convention. Here, Roy Bittan manages to help us forget Mike Garson's absence, and the organ and backing vocals add to the mystical character of the piece. The song is like a gift, with remarkable vocals. Moral and psychic positioning seem to have inspired Bowie's lyrics, which he'd started writing months before recording, but he sings 'Word On A Wing' as if his answers, however explicitly required, could wait a little longer. Just as the journey always seemed more interesting to him than the destination, doubt and expectation turn out to be, at the end of side one, adequate, though partial, solutions. Bowie may not be fully satisfied, but at least he is not totally disappointed.

'TVC 15' is one of David Bowie's many songs in four parts – intro, verses, chorus and bridge. Its introduction, repeated later in the piece, was borrowed shamelessly from 'Good Morning Little Schoolgirl' (the versions by The Yardbirds and Don And Bob[22]), yet Bowie's liberal layout gives it originality. Not quite blues, not quite boogie, this song owes a lot (especially its verses) to 'I Can Help', a global 1974 hit by country singer-songwriter Billy Swann. Four years after Mungo Jerry had an equally successful hit with 'In The Summertime', this song proved that, during the 70s, it was easy to make a fortune just by making a silly pop version of a 12-bar blues. Though of course the 'transition, transmission' part, and especially the chorus with the two oblique menacing chords, are typical of this offbeat artist, as are the tormented arrangements. The original inspiration for the lyrics allegedly came from Iggy Pop who, while delirious, saw his girlfriend being 'swallowed up by her television set'. Perhaps it also refers to the scene in *The Man Who Fell To Earth* where Thomas Jerome Newton slumps dementedly in front of a wall of television screens and feels like he's being attacked by the moving images. Elvis Presley, whom Bowie still found very interesting (and who covered 'I Can Help' in 1975), spent a lot of time in front of numerous television screens, at Graceland or in his hotel suites. Sometimes he used his revolver as a remote.

'Stay', the only openly funky song on *Station To Station*, is another act of bravery. The solid riff played by Earl Slick[23] may have been 'borrowed' by David Bowie (he had already heard it somewhere), but the final chord – a G9 that was typical of James Brown's soul music – was probably suggested by Carlos Alomar. In the verses, Carlos makes good use of a chord progression similar to the one in 'John, I'm Only Dancing (Again)', and plays rhythm guitar tricks in the vein of those that worked so well on 'Fame'. The chorus, swaying to a sensual and devilish groove, is the model for a new genre. Dennis Davis introduces it with an improbable seven-beat drum fill and, thanks to George Murray, a slap bass can be heard for the first time on a Bowie song. David placed 'Stay' in the middle of the album's B-side, making rock and black music's planets collide. Those who thought David Bowie went too deep into soul during the Diamond Dogs tour have to admit that, this time, he's found the perfect balance.

There was only ever one like him – as in the Kinks song, he was 'not like everybody else', and looking back now, we may sometimes wonder if there was even one such marvel – and David Bowie delivers the vocal performance of his life on a song not written by him. 'Wild Is The Wind', the last stop on *Station To Station*, is like a beacon, now digitized for what's left of eternity, lighting up his entire discography. He was obviously inspired by Nina Simone's version of this Dimitri Tiomkin and Ned Washington[24] masterpiece. Because the lyrics of the song are vague but powerful enough for him to find his way round without too much difficulty, and the arrangement uses only guitars (this is the only track to feature an acoustic), bass and drums, all Bowie needs here is his throat to channel the emotion and his voice to articulate it. No keyboards, no flattering strings or charming backing vocals. 'Wild Is The Wind' is all the more commendable and successful as the ballad, typically white, is performed with a black rhythm section which, at that time, grooved like no other (that half-open hi-hat hit at 35 seconds from the end).

Just as he changed his mind at the last minute over the cover for *Station To Station*, Bowie had, at first, envisaged a more theatrical show, before settling on the strong but simple visual aspect of what would become the Isolar tour[25]. Better known as the Station To Station tour, it will cover more than 60 dates in 10 countries, including many he'd never played in before.

His Thin White Duke, a dark and pale echo of Thomas Jerome Newton, will move about against a plain but very effective backdrop reduced to powerful white lighting – neon lights and huge projectors, some operated by technicians, will follow him around the stage. David Bowie drew his visual inspiration (Eric Barrett is responsible for implementing his ideas) from the photographs of Man Ray and the theatre Bertolt Brecht created in the 1930s. It also references *Cabaret*[26], the musical inspired by *Goodbye To Berlin*, one of two semi-autobiographical *Berlin Stories* written by British novelist Christopher Isherwood, which came out as a single work in 1945. When Bowie saw *Cabaret* in London in early 1968[27] at the Palace Theatre on Shaftesbury Avenue, it made a strong impression on him. He met Isherwood in Los Angeles, and his writing and character naturally aroused his curiosity regarding interwar Germany and, more precisely, the aestheticism of the Weimar Republic. Bowie will later recount, not without irony, that Christopher Isherwood advised him to escape Los Angeles and cocaine by moving to Berlin, at the time the 'heroine capital of Europe'. Bowie's sobriety is reflected in his stage outfit. He chooses black trousers and a waistcoat buttoned over a white shirt (a reference to Buster Keaton, he will later reveal). The only colour is found in his blonde hair (with pink highlights) styled by Martin Samuel and the blue pack of Gitanes poking out of his pocket.

Before David Bowie gets to the stage, extracts of *Radio-Activity*, Kraftwerk's fifth album, which was released in 1975[28], will be played. And instead of an opening act, he intends to screen the short silent film *Un Chien Andalou* by surrealist Spanish director Luis Buñuel, who wrote the screenplay with Salvador Dalí in 1929. If all goes well, the film will open most of his American concerts, but not all of those in Europe (it will be deemed inappropriate for minors in France).

The set list, comprising about 15 songs, gives pride of place to material from *Station To Station* – 'Golden Years' is the only one left out because it is tricky to sing live. For the rest, Bowie happily draws from almost all his albums since *Hunky Dory*. *Young Americans* is the least represented (only 'Fame' survives). His cover of 'I'm Waiting For The Man' is also included, as is 'Sister Midnight'[29], which makes a remarkable appearance at the start of the tour. This is an important song because it will allow David Bowie to connect the Iggy Pop wagon to his train.

Since their aborted sessions in May 1975, Iggy is grappling with his own demons and his future isn't looking good. When Iggy finds out that the Isolar tour will be stopping in San Diego[30] where he lives, he decides to visit his friend the day after the show. This is not in vain: at the hotel, David has him listen to 'Sister Midnight', which he's written with Carlos Alomar, and suggests the song be a starting point for an LP Iggy could start recording at the end of the tour[31]. But the English artist knows that he still has to keep an eye on his American friend, who is not easy to deal with. Instead of leaving him to his own devices and to the vultures of the West Coast, and since Geoff MacCormack is no longer travelling with him, David Bowie invites Iggy Pop along on the tour. Jim (or Jimmy) becomes a sort of mascot for Bowie's now slimmed-down touring crew[32]. The two-month-long American tour, which is due to wrap up on 26 March in New York, will achieve great success. Bowie and Iggy's arrest for possession of marijuana a week before will barely cause a stir – they'll be freed after a few hours, after Bowie posts bail.

When the tour stopped in Los Angeles[33], David Bowie organized his move to Europe and appeared on *Dinah!*, hosted by actress and singer Dinah Shore. He sang 'Stay' and 'Five Years' with his band and spoke to the other guests, including actor Henry Winkler (Fonzie from *Happy Days*) and Candy Clark, his co-star in *The Man Who Fell To Earth*, who had never been on a television show before. *Dinah!* aired on 3 March. Bowie's performance on 23 March at the Nassau Veterans Memorial

Coliseum in Uniondale, north of Long Beach, came before the Madison Square Garden concert and was recorded by Harry Maslin for a live radio broadcast (as part of the show *King Biscuit Flower Hour*, on the DIR Network). It won't take long for a bootleg double LP to appear in record stores, but it will take another 34 years for an official version to be released[34].

David Bowie had a day off on 18 March 1976 (between concerts in Boston and Buffalo), when *The Man Who Fell To Earth* premiered in London. In the end, John Phillips of The Mamas & The Papas took care of the musical supervision. Nicolas Roeg specifically asked him to devise an 'American' soundtrack, at the last minute. It includes some pre-existing songs (by Louis Armstrong, Roy Orbison, Bing Crosby...), pieces by the Japanese prog rock musician Stomu Yamashta[35] (mostly extracts from pre-existing albums), and original tracks written by Phillips and performed by a band hastily put together by Mick Taylor, who had left The Rolling Stones in 1974. The master tapes were only found years later, so the soundtrack of *The Man Who Fell To Earth* won't be released until 2016. Unfortunately for them, the sleeve notes don't mention the musicians, so it's impossible to confirm whether bassist Herbie Flowers, guitarist Jim Sullivan and percussionist Luis Jardim (all of whom played with Bowie at different times during his career) did perform on these London sessions, as some have said.

In late March, David Bowie and Coco cross the Atlantic and then the Mediterranean Sea on the SS *Leonardo Da Vinci*, chartered by the company Italian Line. A few days later, they arrive in Genoa, where their friends are waiting for them. Bowie tells an Italian journalist he wants to go to Verona, then Monaco and mentions the possibility of a concert in Rome[36] at the end of May, after those planned in Paris. His musicians and the rest of his team join him just before the tour starts up again on 7 April at Olympia-halle in Munich. It is the first time David Bowie performs in Europe (out of the UK) under just his own name and six further concerts will follow in Germany, which is one more than he gives in early May at the Empire Pool in Wembley, London (the only performances in England). This reveals Bowie's attachment to Germany, whose culture he absorbs and which already seems to him an ideal place of refuge.

Taking advantage of a week off between the show at the Hallenstadion in Zurich and the one in Helsinki, David Bowie, Coco, Iggy Pop, Andrew Kent and Pat Gibbons, the acting manager since Michael Lippman's dismissal (the official programme credits him as 'tour co-ordinator'), celebrate Iggy Pop's 29th birthday on 21 April in Basel. Then they decide to visit Moscow but, during their train journey, they are stopped by the KGB, who confiscate some of David's books, most notably one about Joseph Goebbels (failed author but successful Nazi, Adolf Hitler's minister of information and propaganda). When journalists later question Bowie about the incident, he will mumble a few barely convincing explanations as to why he was reading this. He may not be the only rock star to play with that kind of fire[37], but his questionable claims about the good sides of Nazism (!) or that he intended to make a film about Goebbels' life, would follow him round for the rest of his life.

On arriving at Victoria station in London (after performing in Sweden and Denmark) the day before his first concert in England since leaving in 1974, David Bowie is photographed standing in the back of his Mercedes with the roof open. Adding fuel to the fire, he waves at the 2,000 fans that have gathered to see him and reaches out to them with his arm. In the newspapers the following day, on 3 May, the media liken his gesture to a Nazi salute.

However, the incident doesn't dampen his joy of performing in his home city, in his country, and the 60,000 fans who come to see these London performances give their hometown hero a triumphant welcome. In their reviews, most journalists will emphasize his warmth and emotion, and some of them will write that they saw him cry on stage. As expected, the whole of London jostles for Bowie's attention at after-show parties and, while he finds all of this commotion flattering, he is especially happy to discuss the possibility of a collaboration with Brian Eno.

Released as a single at the end of April (with 'We Are The Dead', a strange choice, on the B-side), 'TVC 15' will almost make the Top 30 in the UK, while *Station To Station* will get to Number 5 in the album charts (and Number 3 in the USA, where it will do noticeably better in the long term). Unsurprisingly, and despite good reviews, *The Man Who Fell To Earth* will never draw much interest from the general public. However, it will be shown in British cinemas in May, riding on the buzz created by David Bowie's return, and receive good press coverage. Over time, *The Man Who Fell To Earth* has become a cult classic and, since the death of its leading actor, it has enjoyed renewed interest that mainly benefits Studio Canal, its distributor. In the spring of 1976, Bowie organized several private viewings for his friends, among them Marc Bolan and his wife Gloria Jones, who were invited to the Isolar tour in Helsinki on 24 April.

In the final scene of *The Man Who Fell To Earth*, fiction collides with reality. Stuck on Earth, now a long-time alcoholic and unable to age, Thomas Jerome Newton, whom David Bowie will say is a better person at the end of the film than at the beginning, asks Nathan Bryce (played by Rip Torn) what he thinks of his album, *The Visitor*[38], which he's just released. Bryce answers that he wasn't impressed and Newton (slightly irritated) declares that he didn't make it for him anyway. In the audio commentary for the DVD of the 1990s reissue, Nicolas Roeg and Bowie both agree, without going into any detail, that the fact that David didn't write the score was a blessing in disguise. Bowie will explain that what he had in mind for the soundtrack appeared on parts of *Station To Station* and even more so on the following album, which would change his direction completely, and truly turn him into … a rock star from another world.

Later on in the audio commentary, David Bowie will declare he's tired of hearing people say that the life of artists resides in their art. He will come to the conclusion that what interests him most is art, and not those who make it. And what he says during the final scene is typically him: referring to some of the props used in the film, especially the rings and his passport, Bowie wonders, almost twenty years later, and using the French word, where all this 'bric-à-brac' went. Then he starts talking about a very dear friend he had in Berlin when he lived there. She had cancer and, to help her cover her head, which was bald from chemotherapy, David gave her the fedora hat he'd worn in the scene, one of the few items he said he'd kept. So, a hat belonging to Newton[39] in this mirror-like film could make a human being's decline in the real world a little more tolerable. In the same way, just under forty years later, by extending the work of Walter Tevis and, as a corollary, that of Nicholas Roeg, David Bowie (who always claimed to have understood the book better than the film) will allow Thomas Jerome Newton, embodied by Michael C. Hall, to make the last months of his own life more bearable. Icarus, who fell to Earth and into the sea in Pieter Bruegel's painting (which Nathan Bryce sees at the start of *The Man Who Fell To Earth*), will fade away to be replaced by the one who, like Lazarus, will rise from the dead.

Earl Slick	Paul Buckmaster
Carlos Alomar	Jay Glennie
George Murray	Stacy Heydon
Geoff MacCormack	Roy Young
Harry Maslin	Buford Jones
	Iggy Pop
	John 'Twink' Alder
	Mat Osman

EARL SLICK[40]

The confusing thing about the Diamond Dogs tour was the change in direction. When the backing vocalists got there, we went from a small band to a larger one and we started playing things that I wasn't expecting when I first joined. The rock side of things gradually faded out. I had no problem with that type of music because, in New York City, I'd had to play all the blues stuff, all the Memphis and Tamla Motown stuff. To perform in clubs there you had to master all kinds of styles, so the Sam & Dave, Otis Redding and James Brown songs were no mystery to me. Actually I had cut my teeth on them! No, what threw me was the feeling that we'd switched horses halfway through a race and I had been caught off guard. It wasn't defined, it wasn't made very clear.

It's funny to think that three of us made most of *Station To Station* at night: it was just David, Harry Maslin and me. Once the rhythm section was recorded, we spent a lot of time doing some crazy stuff. For example, the whole intro to the title song. For the solo, David didn't specifically ask me to play like Chuck Berry, but that was the spirit. I had all these blues licks in my head and they went well with the arrangement. You know, repeating a lick when the chords change is really a blues thing – of course Chuck Berry was the best at that. You have to remember that David knew everything about blues and old rock'n'roll so it was easy for him to give a few indications.

He trusted the people he worked with and had a very clear idea of how his songs should turn out and what we could bring to them. But he never explained lyrics. As a matter of fact they were hardly finished by the time we started recording. Also, I want to say that working with George Murray and Dennis Davis was great. They were the perfect rhythm section for *Station To Station*.

I liked working closely with David at Cherokee. It was a one-on-one situation – I only had to report to him. I'm not comfortable when a lot of people are involved, giving their opinion on what I should and shouldn't play. Personally, unless I'm the one in charge, I never tell others what to do. Maybe people didn't quite get that David wanted something very organic for this album and he had a band that could give it to him. I gave him what he'd asked me to give, this twisted blues played by a white guy. It's my thing and that's what he wanted to hear.

Regarding whatever issues David had at the time, all I can say is that, in the studio he didn't seem to have any problems at all and, if he had, well, it enhanced the work. End of quote. I'm sure you get this. For 'Stay' and 'Golden Years', we actually messed around with riffs, guitar in hand, until the right ones showed up and

David used them as tools for the songs. Also, I heard rumours about those recording sessions. For example, I can't rule out that he indeed dropped in, but personally I didn't see Ronnie Wood at Cherokee!

The split between David and me, just before the Station To Station tour, didn't have anything to do with us. Management, let's put it this way, 'divided and conquered' us and we only realized what really happened six years later, before the Serious Moonlight tour. Before we started rehearsing, we sat down to clear the air, because it had been really ugly and we realized we'd got fucking worked. I'd lost my job and he'd lost his guitar player because of people's idiocy, greed and all that. Power-hungry bullshit! They know who they are. You guys know who you are. If you read this book, you'll know who you are. Nobody's name goes under the bus. (2018)

CARLOS ALOMAR

We really started to work with David Bowie on *Station To Station*, and I have to admit, I was under his tutelage: he introduced me to Kraftwerk, comedy, theatre, architecture. He had books on everything and we discussed many, many subjects... Musically speaking, he wanted this kind of industrial background, like Kraftwerk, this industrial drone beat – but he didn't want to copy anybody. He wanted a thunderous but tight, black rhythm'n'blues section powering this rock'n'roll machine. That was when we called ourselves the DAM trio – Davis, Alomar and Murray. We weren't anything like The Rolling Stones, famous for their loose rhythm section and their jeans and t-shirts. We were black guys in suits. Our metronome was very funky! But still, we liked to flip the beat around. Let me explain that: if you take 'Station To Station', for instance, what we have is a 4/4 beat, then a 6/4 beat, and then a 5/4 beat... So we were constantly flipping these beats around. We would do this kind of thing inside David's music and, of course, if you analyse the songs, you'll realize that we were doing that a lot, but still maintaining that rock'n'roll spirit that he wanted. Most people don't hear that; also because it's so seamless and so tight, you don't notice it.

David's music could be booming without being heavy. We had a tightness that you just didn't hear in conventional rock. People don't say this much, but there are certain political things that happened for *Station To Station* that made it the way it is. You know, disco music just came out at that time and it made a new rule: when you played on a song that went over four minutes, you got paid double. So why do you think the introduction to 'Station To Station' was two minutes long? There are only six songs on that album and look at what they are!

'Wild Is The Wind' and 'Word On A Wing' – these two really are an extension of what was on *Young Americans*. But they have nothing in common with 'Stay' or 'Station To Station'. In fact, the coexistence of these four songs on the same album is what makes it unique. 'Golden Years' and 'TVC 15' are happy songs, light in their own way. They came, incidentally, from jams – we were playing along and the groove was right. But, in those years, we didn't have any concept about what we were going to do. Some may think otherwise, but most of the time we made it up as we went along and, of course, the music evolved. What stayed the same over the years was that Dennis, George and I played around with the songs until we got what David wanted. After that, we taped them in just a few takes. Then I'd help David with the overdubs and only then did we start experimenting. (2016)

GEORGE MURRAY

Carlos, Dennis and I knew each other in New York. I had played more with Dennis than Carlos, but I knew them both. Dennis and I had played with some other local musicians around town: rehearsals, recorded gigs, jam sessions... All Dennis ever wanted to do was play and perform... It didn't matter what, where or what time. Everyone loved Dennis. He was a master of rhythm and he could make anything groove. His sense of humour was always on... Never a dull moment when he was around; he was always in high spirits and there were lots of laughs.

As I remember it, Dennis called me on the phone one day in September 1975 and asked if I wanted to play with him on David Bowie's new album. Dennis said Bowie was changing his band and he recommended me for the spot. I almost missed the call as I had left the house, but returned to retrieve some forgotten item. As I was walking up the drive, I heard my father through the open kitchen window say, 'Wait a minute, here he is!' – I'll never forget that day or Dennis' call.

To be totally honest, I wasn't up with what Bowie was doing before I joined the band. I knew that Dennis and Carlos were working with him and 'Fame' was a hit that was on the radio a lot. Before that, I remember 'Space Oddity', but that was about it. Well, I do remember walking on 6th Avenue in Manhattan one day and seeing David's image from the *Diamond Dogs* album cover on a gigantic billboard. My first reaction was, 'Who the fuck is that?' Little did I know that, one or two years later, I would be working with him.

Recording *Station To Station* in Los Angeles took quite a long time by New York standards. I think Dennis, Carlos and I were there for four or five weeks. I was used to rhythm tracks being recorded first and, after that, the drummer and bass player were usually finished. But David was working on each track individually, so there was time in between as he did other things. There were some distractions as well, as we thought of ways to keep ourselves occupied when we weren't recording. Looking back, I think *Station To Station* was some of the best work we did. I enjoyed recording every track on that album, although I never felt fully comfortable with 'Wild Is The Wind'. But, at the time, I didn't know if David was happy with my playing or not. He and I didn't talk much other than normal pleasantries. But he was concentrating on each song as a whole and had many other things on his mind apart from me.

You know, the first time I met David was at a rehearsal and it gave us a chance to get to know each other musically. The first song he showed us was 'Golden Years' and it was also the first track we recorded for the album. Funnily enough, it was one of the few songs I remember him explaining to us. As he said, many believe that their 'golden years' will occur sometime in the future, during the later years of their life, when they retire. But what he meant was that the memories and 'golden years' are being created right now, in the present, while we're young. I did not realize the profundity of his explanation at the time, or that it was actually a Buddhist concept that David knew about.

I enjoyed the whole experience of recording *Station To Station*. There were a lot of visitors during the sessions: Ronnie Wood and Bobby Womack stand out the most. David composed some music on the spot with them and the overall atmosphere was relaxed and unhurried. And then my concerns about whether David liked my playing or not were resolved the day I was asked to do the upcoming tour.

I remember flying to Ocho Rios from New York in the winter and rehearsing in the living room of this house owned by Keith Richards. This location also gave David a chance to relax and recover from life in Los Angeles... I also remember having our instruments held in customs while the officials determined who we were and that we were not going to sell all the gear to Jamaican musicians for a lot of money and not pay the duty.

The Station To Station tour was very important, as it led Bowie back to Europe. Carlos was the bandleader, but it was different seeing him in rehearsals instead of the recording studio. He had full command of the band and I saw how much David relied on him. One night, Dennis, Carlos and I were fooling around with a riff and a rhythm that caught David's ear. He joined in and wrote 'Sister Midnight' with it[41]. It fit the mood of the evening and the Caribbean setting we were in. The song was supposed to be on the set list of the tour, but I think it was dropped during the dress rehearsals. Or maybe we played it a few times...

To set the record straight, I have to say we did not rehearse in Kingston. I remember all of us taking a chartered bus from Ocho Rios, through the Jamaican countryside to Kingston, because David wanted to record at one of the studios that was noted for the reggae artists who had recorded there. I do not remember the name of the studio[42]. I do recall us trying a couple of takes of 'Sister Midnight', but David could not get the sound he wanted out of the board. So, after a couple of hours, we packed up and left the studio, did a little sightseeing and headed back to Ocho Rios. All in all, a delightful one-day excursion!

We did the dress rehearsals in New York and started the tour in Vancouver. Visually, the shows were incredible – simple but intense. I remember the rows of fluorescent lights behind the band and all the overheads and sidelights were white. When we opened the concert with 'Station To Station' and got to the 'It's not the side effects of the cocaine' line, all the lights came on at full power! The effect that had on each audience, along with the song itself, was unforgettable. The shows got better and better as we went from... station to station! David didn't fly and I remember the tour manager, Eric Barrett, sometimes wondering if he would make it in time for the show. And yes, the tour took David back to Europe and I remember it ending with a couple of shows in Paris. That was one of the best bands I ever played with: Dennis Davis, Carlos Alomar, Tony Kaye and Stacy Heydon. Forty years later, I remember each one of them and can recall each of their faces in my mind's eye. We brought David's music to life, night after night, and there wasn't a disappointing show on the tour. (2016)

GEOFF MACCORMACK

At the same time Gui and I were there Bowie was in Jamaica rehearsing with a new band. He looked a different man to when I'd last seen him in LA. Still not perfect, but nevertheless he'd put on weight, been working out with a personal trainer and had a light tan. We had a great night out together before Gui and I left for New York.

A few weeks later I arrived back in England. It was the middle of January, 1976 and the end of an amazing and enlightening journey, almost exactly three years after it had begun. (2007)

HARRY MASLIN

I wasn't surprised when David called me for *Station To Station* as I did a great job on *Young Americans*. I pulled the whole thing together after Tony Visconti was let go. Of course, one never knows from one album to the next with any artist… But, to be honest, I was pleased. David was a bit tired after working on *The Man Who Fell To Earth*, but he was generally in good spirits. You know, he was already a rock icon and the success of *Young Americans* just helped to spread his fame to, if I may say, wider markets. While much of this album was rhythm'n'blues influenced, most of *Station To Station* was experimental in many aspects. Additionally, while *Young Americans* was geared to create top chart singles, which we accomplished, *Station To Station* was more focused on the purely creative without worrying about singles. Thankfully we did have a hit with 'Golden Years', which helped promote the rest of the album.

To me, the band on this record, is still the most accomplished David ever had in a studio. Don't get me wrong, he's always had great players, but this group had extreme flexibility and versatility of style. So I think the overall quality of *Station To Station*, something quite subjective, has a lot to do with the experimentation, but also with the musicians involved. Also, my general recording techniques were established well before *Station To Station* but, because of the demands of the music, I can honestly say many new techniques were implemented. I was never one to think that there was only one way of accomplishing something in the studio. One of the best things about working with David is that he also has that openness to experimentation. He would try anything I suggested musically without question. Not everything worked, but it was such a pleasure to work with someone receptive to ideas without having to debate the merits. It's easier, more fun and usually more rewarding to 'go for it', rather than discuss it to death first.

David was definitely a workaholic, which I appreciated. He is a serious artist and not a clock-watcher in the studio. We had many overnight sessions. In fact, we had one session that went on all night at Cherokee and, because the studio was booked for another client the following morning, I managed to get The Record Plant[43] to accommodate us immediately after leaving Cherokee to continue the session. That Record Plant session was when both David and I played sax on 'TVC 15'. One might say that was truly a 24-hour session. I believe the album took a good eight weeks to make. David played some guitar, organ, piano, percussion, harmonium and sax. I may be leaving something out… but you get the idea. As you know, David is extremely creative.

As for the lyrics, some were written on the spot... As I recall, 'Golden Years' is a classic example of this. When I was ready to record his vocal, David excused himself to go to the outer office to complete the lyrics. Others were ready to go when I was. There are no hard rules when it comes to David's techniques.

Roy Bittan of the E Street Band left his marvellous musical mark on a couple of tracks, and Ronnie Wood and some other musicians came by and I did roll tape on a couple of jam sessions. But these were never meant to be on the album; just a record of the total music experience of *Station To Station*. You know, some people say cocaine fuelled the album... I can't deny it played a part, but that drug is insidious, a double-edged sword: one side beneficial and the other detrimental. I'll leave the definitive answer up to the listener.

I wish David and I could have recorded more together and, in fact, I started the *Low* sessions with him before it was temporarily shelved. David went through a difficult time immediately after *Station To Station,* and eventually decided that LA and its environment were part of the cause. I think I was an element of that, which I completely understand... I don't necessarily agree, but I do understand. *Station To Station* is one of Bowie's most respected albums and it would still be great to work with David again to try to create some new magic.

I am quite satisfied with the work on the reissue of the album. The new 5.1 and the Nassau mixes are totally mine. I don't think I could have had a bigger part regarding the music. All mixes were submitted to David for approval. He approved most on the first listen and offered input for changes on a couple, which of course were implemented. I also mastered it with Brian Gardner at Bernie Grundman Mastering in LA. I had Brian master the original album many years ago when he worked for Allen Zentz Mastering in Hollywood. I had nothing to do with the packaging. As for hearing the tracks again... I was really quite pleased that they held up sonically. The biggest problem was getting the original analogue tracks copied to the digital format properly. I was not present for this procedure and discovered many glitches as I started to mix, which significantly delayed the process. (2010).

PAUL BUCKMASTER

I can't remember if it was my manager or Nicolas Roeg who called to tell me that David Bowie wanted me in Los Angeles to help him work on the soundtrack of *The Man Who Fell To Earth*. What I'm sure of is that I hadn't seen the film before going. When we started, the tracks didn't have titles, but I remember 'Wheels', the only one that did. It was rather melancholic and was supposed to accompany the images of Thomas Jerome Newton's planet, especially the ones where we see him use this funny vehicle that slides across the desert when he leaves his family... But that's not on *Low*.

We did a few takes at Cherokee with David's band and J. Peter Robinson[44], but we mostly did the writing at his place. We had a TEAC tape recorder, an electric piano and a rather primitive string synthesizer, a Solina. I think we also had an ARP Odyssey synth at some point, which David played quite well. Since the mid-1970s, a lot of theories have blossomed regarding why he didn't end up providing the film score, but I think it was mainly due to the fact that he never finished it. We needed more time, especially to add orchestrations, but film schedules are rigid.

I learned a lot by working with David again, after 'Space Oddity'. He wasn't the same person, but we had some very long conversations about some very serious subjects, which didn't stop us laughing about them! His curiosity and sense of humour were still there! Oh yeah! I'd brought some kalimbas, an African instrument with metal tines that you hit with your thumbs. He loved the sound and one of the pieces was basically made up of kalimba and cello parts... (2017)

JAY GLENNIE

Every member of the team from *The Man Who Fell To Earth* that we spoke to for the book had nothing but praise for David Bowie's time on set. Candy Clark spoke of his professionalism and how he was always ready to rehearse his lines. She also told me that he made a promise to Nic Roeg not to partake in any recreational drugs, which probably added to his restlessness. Buck Henry, who played Oliver Farnsworth, was impressed with his love of literature.

The crew of *The Man Who Fell To Earth* talked about their fond memories of working with David, describing him as polite, a gentleman and a professional, as well as being strange and elusive. Nic spoke of the nervousness of the studio who felt that Bowie was just too weird and out-there which, of course, proved to be ideal casting.

Bowie, in a career of dramatic image changes, never looked more beautiful than he did in *The Man Who Fell To Earth*. Seen 40 years later, his portrayal of an alien stranded on Earth is an extraordinarily nuanced performance, even more so when you consider it was his screen debut.

We were in conversation with David Bowie's representatives in the hope that he would reminisce about his singular work on the film. Sadly, that was not to happen but, with the wonderful memories and tales from the cast, crew and producers who were there, a compelling picture of Bowie during the making of the film has built up. (2016)

STACY HEYDON

David Bowie's management heard about me through Rob Joyce, a roadie on the Soul Tour in 1974, who had submitted my info for consideration to fill the Earl Slick spot. As soon as I landed in Jamaica, I saw that the guys in the band were awesome. Dave was a little bit different, though. Aside from the multi-coloured flaming hairdo, he was somewhat quiet and was much more hands off with the whole audition process. I was also struck by how thin and pale he looked at the time. Apparently he'd just gone through some issues with some kind of affliction and it had clearly taken its toll on him physically. His voice sounded just as the records did though, and his passion for what we were doing was more than evident.

To be honest, I was surprised by how low-key everybody and everything was. Considering they had no lead guitarist for the upcoming tour, they were pretty mellow about the whole thing. To start with, I'm not sure that the guys were into me being there, as I'm certain that they had their own recommendations for one of the most important spots in the band on the world tour. I remember Keith Richards' house was awesome though, right at the top of the hill in Ocho Rios. It was certainly the nicest house I'd ever rehearsed in!

I didn't know any of David's songs musically, although I'd heard them on the radio. The manager had called me about the audition the night before I flew to Jamaica from Toronto, so I had no time to learn anything. I knew I was screwed and not going to impress anyone as I didn't know a single song of David's, a single chord of his material, on the guitar. So we just jammed for half an hour or so, and then it was over. I'd thought I'd completely shat the bed as I didn't know a single chord of his material. To my surprise, the manager came to my bungalow and offered me the US tour! In fact, I was more than surprised, as my experience was very limited; I was only 22 at the time... I'd only played a handful of bar gigs and some smallish shows with local Windsor and Toronto bands by then. Well, I guess I was in the right place at the right time! Slicky and his manager had had issues with David's people and they'd bolted, from what I was told, just a few weeks prior to the start of the 1976 tour, so they'd had to find a replacement pronto.

Yes, we did go to Kingston, but only for a day or two... I remember some dude got shot outside our hotel, in a tree. He might have been trying to break into the hotel or something... Rehearsals took place at Keith's house, then for another five days in Vancouver. We'd had a couple of weeks off between Ocho Rios and Canada because Dave wouldn't fly. He had to get there by boat and he did the same for the European leg of the Isolar tour...

Some people say we rehearsed in LA with Dave, but that didn't happen. I'd met them all for the first time in Jamaica in early January. The only rehearsals that were done in LA were for Iggy Pop's TV Eye tour afterwards.

'Fame' and 'Golden Years' were pummelling the radio at the time and who hadn't heard 'Suffragette City', the *Young Americans* stuff, Mott The Hoople...? By 1976, Bowie was at the pinnacle of the heap. As a musician and as a vocalist, there wasn't much going on. But as a writer and a character creator, he was brilliant. And as an entertainer he was at the absolute top of the heap, making the very most of his God-given talents. His charisma and his prowess at showmanship were second to none. His control of the audience, and of the emotional ride while he took them through various peaks, valleys and emotions, was nothing short of breathtaking. During rehearsals he was a pro's pro – punctual, forthright and gave his all. But during the shows, the beast was unleashed! He was marvellous, whether a little buzzed from no sleep or as fresh as a daisy. His professionalism was quite something to witness.

Opening the show with *Un Chien Andalou* was great. Salvador Dalí was an awesome guy and that flick blew minds. I started the show with freaky, train-like sounds and feedback for five minutes, right after the screen rose amidst the awe and confusion of the audience, night after night. The staging was non-existent – we had a very stripped-down stage, with no colour or props whatsoever. The white lights were brilliant! I'd never seen them before and have not seen them since at a rock show. There was nowhere to hide, nothing to distract the audience – we were right there for the taking, like it or not. Those old arc super troopers were a cruel and unusual punishment in terms of heat and glow. It's a wonder I can still see after those frigging things fried me each and every night.

Aside from that, on the road, we were treated like royalty. The various towns and cities were so very accommodating and mankind in general seemed kind of surreal in a great way at that time. The crowds were mostly women, all dolled up – fashion was the order of the day everywhere we went. The alternative-lifestyle community was also quite well represented at the shows, as David's appeal knew no bounds. Aside from a bomb threat at Wembley, right before one of the shows, there were no incidents on the tour[45]. It was a total pleasure travelling and performing everywhere, including Europe, Canada and the States. It was my first trip to Europe and I kept thinking that I'd somehow been there before. I hadn't, but it seemed eerily familiar to me.

David was our best bud on the tour. I think I was the only one in the band he'd selected a nickname for: Space. Looking back at it, that was quite a compliment coming from a guy who'd thought so much about the correlation between humankind and the unknown. Before the tour started, for fun, we hid his saxophone so he wouldn't be able to play it! That was fun! We weren't together all the time, but we went out a lot after the concerts, at restaurants or clubs. He liked being around people, and like all of us, he loved life. I could not believe how many celebrities wanted to be seen with Bowie night after night. Most of them acted like groupies in his presence. He was that influential that they wanted some of him to rub off on them.

David would ring me up at all hours trying to get hooked up with certain things that he'd run out of... Can you guess what that was? And I'd bust his balls almost every time, then hang up on him! The other lads in the band were awesome! Tony, with his Tequila Sunrises in the morning at the airport; Carlos, with his ultra-clean guitar sounds and that signature smile; George, with his amazing hats, who always let his bass do the talking; and Dennis, with those freaky-looking, fiberglass North drums just shreddin' up the groove on every tune. We lost Dennis only a few months after David's departure, God bless his soul... He was fun to be around and I had many memorable times with him on the road. That rhythm section could not have been better – they could lay down killing jams while they were asleep, they were so good!

As for the audience's reaction, it was astounding. David's command and presence were a brand of entertainment that only a few people have attained. Maybe Sinatra, Presley and Pavarotti could compare to Bowie's raw power of influence... His very presence could generate utter hysteria at any time, anywhere. And, you know, people responded so well to the set list that I enjoyed playing it even more. I had no preference as to which songs to perform, as they were all pretty interesting and appealing to a hungry audience each and every night. For me, the encores were great buzz generators because I knew we'd got through the entire day and were as loose as loose could be. They were kinda like gravy train tracks that we could have a total blast with! (2016)

ROY YOUNG

In the early 70s, after I'd been in Cliff Bennett's Rebel Rousers, I toured a lot in England and I sometimes ran into David and The Spiders[46]. I'd give my concert and then go see theirs. After that, we'd get a drink and have a gossip. Sometimes I'd join them after their show, which was fun. In 1975, David was in Los Angeles about to record *Station To Station*, and he phoned me to ask if I could come to the US. I quickly got a visa, but unfortunately, I forgot my work permit so I wasn't able to go! The following year, when David was in Berlin with Tony Visconti for an Iggy Pop record, he got in touch again. (2016)

BUFORD JONES

After Carlos Alomar became the musical director for David Bowie's band, I started dealing with him most. He took his role very seriously, and during the Station To Station tour, we recorded most of the performances so we could listen to them again and improve what could be improved. The challenge was to put on a show that was just as good as the album that gave rise to the set list, without trying to copy the songs exactly. So I listened to them a lot, but they were so damn good it was really hard to reproduce their spirit on stage. And I found that his music got better, richer, every time he made one of his famous 'changes'. I loved songs like 'Young Americans' and 'Stay', and the songs played during the tour that led to the live album *Stage*.

When I started working with David Bowie, I already knew that most rock stars kept themselves apart from the technical crew, that they simply waved from afar. He was different. He talked to everyone, had meals with the musicians and technicians – he mingled with us. He even came clubbing with us after concerts. In Paris, I remember he introduced me to Peter Sellers! But from the late 1970s onwards, we didn't see each other as much. It got a little harder because he had more security around him. Someone must have thought it was necessary. I sometimes had the feeling that protection mainly came from his close entourage... (2016)

IGGY POP

I was in the hospital in 1975, at rock bottom, and David Bowie was one of the only people who came to see me. I hated the MainMan days, he knew it, but I wasn't angry with him because at the end of the day, he paid a much higher price than I did... Before the Station To Station tour, David had never toured Europe, but what the media didn't get at the time, although they happily denigrated his American period, was that in this business, when the audience and the artist are in total sync with each other, the artist gets this geyser of confidence right in the kisser, and in David's case, I witnessed that.

He was always a very organized person, even before his Ziggy Stardust days. From 1971, he was surrounded by great people, was backed by a big label, RCA, and his intelligence did the rest. So he was able to come back up after hitting the bottom in Los Angeles because he believed in himself. He knew he was good and that people loved him. And that was also when he decided to take control and manage himself. It was a radical change: he went from MainMan's eccentric entourage to a super-small team.

During the Station To Station tour, there were very few of us on the road, a dozen people max[47], including Coco Schwab who always looked after him. She managed logistics. As for the artistic side, I preferred these shows to all the ones he'd done before. They were superb and he had a hell of a great band: wonderful guys from New York, very talented, who believe it or not, had a thing for white girls' asses! David was so professional he did everything thoroughly and systematically. Whatever the circumstances! Whether he had an audience of 15,000 – like at Madison Square Garden – or barely 1,000 – like in Albuquerque or Zurich – he and his musicians were spot on. The shows looked great, the lighting was great – those fluorescent Hollywood lights!

At first, he'd written his songs for a rock band, so they had a sort of heavy feel. But those guys played it light, with a groove that accentuated their weirdness. Carlos didn't have a big Marshall stack and Dennis Davis didn't whack his drums like crazy – they were sensitive musicians. I remember the Berlin concert very well. If memory serves, it wasn't packed[48]. But Berlin audiences can be really tough: they just stood there, didn't say much, didn't do much, kind of checking this shit out, you know. At the end of the show, before the encore, David went back to his dressing room, stripped out of what he was wearing and decided to put his street clothes on. He put on jeans, a thick shirt with rolled-up cuffs and a little jean jacket. Then he got back on stage and did a couple of songs. I don't remember what they were[49], but these two numbers hit a little harder. He wanted a reaction from the audience and they all went for it. I think it was the only time in that whole tour that I saw him shift into a higher gear in response to an audience's apparent scepticism. They played it kind of cool, but they were totally into him. I think David wanted to send a message. At the back of his mind, he already knew he'd be spending time in Berlin, and there was no way he wasn't going to get the city's audience in his pocket. (2016)

JOHN 'TWINK' ALDER

David's fascination with Aleister Crowley[50] clearly stemmed from the fact that, like me, he thought he was an incredible artist. You know, the media has always exaggerated when it comes to Crowley. That thing about him forcing someone to drink cats' blood, we now know it was all made up. I'm not saying he didn't do strange things, but I think he was really the first rock star, even though he didn't have an electric guitar. People like exaggeration. When I worked with Syd Barrett[51], he couldn't have been more normal during rehearsals, focused on the music, on time for sound checks, on time for gigs, very serious. But those who asked me about him weren't satisfied with that. They imagined terrible things, excesses of all kinds and that's how inane stories get passed down through the years. And that seems to be the case with David, too... (2018)

MAT OSMAN[52]

I'm not a superstitious person: I'll walk under ladders, take a plane on Friday the 13th, stroke a black cat. But I do have one ritual that's been with me since I was a teenager. It's not something I'd heard of anyone else doing; rather it's an idea that came to me simply as 'this would be a good thing to do'. Whenever I move house, or even stay in a new place for any length of time, I like to make sure that the first piece of music I play is something whose spirit will imbue the place.

Often it's 'La Vie En Rose' (Grace Jones' or Louis Armstrong's versions, they're both perfect), but mainly, regularly, from New York to Neasden, from Calgary to Kensal Rise, only one tune will do it.

It starts with a riff that rolls like surf and the laziest of finger clicks. A spectre of a mouth organ. It leans back, tips its hat and stretches. The drums tumble down into the beat, there's a trill of maracas and the vocal – *that voice* – comes in, close and low: 'Gol-den years, gollll-d, qua qua qua.' It's so elegant that us Brits need to borrow from the French just to describe it: *insouciant, chic, je ne sais 'qua'*...

The riff has LA's mix of cool and hot, like ice on the palm trees, and Bowie rides it, duetting with himself, playing three different characters before the first verse is out. A confident man, rapping syllables like the start of *Lolita*, three taps of the tongue: 'Last night they loved you, opening doors and pulling some strings.'

Beehived backing singer: 'Ay-ngel.'

Lovelorn doo-wopper, street-corner soul man: 'Come get up my baby.'

Every word is caressed and stroked into place, until we crest the hill into the chorus:

'There's my baby, lost that's all

Once I'm begging you save her little soul.'

Bowie sweeps up through the gears, from Barry White to Nina Simone, in the space of a line, and then we're back into the warm clockwork of the riff.

There are gems scattered everywhere throughout its four minutes and three seconds – that little Alomar riff that pops into the left channel now and again, the steps down as Bowie wrings every note from an end-of-chorus 'g-o-o-ld', a hands-in-the-pocket whistle – but it's the song as a whole, the sheer gorgeous flow of it, the way that it's simultaneously laidback and relentless, that fills each new room in my life with a warmth and a joy and a beauty that colours the rest of my time there.

I know, on reflection, that it's a darker song than it sounds. It's also about isolation and revenge. But, hey, this is Bowie – the man never wrote a song that couldn't be taken more than one way. So I prefer to hear it as an invocation. An invocation of better times, of love and style and music and magic, and of Golden Years for all of us. (2018)

1. David Bowie's words from 1997 were reported by Éric Dahan, a journalist (notably for *Rock&Folk*) who is a friend of the author and also wrote extensively about David Bowie in France.

2. Just because a piece of information is continually repeated over several decades, it doesn't make it true. The confusion between these two addresses comes from the fact that Glenn Hughes always said he lived near a house where the Manson 'family' had committed crimes. People concluded he was referring to the murder of Sharon Tate and her friends on Cielo Drive, close to Benedict Canyon. According to several David Bowie experts (including Paul Kinder of bowiewonderworld. com), Hughes most probably lived on Waverly Drive in Los Feliz, not far from the LaBiancas, who were victims of the second night of killings by Manson's acolytes, on 10 August 1969.

3. A one-day behemoth of an event that took place on the Big O, a race track in Ontario, California on 6 April 1974, while David Bowie and Geoff MacCormack were crossing the Atlantic aboard the *France*. Well organized and very lucrative (there had been more people at Woodstock, but many didn't pay), California Jam turned the business of rock into a highly profitable corporate enterprise, which is now embodied by companies like Live Nation. That day, Deep Purple was on the bill with other major bands including The Eagles, Black Sabbath and Emerson, Lake & Palmer. Their performance, after David Coverdale (vocals) and Glenn Hughes had joined them as replacements for Ian Gillan and Roger Glover, was one of the few that American radio and television actually broadcast.

4. Since then, Glenn Hughes has also said that David Bowie had tried to get Mick Ronson to join Deep Purple when Ritchie Blackmore left, and/or to get Ronson and Hughes to start a band together.

5. These are very likely Oz Studios set up by Ethel Rappaport, Geoff Westen, Jean Janssen and Patti Mitsui. Their original idea was to offer a range of services, from rehearsal rooms to graphic design. The beautiful cover of *Aja*, Steely Dan's album, is the work of Oz Studios.

6. Since we know that later, Iggy Pop and Bowie will influence each other and exchange a lot of ideas, it's interesting to note that it was also in 1975 that David and Angie Bowie were invited to a screening of *Professione: Reporter*, by Italian director Michelangelo Antonioni. In English, the film was called *The Passenger*, like the most famous song on *Lust For Life*. Iggy wrote the song to music by guitarist Ricky Gardiner and it will also appear on the B-side of the single 'Success' in November 1977.

7. Aleister Crowley claimed not to have written this book himself, that it had been dictated to him while he lived in Cairo by an entity named Aiwass, a falcon-headed messenger of the Egyptian god Horus.

8. Edward Waite was a British author who belonged to the Hermetic Order Of The Golden Dawn. His ideas often sparked internal conflict. He participated in the creation of a tarot card game used for divination and he wrote several books including *Devil-Worship In France*. Dion Fortune was also a British occultist associated with The Golden Dawn. After being psychologically abused by the principal of the college where she worked during her studies, she wrote *Psychic-Self Defence,* which David Bowie enjoyed reading in 1975.

9. This film was co-directed by Donald Cammell. His brother David was one of the behind-the-scenes architects of the film adaptation of *The Man Who Fell To Earth.* Donald and David's father was British writer Charles Richard Cammell, who wrote *The Man, The Mage, The Poet,* a biography of Aleister Crowley published in 1962. All signs suggest David Bowie learned about Aleister Crowley through this book.

10. In addition to May Routh, responsible for most of the costumes worn by Thomas Jerome Newton, David Bowie called on African-American costume designer Ola Hudson, who also designed his Thin White Duke outfit for the Station To Station tour. Hudson, who died in 2009, was the mother of Slash, the guitarist of Guns N' Roses.

11. Though remarkable, the version of 'Come On In My Kitchen' by bluesman Robert Johnson – which Mick Jagger sings and plays live on the acoustic guitar one hour and ten minutes into *Performance* – does not appear on the soundtrack.

12. The soundtrack composed by Bobby Beausoleil is now available on vinyl and CD, and Jimmy Page released his music for *Lucifer Rising* in 2012. Mick Jagger's music for *Invocation Of My Demon Brother* was never officially released. Some of the material in this account comes from *Performance* (GM, 2017), a book the author co-wrote with his wife Sophie Soligny.

13. In addition to the authors mentioned in this chapter, in 1975 Bowie also read works by Manly Palmer Hall, Samuel Liddel, MacGregor Mathers, Trevor Ravenscroft, Helena Blavatsky, Louis Pauwels and Jacques Bergier. He reportedly brought several dozen books with him on to the set of Nicolas Roeg's film.

14. During the time they will work together, Carlos Alomar will regularly suggest musicians to David Bowie. For *Outside,* in 1995, he'll recommend Israeli bass player Yossi Fine.

15. Quite expensive and limited to 1,000 copies, *The Man Who Fell To Earth* by Jay Glennie and Darryl Webber (Unstoppable Editions, 2016) is both very informative and thoroughly documented. Paul Duncan's *David Bowie In The Man Who Fell To Earth* (Taschen, 2017) has less text but the photos are of better quality. Susan Campo's *Earthbound,* on the same subject, will also be published in 2017, by Jawbone Press.

16. While he certainly raised some eyebrows, David Bowie is not the first white artist to perform on *Soul Train.* Average White Band and Elton John had already appeared on the programme that same year, the latter performing 'Philadelphia Freedom', his tribute to the music of Philadelphia and to an eponymous tennis team (a sport he always played) led by his champion tennis player friend Billie Jean King. The song was produced by Gus Dudgeon and arranged by Gene Page, who wrote string parts for major soul and rhythm'n'blues acts. Bowie especially liked his work for Barry White. Wanting to capture the sound of Philadelphia, as David did, Elton will end up recording with Thom Bell and the rhythm section of MFSB in 1977. However, only some of the sessions for the planned album

(turned into an EP two years later) will take place at Sigma Sound.

17. They stay at Point Of View, a beautiful home with bungalows and a pool on the north part of the island, perched on a hill over the village of Ocho Rios. They rented it from Keith Richards, who bought it at the start of the decade from Tommy Steele, a teen idol in England in the 1950s and 1960s (and still performing to this day!), whom Ken Pitt was keen for David Bowie to model himself on. It appears that, even though Richards often said he didn't like glam rock, and was no fan of Bowie, he didn't mind taking his money. Apparently, friends of Mick Jagger were not necessarily friends of his...

18. According to members of the band, Roy Bittan was also recommended by Eric Barrett.

19. Although several books on David Bowie claim that he opted for a black and white photo at the last minute after seeing the cover of *Down By The Jetty* (Dr. Feelgood's first album) sent from England by Roy Young, the pianist has told the author that was not the case. The fact that *Down By The Jetty* came out in January 1975, a year before *Station To Station*, casts further doubt on this theory.

20. In 1975 and 1976, four other photographers did memorable sessions with David Bowie. The first was Tom Kelley, who worked in Hollywood and famously photographed Marilyn Monroe nude in 1949. Kelley's photos appeared on the cover of the single 'Fame' in some countries, as well as on *ChangesOneBowie*, Bowie's first RCA compilation, released in May 1976. Andrew 'Andy' Kent shot Bowie for the first time on the set of *Soul Train* and, having become the official (but not exclusive)

photographer of the Station To Station tour, he'll follow the Thin White Duke until the final concerts at the Pavillon de Paris. Kent will publish a book in 2016 called *David Bowie Behind The Curtain* (PSG). Brian Duffy photographed David Bowie on the set of *The Man Who Fell To Earth* at White Sands, between Santa Fe and El Paso. Bowie looked particularly devilish in a black suit and white shirt. Lastly, Terry O'Neill shot a series of photos on the set of *The Man Who Fell To Earth* and during the Station To Station tour. The best ones are in *Bowie By O'Neill*, a book published by Cassell Illustrated in 2019. O'Neill will pass away in 2019.

21. Written by Arlester Christian for his band Dyke And The Blazers in the mid-1960s, this was probably the first song with 'funky' in its title. On Wilson Pickett's version, which Earl Slick often referred to in interviews, Chips Moman and Jimmy Johnson play the guitars. In all likelihood, it's the latter who plays, during the intro, the riff Slick says inspired him. He spins it throughout the whole of 'Golden Years', except in the chorus. The other influence Slick mentioned for this song was 'Outside Woman Blues' by Cream, the riff of which is also very similar.

22. It's completely unthinkable today to appropriate the melody or arrangement from part of a song written by someone else in this way, without asking for permission from the rights holders and their publishers and without paying them royalties. All hell would break loose if any songwriter had the bad idea of including even a few seconds of a song by David Bowie. For 'TVC 15', he happily pilfered two dozen bars from The Yardbirds. But not only that! The version of 'Good Morning Little Schoolgirl' (whose original writer remains unknown) that inspired The Yardbirds and Bowie is not the one recorded by Sonny Boy Williamson in 1937 (like many who sang it after him, he took credit for the arrangement). The intro of 'TVC 15' – especially the piano part – sounds more like a reinterpretation of the song attributed to Don Level and Bob Love who, in the early 1960s, recorded it under the name Don And Bob.

23. It's amusing to note that some music critics at the time attributed this guitar part to Ronnie Wood, who had in fact stopped by Cherokee during recording.

24. Two giants of American music from the previous century. Dimitri Tiomkin was of Russian descent and wrote many film scores, most notably for Frank Capra (*Mr Smith Goes To Washington*, *It's A Wonderful Life*), Fred Zinnemann (*High Noon*) and King Vidor (*Duel In The Sun*). 'Wild Is The Wind' had been written for the eponymous film by George Cukor and Johnny Mathis performs the song in it. Ned Washington became famous around the same time for writing lyrics of songs used in films. Washington worked a lot with Tiomkin, and it is he who must be thanked for the unbelievable 'When You Wish Upon A Star' (music by Leigh Harline), which appeared for the first time in Walt Disney's *Pinocchio* in 1940.

25. An anagram of 'sailor' (which, years later, will be his pseudonym on BowieNet), Isolar is the name of the company David Bowie set up around himself in 1976 after splitting from MainMan. For four decades, those wanting to get in touch with him for professional reasons will have to go through Isolar in New York. The name Isolar appeared officially for the first time on the programme for the Station To Station

tour (sometimes called the White Light tour because of the lighting).

26. *Cabaret* is in fact based on *I Am A Camera*, a 1951 play by John Van Druten, which is an adaptation of *Goodbye To Berlin*.

27. In 1968, Judi Dench played the iconic role of Sally Bowles, reprised in 1972 by Liza Minnelli in Bob Fosse's film adaptation. The music was composed by John Kander to Fred Ebb's script, which was based on a libretto by Joe Masteroff.

28. The German band had been approached to open for the Isolar tour, but the transportation and installation of their equipment, which was bulkier than that of a traditional band, ended up being too difficult to manage.

29. Drafted in rehearsals earlier that year, the song was initially called 'Calling Sister Midnight'.

30. On 23 February at the Sports Arena.

31. During the tour, David Bowie will mention this album project while introducing the song to the audience. And at the risk of giving ammo to those who thought he was always planning everything a long time ahead, Bowie will also tell the audience at the Spectrum in Philadelphia on 16 March that he'll be back in the city 'in nine months, at the Tower Theatre.' His estimation was only off by three months, because he did in fact perform there as Iggy Pop's keyboardist on 19 March 1977.

32. At the time, Barbara DeWitt manages David Bowie's contact with journalists. She stands out as a press officer because she chooses very good journalists to interview him. She will also work for Iggy Pop. DeWitt will die

of cancer in early 2001. She was the sister of photographer Bruce Weber, who'll shoot Bowie in the 1990s.

33. David Bowie played at the Inglewood Forum on 8, 9 and 11 February 1976. Afterwards, backstage, there was the usual parade of local stars. Bowie will perform in this same venue, which had a capacity of 20,000, during his next two tours.

34. To this day, *Station To Station* is the only album to have been reissued as a 'deluxe' LP-sized box set, including CDs, vinyls, memorabilia (badges, a poster, a replica of a backstage pass), an audio DVD containing different remasterings, and a recording of the concert at the Nassau Veterans Memorial Coliseum. The latter won't be released as a stand-alone album until February 2017. In 1991, Rykodisc's reissue of *Station To Station* will include two extracts from this show: 'Word On A Wing' and 'Stay'. A much shorter version of the title song (the longest in Bowie's discography, even longer than 'Blackstar') will also be included in the 2010 box set. The five-CD box set *Conversation Piece*, released in 2021, could be considered a 'deluxe' version of the *David Bowie (Space Oddity)* album, but it doesn't bear the title of the original album(s).

35. During David Bowie's press conference at the George V in Paris in 1973, journalist Hervé Muller asked David Bowie if he knew this musician as he'd just arrived from Japan by train. He said he did, and that he was eager to meet him in London.

36. This concert did not take place, nor did the one in Monaco that David Bowie mentioned in the same interview, and which he said was due to be the first of this leg of the tour.

37. The Rolling Stones, Keith Moon, Jimmy Page, Lemmy Kilminster, Ron Asheton, Siouxsie Sioux, Sid Vicious, The London SS and Joy Division are some of the British rock musicians/acts who made reference in more or less subtle ways, through their words or clothes, to the SS and the Nazis. Strangely, they received much less of a backlash than Bowie.

38. The title of the film David Bowie intends to make with Mark Volman and Howard Kaylan is *The Traveler*.

39. Jay Glennie provided the following clarification for this book: May Routh told him they used several fedora hats for David Bowie in *The Man Who Fell To Earth*. The one he wore in the final scene belonged to Claudia Jennings, who had a small part in the film, and who was the girlfriend of producer Si Litvinoff. So, while David Bowie may have worn in the film the hat he gave to electronic musician Moby (which was stolen and which he later 'found'), it wasn't the one from the final scene.

40. Mike Garson relayed these words from Earl Slick.

41. 'Sister Midnight' was performed in Seattle on 3 February 1976. That same night, David Bowie graced the audience of the Center Coliseum with a long saxophone solo on 'TVC 15'. Some photos, including the ones taken in Paris in May, confirm that Bowie also played a bit of electric guitar during this tour.

42. This was Dynamic Sounds Studios, which were managed by a (then) living legend of reggae: Byron Lee, the frontman of The Dragonaires. Bob Marley and Jimmy Cliff, as well as The Rolling Stones and Paul Simon, recorded at Dynamic Sounds. The latter taped songs for his second solo album there and The Stones recorded part of *Goats Head Soup*, their 1973 album that featured 'Angie'. Byron Lee died in late 2008.

43. After starting the Record Plant in New York in the late 1960s, Gary Kellgren and Chris Stone opened new branches in Los Angeles and Sausalito. In 1975, Tom Waits, The Tubes and The Allman Brothers recorded some great records there. Of the three studios, the one in Los Angeles is the only one still operating.

44. A British studio keyboardist who later wrote many film scores. In the late 1970s, J. Peter Robinson will succeed Robin Lumley in Brand X.

45. David Bowie was under the influence of alcohol during some of the concerts on the Isolar tour, which sometimes affected his performance. On those nights, he was also more chatty.

46. On 2 and 3 September 1972, Iguana, a jazz-rock band from Southampton with whom Roy Young played on stage, opened for David Bowie and The Spiders From Mars at the Hardrock Concert Theatre in Manchester. These two shows marked the opening of the venue. Is it a coincidence that the intro riff of 'I Don't Need No Buddy', a song from Iguana's only album, starts off in exactly the same way as 'Stay'?

47. There were actually about 30 people on the road, which still wasn't many for a rock star in those days.

48. As part of the 1936 Olympic Games, some sporting events (including boxing) were hosted at the Deutschlandhalle, which had been inaugurated the year before by Adolf

Hitler. Jimi Hendrix gave his second-to-last concert there in early March 1970 (with Ten Years After). In *Christiane F*, Uli Edel's 1981 film mentioned in the *Scary Monsters* chapter, the shots of the audience that are shown while David Bowie sings 'Station To Station' were recorded during a performance at the Deutschlandhalle by hard-rock band AC/DC. On 10 April 1976, when the Isolar tour stopped in Berlin, Bowie played there in front of 8,000, although the venue could accommodate 2,000 more. He will return there two years later for Isolar 2, then in 1990 for the Sound+Vision tour and 1996 for the Outside tour. The Deutschlandhalle will be demolished in 2011.

49. 'Rebel Rebel' and 'The Jean Genie', which don't appear on most of the bootleg recordings of the concert.

50. In 2019, Twink And The Technicolour Dream (with Jon Povey) released *Sympathy For The Beast: Songs From The Poems Of Aleister Crowley*, a tribute to Crowley based on his writings.

51. In early 1972, Syd Barrett joined the short-lived Stars, with Jack Monk on bass and Twink on drums. The trio gave fewer than ten concerts in Cambridge and its surrounds, and Barrett struggled with the fact that some of them were worse than the others. He made the decision to stop playing music in public for good shortly afterwards.

52. Mat Osman is the bass player of the British band Suede. Alex Lee, who also played with Suede, is Hermione Farthingale's nephew.

DAVIDBOWIE
LOW

CPL1-2030

LOW

RCA – 14 JANUARY 1977

THE IDIOT (RCA – 1977)

'If we want everything to remain the same, everything must change.'
(GIUSEPPE TOMASI DI LAMPEDUSA, *THE LEOPARD*, 1958)

'From the mid-70s, I lost the habit of coming to the studio with my songs ready. I sometimes had to fight the idea that something familiar was therefore mediocre. It was a trap. Sometimes I have to go against my own mind, disagree with myself, "You can't go to the studio with pre-written songs. Of course you can. Oh yeah? Then go!" In the end, I acknowledged that it was okay to redo something I'd already done, especially if it yielded good results. [...]

'Sometimes I felt like there was no such thing as chance. When I moved to Switzerland, I lived near Balthus, the painter, at a time when I was painting more and more. And I lived near Chaplin's family after I created the Thin White Duke, who was in part inspired by The Tramp and Buster Keaton. [...]

'With Eno it was more about emulation, even stimulation, rather than measurable collaboration. While he was working on the trilogy, adapting to the way I worked, he developed methods he later used with other musicians. What he did with Talking Heads and David Byrne is a perfect example of that. What Eno helped me develop, and what Tony helped me turn into a record, was not a technique for being as different as possible, but a sort of sixth sense for going beyond simply giving the public what they wanted. *The Idiot* helped me come up with a sort of unstable balance that allowed me to create some good things later. I'm better when I work in a minefield. When I forgot that in the 1980s, I became totally unproductive. [...]

'Magma? Oh yes, I remember, but it's a bit hazy. Some members of that band worked on *The Idiot*, right?'

DB (1977[1]/1999/1991)

This chapter about *Low* has been approached in a very different way from the others, for several reasons. The first is that I've already written about this album in a previous book. I tackled it in *David Bowie Ouvre Le Chien*, along with *Pin Ups*. The second is that the interview section of this chapter is the longest in the book. Not because many of the people I spoke to are French, but because they graciously granted me a lot of time. One of them is Laurent Thibault, who was the recording engineer, producer and studio manager at the Château d'Hérouville when Bowie came back there in 1976. I decided to focus on their stories while maintaining a timeline that is as close to reality as possible, while also reviewing the album. In addition, it's impossible to separate the recording of *Low* from that of *The Idiot* by Iggy Pop. In the same way, discussion of *"Heroes"* in the following chapter has to mention *Lust For Life*. The purpose of *Rainbowman* is not to intrude, but it was necessary to include some private information in order to place certain events in context. Also, while I try to deliver only one version of events in this book, the interviewees will tell them according to their own points of view. More than four decades passed between that summer and these interviews, and if some memories are hazy (or in some cases contradictory), they still deserve to be preserved as they are. It's unreasonable to let anyone rewrite history, but the perception of those 'who were there' is paramount.

The making of *Low*, preceded by spending some time in France, and after which David Bowie settled in Switzerland, then in Berlin, is an extremely important moment in his career. The turmoil that governed this period, accentuated by various frustrations and things left unsaid, led me to give pride of place to the interviewees who were also at the Château d'Hérouville. As a result, in this chapter more than any other, the interviewees themselves reveal several pieces of information on the recordings and their work with Bowie, only some of which were previously known.

Our common desire was to relate the facts as truthfully as possible (after their first interview, many got back to me with additional information) and had no particular reason to want to contradict what has been said in the past. Revisionism has become the norm, but I've taken a firm stance against it.

JS

At the first light of dawn on 19 May 1976, David Bowie and his friends (including Iggy Pop, Corinne Schwab, Pat Gibbons and Romy Haag) are at the Alcazar, a cabaret in Saint-Germain-des-Prés in Paris. Romy is a friend David had met the night of his recent Berlin concert, who's travelled from Germany for the occasion. They are all celebrating the end of the European journey of the Thin White Duke[2]. Bowie wanted to play a third show in Paris, but it isn't his fault that KCP[3], who organized the concerts on 17 and 18 May at the Pavillon de Paris, had bitten off more than it could chew and the limited demand for tickets forced it to cancel the concert on 19 May[4]. But RCA had done a good job with the promotion by telling a little white lie – an ad in the June 1976 issue of *Rock&Folk*, published that week, read: 'For the first time in France'.

During his brief stay in Paris, Bowie barely speaks to the press, but he grants some time to journalist Jean Claude Emmanuel, who shoots a story to be broadcast on the news by Yves Mourousi on 18 May. Known as *David Bowie Ou Le Rêve De Natacha*, it gives the French a glimpse of the Thin White Duke in action and they discover Natacha Smolianoff, in her sixties, who lives in the 15th arrondissement of Paris. She knew Bowie in London at the very beginning of his career and then set up a French fan club.

All signs suggest that David Bowie had initially thought of Munich (or maybe Berlin) to record Iggy Pop's first solo album. Between the concerts he'd given in Germany in April, Bowie hadn't had much time to spare, but he did meet up with local musicians in bars and clubs after his shows. If he'd just wanted to duplicate the sound of Kraftwerk or Neu!, he could have simply recorded in Düsseldorf (from where the two groups hail), but that never seems to have been his intention. On 19 or 20 May 1976, besieged by fans at his hotel in Paris, Bowie has his people call the

Château d'Hérouville to ask if he and his entourage could hide away for a bit. But he probably had an ulterior motive[5].

In those days, David Bowie's money problems were far from over. While he did say that Iggy Pop's record would go to the highest bidder (probably a licensing deal – Bowie would still own the masters), he hopes it will go to his label, RCA. Since MainMan has imploded (Tony Defries' company doesn't amount to much without its main artist), and he is still in legal discussions about his parting from Michael Lippman, David pays most of his own bills. At the Château d'Hérouville, a residential studio, food and accommodation will be included in the price. And if RCA is going to release Iggy's album, it will be up to the label to foot the bill. The few days in May that Bowie spends in Val-d'Oise give him the chance to get used to the place again and especially to get to know the new team.

Co-founder of the band Magma with drummer Christian Vander, Laurent Thibault is a bass player, a composer and a producer. He's just taken over the management of the studio and is working with about 20 people, including recording engineer Michel Marie, financial advisor Pierre Calamel and coordinator Chanchan Von Shoeshine. David and Laurent get along so well (the latter has just finished *Macadam*, an album by Yves Simon, which was mixed in Paris at the Studio Davout), that David promises to return to Hérouville in June to record Iggy's album. He is also planning to start working on the follow-up to *Station To Station* as soon as he can.

David Bowie then travels on to Switzerland, to the house Angie has found in Blonay (called Le Clos des Mésanges at 18, chemin de Sainte-Croix). The place is quiet, perhaps a little too quiet for him, but he takes the opportunity to paint and especially to reflect on the two records he is about to record almost simultaneously. In the basement of this opulent house above Lake Geneva, David drafts a few songs with Iggy. A first version of the one called 'Borderline' is quickly put to tape in rough. Since they seem to have played it on instruments designed for children (tinkling piano and baby drums), it sounds vaguely Asian. As agreed, after celebrating Zowie's birthday in Montreux, the wild bunch hit the road again. They take David's Mercedes limousine, which is getting a bit the worse for wear and will have to be replaced that summer[6].

In July, David Bowie will work mainly with Laurent Thibault in the George-Sand Studio (the acoustics are better there and the English-speaking clients usually prefer it to the Chopin). They will concentrate on Iggy Pop's album, but they will dedicate some sessions to David's one too. The songs will remain at the instrumental stage for a long time before they are divided up between the two records. There's been a lot of speculation about the way they were divided up, but it doesn't seem to have been based on quality as some have suggested. Bowie's intention is to showcase Iggy's talent as a lyricist (his forte, he thinks) and he's going to encourage him to sing in a deep voice. Hence, he will tend to give him the heavier songs, which he plans on treating in a rather crude way.

Oddly enough, while Iggy Pop was the drummer of The Iguanas[7] and The Prime Movers when he started playing in bands in his hometown of Ann Arbor, Michigan, he won't strike a single tom on *The Idiot*. Even stranger is the fact that Edgar Froese, keyboardist of the Berlin-based Tangerine Dream, whom David Bowie met after his concert in Berlin in May, although he was invited to come, made his way to the Château d'Hérouville for nothing. David loved his solo work and *Epsilon In Malaysian Pale*, Froese's second album, released in 1975, has spent a lot of time on Bowie's turntable.

Overall, the sessions are serious – they start work on a dozen tracks: some new ones and a few others based on fragments of songs David Bowie has on tape. But the atmosphere isn't as calm as it might appear to be to a casual onlooker. Angie drops by, which dials up the heat on this already scorching summer, and according to witnesses, Bowie's frequent visits to Paris to meet with his lawyers to untangle himself from his brief association with Michael Lippman is taking its toll[8].

Iggy Pop is going to spend a lot of time on his lyrics and will rewrite some of them to reflect his changing mood or situation, or on his friend's advice (for example, David suggested mentioning The Stooges in 'Dum Dum Boys', though Iggy ultimately chose not to). This is how Iggy's infatuation with Kuêlan Nguyen, the partner of singer Jacques Higelin, will turn 'Borderline' into 'China Girl'. Nguyen and Higelin are also staying at the *château* that summer with their son Kên, who is five years old and often plays in the park with Zowie. Under the influence of this illicit affair (Kuêlan did put her finger on Iggy's lips to keep him quiet...), the lyrics will lose their original meaning and become a passionate declaration, probably the most direct love song in all of Iggy Pop's discography.

In late July, the rhythm section of the Isolar tour (George Murray and Dennis Davis) makes a brief stop at Hérouville. While the DAM trio clearly play on *The Idiot*, the dates of their sessions remain uncertain. For example, Alomar may have been recorded in September because there is no proof he was at the *château* in July. *The Idiot* was supposed to have been mixed and completed by the time the sessions for *Low* started, but since David Bowie hadn't given the tapes to his label at that point, they might have continued to work on it. So it's impossible to say who played what on Iggy Pop's album, but half of Laurent Thibault and Michel Santangeli's bass and drum parts probably survived.

In August, because the George-Sand has been booked by British band Bad Company (who will record *Burnin' Sky* with producer Chris Kimsey), Bowie, Iggy Pop and Thibault relocate to the Musicland Studios[9] in Munich, owned by Giorgio Moroder, the Italian godfather of electro-pop. He and his British colleague Pete Bellotte devise hits for American disco diva Donna Summer, including 'Love To Love You Baby', a global dance sensation still huge six months after its release. One hell of a clubber at the time, David Bowie enjoys her music, as does Brian Eno, who is a big fan of hers (not a well-known fact). Iggy records some vocal tracks at Musicland and the young British guitarist Phil Palmer improves or simply replaces some of David's guitar parts that he doesn't think are up to scratch. Apparently, guitarist Ricky Gardiner, who will play on *Low*, was considered for *The Idiot* instead of Palmer, but the first phone call he received about this was also the last.

The decision to use a drum machine on 'Nightclubbing' is not so much meant to mimic the robotic character of certain German bands, but to improve the song by highlighting Iggy's voice with disembodied arrangements. The machine they use is a Roland from that era (almost certainly a TR-77, but maybe a TR-66), customized and with individual audio outputs. It will also be used on 'Art Decade' (on *Low*) and 'African Night Flight' (on *Lodger*).

The choice of Musicland over Konrad 'Conny' Plank's studio near Cologne said a lot about David Bowie's desire to set himself apart from the German bands[10]. Can, Faust and Neu! all worked with Plank and if Bowie had wanted *The Idiot* (and *Low*) to sound like their records, he would have gone to this wizard of German electronic music. In search of similar sounds and productions to those made by Plank, many English-speaking musicians (Ultravox, Eurythmics, Echo & The Bunnymen, Devo, Killing Joke) and even French ones (Rita Mitsouko) will soon be demanding his services. Brian Eno also recorded with Conny Plank, including much of his 1977 masterpiece *Before And After Science*. As for Kraftwerk (who were cutting *Trans Europa Express*[11] in Düsseldorf in 1976), any proposals for collaborative projects with David Bowie will be declined. They always respected each other and loved each other's records (Bowie will pay a direct tribute to founding member Florian Schneider on the B-side of *"Heroes"*), but Kraftwerk never intended to be David's backing band.

In the 1960s, brothers Peter and Thomas Meisel ran a successful label in Berlin called Hansa Musikoproduktion. Having regularly used the Ariola-Eurodisk

Sonopress Studio, located at 38 Köthenerstraße in Kreuzberg, near Potsdamer Platz, they founded their own place (Studio 1) in the late 1960s to record their artists. It was on the Nestorstraße in the Wilmersdorf district. They then took over number 38 (now a protected building) in the mid-70s and developed Hansa Tonstudios. The Meisel brothers opened Studios 2 (the most legendary), 3 and 4, then another Studio 1 when the one in Nestorstraße closed.

Built in the early 1800s and badly damaged during World War II, the building includes a concert hall (the Meistersaal). It is that vast room, with its high ceilings, stage, wooden floor and big windows, that gives the songs cut there a unique sound. While recording *"Heroes"* later on, Dennis Davis will set up his drums there and, in addition to the natural reverb of the room, the stairwell in the building (as at the Château d'Hérouville) will sometimes be used to improve the sound of the vocals or instruments. The building has become known by the nickname Hansa By The Wall, which is often listed on album covers, including David Bowie's[12]. Some say clients of Studio 2 were able to see the Berlin Wall from the windows, but in fact, it could only be seen from the control room.

In late August, David Bowie and Iggy Pop move to Hansa (Studio 1), and Tony Visconti joins David for the first time since *Young Americans*. It's not exactly clear what they work on at that time or what they should have been working on. According to Laurent Thibault, *The Idiot* was already finished, so two theories have evolved. One is that Visconti was in Berlin to work with Bowie using the soundtrack of *The Man Who Fell To Earth*, that is, to listen to it and determine what could be used on his next album. But since the tapes didn't come – Cherokee kept them because of unpaid bills – David Bowie reportedly asked him to listen to *The Idiot* and mix some of its songs. The other theory is that Bowie was disappointed with Thibault's work, so as the Munich sessions were coming to an end, he called Tony Visconti to come and save the day by mixing Iggy's record at Hansa. To add to the confusion, in his 2007 autobiography, Tony will confess he can no longer remember the order of events (was *The Idiot* mixed before *Low* was recorded, or the other way around?). Since David Bowie had been planning on returning to Hérouville to work with Laurent Thibault as his recording engineer in September, the first theory is more likely.

The recollections of the main protagonists often conflict when it comes to the origins of *Low* and how it was made. In his book, Tony Visconti writes that David Bowie phoned him (from Switzerland) in the summer of 1976, probably in early June. The Château d'Hérouville had already been booked for Iggy, and then for him.

David reportedly told Visconti he planned on making his next album in France and that he was going to invite Brian Eno. He wanted to 'apply ambient music techniques to rock songs' and wondered what Tony, who hadn't been asked to work on *Station To Station*, could bring to the table. Having recently purchased an Eventide H910 harmonizer[13], which, as he wrote in his book, could 'change the pitch of a note without changing the speed of the tape, and produce unearthly magical sounds', Visconti easily convinced Bowie that his presence on his next record would be an asset.

The producer reportedly arrived at the *château* in September with the equipment under his arm. One problem: while the Eventide harmonizer was used a lot on *Low* (to modify the sound of the drums, among other things), its effects can also be heard on *The Idiot*, though to a lesser extent. This suggests Visconti already had it when he was at Hansa in August mixing Iggy Pop's album (all or part of it). The plot thickens as Laurent Thibault and Pierre Calamel confirm in the interview section of this chapter that their studio was already equipped with one of these acclaimed devices. As for Harry Maslin, he said he had used it on *Station To Station*! Whatever the truth, the fact is that the effects of the H910, sophisticated (and expensive) for the time, can be heard on *The Idiot* as well as on *Low*.

As with *"Heroes"* the following year, the first week of recording is dedicated to the rhythm section with Carlos Alomar, George Murray and Dennis Davis. Using chord progressions that are fairly basic in structure and sometimes pretexts for jam sessions, they quickly record the foundations for the seven short tracks of the A-side, two of which are instrumental. Roy Young then adds some piano and organ parts, while Ricky Gardiner, frontman of Beggars Opera (a prog rock band from Glasgow), lays down guitar parts.

Another rumour claims that, at the time of the *Low* sessions, David Bowie wanted to work with some krautrock musicians, like the multi-instrumentalist Klaus Dinger of Neu!, and/or Dieter Moebius, the keyboard player of Cluster and Harmonia. But, if contact was made, no one followed up. It's possible these rumours come from the fact that Michael Rother, the guitarist of Neu!, will be asked to play on *"Heroes"*. But unfortunately for him, a few days before the start of recording, he will be told that his presence is no longer required[14].

Brian Eno joins Bowie and his team at the end of the first week of recording. Since playing synthesizer with Roxy Music, which he left in 1973 after *For Your Pleasure*, Eno experiments on solo albums he records alone or in good company. David, who listens to everything, was especially drawn to the charms and textures of the avant-garde pop of *Another Green World* and to the ambient (the term dates from this period) instrumentals of *Discreet Music*, both released in 1975[15]. However, during the glam era, while Bowie asked Roxy Music to open for him in 1972, his songs hadn't resonated well with Brian Eno, who found them not very evocative and just distracting. As a matter of fact, when Bowie phoned Eno, who was co-producing Ultravox's first album in London, he was not over the moon. Brian was only convinced when he understood that David was intending to create a new form of music – one of the titles he was considering for the album was *New Music: Night and Day*, a throwback to *Neu! '75*, the German band's third album, which featured an ambient side and a more rock one – without worrying about the commercial consequences. Actually, Bowie aspires to create a sort of musical collage by juxtaposing culturally opposing elements (an African-American rhythm section supporting relatively traditional rock arrangements, all enriched with synthesizers), an unlikely context conducive to partially planned 'sound accidents'. This time, the intention is to use the studio 'as an instrument'. With *Low*, Bowie wants to delve deeper into what he started with *Station To Station* and risked with *The Idiot*. When Ricky Gardiner asks him for some direction, Bowie urges him to do whatever he wants.

Most of the basic tracks have been recorded when Brian Eno arrives at the *château*, and he notices that Tony Visconti's harmonizer, the effects of which initially left David Bowie dubious, has been used a lot. Eno suggests 'developing the soundscapes' drafted by Bowie, who plays keyboards, guitars and saxophone on the record. They use synthesizers of different brands – ARP, EMI, Moog and EMS's glorious Synthi AKS, which comes in a briefcase and can be controlled with a joystick. They also use a Chamberlin[16], a sort of precursor to the Mellotron, an ancestor of the samplers that will become widespread in the 1980s.

Brian alters the sound of some instruments with his famous 'treatments', which he's tried out with Roxy Music and Robert Fripp (he would put almost any sound through a synth). He also proposes using the card-based method Oblique Strategies, which he invented in 1975 with British multidisciplinary artist Peter Schmidt. The set is made up of over a hundred cards, each with a vague instruction aimed at stimulating creativity in artists who want to work outside their comfort zone (Carlos Alomar will describe it as wacky). Eno will also use Oblique Strategies on *"Heroes"* and *Lodger* and, more than two decades later, he will get them out again for *Outside*.

Brian Eno doesn't stay long at Hérouville for *Low*, but he works on five tracks of the A-side and two of the B-side, which consists of four 'almost' instrumentals (David Bowie sings a few lines on the first and last pieces). According to Tony

Visconti, the mysterious 'lyrics' heard in 'Warszawa'[17] – Eno's biggest contribution to *Low* (he co-wrote it) – were made up on the spot. Brian Eno's fans – and many journalists – will have an annoying habit of exaggerating his contribution to the trilogy and Tony Visconti's name will often be omitted from reviews in favour of his. Yet Eno himself will tend to downplay his own role in interviews as early as 1977. It's also interesting to note that it was not Bowie who invented the practice of placing songs of a similar nature on the same side of an album. *Atlantic Crossing*, Rod Stewart's LP from 1975 has rock songs on the A-side and ballads on the other (as do his next two).

According to many of its clients, the Château d'Hérouville was haunted, an idea which will be confirmed by Ritchie Blackmore, who was there in 1977 recording *Long Live Rock'N'Roll*, Rainbow's third album. We don't know whether it was because of the ghosts of George Sand and Chopin, but David Bowie demanded to change bedrooms because in the spacious one he'd been assigned, there was a corner that was impossible to light (or to heat, nobody remembers...). And like other musicians before and after them, he and Visconti are said to have got food poisoning during the *Low* sessions and were faced with the challenge of finding a doctor, on a Sunday, in the French countryside of the 1970s.

Ultimately, for a tangle of reasons that are impossible to verify, Bowie's team fell out with Laurent Thibault. In his book, Visconti says the equipment at Hérouville became increasingly faulty as the recording of *Low* progressed. David's musicians and entourage also said there were too few staff at the studio and those that were there were not always competent. And because they always tried to be as discreet as possible whenever they stayed somewhere, Bowie and Coco blamed Laurent for allowing a music journalist (from *Rock&Folk*, of course...) to infiltrate the *château* and spy on them. He was apparently posing as a bodyguard or cook. Without meaning any harm, Thibault had also reportedly revealed too much about the making of *The Idiot*, for example telling the press (*Rock&Folk*, again) that a French drummer and bassist had played on it. Maybe it wasn't much in itself, but it was the straw that broke the camel's back and for David, it justified the omission of their names from the cover of Iggy Pop's record.

Much later, when they happen to mention the summer of 1976, Bowie and Visconti will admit that they did enjoy their last stay at Hérouville. Nevertheless, when invited back (in the early 1990s for the musician and in 2015 for his producer), neither of them will want to go. The *château* and its ghosts belonged to a past they had no desire to revisit[18].

In late September 1976, the recording of *Low* continues in Berlin (at Hansa 1), and Tony Visconti oversees the last takes, mainly vocals, captured by house recording engineer Eduard 'Edu' Meyer. Also a cellist, Edu is asked to play on 'Art Decade'[19]. It is also around that time that David, inspired by his proximity to the Berlin Wall, creates the instrumental 'Weeping Wall'[20] from scratch. It is one of two pieces – the other being 'A New Career In A New Town' – to be explicitly inspired by Berlin and Bowie plays all the instruments on it.

In the process of becoming a Swiss resident (he will return to Blonay regularly during his so-called 'Berlin period'), David Bowie allows himself to be drawn into the city of contrasts, which will only become the capital of Germany again in 1990, and moves into Hauptstraße 155, a couple of miles south of Hansa 2. Coco found him this spacious apartment (Iggy will be his flatmate for a while) in the Schöneberg district, which famously inspired Christopher Isherwood when he lived there in the interwar period.

Tony mixes *Low* with David in October and it will come out on 14 January 1977, less than a week after Bowie's thirtieth birthday. Hailed as a masterpiece today, David Bowie's eleventh studio album will draw a mixed response from the press when it hits the stores, but not from the public – it will reach Number 2 in the British charts and Number 11 in the US. It has been said that Tony Defries, even though nobody asked him, advised RCA against releasing it. As expected, *Low* caused controversy among the label's executives[21]. After listening to it (or perhaps just hearing it), some said they were ready to buy Bowie a house in Philadelphia so he could continue to tap the soul vein, while others thought that in time, *Low* would be considered a seminal LP.

At the time of its release, believing that *Low* speaks for him, David will decide not to meet the press. This behaviour ties in with the title of the album, which he chose at the last minute – *Low* for low profile – and with the cover, which features a photo of him, full frame and in profile, again taken by Steve Schapiro on the set of *The Man Who Fell To Earth*. Nicolas Roeg will be one of the first to receive a copy of the album, with a note from David saying this was the music he had in mind for 'their' film. As Tony Visconti pointed out, the name also reflects Bowie's state of mind during its recording: lower than low.

With its opening ('Speed Of Life') and closing ('A New Career In A New Town') themes, the A-side of *Low* is the most delimited of any in David Bowie's discography. On these instrumentals, Dennis Davis' snare drum sound is swollen by the effect of the H910. Carlos Alomar, in the role he affirmed during the Station To Station tour, holds it all together. The heroic melody of the first track is wrapped in layers of synthesizer as delicate as cigarette paper, while Brian Eno and Roy Young make the second one rush without losing its nursery rhyme feel. 'Breaking Glass', one of the few Bowie pieces in which the drummer plays a four on the floor beat (it can't however be classified as disco as the speed doesn't exceed 96bpm), could have been a single had it been more conventional in style, but particularly if it hadn't been less than two minutes in length! The song is treated bluntly and scarred with Eno's Minimoog sounds. The catchy melody hides, as much as it can, the arid nature of the harmonies. It's like a black sheep that's been dancing all its life, but on three legs instead of four.

More of a free-for-all than an actual pop song, 'What In The World' is all over the place, and confirms, again, the elaborate songwriting that made David Bowie who he was. The sudden and unexpected chord changes are in tune with the busy arrangement, the chaotic drums (the snare disappears thirty seconds into the song in favour of tom fills) and the delirious backing vocals. It's no surprise that Iggy Pop's voice can be heard there – according to some who worked on both *Low* and *The Idiot*, 'What In The World' is one of the tracks that could have ended up on either album.

In terms of the melody, structure, arrangements and vocals, 'Sound And Vision', 'Always Crashing In The Same Car' and 'Be My Wife' are the trifecta of the A-side of *Low*. Quite irrationally, the first is the sexiest. It's half instrumental and Bowie gets away with murder by providing both call and response through the lead and backing vocals. 'Always Crashing In The Same Car', with a similar form to 'Fantastic Voyage', which will open *Lodger,* wavers between comedy and drama. Here David allegedly refers to wrecking his car in a hotel garage (in Germany?), the consequence of alcohol. Dennis Davis hits hard and Ricky Gardiner, showcased by the turbulent arrangement, proves himself worthy of Tony Visconti's trust.

It is clear from the intro of the third song in this trio why Bowie had considered Roy Young for *Station To Station* – his ragtime style would have been perfect on 'TVC 15'. Totally offbeat, both sanguine and elusive, rather like the cheap video showing a heavily made-up Bowie (still looking like he's at the end of his tether) shot against a white background, which *Top Of The Pops* director Stanley Dorfman will make in Paris to promote the single[22], 'Be My Wife' – whose title is probably a wink at 'Be My Husband', the opening track of Nina Simone's 1965 album, *Pastel Blues* – is a lucky juxtaposition of two parts. However, except in David Bowie's mind, they had little to do with each other since each claimed to be the conquering chorus of the other, relegated to the rank of common verse.

It's easy for those who are pro Eno to claim that 'Warszawa' is the most majestic piece on *Low* (and in fact in the whole trilogy), because it's true. The title refers to the Thin White Duke's train journey through Poland with his friends in springtime. The resolution of the main chord progression comes after two minutes and twelve seconds, and it is with this very (Italian composer) Ennio Morricone-style major seventh chord – extremely rare in Bowie's musical vocabulary (another obvious one is the third chord – A major seventh – in the verse of 'Absolute Beginners') – that we understand the relevance of Brian's input. On 'Art Decade', he and David share practically all the instruments, while the drum machine grants the piece a krautrock pulse, probably the least covert reference to the genre on the album.

More than four decades after its release, to think that 'Weeping Wall' owes its complexity only to David Bowie's genius would be to forget that in the month it was recorded – October 1976 – he attended the European premiere of *Music For 18 Musicians* by Steve Reich at the Metamusik festival. Bowie probably got the idea for the song's arrangement from the minimalist composer's use of xylophones and vibraphones, just as ten years later, Reich would also inspire a few tracks of Ryuichi Sakamoto's wonderful *Illustrated Musical Encyclopaedia*. In the same way that the lithographs of *Blackstar* will reference the cover of *Low* (and therefore Thomas Jerome Newton), the deepest backing vocals on the title song of Bowie's final album will in part be modelled on those in 'Weeping Wall' and 'Subterraneans'[23].

Bowie was so disorganised with his tapes and cassettes that no one can be sure whether *Low*'s last song, 'Subterraneans', is the only survivor of *The Man Who Fell To Earth*'s recording sessions. But the incomplete mention of 'Peter and Paul' in the credits might be more an offer of thanks – for services rendered unofficially – to J. Peter Robinson and Paul Buckmaster, than proof of their participation. Might the 'unreleased' parts of the soundtrack, probably still stored in David Bowie's archives, ever be released? It's doubtful.

The lyrics of *Low* – absent from the original UK pressing of the album (a fan club leaflet was included), they will appear when his catalogue is reissued in the early 1990s – clearly and succinctly show that David was still being dragged down by memories of his time in Los Angeles and the deep melancholy he felt during his first months in Europe. He makes reference to his gangrenous marriage in 'Breaking Glass' and 'Be My Wife', and to the occultism that was still playing on his mind at least until Hérouville[24] in 'What In The World'. Bowie mentions losing his bearings in 'Sound And Vision' and is obviously referring to his spiritual and moral atrophy in 'Always Crashing In The Same Car'.

Again, there's little point in declaiming, even from the highest cliff, that *Low* is David Bowie's best album (he had so many different personas and lives that to prefer one or more can only be done at the expense of the others), but it is undeniable that its making marked a pivotal turning point in his winding career. Still hurting physically (less cocaine, but more alcohol), tormented by private and financial issues, and consumed by doubt – still troubling him even after the paranoia goes away – Bowie managed to rehabilitate his mind and body, to make music in the manner of an insatiable tinker – whatever people might think or say about him – open and receptive to others. Because, with no disrespect to Iggy Pop (held in the highest esteem here), *The Idiot*, released on 18 March 1977[25], on RCA Records as David had hoped, is, at least in part, a Bowie record. His benevolence, which at the time bordered on devotion, was undeniable, but was also the result of a craving for creating en masse, often in a somewhat disorderly fashion. Later, especially in the twilight of his life, acknowledging the fact that he never made decisions easily, he will confirm this. *The Idiot* (sold with a 'Produced by David Bowie' sticker even though the cover says 'Recorded by David Bowie' and 'Mixed by Tony Visconti') and *Low* convey an artistic duality that David didn't try to hide in 1977. One is his grey side (like Andrew Kent's photo of Iggy on the jacket[26]), and the other, with a fiery-haired Thomas Jerome Newton – like the apocalyptic sky behind him – is his orange. *The Idiot* is distorted and disruptive in many ways – muffled vocals ('China Girl') or erratic ones ('Mass Production'), savage drums ('Funtime') or barely audible beats ('Baby'), guitar groans used as synths and some blunt piano – and on *Low*, anything is allowed (lyrics are optional), even blindfold drunk driving.

While the following decade would be marked by the advent of sampling and computers – generators and triggers of sounds less and less cramped but more and more sanitized – David Bowie remained committed to putting human spontaneity first in *The Idiot* and *Low*. Until the end, he will always make a point of recording with musicians playing together, in the same room, with him standing in front of a microphone: *body and song*.

Despite 'Sound And Vision'[27] reaching Number 3 in the UK singles chart a month after the album is released (in the US it won't make the Top 50), *Low* won't be a great commercial success and won't stay long in the album charts. And it will never be among Bowie's bestsellers, although it will make it to the top of the UK vinyl chart when it is reissued in 2018[28]. But like *"Heroes"*, which will sell even fewer copies that year, it will prove to be enormously influential among musicians and an infinite list of artists and bands will take inspiration from it. And with *Low*, perhaps more than with any of his other records, David Bowie is educating his audience. While most of his peers just want to be popular (in the UK in early 1977, Abba, The Shadows and Frank Sinatra sold the most albums), Bowie puts his fans to the test and leads them into the unknown. He takes them to new heights. Not by provoking them (like Lou Reed with *Metal Machine Music* in 1975), or against their will, but by promising them something new, by making a different kind of rock. Using the same weapons/instruments as the classic rockers they mean to taunt, The Sex Pistols, The Clash and The Damned will give old England a good ticking off (among the new bands he was sceptical of, only The Sex Pistols will make a significant incursion into the charts), but Bowie chooses Europe as the setting for his campaign to exorcise his frustrations and stage his rebirth. By breaking the rules and creating, DIY-style (though clearly assisted by Tony Visconti and Brian Eno), like the krautrockers, a new genre which he would explore further on his next album, and by revealing himself to all as more elusive than ever, he becomes a totally free spirit. The ultimate punk.

Laurent Thibault
BOWIE IN MAY
ART AND METHOD
DRUM'N'BASS
FROESE WHIRLWIND
BAD COMPANY
THE INDIAN
MUNICH
AN ALL-TIME LOW
BEFORE AND AFTER ENO
THE END

Carlos Alomar

Ricky Gardiner

Roy Young

George Murray

Mary Hopkin

Iggy Pop

Tony Visconti

Michel Marie

Eduard 'Edu' Meyer

Albert Koski

Marc Exiga

Kuêlan Nguyen

Pierre Calamel

Chanchan Von
Shoeshine

Cécile Nougaro

Phil Palmer

Paul Rodgers

Chris Kimsey

Barry Gibb

Thilo Schmied

Jonathan Wyner

Pete Keppler

Sonjay Prabhakar

Rob Gentry

Greg McLeod

Ryuichi Sakamoto

Damon Albarn

Ian McCulloch

Nick Lowe

Anthony Agnello

LAURENT THIBAULT
BOWIE IN MAY

This David Bowie story starts after his second show at the Pavillon de Paris – not the third one, as legend has it, because that one was cancelled. He'd invited some friends from Germany and was staying at the Plaza Athénée[29]. But they were hounded by the press and thought the staff were listening in on their phone conversations! That's why we got the call, from Coco Schwab I think, asking if she, David and Jimmy could come and stay at the *château* for a few days, to get away from the crowd. Of course I invited them. They planned to arrive that very evening and asked me to wait for them. So I cut my session short and made everyone go home. We didn't tell anyone David Bowie was coming.

I was waiting upstairs, on my own, when he arrived. He was wearing a suit jacket and a hat. Then came a blond kid, Iggy, who we called Jimmy, and Corinne. David walked around the studio and I remember he did a cartwheel! That stayed with me because he often did that to relax. Anyway, it was crazy he did it on the first day! Then he ran round and round the empty room. He said to Jimmy, 'It's the biggest rock'n'roll studio in the world!' I was thrilled. He was like, 'Okay, we're tired, it's late, see you tomorrow.' And pfft! He was gone. Very brief, it lasted ten minutes.

Over the following days, I continued my work and they stayed in their rooms doing whatever. I hardly saw them at all. Corinne would come and get them something to eat. On the third day, they asked me to stop my session at 6pm and meet them at 7pm in the big room with the fireplace. They'd installed a turntable with a sound system, the real deal. There were some nibbles – everything was ready. I walk around the room a bit and at exactly 7pm the door opens and David, all in blue, dressed to the nines, comes in and says, 'Bonjour!' in French. Without further ado, he takes out an LP and puts it on the turntable. Very direct. 'Take a seat!' he tells me. It was Magma. It wasn't one of the albums I'd done, it was *Mekanïk Destruktïw Kommandöh*. He plays both sides and says, 'Okay, you know this album, but that's just to get us started. Now I'm going to tell you what I like about this record and what I think you could have done better.' Even though I was no longer part of Magma, I listened.

For half an hour, Bowie gave me a lecture on the band, the good and the not so good... It was pretty astounding, and honestly, I wondered why I was there. Of course I was polite, courteous, and I listened to him talk. I was enthralled. And then I started talking too. I was very close to Christian Vander and I talked about the formation of the band, the what and the why. Initially, David acted like he knew everything. But I think that while there were some things he knew – of course – there were others he was less aware of. But he wouldn't say so; actually, he learned a lot from conversations with others. He was always plugged into knowledge! Because that was it with David: if the anode fitted the cathode, things went well. If, on the other hand, the power dimmed, everything stopped, it was over, he'd leave. He always had to be in flux. And our flux that night lasted until 7am! He played a Neu! record for me and others he liked… Then he said, 'Now I'm going to play some stuff you've never heard!'

To be honest, I hadn't heard much of what he played that night, but I didn't dare say so! I didn't want to seem like an idiot, but the German stuff for example, I'd never heard that… When you live in a studio, you can't be up to scratch with everything. Journalists are in a better position. Then he put on a record and I immediately said, 'Oum Kalthoum!' I knew her and I knew that song. He was really surprised… He played another album and bam! I said, 'That's *Le Mystère Des Voix Bulgares*!' He started telling me how they made it and I told him I already knew, which blew him away. Those Bulgarian voices inspired 'Warszawa'!

Then we listened to some other things, like 'Alabama Song' written by Bertolt Brecht and Kurt Weill, and at 7am he said, 'Okay, I'll come back here for Iggy's record and we're going to work together.' That was astonishing, because we'd only talked about music, art and creation. At no point did he say, 'I'm David Bowie, I want this, I want that…' He didn't tell me much about himself. But he did talk a lot about everything else! It was crazy, it was like it had to come out… To the point that once or twice I had to tell him that there were certain things I didn't want to know.

The first day we spent together he stunned me. 'There's a rule you should know: since you'll be working with me, everything you say, everything you do, whether it's lyrics, ideas, notes or whatever, it all becomes mine. That's just how it is. And if you don't like it, you can go.' (2016)

LAURENT THIBAULT
ART AND METHOD

When they returned to Hérouville, it was totally off-the-cuff and they came with no instruments. David had told me that Jimmy played the drums, so I thought they'd bring a kit. Their equipment came later: a Baldwin piano, a Marshall amp, a see-through Plexiglas Dan Armstrong guitar like the ones The Stones used,

Bowie's saxophone, his drum machine, an ARP synth[30], but no drums! Not even a tambourine! Well, we had a few anyway.

So, at the beginning, everything was done with the Baldwin. David didn't explain anything to me. He just said he had some demos on cassette, which he played on his little Philips recorder and listened to with tiny earphones, then he would sit at the piano. I had set up a microphone so he could talk or do some vocals while I was recording the Baldwin. And we went from there. Baldwin and vocals. I think we must have used a click, but I can't remember. I don't have the 24-track tapes anymore. I had rough mixes that I later transferred onto DATs, but I can't find them anymore. I always wondered if someone swiped them... As for my *Low* rough mixes, with the beautiful reverbs from the *château*, quite a few instruments were left out afterwards, including a harmonica[31]. Then drums, guitars and David's lead vocals were added to the tapes of *The Idiot*. I remember he was singing 'Dum Dum Days', which became 'Dum Dum Boys' on the album.

In the studio, in terms of communication, he stuck to the basics. He never said he wanted this or that sound. It was just, 'Record!' His piano would go through the amp, so I'd record the sound of the amp! And if he said, 'Guitar!' I'd record the guitar from the same amp! At one point, I stopped asking questions. I just recorded. He never played for long and only rarely redid anything. When he came into the control room to listen, I'd ask how that went, if he wanted a different sound... He'd stare at me blankly. There was no way to know whether he was laughing inside, mulling something over or thinking about something else altogether. It was as if I was invisible. Most of the time, he'd say the magic word, 'Next!', meaning he was happy with what we'd done. Then '*Répétition!*' in French ['rehearsal']. And bam! That meant it was time to move on to a new song. Jimmy would sit on the floor behind the console, with all his sheets of paper. (2016)

LAURENT THIBAULT
DRUM'N'BASS

One day, David said, 'I'd like you to call in a drummer, a hard-hitting woodcutter, a guy who doesn't think, just plays, very simple.' I thought of Michel Santangeli, whom I'd already worked with on some records, including The Money Spinners'. He wanted him to be at the studio in two days time. So I phoned Michel in Brittany and he asked, 'Is it for Paul McCartney?' I said it was for David Bowie and he said, 'I'm coming!' I told David everything was taken care of and we didn't even mention money! Michel arrived one afternoon, one of the staff told him to come up and I told David he was on his way. Except he didn't turn up! David asked, 'Is your drummer coming or not?' I called down to find out what was happening and they told me, 'He just realized it really is David Bowie. Now he doesn't dare come up.' He came up in the end, but rather shyly. He said hello and David, a bit dryly, said, 'Well go on! Sit behind the drums!' But when he looked at Michel, who was a bit chubby, I saw him think, 'That's just what I asked for.'

I set up the microphones and Michel, behind his drums, was a bit worried and kept asking, 'What are we doing? What are we doing?' I answered, 'You'll see, don't worry.' David got impatient and said, 'Let's go, let's go!' And I said, 'Wait, let me equalize the sound a bit.' And he was like, 'Okay, but be quick.' David was on the piano and a divider separated him from Michel. After five minutes, he said, '*Répétition!*' and started playing something. Michel said, 'Ah yes, okay,' and started playing too. I had to give him headphones because he couldn't hear very well and David got a little annoyed. 'This is taking forever,' he said...

While Michel played, I was trying to get the sound right. After 10 or 15 minutes, David yelled, 'Record!' and we recorded the song. David returned to his place in the control room, sitting cross-legged on his chair, and Michel was standing behind the console between the speakers. We listened to the track and Michel said, 'Okay, I see... So I am going to do that instead, add some tom-toms...' David was looking at him, silent. Michel looked uncertain, so David asked me, 'What is he talking about?' I translated and David said, 'Ah, tom-toms... No. No tom-toms.' Michel tried to explain, 'I mean, because I didn't know the song, I played without thinking... I can do better.' David looked at him and dropped that terrible word: 'Next!' And Michel was like, 'What is he saying?' I explained we were going to work on the next song and he panicked, 'What do you mean the next song? We can't keep that! I just played what came to me. I'm recording with David Bowie here!' David asked me to translate and he looked at Michel and said, 'Next!' So I told him not to worry, that we'd smooth it out later. And we did seven or eight songs like that. Michel started to relax, gain confidence, started to understand what David wanted and almost became familiar with him and his methods.

After recording the last song we listened to everything again. Michel didn't say much, apart from, 'I'd love to have a beer.' David was a good drinker. He was as thin as a stick, but he could hold his drink. And there was always a six-pack in the room. I said to Michel, 'No, not yet, let's wait.' Finally, David said, 'Okay, that's good, you can tell him to go downstairs, we'll do the rest tomorrow.'

That was the first time someone from outside had played on that record, so I wasn't aware how he worked at that point. Edgar Froese would be next... I said to Michel, 'Okay, you can go. We'll continue tomorrow...' But because he had his eye on that six-pack, he insisted, 'Oh, I'm happy to stay. I'll take that beer now, I'll sit in a corner, you won't know I'm here.' I said, 'No, you know, David prefers to be alone.' But he wouldn't budge. 'Oh, come on. I'm with David Bowie for Christ's sake!' David was watching us, and even though I wasn't translating, he must have understood what was going on. Michel ended up leaving and he never came back. There was no need. In the end, the drums on *The Idiot* are just as he played them that day. It only took an afternoon. The record wouldn't be the same had we put more time into it. It was rough around the edges!

One day, David said, 'Okay, listen, it's that time. How long will it take you to put a bass on this?' I must have looked surprised because he asked me, 'You're a bass player, aren't you?' I said yes and, as I was thinking, he said, 'An hour and a half? Would that work...? Good, an hour and a half!' And he split.

I think the first song I played on was 'China Girl'. I'd recorded it, but I hadn't really paid attention to the chord progression. I picked up my Rickenbacker and I thought, given the overall sound, that I'd plug into the amp. We usually did the bass directly into the console[32] because the sound is more precise. But I thought that on the big amp, it would fit in better with the rest. Suddenly, my Ricken' came out with this huge sound. And as I tried to figure it out, I realized the chord progression was quite special, that David had a particular way of composing. I told my assistant, Michel Marie, 'Okay, now I'm going to play something and maybe David will keep it.' And when I thought I'd almost mastered it, I said, 'Great, now I can do it right!' Of course, that's when he came back. 'You're done,' he said, 'Can I listen?' And I was like, 'Yeah, I played around with something, but...' And he interrupted, 'Can I hear it?' We listened and he asked, 'Can we put this bit back? Okay, so there, I'd like it if you could just do 'dum-dum-dum-dum.' That seemed strange to me, but I did what he asked. 'That's good,' he said. 'Tomorrow you can play on another song.'

So we went on like that. For some songs he didn't tell me anything, and he redid two himself I think, including 'Funtime'. 'That one,' he explained, 'I don't see it like that. Can I try with your bass?' And he played the part on 'Funtime' in one or two takes. That's the one on the record. Later, in Munich, he redid the bass on 'Nightclubbing' with a synth because he wanted a simpler sound. Neither Michel nor I played on 'Sister Midnight'. For that one, we received a tape, but we redid the piano, the guitars... George Murray played bass, Dennis Davis is the drummer and

Carlos Alomar replayed a few of his guitar parts... What was on tape didn't work. Michel played on 'Dum Dum Boys' since I'd also recorded the Baldwin on it. But later, Dennis came to Hérouville to redo Michel's drums and George, an amazing bass player, replaced the bass. They stayed for two days in July – that was quick!

Even though he was always there in the studio, Iggy got even more involved during the vocal takes. To the point that David didn't come during the day anymore. I cut the vocals alone with Jim. David didn't show up until around seven or eight in the evening and then stayed until dawn. He didn't direct Jim's vocals. He let him do his thing, he wasn't even there. Usually, Jim left around midnight and I'd stay with David. Unless there was a beautiful girl around, he worked until late... Jimmy seemed thrilled about the collaboration. There were never any arguments. (2016)

LAURENT THIBAULT
FROESE WHIRLWIND

One day, David told me that Edgar Froese was coming to the *château*. I didn't know who he was at the time, but my assistant told me he was the keyboard player of Tangerine Dream. Magma's roots were more on the side of Stravinsky, Coltrane and, as far as I'm concerned, rock. In the studio, I mostly knew the artists I recorded and the ones they told me about. For example, when Iggy Pop came, I'd never heard The Stooges' music. I was almost annoyed because they'd described him as this guy who rolled around on the floor during his shows... But when he started singing, I was blown away. He is a real crooner! He has a beautiful voice, even better than David's. After two days he asked me, 'What do you think of my voice?' And I was thinking, 'My God, I hope he doesn't ask me about his records!' I thought it best to be honest so I said, 'You remind me of Jim Morrison and Frank Sinatra at the same time.' He was happy with that and he told me it was the best compliment he'd ever received!

Okay, so Edgar Froese: we saw this Goth, Viking, arrive – with a big beard, dressed in a big wolf fur coat, even though it was summer and it was boiling! The girls took care of him because we were in a session and David let him know we'd see him later, at dinner. That night, we ate in the garden as usual, by candlelight. It was just David, Edgar Froese across from him, and me next to Froese, opposite Jimmy, who didn't say a word... I could see David's reactions very well from where I was sitting. Froese said to him, 'I was surprised you called me to play. So I looked into what you do... I mean, sure... I listened... There are some interesting things...' David didn't say anything. He fiddled with his napkin. Froese continued, 'As I was saying,

I was surprised you thought of me. And I wondered what I had to offer. But then I thought it's not for you, right? It's for Iggy...' David turned to Jimmy and said, 'After dinner, play some things for Mr Froese...' I could see that Edgar was starting to piss David off, who had nothing to say to him. He'd probably contacted him because of Tangerine Dream, but this uninteresting and slightly disagreeable introduction seemed to have upset him. So David sent us to the studio.

He told me, 'Play him this and that...' I can't remember the songs. Then Froese said, 'What's this? Oh come on, what am I going to do with that? Yeah, maybe... Can you play the tape again? Yeah, yeah, what a weird thing...' After about half an hour, David arrived and asked us if we'd been listening to the music. Froese said yes and that he was ready to get started, but David explained he needed to work on his own for a bit longer, and insisting that Froese must be tired from his trip, he sent him to bed! With David, I got used to people leaving as quickly as they'd arrived. We never saw Froese again. The next day, when I arrived around 10am – we'd gone to bed at 5am – he just said, 'The German is on his way home!' (2016)

LAURENT THIBAULT
BAD COMPANY

During the recording of *The Idiot*, Bad Company was rehearsing in the other studio downstairs. At the dinner table we had Bad Co and the four of us – Bowie's group – meaning David, Jimmy, Corinne and me. During sessions, David would close the window that opened onto Bad Co's area, but sometimes he opened it so he could listen to the blues. He'd produced Mott The Hoople, so he knew Mick Ralphs, who'd been their guitarist. They chatted for a bit. But when David came back across the courtyard, he didn't see the guys from Bad Co making fun of his dandy look behind his back. He'd clashed with the group's roadies once or twice. (2016)

LAURENT THIBAULT
THE INDIAN

One time, during *The Idiot*, something strange happened. Our hours were very demanding. We were in perpetual motion, we weren't getting much sleep, or sometimes none at all! Jim was just about coping, David too, but Michel and I were exhausted. One night, David couldn't find what he was looking for. We were going around in circles; it wasn't working. We were tired, so we tried to do something funny to lighten the mood. We had some red and white electrical tape. I don't know why, but I started to put the red tape on my cheeks, to look like an American Indian. David had popped out the room, but when he came back, he saw me and didn't say a word. As a joke, Michel decided to put the feather duster we used to clean the console on my head, to make me look like an Indian chief. We were just being silly.

Then David asked me if I had a china marker. I had no idea what he was talking about. He got mad, which was rare, and said, 'You know, every studio has a china marker!' I said, 'Just describe it to me!' And he said, 'It's a sort of white pen used to write on the console.' And I said, 'Oh, yeah, okay, I didn't know it was called a china marker!' And he added, 'Mark the channels on this fucking console, so I know where the tracks are!' So I said, 'Wait, we have special tape for that. You stick it on, write on it, and peel it off at the end.' That irritated him. He scribbled down a few things and left. I said to Michel and Jimmy, 'Shit, it's my fault, I shouldn't have dressed up as an Indian chief, I lost it.' David came back half an hour later as if nothing had happened and we continued the session until five or six in the morning...

The atmosphere during *The Idiot* was odd, but it was basically okay and pretty productive. But *Low* was different. Articles started to come out in the British press and Tony Visconti was saying unpleasant things about the *château* – that the food was disgusting, that nobody took care of them, that ghosts were pulling at their feet, that they'd been poisoned... Tony hated cheese and moaned whenever we served it. And eventually he fired me because of an alleged technical fault but, in truth, he was the one who didn't press the right button. And when I came to 'fix' the problem, David asked, nastily, 'Show me what you did? Oh, Tony, so it wasn't a technical fault, you're the one who didn't press the right button.' Tony became even angrier. But I don't blame him. He was the producer and he was probably pissed off that he hadn't been part of *The Idiot* from the start. (2016)

LAURENT THIBAULT
MUNICH

After Bad Co had rehearsed for about 20 days and needed the studio, David had to leave. He told me, 'We're going to continue in Germany; I'm going to find a place and I'll call you so you can join us.' I didn't know what to make of that, but because his label hadn't paid, I kept the tapes and I didn't worry about it. One day, I was told, 'There you go, here's your ticket. You're going to Munich.' I had only one request: to be back in time for Jacques Higelin's album, which we were supposed to

When the musicians from Philadelphia decline to work with him at Sigma Sound in 1974, David Bowie has to bring in his own, foremost of whom is pianist Mike Garson.

The skin on his skeleton, his quivering nostrils, his brain taken over by bitter blades – he basically turned himself into his art. The height of the risks Bowie took equalled that of his ambition.

He'd painted white stripes on his sweater and trousers,
a style inspired by his Riot Squad days. He will recycle it for
the Outside tour, then in the video for 'Lazarus'...

With his haunting litanies, the Thin White Duke sings of magical
moments, dredging the ocean and bewilderment...

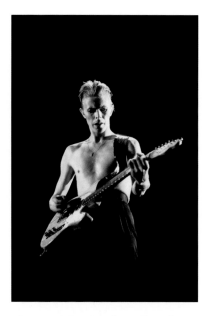

Photos from Paris in May 1976 confirm that Bowie played
a bit of electric guitar during the Station To Station tour.

Bowie manages to rehabilitate his mind and body, to reinvent
himself as an itinerant musician, insatiable and – whatever people
might think or say about him – open and receptive to others.

The covers for *The Idiot* and *"Heroes"* make reference to the work of painter Erich Heckel. In 1977, David Bowie visits Victor Vasarely. He'd fallen in love with his graphic art in 1969.

For the Isolar 2 tour, David Bowie decides to liven up the set list with a healthy dose (six songs!) of *Ziggy Stardust*, the album that widened his audience six years before.

David Bowie's life right up until the 1990s will never be simple, but Berlin will undeniably bring him some stability, as he hoped.

In early 1978, David Bowie agrees to play the role of a German officer in *Just A Gigolo*, in part because filming is taking place in Berlin. That same year, the 'lodger' will leave the city for good.

Since his fans and a whole generation of musicians are now paying tribute to him by imitating him, Bowie concludes that his handsome face and his incredible figure distort the relationship he has with his audience...

In Los Angeles in 1980, David Bowie performs two songs live on *The Tonight Show* with Johnny Carson... Wearing a red Harrington jacket, and with a similar haircut, he evokes James Dean.

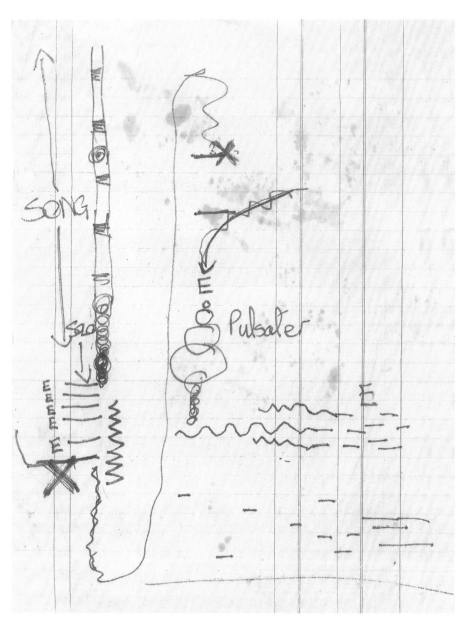

'I kept a genuine work of art: it's a drawing by David to illustrate the end of "Waiting For The Man". Instead of noting the chords, he drew the meaning of the song and I used that as my sheet music.'
Robin Lumley

start recording at the end of August. That's roughly when I stopped working with David. When I got back, somebody working at the *château* came to pick me up at the airport and told me that Jacques had started without me at la Bergerie. He thought that since I'd left with David Bowie, I wasn't coming back. I was pissed off because we had planned to work on *Alertez Les Bébés!* together...

We didn't go out much at Hérouville but, in Munich, we went to these little restaurants. David took me to some strange places, including an incredible bar full of businessmen with briefcases. We had to go down to the basement and there was a transvestite at every table, with outrageous make-up. Okay, so it was strange but not all that exciting. We sometimes went to the club in the Sheraton Hotel, but there were only Americans there – it was incredibly sad. And also to this restaurant at the top of a tower, and it revolved!

There's this really funny story about sauerkraut. One afternoon, David said, 'I'll introduce you to the most typical German dish.' We ended up in this restaurant and they brought us this amazing sauerkraut. And I said, 'But that's not German, that's Alsatian!' David grabbed his napkin and said, 'Fucking French people, you're all the same! You think you're the kings of the world, that you know everything. Everything that's good is French, and everything else is shit...' Corinne burst out laughing, and said, 'But it's true, sauerkraut is French!' We'd see Coco in Munich sometimes, then she'd leave again. Probably because she was dropping off David or something. Corinne was invisible from an artistic point of view. However, she was always there in terms of logistics, support and organization. As soon as we went out, she was there. All the meals were ready. But she never set foot in the studio.

You know, I worked with David Jones, not David Bowie. He didn't play that character in our sessions. In fact, when he listened to his songs, he'd refer to Bowie as 'he'. We walked around Munich quite a bit, but no one ever guessed who he was. As soon as he took his Bowie 'hat' off, he was unrecognizable. While French artists went to great lengths to be the same on stage and on the street, he was the opposite. Like other Brits, he needed to blend into daily life, to see, to feed himself, to get ideas... He knew how to be invisible. (2016)

LAURENT THIBAULT
AN ALL-TIME LOW

We're in Munich, we've finished Jim's record and David says, 'Laurent, if you hadn't been here, we wouldn't have done so well!' I don't know what to say. He explains,

'I'll be coming back to the *château* for my album. RCA really wants me to hire a producer. If it were up to me, we'd make it like we made *The Idiot*. But Tony Visconti will be there.' When they came back to the *château*, the *Rock&Folk* thing happened and David was fuming. I ran into Tony, who'd arrived just after them, on the stairs that went up to the studio. He was with Michel Marie, who said, 'There's Laurent!' And the first thing out of Visconti's mouth was, 'You're the one who played the bass on *The Idiot*?' I said I was and he continued, 'What's your instrument?' 'A Rickenbacker,' I said. And he was like, 'Oh, that's weird, because I mixed the record and the bass sounded like shit.' I thought that was weird because I felt like the sound had been good. What a great first meeting!

When we started the sessions for *Low*, I quickly realized that Tony had it in for me. It must have been because of *The Idiot* – he'd wanted to be at the console from the start rather than a French recording engineer... At that point, I didn't understand why he was saying he'd remixed the record, because I'd already mixed it and everyone had seemed happy with the result. Then Jimmy told me that at Hansa, Tony had been waiting for the tapes of *The Man Who Fell To Earth* so he could work on them, but they never arrived. They only had the ones of *The Idiot*. So Tony had asked to hear them, decided they didn't sound great, and offered to remix some of the songs. Iggy never told me which ones.

After all these years, I still think *The Idiot* was like an incubator for *Low*. But David had it released after, which was fair game! There are some songs that were planned for *The Idiot* but they didn't use them and they ended up on *Low*. Only their names have changed. Others didn't make the cut, like the one called 'Iggy Pop', which was really funny. In fact, they spent some time in Germany before making *Low*, to see what they could get out of the film soundtrack. And they erased some tracks, which was crazy! Michel told me that on one of the songs, the only thing they kept was the bass drum!

As soon as we started working with the musicians, we used the famous Eventide harmonizer that 3M, then based in Cergy-Pontoise, had lent us. At the beginning, we roughed out the tracks. Tony was doing what he had to do and David was muttering behind him, but not saying much. I didn't feel like opening my mouth either. Initially, I made a few comments, and Tony politely and kindly explained that my opinion didn't matter. Things weren't going well and David was well aware of it. A few days later, Tony told me, 'Okay, I'm the producer and you're the recording engineer. I don't need you. You can go. If there's a problem, I'll call you.' I looked at David but he didn't say anything.

Little by little, Tony found his bearings in the studio and called me less and less frequently. Michel was like, 'It's over, you're toast!' Mary Hopkin came to sing on the record and you could see David's face getting longer every day. Jimmy made himself increasingly scarce at sessions – I know because we spent a lot of time talking. Everything David had told me he dreaded was starting to happen. When Angie came by, they went to see *L'Homme Qui Venait D'Ailleurs*[33] in Paris. They were planning on taking the limousine – David dressed up as Bowie for the occasion and did the whole star routine. But they couldn't get the limo to start so they had to take a cab. It was a Peugeot 504 diesel I think, which was much less glamorous! (2016)

LAURENT THIBAULT
BEFORE AND AFTER ENO

Brian Eno didn't help my relationship with Tony Visconti. He got along well with David, which Tony didn't like. Before working on 'Warszawa', Eno said to him, 'Listen, when I record I prefer to be alone. Laurent will come to plug some things in for me and that's it.' I went up and Brian said, 'See, I do things in a simple way. I'm not a keyboardist, I play with one or two fingers. I'm going to record plenty of tracks… I have some idea of what I want to do, but it's not very clear – actually, I don't really know where this is going. So, plug me in, set up the tape recorder on a loop or show me how to do it.' I was the only one to hear that. Neither David nor Tony were there. Brian wanted to give them a finished product.

I think David really wanted to be involved in the production of *Low*. He cared about it deeply; it was visceral. He feared Tony would lead him towards something more conventional. Even outside the studio, the mood was uncomfortable. We'd lost the friendly atmosphere of *The Idiot*'s sessions, when we only listened to David. (2016)

LAURENT THIBAULT
THE END

How were they when they left Hérouville? Very upset. Tony wasn't talking to me anymore. About 75 per cent of what we recorded in France can be found on the album. The only track they did at Hansa was one of the few that survived from the film – 'Subterraneans', the last piece on the album. I also think they'd planned to add more vocals but, because of the deteriorating atmosphere, David kept it simple…

In fact, the record wasn't supposed to be called *Low* at first. It became *Low* because he wasn't able to create the record he'd wanted, so he got depressed. I saw his fights with Angie, the problems with Tony – they certainly weren't patting each other on the back... A real contrast to the recording of *The Idiot*. The only common point was Jimmy, although he stopped coming to the sessions. Even Corinne was absent. She didn't come to the studio during *The Idiot*, but we felt her presence. At the end, David had given me a big hug and they had written something in the guest book.

While they finished recording *Low* at the *château*, the friendly mood was gone. David wasn't cold with me but, without knowing exactly why, I could see something was off. I kind of felt like I hadn't been good enough, like I'd let him down. After that, I never saw or talked to David Bowie again. Pierre Calamel asked me to respond to Tony Visconti's accusations in *Melody Maker*. David ended up calling the *château* to ask us to stop arguing!

You know, I've always wondered about the day I dressed up as an Indian chief – when David left the room, did he call Tony to tell him he was working with incompetent people and to ask him to come to the studio? I was told that he didn't call Tony... But I guess I'll never know. At the time, the mood was weird, so David couldn't blame me for going a bit crazy. Especially because it didn't get in the way of our work. In the studio, a situation can escalate quickly for no obvious reason. We can be tired, exhausted even. There are days when we chase our tails and others when we work at speed. (2016)

CARLOS ALOMAR

To get the best out of them, you sometimes need to remove musicians from their usual environment. At the Château d'Hérouville, there was nothing else to do but music. No visits from friends, no phone calls, not a single shop nearby, no reason to go out. We didn't know anybody, we were in the middle of nowhere. We ate, we drank and we slept music. We could barely tell the difference between day and night. The concept of the first two albums of the trilogy partly came from the studio, an external element, but also from Tony Visconti's now-famous harmonizer, technology that was suddenly available to some producers. Personally, I don't really have a preference for a particular studio. I find them all fabulous because they are places where you can record! Let's not forget that, at the time, it was important for David to say, 'Fuck you!' to his record company. It was intentional, he was fed up! He was wondering, 'How much success do I have to have before I get the A-star treatment?'

Station To Station had been a successful album and David needed to be on the road. Don't forget, there was still a lot of tension between him and his former manager, and he had to make money. But, after a while, RCA asked him to come off the road, go back into the studio and do another LP. David told them, 'You've got at least two follow-up singles on *Station To Station*. Why am I killing my album? Why don't you release them[34]?' So there was a lot of frustration. He thought, 'Okay, they're only going to release one single from my next album and then they'll ask me to record another one.' Being a bit provocative, he decided to make a record with short songs on the A-side, which weren't exactly the right format to be singles, and instrumentals on the other side.

Here is what you have to know to understand David's humanity. You have to remember that, before the so-called Berlin period, I got called to help David with Iggy Pop. And we did *The Idiot*. And, at the time, David's need to help Iggy was what created this ability to extend himself, outside of himself, to his friend. And David was so involved he didn't just dedicate time to *The Idiot* and then *Lust For Life*, he went on tour with him for a little while. And Iggy was feeling great, he was getting his energy, getting his confidence back, and he didn't want to do drugs. Why? Because the music was so good that he didn't need them anymore. And actually, that was reciprocal because, for the *Low* album, who went into the studio with David? Iggy! And so the extension of David's humanity towards Jimmy and then, in return, Jimmy's humanity to David, that was crucial.

Most of the songs on *Low*, like those on *"Heroes"*, perfectly reflect David's state of mind at the time. He was saying, 'If you want to know me, know me during these periods – who I am is reflected in the music.' If you want a true human experience, don't look for anything bright and happy. That is not the human condition. The human condition is in the dark, electronic pieces, in 'Art Decade', in 'Weeping Wall'. These tracks hold a tapestry of emotion that is so dark... That's where the true human experience lies. (2016)

RICKY GARDINER

Although I have no evidence that he, alone, was responsible for my appearance on *Low*, I know Tony Visconti was involved. To tell you the truth, I didn't know much of David's music at the time, so I was neither a big nor a small fan of his music. Curiously enough, my memories of the *Low* sessions mostly involve the other musicians, although I do remember Bowie doing Marc Bolan impressions and his apparently spontaneous rendering of the vocal of 'Sound And Vision', which was most impressive! This album was the first part of a trilogy that is often called experimental but, for me, the recording was completely conventional... It was during the mix that things happened. You know, I found David very easy to work with and I enjoyed being part of this project. I'm not someone who looks back too much, but it definitely remains one of the high points of my career. (2016)

ROY YOUNG

I enjoyed the *Low* sessions, especially because the mood was very relaxed and I knew David dug my boogie-woogie piano style. That's what he knew about me, and what he wanted to hear. I have some very clear memories of the atmosphere at the *château*: it was a scorching hot late summer, there was a swimming pool and David's son was there. I babysat for him a little, to relieve the nanny. I remember that Zowie was running around with a boat and there was no way I was going to let him out of my sight – he could have easily fallen into the water.

I also remember getting Bowie stinking drunk! Don't forget he was quite a strange character and, personally, I was a bit of a boozer. I was downing gin and tonics. I usually kept my glass on the piano and someone would fill it when needed. David was in the control room, looking at me. Suddenly, he got up and said, 'Me too. I'll take a drink each time you do!' He was soon really drunk and I was a bit embarrassed because he quickly got to a state where he could barely stand up. Take after take, Tony Visconti kept asking him what he thought and at one point, we noticed he couldn't answer any more – he was fast asleep, sitting cross-legged in his chair. We put him to bed. A few hours later, there was a knock at my door. David wanted to drink more, and after that, he wasn't capable of getting back to bed. He ended up passing out on the stairs. The next day, I asked him how he was doing, and he pulled up his shirt to show me his bruises. The steps had made his back look like a keyboard!

The *Low* sessions weren't the only ones I did for him, but they were the only ones that were released. When I emigrated to Canada years later, I needed a recommendation letter and David wrote me one. Because the style of the trilogy was very different from what I usually did, I often wondered why he'd wanted me on the project. But something told me that his passion for Little Richard may have played a part in it. Knowing I was familiar with his repertoire and knowing my piano style, he may have wanted to come full circle. I still play in the style of Little Richard, because it's what I do best. Before they saw me on stage, a lot of Americans used to assume I was black... (2016)

GEORGE MURRAY

Dennis Davis and I were on the same flight from New York to Paris for the *Low* sessions. David's manager, Pat Gibbons, had given us $100 and the address of the studio with these instructions: 'Before leaving the airport terminal, change the dollars to francs and pick up your luggage.' In other words, no one is meeting you; you're on your own. 'Next, go out to the taxi line and give the cab driver the piece of paper with the address.' Okay, Dennis and I don't speak French, the cab driver doesn't speak English and we had no idea where this place is. We were very nervous during the ride, but relieved when, about an hour later, we arrived at the *château* and saw David and Brian.

These sessions were different from *Station To Station*'s because we were isolated. We were about an hour outside Paris, in the French countryside. There were no distractions, because there was nothing outside except farmland and a small village. There was the house for sleeping, eating and watching TV. I remember a French channel and an English channel...

When we played, we opened the shutters and really went for it, as loud as we wanted – there was no one around to hear! David was experimenting with electronics and synthesizers during these sessions. One day, Dennis, probably looking for something to do, turned on the drum machine and started playing along. It was a hot day, the studio shutters were open, and outside it sounded like there were three or four drummers banging at once!

The rhythm tracks on the A-side of *Low* are solid, real good work. 'Breaking Glass' was based on a riff Dennis showed me back home and we used it when playing with other musicians. I embellished it and modified it a little and we showed it to David during one of the sessions. He took it and wrote 'Breaking Glass' around it and he shared the writing credit with Dennis and me. I didn't realize how generous of him that was at the time, but I do now – I still receive performance royalties in the mail!

We recorded these tracks first and, when David thought he had enough material, Dennis and I left. I think he wanted to work independently with Brian and Tony. Unlike the *Station To Station* album, I heard less of the songs while I was there and the finished product surprised me. It was not what I expected. The music was more artistic, less commercial, and it took a while to get used to. But it also made me realize that David was more artist than rock star and I was part of something very different from what I had been accustomed to. I don't know if he was reinventing himself though... I thought he was taking the opportunity to write, record and produce what he wanted, as he was nearing the end of his contract with RCA. (2016)

MARY HOPKIN

I was at the Château d'Hérouville just outside Paris, where David, Tony and Brian Eno were recording the *Low* album. I was down in the dining room where we spent half the day. The phone rang and it was Brian up in the studio saying, 'Can you come up and do a little backing vocal?' So up I went. Brian and I went into the booth and he said, 'I've just got this little riff as a backing vocal to "Sound And Vision".' He sang it to me in falsetto and we recorded it in unison. It was the 'do-do-doo' part. People always assume it's just me, probably because he sang it in falsetto, so we sound alike.

It was meant to be a very quiet vocal, way in the background, but when the time came to mix it, David came into the studio and pushed the faders right up to the limit so it blasted out. I was so embarrassed, because I thought, 'Oh, it's so twee and awful.' It really was a twee little part! It was meant to be an echo in the distance, but David insisted on having it right up front. And it has since become an iconic theme, all thanks to Brian. (2019)

IGGY POP

I can recognize talent: we started working together because I needed a writing partner, and he was the best around. It's as simple as that. I had to get rid of Defries and company, and it made sense to go back through the door where I'd entered. That door was David. In the summer of 1976, we started recording *The Idiot* in France, then we went to Germany for a while. We continued to work on the record in Munich and saw the Black Forest in David's limousine, which was amazing. Then we mixed the album at Hansa with Tony Visconti. That fall, we decided to stay on a bit longer in Berlin. Before the fall of the Wall, the city was really 1920s. We lived like Berlin hippies – a bit dirty, bitter, always grumbling, our noses buried in books. It was a really exciting atmosphere.

I knew *The Idiot* and *Lust For Life* would be important records. I see them as David Bowie's dark side, revealed by Iggy Pop and enhanced by the combination of our personalities. The lyrics are my interpretation of life with him and mostly only talk about what we did. He was very inspired and the quality of his work pushed me to do better. His contribution as a musician shouldn't be overlooked either. He played some wild guitar there. The musical bond we established during *The Idiot, Lust For Life* and *Blah-Blah-Blah* was really strong, and I don't care if people think he was using my records to test the water before diving headlong into his.

As for the rest, especially his involvement, he had personal reasons for it, but it's good that he took those feelings and reflections with him. And because your book is about his music, you can understand that I'd rather not comment. Likewise, people often said I played a role, on *Low* for example. To confirm that would be very arrogant of me. The truth is, I just happened to be there. You know, what happens during the making of a record of course depends on the context, the entourage. I was there, as were Tony Visconti and Brian Eno, who of course played a greater role than me. Well, as you know, my voice can be heard on a couple of songs, but I didn't do anything spectacular! Some people have also said that, back then, David wrote songs not knowing whether they'd be for *The Idiot* or *Low*, but that wasn't the case. I can assure you he knew quite well what he wanted to keep for himself! I'm not saying he gave me his least good songs, but he kept the ones he thought would suit him best.

I have great memories of the Château d'Hérouville, which was a really funky place. I really enjoyed working with Laurent Thibault, a really great guy, as well as his wife who was an amazing musician, organist and impeccable singer[35]. Okay, so the French had this habit of not clearing the table after a meal, so the smells would linger throughout the day. Sometimes the equipment was unreliable, but aside from that, it was great. Jacques Higelin was also staying at the *château*, at la Bergerie. But he was rarely there. I knew his girlfriend at the time, Kuêlan Nguyen, who directly inspired a few of the lines of 'China Girl' – before I met her, the subject of the song was more geopolitical. (1999/2016)

TONY VISCONTI

David Bowie is never hard work for me. I love music with no boundaries. He is such an expert when he changes styles that I never think he is taking on a challenge he won't do well at. He always works quickly in the studio, because once he has a thought, he pursues it rapidly and I have always been able to match his speed. When he's done, he doesn't hang around the studio. What David can do in three hours, would take most musicians who compose in the studio days and days.

He's not a control freak at all. Say, with a guitarist, David would discuss in vague or specific terms what he is looking for, but then we expect the guitarist to take it to a more advanced level. The same applies to drummers, bass players, all kinds of musicians. David has a knack for selecting the right musician for the right job, which is a prerequisite for being a good producer. Once a musician is given the direction, both David and I are completely open as to what might come from the performance, especially if neither of us thought it up. We both love the 'zen' of creative accidents. Sometimes a musician might accidentally make a mistake, but with great panache – that mistake might be just wonderful and we use it! Most producers erase mistakes and want musicians to play exactly as they are told. David is not like that, although if he wants something played exactly so, he's not afraid to say that. Neither am I. From *Space Oddity* onwards, he and I have surrounded ourselves with excellent musicians who we respect and who we don't feel like muzzling.

Yes, initially, David was a bit thrown by what the harmonizer could do! We kept it in the mix, but sometimes he'd ask me to reduce the effect while he was working, especially on the snare drum. Dennis Davis found it very stimulating. He modified his playing depending on the sound alterations made by the equipment. He played around with it! (2015/2017)

MICHEL MARIE

I came to Hérouville because in 1967–8 I was in a band, Les Zorgones, with Laurent Thibault and some other friends from secondary school and uni. This was pre-Magma. We were a phenomenal flop. We were alternative... Which is a shame, because Aphrodite's Child played in the same style, and they had a massive hit with 'Rain And Tears'!

What can I say about the sessions with Iggy and Bowie? We were trying to do everything at once – it was chaos, but in a good way! Some days we recorded Iggy's album, and others we laid the foundations for David's. It was a permanent laboratory, not at all organized like with The Bee Gees, who I worked with later[36].

In the summer of 1976, things were already heating up at Hérouville because of financial issues; there were always problems like that during Laurent Thibault's time there, but he had nothing to do with it. The studio was bankrupt when he took it over so it belonged to the commercial court. The money went back to the court as quickly as it came in. It was a nightmare to manage because they had to pay the permanent staff. It wasn't like the madness and luxury of the old days when

Michel Magne was there. It had become complicated.

I was a studio assistant in those days but I ended up working the console with Tony Visconti! It seemed like Bowie, who was anything but stupid, had realized there were treasures in those dozen songs he'd co-written with Iggy and he wanted to use some of them... 'China Girl' was released again a few years later, sung by him... During Iggy's record, well...Iggy...we were often looking for him. He drank quite a bit and, when we couldn't find him, Bowie would lose his patience and to avoid letting the production money go to waste, he'd work on some of his own stuff. After a while, we always ended up finding Iggy. He'd be on his 37th beer and we'd have to make him sing! We'd sit him in a chair with a microphone in his face and headphones over his ears...

Tony Visconti is convinced he brought the Eventide harmonizer used on *Low* with him, but we already had one. The day we got it, we were all pretty excited. The *château* had some good equipment. Also, I loved the way Bowie worked. With him, the first draft was the one that mattered. In that sense, he was a true experimenter. He had some very interesting ideas, which he'd sometimes swiped from others, but which he'd develop really well. He never forced things: if he felt like it wasn't working, he didn't insist.

Tony, as producer and recording engineer, managed extremely well: he knew exactly where he was going, but sometimes it conflicted with David's direction. He was into more modern musical concepts. Outside the studio, Bowie was listening to Kraftwerk and Neu! for hours. Neu!, his favourite band at the time, were sort of pre-punk. That wasn't really Visconti's thing. There was a big difference between what Bowie loved and the life he led. He didn't seem to have any money issues, he could spend what we earned in a month in one night out, but he was fascinated by obscure things.

At Hérouville, breakfast was at 11am and served as lunch! David kept regular hours. We'd start after 10am, sometimes not until midday, but then we worked until late at night. There was a break for dinner and after that, we could go on until 3am. Sometimes we weren't working at all – we'd be chatting about this and that or we'd be waiting for Iggy to sober up and sing! Sometimes someone would say, 'Oh well, we can do this tomorrow, no worries!'

Personally, I don't remember there being any problems during recording. When the disagreements started, I'd gone on holiday. The only problems were over the food. But that rumour about Bowie's food poisoning is bullshit! On the other hand, even though we told him to be careful in the sun, we sometimes found him sitting on a chair by the pool, in the scorching sun, with sunburn! I think he even got sunstroke at one point, but his condition had nothing to do with the food. The doctor came and we were all laughing, because we were starting to get to know his character. We'd warned him, but he just did what he wanted, as an Englishman! I wasn't fooled: I could see everything that happened by the pool from my bedroom window. (2017)

EDUARD 'EDU' MEYER

I met David Bowie when he came to inspect Studio 2 at Hansa, on Köthenerstraße. He was very pleased when he saw the big Meistersaal with its special connection to the control room. Neither Tony Visconti nor David told me why they were in Berlin. They didn't talk about the Château d'Hérouville much, but it sounded like they'd had a problem with a journalist and too many flies on the food at breakfast! When they got to Hansa, some work still had to be done on 'Warszawa', 'Weeping Wall' didn't exist yet[37] and 'Art Decade' didn't have a cello part. Tony and David knew I was a cello player and they asked me to do an overdub. Tony wrote down a score for my part and I actually played eight distinct tracks on the song.

I thought the idea of having one side of the album with songs and the other with instrumentals was interesting. And I noticed that Brian Eno and David operated as good friends during the session and influenced each other while checking out the instrumentations. Brian Eno was the leader in decision-making. As for Tony Visconti, he was the wise guy in the sessions and, whatever he proposed, was done in one way or another. The final decision, of course, was directed by David himself. He knew what he wanted, nothing scared him – for example, he insisted on playing the vibraphone and xylophone parts himself. He was very hands on and worked with extreme diligence. Same for the vocals, which he recorded beautifully.

David and I got along well at Hansa, so we spent time together outside the sessions. In 1981, I was the recording engineer on *Baal*. Those songs were taped with classical musicians and arranged by Dominic Muldowney.

In June 1987, when he played at Nürburgring and at the Reichstag[38], David came to the studio again. To keep his band and technicians busy, since they were being paid, he organized a 'fake session' at Hansa 2. He'd decided to redo 'Time Will Crawl', a song on *Never Let Me Down*. When I told him I was ready to record his vocal, he smiled and started to explain – that we had just finished his fake session. No one asked me for the tape, so I took it home and kept it! (2017)

ALBERT KOSKI

In the early 60s, I was a photographer's agent and I spent a lot of time in London. I represented David Bailey, Brian Duffy, Terence Donovan and my job was to fight on their behalf to resolve their copyright issues – believe me, it wasn't easy. Today, as soon as a photo is printed in a magazine, the photographer receives something, but that wasn't the case back then. Almost every night in London we ate in the same place – an Italian restaurant in Soho where musicians used to hang out too. Later on, I was dating this girl whose sister was going out with Mick Jagger, so we saw a lot of each other. It was Mick who introduced me to David Bowie. We spent some nights together – let's just say they were a bit mad, wild, pretty crazy! As for me, because I liked girls, I didn't necessarily go along...

I ended up working in the music industry because in the early 1970s I had the opportunity to go on tour with T. Rex. It was hysteria. Every night, Marc Bolan played in front of 3,500 crazy girls and whenever he touched his hair, they'd throw their knickers at him! I thought that was interesting – not the knickers, but the idea of hiring a venue, doing some promotion, paying an artist, basically managing a whole show and earning money that way. I started in Paris, with a Temptations concert at Pleyel! The first one I did at the Pavillon de Paris was with Alice Cooper[39] and the stage set was only built the night before! David played there for the first time in 1976.

To be honest, we got along, but we weren't that close. Iggy Pop was there too, and I remember a dinner at the Élysée Matignon. It was me, David, Coco and Danièle Thompson. Iggy suddenly barged in on us in what you could call a rather advanced state and, from David's face, I realized things were going to get complicated. In fact, ten seconds later, Iggy started hitting on Danièle, who wasn't having any of it. I wasn't too happy about that, and when David took charge and showed him the door, Iggy left! Although honestly, I was a bit annoyed because I knew he was amazing. He came back, he apologized and we moved on. As for David, I know that in 1976, things were difficult for him in terms of drugs and all that, but from what I saw, I can say he knew how to behave. Not like Lou Reed, for example, who'd get into these sorry states... (2018)

MARC EXIGA

David Bowie was absolutely not a bling character! It might seem strange to point that out, but he was a very polite person. He knew how to behave. That said, he did bail on us once, at the last minute, when he refused to go on a Guy Lux show! I always thought our press officer had been a bit naïve to think David Bowie would commit to that kind of programme. But that time we rented the Paradis Latin, a cabaret next to the Jussieu Campus, after one of his concerts, he was happy to come!

Usually, in those days, people who worked in film thought people in the music industry were gypsies, second-class citizens. We were used to it and it didn't surprise us anymore... However, the film people wanted us to work with them on the launch of *The Man Who Fell To Earth* and the premiere in Paris because, for the French media, Bowie was just a musician and had no film career to speak of. So they asked us to send them journalists, but we weren't much more involved than that. And when *Just A Gigolo* came out, I don't think I was with RCA anymore. (2018)

KUÊLAN NGUYEN

During *The Idiot*, David Bowie seemed like a friendly guy, charming and complex. He was one of those very rare artists who was capable of forgetting about himself and taking an interest in other people. I have memories of that life – some are happy, others are troubled. He and Iggy Pop were good friends who exchanged books, music and spent their evenings together talking and laughing. I had the privilege of attending the sessions for 'China Girl' and the birth of some of the songs. When David covered it in 1983, it caused an ambiguity that didn't previously exist in my relationship with the two men. But I was relieved to learn that, by singing 'China Girl', David had been able to help Iggy pay his taxes and, ultimately, I was glad when such a brilliant and intelligent song became a big hit. Without David, and despite Iggy's extraordinary performance and the mysterious mood of the original recording, it probably would have stayed not so well known. In any case, I'll never forget this tribute of an American guy to a little Vietnamese girl still recovering from her war wounds[40]. (2014)

PIERRE CALAMEL

My job at Hérouville was to take care of finances and to make sure things ran smoothly. Meaning I had to make sure we got the money in exchange for the tapes! Sometimes it was hard, but we always got there in the end. One day, I got a call from Pat Gibbons, who booked the sessions for Bowie. Later on, he managed to kick our asses at tennis, even though he had a bottle of Jack Daniel's to hand in the corner of the court. We had a tennis court at the *château* that was made of concrete!

The funny thing is that they arrived in a big black Mercedes with a driver who looked like a Serbian war criminal, very strange, always dressed in black[41]. About 50 per cent of the time, that big car they kept in the courtyard just wouldn't start. Each time they were about to go somewhere, it was an anxious moment, and they often had to call the Aronde or the 403 at the last minute. Those were the only two taxis at Pontoise station. Bowie often had to go to the Hotel Raphael to meet some people for difficult conversations. He was always having to deal with these issues, and it made the atmosphere rather tense.

But, you know, David Bowie was a real gentleman. He never said anything mean to us. After the Plaza Athénée, which he'd had to escape because people were throwing themselves at his feet and asking him to walk all over them, he appreciated the *château*. The night he arrived, he came back down to eat some Camembert and ham. We talked for quite a while…

Sometimes I'd have to play security guard at night, going around with my flashlight to make sure everything was all right, that everything was in order. My big worry was that the female staff would let themselves be seduced by the guests. That wouldn't have been great for our reputation. One time, I found Bowie in his raincoat, a green waterproof like the ones British schoolchildren wear, its belt loose, wandering totally lost between the two wings of the *château*. I led him back to a path he recognized. He was haggard, definitely stressed out, not doing great. Anyway, he was a curious guy. He talked about himself in the third person! One time, I went into the control room as David was finishing something up and he said, 'He did a good job!' À la Alain Delon!

Initially, I had the feeling that Bowie had come for a sort of test with Iggy Pop. Laurent had managed to get his Breton drummer friend to play on *The Idiot*, but one of David's musicians replaced him. One time, I don't remember why, Bowie was very harsh with good old Carlos Alomar. Then there was the Edgar Froese incident. Not only did Bowie make him come all the way from Germany for nothing, but he left him baking in the sun all afternoon, sitting to attention, waiting. They brought him a parasol, gave him something cold to drink… They ended up walking him back to his car without him ever playing a single note.

At one point, Bad Company and Bowie were at the *château* at the same time together, but it wasn't exactly an *entente cordiale* between the two clans! I wonder whether Corinne Schwab didn't have something to do with it… When they ran into each other for the first time, one of the musicians said, 'Hello, I'm in Bad Company!'

and she said, 'Hello, I'm in David Bowie!' And that was it. Mick Ralphs was their only common link. He was a nice guy who'd played with Mott The Hoople. Mick got along well with David Bowie and his team. Other than that, they sat at opposite ends of the table. Luckily, it was beautiful outside!

When they came back in September, Visconti said he wasn't happy with what Laurent had done on *The Idiot*. Of course, he didn't take it very well. After Tony badmouthed the studio in *Melody Maker*, we were asked to give a response and I wrote a quarter of a page. I guess Tony doesn't have good memories of the *château*. That said, he didn't have an easy time with Bowie either...

When David left after *The Idiot*, he wrote a cheque for the amount he owed us. I gave him the tapes, but we soon realized it was a bad cheque. So we met with Jean-Claude Delaplace, our third partner, who was already struggling with the bank, and Laurent, who didn't know what to say. It felt like we didn't have a choice: as they were supposed to come back, we had to pretend nothing had happened. When they came back for *Low*, I remember we were all gathered around the pool. Bowie came over to me, shook my hand and the first thing he said, without specifying what he was talking about, was 'Thank you! Truly!' I realized he'd appreciated our attitude, and I knew full well that sooner or later, we'd get our money. (2017)

CHANCHAN VON SHOESHINE

When David Bowie came to Hérouville, I was 20 or 21 years old and I was a sort of coordinator. And I cut people's hair! I'd been doing it for a long time and because there was nothing anywhere near the *château*, I was the one who did everyone's hair! I did Sapho – I created all those extravagant hair styles she's had. Later, I worked in film and for fashion shows. I did Higelin's hair for the album covers of *Caviar* and *Champagne*. I also styled Catherine Lara's hair. She was the one who first called me Chanchan.

That summer, it was obvious that Bowie was trying to quit drugs. And Iggy wasn't taking much either, especially because David wouldn't give him a penny for it. You know, everyone put Bowie on a pedestal, treated him like a god. I wasn't interested in that kind of relationship and I think that might be why I was the only girl allowed to set foot in the studio! Bowie didn't like girls going up there. I didn't want to seem like a groupie.

Taking care of Bowie's entourage – with his musicians, his assistant Coco, his wife Angie who also dropped by – wasn't easy. He was the type to snap his fingers in the middle of the night and say, 'Okay, let's go record!' I'm sure he would have loved it if we all did his bidding... I was like, 'No! We need to have a different sort of relationship.' He liked that I stood up to him. There was no way he was going to walk all over me. From then on, we got along quite well and he nicknamed me 'Shoeshine' because I certainly wasn't shining his shoes! I thought that was funny. And then I just kept the nickname, to remind me of that time in my life. I became Chanchan Von Shoeshine.

David wanted to meet Claude Nougaro, whom he thought was a very interesting singer. Because I was good friends with his ex-wife and daughter Cécile, I told him I'd talk to them. Claude was on tour at that point, but David asked me to invite the girl and her mother to lunch with him. He was a really sensitive, warm person when you knew how to handle him. He was even nicer after his son Zowie arrived. There were other children; it was the holidays... Of course I also remember Bad Co, a band that took up quite a bit of space... Between the musicians and the roadies, I had my hands full! I thought their sharing the space with Bowie went quite well, even though they kept themselves to themselves. Then I had a little fling with Mick Ralphs... It could have lasted, but for me, it was too difficult to manage emotionally... Later, I remained friends with Paul Rodgers and his wife. You know, it was a magical time for me. Enchanting! (2017)

CÉCILE NOUGARO

I knew Chanchan, who was friends with my mum. She was a very colourful character, very friendly, and made a lot of noise with all her bracelets! She was disarming, and had a child-like side... In those days, I was living in the country, in Seine-et-Marne. I was going through adolescence and acting a bit like a savage... Without really knowing why, I really liked Bowie's voice. He sounded kind of like an alien to my ears. His music surprised me, as it probably surprised a lot of people, and when I listened to it, I felt a kind of fascination and also comfort. Hearing him made me feel like life could be breathtaking. To be honest, having grown up in an artistic environment, I always had a hard time with anything bland, so David Bowie's songs delighted me. Adolescence is a bit like spring and I discovered his records at a time when all my senses were awakening...

One day, Chanchan came over and, because she knew I was a fan of Bowie, who was recording at the *château*, she suggested I stop by sometime. It was the summer holidays, the weather was nice... My mother wasn't too keen, but in the end she agreed. I thought it was going to be an unbelievable experience, but actually, things just happened naturally. I was very shy and, at the thought of meeting him, I felt a surge of panic. I was dreading that moment because on top of everything, I didn't speak English very well... I remember that first lunch together. The amazing thing was that there weren't a lot of people at the *château* that day; everything was calm... Since childhood, I'd been used to seeing people fawning over my father and I absolutely did not want to come off as a starry-eyed girl who'd fallen for him. I didn't want to look at this artist, who meant a lot to me, all wide-eyed and with an inferiority complex. I kept to myself and I think that was the best thing to do. I knew that he'd chosen Hérouville to be left alone, and I wasn't going to ruin that.

A table had been set up in the garden, in front of the kitchen, and we ate outside. We were sitting next to each other and he immediately asked me what I liked about his music. I was into his soul period and so I talked to him about *Young Americans*, which I especially loved. I saw that he was very receptive and was making an effort to try to understand me. And so just like that, we talked about his records. Tony Visconti was there too, and he was very nice. The whole scene seemed somewhat surreal, but actually it wasn't, not all that much. You know, I had trouble associating David Bowie with rock music. When I was younger and listened to 'When I Live My Dream', I'd envisaged a sort of very curious troubadour travelling through time. In May, I'd seen him in concert at the Pavillon de Paris, the end of the Station To Station tour. Of course someone had taken me!

At the *château*, I felt like something was bothering him, he was quite subdued. Plus, I was there while Angie was visiting, so there was trouble brewing! The other funny thing was that my bedroom was in the right wing of the *château* and, at night, I could hear them playing. I could hear snatches of song. I clearly remember first hearing 'Nightclubbing' that way, as well as 'Warszawa'. And I remember Jacques Higelin; there was a fight one night... And Chanchan, who had a boyfriend in Bad Company. It was a hot summer, in every sense of the word. (2018)

PHIL PALMER

I'd just worked with Tony Visconti[42] and a week later, one night when I was still living with my parents, the phone rang. I went to get up, but my mum picked it up before me. She gently knocked on my door and whispered, so as not to wake my father, 'There's a certain Mr Bowie on the line for you...' I was sure someone was pulling my leg, but I got up anyway and it was really him! He'd heard good things about my guitar playing, he was in Germany recording an album with Iggy Pop, and wanted to know if I could join them as soon as possible. Two days later, I arrived at Musicland with my guitar.

I was impressed from the start: David Bowie looked strong, confident, like a sort of super hero. His mannerisms and the way he moved permeated the studio. His personality, combined with Iggy's, created a sort of explosive cocktail and it looked like they brought out the best in each other. In fact, their artistic bond was such that it wasn't easy to work alongside them. They were patient with me, but I didn't always feel super-comfortable around them. The sessions took place at night because the band Thin Lizzy used the studio during the day. In fact, I can't remember ever seeing David or Iggy in daylight hours!

When you got there, the first thing you noticed was Phil Lynott's bass guitar, his black Fender Precision with its chrome plate that still had traces of white powder on it! The first song I played on was 'Nightclubbing', and I served as a bit of a guinea pig for techniques that David later applied to *Low*. He'd describe a situation to me and ask me to react. Like, 'You're walking down Wardour Street... Play the music you hear coming out of the clubs you pass.' I tried to find out more by asking what key or genre I should play, but David made it clear that that wasn't important. So I recorded my parts for this song and for others, a bit on instinct, hoping it would work. They were usually happy after two or three takes and I realized it was okay when, after desperately trying to read their lips behind the glass to find out what they were saying, I would hear in my headphones, 'Okay, next song.' (2016)

PAUL RODGERS

Ah, that famous summer! When we arrived at the Château d'Hérouville, the studio windows were open and David Bowie was working in there with Iggy Pop. We heard bits of what they were doing... I immediately loved Bowie – he was always a gentleman with me. The first time I met him – it wasn't in a very musical setting – we were smoking the same spliff and I remember he pointed out that we could see sparks flying! I'm extremely touched to hear that I was one of his favourite singers... He wasn't just an innovator, he went deep! And we had something in common: we've both recorded with Queen! 'Under Pressure' is an incredible song. It seems simple, but it's very sophisticated.

Bowie and I both learned a lot from the blues because it's the most expressive musical genre. The blues don't cheat – on a purely sexual level, on a dance or emotional level – whether you're describing a problem with your girlfriend or something happy. You know, the Brits don't show a lot of emotion. When I was growing up in Middlesbrough in the 1950s, we tended to hide our feelings, but blues helped us lose our inhibitions and David did that better than all of us. (2017)

CHRIS KIMSEY

I'd never worked with Bad Company before *Burnin' Sky* and I'd never set foot in Val-d'Oise! I'd heard about the studio but, when I got there, I asked to change the monitors because I didn't like their sound. I got Bad Co to bring a pair of JBLs and I've still got them actually! It wasn't all fun and games though, because Paul Rodgers had some personal problems and was drinking a lot… Things would occasionally be thrown out of his bedroom window on the first floor! I remember we used to have the weekends off and Mick Ralphs was really good at arranging alternative entertainment. One evening, we all put on costumes and went to the Café de la Paix in Auvers-sur-Oise. Some were dressed as girls and jammed for most of the night for the people from the village, who were all invited. They played anything that came into their heads, except rock.

I do remember the tour manager, Phil Carlo, driving the band and me to Paris in a bright yellow Transit van. After spending the night at a club, we returned to Hérouville at daybreak and Simon Kirke, the drummer, was so drunk he had to crawl from the van to the *château*. No one could pick him up! The band definitely let their hair down on the weekends… And yes, it's interesting to note that we were in Hérouville at the same time as Bowie and Iggy Pop. I can't recall any friction with them, but they left soon after we arrived… Tony Visconti wasn't around, that I'm sure of… But I remember Laurent, he was a great guy. Of course, with an album title like *Burnin' Sky*, we couldn't help recording the sound of a storm and also the village church bell, which was really close! (2017)

BARRY GIBB

I never met David Bowie, which is one of my greatest regrets. We got into rhythm'n'blues around the same time he did, and 'Fame' and 'Golden Years' were quite successful. Really great songs. As a matter of fact, those songs, like the ones on *Saturday Night Fever*, were made under the influence of substances we probably abused! When we got to Hérouville we knew he'd worked there a few months before. English bands all told each other about that studio, because it made financial sense... David Bowie's death was a tragedy and, like it or not, it marks the end of an era. (2016)

THILO SCHMIED

It's hard to establish a timeline for the summer of 1976. The difficulty comes from the fact that, without ever officially admitting it, David and Iggy Pop did actually divide up the songs they were making between *The Idiot* and *Low*. Some only found their final place at the lyrics-writing stage. The few people who were there at the recordings can confirm that. We also have every reason to believe that some songs were written in Munich. Also, while Brian Eno's fans talk up his involvement in *Low*, Iggy's role in the making of *The Idiot* is sometimes downplayed...

Tangerine Dream is not a band that immediately springs to mind when we talk about David Bowie's time in Berlin, but Edgar Froese was the one who recommended Hansa to him in April 1976[43]. 10th April was a very important date for Bowie and his relationship with Germany. It was the day he met Romy Haag, who'd come to see him in concert at the Deutschlandhalle with a group of drag queens. They hit it off and spent the night at her club – then he ended up at her place! We all know the story now: the next day, David turned up very late to the first of his two shows at the Congress Centrum in Hamburg[44]. (2017)

JONATHAN WYNER

Of all the David Bowie records of Rykodisc's *Sound+Vision* reissue campaign that I've worked on as a sound engineer, *Low* is the one I consider the most sonically exciting, because of the way the technology infuses its sound in such an adventurous way. It's one of the greatest albums of all time; it changed the history of music. It's clear that starting with *Low*, David Bowie and his producer were saying, 'Okay, let's try this! People don't do this, and there's no reason why it should work, but we're going to give it a go, you never know.' (2017)

PETE KEPPLER

His body of work was so rich and varied that I have no idea what 'David Bowie's best record' even means. For fifteen years I sometimes thought it was *Low*, but I'm not sure I've ever listened to the B-side in its entirety! I love the A-side and knowing that Iggy Pop was in the studio with David makes it even more special. (2016)

SONJAY PRABHAKAR

A friend of mine works for an advertising agency and, when they took over the launch campaign for Sony's Xperia Z phone in 2013, they got in touch with me. Apparently, several people had already been asked to remix 'Sound And Vision', the song that was meant to go with the ad campaign, but no one had come up with anything satisfactory. Being a jingle writer, I was lucky enough to be offered this project.

Because they didn't want the original version, the task was simple: make something new with something old. So I received the separate tracks and what I discovered was madness. Obviously, it all sounded super vintage with that incredible, slightly disco groove played by the drummer. Because people in publicity are always in a hurry, I didn't have much time to remix it. They sent me everything on a Friday night and they wanted it back the following Monday. I received the tracks after going for a drink with some friends and then I did nothing but listen to that song until 4am. It was fascinating to be able to dissect a legendary recording!

To be honest, I'm not a Bowie fan and I didn't know much about his life or career, but when I opened the vocal tracks, I found out it was an incredibly sad song. I had a friend who was a super-fan, who lived quite a long way from me, but he wanted to come over! He told me where Bowie was at during that time – not in the best place, apparently. So, for the remix, I imagined Bowie, down in the dumps, showing Tony Visconti this song he'd just written. He played it for him on the piano, like that, just to get his opinion. I wanted to do it as if this version was a demo that had been rediscovered later. That's why I gave the piano a vintage sound. Of course, it's not the one that was on tape, which was more honky tonk. Because they'd told me to do whatever I wanted, I had someone play it again. I started by making two or three more conventional remixes before choosing a very stripped-down version, for which I hired pianist Rob Gentry. It's a very simple arrangement that goes back to basics in terms of harmony. And that's the one they kept!

Discovering the various elements of the multitrack tape was a fantastic experience. I don't know how it was made nor at what time of day those recordings were done, but, again, the groove is amazing. I listened to the tracks individually, and honestly, they were all crazy! Roy Young's piano, Mary Hopkin's voice and the descending synth line in the intro, it's mind-boggling in terms of music and the quality of the takes. (2016)

ROB GENTRY

I've been a David Bowie fan since I was ten years old! I still remember the moment I found the cassettes my dad had recorded from his vinyl albums, so I could listen on my Walkman – *Space Oddity*, my favourite tracks being 'God Knows I'm Good' and 'Letter To Hermione', and *Aladdin Sane*, with Mike Garson's piano solo on the title track, were among them.

To be honest, it was such a joy to be able to solo tracks and hear parts individually, especially how the various components interact to form the final mix. It's always surprising to hear things you're not expecting to hear. The original piano, for example, is a fairly busy, jangly part that I'd never really heard before. Many of the parts sound out of place when soloed, but once everything is in, it's fantastic. The harmonizer drum parts were very cool to hear solo as well.

The crazy thing about this song is that there's not that much movement harmonically but, as an arrangement and performance, it's certainly quite intricate. As our version was much sparser, we used a pedal note in the left hand to build the tension, and then some slightly different chord inversions compared with the original. Well, I was happy with the result, and I heard that the man in question also liked it. (2016)

GREG MCLEOD

This animated film about the recording of *Low* at Hérouville, with David Bowie, Tony Visconti and Brian Eno, that has gone viral on YouTube, was commissioned by Adam Buxton[45], who was doing at talk at the V&A museum as part of the *David Bowie Is* exhibition. Adam and I grew up listening to Bowie and we still love his stuff. Adam is a massive fan and a bit of a Bowie geek! And he imitates his voice incredibly well. He did all three voices in the film and managed to capture Bowie's perfectly.

Low is one of Adam's favourite albums and the unique context of its making provided the necessary material for the dialogue. Personally, I never met David Bowie, but he was a very visual person and very distinctive. So animating him was quite easy. The deadline was very tight, so I animated this in double-quick time.

I didn't get as many jokes and visuals in as I would have liked. However, I was really happy with the end product and I loved working with Adam. (2016)

RYUICHI SAKAMOTO

Low and *"Heroes"* are my favourite Bowie albums. They both embody the perfect balance between the pop side he mastered so beautifully, his spirit of experimentation, his intelligence and his darkness. They're also the best collaborative recordings ever by Brian Eno, who has released quite a few! You can hear their true friendship on these adventurous records. They changed the course of rock and popular music as a whole.

You know, I think artists should always try to surprise themselves rather than surprise their audience. That's the difference between *Low* and *Tin Machine*. (2016/1990)

DAMON ALBARN

Low is my favourite David Bowie record. Too much modernity is rarely a problem... I sometimes feel like it's mostly musicians who like our album *13*. It's as if, for them, the debate was elsewhere. I spent some unforgettable moments with members of the band Can, who urged me on, arguing that Blur was just the beginning for me. The further I go, the more I realize how far I have to go. You know, I thought I was going mental when I heard that Bowie really loved *13*. He left me two messages, but I never took the time to answer. It's shameful! (1999)

IAN MCCULLOCH

With Echo & The Bunnymen, we always tried to avoid falling into time traps with the sound. For instance, we were always very cautious when it came to using certain snare drum sounds that could have dated our music. Will Sergeant, our guitar player, fought hard against that. Sometimes we fell in love with particular sounds, especially those on *Low* by David Bowie, but we never wanted to reproduce them for fear of being laughed at later... I followed the artists I love and I still enjoy watching them evolve, change. Maybe I'm a bit naïve. As a kid, I dreamed of singing, like David Bowie, but I never thought for a second I could get paid for that! (2001)

NICK LOWE

Bowi, my 1977 EP, was an allusion to David Bowie who'd just released *Low*, the first album of his trilogy. To be honest, even though I have a lot of respect for him as an artist, I've never been a big fan of his music. It was a dig, but nothing mean[46]... (2011)

ANTHONY AGNELLO

Yes, I developed products for Eventide, but that doesn't mean I can comment on how people used them! I imagine Tony Visconti can speak about the H910 in detail. The gear that I designed was used by many producers and recording engineers, but I never tried to discover where, when or how. What I do know was that Tony's use of it on *Low* was obvious, while sometimes my harmonizer was used in barely perceptible ways. I know Tony Visconti, but I never met David Bowie... (2018)

1. David Bowie's words from 1977 that appear in this chapter and the next one were collected by Philippe Manoeuvre and Jonathan Farren. The entire interview was published in issue 128 of *Rock&Folk*.

2. Since we know it took place after one of his concerts in Paris, and David Bowie was at the Alcazar on 18 May, the famous private party at l'Ange Bleu, near the Champs- Élysées, where Ralf Hütter and Florian Schneider (of Kraftwerk) received a standing ovation, probably happened on 17 May.

3. KCP was the company of concert promoters Albert Koski and Christophe Cauchois. They put on shows at the Pavillon de Paris between 1975 and 1983. The Pavillon was then replaced by Le Zénith.

4. Throughout the European tour, David Bowie performed in venues of various capacities, with between 5,000 and 30,000 seats, that weren't always full.

5. As the preamble to this chapter suggests, the adventures of David Bowie at the Château d'Hérouville in 1976 were marked by confusion from the beginning. While the author presents the version of events recounted by Laurent Thibault, it has sometimes been said (and written) that in May, having learned that the Thin White Duke was being harassed by fans in Paris, one of the managers at Hérouville phoned him to offer the *château* as a refuge. Logically, RCA France, with whom Bowie had a cordial relationship, could have also taken care of this hosting issue.

6. When Bowie was on the road in those days, the convoy was made up of several vehicles, including a Ford Transit that carried his gear

and a trunk containing the dozens of books he refused to be parted from.

7. Obviously no relation to Iguana, the Southampton band mentioned in the previous chapter.

8. Tony Visconti also played a non-musical role that summer. With David Bowie distracted by legal problems, Tony was usually the one to cheer him up and get him back on track with his art. Visconti was the co-producer of the famous trilogy, a term that will be overused after the release of *Lodger*, its third instalment. The author prefers the term 'European trilogy' to 'Berlin trilogy' because the Château d'Hérouville is in France and Mountain Studio in Switzerland.

9. Located in the basement of the Arabella-Hochhaus building in the Denning neighbourhood, this studio, which opened in the late 60s (and will close in the early 90s), was the one where Marc Bolan and T. Rex recorded most of *Zinc Alloy And The Hidden Riders Of Tomorrow – A Creamed Cage In August*, their last record co-produced by Tony Visconti. T. Rex were probably among the first English-speaking clients of this studio, where recording engineer Reinhold Mack trained before recording Deep Purple, Electric Light Orchestra, Queen and Sparks. David Bowie and Iggy Pop's sessions at Musicland won't be mentioned on the cover of *The Idiot*.

10. In 1976, with *The Idiot* and, surely, *Low* in mind, David Bowie reportedly visited Conny Plank's studio at an old farm in Wolperath, about 25 miles east of Cologne. Plank, who thought excessive drug use was incompatible with making a record, reportedly refused to work with Bowie for that simple reason. So it's

unlikely that he and Eno managed to record any demos there before deciding to work at the Château d'Hérouville.

11. In the title song of their sixth album, to be released in March 1977, Kraftwerk will pay tribute to David Bowie and Iggy Pop ('From station to station/Back to Düsseldorf city/ Meet Iggy Pop and David Bowie'). They probably met up with them on 8 April during the Station To Station tour's stop in their city.

12. When David Bowie and Iggy Pop were there, Hansa still had two locations and there were several studios at the second one.

13. The model that Tony Visconti used was designed by Tony Agnello, chief engineer and co-founder of the American company Eventide, one of the first to manufacture digital sound processors which, at the time, still contained plenty of analogue components. The name of this harmonizer released in 1975 is a tribute to The Beatles song 'One After 909'. In the late 1980s, David Bowie will ask the post-production team on *The Hunger* to use Tony Visconti's H910 to alter his voice in the film.

14. Michael Rother is interviewed in the following chapter because all signs suggest David Bowie had wanted him to play on *"Heroes"*. However, he claims to have received phone calls from Bowie in 1976 as he was finishing *Low*. Would David have phoned Rother several months before starting sessions for *"Heroes"*? It wasn't exactly his style – he usually got a team together at the last minute – but of course it's possible.

15. Two other albums Brian Eno worked on that David Bowie liked very much are *(No Pussyfooting)*, recorded with guitarist Robert

Fripp and released in 1973, and its successor, *Evening Star*. Apparently, there was also talk of Brian Eno going to the Château d'Hérouville during *The Idiot*, along with Robert Fripp.

16. According to Laurent Thibault, the Chamberlin on *Low* was bought especially for David Bowie and cost the studio a fortune. The instrument, nicknamed 'le chant de Berlin' ('the voice of Berlin') that summer, will later be used by the band Magma, then sold in the mid-1980s.

17. Welsh singer Mary Hopkin, who was very popular in the late 1960s, notably thanks to her cover of 'Those Were The Days' (an adaptation of a Russian song produced by Paul McCartney). The original song, with its Russian lyrics by poet Konstantin Podrevsky (quite different from the English lyrics later penned by Gene Raskin for the English hit) was banned in the USSR in 1927 for its nostalgia. The music was composed by Boris Fomin, who worked in the musical tradition of *Russian romance* – which was itself denounced as a 'counter-revolutionary' genre by the All-Soviet Conference of Musicians in Leningrad in 1929. Hopkin was married to Tony Visconti at the time and went to the Château d'Hérouville that summer with their two children. Jessica was not even three months old and Morgan (born Delaney), wasn't yet four. A few notes played by Morgan (with some vigour) on the studio piano reportedly inspired Brian Eno to write the start of the melody of 'Warszawa'. Morgan and Jessica, who was a member of the band Holy Holy, are both professional musicians.

18. While in Berlin in 2018, Brian Eno turned down an invitation from Thilo Schmied, the director of Berlin Music Tours, to visit Hansa again. Born in East Berlin the year *Aladdin Sane* came out, Schmied has worked in several different musical fields. He's an expert on the Berlin scene and, since 2005, has been organizing visits to locations related to David Bowie (and Iggy Pop), including the Hansa Tonstudios. Thilo provided a lot of information for this chapter and the next.

19. Contrary to another rumour, this song based on a piano melody found by David Bowie has always been attributed to him alone, and never to Brian Eno as well. However, Eno is responsible for a good part of the instrumentation. 'Warszawa' is the only piece on *Low* co-written with Eno.

20. Most in-depth books published about David Bowie mention the similarity between the melodies of 'Weeping Wall' and 'Scarborough Fair'. However, it would be grossly inaccurate to attribute the song to Simon & Garfunkel, since it's a traditional folk song whose lyricist and composer remain unknown. Like the hundreds of thousands of British children born soon after the war, David Bowie probably first heard this Medieval ballad sung by Audrey Coppard on her 10-inch record *English Folk Songs*, released in 1956. This doesn't mean Bowie didn't love Simon & Garfunkel, whose song 'America' he will cover with humility and panache in 2002 at the tribute concert in New York for the victims of September 11. The band 1-2-3 played 'America' (and 'The Sound Of Silence') on stage from 1967 onwards. It's also interesting to note that some Anglophone authors, looking for real or imagined parts Bowie took from English and American songs, have not always spotted those taken from French songs. During the ten or so weeks he spent in Hérouville in 1976, David Bowie could very well have heard 'D'Aventures En Aventures' ('From Adventure to Adventure') by Serge Lama, whose vocal

melody is strangely similar to that of 'Tiny Girls', which Bowie composed for *The Idiot*.

21. While visiting David Bowie in Switzerland for the first time in the late 80s, Reeves Gabrels will see a framed letter from RCA hanging on the wall, sent after the label had listened to *Low*, registering their disapproval. Some have taken this to mean that the label refused an initial version of *Low* and Bowie reworked it to their taste. However, this is not the case. There was only ever one *Low*: the one that disappointed the label but is now considered to be one of the most important albums of the second half of the twentieth century.

22. Released in June 1977, the single 'Be My Wife' will be conspicuous by its absence from the charts on both sides of the Atlantic.

23. This is also the title of a semi-autobiographical novel Jack Kerouac published in 1958.

24. In his autobiography, Tony Visconti will explain how he decided to take the famous room David Bowie refused at the Château d'Hérouville, which was allegedly haunted and had a corner that seemed to suck in light and heat. He thought it could have spawned the ghosts whose spirits wandered the halls. However, Tony didn't have any surprise encounters there! In the same vein of delirium, when *Low* came out, some people said they could hear demonic incantations in the vocals of 'Warszawa'.

25. *The Idiot* will stay in the British charts for three weeks and climb to Number 30. In the US, it will settle for a more modest Number 72.

26. Yet more proof that David Bowie never missed the chance to borrow from works he liked, the name *The Idiot* has several origins. First, we know that Bowie discovered Fyodor Dostoevsky's book in 1968, and that he loved it. Later, he saw a painting by German painter and sculptor Hanno Edelmann called *Der Idiot*. The character depicted in it reminded him of Iggy Pop, so he thought this would be a good title for the record. In the end, at David Bowie's suggestion, Iggy posed like the character in Erich Heckel's painting *Roquairol* for the album cover and, in fact, they'd initially thought of using the painting itself. Heckel was one of the founders of the Die Brücke movement and Bowie was fond of his work.

27. In 2013, Sony will use 'Sound And Vision' for a television ad for one of its phones. Sonjay Prabhakar will remix the song and have Rob Gentry replay the piano. That same year, the McLeod brothers will make a hilarious animated short based on the 'Warszawa' recording sessions at the Château d'Hérouville.

28. It's scandalous, but Parlophone has still not reissued *Low* in the form of a box set like *Station To Station*. This shows the width of the gap between what the public would like to buy and what those in charge of David's catalogue think should be released – will we need quite so many 'derivative products' from *Space Oddity* in 2019? The Rykodisc reissue of *Low* in 1991 will add unreleased pieces 'Some Are' and 'All Saints' as well as a dreadful remix of 'Sound And Vision' by David Richards. Bowie apparently considered 'Some Are' the best track among the ones he'd scrapped from the original trilogy. It was written by Bowie and Eno, but its recording, like that of 'All Saints', is impossible to date. It has a lot in common with 'Warszawa' (especially the vocals) and will also appear

on *iSelect*, the compilation David Bowie will conceive in 2008. 'Some Are' will be the title of the second movement of *'Low' Symphony* by Philip Glass in 1993. 'All Saints', a noise factory with krautrock accents, also written by Bowie and Eno, is more dispensable. In 2017, the box set *A New Career In A New Town (1977–1982)* will unite the three albums of the trilogy (*Low*, *"Heroes"* and *Lodger*) and also feature the double live album *Stage* and *Scary Monsters*.

29. Some music journalists believe that David Bowie didn't stay at the Plaza Athénée in May 1976 but at L'Hotel, 13, Rue des Beaux-Arts in Saint-Germain-des-Prés. However, it is possible that he stopped by the hotel on Avenue Montaigne while in Paris. Most of his team was staying at the Relais Bisson, 37 Quai des Grands-Augustins.

30. Probably the Odyssey model.

31. Actually, there is a harmonica on *Low*, played by David Bowie on 'A New Career In A New Town'.

32. 'Direct instruments' are plugged 'directly' into the mixing desk. In those days, guitars were usually recorded using a miked amplifier.

33. The French title for *The Man Who Fell To Earth*. It was a private screening because the film didn't hit the cinemas until the following year.

34. In fact, RCA got four singles (out of six songs) from *Station To Station*. 'Stay', the third, came out in April 1976 before the end of the Isolar tour, but didn't do well in the charts. 'Wild Is The Wind' will be released in 1981.

35. Iggy Pop is referring to Jacqueline Thibault, Laurent's wife at the time, a musical artist also

known as Laurence Vanay. She recorded at the Château d'Hérouville and lived and worked there, in all sorts of roles, over the course of a decade. Jacqueline Thibault has mixed with most of the English-speaking musicians who stopped by the studio, and therefore David Bowie. In the booklet of *Galaxies*, her first album, which Lion Productions recently reissued (along with her whole calatogue), she says she signed a confidentiality agreement with Bowie in 1976, which forbids her from talking about anything to do with his time at the *château*. This practice will go on throughout the next four decades: before *The Next Day* and *Blackstar*, David Bowie's last two albums, his musicians and technicians will have to sign a similar contract. The song 'Mon Vaisseau De Pierre' ('My Stone Ship'), on *La Petite Fenêtre* ('The Little Window') is Jacqueline's tribute to the Château d'Hérouville.

36. Contrary to myth, The Bee Gees did not go to the Château d'Hérouville in early 1977 to record the soundtrack of *Saturday Night Fever*. They were there to mix a live record, but technical difficulties led to them composing some songs that Robert Stigwood, their manager, would later suggest they use for the film. Interviewed by the author in 2017, Blue Weaver, the band's keyboard player, said, 'Honestly, the studio was in terrible shape. The equipment was poorly maintained. For example, we could only use certain channels on the mixing console, which were the only tracks that worked well. The others had a muffled sound because of the worn-out reading head. We got some equipment shipped from Miami. So, while we were waiting to mix the live album, we wrote some songs because we didn't have anything else to do. The Gibb brothers often sang in the stairwells because they loved the sound of this natural reverb. The first song born

there was "If I Can't Have You". Almost none of the soundtrack was completed at the *château*. While "Night Fever" was indeed recorded there, as well as some other demos, the famous versions were almost entirely re-done in the US. The final songs sound very different from what we recorded in France.'

37. This statement contradicts Brian Eno's plausible account from June 1978 (as told to Glenn O'Brien from the *NME*), that 'Weeping Wall' was started by David Bowie, for the soundtrack of *The Man Who Fell To Earth*, in Los Angeles.

38. David Bowie will perform at Platz der Republik in Berlin, outside the Reichstag (where the Reich assembly sat), on 6 June 1987. Contrary to many accounts, he will play on the opening night of a three-day festival to celebrate the city's 750th birthday, not at the end. Eurythmics and Genesis will headline on the following two days. On a personal level, the show will be very emotional for Bowie because, a decade before, he'd lived nearby. Part of the audience will stand on the other side of the Wall that night, so David Bowie will send them a message in the form of a poignant version of "Heroes". The Berlin Wall will fall two years later.

39. This concert took place on 16 September 1975.

40. This interview comes from *David Bowie Ouvre Le Chien*.

41. This was Tony Mascia, David Bowie's driver and bodyguard, who played exactly the same role for Thomas Jerome Newton in *The Man Who Fell To Earth*.

42. In the interview he gave for this book, Phil Palmer said he thought Tony Visconti suggested his name to David Bowie for *The Idiot* sessions. Although it's mentioned in several books (but not in Tony's), this information is to be taken with a pinch of salt for at least two reasons. The first is that Visconti worked in Berlin, on the (re)mix and possible last takes, after Palmer did. However, Visconti could have recommended Palmer to Bowie when he called him to ask him to come and mix the album. The second is that there is a lack of clarity surrounding Palmer's first collaboration with Visconti and his alleged recommendation to David Bowie. In the same interview, Phil Palmer said he played on an album by Ralph McTell at Good Earth, produced by Visconti, before he was asked to work on *The Idiot*. But according to the liner notes, McTell's records that feature Tony's name (*Not Till Tomorrow, Easy*) were recorded before he started his own studio, and the first one that Phil Palmer played on (*Slide Away The Screen*) was released in 1979.

43. In a rare interview about David Bowie with *Berliner Zeitung* in January 2013, Froese will say he'd also advised Bowie on his detox treatment, which he started in earnest in the autumn of 1976, after moving to the Schöneberg district of Berlin with Iggy Pop and Coco Schwab. At first, they lived at Schlosshotel Gerhus, in southwest Berlin, not far from the Grunewald forest.

44. According to members of the audience, David Bowie gave (at least) the first of these two concerts under the influence of alcohol. He introduced Dennis Davis twice and said he thought he was playing in a hospital. Even more shocking was when he went to sit among the crowd for a few minutes to listen to his band. The audience was speechless!

45. British comedian, author and radio host Adam Buxton is well known as a Bowie geek. Buxton created *Bug*, a series of funny but educational shows celebrating the wonderful world of music videos. His *Bug: David Bowie Special* is still a big hit on both sides of the Atlantic and includes this animated film about the making of *Low*. Buxton has also worked with Chris Salt on other shorts. In the hilarious *Cobbler Bob*, Bowie appears in the form of a Lego mini-figure (as does Angie).

46. In 1978, Nick Lowe released 'I Love The Sound Of Breaking Glass', co-written with two members of The Rumour, which a lot of people saw as a parody of a song on *Low*. It came out as a single and appeared on his LP *Pure Pop For Now People*. Indeed, 'I Love The Sound Of Breaking Glass' does seem to make reference to two songs from the A-side of *Low*.

"HEROES" DAVID BOWIE

RCA International

DAVID BOWIE
heroes

RCA

"HEROES"

RCA – 14 OCTOBER 1977

LUST FOR LIFE (RCA – 1977)

'Never touch your idols: the gilding will come off on your hands.'
(GUSTAVE FLAUBERT, *MADAME BOVARY*, 1857)

'Since *Ziggy Stardust*, I no longer think I'm the king of the world. Ziggy was a bit of a super-god. But turning 30 was the best thing that happened to me. Everything changed. All of a sudden, I was no longer in the grip of that furious ambition that had tormented me as a young man. Now when I make a record or something else, it's for my own pleasure. Whatever the result, pfft... it doesn't matter.

'I think most rock stars are deeply childish. I think I have an advantage: I never thought of myself as a rock star. David Bowie is David Bowie. I was always happy to be the outsider. I never could have tolerated living as a rock singer! It's all a superficial clique, based on knowing glances; not to mention that the concept of the world of the rock star is totally restrictive. What do they know about what happens outside of rock? Personally, in private, I've never been interested in rock. I only listen to it for analytical purposes, to look for ideas; I don't particularly enjoy it. That's it. I think fans feel an excitement I no longer experience. Of course I still think rock is an interesting phenomenon and an excellent way to work. But if I'd been a better painter, I would have done that. Only I wasn't good enough! So I thought, "Rock seems to be the new way to express ideas. Interesting." And from there, I used it to express mine. I wouldn't give my life for rock'n'roll. No way!

'I love Berlin because of the friction. I've written in all the Western capitals and I got to a point where there was no friction between these cities and me. Things would start to get nostalgic, vaguely decadent, and I'd leave for another place. Now I simply can't write in Los Angeles, New York, London or Paris. There's something missing. And Berlin has this strange ability to make you write only important things. Either that, or you shut up and don't write anything at all. [...]

'Sometimes I feel like a song lacks integrity. So I give it another chance by speeding up or slowing down the tempo, or stripping down the arrangement. In the past, I'd often make this type of decision based on Brian Eno's advice. One time, we listened to some records at the wrong speed, just to see how they sounded. I remember playing him a 1932 78rpm by the Berlin Symphony Orchestra at 16rpm: the *Tannhäuser Overture* from Wagner's opera. It was just magical! A new kind of ambient music. And we said, "Let's copy that with our synthesizers!" In the end, we never did. It's a typical example of a piece that disappeared before it even existed!'

DB (1977/2003)

Having never been in David Bowie's head – some kind of hard drive with almost infinite storage capacity, which couldn't be reformatted because of time, fragmentation and the volume of information on it – it's hard to know what pact he had made with himself when he decided that the best thing he could do in early 1977 was to go on tour as a lowly backing musician (keyboard player) for Iggy Pop. Bowie's life right up until the 1990s will never be simple, but Berlin will undeniably bring him some stability, as he hoped, until March 1978 when he embarks on a world tour.

In Berlin, he will be practically anonymous, enjoying Iggy's company and being looked after by Corinne Schwab. He will dedicate his time to his favourite activities: reading, painting, visiting bookshops and art galleries. He will also enjoy antique shops and museums. The Brücke-Museum is only 30 minutes away by bicycle from 155 Hauptstraße and Bowie will regularly use this mode of transport, which is ideal for capturing the mood on the street, both literally and figuratively. During the day, without attracting any attention, he will sometimes shop at KaDeWe department store, then at night he will give himself up to Berlin's many temptations. Not exactly ideal for detoxing, they will give him the morale boost he needs. Cafés, beer halls, discotheques, gay clubs and cheap or smart restaurants – the list of establishments he patronizes at this time is as long as Iggy Pop's right arm on the cover of *The Idiot*. And so, as he wanted to get better, his decision to jump back into the lion's den of touring, going from city to city in the UK and USA and mixing with the media and other parasites, did seem like a strange idea. But, in truth, David Bowie will find salvation in workaholism. He knew full well how idleness could worsen his still precarious state.

In terms of record releases, 1977 was David Bowie's busiest year: in addition to the first two volumes of his European trilogy (*Low* and *"Heroes"*) he generously contributed to Iggy Pop's first two albums *The Idiot* and *Lust For Life* (which he produced), co-writing most of the songs. While he'll make a point of telling the media that he was not managing Iggy, Bowie will 'advise' his friend at least until the summer of 1977. And if he agreed to play live with Iggy, it wasn't just to keep an eye on him, but because he really believed in his art and wanted people to know. Last, but not least, it's thanks to Iggy Pop that David Bowie started flying again – he would have done (almost) anything for him.

Tony and Hunt Sales, the sons of Soupy Sales, a popular comedian and TV personality in the US in the 1950s, met Iggy Pop in Los Angeles in 1974, when he was hanging out with Ray Manzarek of The Doors. The year before, as the rhythm section of Utopia, Todd Rundgren's prog rock band, the brothers had been introduced to Bowie at Max's Kansas City and had vaguely stayed in touch with him. When Bowie tells Iggy he should ask them to play bass and drums in the band that will accompany him on his upcoming tour (thirty or so shows are planned between 1 March and mid-April), Iggy agrees wholeheartedly[1]. He is equally happy that Ricky Gardiner, who did a great job on *Low*, will join them on guitar.

After a few days of rehearsals at the end of February, in the studio[2] of keyboardist Peter Baumann (founding member of Tangerine Dream, which he'll leave that year), Iggy Pop and his musicians perform at the Friars in Aylesbury (at Vale Hall), another of David's suggestions. It is the first in a series of six British shows, the last two of which, sold out, will take place at the Rainbow. In London, the new wave movement is in full swing and Bowie catches up with Marc Bolan. A while later, the two of them will record a few demos, including 'Madman', which will do the rounds as a pirated single until 1979, when the band Cuddly Toys cover it. The Vibrators – whose first album, *Pure Mania*, will be released that June – open for Iggy and make the grade in front of an audience as punk as they are.

David Bowie has just turned thirty, an age these young musicians with spiky hair and dangling safety pins consider ancient, and prefers to stay in the background, stage left, backing up Iggy, whom everyone calls the godfather of punk. Once outrageous, he now masters the art of blending into the times: his record sales are far from remarkable, but he maintains his reputation as a whirlwind influencing the times instead of experiencing them. Backstage after the shows, young bands rush to receive his blessing as much as Iggy's. Among them are Johnny Rotten, Johnny Thunders, Brian James and Howard Devoto, the frontman of Magazine.

Organized by Bowie's tour people, the journey continues in Canada and on to the US in mid-March. Having more or less conquered his fear of flying, Bowie takes the plane again. The next time he will take a trip by sea will be simply for the pleasure of it. In New York, Bowie runs into some old acquaintances – he goes to a Patti Smith concert with David Johansen and Cyrinda Foxe, and some of The Rolling Stones, including Ronnie Wood, will be at Iggy Pop's show at the Palladium. He is happy to be back in the city, where he is planning on recording soon. They give one performance after another in medium-sized venues that are easy to fill – the tour stops at the Tower Theater in Philadelphia and the Civic Auditorium in Santa Monica. Blondie (led by Chris Stein and Debbie Harry) open the shows for them, though their set isn't to everyone's liking. The American audiences appreciate Iggy's repertoire, more than half of which is borrowed from The Stooges, interspersed with songs from *The Idiot*. The band performs valiantly and, in addition to a few songs from Iggy's next album, they sometimes play 'Fame'. In Cleveland, the band Devo, from nearby Akron, give a demo tape to David Bowie, hoping he'll be interested in producing their first LP. He will love their art punk and will describe them as 'three Enos and a couple of Edgar Froeses' to Ian Birch in 1978.

Iggy Pop and his musicians are invited to appear on some television shows, and they perform two songs ('Funtime' and 'Sister Midnight') on *Dinah!* in Los Angeles in April. During the programme, broadcast in May, Iggy and David give a surreal interview in which they refer to punk as nihilist rock. Bowie, Iggy Pop and Coco Schwab then travel to Japan, officially on a holiday, but they will give a few interviews about *The Idiot* and David will agree to answer some questions about *Low* and *The Man Who Fell To Earth*. He will also take advantage of his stay in Tokyo to hold a photo shoot with Masayoshi Sukita. The cover of his next album will come from this session, for which he wears different black leather jackets. The shot he will choose is a nod to *Roquairol*[3] but, in the others, Sukita thought David Bowie looked like British actor Bruce Byron in *Scorpio Rising*, a short film by Kenneth Anger from the 1960s. In 2012, in the photographer's book, published by Genesis, David Bowie will explain that posing with his hand in front of his face, looking at the palm of his hand, was a reference to the scene in *Un Chien Andalou* when Salvador Dalí watches hundreds of ants swarm out of his own hand.

As soon as they return from Japan, David Bowie and Iggy take over Studio 3 at Hansa. Iggy's touring band – now including Carlos Alomar – already knows some of the new songs (having played them live or at sound checks during the tour), so sessions for the follow-up to *The Idiot* will last just over two weeks, in June. As an instrumentalist, David will not be as noticeable on this record – he will mainly play keyboards – which, thanks to an advance from RCA, he funds under the name of

Bewlay Bros. With this company, he is also planning on producing films, in which Iggy and Marc Bolan (together or individually?) might feature.

Iggy's new album will again state 'Recorded by David Bowie'. Alone, he wrote four of the nine songs (which he first demoed on his own) and his name will also appear in the credits of 'Turn Blue' (drafted in Los Angeles with Geoff 'Warren Peace' MacCormack two years before), 'Neighbourhood Threat' (co-written with Ricky Gardiner) and 'Fall In Love With Me' (the only piece co-signed with the Sales brothers). *Lust For Life* is less experimental and more rock, and British recording engineer Colin Thurston[4] and Edu Meyer are partially responsible for its unique sound. A very creative individual, Edu will suggest recording Iggy Pop's vocal through an amp, notably on 'Success'.

'Some Weird Sin' and 'Tonight' are strong tracks that were previously tested live, but 'Fall In Love With Me' is the unconvincing result of an experiment David Bowie will repeat on his next record (and probably with some of his bands later on): he's asked his musicians to swap instruments. 'Sixteen', the only song on the album credited only to Iggy, is much better.

Sukita took some beautiful photos of Iggy Pop when he was in Japan, but it's a black-and-white shot by Andrew Kent (dating from the UK tour), showing him smiling, that will be used for the cover of *Lust For Life*, the only album made entirely in Berlin by Iggy Pop or David Bowie during their German parenthesis. *Lust For Life* will come out at the end of August and will do fairly well in the charts, despite RCA committing professional misconduct by not releasing 'The Passenger' as a single. This song, written by Ricky Gardiner, was a potential hit that would probably have boosted sales. *Lust For Life* will remain Iggy Pop's best-performing record in the British charts for decades – reaching Number 28 in the Top 30 soon after its release – only to be beaten in 2016 by *Post Pop Depression*, the album he will record with Josh Homme of Queens Of The Stone Age (which will get to Number 5).

In the US, it will be a different matter – Elvis Presley's death on 16 August 1977 means that, until Christmas, most of RCA's resources will be put into making and selling compilations and hastily reissued albums. To improve sales of *Lust For Life*, Iggy Pop will give another series of concerts in the autumn, with Stacy Heydon on guitar instead of Ricky Gardiner. Busy promoting *"Heroes"* and aware of the dangers of the road in terms of temptation and excess, David will give up his piano stool to Scott Thurston, who played with The Stooges in 1973 and 1974, and will later join Tom Petty's Heartbreakers as a multi-instrumentalist. Released in May 1978, three years after Bowie visited Iggy in the mental institution where he had committed himself, *TV Eye Live 1977*, taped during the tours that preceded and followed the recording of *Lust For Life* (Bowie plays on four of the eight songs), will be the ultimate testimony of their European collaboration.

For reasons known only to them, the relationship between David Bowie and his friend will become strained again, shortly after the release of Iggy's second album of the year (the third one being *Kill City*). Some will assert that Iggy messed it up for himself again, while others will claim that David was sick of playing the Good Samaritan. RCA, which was much less interested in Iggy Pop without his advisor, will release him from his contract in the summer of 1978. He and David Bowie will work together one last time in the mid-80s.

In late winter 2015, as he is putting the final touches to *Post Pop Depression*, Iggy will record a song in a deep baritone, in the vocal style which David Bowie expected of him in 1977. Its title, 'German Days', is more revealing than its lyrics. The year Bowie died, Iggy Pop will tour with Josh Homme to promote their album. They will only play half a dozen songs from it, but twice as many from *The Idiot* and *Lust For Life*. *Post Pop Depression* will be nominated for a Grammy in December 2016 in the Best Alternative Music Album category. But, more fittingly, the record that will win that year will be *Blackstar*.

In late June and early July 1977, David Bowie and Iggy Pop spend some time in Paris. They stay at Hôtel Plaza Athénée and, on RCA's request, David agrees to pose for promotional photos and give some interviews. With unwavering devotion, television presenter Yves Mourousi dedicates another news segment to him. With American actress Sydne Rome at his side, Bowie attends the premiere of *L'Homme Qui Venait D'Ailleurs* and the couple will talk about *Wally*, a film project about Austrian painter Egon Schiele[5], which will never come to fruition. David, whose passion for painting and graphic arts is less and less a secret, uses his time in France to visit visual artist Victor Vasarely at his home in Annet-sur-Marne (about twenty-five miles east of Paris). He is accompanied by photographers who will shoot him in front of Vasarely's works. Calvin Mark Lee had advised Bowie to take inspiration from his universe for the cover of *Space Oddity*.

Soon after, Tony Visconti arrives at Hansa from Canada where he's just finished *Bad Reputation*, Thin Lizzy's eighth album. He is a week late. David Bowie was even more impatient with others than he was with himself and he'll be angry with Tony for not having joined him sooner, especially since he is late because of a band Bowie is not very fond of. Brian Eno is already in Berlin, ready to make his mark on the recording as he was asked. He is staying with David and is a little surprised by his frugal diet – David usually swallows a raw egg in the early mornings after returning from the studio. Eno is well aware of their differences on many levels, but the recording of *"Heroes"* will confirm for him that their collaboration is based on the quality of a real exchange.

To start, Brian Eno explained he intended to abolish the traditional hierarchy governing the concept of rock music, especially the supremacy of the main melody carried by the vocals. That way, the songs can be recorded together (another particularity of the album) without the musicians knowing what the vocals will sound like – David will only have to worry about them right before recording them. Just like at the Château d'Hérouville the year before, the first sessions are devoted to rhythmic takes based on raw chord progressions provided by Bowie. George Murray and Dennis Davis spend just under a week at Hansa playing on seven of the ten tracks of the future LP. By the time they leave Germany, they will only have a vague idea of how the songs will turn out, but they were glad David explained some of their themes, especially for the title song[6]. Bowie and Eno play some keyboard parts live with the musicians, but most will be added over the following days.

The same thing happens with Robert Fripp. When David phoned him, the King Crimson frontman warned him that his band was dormant and that he hadn't played rock guitar in a long time[7]. Far from being dissuaded, Bowie was further convinced that Fripp was the right choice. He picks up his guitar the minute he steps foot in the studio, just before midnight, having just flown in from New York. He is going to record quickly, relying on instinct and often without hearing all the other tracks. Robert Fripp will only spend a few hours at Hansa, but he will make his mark in crucial ways on the album, his sound made even more gripping by two basic pedals (distortion and sustain) and the treatments imposed onto his instrument by Brian Eno. Above all, and especially on "Heroes", Fripp will prove a master of feedback, and extract melodies from his guitar which are vital to the arrangement[8].

Once again, Eno will play his Synthi a lot throughout the record, and David Bowie will use the Chamberlin and Solina. As on *The Idiot* and *Low*, his keyboards will sometimes be recorded through a guitar amp. Also appearing on the album is Antonia Maaß, the singer of Messengers, a Berlin jazz-rock band who are working at Hansa that July on their album *Children Of Tomorrow*. In the evenings, they perform at the Eierschale, a now-defunct club in Breitenbach Square, where Bowie's musicians sometimes have a drink and a jam. They became friendly with Maaß, and her voice will stand out in the backing vocals of 'Beauty And The Beast'. She also translated the lyrics to the German version of *"Heroes"* (*"Helden"*), while Coco took care of the French version (*"Héros"*). The vocals for *"Helden"* will be recorded in Montreux, and Antonia Maaß will be there to coach Bowie.

The mix of *"Heroes"*, which started in Berlin, will be completed in Switzerland. Located at 8, Rue Du Théâtre, less than five minutes by car from his house in Blonay, the Mountain Recording Studio (its name complete without an 's' at the end, unlike the English and American studios) was still being managed by the founders, Alex Grob and Anita Kerr, when David Bowie discovered it. John Timperley, the in-house recording engineer, will leave Mountain in 1977, so Tony Visconti will work with David Richards (brought from London as an assistant by Timperley) and the young assistant Eugene Chaplin, son of the creator of The Tramp, whose family live nearby. After *"Heroes"*, they will both work on its follow-up. Between 1977 and 1995, David Richards, based in Switzerland, will be David Bowie's sound engineer on most of his recordings in Montreux, in London and in New York.

Mountain Studio, located in the same building as the casino that had been rebuilt after a fire in December 1971, is the work of Tom Hidley, an influential American acoustician who designed, among other studios, the Record Plant in Los Angeles. He is the one who suggested encasing the control room's huge speakers in a wall of stone specially imported from California! Queen will buy Mountain at the very end of the 1970s, and work there regularly, starting with *Hot Space*, their tenth album, released in 1982.

In 1977, Marc Bolan is again riding a wave of success. Since T. Rex's decline, which started four years earlier, his records have gone unnoticed or, worse, been slammed by the critics. But in 1975, he and his partner Gloria Jones had a son and, since then, Bolan has been doing everything he can to jump-start his career again. In March, when their twelfth and last album, the unexpected *Dandy In The Underworld*, was released, T. Rex was on tour with The Damned opening for them. Many punk bands, whose members grew up with Bolan's hits, do not see him as a has-been (although he will soon turn thirty!), and accord him a legitimacy he didn't expect. They even consider him a mentor. (In his interview with *Rock&Folk* in 2019, Iggy Pop will joke about the number of 'godfathers' there were knocking around at that time – Lou Reed was another.)

When Granada suggest producing a series of music TV shows called *Marc*, with Marc Bolan as the host, he sees the chance to restore his reputation, to return the favour to the mad young dogs nipping at his heels, and he readily accepts. Granada will broadcast six episodes in one month, starting in late August and featuring Radio Stars, The Boomtown Rats, Generation X and Eddie And The Hot Rods[9]. For the last episode, Bolan wants to end on a high, so he invites David Bowie to sing "Heroes". Since the show will air the same week the single is due to come out (which will stagnate around Number 25 in the British charts and at 125 in the US), David agrees to play even though he isn't exactly thrilled that Herbie Flowers and Tony Newman – mutineers on the Diamond Dogs tour and now T. Rex musicians – will also be on set.

For the occasion, Bowie and Bolan have drafted a few songs together, including 'Sitting Next To You'[10], which they intend to perform at the end of the show. A sign that the balance of power between the two is definitely not in Marc's favour any more, he trips over a cable as David starts singing and disappears off camera, provoking general hilarity in the audience. Due to a lack of time, the scene will be kept and it will wrap up the programme. But on 28 September, the night it airs, no one will be in the mood to laugh. Twelve days before, Marc Bolan was killed instantly when the car he was travelling in hit a concrete fence post, ending up in a tree. Gloria Jones was driving him home after dinner through Barnes (near Olympic Studios), when she lost control of their Mini 1275 GT. The media coverage of Presley's death will overshadow that of Bolan's around the world, but not in the UK, where his demise will deeply affect the music lovers who've grown up to the sound of T. Rex. Many will say that glam rock died with him that day. David Bowie will attend Bolan's funeral and, when he finds out that Gloria (who was not married to Marc) and their son Rolan might end up in financial straits, he will offer to provide for them, without ever mentioning it publicly, for as long as they need.

Since it turned out that the city still haunted Bowie, the lyrics of 'Beauty And The Beast' can be seen as a kind of snub against the psychic oppression he had experienced in Los Angeles. The tone of the song is quite vengeful. The cadence of the Euro-disco beat is lively (127bpm, which is 20 more than 'Fashion' on *Lodger*) and the robotic illusion is accentuated by the fact that the track, with no verses or chorus, is largely based on a single chord/riff. The only harmonic variation comes at more than two minutes in and Dennis Davis ends it with a flurry of tom-toms that lead to a path made difficult to navigate by Eno's synthetic crackling and Robert Fripp's shards of sound. Finally caught in Bowie's net, Fripp has no choice but to give it his all, which is what he also does on 'Joe The Lion', another typical Bowie song (and therefore atypical), deranged both vocally and contextually, reflecting the subject that initiated it: performance artist Chris Burden's famous crucifixion on the back of a Volkswagen Beetle[11]. The juxtaposition of an arpeggiated texture that sounds like a sequencer and a few bluesy licks – is it Fripp? No, it's Alomar! – heralds Nile Rodgers' and Stevie Ray Vaughan's sleight of hand on *Let's Dance*. It increases the strangeness of this song – its tempo is barely slower than the previous one – which climbs over another strange bridge, from which Bowie escapes screaming.

Was David trying to appear more romantic than he actually was when he claimed that the title song of his twelfth album had come to him after seeing a couple steal a kiss at the foot of the wall of discord, towered over by a mirador, from the control room of Hansa 2 Studio? (He even said it was Tony Visconti and Antonia Maaß.) Discreet on the matter for more than four decades, Maaß points out that Bowie couldn't have seen her kiss Visconti when he wrote the lyrics, because their summer fling hadn't started then. David has also implied that, because Tony was married to Mary Hopkin at the time, he'd chosen not to reveal the couple's identity. We now know that his visits to the Brücke-Museum brought out his poetic side, and that he'd fallen in love with *Liebespaar Zwischen Gartenmauern* [Lovers Between Garden Walls] by painter Otto Müller, who had been persecuted by the Nazis along with Ernst Ludwig Kirchner. As for the lines mentioning dolphins, this is a reference[12] to *A Grave For A Dolphin* by Italian writer Alberto Denti di Pirajno. Bowie will say he loved this collection of short stories in the preface to *I Am Iman*, a book his second wife will publish in 2001.

Put simply, "Heroes" is an epic, partly autobiographical narrative set to music, in which the author wants to believe in his own rebirth. He lets his fears and mistakes shine through and sings of absolute hope, by way of an idealized love unfolding in the heart of a divided city.

Of course, the quotation marks around the name of the song (and the album) prove that literal meanings were not Bowie's speciality – he uses them to bring a touch of irony to a song that is more dramatic than it appears, in an effort to avoid grandiloquence. Musically, "Heroes" owes a lot to 'I'm Waiting For The Man' (with that same eighth-note rhythm on the piano) and a desire to stand out at all costs seems to have dictated most production choices. Tony Visconti always said he was impressed by the impeccably steady tempo Dennis Davis was able to keep. Dennis is particularly stunning on "Heroes", as he hardly deviates from 113bpm. While he played with David Bowie, Davis never recorded to a click. As for Fripp,

Tony recently explained that he'd suggested keeping all of his guitar parts instead of choosing just one (they only appear between the lines of the verses in the first half of the song, but are everywhere as soon as Bowie sings in a higher octave).

"Heroes" may be the most conventional song on the album, but it remains an incredible laboratory of ideas, demonstrated by Eno's radical treatment of Fripp's guitar (through analogue filters) and the way he draws from his Synthi and VCS 3 those droning sounds that only vaguely follow the chords. David Bowie's Solina emulates real strings, and the 'cheesy' brass sounds come from the Chamberlin. Because there was only one track left when it was time to record the main vocal, Tony Visconti introduced his three-microphone technique: he set one up in front of Bowie and two others further away, ready to 'open' depending on the volume of his voice. It sounded natural as long as David didn't push it, and it reverberated more and more as the backing vocals also intensified, giving the last third of "Heroes" its epic character[13].

While the lyrics for many songs on the album, including 'Joe The Lion', were partly improvised (or assembled on the spot from various notes) in a free-style technique Tony Visconti said was borrowed from Iggy Pop, 'Sons Of The Silent Age' is the only one that was reportedly 'almost' finished by the time David Bowie showed it to his musicians. In fact, he even considered it as the title of the album. This is easily believable because, in a way, it harks back to the classicism of *The Man Who Sold The World*. This impression is reinforced by the cockney accent, deployed freely on the track, which made his vocals sound unique. 'Sons Of The Silent Age', a possible reference to the punk generation and given an early Roxy Music colour by its filtered saxophone, is carried by a real chorus, with richer vocal harmonies than on the first two tracks of side A (with Antonia Maaß) which are reminiscent of Flo & Eddie.

While listening to 'Blackout' – the lyrics (or at least the title) were probably inspired by the power cut that plunged New York into darkness on the night of 13 July 1977, causing a wave of looting and riots – it's easy to wonder whether Eno and Peter Schmidt's set of cards had turned David Bowie into the most oblique of strategists. In this song, again, Bowie does exactly as he pleases – his only rule seems to be that there are no rules. At one minute and twenty seconds in, we notice, without necessarily minding, the total absence of landmarks. Agreeing to get lost in speculation is the only way to reach the end of this brutal and tricky song that Robert Fripp, like a mechanical drilling machine and with all the application and determination of a man on a mission, throws his whole body into, making those high notes shriek.

In order to further heighten the sense of instability, the B-side of *"Heroes"* opens with a song whose sketchy vocals (the title of the song repeated, and that's it) are put through a cheap synth. It was chosen over a real vocoder[14], although they were already available at the time and widely used by many krautrock bands, including Kraftwerk. Bowie confirmed that the name of 'V-2 Schneider' was a reference to Florian Schneider, one of Kraftwerk's founding members, and the V-2 missiles developed by the Germans in World War II (which had, incidentally, gutted London). The rhythm section, probably intended to be relentless (Dennis Davis did listen to Kraftwerk before delivering his own motorik beat), is made unruly by George Murray's bass. As a result, it gives the track a pulse that is both sensual and disconcerting.

Brian Eno's influence can be felt in the austerity of 'Sense Of Doubt', the first of three full-length instrumentals of the album. It was very likely written with the help of Oblique Strategies[15] and makes use of synthesizers to generate noises. Four descending low notes – which inspired film-score composer Jóhann Jóhannsson's theme 'The Beast' for the film *Sicario*, directed by Denis Villeneuve in 2015 – threaten sustained chords and space bells, which are rescued halfway through by a harmonic resolution already heard on *Low*. 'Sense Of Doubt' finally lands on its feet (thanks to a major chord!) then, after synthetic easterly wind and a sound effect similar to the one heard in the opening scenes of *The Man Who Fell To Earth*, it blends into 'Moss Garden'. This is the most 'Japanese' piece in David Bowie's discography (co-written, like the following track, with Brian Eno), even more so than 'Crystal Japan', which he will record two years later. Its title evokes the traditional moss gardens Bowie had visited on his recent trip to the Land Of The Rising Sun. The defining feature of these gardens is that nature is idealized and artifice restricted. These principles are applied to the music by Bowie on the koto and by Eno, grand master of synth pads, which vaporize on contact with ozone.

The sense of being uprooted felt by the Turkish immigrants living in the Neukölln district of Berlin – separated from his own (Shöneberg) by a state park – inspired the harshest instrumental on *"Heroes"*. Even though he missed an 'l' in the song title ('Neuköln'), we know David Bowie took the subject of immigration very seriously, as we can hear by the moaning saxophone at the end of the track.

Punk, new wave, ska, reggae – 1977 was the year of all musical flavours, and Bowie didn't miss the chance to fill his shaker of a head with them. Drawing comparisons between Bowie's songs and those he might not have been impervious to is not the subject of this book, but 'The Secret Life Of Arabia'[16] clearly grooves to the beat of at least one highly popular track of the day, with a rather fitting title: 'Cokane In My Brain' by Dillinger. It's not surprising to discover that this single from the Jamaican singer's first album had been a big hit in the Netherlands, Belgium and... Germany. To cut through the mix and give the track its groove, George Murray's bass on 'The Secret Life Of Arabia' is louder than on any other song on the album. In a detached manner, David Bowie flaunts his talents as a vocalist, and the top-notch quality of the song owes a lot to him. Echoes of the ending will be heard on 'Inbetweenies', on Ian Dury And The Blockheads' stunning second album released in 1979, *Do It Yourself*.

While he'd barely lifted a finger to promote *Low*, David Bowie launches a genuine media marathon that autumn for *"Heroes"*, covering Europe and then America. The French and German versions of the title song are released in their respective countries and British director Nicholas Ferguson[17] shoots some minimalist videos for "Heroes" and 'Sense Of Doubt'. Wherever he goes, Bowie appears on radio and television shows, grants long interviews and graces the covers of music magazines. In France, he shines on the set of *Les Rendez-Vous Du Dimanche* [Sunday Meet-ups] hosted by Michel Drucker, and takes part in a radio show during which Henri Leproux phones in to ask him if he remembers his time at the Golf Drouot.

In London, Bowie sings "Heroes" on his fourth appearance on *Top Of The Pops*, the first since 'The Jean Genie' in 1973. In New York, he attends a Devo concert at Max's Kansas City and introduces their second set[18]. He is also interviewed by Flo & Eddie at the Plaza hotel for the Canadian television show *90 Minutes Live*.

In stores on 14 October, *"Heroes"* is going to be well received, especially by *Melody Maker* and the *NME*, and will cause more of a sensation in the British charts (at Number 3) than in America (not even in the Top 30). Nevertheless, sales will remain modest[19]. Ironically, when it comes out in November 1982, 'Peace On Earth/Little Drummer Boy', a duet recorded with Bing Crosby at the end of 1977 and aired massively on both sides of the Atlantic over the Christmas holidays, will be a resounding success and remains, to this day, one of David Bowie's bestselling singles. Bing Crosby will die a month after Marc Bolan – Bowie, who didn't mind using dark humour, will wonder aloud whether, hero or not, singing a duet with him at that time had been very prudent.

Carlos Alomar	Thilo Schmied
Robert Fripp	Ian 'Knox' Carnochan
George Murray	Robin Mayhew
Tony Visconti	Iggy Pop
Eugene Chaplin	Ricky Gardiner
	Michael Rother
	Hans-Joachim Roedelius
	Irmin Schmidt
	Jean-Hervé Péron
	Nicolas Godin
	Albert Koski
	Marc Exiga
	Reeves Gabrels
	Matthew Fisher
	James Williamson
	Elvis Costello
	Philip Glass
	Martin Gore
	Neil Tennant

CARLOS ALOMAR

If you listen to "Heroes", I will ask you to consider this as part of what I was trying to do. We have this thing in rock'n'roll called signature guitar lines. One of the best-known examples is the one in '(I Can't Get No) Satisfaction' by The Rolling Stones: if you take that line out, there's no song. Same thing for 'Stay' – if you take out the funky riff, there's no song. These are classic lines. But on "Heroes" [he sings the intro melody line], how could that be a classic line? [then he sings the bass line] Well, it is a classic line! Dude, on "Heroes", every line is a classic line – there are at least 12! And it's a simple song. Do you know why we did that? Because the chord progression repeats itself over and over and over again... The harmony is static, so we had to create classic guitar lines to make it more exciting. That song is like a staircase that we just kept building. It sounds like it's accelerating, but it's not. And when you think it repeats itself, it's adding layers and it changes. Musically speaking, we have to have an emotional attachment to the chords. The same goes for the lyrics. David repeats, 'We can be heroes' and, then, boom, 'Just for one day'. It grows in power and, of course, these things are planned. The vocals were recorded at the end of the sessions but, of course, he tried ideas almost every day. On *"Heroes"*, the rhythm tracks were recorded quickly, usually two or three takes, because – and this is another one of my golden rules – the studio is not a place for rehearsing. When I get to a session, all the recording engineer has to do is press the red button.

David and Iggy were really close friends in Berlin and it was clear from the neighbourhood and apartment they chose to live in, that the most important thing for them was to be together. They were living in poverty, man, and that flat was cheap, because that was all they could afford. I went to have dinner with them and we went to the local pub – there was no record company to wine and dine us. Just like in Hérouville, there was only music. All they could do was write songs. You're away from everything – the environment is music. That must have given pause to anyone who only saw David Bowie as a businessman, ostentatious or whatever. The blow was gone – they both drank from time to time and there was a lot of smoking, but that was it. (2016)

ROBERT FRIPP

Before and during *"Heroes"*, David Bowie told me *(No Pussyfooting)* was one of the albums that had influenced him the most. A bit like The Velvet Underground with their first LP, I sometimes feel that *(No Pussyfooting)* had more of an impact on musicians than on the public! Whenever I play on someone else's record, I always try to blend into the music rather than stand out, which I think would be arrogant. I play what the tracks require of me. But, you know, David Bowie inspires you to be good, as does Brian Eno.

Right up until we started the *"Heroes"* sessions, I was a bit anxious and I was wondering whether I'd show up. I hadn't touched my guitar in quite some time and I wanted to warn David before I got to the studio. He asked me if I could play basic rock and, as soon as I got there, I plugged in my guitar and off I went! I think I started with 'Beauty And The Beast' and I played on it without knowing the song. I did the whole album like that, in a very intuitive way. And people still talk about it more than twenty years later[20]... (2000)

GEORGE MURRAY

I remember walking into the studio and being able to see the Berlin Wall out of the window. It was literally across a small courtyard. But the significance of the studio's proximity to the Wall and all that the Wall represented was lost on me at the time. I had been to Berlin before and knew the city was divided into sections. Again, significant, but I didn't give it much thought. But, like 'Golden Years' on the *Station To Station* album, David took the time to explain the significance of "Heroes", the first track we recorded for the album. Two people in love, separated or overshadowed by the Wall and all its implications, and it didn't matter to them one bit – they were heroes. This was 1977, but it wasn't until 1989 when the Wall came down that I had a better understanding of David's vision. He was ahead of his time once again.

"Heroes" seemed to be an extension of *Low*, but more sophisticated. Two of my favourite songs are on this album: "Heroes" and 'The Secret Life Of Arabia'. "Heroes" for the sound of the bass – a Rickenbaker that I found at the studio, with a very bright sound that I ran through an MXR Flanger, and I used a pick. And 'The Secret Life Of Arabia' because of the bass line and the overall groove – it was strong and powerful and was not overshadowed by the electronics or effects more evident on other tracks.

I think David chose the environment to match the circumstances or objective: *Station To Station* in Los Angeles, with all the distractions and implications they wrought; *Low* at the *château*, in the middle of nowhere, so we could get the work done; and *"Heroes"* in Berlin – the representative centre of the tensions between Eastern and Western Europe and a thriving artistic centre at the same time.

David and Tony Visconti were obviously comfortable working together and seemed to share the same goals. The discussions were free-flowing and sometimes opinions and input were sought from Dennis, Carlos and me. That went a long way towards making me feel part of the project instead of just a band member. However, I was disappointed not to have met or recorded with Robert Fripp. I knew some of his work, had some of his recordings and was impressed with how he layered his sound. I found out he was on *"Heroes"* when it was released! I think his guitar parts on the title song are classic and add a dimension, depth and emotion that are unique to him and the song. (2016)

TONY VISCONTI

After Brian left Berlin we added some percussion to some tracks; all this was typical of how David worked. His ideas were spontaneous and he liked them executed quickly to see how the notion played out. In David's mind *"Heroes"* cried out for a cowbell, but it was too late to order a box of percussion from a rental company. We couldn't find a cowbell anywhere in the studio, but we found an empty tape platter (in those days it was a German recording preference to put a tightly wound reel of tape on an open platter with the top of the tape exposed). Because we had a limited number of tracks David and I overdubbed the percussion elements of 'tape platter' and tambourine standing side by side.

If I've given the impression that this was the album finished, nothing could have been further from the truth. Not a single vocal had been recorded, or a melody and lyric written until just David and I remained at Hansa. This was no easy task and there were long lulls when David had to concentrate on writing. He'd arrive at the studio with a partial lyric, and we'd start recording his vocal with what little he'd have. I would record the first two lines, then he would hold up his hand for me to stop, listen to the playback, and then he'd write another scribbled couplet on his pad atop the studio piano. I could hear him off mic mumbling a few alternatives then walk up to the mic with something to sing. When he had something he'd ask me to 'drop in' his voice immediately after the first couplet. As tedious as this might sound, he'd usually finish writing the song and performing the final vocal in under two hours.

Many of the songs on David Bowie's records have only needed a single lead-

vocal take. As we were working on both 8-track and 16-track tape, we didn't leave many tracks open for lead vocals. Sometimes, and this was the case for the vocal on "Heroes", we had only one track left! In those days, you couldn't keep a vocal in a folder the way you can with digital recording. If you thought the artist could sing it better, you would have to erase the previous vocal forever! David was used to this system and was a great singer due to this technical discipline. He knew the consequences. He sang so well, it would often be a difficult decision to make. Could he sing it even better or will it get worse? Should we stop here and say, 'Yes, this is the best vocal'? It was always a nerve-racking, butterflies-in-the-stomach experience. This element of tension and expectation is missing entirely from today's digital recording. Back then, it was taken for granted that an artist had to be a great singer to get a recording contract. Don't get me started on how things have changed...
(2007/2015)

EUGENE CHAPLIN

When I was young, I trained as a stage manager at the Royal Academy of Arts in London, and had some basics in sound design because that was part of the job. I was working at the Montreux Casino when Mountain Studio had just opened, and they hired me because I already had some experience. The Rolling Stones recorded *Black And Blue* there, we had Emerson, Lake & Palmer and Yes. When we found out David Bowie was coming with Tony Visconti, we didn't really know what to expect, because we had this idea of him – that he was androgynous, a big druggie, all that – and we thought it might be difficult.

The day he was due to arrive, this guy showed up at the door wearing a cap, unshaven, and we told him we couldn't let him in because we were waiting for someone important. He said, 'Oh yeah? I'm David Bowie.' A hell of a start! I never usually joined fan clubs, but when I was at the Royal Academy, I'd bought *Aladdin Sane* and inside there was a leaflet you could send off to join Bowie's. And I had! I never would have thought that years later, I would end up in the studio with him.

Some parts of *"Heroes"* were added at Montreux, though most of the takes were done at Hansa. However a lot of vocals were done at Mountain, as well as a good part of the mix. Robert Fripp recorded in Berlin. I know because David often joked about the relationship between Fripp and Eno. During the *"Heroes"* sessions, I learned something from Bowie: never hesitate to leave a song unfinished – go on to another one and come back to it later in a better mindset. (2016)

THILO SCHMIED

During those 20 or so months when David Bowie spent a lot of time in Germany, it's quite possible he made a few demos, especially for *"Heroes"*, at the Audio Studios in Berlin, where Tangerine Dream worked. As for Edu Meyer, he was definitely the assistant recording engineer on *Low*, but not on *"Heroes"*. It was summer, he was on holiday, so Peter Burgen replaced him. Peter was always around in those days. He also worked a lot on *Lust For Life*, for which he even sang backing vocals.

The 'Berlin trilogy' is an enduring myth because the term appears on the plaque the City of Berlin have fixed on the building where David lived. Since we began the Berlin Music Tours, my team and I are constantly having to say that this term is not historically accurate, but no one listens! People should stop saying that *"Heroes"* was done in Berlin, as it was mixed, at least in part, in Montreux – that information has been on the back of the album jacket since it came out!

Peter Burgen and Antonia Maaß are wary of giving interviews, and I don't blame them. The few times they have spoken, their words were reported inaccurately and, most of the time, they're briefly quoted in books or articles about Bowie or the city. And their memories of what happened in the studio or outside it don't necessarily match the memories of other people... Some Bowie fans have criticized Antonia for her poor adaptation of the lyrics of "Heroes" but, actually, David couldn't properly pronounce some of the lines, so she had to use words he was familiar with.

Speaking of Berlin, Iggy Pop told some funny stories. For example, that young Berliners refused to talk to him or that they didn't speak English well enough to talk to him. So in bars he often chatted to older folks, and they'd tell him all these stories about the war and the old Berlin. Like life with its ups and downs, what David and Iggy experienced in Germany wasn't all rosy. At one point, they realized that sharing a living space had its downsides. David kicked Iggy and his girlfriend out of the apartment on Haupstraße. They moved into another one at the back of the building! For David, Berlin was also important on a visual level, because he deepened his knowledge of Die Brücke, the group of German expressionist artists, especially Erich Heckel's work. At the Château d'Hérouville, David had a catalogue from the Brücke-Museum. He'd gone there while he was in Berlin during the Station To Station Tour. Several pages were dedicated to Heckel.

It's such a shame that Brian Eno refuses to talk about that time – he says he doesn't like to look back. But he definitely played a major role in these albums, though despite what some think or say, he didn't produce or even co-produce them.

The photos of Robert Fripp at Hansa with David Bowie and Brian Eno suggest he spent quite a lot of time there, but we know that's not the case. Carlos Alomar, George Murray and Dennis Davis were in Berlin for less than a week, and Fripp wasn't around for long either. (2017)

IAN 'KNOX' CARNOCHAN

The Vibrators opened for Iggy Pop in 1977 because we were on Epic Records and had a good agency. I heard that Iggy and Bowie listened to our first album, *Pure Mania*, and thought we were a suitable support act. Also, we were the right kind of band, as punk was very much happening. Personally, I loved Bowie, but I didn't go for The Stooges when they first came out. A bit later I really got into what they were doing. I guess it was the most manic stuff because, before then, there was metal and The Velvet Underground. But metal had terrible lyrics. The slow Stooges stuff I didn't get straightaway...

We knew Bowie was going to be on stage with Iggy, but it was quite surprising. He was low-key on stage; he dressed and looked very much like a student. It was Iggy's show after all and they were both very professional. Of course we loved *The Idiot* – the bass drum and Iggy's voice sounded really good. I think in the studio he did his vocals through a Fender Twin Reverb amplifier, which helped to make them very authoritative and convincing. Each night after our set, we'd watch theirs and Ricky Gardiner also wowed us. I'd be lying if I said we spent a lot of time with them, because they were busy! But Iggy did some photos with us and, another time, David came and chatted with the band for a few minutes down the back of the venue, during the sound check. In any case, it looked like he and Iggy very much enjoyed each other's company.

I think on the whole tour – fewer than ten dates – we only had thirty seconds of sound check! We were squashed right up at the front of the stage. We didn't complain though – it was fantastic to be doing the tour. It has to be one of the greatest tours ever in many ways! Also, one time, we were at a restaurant, eating before a gig, and Tony Sales, Iggy's bass player, joined us. When we came to pay the bill, Tony had already paid it. So very nice of him!

I never bumped into them afterwards, but I did see a couple more Iggy shows. The Vibrators' song 'Automatic Lover' is about going to an Iggy show in either Berlin or Hamburg, when the girl I was with had a gun. I think it was just a gas pistol, but she had it at the concert so I definitely had to make sure she wasn't going to shoot

Iggy. There's often a lot of madness around these bands. I had been drinking with her earlier in a bar and probably – stupidly – thought it was cool that she had the gun out on the table in the bar. Rock'n'roll! (2017)

ROBIN MAYHEW

In 1977, David did an incognito tour with Iggy Pop, playing keyboards. I had produced the album *Pure Mania* for the punk band The Vibrators and they had got the support act gig. I was doing their sound at some venue and David came and sat with me at the soundboard during the sound check and we chatted for a while. That's the last time I saw him. (2016)

IGGY POP

In 1977, life got a bit more...um...tumultuous, and we decided to make *Lust For Life* quickly. I wrote all the lyrics in a week and recording lasted about 10 days... We lived off cheap draught beer, German sausages and cocaine. Things were quite simple in the studio with David. When we disagreed, which was always, I'd wait until he was done working on the tapes. Sessions lasted 12 hours, but he often worked for much longer than that, until he collapsed. Then I'd show up: those were going to be my twelve hours and the recording engineer just had to deal with it. And after David did his best to mess up my ideas, it was my turn to mess up his! He'd fire back: 'You're just a shitty American rock singer who's really naïve and just follows the latest trend.' I'd say, 'Do you really think for a single second that we took your fag ballads seriously, your fucking stories about guys lost in space?' So we would argue a lot but, at the same time, we respected each other, which was stronger than anything else. We both needed conflict in order to create.

We really thought America would love *Lust For Life* and that it would shake Europe up like an earthquake, but none of that happened. David used my first two albums as sketches for *Low* and *"Heroes"*. He already knew the musicians, the engineers and the studios. He's clever, you know. In the end, he'd had enough of me; he didn't want to make another record together. He suggested releasing a live album to complete my own trilogy. I wasn't thrilled with the idea, but I couldn't do much about it since I was under contract with his company. On *TV Eye Live* 1977, the compromise was to bring together some songs with him that were more polished, and others without him, which were messy and noisy.

David and I loved Berlin as it was then. That kind of security zone between the European superpowers, between East and West, hadn't changed much since the war... Close to where we lived there was a cinema that sat just over 250 people and they played films from the 1920s. We spent hours in little shops like they used to have, with a window on the street and the merchant's living quarters that gave out onto the back courtyard. We'd buy amazing wines there and 1940s-style shirts from second-hand clothes dealers who always had crazy stories to tell. The people of Berlin contributed greatly to the warm atmosphere, but most of them didn't have central heating! There are bits of all that in *Lust For Life*. I caught whatever was in the air; the lyrics flow from there. During the recording, after living with David, I rented an apartment behind his and I used to buy some coal from this guy on the street with an enormous sack on his back. I put it in the stove and it smoked but, frankly, it didn't make it much warmer! David had central heating...

Sometimes I didn't agree with him while we were recording, but we weren't competing with each other, just collaborating. Berlin was a culture shock for me, but London had been one too a few years before. At the start of the 1970s, American plumbing was much more advanced than in Europe[21]. I was used to turning on the hot water and having it arrive right away, not waiting around for it to get barely warm! Okay, so it was worse in Germany. But seriously, we could see that they had a really strong culture. When I left the US, popular culture had already been violated: we used to say, 'Elvis Presley!' and the system would answer, 'Perry Como!' But when I got back from Berlin, the country I'd been missing had disappeared! Gone! Television had become the primary source of inspiration for the new comedians. Before then, they'd made jokes about life. That says a lot about the drift of a society.

I was incredibly lucky that David gave me the chance to experience European culture, especially in the way he did it: we were in the best of contexts and everything was interesting. I wasn't always aware of what was going on because I was often stoned, but I was releasing records and I performed all over the place... I ended up on stage in Copenhagen... Okay, sometimes there were hardly more than 150 people in the audience, scratching their heads, wondering what the hell I was doing there. But I got it right during that period, and things in the end worked out for me. All that only lasted about a year and a half, but I think it was a much more important time than London in 1972. See, I was glued to David, and he introduced me to all sorts of people: David Hemmings, Mick Jagger and Keith Richards. He brought them to my concerts and Keith would give me stuff and whisper in my ear, 'There you go, be a good boy, take this.'

I've already talked about how, in the apartment in Berlin, some songs came to us. One time, we were waiting to watch an episode of *Starsky & Hutch* and it was preceded by a series of beeps, a sort of theme with a beat that sounded like Motown. David, who was sitting on the floor in front of me with his ukulele, immediately found a chord progression that went with it and he said, 'There you go, write some lyrics to that. You can call the song 'Lust For Life'' ²². And Hunt jumped at the chance to bash out this wild beat! David taught me a bunch of things I still use and sometimes I think that I behave better in society and in life partly because of him. (1999/2016)

RICKY GARDINER

The tour I did with Iggy Pop and David Bowie? Well, I understand that memory is a construct. However, I remember the two little boys, for such they were, running up the hotel corridor, knocking on my door and asking if my wife, Virginia, was coming out to play. I do not think they were joking. I also remember Hunt and me laying back on a track so much that it, imperceptibly, slowed down. I do not remember which track it was... or which gig. Then I seem to remember that Hansa could be divided into different spaces by the judicious arrangement of the curtains. It was a huge space!

Berlin was very strange then... It had been the capital of Germany, but was now an island of so-called plenty, surrounded by the grey decay of East Germany, with colourless posters advertising holidays in Poland... Very strange!

Writing with the two boys was easy, plain sailing. David had a small upright piano and I had my unplugged Stratocaster and Iggy had a recording device that was beyond description. Working with the boys, I took as much space as I needed... but I'm not greedy. Funnily enough, my favourite Bowie album isn't in the trilogy. It's *Outside*, a bit like its heir. (2016)

MICHAEL ROTHER

Brian Eno came to see Harmonia in concert in 1974 in Hamburg and he said he knew most of the krautrock bands and often spoke about them with fellow musicians, including David Bowie. We didn't pay much attention because, at the time, Hans-Joachim Roedelius, Dieter Moebius and I were busy getting the Harmonia project running. It wasn't easy – we weren't popular. More precisely, we were totally unsuccessful; it was a disaster! But not on an artistic level.

The funny thing is that Klaus Dinger, my partner in Neu!, was a big David Bowie fan and he introduced me to his music. He would listen to Bowie at home, in the car but, to be honest, I didn't pay much attention at first. Like other German musicians of my generation, I was focused on what I was doing, which closed me off to others. Knowing David Bowie's passion for krautrock, I wasn't all that surprised to receive a phone call in 1976. I was asked if I'd be interested in playing on an upcoming record of his. I told this person – I don't know who it was – that I was up for it, but I wanted to get in touch with David himself to talk about what he had in mind, what we could do together.

So he phoned me and what I remember is that we were enthusiastic about the prospect of working together. I also made some suggestions, like hiring Jaki Liebezeit[23] on the drums. After that, some other guy from his organization wanted to talk to me about money, contracts, and I think that that's where it went wrong. At the time, fees and percentages were the least of my concerns, and I told this person not to worry about that. That as long as the music was good, the rest didn't matter. I said it wasn't necessary for me to sign a 20-page contract before going to the studio. I just said, 'Let's make music and we'll see.'

The next thing was, I received a third call, a very short one. The voice said, 'David asks me to tell you he has changed his mind, he doesn't need you.' I thought that was strange; it didn't sound like what David Bowie had told me a few days before. I threw myself into my second solo album[24]. I was disappointed, of course, but I had no way of reaching David Bowie to know what had made him change his mind so that was the end of the story. I was stunned to learn, a few years later, that he said in an interview that I'd turned him down, that I'd refused to play on his album!

I remember that David was willing to contribute a quote for the liner notes when part of Neu!'s catalogue was reissued in 2001. The record company went through his management and he wrote a few notes about Neu! But, in the text he sent, he mixed up my name with Klaus Dinger's. I told the record company it didn't make sense to print this, that they had to ask him to correct it. They said, 'No, he's going to send us packing.' They finally did it and he was very polite, very friendly, and said, 'But of course, where has my memory gone?' I think we even exchanged emails, because I remember that he apologized to me. In the end he contributed a very nice quote.

I have very strong reason to believe that Neu! inspired the name "Heroes" because, in 1976, David Bowie told a German music magazine that 'Hero' and 'After Eight' were his favourite tracks on *Neu! '75*, our third album. It's not too much to think that 'Hero' must have somehow left a mark on his brain and in his heart[25]. I'm not a Bowie expert, but I've carefully listened to *Low* and *"Heroes"*, and I have to say I was very impressed by the title song of the second, which I thought was particularly good. I really like the video on YouTube where Tony Visconti talks about "Heroes" and opens up the tracks to explain how the song was recorded. I also always thought that 'Always Crashing In The Same Car' had an interesting title and I really like 'V-2 Schneider'. On those two records, it all made sense – it felt like Bowie was recycling some German music elements, but made them personal to him. Nowadays, I hear a lot of influences from Neu! or from other German bands in the work of English-speaking artists, even the younger ones! That doesn't bother me if they pick up ideas, but I wish they were more ambitious. It's not enough to take a drum loop from a Neu! album and play guitar over it to recreate that spirit. David Bowie was much more subtle, and what you hear on those records are echoes of krautrock, but with his own signature. It remains, above all, very interesting music.

So I never managed to meet Bowie. However, during that brief email exchange over the liner notes, he asked me to let him know if I was ever in New York. I'm a bit sad about not having had the chance, because I would have loved to discuss music with him. And I never saw him on stage either. You know, I enjoy a quiet life in a village in Lower Saxony and only rarely go to concerts. That's where Harmonia started in 1973. But I do love to travel and I'm pleased that my music comes with me. I like to think David loved that too. What happens on the road stays with us, in our system. I kept an eye and an ear on what he was doing, but anyway, he was so famous, he was everywhere! I don't listen to the radio much either. Most of the time, unless I'm into something or someone, the absence of information suits me well. I love music so much that, whenever there is some around, at least 40 per cent of my mind is already connected to it and I cannot do anything else. And I never ran into Brian Eno again either. Some friends who saw *The Ship*, his recent sound installation in Hamburg, gave me news of him. These days, whenever I'm in Forst, I prefer to listen to the sounds of nature while I'm watching the Weser flow by. (2016)

HANS-JOACHIM ROEDELIUS

When David Bowie talked about his love for krautrock in the mid-1970s, I wasn't really familiar with his work at the time because I had to learn a lot to be able to do my own thing, but I knew about him. Brian Eno came to our place in 1976[26] to tell us that the two of them were blown away by our understanding of contemporary music and the way we tried to do our own thing. I loved *Low* and then *"Heroes"*, but

I always felt like these records were a long way from my universe. I was never a fan of Bowie or other 'heroes' of that genre. Mine were Hapshash And The Coloured Coat, Third Ear Band, Captain Beefheart and Can.

I don't know what David Bowie liked about krautrock or whether the genre just pushed him to experiment, but I know for sure that he and Brian Eno were very much influenced by Harmonia, Cluster and, of course, Can. Eno didn't play anything of the trilogy he recorded with Bowie for us – the final instalment was *Lodger* and it was recorded in Switzerland after he'd worked with us. But he did play us some songs from *Before And After Science*[27].

I often saw David Bowie in Vienna, where I lived, and I went to see him in concert many times. But he never suggested we work together; I honestly don't think he would have asked me to collaborate at all. Whenever we met, I felt like he was well aware our respective approaches to composition were totally different. He did ask Michael Rother for a collaboration though, but it didn't happen. (2016)

IRMIN SCHMIDT[28]

What was fascinating about David Bowie was his ability to continually reinvent himself, to be mysterious, and the impression he gave of never aging. It's like he was the very embodiment of his music, which is impressive. He had this Dorian Gray side, so I didn't think he'd ever die. When I think about him I think about *Der Mann Ohne Eigenschaften* [The Man Without Qualities] by Robert Musil[29].

While people often talk about the impact krautrock had on Bowie in Berlin, I tend to hear it more in some of his songs from the early 80s, especially 'Scary Monsters', which always makes me think of 'Mother Sky'[30]. And he never denied the similarity. He was open to all styles and he knew how to take advantage of them – folk, rock and even French chanson! He was the definition of a post-modern artist.

When he lived in Berlin at the time of *"Heroes"*, I didn't really know he was drawn to bands like Can, Neu! and Kraftwerk. We were deep in our thing and had no idea what was happening around us. I never cared to know who was interested in Can but, in hindsight, it's satisfying to think that we might have had an influence on the music of our times and its most illustrious figures.

I saw Bowie on stage in London, if I remember correctly, but didn't get the chance to meet him. I'll always think of him as someone who exuded kindness, with real nobility and a touch of mystery. He knew how to keep his secrets and he took them with him. (2017)

JEAN-HERVÉ PÉRON

When I hear Bowie's name, it reminds me of a story that some musician friends told me about them eating at the same restaurant as him one day. They hadn't noticed him there, but he came up to their table and asked if he could join them. They saw he'd just come from a table full of music VIPs, but David Bowie told them he was bored and wanted to finish his meal with them instead, as they seemed to be having fun. Mr Bowie didn't beat around the bush! I'm like that too – direct.

At the risk of disappointing you, in the early 70s, when I started playing with Faust, I didn't know anything about David Bowie's love for krautrock. He meant a lot to me as a musician, but Faust voluntarily shut itself in a sort of bubble and, even today, I have trouble believing that German music, and therefore our band, could have had an impact on such incredible giants as Bowie and Eno. I only know it because I read about it later. We heard about others – Can and all that – but we'd decided to stay in our zone.

David Bowie haunted me, as did Lou Reed and Frank Zappa, who was one of the first to write lyrics that were critical of American society, and whose music deviated from the well-trodden paths of rock and pop. But, at the same time, I was suspicious of show business. One time in 1973, we were at The Manor, Richard Branson's studio,[31] with Mike Oldfield, and there were quite a few VIPs there, including Keith Richards. Branson kindly introduced us as a 'revolutionary new band' and Richards, contemptuously, just said, 'Keep rehearsing.'

Unfortunately, I never met David Bowie, but some of my friends knew him and always said nice things about him. You know, Faust may have started a revolution, but only one, while staying on the same path. David Bowie initiated several! From the outside, that's what it looked like. One day, he was like a chick with feathers, another, he was as mysterious as a Martian. Yet another day, he was stunningly elegant... I think that's what fascinated me the most about him. I was almost jealous. He had many strings to his bow and he was shooting arrows in all directions. In the days of his trilogy, he may have been influenced by us and other Germans, but what I can say – and I'm ready to swear to it – is that he never needed to copy anybody.

Faust's golden rule was to set off on our own new paths, even though it was impossible for us to be completely cut off from the outside world. There was nothing elitist about that and it wasn't contempt for others, but we had voluntarily shut ourselves off since the Wümme period[32]. As for me, I had so much music in my head that I didn't naturally lean towards what others were doing. It's probable that, as well as our sound, David Bowie appreciated our spirit of absolute freedom, coupled with real risk-taking. But I didn't gravitate towards his songs or records. I was often exposed to his music by an intermediary, a friend for example, who suggested I listen to such and such a thing. And, each time, I was floored. When I heard bands like The Rolling Stones, because it was impossible not to, it didn't pique my curiosity. But Bowie was another story. I sometimes wondered, while listening to his music, 'Why didn't we think of that first?'

I never saw him at any of our concerts or on stage – I either didn't have time or I wasn't able to! And you know, I never stopped being drawn to the unusual, to the unexpected. Perhaps David Bowie's problem was fame. That time he joined my friends at their table says a lot about the kinds of trappings of success he was trying to escape. (2016)

NICOLAS GODIN

EMS's VCS 3 synth, which Brian Eno used a lot, is a pretty small modular synth with a sort of patchboard matrix where pins are inserted, into which he plugged a control keyboard, the DK1. Phil Manzanera had asked EMS to make him a pedal version of the VCS 3, but he never managed to get it to make the same sound twice! There's also a briefcase model of this synth, the Synthi AKS, that David Bowie and Eno used a lot on *Low*, *"Heroes"* and *Lodger*. Pink Floyd, Tangerine Dream, Depeche Mode and The Who are among the other famous users of the VCS 3. They still make it in England... (2018)

ALBERT KOSKI

All those rumours about David Bowie's alleged statements on Nazism, the far right, all that, was nonsense. Yes, he loved everything about Germany, but it was mostly because of the arts, expressionism, the films, the whole visual side. And he wasn't the only one! French directors François Reichenbach and Luchino Visconti thought the Nazis in uniform looked very beautiful. I'm Jewish, you know, so I could have taken offence... (2018)

MARC EXIGA

Personally, I always thought record label people were a bit like the lackeys of capitalism, and our mission was to serve those who'd signed a contract! Our job was to make an effort – never enough according to the artists – to make them profitable and increase their fame. But, in reality, we were just employees of that monster. So there were things we could do, and others that I thought we shouldn't do. I made a point, and especially with Bowie, to approach the artist in the most pragmatic way possible, without trying to use our position or label to interfere with his entourage or personal life. It might have been a tall order, but I had this sort of code of ethics. That's how I did my job. So long as my presence was necessary, and it was wanted, I'd be there. But if not, it could have become too much. Not that we had to deal with Bashar al-Assad or anything, but I always felt that there was a sort of red line one should not cross. It was better to follow a sort of code of conduct, if only to keep the artist from saying, as they're leaving, 'Actually, what's-his-name, he's nice, but he's always breathing down my neck and I can't stand it anymore. So when I come back from Paris, you'll give me someone else, okay?'

Of course I remember Pat Gibbons, actually Pat Gibbons III – it was a dynasty... Okay he was charming and I shared quite a few meals with him, but I felt like it was more like David Bowie was managing him than the opposite. Gibbons was a sort of letterbox that presented his artist with various options. David would say yes or no, and Pat's job was then to confirm what Bowie had decided to do or not to do. Pat was nice but, if I'd been an artist, I don't think I would have hired him as my manager...

In France in the 1970s, David Bowie didn't sell a whole lot: the best-selling album was *Young Americans*, which benefited a bit from the success of 'Fame' and 'Golden Years'. But it was very impressive to see how much stronger his reputation was than his commercial impact. Despite everything, the rest of the world showed us that sales in France were decent. I think our country was a good place for him. (2018)

REEVES GABRELS

For one song on *Earthling*, David wanted to have the piano sound of "Heroes", so he decided to sample it from the original multitrack tape. It had been damaged and we had to 'bake' it[33] to play it on an analogue tape recorder we'd rented for the occasion, so we could transfer the tracks onto a digital format. So I listened to each track while looking at the original recording notes, and discovered exactly what was on tape. I wanted to check, among other things, that, as everyone has been saying since 1977, Robert Fripp played his iconic part from start to finish, and in one take.

In fact, there are three guitar tracks by Fripp, two of which are quite messy. And I love Fripp's work! What we hear on the song mainly comes from the good one!

But the rest, the melodic guitar lines leading to the C part, for example, was played by Carlos Alomar. Carlos is much more present on *"Heroes"* and *Lodger* than one might believe. People usually think that the more aggressive, saturated sounds come from other guitarists, but that's not always the case. (2017)

MATTHEW FISHER

A few years ago, I realized *"Heroes"* was produced by David Bowie and Tony Visconti. I don't know why, but in my mind, Brian Eno had made that record. But in fact, his name does not appear on the centre label. So I got that David and Tony were responsible for this production and I actually emailed Visconti to congratulate him. (2016)

JAMES WILLIAMSON

In 1976, while I didn't exactly know the nature of their deal – whether David Bowie, who had money and success, wanted to take Iggy under his wing, or whether he really needed an artistic partnership – it is clear to me that David held out his hand to Iggy and ended up doing what he'd had in mind for a while: to tame that crazy artist by becoming his producer, and without having to deal with his impossible band! When his two albums came out, I didn't think much of them, but some of the songs from *The Idiot* and *Lust For Life* are important and have undeniably stood the test of time. As for Iggy's real contribution to these songs, the matter is controversial and it's likely that Bowie was in charge. But, at the same time, it was probably what Iggy needed. He was fragile and David helped him get back on his feet. Later, the success of Bowie's version of 'China Girl' put quite a bit of butter on Iggy's bread. I know what I'm talking about, because after David covered 'Don't Look Down'[34] on *Tonight*, even though I wasn't making music anymore, a lot of money appeared in my bank account!

Over the past few years, 'Search And Destroy' has featured in several films, series and ads and *Raw Power*, which owes a lot to Bowie, has become the foundation of The Stooges. In 1972, we had no other ambition than to make music we thought was good, believing the world needed it. It turns out that it took the world a bit longer than expected to figure it out... (2017)

ELVIS COSTELLO

We recorded *Armed Forces* in six weeks at the Eden Studios in London, with the barely veiled idea that it could be our *Sgt. Pepper*. It was my first road record, written while looking out the window of a coach, 'live from the American dream', both physically and morally, by gleaning words off posters. But my bad touring musician habits started to get the better of me. My marriage broke down. I drank a lot, I did drugs... It wasn't bad at first, but it ended up bringing me down. And we were totally captivated by *Low* and *"Heroes"*; we listened only to that, drooling with admiration. (1998)

PHILIP GLASS

I've always been in touch with David Bowie. I remember he phoned me in 1976 when I created my first opera, *Einstein On The Beach*. After reminding me he'd attended a concert by my ensemble at the Royal College of Art in London in 1970, he mentioned the new direction his music was taking, and I was happy to hear that he was working in an experimental way – that was what made his work valuable in the world of pop. It so happened that we liked the same artists, including John Cage and Marcel Duchamp and, having gone to art school like a lot of British rock singers, David knew the importance of innovation.

At the time, you could make art in popular music – Hollywood hadn't reduced everything to a sideshow – and so he applied this idea of the avant-garde to rock. *Low* and *"Heroes"* nevertheless surprised me a lot because not only did his music deviate from the usual format of rock material, but it was much more inventive than what people were writing in prestigious music academies. To the point where some of what I found in these two albums directly influenced the opera *Satyagraha*, which I composed in 1979.

David Bowie hears music in an organic, visceral way. He writes in the studio, following his instinct, and has no theoretical knowledge of polytonality and its importance. It's like with George Gershwin. Whenever I hear one of his pieces, I don't care that historians consider him a second-rate composer because, for me, his music is of the highest order. People who've spent years studying music theory are not capable of writing melodies like the ones you hear on *Low* and *"Heroes"*, which are both very common and very strange. I immediately wanted to do something from these records, which I think are the most interesting in electronic avant-garde music. When I phoned him fifteen years later to tell him I wanted to compose symphonies based on the themes from *Low*, *"Heroes"* and *Lodger*, David was thrilled. The project is no doubt as good for his image as it is for mine!

Still, many 'serious' orchestra conductors will probably refuse to conduct these symphonies because they're associated with David Bowie's name. It's heartbreaking, because these people could learn a lot from his passion for art and his undying curiosity. I suggested to David that we work together on the symphonies, but he told me he'd prefer not to get involved, and that I could have all the artistic freedom I wanted. He did come to some rehearsals and told me he especially liked the *"Heroes" Symphony*, precisely because it deviated the most from the original material. (1993/1997)[35]

MARTIN GORE

The record I'd take to a desert island? It would have to be a David Bowie album, but which one? Let's say *"Heroes"*. Dave [Gahan] sees him a lot in New York, their children go to the same school. I think he's recording at the moment, right? (2012)

NEIL TENNANT

We have a studio in Berlin right now, and one in London. The city makes us productive and we work later into the night. Today's Berlin is no longer the one David Bowie knew in the 1970s. That Weimar Republic vibe, all that. But we did go and have a coffee at the Neues Ufer bar, where he liked to drink... There are photos of him on the walls. (2016)

1. David Bowie had listened to some of Iggy Pop's demos on which the Sales brothers played and sang (backing vocals). These songs – released on *Kill City* – apparently gave him the idea to call them. The Sales brothers' vocal contribution can be very clearly heard on the song 'Success' on *Lust For Life*.

2. He was renting a room in the former UFA (Universal Film AG) film studios on Viktoriastraße, where Nazi propaganda films were shot. Peter Baumann recorded *Romance 76*, his first solo album, in this studio/rehearsal room, which he called The Victoria (The Vic).

3. A common thread (or rather a conductive thread) in the life and career of David Bowie was the theme of madness. Stimulated by the mental illness of his half-brother Terry, it found new life on the cover of *"Heroes"*. This other reference to Erich Heckel's painting betrayed a worry that wasn't just aesthetic. In fact, *Roquairol* is the name of the crazed character in the four-volume novel *Titan*, by Johann Paul Friedrich Richter, a German romantic writer from the early 19th century. A fan of *Titan*, Heckel also took inspiration from his friend Ernst Ludwig Kirchner for his canvas. A German painter, printmaker and sculptor, as well as a founder of the movement that became Die Brücke, Kirchner, who Bowie was also interested in, suffered from serious psychological problems and died in Switzerland. On the eve of World War II, desperate over Hitler's politics, he shot himself in the heart.

4. In the spring of 1977, Tony Visconti was asked to produce *Hit And Run*, the third album by British hard rock band Dirty Tricks. Sessions took place in his London studio (Sound House) near Hammersmith, as well as at the Zodiac Sound Studios at 59 Dean Street in Soho, which he bought that same year and which will become Good Earth. Colin Thurston, the recording engineer at Zodiac, was Visconti's assistant on *Hit And Run*. In fact, Tony Visconti had known Dirty Tricks since 1976 – *Night Man*, the band's second album, was partially recorded at Sound House. On the jacket, he was thanked for having made his studio available, and nothing more. After *The Idiot*, Colin Thurston will be Visconti's assistant on *"Heroes"* (in Berlin) and will later produce many important records in the 80s, including the first by Duran Duran, Talk Talk and Human League. He was also responsible for Magazine's second album (recorded at Good Earth) and the third and last LP of The Only Ones: *Baby's Got A Gun*, released in 1980. Thurston will die in early 2007, after a long illness.

5. David Bowie first heard about this early-20th-century painter from Owen Frampton – he was one of his favourites. *Wally*, the nickname of Egon Schiele's first muse (and probably his great love), was going to be directed by Clive Donner. During his session with Sukita for the cover of *"Heroes"*, Bowie struck some of the poses the painter famously depicted.

6. George Murray's interview in this chapter undermines the recurring theory about the genesis of "Heroes", proving that David Bowie didn't have all that much 'artistic haze', especially regarding the subjects he wanted to tackle in some of his songs. While he completed most of his lyrics just before recording them, by continuing to use cut-ups and other random methods, he almost always had in mind several guiding ideas and often titles before entering the studio. However, he wasn't usually interested in letting those around him know

what his songs were about. People who pretend to know are liars.

7. Robert Fripp wasn't all that rusty on his instrument. Before and after sessions for *"Heroes"*, he played on Peter Gabriel's first two albums, perhaps his best, which came out in 1977 and 1978. He also produced the second one. Keyboardist Larry Fast is also on these two records, and the pianist on the second one is Roy Bittan.

8. After *"Heroes"* came out, many guitarists were convinced that Robert Fripp had used an Ebow and went out and bought one for themselves. It is a sort of electronic bow that causes the strings to vibrate, like a 'resonator'. This piece of equipment has been manufactured since the 1960s, but Fripp did not use one on the title song. He achieved the iconic feedback sounds and varied the pitch of his notes by moving closer and further away from his amp.

9. This day of shooting (9 September) was reportedly chaotic. Since the show was being filmed in Manchester at the Granada Studios, some guest musicians arrived from London on a morning train. Some participants were filmed that same day (including Generation X, even though they were late), but not Eddie And The Hot Rods (who simply went by the name The Rods that summer). In fact, the band from Canvey Island spent the day waiting to be filmed, only to be told that they would have to come back the following week because David Bowie and Marc Bolan had taken up too much rehearsal time, and that the union hours of the technicians were very strict. And come back they did, because in episode six of *Marc*, The Rods are seen singing their hit of the day, 'Do Anything You Wanna Do'. At the time, the band had two guitarists (David Higgs and Graeme Douglas), but only the latter appeared on TV. The day of the initial planned filming, Higgs had missed the train to Manchester, and he didn't travel with them when the band returned either. The night of 9 September, David Bowie and his entourage were on the train back to London. After picking up some food and wine from his compartment, he went over to sit with The Rods and spent part of the trip talking to them about everything and nothing. Barrie Masters, the frontman, will talk to the author about that special day after a concert in Le Havre in 2010.

10. 'Standing Next To You' and 'Sleeping Next To You' are the other two names of this song, which was never officially released and has often been pirated.

11. That same year, Laurie Anderson also paid tribute to Chris Burden in 'It's Not The Bullet That Kills You – It's The Hole', which appeared as the A-side of her first single, released for an installation at the Holly Solomon Gallery in New York.

12. Photographer Vernon Dewhurst – interviewed earlier in this book – explained that British artist Clare Shenstone was a good friend of David Bowie. She was a witness at his first wedding and he will ask her to paint a portrait of Iman years later. Shenstone spent some time with Bowie in Berlin in 1977 and she told him she had a dream about swimming with dolphins… David owned one of her works, a portrait of Francis Bacon, to whom she was close.

13. In 2016, Eventide will release *Tverb*, a plug-in designed with Tony Visconti to reproduce his technique of the three microphones, which could be placed anywhere in a virtual Meistersaal.

14. A technique that the French electro-pop group Air will use 20 years later. In the song 'Sexy Boy' on *Moon Safari*, Jean-Benoît Dunckel's voice goes through a rapidly spinning Leslie, like Ozzy Osborne's voice in 'Planet Caravan' by Black Sabbath. Similarly, Nicolas Godin plays the bass on 'Sexy Boy' on the Minimoog and puts it through a Talk Box, an effects unit with a plastic tube that makes it possible to alter the sound of an instrument with your mouth. It's been a very popular device since the 1960s and Peter Frampton made it even more popular in 1976. His Talk Box could be heard prominently on some of the songs on his *Frampton Comes Alive!* album.

15. David Bowie and Brian Eno each drew a card without telling the other what was on it. Bowie's urged him to 'emphasize differences' and Eno's said to 'try to make everything as similar as possible'. This antagonism largely contributes to the singularity of 'Sense Of Doubt'.

16. However, this title obviously refers to *The Secret Lives Of Lawrence Of Arabia*, one of the first serious biographies of Thomas Edward Lawrence, which was published in the 1970s. It's funny to note that the titles of at least three books in English about Lawrence published after 1977 contain the word 'hero', a term commonly used by admirers of this mysterious and controversial figure.

17. In *Best Of Bowie*, the 2002 DVD compilation released on EMI, the video of "Heroes" will be attributed to Stanley Dorfman. It appears that Ferguson and Dorfman directed it together in Paris. (In 2019, Nacho, a British videographer living in Hong Kong, will edit a 'new' version of "Heroes" from footage of the original shooting.) The videos of 'Beauty And The Beast' and 'Blackout', never officially released, were most probably directed by the same team. In late 1977, Ferguson alone will direct the video of 'Mull Of Kintyre' by Wings, Paul McCartney's band. The song will be Number 1 in the charts in December and will hit the same position in the Top 100 Bestselling Singles Of The Year. "Heroes" won't make it, but 'Sound And Vision' will, at Number 31, way behind singles by Leo Sayer, Donna Summer, The Bee Gees and Queen.

18. Contrary to what is often assumed, David Bowie spoke at Devo's concert at Max's Kansas City on 14 November 1977, and not on 25 May, because he had just returned from Japan then and was in Berlin preparing for the *"Heroes"* sessions.

19. Like more than 15 of Bowie's studio albums and several compilations, *"Heroes"* was certified gold in the United Kingdom (only *Blackstar*, *The Next Day*, *Let's Dance*, *Scary Monsters*, *Ziggy Stardust* and *Hunky Dory* will be certified platinum). However, *"Heroes"* has still not been given its own special reissue, only appearing in the box set *A New Career In A New Town (1977–1982)* in 2017. In 1991, Rykodisc will re-release it with 'Abdulmajid' as a bonus track and a not-so-tasty remix of 'Joe The Lion' by David Richards. The song "Heroes" won't reach Number 1 in the British charts until late 2010, when it is covered by the finalists of the horrible television talent show *The X Factor*. In *Rainbowman*, the author has made the choice not to mention or list the (rarely good) covers of David Bowie songs, but it's interesting to note that, when, in 2014, Swedish DJ Alesso and singer Tove Lo deliver their pathetic electro-pop version of "Heroes" – aptly renamed 'Heroes (We Could Be)' – they'll manage to take it to Number 6 in the British charts.

20. While promoting *"Heroes"*, David Bowie will say he planned to sing on *Exposure*, Robert Fripp's first solo album, released in 1979. He won't, but three musicians who worked with Bowie – Brian Eno, Sid McGinnis and Tony Levin – will appear on this record.

21. The plumbing issue (in London) also baffled another American, Tony Visconti, who mentions it in his autobiography.

22. David Bowie's passion for painting was so strong at the time that it must be noted that *Lust For Life*, which he suggested, was the name of a biographical novel by Irving Stone about Vincent Van Gogh, published in 1934. It was made into a film by Vincente Minnelli in 1956.

23. Phenomenal drummer of German band Can, he mastered all styles and, like Dennis Davis, he was known for making almost any music groove, even the most intellectual kind. Jaki Liebezeit died in 2017, the same year as bass player Holger Czukay, another founding member of Can.

24. This clarification helps us date David Bowie's initial phone call. *Sterntaler*, Michael Rother's second solo album, came out in 1978 and was probably recorded in the second half of the previous year. So it is more likely that Bowie phoned Rother in 1977 (not in 1976).

25. In interviews before his death in 2008, Klaus Dinger rarely mentioned his passion for David Bowie. He barely touched on the fact that Bowie had asked him to work with him in the 1970s. However, he knew that Bowie had a soft spot for La Düsseldorf, the band Dinger started after Neu!, and had liked their first album. While "Heroes" is nothing like 'Hero', its beat has a lot in common with 'Silver Cloud',

an instrumental from La Düsseldorf's first album (produced by Conny Plank), which also came out as a single in 1976.

26. In early September 1976, Eno worked with Harmonia at their studio in Germany. The result of these sessions only came out in 1997 under the title *Tracks And Traces*. Eno also recorded with Cluster, the duo made up of Hans-Joachim Roedelius and Dieter Moebius. They released *Cluster & Eno* in 1977 and *After The Heat* the following year. It has often been said that the *Low* instrumentals were influenced by Eno's work with Harmonia. This could be true but, as Moebius has pointed out, some krautrock musicians, although claiming to be impervious to English and American bands, had still managed to stay up-to-date with what David Bowie and Roxy Music were releasing in the early 70s.

27. Cluster and Jaki Liebezeit contributed to Brian Eno's fifth album, partly recorded at Conny Plank's studio near Cologne. Around that time, Eno admitted that his collaboration with David Bowie on *Low* and *"Heroes"* had put wind in his sails and money in his bank account.

28. Irmin Schmidt is one of the founding members of Can, an influential krautrock band from Cologne.

29. Twenty extremely different characters coexist in this unfinished novel by the Austrian author. *Der Mann Ohne Eigenschaften* is made all the more mysterious by its lack of resolution and is now considered a classic of 20th-century literature.

30. Written by Can in 1970 for the film *Deep End* by Jerzy Skolimowski, 'Mother Sky' lasts for almost 15 minutes and appears on the band's album *Soundtracks*, released that same year.

Several sources indicate that David Bowie
started listening to krautrock in the early 1970s.

31. The band recorded *Faust IV* there, their
first album for Virgin, the label co-created by
Richard Branson. Virgin owned The Manor
(Studio) near Oxford. Mike Oldfield will make
his famous *Tubular Bells* there. The Manor was
one of the first residential studios in the UK.

32. Faust recorded their first albums in
Wümme, east of Bremen, where they practically
locked themselves in between 1969 and 1971.
Polydor had given them a hefty advance, so
Faust set up their own studio in a former school
building outside the city.

33. A well-known practice among recording
engineers working on remasterings, 'baking' an
old tape helps preserve as much information as
possible before playing it, usually one last time,
before a digital transfer.

34. Co-written by Pop and Williamson, 'Don't
Look Down', whose original version is totally
different, will come out on *New Values*, Iggy
Pop's 1979 studio album. It will be his first
since the David Bowie period (between 1976
and 1978).

35. Words reported by Éric Dahan.

LODGER

RCA – 18 MAY 1979

STAGE (PARLOPHONE – 8 SEPTEMBER 1978)

WELCOME TO THE BLACKOUT
(LIVE LONDON '78)
(PARLOPHONE – 21 APRIL 2018)

'The disagreeable manservant, whom I had hoped never to see again,
opened the door...
"What name?" he asked, though I felt sure that he remembered it well
enough. He spoke in English with a bit of a cockney twang.
So he had remembered my nationality.
"Jones," I said.'
(GRAHAM GREENE, *DOCTOR FISCHER OF GENEVA*, 1980)

'I never hoped that people would understand immediately what I was doing. If that were my wish, I'd jump onto the first moving train, without getting off, and I'd make a lot of money. What I do isn't necessarily a financial success in all cases. But it's interesting and sometimes important. I never felt part of mass consciousness. If you asked me what I, David Bowie, could do for people, I'd say, "Nothing." NOTHING. All I can do is create something for myself, and for myself alone. And maybe that will affect X number of people. It's just that I can't picture those people. The only one I see is me. And if it does something for me, it'll do it for others, because I'm not different. I'm like you. Punk rock? It's delightful. Is it a new wave? No, it's an old wave. I think the most interesting of all these bands is Television. I love Television. All the others are amusing. […]

'In France they talk to me about *Low* because of the Château d'Hérouville, in Berlin it's *"Heroes"*, but I'd love to talk about *Lodger* – except that for the media, it's from nowhere. Well, I guess it's my fault, as I opened it up to many genres, even reggae! So it's not easy to analyse, which I think baffled the press. They thought they were hearing a conventional album, which from me, might have been the ultimate provocation! And those who thought I was trying to fit into a mould didn't really listen to *Lodger*. There is not a single normal song on that record! […]

'I don't think you can recommend anything to someone who's going through depression. I'm afraid there's no way to save people from their feelings of insecurity, their fear of really having to get to the bottom of the abyss in order to start seeing the positive aspects of life. The only reassuring thing you can tell someone is that they haven't seen anything yet, that it could get worse in a heartbeat. But that's just my personal experience. It's pointless to resist, you have to drop to the bottom of the chasm and then, if you're lucky, you can climb out again.

'I know, deep down, that I'm a late-19th-century man, that writing and reading are at the heart of my psyche, that my very life is just a long conversation with *oeuvres* from the past and that the dialogue is not over yet. Even if I'm more and more interested in the expressiveness of words than their meaning. […]

'Um, personally, I never hear mistakes – just interesting choices!'

DB (1977/1991/1997/2002)

It's not as if he hadn't warned us. That he would lie sometimes or, more exactly, that he would bend the truth. Not necessarily to his advantage, but according to the movement of the sands of his mind, which knew no rest. During interviews in 1977, David Bowie often joked about his soul phase and said he was surprised 'Fame' worked so well, even though it came from a jam session. Without even checking his notes, he'd scrawled the lyrics down quickly, on a coffee table at Electric Lady Studios. As if he thought that success didn't exactly reward his years of effort. In truth, he was proud and loved that song which, like 'Let's Dance', he played on stage until the end, and not just to please the audience.

He also admitted to some journalists (not necessarily the same ones – he liked to divide and conquer) that his Thin White Duke, although he eventually loosened up a bit over the concerts of the Isolar tour, was a relatively cold character. It amused him all the more because he considered himself to be quite the opposite in real life. Also, he didn't hate being told that Raw Moon, the DAM trio as Carlos Alomar still calls them, might have been his best band. They were bubbly, instead of him and he, who never sweated on stage (as Tony Defries pointed out), was perfect as the black and white dandy, standing like a Mikado stick against this fluorescent backdrop.

As for the trilogy, which he called a triptych, he reportedly spent 25 years not knowing what to do with it, or what to think about it. Other than that it did badly. While being interviewed about *"Heroes"*, Bowie told some of his interlocutors that *Low*, which had no muse, was a lot like him ('my DNA'). With others, he wondered aloud what he'd wanted to do with those records, going so far as to blame Brian Eno for their lack of humanity. Some lyrics, written in what he sometimes called a comatose state, also worried him. He lamented their emptiness. And to refute those who showered him with praise (although in 1977 there were fewer of them), David Bowie sometimes lashed out at *"Heroes"*, or more precisely, at who he was when he recorded it – a British musician damaged by drugs and confused by alcohol, landed in Switzerland, with a refuge in Berlin and a desire to leave for New York, by way of London. A godfather of punk, like Marc Bolan, Lou Reed and Iggy Pop. A 30-year-old icon, but one who said he didn't care about fame, or that he wasn't made for it. But by the 1990s, when American composer Philip Glass, whom he greatly respected, turns *Low* and *"Heroes"* into symphonies[1], Bowie will stop changing his mind (at least on this matter) and will agree with those who see them as pivotal records.

At Meltdown in 2002, he will play *Low* in its entirety (followed by *Heathen*). It's his only 'classic album' to have received such a treatment. As for *Lodger*, the last of the trilogy, appreciation of it varied widely after its release. It divided the media and the public, who often saw it as a third leg. Some of those who played on it have continually revised their evaluations upwards or downwards depending on the circumstances and especially – which is in the nature of musicians – on whether it would favour them or not. Not even Bowie's opinion has been consistent on this subject.

Others saw *Lodger* as an absolute masterpiece. Tony Visconti always thought the world of it – it is on his initiative that a remixed version now exists, in the box set *A New Career In A New Town (1977–1982)*, released by Parlophone in 2017. *Lodger* is the only record from the triptych on which Brian Eno worked on more than half the songs, but it was still co-produced by David Bowie and Tony Visconti – tired of reading (and hearing) that his Berlin period was the most interesting because Eno was producing his music, Bowie would set the record straight at the turn of the new millennium.

The end of winter 1977 is complicated for David Bowie, and not just because of his family life. 'Beauty And The Beast' has been released as a single in January, and although it has a Masayoshi Sukita[2] photo on the cover, it won't get above Number 39 in the British charts. And while he saw it as a welcome diversion, *Just A Gigolo*, the film by British actor and director David Hemmings, in which Bowie is starring as the male lead, will not meet his expectations. He has agreed to play German officer Paul Ambrosius von Przygodski in part because filming is taking place in Berlin and he loves the idea of working with Sydne Rome and Marlene Dietrich (although in the end, he will never meet the latter, as the scene in which they both appear will be filmed in two different cities).

On and off set, Hemmings and his team pamper David. They enjoy his company and worry about his lack of appetite and his excessive smoking (more than three packs of Gitanes a day...). Between takes, to kill time, he takes up lino cutting. Nobody remembers whether Bowie was asked to work on the film score, but all signs suggest that, if that had been the case, he would have accepted. His contribution to the music will be limited to a hummed part in 'Revolutionary Song', co-written with Jack Fishman, the film's musical director, and attributed to David Bowie And The Rebels on the cover of the soundtrack. The press release for *Just A Gigolo* will report that he wrote this song on set and recorded it himself while playing all the instruments. However, the piece, as heard in the movie, seems to have been significantly enriched after he delivered the tape. A financial flop when it comes out, *Just A Gigolo*, like all the projects David Bowie was involved in, will be viewed more favourably after his death. He spoke very highly of it while he was shooting it, but knowing that as an actor he'd gone from an important work (*The Man Who Fell To Earth*) to a sort of dud, he will later say about it, 'It was my 32 Elvis Presley movies rolled into one.'

Until February, whenever his schedule allows, Bowie goes to Conny Plank's studio to take part in sessions for *Q: Are We Not Men? A: We Are Devo!,* Devo's first album. The production will be attributed to Brian Eno, but David definitely played a key role in the making of the record[3], although his name will not appear on it. During these takes in Germany, Eno plays some synth and records backing vocals with Bowie. Ultimately turned off by the idea of having a recognizable outsider work on their album, Devo will keep a few keyboard notes, but no traces of David's contribution. Witnesses confirm he got involved in the mix, especially since, according to some, Eno left before the end. After Iggy Pop, Devo is the only band David Bowie publicly (and seriously) declared he wanted to produce. His management will probably be approached regularly by singers and bands until the end of his life. The last record to carry the words 'produced by David Bowie', other than his own, will be Iggy's *Blah-Blah-Blah* in 1986. Coldplay, who will receive a particularly scathing refusal in the 2000s, will be honest enough to let it be known. They will ultimately settle on... Brian Eno.

His interviews with the media in early 1978 give Bowie the chance to mention other film projects and drop names of directors he would like to work with. He also talks about his painting, which he thinks is mediocre compared to that of the artists he admires and who inspire him. And when RCA reveal the dates for the next world tour (the first on such a large scale), his fans rejoice. Rarely short of witty remarks (or what he considered to be kind words), it amuses Bowie to say that it's primarily for financial reasons that he is preparing to hit the road again soon; although partially restored, his situation in this regard is far from spectacular (he pays most of his bills with RCA's advances) and, despite his great fame, he has never been a huge seller of records and knows that concerts are by far his most lucrative activity.

And then, during this time of musical upheaval, David Bowie wants to show what he is made of. *Low* and *"Heroes"* made him look experimental, and he is eager to see whether he will be able to fill venues with his 'new music'. But he isn't stupid and knows it's the right time to set the record straight. Bowie decides to liven up the set list with a healthy dose (five songs!) of *Ziggy Stardust*, the album that widened his audience six years before. During the two previous tours, he and his musicians always noticed that many fans had remained stuck in the glam era, often with orange hair and lightning bolts across their faces. The fans loved David's hair and wardrobe changes, but by reproducing Ziggy Stardust or Aladdin Sane's look, they continued to remind him of the value – in their hearts, eyes and ears – of his records from the first half of the decade.

Eager to offer something new, David Bowie is going to strengthen the DAM trio[4]. Unsurprisingly – given his impatience and versatility when choosing collaborators – the band that will accompany him from 29 March to 12 December 1978 won't be exactly the one he had in mind at the start. His first choice of lead guitarist, a crucial position in Bowie's bands until A Reality tour, was obviously Robert Fripp, the only virtuoso he said he liked. The reasons Fripp turned him down haven't been widely discussed, not even by him, but it seems that if the idea of playing *"Heroes"* live didn't put him off, having to learn a whole new repertoire (and not his own or King Crimson's) seemed like too tall an order and maybe even a little scary. Since the start of his career, Robert Fripp has been a methodical and rigorous guitarist, who never climbs on stage without being sure that he controls all aspects and parameters of his performance. Of course, he had nothing but admiration for David Bowie, at least as a musician – he wrote it on his blog – and he still considers his contributions to *"Heroes"* and *Scary Monsters* as two highlights of his very rich career (which he's recently decided not to discuss with the press anymore).

It is no secret that Brian Eno was also asked to participate in this tour[5]. The reasons for his refusal were probably very similar to Fripp's. The fact that Roxy Music's ex-synth player, the great transformer of sounds, is not the most gifted instrumentalist probably discouraged him from prolonged stage performances... Besides, being the stooge of a singer so much more expressive and demonstrative than himself probably wasn't all that appealing. In the creative atmosphere of a

German or Swiss studio, Eno must have felt, to some extent, like he was on an equal footing. But not on stage – a forbidding playground for those who lack confidence and where, as a performer, David knew few rivals at the time. Until the start of the tour (and even during it), Bowie will entertain the hope that Brian might join him for two or three important performances, but he never will[6].

Although we know that Ricky Gardiner and Stacy Heydon's names were put forward, Brian Eno is the one responsible for the choice of lead guitar player. In mid-February, Brian saw a Frank Zappa concert in Cologne and noticed American guitarist Adrian Belew in his band. He dutifully called David Bowie the next day and mentioned his discovery of a very rare bird. Not only is Belew excellent, he is so good that he stands out next to one of the masters of the instrument, which of course intrigues Bowie. That night, Zappa was playing in Berlin and David went to the show with Iggy Pop and Corinne Schwab. During a brief conversation, Adrian Belew told him he loved his music so Bowie, not the type to beat around the bush – especially when he was looking for musicians – asked him to join his band. It is said that Frank Zappa, who was no fool, wasn't thrilled about Bowie's offer to his guitarist and that insults flew in a restaurant later that night. In 1978, Adrian Belew, a generous and eccentric musician, starts working with David Bowie and he will be as talented in the studio as live. He will later play with Talking Heads and Tom Tom Club, and finally in King Crimson, for whom he will be second guitarist for more than three decades (Bowie introduced Belew to Robert Fripp at a Steve Reich concert).

On synthesizers and keyboards, David initially thought of recruiting Larry Fast from New Jersey. Fast is unavailable, so he recommends Roger Powell of Todd Rundgren's band Utopia. On the piano, David considered an old acquaintance: Sean Mayes of Fumble. A few months before, Mayes was surprised when Tony Visconti (bass player on the session) asked him to record, at Good Earth with Ricky Gardiner, the playback tape of *"Heroes"* for Bowie's appearance on *Top Of The Pops*. He is even more surprised when he is asked to go on tour! At the time, Fumble provides background music for the musical *Elvis!* at the Astoria Theatre in London. Sean Mayes, in agreement with his colleagues, will be quickly replaced there.

Even more unexpected, the last recruit proves to sceptics that David Bowie could be very determined. When the Diamond Dogs tour morphed into the Soul tour, thinking a violin would bring a touch of originality to his music, he'd already tried (unsuccessfully) to poach Eddie Jobson, who played the instrument in Roxy Music. Of course, David had also noticed the presence of a violinist, Michael

Karoli, in Can, another band he liked. So, in 1978, he invites multi-instrumentalist Simon House to join his band. A former member of High Tide and Third Ear Band, this quiet Englishman is going to leave Hawkwind but will later play again, twice, with that space rock group, led by Dave Brock. House is a very competent musician, whose violin will give a distinctive colour to the sound of the tour and to Bowie's next studio album. He will also be one of the three mandolin players on 'Fantastic Voyage'.

Dallas is the city of ShowCo, the company that has been providing sound equipment and services for David Bowie's US concerts since 1974, so that's where (in Irving, to the east of the city) they start rehearsals in mid-March for the Isolar 2 tour, also known as the Stage tour. Carlos Alomar is again the musical director and he will help the band learn some thirty songs.

Arguing he is now himself, and no longer needs to embody a persona, Bowie opts for a relatively simple look, less austere than that of the Thin White Duke. He calls on Natasha Korniloff, who hasn't dressed him since *The 1980 Floor Show*. His basic tour outfit will be a white t-shirt and oversized trousers. At the start of the show, David will usually wear a jacket (in light oilskin), then a Hawaiian shirt (like Adrian Belew), as well as a magnificent fake snakeskin jacket. His hair will be short, parted on the side, and the captain's hat he will wear towards the end of the shows will earn him the nickname Sailor. In terms of lighting, David Bowie will amplify the concept from the previous tour and add impressive neon lights on each side of the stage.

During this marathon tour, he fully embraces the experimental character of his two previous albums, from which he plays ten songs – the show starts with 'Warszawa', which Carlos Alomar conducts with a baton, then the instrumentals 'Sense Of Doubt' and 'Art Decade' are played respectively in the first and second thirds of the set. And David caters to his oldest fans by giving them, on his brightest stage ever, some fairly close-to-the-original versions of five (out of eleven) songs from *Ziggy Stardust*.

The tour launches on 29 March at the Sports Arena in San Diego, a venue with a capacity of 12,000 people (it's still standing to this day, although it is now called the Valley View Casino Center), who all have the pleasure of finding a more relaxed Bowie. From the second song ("Heroes") onwards, he even smiles at them. The audience enjoys the pops of colour that light up at certain moments in the show and, despite David's efforts to appear normal, they feel like they are watching a new character take shape. An actor in his spare time, a painter when his schedule allows it, David (who then describes himself as a 'generalist') remains – above all – a prodigious performer. No audience member, musician or journalist can resist him.

Of the 30 concerts in the US, the most notable are those that take place in the larger cities but, overall, they are successful. Part of the set list harks back to the time when bisexuality was the backbone of Bowie's career, but the average American audience – even the younger generation – seem to prefer the ostensibly announced conformism and masculinity. Moreover, the fact that he's included a 15-minute interval between the first and second halves of the show gives audiences in the most capitalist country in the world the feeling that they are really getting their money's worth (in a manner of speaking, as they are actually spending more on merchandise during the break).

The mood backstage is positive, but David Bowie is still suffering from some of the bad habits he's developed, which sometimes affects his state of mind. The musicians interviewed for this book preferred not to revisit what they now consider mere details of their story with Bowie but, at the time, Adrian Belew and Sean Mayes complained about the distance David's protective entourage maintained between them and him (although they were only ever following his instructions).

In the US and in Europe, shows from the Isolar 2 tour will be filmed (most often in part) for television programmes[7]. One might assume that David Bowie's ties with the city will lead Tony Visconti to record most of the live double album *Stage* at the Spectrum in Philadelphia on 28 and 29 April (the album will also include some songs recorded the following week in Providence and Boston). Once again, to pull the rug out from under the bootlegger's feet, RCA plans on releasing it as quickly as possible. But, in truth – and Visconti confirms this in his autobiography – the initial idea was to film the concerts at Madison Square Garden (on 7, 8 and 9 May), which was Bowie's favourite venue on the continent[8]. However, the filming fee at MSG was exorbitant[9], so they fell back on the Spectrum.

Stage was recorded using a mobile studio belonging to RCA and, since Tony had been incensed by the poor quality of the recording of *David Live*, he wanted to supervise each step of the process for *Stage* – mostly the microphone placement (including those over the audience) to allow more control during the mix at Good Earth. According to Visconti, this double live album, unlike its predecessor, doesn't contain any fixing. Only 'Station To Station' gets a little touch up, because the beginning and end of the track were taken from the Boston concert and the middle from the Providence one. As Visconti said in the liner notes of the 2005 reissue of *Stage*, it had only been possible to merge recordings from two performances because Dennis Davis was so excellent that he used to play at the same tempo from one show to the next.

This album has been one of Bowie's most controversial since its release. While the sound was recorded correctly, the noise from the crowd during and between songs is very low in the mix. But the purists' main gripe against *Stage* is its running order, which is different from the live performance. The idea David approved during the mix was to create an (almost) chronological order, but people who liked the original set list strongly disagreed with this. It won't be until the aforementioned reissue, when Tony Visconti remixes the record (and adds 'Stay' and 'Be My Wife' – left out of the original vinyl edition due to lack of space), notably in 5.1, that an official recording of a typical performance from the Isolar 2 tour, as the audience experienced it at the time, will become available. Since the bootleggers respected the original set lists, their records will continue to sell alongside the official version over the decades[10].

To this day, the Isolar 2 tour is the only one that a David Bowie musician has documented in a book. Sadly, Sean Mayes' *Life On Tour With David Bowie – We Can Be Heroes*, will be published posthumously, by Independent Music Press in 1999. It will be filled with anecdotes about life on the road and the recording of *Lodger*. Like Tony Visconti in his autobiography, Mayes will reveal details about the show at Madison Square Garden – on and off stage – and events in the VIP area with Andy Warhol, Dustin Hoffman and Mick and Bianca Jagger. As the American leg of the tour came to a close in New York, performances by the Ringling Bros. and Barnum & Bailey circuses were taking place at MSG (from 28 March to 3 June) and the wild animals were housed backstage. Taking place between circus performances, these concerts are the only ones where Bowie and his musicians ran into chimpanzees and elephants before and after the shows.

Iggy Pop's first live album comes out in May, as does *Prokofiev's Peter And The Wolf*. This narration, by Bowie over the music of the Philadelphia Orchestra, directed by Eugene Ormandy, confirms that David's thirst for experience is impossible to quench. The offer came from Ralph Mace, who was then in charge of Red Seal (RCA's classical label), and Bowie will say he accepted it to please his son, of whom he was preparing to take full custody. Unsurprisingly, David excels in the role (turned down by Alec Guinness and Peter Ustinov – the latter will finally do it ten years later, as will Sting in the 1990s) and the record will get positive reviews. *Prokofiev's Peter And The Wolf* has been reissued quite a few times since 1978 and the original green vinyl version remains a collector's favourite.

The European leg of the tour starts in Germany on 14 May, then David Bowie makes a brief appearance at the Cannes Film Festival, where *Just A Gigolo* is being screened. Not as part of the official selection, but in the hope of finding a distributor. The shows on 24 and 25 May at the Pavillon de Paris are sold out and, after the second, David and his band have a great evening at the Palace, which Fabrice Emaer has just reopened (hoping the place will become the Parisian Studio 54). They then perform in Northern Europe and, in mid-June, before the first concert of the tour in his home country, Bowie attends Iggy Pop's gig at the Music Machine[11] in Camden (London). The venue is a temple of punk rock and Johnny Rotten – The Sex Pistols are already a distant memory – is in the room that night.

David Bowie performs outside London for the first time in five years and the Newcastle, Glasgow and Stafford audiences do not hide their appreciation. The tour wraps up in the capital with three shows at Earl's Court and David Hemmings films two of them for a project that will never come to fruition – he is fascinated by the world of pop and rock music, and the scene from Michelangelo Antonioni's *Blow-Up*, in which he rubs shoulders with The Yardbirds, is still on everyone's mind. Hemmings wanted to make a sort of music documentary, mixing live footage with scenes shot backstage and on the road. In the end, disappointed with the cut Hemmings will show him, Bowie will put a stop to the project. In the 1990s and 2000s, when music DVDs become popular, most of the concert films will look similar to what Hemmings had in mind in 1978. There is no official visual documentation of this tour but, from the next one onwards, they will all be filmed and sold (and reissued) in VHS, Laserdisc, DVD and Blu-ray.

'Alabama Song' by The Doors is one of the songs David Bowie played for Laurent Thibault at the Château d'Hérouville in May 1976. Since the beginning of the decade, Bowie has often spoken about his passion for Bertolt Brecht's songs put to music by Kurt Weill ('Time' on *Aladdin Sane* could have been written by the two Germans). David particularly loves 'Alabama Song' from *Little Mahagonny*, which was a sort of short and preparatory version of *The Rise And Fall Of The City Of Mahagonny*, the experimental opera they made in Leipzig in 1930. Elisabeth Hauptmann first translated the words of the song into English and this is the version that Jim Morrison's band covered in 1966, after a few modifications. In July, Bowie gathers his musicians at Good Earth and Tony Visconti co-produces a reinterpretation of the song as they play it on tour. Wonderfully performed and arranged, 'Alabama Song' (the A-side of a future single and a bonus track of the Rykodisc reissue of *Stage* in 1991) is another testament to David Bowie's artistic boldness. By asking Dennis Davis to play 'against the beat' (quite a technical feat), he throws the song off balance, but the result is unique and particularly catchy.

This audacity impresses his musicians, especially those who are recording with him for the first time. Thirty-seven years later (again in the presence of Tony Visconti) in a New York studio that will close forever shortly after, drummer Mark Guiliana will play an equally complex and quirky beat on 'Blackstar' without realizing that, most likely, he is following in Davis' footsteps.

In September 1978, Bowie's musicians are invited to Montreux for his next album. During the summer, he moved out of his flat on Hauptstraße, without returning all of the keys – indeed between 2013 and 2015, a set of keys for Number 155 will be displayed in the Berlin section of the *David Bowie Is* exhibition. Until the beginning of the 1990s, while keeping a pied-à-terre in both New York and London, Switzerland will be his base and his official home. That September, are all Bowie's musicians at Mountain Studio? No. Since David Bowie requested Brian Eno's presence again on synthesizers (and for his random methods), Roger Powell remained on the sidelines. Even though they prefer not to discuss it, the other members of the band are not happy about his absence. For them, playing on a Bowie record is a kind of achievement and they think it's unfair that Powell is missing.

Paradoxically, and even though he intends to give Eno more latitude (he will co-write six of the ten songs), David Bowie feels the need to let his own imagination run wild, to return to a sort of basic narration without always using cut-ups, and to tackle social issues. Minor artistic accidents continue to interest him (one of the titles considered for the album, possibly whispered in his ear by Brian Eno, will be *Planned Accidents*), but he does not want them to stand in the way of a certain naturalness. Thus, when Bowie plays a demo of 'All The Young Dudes' backwards on his tape recorder (looking for bits and pieces of songs he never used) and 'hears' a melody that will become that of 'Move On', he decides he won't repeat the trick. In the studio, he will say he wants to create rawer material, with less polishing and rounding of corners. He will take to heart one of his precepts from the making of *Just A Gigolo*: 'Let's hurry up and film this scene before it gets better.'

Mountain is nothing like Hansa's Meistersaal. The room where Bryan Ferry worked on *The Bride Stripped Bare* is less spacious and the natural reverb is practically non-existent. Having ten or so musicians recording there together (Eno and Bowie will often play with them) at the end of summer, even in Switzerland, is a challenge in itself and the air-conditioning will soon reveal its limitations. However, the rhythm tracks are again recorded quickly, in less than a week.

Most of the time, the band played chord progressions without knowing where the verses or choruses were (or if there were any) and Tony Visconti is in charge of assembling these various parts with David Bowie. Nowadays, computing technology enables manipulations of this type to be performed in a matter of seconds, but they were much more tedious in the 1970s, because the tape literally had to be cut and the pieces stuck back together. Carlos Alomar, Sean Mayes and Simon House then take care of the overdubs. Adrian Belew said that, like Robert Fripp on *"Heroes"*, he played his guitar parts over basic tracks that were sometimes harmonically 'blurred', which implies that he wasn't present at the start of the sessions.

Brian Eno will use Oblique Strategies again and give directions to the musicians but, by their own admission, those who've worked on previous albums will pay him less and less attention and even be annoyed by his method. By way of experimentation, David and Brian will take great pleasure in making use of 'mistakes'. These will usually be harmonic twists caused by the fact that, at the time of overdubbing, some parts were missing an evident tonic or root note. Although they are very innovative in terms of structure, several songs as a result will sound less spontaneous than others, and arrangements will add to their eccentricity. World music might not be the right descriptive term, but it's obvious that David Bowie's travels, on tour and privately, and his temporary association with other cultures impacted on songs like 'Yassassin', 'Move On' and 'African Night Flight'.

Before recording, Bowie and Eno talked a lot – they wanted the final part of the triptych to make an even bigger splash than the others. The lack of instrumental tracks showed they were going back to basics, limiting destabilization but without resorting to conformism. But between *"Heroes"* and *Lodger*, Brian Eno had worked with other musicians, particularly Talking Heads, the American new wave band that was slowly but surely climbing the ladder of success. Listening to *More Songs About Buildings And Food*, David Bowie couldn't help but notice that the band's second album owed a lot to the production of Brian Eno, and therefore to Brian's experience of working with him at the Château d'Hérouville and in Berlin. David, who borrowed freely and openly from others, was certainly not in a position to take offence. But Brian will raise his eyebrows on listening to *Lodger* on its release in May 1979, and particularly the song 'D.J.', which David sings – and he didn't even deny it – in the style of David Byrne, the frontman of Talking Heads. This transfer of skills worked both ways, as *Scary Monsters*, Bowie's last album for RCA in 1980, would bear the touch of Eno, even though he didn't work on it.

The making of the album will be characterized by another exchange of good practices. Right after he arrived in Blonay (the other musicians were staying at the Trois Couronnes Hotel in Vevey), Brian Eno played *Nite Flights* for David. One of the key features of the sixth (and last) album by the American trio Walker Brothers, released two months before, is that its members (who were definitely not brothers) shared the writing of the songs. Scott Walker, who has fascinated Bowie ever since he was introduced to his work a decade before by Lesley Duncan, wrote the first four tracks of the album, which David finds rather surprising. Walker undeniably inspired him as a vocalist, but when he heard 'Fat Mama Kick' and 'The Electrician', David quite rightly thought that Scott Walker had been seduced by the charms of *Low* and *"Heroes"*. David Bowie will return the favour, but in his own way: not by emulating Walker emulating him, but by increasingly adopting a baritone voice like his.

Those who saw one or more concerts of the Isolar 2 tour noticed that David was less and less able to hit high notes like he used to (in 'Soul Love', for example), though he could still do it in the studio. Bowie smoked several packs of cigarettes a day for almost three decades (much to the displeasure of his friends and relatives) and, in concert in 1978, he is no longer capable of using the full vocal range that was his five years before, and so will adapt his future compositions to this new reality. Until his death, David Bowie will maintain a good set of lungs (Tony Visconti, the last to record his voice, will confirm it when *Blackstar* is released) but, from 1983 onwards, Bowie will sing his more vocally acrobatic classic tracks one or two semitones lower. 'Life On Mars?', with Mike Garson on piano, which he will perform for the last time at the charity fundraiser event Fashion Rocks in 2005, will be three whole tones lower than the original version.

When *Stage* is released on 8 September 1978, in a gatefold jacket with three variations of a photo taken in Chicago[12] by Gilles Riberolles (a member of the French band Casino Music who also writes for the rock magazine *Best*), rumours about Bowie's departure from RCA are running rampant. Apparently he insisted to the label – in vain – that this double album, which will barely make more ripples in the British than the American charts, should count as two records, therefore bringing him closer to the end of his contract. But David will have to wait until the beginning of the 1980s to finally break free. Overall, the public and media respond positively to *Stage*, but many fans (and band members) make themselves a cassette tape with the songs in the right order[13].

On 21 April 2018, as a limited edition for Record Store Day, Parlophone will release *Welcome To The Blackout (Live London '78)* on triple vinyl. It will be available on CD a couple of months later. This second official live album of the Isolar 2 tour, with a Masayoshi Sukita photo on the cover (taken at Madison Square Garden or in Japan – but not in London as Sukita wasn't there), was recorded by Tony Visconti on 30 June and 1 July 1978 at Earl's Court and mixed by Bowie with David Richards in January 1979 at Mountain Studio[14]. 'Rock'n'roll Suicide', 'The Jean Genie' and 'Rebel Rebel', although regularly played on this tour – as attested by many bootleg records – are absent from *Stage* or *Welcome To The Blackout (Live London '78)*. However, 'Sound And Vision' appears on the second album – it looks like it was only performed once, on 1 July, during the tour.

After just under a week of rehearsals, Isolar 2 starts up again in Australia on 11 November in Adelaide. It is Bowie's first time there, and the public and media are eagerly awaiting him. The English musician will develop a special relationship with this country and even buy a flat in Sydney a few years later. Surprised to have been called back, Roger Powell, who'd returned to Utopia for a series of concerts, misses the first two performances and is replaced by Dennis Garcia. A former member of The Mixtures (an Australian band known in the early 70s for their cover of Mungo Jerry's 'In The Summertime'), Garcia is a local pioneer of the synthesizer. David Bowie may have heard his *Jive To Stay Alive* LP, released in 1977.

During his trip down under, David listens to Dire Straits on a loop and will run into some friends – Peter Frampton and Bette Midler – who are also performing there. Frampton, who'll play lead guitar on the Glass Spider tour, is high on the success of his album *I'm In You*, and the live album that came before it, which is still doing well in the global charts thanks to a breathtaking version (released as a single) of 'Show Me The Way'. Bowie didn't have any support bands in 1974, 1976 or during the American and European legs of the Isolar 2 tour but, in Australia, The Angels open his concerts. They are a local band that have made a name for themselves with their LP *Face To Face*. Seven performances before an audience of several tens of thousands of people each night[15] will increase their fame tenfold.

After two shows in New Zealand, David Bowie sings in Japan for the first time since 1973, and meets up with Sukita and Kansai Yamamoto. The tour ends in mid-December with two concerts in Tokyo, including one at the famous Nippon Budokan. With a capacity of 15,000 people, this temple of martial arts became a music venue when The Beatles gave four concerts (in two days) there in 1966 and, since then, various major bands have followed suit and even had their performances recorded and/or filmed there.

As the decade came to a close, some of Bowie's musicians started to feel like a page was about to turn. Rock hasn't yet become a massive industry, MTV and the degrading music channels don't exist yet, but all the signs are pointing to the fact that the days of a certain amateurism are numbered. While many contracts are still being sealed with a handshake and half of the fees are taken care of in cash (or sometimes something else), change is definitely on the way.

On the road since the end of March, some members of David Bowie's band were surprised that, although closely guarded, he was relatively easy to access. Some of them have been invited to spend time with him: in his hotel suites, at a restaurant, in clubs. This will still be the case five years later on the Serious Moonlight tour, but the assassination of John Lennon will change the situation and the overprotection of celebrities will become the norm.

In the 1980s, David Bowie and his art will change drastically, and the pace of the release of his albums will slow considerably. Although he won't totally withdraw from public life or become a hermit, unless he is on tour, Bowie will only make appearances at events he's selected well in advance. He will spend most of his time working, often painting at his house in Switzerland where his anonymity is respected. For over ten years, London and New York – the main centres of his work – will welcome him frequently, but only as a visitor.

In February 1979, David Bowie returns to England and gives a few interviews to promote *Just A Gigolo*, which needs all the help it can get. He reconnects with his home town and tells journalists he might settle there, or at least complete his album in London. He catches up with the music scene and attends a Human League concert, where he makes friends with the band, particularly their frontman, Phil Oakey.

Eventually, it is in New York the following month that Bowie will put the finishing touches to *Lodger*. Unfortunately, they are relegated to Studio D at Record Plant. It is small and, according to Tony Visconti, underequipped. As a result, they won't be fully satisfied with the mix. Even so, David will count *Lodger* as one of his favourite records until his death.

In 2012, the curators of the *David Bowie Is* exhibition at the Victoria And Albert Museum in London will ask Visconti to put together a mash-up – a soundtrack made up of elements from the multitrack tapes of Bowie's albums – to play in the largest room. Some reel-to-reel tapes will remain at Human, Tony's studio in New York so, in between sessions for *Blackstar* in 2015, he will be able to remix *Lodger*. As one can hear when listening to this new version in the box set *A New Career In A New Town (1977–1982)*[16], it is true to the spirit of the original. Limiting himself to brightening up *Lodger*, Tony focused his efforts on improving the drum sound and making Bowie's voice more present, and brought out a few buried keyboard parts.

All David Bowie fans know that in 2013, with *The Next Day*, he will pay tribute to *"Heroes"* and the video for 'Where Are We Now?' will be dedicated to his time in Berlin. But towards the end of his life, he will make other veiled references to *Low* and *Lodger*. At the Black Ball charity gala in 2006, as part of his last live appearance, Bowie will sing 'Fantastic Voyage'. Was it because he had a soft spot for the opening song of *Lodger*, or because he thought the title summed up his journey rather well? No one will ever know, but he'd probably be glad that we're still asking that question. This offbeat ballad opens David Bowie's thirteenth studio album. It is one of the most splendid of his entire discography and he performs it in a remarkable way. Whether speaking of having survived his deep-seated rootlessness, or of the fate of humanity as we face our self-destructive tendencies, the gravity of the subject is admirably counterbalanced by a stunningly playful orchestration. The famous mandolins bought in a music store in Montreux (played by Tony Visconti, Adrian Belew and Simon House) contribute to the apparent lightness, and the third chord, minor after two major ones, sways the melody towards drama.

Perhaps David and Tony[17] intended to be provocative by placing 'African Night Flight' second on the album. This track, not really a song (it's the most experimental of the collection), is animated by jolting sounds that are typical of Brian Eno. It's possible that David Bowie's trip to Kenya with his son earlier that year partly inspired the mood of this track, which he delivers in spoken word almost in the voice of a griot, typical of some African religious chants. Knowing that Bowie wasn't the type to go to a country, or continent, without doing a lot of research beforehand, it is probably safe to say that he'd taken an interest in Britain's colonial past in Africa. 'Asanti' – the first of three African words sung, like an incantation, by the backing vocalists – means 'thank you' in Swahili. It also evokes the Ashanti, a tribe that imposed its political supremacy over Ghana in the 18th and 19th centuries, until the British colonists, after claiming they were only interested in the coast of the country, decided to exploit its gold deposits and unleashed a series of armed attacks. 'African Night Flight', a montage of different parts, most of which are submitted to the isochronous oscillations of a piano 'treated' by Brian Eno, is, to say the least, unusual. It's also surprising to hear that, as Bowie has claimed, this piece evolved from a jam in Switzerland on 'Suzie Q', the standard by American rock musician

Dale Hawkins (written with Robert Chaisson).

But it is clear that the 'All The Young Dudes' 'accident' – the tape played backwards – gave rise to 'Move On'. With its haughty chorus, the song pins down a mobile Bowie (an impression reinforced by Dennis Davis' beat, like a cavalcade of horses) who doesn't attach himself to places or people and favours the journey over the destination.

Tony Visconti is right when he says that not all experiments were successful on *Lodger*, but 'Yassassin'[18], featuring a pseudo-oriental chord progression bending to the constraints of a quite stiff reggae[19] beat, is a real success. The lyrics are clear, and so is the marriage of styles. It was Bowie's way of tackling the subject of racial integration, in this case of the Turkish community he'd become familiar with in Berlin. The inspiration here surely didn't come from Switzerland, so we can imagine he'd been thinking about it for a long time or that he'd drafted a few words regarding the matter some years before. Simon House plays an enthralling violin part that sounds like it was recorded on a market day in Ankara, even though he'd probably never set foot there. It may not be straightforward, but 'Yassassin' is one of the rare examples of David Bowie's foray into reggae. The two others will be found on *Tonight* in 1984, when he covers 'Don't Look Down' by Iggy Pop and James Williamson and, in a duo with Tina Turner, the title song of the album (written with Iggy for *Lust For Life*[20]).

The krautrock musicians interviewed for this book may have claimed they weren't influenced by English-speaking rock bands of the time, because of their immersion in their art, but one can't help but think of Roxy Music's first recordings when listening to 'After Eight' by Neu! or 'Monza (Rauf Und Runter)' by Harmonia[21]. These two tracks are especially reminiscent of 'Virginia Plain', Roxy's first hit in 1973, when Brian Eno was still helping to shape the band's sound. So it was a fair exchange when, five years later, these German records, to which punk owed a lot, inspired Bowie and Eno's musical mood and, in particular, the drum beat of 'Red Sails'. The dizzying melody is akin to those composed by Ron Mael for Sparks, the American duo whose fifth album, *Indiscreet*, was produced (surprise, surprise) by Tony Visconti in his first London studio in 1975. It's quite possible that the name 'Red Sails' was a reference to 'Red Sails In The Sunset', a song written in 1935 by Wilhelm Grosz and Jimmy Kennedy and made famous in 1951 by Nat King Cole. But the analogy stops there, because David Bowie's song, tumultuous and pierced by an equally ear-shattering solo by Adrian Belew, is anything but a ballad.

In the late 70s and early 80s, anyone who felt like writing about a club DJ in a song would have done it to a disco beat[22]. But not David Bowie, who on 'D.J.' has allowed Dennis Davis to hit his bass drum anywhere but on the beat. And George Murray, in the spirit of disco, showed he could hold his own to Bernard Edwards, the bass player and founding member of Chic. With its piano à la Velvet Underground (probably played by Bowie) and its 'treated' scratchy guitar and violin parts, this stunning pop song, co-written with Carlos Alomar and Brian Eno, happily eschewed the fashions of the time. The strength of the chorus will prompt RCA to release 'D.J.' as a single but, even though it was boosted by a video directed by David Mallet[23], the song will only make Number 29 in the UK in June, and will never reach the Top 100 in the *Billboard*.

Even though David Bowie will still look like Dorian Gray at the beginning of the 2000s (mortality seemed to obsess him less and less over the last decades of the century), he was not indifferent to the passing of time while recording *Lodger*, as 'Look Back In Anger' demonstrates. The song is a thinly veiled contemplation of his past, to a vigorous beat by Dennis Davis at the top of his game (he doubled his drum part with congas) and judiciously enhanced by Beatles-style backing vocals. Carlos Alomar gives a remarkable performance (a sort of 'rhythm guitar solo' based on chords in the style of John Lennon) that he will replicate with panache during the Serious Moonlight and Glass Spider tours.

As for Adrian Belew, he maintains the turmoil in *Lodger*'s lightest song. 'Boys Keep Swinging' is a jovial hymn to masculinity, a forced jam in fact, on a chord progression similar to the one in 'Fantastic Voyage'. The song will owe part of its success to David Mallet's video, in which Bowie plays all three drag queens/backing vocalists. At the end of the clip, one after the other, they remove their wigs and lipstick, smearing it with the backs of their hands. David had seen Romy Haag make the exact same gesture at the end of her show in her cabaret in Berlin.

Two months before *Lodger* came out, David Bowie revealed an open secret: he was offering to produce Scott Walker. His American hero will politely refuse and they will never work together. However, Bowie will be the executive producer of *30th Century Man*, Stephen Kijak's 2006 documentary on Walker. On *Lodger*, David is happy to simply give Walker a wink by singing 'Look Back In Anger' in his style. The song will be released in August on the A-side of a single that will only be available in the US and Canada.

On 'Repetition'[24] David Bowie's lead vocal is reminiscent of Lou Reed who, a bit later, he will very seriously (and in a rather vehement way) consider working with again. A tragic variation on the theme already covered in 'Boys Keep Swinging' (here a man reaffirms his masculinity by hitting his wife), 'Repetition' develops over two chords and is not the richest on the record in terms of melody and harmony. Its steady pace (125bpm) contrasts with that of 'Red Money', the closing track on the record, which lags a little despite Carlos Alomar's riff and consistency. This variation on Iggy Pop's 'Sister Midnight' allows us to better understand how Bowie very often worked from the mid-70s to the end of his career. Usually in rock and pop, the rhythm tracks and basic arrangements are developed to suit the melodies, which are in turn defined and supported by the chords. But David Bowie usually wrote his melodies last, making his songs sound out of step with themselves. Also, some of them revolved around a gimmick, while in others, it wasn't always easy to know which part was the verse and which the chorus. Sometimes he created a bridge – or two, as he did for 'Word On A Wing' and 'Teenage Wildlife' (on *Scary Monsters*), which are similar in form. Referring to musical notes – sometimes old ones – that he kept on cassette (then on DAT), David modified several songs, just before recording them.

Unlike those of *Station To Station* and *Low*, the cover of *Lodger* does not show a photo from *The Man Who Fell To Earth*. Anyone seeing the jacket on the album's release on 18 May 1979 might think that David Bowie, who Nicolas Roeg predicted would be haunted by Thomas Jerome Newton for a long time, had finally left him behind. But that wasn't the case. In early 1979, when Bowie called Brian Duffy to ask him to organize a photo shoot for the cover of *Lodger* (he was able to confirm its title), he told him he wanted to be represented as a 'falling man' photographed from above. He wasn't an alien, but an average guy dressed in a normal way (although wearing a string vest, like a punk, under his jacket). A nobody, in short, no happier or unhappier than anyone else, going about his pre-planned life – and whose fall symbolizes abandoning himself to destiny. Unlike an 'owner' who stays at the same place, who puts down roots, this 'lodger' has nothing to his name but the comb he is holding in his right hand.

David Bowie, quintessentially contradictory and maybe already defiant, has actually started to keep everything that is his. To collect and store objects, souvenirs and also art, in the form of books, films, paintings and furniture. Was he already thinking of showing off his treasures in one of London's most exclusive museums? Who can confirm it? Who can deny it? It is the dawn of the 1980s, which will not be his decade, and the only way Bowie can embrace it is by bursting the mirage of total glory into a thousand pieces. The 'lodger' is teetering on the edge with a fear of too much stability – falling is living life to the full. After Los Angeles, Berlin was a rather decadent setting for his voluntary rehabilitation and had made its mark on him. But wasn't he going to die of boredom in Switzerland, the heart of a sterile bourgeoisie?

A fan of Derek Boshier, an artist (painter, illustrator and photographer) associated with British pop art, David Bowie suggested to Duffy that he should design the cover of *Lodger* with him. Despite never really organizing all of the other images that swirled around in his head (dozens of ideas for films came to him and fuelled his conversations over the years), Bowie was always the craftsman of his own visual identity. While the slogan used for the publicity campaign for *"Heroes"* (*There's old wave, there's new wave, and there's David Bowie*) can be attributed to a marketing person at RCA, the one for *Stage* was the musician's own suggestion. He borrowed the idea, like the album's title, from William Shakespeare – 'All the world's a stage...' Despite his best efforts to go unnoticed, Bowie proved, until the end of his life and beyond, that his world was indeed a stage. And it was mobile, like the revolving one they will use at Live Aid in 1985. He gave off a sort of aura, a more-or-less perceptible halo, a unique and captivating atmosphere that, like a thousand magnets, attracted other creators.

On the day of the photo shoot for *Lodger*, those who worked with him were well aware of this effect. David Bowie, in any studio, was certainly not the source of every idea, but he encouraged his collaborators to do whatever the art required, sometimes to the detriment of their convictions and even his own. Albert Koski went further in conversation for this book, calling him a mind magician, a sort of mentalist. In *Duffy Bowie: Five Sessions*, Kevin Cann points out that the deformities on Bowie's face in the photograph (made with nylon threads taped to his skin) are supposed to illustrate the fall and are a reference to a self-portrait by Egon Schiele. Like the shapeless haircut, they're also testimony to a desire to damage his image as a sex symbol. Encouraged to do as he sees fit, Boshier will represent the concept of a traveller, a man who can't stay in one place, by adding a postcard to the design. Only David's legs and feet will be visible on the front cover, the first without his face. Duffy will have to accommodate another radical idea from the artist[25]: to use a Polaroid snapshot and not a real photograph taken with a much more advanced camera.

Instead of seeing a falling man, a lot of people saw an injured David Bowie in the image – perhaps even one who'd committed suicide – and they searched for meanings in the smallest detail. Maybe there were some to find. Everyone is free to see what they want in any work of art because, after all, that's the point of it, right down to packaging. Bowie was always keen to stimulate the imagination of those he worked with and they always bent over backwards to interpret his desires, even though he deliberately gave them only a very sketchy idea of what he wanted. The morning of the photo session for *Lodger*, David claimed to have scalded himself with hot water or coffee, so he turned up with a bandage on his right hand, which he decided he would keep for the shoot. When he sings 'Life On Mars?' at Fashion Rocks years later, he will again have a bandage, on his left hand this time, very prominently displayed. Was it a reference to that session or to the person he was then? Maybe it was both.

David Bowie wasn't one of those musicians who, when they're about to play their new record to their friends, rub their hands together anticipating the praise. In the spring of 1979, a few days before *Lodger* came out, he meets Sean Mayes in London and plays *Lodger* to him. He is anxious and admits he is worried that the public and media will give it a lukewarm reception. Tony Visconti said that, between the mix and the release of his albums, Bowie was depressed. Once again, his fears would be justified. 'Boys Keep Swinging', released as a single in late April, will take him into the British Top 10 (for the first time since 'Sound And Vision' two years before), but *Lodger* will hardly perform any better than *"Heroes"*, a disappointment for a musician of his stature (it will make a fleeting appearance in the British Top 5 and won't get above Number 20 in the US).

Rehabilitated every time the catalogue has been reissued since the 1980s, the famous 'Berlin' trilogy wraps up with an LP that has little to do with Berlin and, aside from a few motorik beats from Dennis Davis, who never would have heard of Neu! or Can had he not crossed the Atlantic, not much to do with Germany. And if Davis did actually listen to some of these bands before getting down to playing his parts, it was probably only briefly...

As for Brian Eno, feeling he's travelled as far as he could with David Bowie on these three albums, he will take his unorthodox methods elsewhere. On those rare occasions he will mention *Lodger*, he will not always be very flattering about it, although it must have topped up his income quite a bit. Ironically, while Eno has a lot to do with the quality of the LP, he may also be responsible for the excellence of its successor: Bowie's first and best album of the 1980s. In fact, David was not thrilled when members of his teams talked too much in music magazines or in books about him and his work, even if they didn't mean to be malicious. By hitting the rocks, did Eno make the sparks that will push Bowie to return to the studio less than nine months after the release of *Lodger* with, in an unusual move, some pre-written songs, including a future Number 1? If Pete had wanted to show Dud what he could achieve without him, that's exactly how he would have done it.

Carlos Alomar	Larry Fast
Adrian Belew	Roger Powell
George Murray	Albert Koski
Tony Visconti	Marc Exiga
Eugene Chaplin	Gilles Riberolles
	Jay-Jay Johanson
	Nicolas Godin
	Marc Minelli
	Phil Manzanera
	Page Hamilton
	Chris Frantz

CARLOS ALOMAR

Whenever I think of David performing, a storm of images swirls in my head. As for 1978, what I remember today is him playing in the rain at a concert in Melbourne[26]. Anyone else would have been more careful, and some rock stars of his stature would have even cancelled the show. Not only did he do it but, instead of complaining, David had fun. From where I was standing, I usually only saw his back, but I'll never forget that image of him, his face dripping wet, his hands held up towards the sky. He was the ultimate performer. Of course, to wind down after a show, he was usually the first to start partying. But often, very late at night or early the next morning, he'd listen to the recording of the concert to see whether anything could be improved. I also remember the one in Auckland, New Zealand, where we broke a record with the audience[27]!

I think there is a very nice blend on *Lodger*. We approached the songs in a really interesting way. Even 'Yassassin'! Initially, I thought: 'Okay, I don't get it. I mean, why don't we just turn this into a nice reggae song?' Eventually, we ended up with that mix of reggae, Mediterranean and funky flavours and, depending on how you listen to it, it could be in either style. And you might really wonder what those lyrics are doing there! You know, I talked to him, on occasion, about lyrics and their meanings... But, as you know, he didn't have just one favourite way of writing them, but at least two or three! That's where the disjointed things came from. Once I was reading a paper and he asked me to look for the most interesting descriptions I could find. And there was a line that said, 'Sandpaper across my eyebrow'. And he asked, 'Who wrote that? It's a great line. I should definitely use it on my next record.' Words, for him, didn't have to mean things like you think they do. He was more interested in the visual power of words than in their actual meaning. What's for sure is that he was the only one who knew what his lyrics were really about, and he loved the fact that the audience understood what they wanted to understand. People who have tried to analyse them got lost in conjecture. Sometimes, there's no need to complicate things...

As musicians we have this ability to convert emotions into works of art. David taught me that better than anyone. He would say, 'Carlos, if you see something, write. If you feel something, write. If you love something, write. Write, write, write.' Working with him encouraged me to pass on the knowledge I acquired while we were doing these records. The trilogy allowed me to take the road less travelled, out of my rhythm'n'blues, out of my rock'n'roll methodologies, and then I started exploring what could be done with computers and other toys designed to create soundscapes. Honestly, the trilogy changed my life. How did we do that music? I don't know. It came from nowhere. It might well be why I'm feeling so young today, why I'm still curious! When I'm playing laser harp or Wavedrum, I'm like a kid in a candy store and I know that I owe that to David Bowie. (2016)

ADRIAN BELEW

What struck me when David poached me was his confidence. He looked a bit like a naughty boy who couldn't help getting into trouble. He didn't even flinch when he bumped into Frank Zappa in that restaurant we went to, to talk about the tour! I was aware of what I'd learned with Frank, but I felt like with Bowie, especially live, I would have more freedom. And I wasn't wrong. He let me try things out and I soon realized that technical skill wasn't his thing... He looks for originality, character in his musicians. With him, you can be off-track for a while, as long as it doesn't affect the overall performance. Frank taught me a great deal, but everything was planned ahead of time.

David himself has a very interesting way of approaching the guitar. He is absolutely not into 15-minute solos... Sometimes he wants his guitarists to be like synth players. I mean, he wants textures from them – things that, on a record, aren't always easy to hear. That's why Robert Fripp did such a good job with him.

On *Lodger*, Bowie and Visconti were deep into experimentation. I was amazed when I realized that most of the tracks had been recorded with effects. There was no turning back! You had to build something based on what was on the tape and, if there was a problem, you couldn't erase anything, you had to work around it. Many songs on *Lodger* owe their uniqueness to that practice. Like others who played on it, I was very surprised when I listened to the finished record. We'd filled the tracks, and it had become something else!

I was also thrilled when David called me again because I didn't feel like I'd really got to know him during the tour. We had some conversations but, most of the time, it was impossible to get close to him because of his entourage. I was often surprised by the way he worked and I think he was under Eno's influence a lot. You know, Brian could be very persuasive without necessarily talking much. There was definitely some kind of challenge between the two of them, not to say competition, but most of the big decisions were taken after Brian had left.

I was really disappointed not to be on *Scary Monsters*, but David called me back for the Sound+Vision tour. There are two ways of looking at it – you can either be offended not to be invited, or you can come to understand that, for David, music comes first and the decision of who works on it is based on that. Who knows, he might even call me for his next album! But I think he has a really good band at the moment, right? (2003)

GEORGE MURRAY

Montreux was a beautiful city and the studio was a short walk from Lake Geneva. I could see it from my bedroom window and I had never stayed any place as relaxed, friendly and just plain pretty. David had taken up residence there and looked healthy and happy. He would drive himself to the studio and around town in a red VW Golf sedan. No flash, no fanfare, no entourage, pretty much just us – David was one of the local 'lodgers'.

The last album of the trilogy doesn't have an instrumental side, but many of the songs are very surprising. Some, like 'Fantastic Voyage', have excellent melodies and others, like 'Boys Keep Swinging', are pretty funny… And there was this reggae thing, 'Yassassin'. I remember the music just flowed from us. David had some songs pretty much worked out or had little pieces of things he wanted us to play. The technique was pretty much the same: strong rhythm tracks, good melodies with synths, guitars, and effects on top.

I was just listening to the album to refresh my memory and the last track, 'Red Money', is the same riff that Dennis, Carlos and I put together during the 1976 tour rehearsals in Jamaica, the one David turned into 'Sister Midnight'[28]. 'Fashion' has similar origins… On *Lodger* and the two previous albums, I was impressed and surprised at what David made the final tracks sound like…

Life during these sessions was normal. We pretty much started at a normal hour and finished at a normal hour. In 1978, working with David was almost like a regular job!

One day when we weren't recording, Dennis, Carlos and I decided to take a drive into the mountains. Well, we're city boys, not very much accustomed to the mountains; and, since we lived in New York City, we definitely didn't have to drive much. So we start out – it's a beautiful day, brilliant blue sky, clean, crisp air – it was perfect… After a while, we notice that the road is starting to get narrower and there is no oncoming traffic. Do we stop and turn around? No, we just keep going. We pass a man by the side of the road and we wave to him. He waves back, but has a very puzzled look on his face. Do we stop and turn around? No, we just keep going, except now we're heading downhill and picking up speed. We finally do stop, just before a dead-end barrier – if we'd missed it, we would have gone off a cliff! We then have to drive backwards, because there is no room to turn around. We pass the same man on the way back and he waves, but this time he has a big grin on his face. (2016)

TONY VISCONTI

After a seven-month hiatus David called me and said we would finish *Lodger* in New York, with just David, Adrian Belew and myself. We recorded some new jams with Belew on drums, me on bass and David on guitar, but nothing came of it. Instead, we settled for some Belew guitar overdubs and I replaced the bass on 'Boys Keep Swinging', the experimental track where the band had switched instruments[29]. Carlos Alomar played the drums quite well, but Dennis Davis – who is left-handed – never played a satisfactory bass part on George Murray's right-handed bass. I played an over-the-top bass part on the song, in the spirit of 'The Man Who Sold The World'.

David was never happy with the mix of *Lodger* and, in 2015, between sessions for *Blackstar*, I spent quite a lot of time in my studio. I never hid the fact that it was probably my favourite record of the trilogy and, once I'd finished the digital transfers, I really enjoyed listening to all the tracks again. In particular, I got to study all of Brian Eno's hacks, his sounds, those noises he liked to record on tape. 'African Night Flight' had one he pulled out of a simple drum machine I had at the time. He called it 'Cricket Menace'[30]! I noticed that some of the tracks still sound really weird on their own, but they work very well all together.

I don't remember much of Switzerland because Montreux wasn't a very exciting town but, listening back to *Lodger* reminds me of the time we spent on the album in New York, in one of Record Plant's studios, which wasn't the best one. So I remixed half the record in my studio before playing anything to David. When he'd heard what I'd done, he was blown away! He gave me the green light and I can't wait to remix the other songs[31]. (2007/2015)

EUGENE CHAPLIN

When David Bowie and Brian Eno were in the same room, the mood was pure creation! Some songs had blurry outlines and Eno acted kind of like a professor with his students. He had his set of cards to hand and he sometimes told the musicians which chords to play, pointing to their names on a blackboard. He would get some material that way, then David would do what he wanted with it. For the lyrics, I saw him cut out letters from magazine pages and arrange words with them. I was very young, but I was impressed by the fact that I had a real artist in front of me who, once again, was challenging himself.

One morning he came to the studio with a Wasp synth[32]. I thought it sounded absolutely terrible – it was for children – but he liked it and put some on the album. He'd sometimes compose a really beautiful melody, and the next day he'd completely destroy it, rebuild it better and get a much better result. I'd never seen anyone work like that before.

The rhythm tracks for *Lodger* didn't take long! It was a good thing because the drummer was playing so loud! After the sessions, we sometimes went to clubs in Montreux where bands were playing. Dennis Davis jammed with them a few times but, as soon as he started playing, you couldn't hear the others! There was that famous time when the musicians swapped instruments – that was experimental! People wondered a lot about the Bowie-Eno-Visconti process, but in the end it worked – especially because David had the last word. Tony was responsible for the sound quality. For example, he was the best at arranging and recording backing vocals, he had a really incredible ear. Eno was there as a sound designer. He'd give his ideas and then he'd go for a walk. He didn't stay long for *Lodger*. He wasn't there in the final stages.

I invited David over to my family home and introduced him to my sisters and mother. In terms of his private life, things were complicated for him. He'd arrived in Switzerland, he'd divorced – but at our house, he felt comfortable. We even went on holiday together! We went to my sister's in Bourgogne. David had this traditional side that was very endearing. We saw a lot of each other when he lived in Blonay, but a little less after he moved to Lausanne. In the early 1980s, David often came over with Eric Idle and Iggy Pop. We talked a lot about literature because he was constantly reading. He'd fallen in love with *Doctor Fischer Of Geneva* by Graham Greene, who also lived nearby. In Switzerland, people are quiet and discreet and I think David liked that they left him alone. Later, after marrying Iman, he gave me a call and then introduced me to her. I thought that was very nice of him... (2016)

LARRY FAST

David Bowie and I were like two planets – I was the smaller one – that orbited around each other and sometimes came close without ever colliding. But we narrowly missed each other in 1978 and 1979... I was told about David very early in my career. It was early days for Yes and I knew Rick Wakeman. I actually met the band in 1971 when they were touring to promote *Fragile*, their fourth album. Wakeman had just joined Yes and had already worked with Bowie. As for myself, I was only marginally aware of his music. I was excited about space exploration and I remember having heard 'Space Oddity' at that time, and thinking to myself that no Apollo mission had turned out the way it does in the song! But, you know, I was really into technology, new keyboards and stuff, and I loved the Mellotron sound on that song... Later, I realized that Wakeman had a big impact on *Hunky Dory*.

Then, in the mid-70s, I played with Nektar, a British prog rock band based in Germany. We sounded a bit like Pink Floyd, with Beatles and Jimi Hendrix influences... By going to Hamburg, the musicians had made the same journey as The Fab Four, but they'd stayed there! Then, because people in the US liked Nektar, they decided to spend some time there and I went with them as their keyboardist. Since I was the only American in the band and knew New York well, I was a bit like a tour guide. For a while I also lived with Derek 'Mo' Moore, the bass player and *de facto* bandleader.

One day, the phone rang and it was David Bowie! I never found out how he got my number; I guess he knew one or more members of Nektar. He was looking for a keyboardist and wanted to know if I was interested. I was about to go on tour with Peter Gabriel, so I had to turn him down. It was a difficult decision, but I stayed loyal to Peter and it was the right thing to do – over the following years, he gave me some wonderful opportunities[33]. I suggested David take Roger Powell instead. I'd known him since the days when he worked with Robert Moog, the guy who invented the synthesizer of the same name. I knew Roger's music and what he was doing with Utopia. Todd Rundgren was not touring at the time and I thought that Roger would be great, so I made the recommendation. Actually, you remind me that I should get in touch with him, and I will...

Two years later, I had to decline David's invitation again when he asked me to play on *Saturday Night Live*[34]. In May 1978, through Brian Eno and Roger, I went to the Madison Square Garden show during the Isolar 2 tour and I finally met David Bowie! It was nothing more than a quick handshake, but we did speak on the phone after that. And then I ran into him again five years later on the Serious Moonlight tour[35]. I was playing with Peter Gabriel and he was sharing the bill with David. We had fun backstage and I actually took that photo of Peter and David, just before we went on stage. Actually, we joked about the fact that we still hadn't managed to play together! I never saw him again after that. I remained interested in his music, but I have to say that I still haven't had a chance to listen to *Blackstar*. I'm busy with a film project, and when I'm working on something, I tend not to be interested in anything else. (2016)

ROGER POWELL

I was living in Woodstock, New York, doing tours and recording with Todd Rundgren's Utopia. I started with them in 1974. I believe it was some time in February 1978 when I got a phone call one night from someone named Coco. She said she was David Bowie's personal assistant and they were putting a band together for a world tour. At first I thought it was a prank phone call – like somebody playing a joke on me! They needed someone to cover Eno's parts on *Low* and *"Heroes"* – you know, all the synthesizer stuff. Eno had some health issues and wasn't going to do the tour. Actually, I got the job indirectly. David contacted Peter Gabriel about Larry Fast, who played keyboards with him, and Larry recommended me. We were good friends and he had other commitments. I got pretty excited about the whole idea! David Bowie was a big star and this was a great opportunity. I had to set up a leave of absence from Utopia, but that worked out and I took the job.

I'm not sure if David Bowie knew about my work, but I guess he did. I'd put out a solo synthesizer album in 1973 called *Cosmic Furnace*. Maybe he'd listened to that or knew about Utopia. I was one of the early guys into electronic music and synthesizers. Bowie *must* have checked me out before I could be in the band and figured I could handle the synthesizer parts. We met up in Dallas for the rehearsals. We only had two weeks to practise everything! The first week was just the band, and then David came in. Thinking back, it was perhaps a bit foolish, but I was expecting a more flamboyant person – you know, make-up, dyed hair, rock star outfits, the whole thing. Not the case though – he looked very casual and stylish, just a natural and unassuming gentleman. I wouldn't say I was deep into his music, but I followed what he was doing and had some of his records, mostly from the *Space Oddity* period and beyond. I was fascinated with all the different musical styles and directions going on. To me, each record sounded different from the previous one – constantly evolving – with cutting-edge songwriting and production. His voice was very distinctive and unique, with that deep baritone vibrato. I was impressed how he'd shape his voice in different ways to fit a song.

In rehearsals, Bowie was typically pretty relaxed, but also serious about his own performance – you know, polishing his singing and stage moves. He was heavily involved with the lighting design as well. This tour was notable for the intense stage lighting – we had walls of fluorescent tubes and huge sky-beam searchlights, like you used to see at car dealerships. Sean Mayes used to wear a black vinyl jacket on stage until it got scorched by the searchlights because he was sitting so close to them! One time, when the band was running through a song, I remember David sitting in the audience calling out instructions to the lighting crew. He thought up a cool idea for having the spotlights chase each other – kind of like a game. He was always tweaking the show to make it better.

It was okay for us, the musicians, to add our own touches, as long as we played the signature riffs and core parts from the originals. We were free to add things here and there if they didn't get in the way. I had to come up with a lot of my own parts for the second half of the show, which was mostly stuff from *Ziggy Stardust*. Our work was made much easier thanks to Carlos Alomar, a very charming person as well as a phenomenal musician in all respects. I can't imagine anyone not getting along with him! He already had a lot of experience with David and the rhythm section, so he was the ideal musical director. He was a really easy-going guy, but he still kept things moving along. Of course, he was totally on top of the material – he helped us all get our parts down and come together as a band.

I think it's amazing we put that show together in only two weeks. Carlos made that happen. I didn't know any of the other band members before the rehearsals. We all became friends right away! There was a lot of respect for each other as musicians. It really was an incredible band and I think you hear that on the recordings. Everyone was first-rate, but Adrian sort of stood out for me. I liked his kind of twisted approach – it added a lot of energy to the show. No wonder David grabbed him from Zappa's band! We had a lot of fun with the train sounds for the intro on 'Station To Station'. I made the chugging sounds of the engine – starting slow and then getting really fast and distorted – and he did the wailing of the whistle and other wacky noises. I remember he was using two Roland Jazz Chorus amplifiers cranked way up to get this manic swirling feedback. David liked it, so we used to stretch it out and go nuts with it.

The most impressive things about David Bowie were his voice and his stage presence – simply brilliant, as everybody knows. It was a long tour, with over seventy shows[36], but he put everything into it and gave a stellar performance every night. Very professional and a tribute to his stamina. He obviously loved performing so much. We had sell-out crowds nearly everywhere and he really connected with the audiences. The concerts must have been pretty memorable for them.

I remember when we played the Apollo in Glasgow[37] on Eric Barrett's birthday. He was our Scottish road manager. He had also worked with Jimi Hendrix during the early 1970s and a lot of other well-known acts. Anyway, they served him haggis as a special treat for his birthday dinner. Maybe you know about haggis – it's a traditional Scottish dish made with a sheep's stomach. They stuff it with other organs and cook it in blood. Yikes! We wondered if he'd even try it, but he sort of couldn't refuse – I mean you don't want to offend the cook, right? I was just glad they served regular food to the rest of us...

Then there was the famous power failure incident. We were playing this big sports arena in Marseille[38] and, all of a sudden, the light and sound system went dead. Some people have said it was only the sound system but, as I recall, everything went out – it was dark and silent. I don't think we were very far into the first set. The power box was actually smoking and the crew didn't think it was a quick fix. Somebody thought there might be crowd trouble – they didn't get bands there very often, so the audience was really fired up for the show – so we got hustled offstage and went back to the hotel. We felt bad for the audience, but we figured we were done for the night and started to relax. A few of us got together and ordered room service – a big meal plus various adult beverages. I believe other substances were possibly consumed... We didn't think we'd be playing again, so what the heck? Then we got the news that one of the tech guys had pulled off a miracle and had rewired the blown power box. By then, we were... uh... shall we say less 'clear-headed' than normal for performing, but of course we went back and finished the show. I think we had to cut a few songs because of a curfew, but it all went well in the end. Most people had stayed there watching an empty stage and went crazy when David came back on!

I know that Sean Mayes, who sadly passed away in 1995, said we slowed the tempos for the recording at the Spectrum in Philadelphia. I don't remember doing that, but he was always taking notes, so I'd rely on his recollection. Perhaps the idea was to have other tempo choices to pick from for an album. I listened to the 2005 *Stage* CDs the other day and thought we played the songs rather fast, to be honest. I'm not sure which venues the songs were taken from.

After the Stage tour, I didn't work with David again, although I would have liked to. Utopia was my full-time gig and I started creating music software too, which led to a whole second career for me. We did meet and chat for a little while backstage during the Glass Spider tour[39]. This was around nine years later, at the Denver show. It was great to see him again and catch up on things.

It was an extraordinary adventure to travel the world and perform with David Bowie. He was one of the most gifted artists on the planet and I learned a lot from him about professionalism and creativity. He was such a fantastic musician, composer and performer, as well as scholarly about any topic you could think of. And really funny, with that dry British sense of humour. He treated everyone on the tour with great respect – always friendly and supportive. Now, you might not expect this from a big celebrity, but he spent a lot of time just hanging out with the band and crew. We'd have meals together and go places together pretty often. He knew how to bring out the best in people and we all tried to work as hard as he did. I will always admire him for those qualities and treasure those times.

Oh, and I remember visiting the zoo in Sydney: I got invited to join David and Coco and Bette Midler, who happened to be in town[40]. I didn't know that he and Bette were good friends. The really funny part was seeing David and Bette imitate the animals. At one point, we were watching some ostriches and David and Bette started acting like them, running around chasing each other! He had a really whimsical side and that's an image you don't forget!

I met Tony Visconti while we were making a studio recording of 'Alabama Song'. Well, I think he did a super job of mixing those shows. Working with David for such a long time had to help. It's a big challenge to mix live concerts of a seven-piece band and singer. Tony captured the power and tightness of the rhythm section and managed to highlight each instrument's unique parts at just the right spots. David's voice is big and full and projects just like it did during the shows. The result is very faithful to the spirit of the live performances. No question – the guy is legendary, absolutely a master of sound craft.

I wasn't invited to Montreux for the *Lodger* sessions and obviously it was a big disappointment for me as I was really looking forward to it and wanted to be on a David Bowie studio record. Eno was going to handle all the synthesizer work for *Lodger*. But I was the only guy from the band who wouldn't be there. I guess it kind of made sense given their collaboration on the two previous records, but I wasn't too happy about it. I'm still somewhat puzzled why I am credited on the album[41]. Funnily enough, Adrian Belew told me later how the sessions went with

Eno. He said it was sometimes an odd experience and told me a little about the musical experiments during the recording process... Like having Adrian record parts without learning the songs beforehand. He just made stuff up – played freestyle – and pieces were edited together for the final track. I also heard about Eno pointing at the chords. The band never knew which one would come next – sort of spontaneous composing! Or he'd ask guys to swap to instruments they weren't used to playing – that had to be unnerving. Eno was trying to stimulate the musicians with unusual things like that. It's kind of his trademark approach, as you know.

As for the trilogy, I think it's hard to give a simple comparison of any of these records – they all contain such a diverse collection of material. The Eno influence was, of course, enormous on these albums – a big departure from earlier production methods. On *Low* and *"Heroes"*, you hear more prominent synthesizer sounds and effects, and the instrumental-only cuts could be part of a movie soundtrack. But even with the experimental techniques, there were hit singles and structured songs on each of the records. To me, *Lodger* is just an evolution from the previous ones – maybe a little more accessible musically and not as dark sounding. (2016)

ALBERT KOSKI

We really got to know David in 1978 during a holiday in Saint-Martin – the French side – where he came with his son and secretary. He told me about his life, I told him about mine and we had some great times together. We talked about this and that and not necessarily about work... One day, however, a subject really caught his attention: I had this project that was a bit crazy, with UNESCO, to organize a double concert on the pyramids in Teotihuacan, Mexico. David Bowie would be on one and Paul McCartney on the other. It was almost ready, but then unfortunately, Mexico got a new president and it fell through. It's a shame because the idea, since the area wasn't cordoned off, was to have a million audience members... David was really excited.

Our relationship was primarily professional with a few nice private moments here and there. That's how I ended up spending a few days on his boat... What stunned me the most, and I guess I'm not the only one, was his erudition. He appreciated the fact that, since I had a design background, I gave a lot of importance to visuals: the posters, the tickets. I knew the whole team of illustrators from Push Pin Studios in New York: Milton Glaser, who'd drawn Dylan with colours in his hair, Seymour Chwast... Working with these artists really gave me an eye: without them, I might have never bought the Basquiats. At one point I had 11 of them and people would ask, 'What's this shit?'!

In the 1970s, Bowie had a lot of support in France. RCA went out of its way for him, he had support in the media, like Yves Mourousi... Everyone loved him... He also had the radio on his side. Initially, I was with Europe 1, because I got along well with Maurice Siegel. When Jean-Luc Lagardère came, I went to RTL and they were great. But from the start, a lot of people were trying to stab me in the back. Obviously I was trying to do things well. There was a whole production; at one point, I had four press officers, it was a big company. People never talk about that. The media and the fans only care about the artist – the only thing they want is to go backstage and, in Bowie's case, I can tell you there was plenty of interest! Contracts worked on handshakes, we didn't really write anything down. I'd started on Wall Street, so I knew that once someone said something, they couldn't take it back. With the Brits and with the Americans, it was simple: we sent them half the fee and gave them the rest the night of the concert. In France, we were kind of pioneers because there was nothing set up. In Germany and Sweden, they were already better organized.

In 1978 in Marseille, we had this power outage. There were two of these British generators no one knew, and one of them went haywire. Bowie's roadies started yelling and there must have been 15,000 people stamping their feet. Luckily, Pat Gibbons, the manager, was a really cool guy and we got along well. In those days, there were very few venues that could hold that many people, and even fewer outside Paris. We could only find hangars! Because we wanted it to be nice, we got a truck down from Paris with black curtains, another one with chairs, basically whatever we needed to turn an exhibition hall into a concert hall. And so there, while we were this close to catastrophe, a little local guy showed up. He seemed to know what he was doing and he said, 'Okay, I can't promise anything, but I'm going to try and fix it...' The Brits' first reflex was to send him packing, but I thought this guy was a godsend and I let him do his thing. About a quarter of an hour later, it was all working again!

I called the hotel, they all came back, and it was one of the best shows of the tour. You know, in the South of France, we got ripped off by everybody: the guy who rented us the venue, the one who checked tickets... Some of the booking agents at the time were crooks who later went into football. We really had to have security, the best there was. We sometimes had to grab people by the feet to shake them a bit, and bank notes fell out! That was the sort of thing that made Pat laugh!

Most French organizers tried to rip off any English artists who didn't watch out, especially outside Paris. In Paris, the Pavillon allowed us to do a few things, but the authorities were wary of the 'long hairs' and there were always problems with the cops, the prefect, all that. Honestly, under Giscard d'Estaing it was complicated but, at the same time, it made things exciting! (2018)

MARC EXIGA

One thing that really stood out for me in 1978 was Bowie's stage outfit. I remember he arrived with these sort of huge baggy trousers like the Turks wore. I'd already seen a lot of artists live, but this was the first one I'd seen dressed like that. I would have been less shocked if he had made music with a hookah, or covered songs by Fairuz or Oum Kalthoum... It's easier to understand looking back: He was such a unique individual, experimenting with every imaginable facet of his presentation, things that others wouldn't even think of trying... (2018)

GILLES RIBEROLLES

You know, I was absolutely not a photographer, I was just a freelance writer at *Best*. But I'd realized it was a good idea to take photos too while I was reporting on an artist or band. Images paid just as much, so I doubled my income! So, when it was possible, I took the photos for the articles I wrote.

In the spring of 1978, they sent me to Chicago to cover a concert of the Stage tour. I showed up with my big camera fitted with a long zoom so, logically enough, I was turned away at the entrance! It didn't put me off though – I hid everything on me as best I could and I managed to get in. Of course, as soon as I got out my camera, security asked me to put it away and go to the back of the venue. But, in the end, thanks to the long zoom lens, I managed to take some shots before they noticed again and asked me to stop – either that or they kicked me out! Anway, because of the zoom and the lack of lighting, the photographs had a special grain, and some of them ended up in the magazine[42]. One day, I got a phone call from a young guy, a certain Pat Gibbons, Bowie's manager! He wanted to buy one from me. It was as simple as that. I want to point out that I was dealing with honest people because, ever since, each time the photo has been used for a reissue, they've paid me. And recently, they asked me if I had some more... (2018)

JAY-JAY JOHANSON

Of all the concerts I've never been to, this is the one I would have loved to see most of all. Bowie came to Stockholm on the Isolar 2 tour in June 1978, but my parents forbade me to go. I was nine years old. So, I had to wait until the album *Stage* was released later the same year. I had read the reviews of the tour in magazines and talked to older friends who'd gone to see the show.

To open the show with the electronic instrumental 'Warszawa' is just genius and sets the mood for the entire listening experience, and then to dive head first straight into "Heroes" is pure magic. We get more art rock in 'Sense Of Doubt' and 'Art Decade', just before the best version ever recorded of 'Alabama Song'. The double album is worth every penny just for this track! And then comes the fantastic 'Station To Station', here with its even longer noise intro. And let's not forget the bold violin on 'Ziggy Stardust' playing Mick Ronson's brutal guitar hook!

The 2005 reissue is, of course, much better than the first release of *Stage*: the correct running order, no fades between the songs and the full set. We can only hope it will be released on DVD one day, because the clothes David Bowie wore on this tour, and the neon stage lights, were as unique as the music itself.

It's difficult to imagine that this show was the creation of a 30-year-old David – so rich, so obsessive, so ahead of its time and absolutely fabulous. It's the best live album ever recorded. (2016)

NICOLAS GODIN

For me, *Lodger* stands out because I never understood what David Bowie was trying to do with it. Up until this album, it seemed that, for him, each concept having been fixed beforehand in his mind, the records showed tremendous consistency. The first two volumes of the famous trilogy are conceptually clear: strange but brilliant songs on the A-side, and great ambient instrumental tracks on the B-side. But Tony Visconti didn't record them all too well. I always thought the production of the three albums was very avant-garde, but I never thought it was brilliant in terms of recording and mixing.

Lodger doesn't have the same power as *Low* and *"Heroes"*, the two classics that came before. It's the exit album from the Berlin period, the black sheep of the family... Sure, there are some strange songs on the A-side, but instead of turning to the expected ambient tracks, Bowie brings out the big guns in the middle of the B-side, a sort of hit trilogy within the trilogy: 'D.J.', 'Look Back In Anger' and 'Boys Keep Swinging'. Yes, his songs were unstoppable, and his voice was unique and disarmingly poised. His huge and fascinating charisma could sometimes overshadow his musical brilliance. And yes, record after record, he challenged himself to provide sounds that went against what he'd been doing just a few months before. But to manage to make singles with such an avant-garde production... That's the mark of Bowie's greatness. Dissolving the line between the mainstream and the underground is the crowning feat of his immense talent.

Lodger came out at a pivotal time in pop-rock music production, at the end of a decade, before the next one even began. And that's where I also think Bowie was most beautiful. The style of that period, with punk and before the surging 1980s and the MTV look, was a perfect balance in terms of proportions, clothing and hairstyles. For example, on the jacket of *Lodger* and in the 'D.J.' video, Bowie's appearance, his allure, is stunningly modern[43]. He was so charismatic he could afford all those sartorial excesses while maintaining absolute class. He had an undeniable elegance.

In hindsight, I think that, instead of a trilogy, it makes more artistic sense now to talk about two diptychs: *Low* and *"Heroes"*, then *Lodger* and *Scary Monsters*. *Lodger* is a call towards *Scary Monsters* and this diptych represents a specific path that very few artists go down. It's hard to express, but I think these two records are beyond references, 'beyond dreams' I dare say, which is what I think makes them unique and mysterious. Bowie didn't want to be glam, soul or krautrock. It felt like he was finally removing his mask, which is what makes *Lodger* special to me. Its 'non style' reveals something much more intimate than what his characters got us used to. As if, for once, David Bowie was spurning all influences. (2016)

MARC MINELLI

Lodger saved me from disaster, it changed my life, showed me there were images beyond the alienated neighbourhood where I was living. It was the precursor to my music and future encounters, it helped me get dressed, reminded me why I'd loved *The Idiot* so much, gave me the strength to lift my head when it was full of an amorphous, shapeless rock'n'roll.

Lodger was as much a life buoy as it was a ticket to new destinations. It gave me the will to move, to pack my bags whenever I felt like it... Musically, it hooked me up with heroic backing vocals, tortured guitars, ultimate swing and the marriage of different styles. I was always surprised when I read that some consider it the weak link in the chain. For me, it's the opposite! *Lodger* is the David Bowie record I'd take to a desert island.

Initially, I really hated the album cover. I was thinking of *Low* and *"Heroes"* and, of course, that postcard meant absolutely nothing to me alongside music which I had held to be the pinnacle of good taste and elegance, with pride of place in my ultimate record collection. This was not without a touch of snobbery – I am from Normandy, after all. Bowie looked deformed and those old photos inside looked out of place... I learned, like I learned everything else – death, birth and everything in between – about the passing of time, which always swings in the same direction, like a killer wrecking ball.

For me, 'Look Back In Anger' and 'Red Sails' are monsters. On the first listen, they had as much an effect on me as 'Heartbreak Hotel' or 'My Generation'... However, after all this time, they've remained mysterious and rich and they make me rediscover this album every time I listen to it, and I've been doing that for decades!

I'll never tire of this confident, kind and slightly hysterical performance. For me, it represents life and humanity at its best, an adult who kept his childlike soul and his openness, a character with enough perspective to describe without judging. *Lodger* taught me what a masterpiece is. It'll always have a special place in my world. I can refer to it for all sorts of reasons, musical or otherwise.

It allowed me to understand what a singer, composer or arranger is... I immersed myself in it when I conceived *Electro Bamako* in an 'African computer' style. This record gave me many different choices. It's colossal, maybe even scary! (2018)

PHIL MANZANERA

I never stopped being interested in David Bowie's music. I followed it all: the soul days, his partnership with Brian Eno... We knew what he was up to, partly because Ian, the brother of Bill MacCormick, who I played with in Quiet Sun[44], was an *NME* journalist and kept us updated. Each of his albums, each of his artistic U-turns, was a pretext for scrupulous decryptions and long conversations. Of course, his Berlin days, with Eno, were particularly interesting. Curious by nature, David was simply fascinating as a pop star, in every way. He wrote fantastic melodies, which his voice, fantastic too, really emphasized. And if I happened to miss something in Bowie's music, Ian would help me decode the message. With Roxy Music, we always appreciated that he came to see us whenever he could. (2016)

PAGE HAMILTON

From a guitarist's perspective, it's very hard to say which is the best part of David Bowie's discography. But I do have a weakness for the Robert Fripp/Carlos Alomar duo on 'Joe The Lion', 'Scary Monsters', "Heroes" and 'Teenage Wildlife'. They really killed it. Some of my favourite arrangements in Bowie's songs come from the partnership between these two guitar giants. When he played with David, especially on the trilogy, I think Carlos was really the soul of the band. As for Robert Fripp, he's an alien... like Bowie! (2017)

CHRIS FRANTZ

We were playing at CBGB – Talking Heads were a very young band, still a trio – and just before we got on stage, someone said, 'David Bowie is in the audience!' We did our show and then we thought, 'Now we get to meet Bowie.' But we were told he'd already slipped away! He left because there were a lot of fans around, probably more than he wanted to deal with. When we started working with Brian Eno, after he finished recording with David and Devo, we found out that Bowie considered us to be an important influence on him, which did come as a surprise to us, but a pleasant one. However – and this interview gives me the chance to set the record straight – I want to say that we picked Brian Eno as a producer for his own solo work, his early albums on Island that we loved. But of course the Bowie connection didn't work against him! (2018)

1. In 2019, Philip Glass will complete his own trilogy with *Glass's Lodger Symphony*. The London Contemporary Orchestra will perform all three symphonies at the Royal Festival Hall in London in May of the same year. Available on CD (*Symphony No 12 "Lodger"*) since 2022, it will get a lukewarm reception from the public and critics.

2. Since punk and new wave normalized the use of illustration on singles, most of David Bowie's will be released with jackets from 1978.

3. It's very likely that David Bowie had planned on releasing Devo's first album on Bewlay Bros., his own label, which in the end never existed (it was just a production company). Bowie advised Warner US to look into Devo because they were interested in distributing Bewlay Bros.. So it's plausible, since at the time he was acting in the same way for his own recordings, that Bowie started to fund *Q: Are We Not Men? A: We Are Devo!* with his own money before handing it over to Warner (and being reimbursed!). The situation was complicated by the fact that Devo, in London in the spring of 1978, seems to have signed with Virgin before the contract with Warner was finalized. In the end, an agreement was made so that the record could come out in August that year: Virgin released it in Europe and Warner in the US and the rest of the world.

4. Thinking that something positive could come from destabilizing a band that had more than proven itself in 1976, David had reportedly considered letting go of Carlos Alomar.

5. Contrary to what's often been said, it's highly unlikely that Brian Eno refused to go on tour with David Bowie in 1978 for health reasons.

Nor was he the one who recommended Roger Powell to replace him.

6. In *David Bowie: I Was There* (Red Planet, 2017), a collection of testimonies from fellow musicians and audience members who saw Bowie live, Donna Sullivan will write that Brian Eno was on stage on 25 June 1978 at the second of three concerts of the Isolar 2 tour at the New Bingley Hall in Stafford, England. She may be right, but no other witness has confirmed this.

7. Sometimes David Bowie will give special concerts, usually short ones, for television. This was the case for example in late May 1978, for the German music show *Musikladen Extra*, an offshoot of *Der Musikladen*, which aired from the early 1970s to the mid-1980s. *Der Musikladen* had taken over from *Beat-Club*, the famous show from the 1960s.

8. He will give the concert for his 50th birthday there in 1997.

9. In time, this practice spread to all prestigious venues. The Damned, for example, wanted to film the show they gave at the Royal Albert Hall for their 40th anniversary, but unfortunately they didn't have the money.

10. It appears that, in the late 70s, when David Bowie's financial situation improves, without yet being as healthy as it will be in the 80s, he and RCA will have bootleggers in their crosshairs. With the support of the whole industry, they will instigate several lawsuits. Twenty years later, when illegal downloading causes the fall of the entire music industry (closure of labels, studios, record stores and a good number of songwriters and technicians going broke) and does more damage than that caused by the bootleggers of the 70s and

80s, Bowie will change his mind. By then a multimillionaire, he'll sometimes say in his final interviews, not always joking, that 'free' music was 'an incredible thing'. After his passing, the intensive commercial exploitation of his back catalogue (acquired by Warner in 2022) will tell, again, a different story.

11. The venue, which can accommodate 1,500 people, is now called Koko. Artists and bands of medium stature continue to play there, and the more prestigious groups sometimes hold showcases at Koko. That's where Coldplay will launch their album *X&Y* in 2005.

12. The tour stopped at the Arie Crown Theatre on 17 and 18 April.

13. In November 1978, RCA will release an EP of songs from *Stage* including the long version of 'Breaking Glass', as played live that year, on the A-side. David Bowie and his label thought it had the potential to do well in the charts, but certainly not as the super-short version from *Low*. Unfortunately, they were wrong: 'Breaking Glass' didn't even make the top half of the British Top 100. In the 1960s and 1970s, few short songs got to Number 1 in the British or American charts. Two memorable exceptions were 'From Me To You' by The Beatles in 1963 and, in the US, 'The Letter' by Wayne Carson Thompson, made popular four years later by The Box Tops (with Alex Chilton on vocals). Both were under two minutes in length.

14. The fact that David Bowie mixed this record back in 1979 might imply that it was supposed to be released then. It doesn't seem likely that Bowie or RCA would have thought it wise to release two live albums from the same tour, a few months apart. However, it's highly probable that it was meant to be the soundtrack to the concert film David Hemmings had started working on.

15. Bernard 'Doc' Neeson, the singer of The Angels, will pass away in 2014. He said he'd fallen in love with David Bowie, who'd come to see the band during their sound check, and had lent them much of his equipment. Before the end of his career, Bowie will return to Australia for a further three tours.

16. Of the two bonus tracks on Rykodisc's 1991 reissue of *Lodger*, 'I Pray, Olé' is a bit of a surprise, especially since we know that David Bowie will make a point of choosing them himself. In fact, it's impossible to date this piece. Its presence on the record suggests it was an unreleased track from sessions for *Lodger*, which is possible, except that none of the people in the studio – in Switzerland or the US – remembers working on it. However, it could easily have been an abandoned work in progress without a title or vocal melody when musicians played on it. The credits in the Rykodisc reissue state that George Murray and Dennis Davis are the rhythm section, but it's not that obvious. Was 'I Pray, Olé' (with or without the accent, which appears on the CD, but not on the cover) drafted in 1978 even though the copyright indicates 1979? Did Bowie make this unreleased song from old tracks supplemented with new ones? Is it a reworked piece that had gone wrong? Is it a late 1980s creation or even something from the start of the following decade? Only two things are certain: the chord progression borrows heavily from Roxy Music (if Eno played on it, as the notes suggest, he was bound to have noticed) and, once again, the 1991 mix is awful. The second bonus track on *Lodger* will be the 1988 version of 'Look Back In Anger'. Since the Rykodisc reissue has been out of print for some time, 'I Pray, Olé', as of 2022, is no longer officially available.

17. Back when running time was limited on each side of a vinyl record, Tony Visconti, like Ken Scott before him, had a say in sequencing the albums.

18. The liner notes say this word means 'Long Live', but since David Bowie claimed he didn't know what it meant when he wrote the song, this clarification has always seemed strange. 'Yassassin' will come out as a single in July 1979, but only in the Netherlands and Turkey.

19. Like punk and new wave, reggae will become popular in the late 1970s, and highly commercial under the aegis of Chris Blackwell, who'll make Bob Marley a global star. Ska, which is not an offshoot of reggae but a precursor genre, will also be very popular at the turn of the decade.

20. The beat during the first half of 'What In The World', as played on the Isolar 2 tour, was also undeniably reggae. It started at 95bpm, then went up to 125bpm, as in the original version.

21. 'After Eight' is on Neu!'s third album, released in 1975, and 'Monza (Rauf Und Runter)' is on *Deluxe*, Harmonia's second.

22. In early 1982, the American band Indeep (one man and two women) will also make an obvious reference to DJ-ing (and make the world dance) with the successful 'Last Night A DJ Saved My Life', written by Mike Cleveland.

23. David Bowie met him on the set of *The Kenny Everett Video Show*, a musical comedy show that aired on ITV. He was its creator and director. This show will be broadcast between 1978 and 1981 and Bowie sang 'Boys Keep Swinging' on it in April 1979. The performance was quite surreal, and he can even be seen playing a violin he ended up breaking! Mallet directed the three videos from *Lodger*, including the one for 'Look Back In Anger', in which Bowie appears as a disturbed artist, scared by the idea of getting old. Their partnership will span two decades and, in addition to the music videos, David Mallet directed the films of the Serious Moonlight and Glass Spider tours, but not the 1984 documentary *Ricochet* sometimes attributed to him.

24. As Laurent Thibault explained, '*Répétition*' was one of the French words David Bowie used while recording *The Idiot*. The title of this song is not in the lyrics and it is the same for 'African Night Flight'.

25. He will experience a similar artistic misadventure with *Scary Monsters* in 1980.

26. On 18 November 1978 at Cricket Ground. Three weeks before, some fans started camping out near the stadium, which held 40,000 people. It will be almost full on the night of the concert. David Bowie doesn't talk much to the audience that evening, but he says, regarding the pouring rain, 'If you're crazy enough to stay, we're crazy enough to play.'

27. On 2 December 1978, more than 40,000 people went to the show at Western Springs Stadium.

28. The rhythm tracks of 'Sister Midnight' and 'Red Sails' are identical (and played at the same tempo: 106bpm). These are almost certainly the ones the DAM trio recorded for *The Idiot*,

probably not at the Château d'Hérouville but in Jamaica.

29. David Bowie's musicians have often told this story, with variations. Some said they got their instrument back before the final take.

30. In 1975, Brian Eno produced *Lucky Leif And The Longships*, the sensational second album by South African author and musician Robert Calvert, recorded with some members of Hawkwind. Two songs were added to its CD reissue in 2007, including 'Cricket Lovely Reggae (Cricket Star)'. This song was recorded between Calvert's first two albums, but its name might have appealed to Eno. Simon House played on this record and the liner notes say, 'Arranged by Calvert, Rudolph and oblique strategies'.

31. Tony Visconti spoke to the author – who was in New York for a preview of *Lazarus* – when he visited him in his studio in early December 2015. That day, Visconti didn't say a word about David Bowie's health. It wasn't until after Bowie's death that his fans realized why recording sessions for *Blackstar* had been so sporadic.

32. A basic and inexpensive synthesizer the year it came out (in 1978). It was designed by Chris Huggett. Like the Stylophone, the Wasp has a fixed keyboard that just needs to be touched lightly to make raw, but interesting, sounds.

33. Between 1977 and 1985, Larry Fast will play on Peter Gabriel's first four solo albums and on the soundtrack he'll compose for the film *Birdy*.

34. On 15 December 1979, David Bowie will sing three songs live on the set of the NBC show. His band will be Carlos Alomar, Stacy Heydon, George Murray and Dennis Davis. Jimmy Destri of Blondie will play keyboards that day instead of Larry Fast, who'd been Bowie's first choice. This appearance on *Saturday Night Live* will also go down in history thanks to Joey Arias and especially Klaus Nomi, the backing vocalists. Nomi will release his first (and best) album two years later. His success will be significant but short-lived, although Nomi will become a new wave and synth-pop icon, especially – and paradoxically – in the eyes of those who were not born when he had his heyday.

35. On 7 August at the Commonwealth Stadium in Edmonton (Canada's biggest stadium), in a heat wave, before an audience of 60,000 people, The Tubes and Peter Gabriel will open for David Bowie. Larry Fast (as well as bassist Tony Levin, who will play on *The Next Day* in 2013) was in Gabriel's band then. He also opened two days later in Vancouver.

36. There were 75 shows.

37. That year, David Bowie played there for three nights in a row, from 20 to 22 June.

38. On 27 May at the Palais des Sports. The blackout occurred about twenty minutes into the concert.

39. Roger Powell is referring to the concert on 12 August 1987 at the Mile High Stadium. The interview with Marilyn Manson in Michael Moore's 2002 film *Bowling For Columbine* will take place in that stadium.

40. David Bowie performed at the Sydney Showground (Moore Park) on 24 and 25 November.

41. The presence of Roger Powell's name in the notes of *Lodger* (he reportedly played on 'Repetition' and 'Red Money') is not the only anomaly. The saxophone part in 'Red Sails', long attributed to a certain 'Stan', is credited to Stan Harrison in the most recent reissue of the album. The problem is that while Harrison will indeed work with David Bowie, he won't meet him until five years after *Lodger* was recorded, during the sessions for *Let's Dance*.

42. The article and photos were printed in Issue 119 of *Best*, in June 1978.

43. The jumpsuit he's wearing is designed by Willie Brown.

44. Quiet Sun is the prog rock band from Canterbury in which Phil Manzanera played before Roxy Music. In 1975, while recording *Diamond Head*, his first album, Manzanera was also working on *Mainstream*, the only LP by Quiet Sun, with Bill MacCormick on bass (for which Quiet Sun reconvened, having been dormant since early 1972). Brian Eno also plays on these two records. Bill's brother Ian, who went by the surname McDonald, wrote some lyrics for 801 (another great band with Phil Manzanera, Brian Eno, Bill MacCormick and Lloyd Watson) and, as an author, is known for *Revolution In The Head*, his important yet controversial book about The Beatles. He died in 2003 and never wrote, as he had planned, a book about David Bowie.

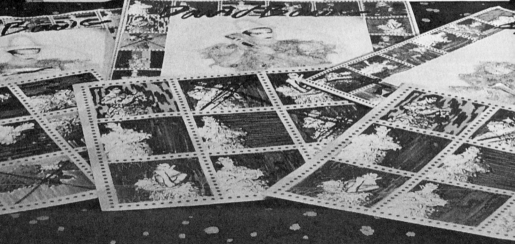

SCARY MONSTERS (AND SUPER CREEPS)

RCA – 12 SEPTEMBER 1980

'I always say that I only wish to have three sorts of people as my friends: those who are very rich, those who are very witty and those who are very beautiful.'
(CHRISTOPHER ISHERWOOD – *MR NORRIS CHANGES TRAIN* – 1935)

'It's always a pleasure to work with Tony Visconti, an Italian from New York! I mean, he has a sensitivity for songs, sympathy and empathy for the right melody, and he knows how to arrange them. He is also a fabulous musician: his string parts are incredible and he's a sublime bass player. He knows me. He's one of those people who understands how much I really know what I want before entering the studio. And he knows how to help me and create a comfortable environment that makes me prolific and effective. Take Eno. I don't really know why he's a good teammate, because he doesn't know how to play anything. Everything basically comes from the way he speaks. He establishes and expresses his parameters with certain words, he articulates new methods, but his actions are common. It's very interesting. [...]

'I'm not a singles singer but an album artist. Whoever my core fans are, I'm sure they'd agree. Everything Tony and I do together is identifiable somehow. The songs I worked on with him undoubtedly bear our hallmark. But I hate it when people say they sound the same.'   DB (2002/2003)

Like *The Man Who Sold The World*, neither *Lodger* nor *Scary Monsters*, its successor, was followed by a tour. It's one of the reasons that prompted Tony Visconti to follow Woody Woodmansey's suggestion in 2014 and 'play live the album David Bowie never promoted'. Having got back on his feet in 1978, the musician will not tour again until the year *Let's Dance* is released. However, he will not be idle, but will let himself be guided by his instinct again, considering many artistic propositions but only taking in some of them, depending on encounters, circumstances and desires.

So, on April 1st, 1979, Bowie performed at the First Concert Of The Eighties in New York, a benefit show organized by WKCR. This non-commercial radio station, which is still run by students at Columbia University (and now airs online), made a great contribution to popularizing alternative music trends. That evening, Steve Reich, Philip Glass and John Cale were also on stage at Carnegie Hall. Apparently, Nico had been invited to sing with Cale, but she was replaced at short notice by David, who played viola on 'Sabotage'[1]. When *Lodger* came out, even though it didn't enthuse RCA any more than *"Heroes"*, Bowie appeared on a number of radio and television shows in London and, at the end of the summer, after learning that Iggy Pop[2] wasn't progressing well with his fifth album, David went to Rockfield Studios in Wales[3].

These sessions didn't go too well and the memories of those who agree to talk about them are, once again, fuzzy. Having been asked to come along, together with Coco Schwab, in the hope that his presence might improve the vibe, David Bowie will only manage to raise tensions and make James Williamson – producer of *New Values*, the successor to *Lust For Life*, released in April – fly off the handle. Iggy and David write a song on the spot and put it on tape with the musicians on hand. It features some members of Simple Minds, who happen to be recording there, on backing vocals, but 'Play It Safe', despite its drum part by Tangerine Dream's Klaus Krüger, is a bit too aptly named and not at all memorable.

Luckily, sessions will be more productive at Good Earth, Tony Visconti's studio in London[4], where Bowie goes after returning from Wales. Invited again on to *The Kenny Everett Show*, he agreed to David Mallet's request to perform 'Space Oddity', on the condition that he does a different version. At the start of the new decade, wanting to cut a few ties with the past (he began to take apart his image on the cover of *Lodger*), David revisits the song that made him famous ten years before in an ultra-minimalist way – laying down a basic rhythm track and simple piano chords under his vocal and 12-string guitar. Another version of 'Panic In Detroit'[5] is also taped by Visconti, but the mood in the studio isn't great. Bowie is annoyed by the presence of bassist Zaine Griff. At the time, this New Zealander is working with Tony, who is impressed by his writing and his elegance. The problem is that Griff, who surfs on the new wave (that heralds the New Romantic movement), is one of those fans who show their appreciation by physically imitating their idol. But this idol, however, had issued a warning. In 'Boys Keep Swinging' on *Lodger*, David Bowie sang two lines with a certain amount of contempt: '*They'll never clone ya/ You're always first on the line.*' While one might think him indifferent to plagiarism, or far above all that, Bowie frowns on being openly copied.

Later that year, Gary Numan will be treated even worse. For some time already, against a backdrop of military and synthetic electro-rock, the English singer-songwriter who started his musical career as the frontman of Tubeway Army, has been rehashing some of the dystopian themes developed by David Bowie. In addition – and this is probably where it really hurts – he has been quite successful with it: in July, *Replicas*, Tubeway Army's second album, topped the charts along with the single 'Are "Friends" Electric?'. Two months later, Numan had equal success with his first solo album, *The Pleasure Principle*, and 'Cars', the first single from the record. Moreover, in terms of clothing and hairstyles, Gary Numan – on stage, in his videos and on the street – shamelessly borrows from Bowie.

The day *The Kenny Everett Show* is filmed (it will be aired on 31 December and called *Will Kenny Everett Make It To 1980?*), David spots the one he considers a poor imitation of himself among the attending VIPs. He halts shooting and demands the clone be expelled. In his defence, it must be noted that Numan also drew inspiration from Kraftwerk and Ultravox, whose frontman was then still John Foxx. He will have Number 1s only for a short time but, by harnessing all facets of electronic music and searching beyond the boundaries of the genre, Gary Numan will forge a respectable and consistent career. After turning to industrial rock, he will become an influencer in his own right, and Trent Reznor and Marilyn Manson will not stop singing his praises. Inspired by David Bowie and Roxy Music, the New Romantics and their more or less direct synth-pop followers, like the glam stars before them, will focus a lot on appearances. In the early 80s, these very well-groomed young people, colourful in appearance (and equipped with as many synths as they have guitars), will fuel the debate and even revive the sexual ambivalence that had worked so well, at least as a detonator, for Bowie. The press (who didn't see it coming) won't always be kind to Adam And The Ants, Culture Club, Hazel O'Connor, Duran Duran, Classix Nouveaux, Visage, ABC, Japan, Eurythmics, Spandau Ballet, Depeche Mode and friends, but some of these acts will proudly stand up to the old guard, who they will often stare at from the heights of the charts throughout the decade.

In December 1979, David Bowie is back in New York to film an episode of *Saturday Night Live* on NBC, to be broadcast in early January[6]. Martin Sheen is hosting, and David performs three songs in extravagant clothing that contrasts with the more serious outfit he wore on *The Kenny Everett Show*, or his last tour attire. Again he has hired Mark Ravitz for the staging and costumes of this performance, under the influence of Dada theatre and the founders of the Cabaret Voltaire in Zurich. His two backing vocalists (Klaus Nomi and Joey Arias, whom he discovered as human mannequins in the window of the Fiorucci retail store on East 59th Street) bring him to the middle of the stage and he starts by singing 'The Man Who Sold The World' wearing a rigid jacket. It is partially inspired by the outfits made by painter and stylist Sonia Delaunay for the actors in *The Gas Heart*, a 1922 play by Tristan Tzara, and also by a tubular costume Hugo Ball wore while reciting *Karawane*, a 1916 poem.

For 'TVC 15', Bowie wears women's clothes (long jacket and skirt and shoes), and looks like a 'Chinese air hostess' he will later say; while for 'Boys Keep Swinging', he attaches to his chest a sort of papier-mâché dummy that he animates in front of his green outfit. The trick makes him disappear, only his head remaining visible. The DAM trio is David's band on the show, and Stacy Heydon is temporarily back on guitar. Blondie's Jimmy Destri – a passionate fan of Bowie's music – plays keyboards, replacing Larry Fast who was not available. In late 1981, not long before Blondie's split, Destri will release *Heart On A Wall*, his only solo album to date, featuring Earl Slick, Carlos Alomar and Michael Kamen (on keyboards and production).

Those whose life is sad like a prefilled form, who are incapable of rising above their own existence and who are happy to judge others, sometimes accused David Bowie of being an opportunist. When he goes to see *The Elephant Man* in New York just before Christmas, however, little does he know that John Merrick is going to offer him the chance to deliver one of his most beautiful performances as an actor. That night Bowie is introduced to Jack Hofsiss, the director of the play, and he tells the lead actor Philip Anglim how impressed he's been with his performance. Unlike John Hurt in David Lynch's film a year later, Anglim plays Joseph Carey Merrick (his full name), an Englishman who lived in Victorian times and whose facial growths and physical deformities earned him the nickname 'elephant man', without prosthetics or special make-up. A moderate success when it premiered in London in 1977, Bernard Pomerance's play is doing fairly well in New York but, still, Hofsiss is convinced it would do even better with a more charismatic lead. After a few months' reflection, he will offer the role to Bowie, whose performance in *The Man Who Fell To Earth* convinced him that he might be the right man for the job.

'Being' John Merrick will take David out of the music world for more than six months, but he will accept the role for at least two reasons. First, playing Merrick is as much a physical feat as an artistic one (the press will salute Bowie's 'without artifice' performance, which was wrongly considered 'innovative') – aside from the acting itself, the role requires altering his voice and speech, and especially adopting a posture to simulate the deformity. The second reason is that it is a challenge worthy of David Bowie, something that resonates with him at that time. Since the beginning of the 70s, he was fully aware of the importance of his physical appearance in the development of his career. Since his fans and a whole generation of musicians are now paying tribute to him by imitating him, he concludes that his handsome face and his incredible figure distort the relationship he has with his audience, some of whom are attracted to him for reasons that have nothing to do with art. From 1979 until 1984, when he chooses a flattering image again for the album cover of *Tonight*, David Bowie will deliberately leave behind his image as a 'poster boy' for bug-eyed girls on his official photos. And in his acting choices, he will never refuse a role that involves compromising his appearance.

After a trip to London to research John Merrick and a month of intense rehearsals, the first performances of *The Elephant Man* with David Bowie will take place in the middle of summer 1980 at the Auditorium Theatre in the Denver Center For The Performing Arts, then at the Blackstone Theatre in Chicago. Before returning to Broadway, Hofsiss and the producers of the play think it wise to try it out in the provinces. With this experience in his pocket, Bowie plays the role for three months at the Booth Theatre in New York (222 West 45th Street), and his performance, as well as his commitment and professionalism, is appreciated by all. Strangely though, the audience will be mostly made up of theatre-goers rather than rock fans. Unlike most of the actors who played the role[7], and even though the press declare him to be the perfect John Merrick, David will not receive any awards for his performance. Philip Anglim will later take up the role again, so David will not appear in the television adaptation Jack Hofsiss directs in 1982. If the play with Bowie as Merrick was shot in its entirety, the footage remains in the vaults[8].

One of the many things David Bowie and Tony Visconti had in common was that at several points in their careers, they both put their jobs first. When Bowie's divorce is finalized in February 1980, he decides to throw himself into his next record. At the same time, Tony is very affected by the imminent end of his marriage to Mary Hopkin, and joining David in New York means leaving his wife and children (who live in England) again. But, as he wrote in his autobiography, 'the job won out.' Two factors will urge the pair to choose Power Station Studios. Firstly, this old power plant on 441 West 53rd Street in Hell's Kitchen, Manhattan, was renovated by Bob Walters and Tony Bongiovi, Jon Bon Jovi's cousin. This American sound engineer learned the ropes with Jimi Hendrix, then, in the mid-70s, when David Bowie was living in the US, he co-produced Gloria Gaynor's first three records. David loved her first hit songs, including 'I Will Survive' and 'Never Can Say Goodbye', which bore Bongiovi's signature. Having fantasized about the Motown sound, Tony Bongiovi has unlocked most of its secrets and also knows how important it is to make high-quality equipment available to his clients. So, after the disappointing experience at the Record Plant, where all work on *Lodger* was finished off, David Bowie and Tony Visconti are thrilled to work there. Secondly, when they find out that Chic have been recording most of their hits at the Power Station since its opening in 1977, even though neither of them have yet met guitarist Nile Rodgers or bassist Bernard Edwards (the two founders of the disco band), they know they have landed in the right place[9].

Only one thing casts a shadow on their enthusiasm: over the phone, Bowie was impatient and asked Visconti to drop everything and join him. He said he had some new tracks ready and he wanted to start recording quickly before they evade him. When he arrives in New York, instead of finished songs, Tony finds David only has short chord charts and a few rough drafts that the DAM trio has to mess around with for quite some time before getting anything coherent or usable. Affected by his personal problems and 4,000 miles from his family, the most English of all American producers completely loses it, despite being in his home town. Four years before in France, Visconti had to raise Bowie's spirits when he was downcast by the legal problems with his ex-manager. This time, it is David who is going to comfort him. Tony realizes that this record they are about to make is their ninth (and their fourth in a row) together. Of course he has no idea what the future will bring for either of them, but he knows how lucky he is to be working with an artist he respects and who, as a man, is offering him support. With this in mind, Tony Visconti immerses himself in the album. They tackle it using the same model they had in mind for *The Man Who Sold The World* – The Beatles' *Sgt. Pepper*. In the 2017 liner notes for the box set *A New Career In A New Town (1977–1982)*, Tony will specify that *Scary Monsters* was more like their *Revolver*. Either way, and even though they aren't to know it will be their last album together before a two-decade break, they both intend to invest everything in it.

Unlike Berlin or Montreux (where David Bowie decided not to record, even though he gets along better and better with David Richards), New York is a hotbed of musicians, like Los Angeles and London. The basic tracks, with only working titles (George Murray and Dennis Davis don't yet know they are recording with Bowie and Visconti for the last time), will be enriched by passing instrumentalists. Since Bruce Springsteen and the E Street Band are putting together *The River* in the next studio, David asks Roy Bittan, who did a great job on *Station To Station*, to play piano. Tony still recalls an amusing anecdote about their time at the Power Station – Dennis Davis's musical knowledge was limited to jazz so, when he met Springsteen in the lounge there, he asked him which band he played with!

At least two covers are recorded during these sessions: 'I Feel Free' by Cream[10], which Bowie especially loves and has often played live with The Spiders From Mars, and 'Kingdom Come' from the first solo (and eponymous) album by Tom Verlaine, the frontman of Television[11], one of David's favourite American art punk bands. After shouting from the rooftops how much he loved Tom Verlaine, it was time to take action – in truth, David Bowie would have loved to collaborate with him, but it never happened. Carlos Alomar is the one who suggested covering this particular song. Verlaine has been invited to play on this version, but he will spend his day at the Power Station trying to 'find the right sound' by plugging into every amp that has been rented at his request. He is no more satisfied with the result than he was when he tested a dozen pedals. In the end, whatever he (might have) committed to tape will not appear in the mix.

Strangely enough, even though Adrian Belew was asked to play on *Scary Monsters* (he had supposedly been paid upfront), his presence will ultimately not be required. An organ part played by Jimmy Destri did not survive the mix either. On the other hand, Chuck Hammer, a guitarist Bowie spotted live alongside Lou Reed a few months earlier, didn't come to the studio for nothing.

A little less than three weeks after the start of the sessions (they have been working on a dozen songs), David Bowie, in an unusual move, decides to postpone his vocal takes and the last overdubs. He suggests to Tony Visconti that they complete the record in London, at Good Earth Studios. He also promises that most of the melodies and lyrics will be ready by then. Bowie hasn't recorded in his home town since *Diamond Dogs* and, when he arrives at 59 Dean Street, he feels more at home than expected. The mixing console is a Trident, like the name of the studio a few hundred yards away that he used so often between 1969 and 1973...

Tony first calls Andy Clark, a versatile British keyboardist who once played with Be Bop Deluxe. Because Bowie has always been a fan of The Who (which he clearly demonstrated on *Pin Ups*) and since he is in London, he can't resist the temptation to invite Pete Townshend to play on 'Because You're Young' (a song he will revisit in part with 'New Killer Star' in 2003). As its title indicates, 'Because You're Young', perhaps the most questionable track of the batch – the line between a well-crafted chorus and a pimped-up one can be very fine – addresses (again) the subject of the passing of time and its ability to heal wounds. Strangely enough, while it is known that Pete was fond of David, he doesn't mention this participation in *Who I Am*, his amazing autobiography published by HarperCollins in 2012. But he recalls a Who concert at the Royal Albert Hall on 5 July 1969, when he asked David Bowie to babysit his son Simon (then nine years old) during the show. Townshend also suggests that after this unusual babysitting session, just after The Who had released *Tommy*, the idea of a concept album based on an imaginary character would have been born in the spirit of Bowie...

The session with Pete Townshend doesn't exactly go smoothly, partly because of the flowing red wine. Townshend[12] will say later that he didn't feel comfortable that day – David and Tony were so close when they were working together that it was sometimes hard for an outsider to feel part of the process. However, the guitar part he recorded, including signature windmill chords, was kept. The same goes for most of the tracks Robert Fripp laid down on six of the ten songs on the record. Like George Murray and Dennis Davis, Fripp didn't know that this performance would be his last in a studio with Bowie, but maybe he suspected it.

As for the backing vocals, David and Tony both wanted to capture the spirit of the girl bands of the 1960s[13], so they recruited Lynn Maitland[14] and Chris Porter. At the time, Porter is the assistant recording engineer at Good Earth (he also helped build and decorate the place) and he will later become the chief recording engineer. As a producer in his own right, his name will appear, in the years to come, on the backs of albums by Elton John and George Michael, among others.

In February 1980, the single 'Alabama Song', with the sparse acoustic remake of 'Space Oddity' on the B-side, stopped just short of the British Top 20, but many fans jumped on it because the jacket was a mini poster folded in four, featuring a photo (taken on the set of a Dick Clark television show in December) of David Bowie in a Willie Brown[15] outfit inspired by Le Corbusier. Since the start of the year, RCA executives had finally realized they were about to lose their most important artist since Elvis Presley. The 'war of succession', involving many record companies, will last a couple of years and, not surprisingly, Bowie will take his time before signing his name at the bottom of another contract. In fact, when he starts recording the successor to *Scary Monsters* (and deals with the associated costs), David will not have a label to back him up. To show what they are still capable of, RCA will launch a memorable marketing campaign to promote the new album and the half dozen singles (and an EP) that David will release between 'Alabama Song' and 'Peace On Earth/Little Drummer Boy' in November 1982.

In addition to funding videos and buying ad space on television and in print, because David Bowie was on his way to becoming one of the most collectable rock stars of his generation, RCA will bet on new mediums – singles with different visuals, maxi-singles (with or without extended versions of songs), coloured vinyl records, picture discs and cassette singles (called cassingles at the time). Following RCA's lead, since remixes were all the rage, every record company tasked with selling Bowie's work will play this very lucrative card. Much later, like any singer-songwriter living off his art, David Bowie will not be spared illegal downloading and institutionalized streaming by the modern-day crooks who are the only ones to make a profit out of it. For vast numbers over the past 20 years, it's become the normal way of acquiring and listening to music.

Bowie's records, however, available in several formats, will keep selling at a decent pace. Reissues will multiply after 2013, when EMI collapses. Parlophone will become an imprint of Warner Music Group and continue to distribute his RCA albums (he will be the sole owner of his master tapes by then). Unsurprisingly,

Bowie's death and a renewed interest in vinyl records will contribute to collector fans being offered more and more 'new' products[16]. Since they are very often sold as limited editions, it isn't unusual to see reissues being resold for crazy sums of money (sometimes much higher than the original record's price), especially at record fairs and on auction websites. But it would be stupid to rebuke Warner Music Group and Sony Music Entertainment (which will distribute David Bowie's recordings, starting with *Outside* in 1995) for the overexploitation of the back catalogue, especially on Record Store Day – which in no time went from being a nice event to a ruthless commercial operation – as, evidently, Bowie's heirs also profit from these sales. In defence of those who are in charge of his legacy, even though it's not being sold for public good, it's worth noting that David keeps on fascinating young music lovers. Growing up, most of them only knew their parents' unappealing CDs, so it is good news that they see these new vinyl records and box sets as having some kind of soul.

In the early 1980s, the luckiest David Bowie fans get their hands on three different editions of the single 'Ashes To Ashes'. The fastest ones will find a sheet of stamps inserted in the jackets of the first 100,000 British singles – there will be four different ones to collect. RCA wanted to make an impression with the packaging but, for Bowie, music is what matters. After being ahead of his time, sometimes in spite of himself, for almost ten years, he will state that the songs on *Scary Monsters* perfectly capture the sound of the passing of the decade from the 1970s to the 1980s. That is proof that he was a better singer-songwriter than he was a music critic. As a matter of fact, while 'Ashes To Ashes' has all the elements to become a classic, it is actually far ahead of its time. To this day, it still doesn't sound like anything that came out before it, or after it.

On first hearing, 'Ashes To Ashes' is disarming in its clarity, while remaining as deep as the faith its creator had in his art. One can try to probe its nooks and crannies, use a stethoscope to listen to what's going on in the background, analyse its shape and identify its embellishments, but with each listen, this song seems to have something new to say. It's about the past, loneliness, childhood, moral insecurity, drugs and especially Major Tom, of 'Space Oddity' fame. While he was thought to be lost, forever floating in a faraway galaxy, here he reappears and confirms that, at least in David Bowie's mind, he was in fact the first in his series of personas. And because nobody knows, in 1980, what's to come and even less what the end will look like, he will perhaps turn out to be the most important.

'Rebel Rebel' had allowed Bowie to shut the door on glam rock without so much as a backward glance; with 'Ashes To Ashes', he will officially put an end to the 1970s. Did his partnership with Tony Visconti ever work better than on this album and, hence, this song? There are as many answers to this question as there are lovers of the music these two created. Inventive keyboards perfectly spread in the stereo field, a titillating bass line, acrobatic guitars and, above all, that chorus, sung in a lower key than the verse, a nonsense that Bowie sweeps away with astute backing vocals... The listener is spared nothing because the musician left nothing to chance. With 'Ashes To Ashes' he puts the pressure on, but all his cards are on the table. Nevertheless, this shot of growth hormones deepens the mystery of his own legend.

Scary Monsters comes out on 12 September 1980, less than two weeks before the Broadway premiere of *The Elephant Man* with David Bowie in the lead, and proves to be no more a concept album than its predecessors. But by choosing to bookend his field of investigation, with the same song approached in two different ways, he encouraged it to be seen as more than a simple string of songs. Bowie knew how to rummage through his attic better than anyone (are there enough unreleased songs lying around the archives to fill an album worth releasing? We'll know soon enough...) and for *Scary Monsters* he decided to revisit 'Tired Of My Life', already known to fans in the form of a 1970 demo. Most of them are surprised to find it here in a fleshed-out version with a different name – 'It's No Game (Part 1)'. They may also be stunned to hear, at the start of the track, a few lines sung/spoken by a Japanese girl[17], with a machine-gun flow, who finally shuts up to give way to a very angry David Bowie. Strangely enough, the causes of his wrath are the same ones he will mention in interviews at the beginning of the 21st century: ignorance, inaction in the face of cruelty and stupidity, 'pandemic' migration...

Like many of Bowie's songs, including 'Ashes To Ashes', 'Up The Hill Backwards' had a different title[18] when it was made, but it already had that 7/4 beat, which rock music lovers who don't know much about music theory (it is actually a variation of the 3–2 clave) usually associate with the famous Bo Diddley shuffle. The unique feature of this song, which has a nursery-rhyme melody (like some tracks by Lou Reed have), is that David Bowie never sings alone. Visconti and Maitland support him vocally from start to finish, giving 'Up The Hill Backwards' – whose lyrics include references to the seismic shock caused by his divorce – the feel of a military march. The finale is joyfully disturbed by Robert Fripp, who spins through the high notes and sounds like he's searching in vain for the meaning of it all. Although Bowie always encouraged an open interpretation of his lyrics and never revealed all their arcana, it's certainly not out of place – because he was probably still harbouring some psychological rancour – to hear veiled references to his American years of black magic, white powder and bad temper in the lyrics of the title song of the album. Of course those days were long gone, but they haunted his past and still stung.

While promoting the album, Bowie will sometimes claim that living alongside the New York jet-set crowd as well as the homeless in Manhattan was the initial inspiration for 'Scary Monsters'. The song has the most upbeat tempo of the album (140bpm) and the verses showcase one of his talents as a composer – knowing how to create, on a very simple chord progression, a melody with precisely controlled variations in pitch, undulating like the surface of Lake Geneva when the Foehn wind blows down off the mountains. Fripp's guitar roars throughout the song and, in Brian Eno's absence, Tony Visconti punctuates it with cheap synth sounds (the famous yapping of the 'monsters' comes from the Wasp) and inspired finds (George Murray's gated bass[19] sounds like a sequencer).

David Bowie drew most of his logic from multiple contradictions. In the bridge of 'Fashion', a slap in the face for trends he prided himself on ignoring, even though he started several himself (and will marry a model a decade later), he begs his audience to listen to him, and not to listen to him! Annoyed by mimicry, yet unleashing on the world a flood of images to copy, and knowingly provoking adulation, he doesn't mind being adored or having his footsteps followed, but at a reasonable distance. 'Fashion' has been in his head since rehearsals for the Station To Station tour, when the DAM trio played an embryonic version of it (hence the working title 'Jamaica'). At one point, it was on the verge of being rejected from the album, because Bowie couldn't write the lyrics.

'Fashion' is the most techno song on the album, even though this musical genre does not exist in 1980. But the word refers to production choices that were radical at the time – Dennis Davis plays to a drum machine pattern that stayed in the mix, and the 'whoop' on the offbeat is the click generated by Andy Clark's sequencer, which was also kept. While George Murray's bass line would be perfect for disco (despite a rather slow tempo of 110bpm), Davis stands out significantly from the genre, mainly because of his tom fills highlighted by Visconti. Carlos Alomar plays it safe by strumming a funk pattern, while Robert Fripp spreads himself equally between genetically modified art (in the intro), being scathing and mordant (as he carves out some funky chords, as if with a box-cutter) and trumpeting blasts (when he comes in after the bridge).

'Teenage Wildlife' is most probably an assemblage of parts composed at different times. It is offered as a starter on the B-side of *Scary Monsters*, even though it's really the main course. Again, something that can be called a verse develops, at least when the song begins, on the chord progression of 'I'm Waiting For The Man' (and therefore of "Heroes", which also came from it). But while David Bowie's vocal grew gradually in power on the title song of his second 1977 album, it is incandescent from the start here and it remains heated throughout the nearly seven minutes of the song. From the viewpoint of his 33 years, as if he were in the twilight of his life, he looks back on past grievances, with or without condescension (throwing spikes at MainMan and those 'new wave boys' who failed to impress him) and takes advantage of an arrangement which is convoluted to deliver messages that are not. Bowie knew his way around a song, so he could easily make the backing vocals, perfectly crafted here, help swallow the pill of reckless harmonic twists. For example, it happens at two minutes and forty-two seconds in, when he opens a sort of bridge (a pre-chorus actually), well aware that very few others, apart from him, would have the guts to cross it. And because Dennis Davis gives him confidence with a drum beat which is ultimately nailed down with a kick drum hit on every quarter note (despite the drummer's precision and rigour, it doesn't sound like disco), David repeats the trick further into the track. Roy Bittan, who is happy just to emphasize the harmony, has no rival in this field and his restraint contrasts with the sonic eruptions Fripp no longer tries to suppress.

Like 'It's No Game', 'Scream Like A Baby' is a holdover song recorded by The Astronettes at Olympic in 1973 under the name 'I'm A Laser' (for an album that was shelved). But thanks to Tony Visconti's new wave arrangements, it found itself a home on *Scary Monsters*, even though the melody and structure of its chorus (a libertine chord progression that would have nauseated anyone – who, except him, would have thought of that fourth chord?) recall the writing methods Bowie was pioneering ten years before. As for Andy Clark's 'descending' synth part[20], which comes in for the first time at 44 seconds, it may well be a nod to the one at the beginning of 'Speed Of Life' on *Low*.

Due to the nature of this book, a good portion of the material comes from those, mainly in the music world, who worked with David Bowie decades ago. Over time, grievances have faded and most wounds have healed. For some of them – most notably Tony Visconti and Mike Garson – working with Bowie hasn't always been easy. Photographer Brian Duffy knew a thing or two about that. When in June 1980, Bowie asks him if he'd like to shoot him for the jacket of his next album, Duffy has no idea that his work is going to be altered again. The year before, the high-angle shot he'd envisioned and fine-tuned for *Lodger* had been turned down. David had instead chosen an unlikely Polaroid snapshot used by Derek Boshier in a radical way.

Brian Duffy passed away in 2010 so he can no longer say whether 30 years earlier, while he was about to put an end to his career, it was over the phone or in person that he recommended Edward Bell's work to Bowie. It's likely that, during this conversation, names of other visual artists came up, but because Bell had his first exhibition starting at the Neal Street Gallery²¹ near Covent Garden at the time, David Bowie went to the private view. In 1980 Bell was starting to make a name for himself thanks to his colourful portraits based on photographs and, soon after the gallery owner introduced them, David asks him to design the cover of his upcoming album. Bell eagerly accepts, but says he needs photographs to work from. When he turns up at the photo session (in a studio near the British Museum), Edward Bell is surprised to find that Brian Duffy is already at work: he is shooting Bowie from every angle in a splendid clown costume that Natasha Korniloff has made for him. Bell doesn't like the outfit – he photographs David himself (with his Pentax camera), but only after suggesting he drops the *commedia dell'arte* clown look, loses the ridiculous cone hat, messes up his hair a bit and lowers the top of his costume.

A couple of days later, when Brian Duffy gives Edward Bell one of his shots and asks him to colour it, the tension between the photographer and the visual artist raises a notch. Bell explains that he already has a clear idea in mind for the cover. So he paints Bowie's face and upper body from a photo he's taken himself, in comic-book style. He then tears off the surrounding blank paper and lays the illustration over a Duffy photo, so that only the right and left-hand sides of the photograph remain visible. To balance the image, Edward Bell uses the musician's shadow (from Duffy's photo) in the background. When, a few days later, David approves the finished artwork, Brian Duffy, who is also present, is a bit less enthusiastic. Much later, Bell will admit that at the time he didn't realize how frustrated Duffy was. He will state he simply approached the job as best he could, that is to say using his own ideas.

Like *Scary Monsters* and 'Ashes To Ashes', its most popular song, the visual for the album captures a moment in time – it's a snap shot of the artist at the end of an era. David Bowie has once again chosen to let one of his collaborators express himself fully (at the risk of offending another) – for him, getting the right result brushed all other considerations aside. It may not have been his idea, but reproducing vignettes from the covers of his albums from the 1970s on the back of *Scary Monsters* was definitely an explicit message to RCA. Either way, it was David who wanted his hair to be red, as he saw it as a symbol of the past decade (he told Bell he was known as the 'red-haired bisexual' in America). Bowie will hire Edward Bell[22] again in the early 1990s, but Duffy will never work with him again. Masayoshi Sukita will be less touchy (and will be paid a second time!) when, 33 years later, for *The Next Day*, Jonathan Barnbrook simply places a white square over the cover of *"Heroes"*.

When *The Next Day* comes out, emotions will be even more vivid because in the lyrics and video of 'Where Are We Now?', the single released two months before – a candid evocation of his Berlin period – Bowie will openly, and for the first time, give himself up to nostalgia. For a long time he will try to convince people that it wasn't his style, but the exhibition *David Bowie Is* at the V&A in London will prove the opposite once and for all. As a result, most observers forgot to point out that, because of the shadow, the sleeve of *Scary Monsters* already referred to *"Heroes"* and Dalí's famous pose contemplating his hand in *Un Chien Andalou*. Bowie never drew a line under his artistic past, quite the contrary. When he hired Brian Duffy, requested Natasha Korniloff's services or insisted on having red hair, he was picking elements from his past that he took a mischievous pleasure in injecting into his work in progress, whether it was obvious or not. After *Aladdin Sane*, time started to pass at lightning speed and, even though it will only have a tenuous grasp on his insolent Dorian Gray beauty throughout three decades, one can't help but see in the cigarette he holds in his fingers on *Scary Monsters* a reference to the one he was singing about in the first line of 'Rock'n'roll Suicide' eight years before – 'Time takes a cigarette'. As for its consumed part – the ashes – could it be anything other than a symbol of perpetual rebirth?

Natasha Korniloff's clown (or Pierrot) costume turned out to be a good investment: David Bowie wears it on the cover of 'Ashes To Ashes' (this time, the photo really *is* Duffy's and the stamps around it have been colourized by the musician) and in the video directed by David Mallet. In 1980, MTV hasn't started airing yet, but 'Ashes To Ashes' will still have a huge impact on traditional networks. It costs RCA a fortune and it is the first that Bowie story-boards entirely on his own – from then on, he will get more involved in his videos. He can be seen dressed as a clown on Pett Level beach (near Hastings), but most of the scenes were shot in a studio.

The video for 'Ashes To Ashes' feeds on David's story and alludes to Major Tom twice. When he appears in the padded cell (there is always a reference to madness), he's sitting on a stool wearing platform boots, like in Mick Rock's photo on the back of the RCA reissue of *David Bowie* (the album had become *Space Oddity* by then). At the end, the scene with his mother (not his real mother of course) is a recreation of a part of George Underwood's artwork for the back of the original album. The segment where Bowie is sitting in the kitchen refers to *The Man Who Fell To Earth* and the sci-fi vibe is also present when he appears on a drip in a setting that alludes to the work of Swiss artist H.R. Giger (his contribution to *Alien*, Ridley Scott's film, had impressed David). Polarized, like much of the video, the chorus scene that shows him walking in front of a bulldozer with Steve Strange[23] and three of his friends (two of whom are dressed as operetta priests like him) is the most memorable. The machine hadn't initially been planned, but Bowie felt like using it once he saw it on the beach.

Over time, even more so after music channels started to appear, David will make full use of music videos. He will see them as a valuable commercial tool, but also as an artistic medium. As expensive as it is surreal, the video for 'Ashes To Ashes' is not, however, the most expensive in the history of rock and, of course, not the first. During the decade to come, when record companies will devote huge amounts of money to music videos, David Bowie will be one of the first to benefit. In 1984, two years after Michael Jackson will hire John Landis to turn 'Thriller', the title song of his sixth album (which will break all records of cost and income), into a genuine short film, Bowie will have Julien Temple direct *Jazzin' For Blue Jean*, a long-form video (about 20 minutes) to promote 'Blue Jean', the first single from *Tonight*.

David Bowie's detractors saw him as a clever strategist at best, and the king of scoundrels at worst, but he was far from able to predict the future and even less the success of 'Ashes To Ashes', which will surprise everybody. The song will stay at the top of the British charts for a week in August (the previous one to have done so well was the reissued 'Space Oddity' five years before) and will be the fifteenth best-selling single of 1980.

During a trip to Japan in March, Bowie was joking about the fact that his music wasn't played enough on the radio and said he preferred it to air on television, a medium that suited him better. He was there to shoot television ads extolling the virtues of Crystal Jun Rock, a local alcoholic beverage made with sake, but he also spent a day in Kyoto being photographed by his friend Sukita. And since he'd also been asked to flex his musical talents, David Bowie delivered 'Crystal Japan', a quasi-instrumental piece that was originally called 'Fuji Moto San', on which he played all synthesizers. The falsetto voice here is Tony Visconti's and the date and place of recording remain unknown. Very close in spirit to some of the tracks on the B-sides of *Low* and *"Heroes"*, it was probably cut in 1979 at the Record Plant, and not the following year at the Power Station. Whatever the case, 'Crystal Japan' confirms that Bowie could produce some perfectly good ambient music without Brian Eno. The song came out on the A-side of a Japanese single in 1980, then on the B-side of 'Up The Hill Backwards' (the fourth and last single taken from *Scary Monsters*) in March 1981[24]. Unsurprisingly, as it was released six months after the album came out, 'Up The Hill Backwards' won't make it into the British Top 30. In the US, the song will become a maxi-single with another sheet of collector's stamps. 'Fashion' and 'Scary Monsters', released as the second and third singles in September 1980 and January 1981 respectively, reached Number 5 and Number 20 in the UK.

In September, David Bowie is in the US giving interviews about his double career as a musician and theatre actor. In Los Angeles, he performs two songs live on *The Tonight Show* with Johnny Carson[25], and is spotted at Hurrah in New York, where he attends a concert by The Psychedelic Furs. It is in this music club at 36 West 62nd Street that David Mallet will shoot the video for 'Fashion', meant to boost sales of the single. It's also where David will be filmed for the live scene in *Christiane F. – Wir Kinder Vom Bahnhof Zoo*, an adaptation by German director Ulrich 'Uli' Edel of a book about Christiane Vera Felscherinow (in the first person, but actually written by journalists who interviewed her), a teenager who grew up in West Berlin and got into drugs and prostitution in the mid-1970s, played by Natja Brunckhorst. Felscherinow lived in the Neukölln district of Berlin, was a fan of David Bowie and reportedly took heroine for the first time during his Isolar tour show there. So, of course, it will be 'Station To Station' – the *Stage* version actually recorded in Boston and Providence during the American leg of the Isolar 2 tour – that we will see Bowie perform in the film in the spring of 1981. He will authorize the use of several of his songs for the soundtrack, mainly from the trilogy. In the film, he has the same look as on the Johnny Carson show. Wearing a red Harrington jacket and jeans, and with a similar haircut, he evokes James Dean. His presence in the film will draw his fans to the cinema (especially in Europe) and, in time, *Christiane F. – Wir Kinder Vom Bahnhof Zoo* will become a cult classic. The soundtrack was also released in the spring and quickly reached the Top 5 in Germany.

It is a beautiful New York autumn for David Bowie. His performance in *The Elephant Man* on Broadway is being lauded by the public and critics alike, and knowing that *Scary Monsters* is a bestseller in his home country thrills him. The Police will knock him off the top spot after a couple of weeks, but the album will stay in the charts for 30 more, doing almost as well as *Diamond Dogs*, his previous Number 1 album. He feels comfortable in the city and tells journalists he plans on getting back on stage as soon as possible to promote his new songs. David attributes the fact that the record is called *Scary Monsters* at a time when he is playing a 'monster' on Broadway[26] to synchronicity.

In early December, Bowie gives an interview to British journalist Andy Peebles, who's been sent to New York by Radio 1. He talks about his music, the play and his past work with his 'neighbour' John Lennon, who's just released a new album (with his wife Yoko Ono) called *Double Fantasy*. Peebles goes on to interview Lennon, who in turn talks about his collaboration with Bowie and has only good things to say about him. Actually, Yoko and John are planning to see *The Elephant Man* a few days later. However, they will not get the chance.

In 'It's No Game (Part 1)', which opens *Scary Monsters*, Bowie makes direct reference to fascists in order to get something heavy off his chest and shut down rumour-mongers. As a disturbing premonition, he also addresses the subject of death: *'Put a bullet in my brain/And it makes all the papers.'* On 8 December, just before 11pm, John Lennon is assassinated outside his building by a crazed fan. In just one night, although the internet doesn't exist yet, the terrible news will make its way around the world. Shocked, sad and furious, David Bowie paces back and forth in an apartment he is renting after having stayed at the Carlyle Hotel. Coco is there with May Pang; she didn't know where to go so they've taken her in. Bowie, who always has a thirst for understanding, is faced with something he simply can't understand. What is still just a crack isolating him from the rest of the world, is going to turn, gradually, into a chasm. Lennon sought normality and refused to hide, but it only worked for a while. David is starting to question whether it will work better for him. He is going to have to slip away before someone wipes him off the map.

The killer[27] went to see *The Elephant Man* a few days before. On the programme for the show that the police find in his apartment, the name of the lead actor has been circled. Wounded but not destroyed, David Bowie will perform the play as planned until 4 January without asking for any special protection. But he will decline to extend his contract and will not appear again on stage, before his public, until 18 May 1983.

Carlos Alomar	Mark Ravitz
George Murray	Hazel O'Connor
Chuck Hammer	Zaine Griff
Chris Porter	Joe Jackson
Tony Visconti	John Cale
	Chris Frantz
	Frank Darcel
	Kent
	Brian Molko
	Chris Martin
	Sophie Soligny

CARLOS ALOMAR

Scary Monsters was very important for us all; actually, it's my favourite David Bowie album. By then, the DAM trio had completely got used to the idea of being David Bowie's rhythm section. Personally, at the same time, I was also working with other people and that did have an effect on what I was doing with him. I was able to bring all these different influences to the studio. We knew exactly what we wanted to do and how to do it. The ideas flowed really easily, because we were mastering our methodology perfectly. The number of ideas we had at that particular time was crazy. David was very receptive to our suggestions and the reason there are two versions of 'It's No Game' on the record is because he couldn't decide which one he preferred. We played a fast one with this Japanese lady singing in a very fast cadence, smashing everything into one minute when it should take three, and a slower one[28]. On the first one, he yells like he's in primal scream therapy, but the other one allowed him to place his voice better.

Scary Monsters also has gigantic anthems – 'Because You're Young', for example – take out your lighters, I can see it on tour! 'Fashion' was supposed to be kind of like the new 'Fame', but with a faster tempo. Also the groove had changed. So it's still funky, but a bit less 'dirty' – pretty much in line with what DJs were playing back then. Let's not forget that musical styles evolve; the speed of the songs, especially in the clubs, changed. 'Fame' worked well in 1975 and 'Fashion' perfectly matched the 1980s. It was often more exaggerated when we played the songs on stage: with the excitement and enthusiasm of the moment, we tended to speed up the tempo.

On *Scary Monsters*, all the songs are positive, all the songs have power. You know, we used to record some magnificent rhythm tracks for David, but when I went back to the studio, like a few days later, to listen to how the songs were coming along, I often found that he'd thrown in a surprise! Of course, putting in a disruptive element – Robert Fripp in this case – added to the magic of his music. David sometimes expressed more with the harshness of his songs than with the lyrics. It's obvious in 'It's No Game (Part 1)', where the guitar is quite jarring throughout. And it works even better because he sings about a society altered by tension. If I said to him that something might not work, he would say, 'It's going to work because it's on my record.' Well, that confused me a bit at first, but I ended up admitting he was always right. (2016)

GEORGE MURRAY

Considering David's history of changing musicians, concepts and direction, I thought he might get rid of us at that time, since Brian Eno was not part of the album. But he didn't and I was glad to be called at least one more time. We recorded at a new studio – the Power Station – and, technically, it was excellent. The tracks feel a little different and, for me, they were not as easy to record as all the others. But I still have a favourite on this album – 'Ashes To Ashes'. This is one of the tracks where David asked Dennis to play the beat backwards. Dennis simply said, 'OK,' and counted it off. I was hoping I wouldn't lose the one during the take that he kept for the album. I also think David was telling us something on 'It's No Game (Part 2)', the last song on the album. At the end of the track, the recorded sound of the tape end spinning on the reel for about 30 seconds is classic…You know, I was always impressed with David's talent and ability to write songs and some here are really great pieces of work. Listening to them after all these years they sound even better and still impress me.

New York is a 24-hour city and *Scary Monsters* was recorded right in the middle of it, at the Power Station. It stands to reason that the recording hours were later and longer. I moved to Los Angeles in 1979, so going back to New York felt a bit odd. I was staying at a hotel on 7th Avenue in Manhattan and, as luck would have it, certain parts of the building were being renovated. So, as I was trying to sleep, the carpenters and electricians were working the other side of the city's 24-hour clock. I remember being sleepy a lot during these sessions!

The DAM trio was the foundation – as solid as a block of concrete – of that entire era of David's creativity and style. We gave him a unique sound, spirit and soul for those experimental years – from 1975 to 1980 – of his long and varied career. Yes, I think we were one of the best rhythm sections and one of the best bands David had. For me, it was exciting, fun and we always had the groove! I hope he enjoyed the ride; we did it all for him. The last time I remember seeing David was our last night for the *Scary Monsters* sessions. There were warm goodbyes and, at that moment, I didn't think it was over. Now that he's departed, I kind of wish I had seen him again. In any case, I am glad to have worked with him. I had the good fortune to play with Dennis and Carlos, to travel to places I probably never would have seen and to have many unique experiences. I became a Buddhist while working with David, thanks to Carlos and his wife Robin and I'm still a practising one to this day. I have memories of our conversations and activities together. Talking about

Buddhism with David on a plane, somewhere in the middle of the night, is one of those memories. I have some of his songs in my iTunes library that I listen to, not just because I played on them, but because they are inspiring pieces of music. After all things are considered, my greatest treasures from working with David are my memories of the golden years. (2016)

CHUCK HAMMER

In November 1978, I began working as a guitarist with Lou Reed. At this time I was also developing a series of experimental textural guitar recordings known as *Guitarchitecture*. I met David Bowie in October 1979 while on tour with Lou in London. We were playing a series of concerts at the Hammersmith Odeon and during one of these I looked up and noticed David sitting on the side of the stage on an amplifier crate. Afterwards, David joined us for dinner and it was then that we first had the chance to talk. I had been an avid fan of his prior three records as well as of his earlier work. I mentioned to him that his music had been a big influence on me as a guitarist. David responded by saying, 'Well, Chuck, we might be working together.' A few moments after this dinner conversation, a fight broke out between Lou and David. I was sitting right next to David and across from Lou. Lou had asked David if he would be interested in producing his next album and David replied, 'Yes, if you clean up your act…' He was referring to Lou's 'involvement' with Scotch. Hearing this, Lou slapped David hard across the face and the dinner party instantly broke up with David's bodyguards emptying the room.

Upon returning to New York in January 1980, I forwarded a cassette recording of the experimental *Guitarchitecture* tracks to David via his manager. A few weeks later, in February, I received an unexpected phone call from David's assistant, Coco Schwab, while I was recording at RCA. Coco said that David loved the cassette and asked if I would be interested in working on his next album, to be recorded at the Power Station in March! So, from my perspective, this was the beginning of *Scary Monsters*.

Up until the moment when I first noticed David sitting on the side of the stage in London, his image in my mind had been entirely influenced by his album covers, his music and his exquisitely stylized press photos. It was a surreal experience to see him casually sitting there. As I walked past him, leaving the stage, I lightly touched his shoulder to say hello. It was at that moment that he first became human and approachable – a person, not an image.

I must add that, during this era, I held David's music in the highest regard. Although I was already working with Lou at an advanced professional level, I was also a huge Bowie fan. Going all the way back to *Space Oddity*, I listened intently to his work, so I was keenly aware of the arc and path of his recordings. From a guitarist's point of view, I was already on a collision course with where David was coming from, simply because of the deep influence his earlier recordings had on me. The question was how to take it a little bit further, and it was with my experimental *Guitarchitecture* tracks that I was working towards this expanded textural vocabulary. The idea of layering and multitracking guitar parts to orchestrate a guitar texture was my prime focus during this time.

One of my first impressions of David Bowie was how incredibly polite he was. As I arrived to record the tracks for *Scary Monsters*, David phoned the studio to say that he would be ten minutes late: as it turned out he was only five! He walked into the control room wearing a full-length leather coat with an oversized wooden cross around his neck. He was carrying a clipboard and drinking out of a milk carton. The first thing he said to me was, 'Chuck, it's great to see you again. The tape you sent me is all I listen to.' His level of politeness and openness really set the tone for the session. I felt I was in the presence of a collaborator and it created an environment where I could experiment in any direction. The session was done privately at the Power Station with just David, Tony Visconti, an assistant tape op and me. They played me a stripped-down basic track that would eventually become 'Ashes To Ashes'. The sub-mix they chose was a sparse, basic instrumental track containing only bass, drums, rhythm guitar and a minimal sketch keyboard part without vocals – or perhaps David chose not to let me hear any. So it allowed room for me to imagine adding a wide range of possible guitar textures. After listening, neither David nor Tony said anything, politely waiting for my reaction. I noticed a few similarities with one of the experimental tracks from my cassette tape used as a reference point. Certain sections within David's basic track seemed like they could be developed with layered guitar-synth textures. Those sections would later turn out to be the vocal choruses of 'Ashes To Ashes'. I suggested that we try to multitrack the GR-500[29] as a textured guitar choir with stacked, sustained chord inversions. David was very open to the idea and simply nodded his head in agreement. He and Tony had already prepared a basic chord chart for the song. I began to overdub a series of four discrete stereo tracks of layered chord inversions. Each pass was recorded with slightly different tape echo, harmonizer and GR-500 settings. As the sustained tracks were built up, they began to sound like a guitar choir.

Between takes, both David and Tony walked into the main studio from the control room. Tony made a few tonal adjustments to the JC-120 amp settings prior to each take. I recorded a few additional takes running the song down from end to end, adding guitar-synth textures where I felt they would help develop the track. Honestly, I don't know how I could have worked more freely! The second song we recorded was 'Teenage Wildlife' and it was much more complex in terms of containing multiple sections. Tony suggested that we actually record each section separately, like a suite, using different GR-500 and harmonizer tones for each one. Their basic track already had a solid chordal presence, so I began to build up layers of single note lines using the GR-500 set to solo mode.

Robert Fripp also appears on the song in a major way but, at the time, Tony and David did not play his tracks nor mention it during my session. It was a clever production strategy on their part, as they simply left it open for me to build as much density in the lines as I wanted. Since I had no idea that Robert's brilliant tracks would also be in there, I kept developing and layering the lines as we worked through the song sections. Tony made extensive harmonizer adjustments about three-quarters of the way through the song, where he wanted more density. He was deeply involved in guiding me through each section, which also had no reference vocals. Eventually they mixed our guitar tracks together, varying the density of the layers, like a small guitar orchestra in certain sections, depending on how thick they wanted it to sound.

While recording those songs, the focus was very much on the present moment. I think we were all aware that we were attempting to make a piece of art, that we were consciously trying to advance the language of music from a textural, layered perspective, both vocally and with the guitars. We were looking to create something that had never really been done before – building on David's previous work while attempting to extend it. We were working quickly and instinctively in real time. During the initial playback of the layered guitars on 'Ashes To Ashes', when we first heard all the parts sub-mixed in the studio at full volume, we were all in a state of happy shock. I think it was immediately obvious to the three of us in the control room that we had recorded something beautiful and new. We were working, but David was smiling, and there was a triumphant sense that something major had been accomplished. During my guitar tracking, David did not play an instrument, though he took a keen interest in the technology I was working with and asked me to show him the range of tones and textures.

By 1979, by the time *Scary Monsters* was recorded, Bowie's music had become deeply influential within the art world. From my perspective, I had a sense of where he was heading, and it was natural to be able to extend it, because all his previous work, starting with 'Space Oddity', was ingrained into the contemporary DNA. Yes, I was impressed by the quality of the songwriting on *Scary Monsters* and especially the way in which the songs are inextricably linked into the textures and the broader concept. They function almost as a complete song cycle. His vocals and lyrics are multi-layered; the narration 'undervoice' in 'Ashes To Ashes', where he dryly speaks the lyrics layered underneath the main vocal, his integration of the Japanese vocals, his references to his earlier songs... I was always wondering where he got those crazy ideas! (2016)

CHRIS PORTER

I was a late starter in the studio engineering game at 26 years old. This was quite unusual. At that time, people would generally start 'assisting' in their early or late teens. Consequently, I like to think I climbed up the 'studio ladder' more quickly than was usual!

Tony had been in New York recording the rhythm tracks for *Scary Monsters* for a few weeks, so we knew that he and David would be coming back over to Good Earth to record vocals, other overdubs and to mix the album. While we were used to working with high-profile acts at Good Earth, there was an air of unusual excitement at the prospect of recording with Mr Bowie. Kit Woolven, who was chief engineer at the studio, had worked on *Lodger*, but, as I remember, he was co-producing Thin Lizzy's *Chinatown* at the time. So I, by default, and due to a lack of other personnel, assisted Tony through this stage of the production.

Having grown up in the 1960s and 1970s, I was a big Bowie fan and very intimidated by the prospect of working with him. You know the saying 'never meet your idols'? Well, it didn't apply to David. I remember welcoming him at the foot of the stairs that led to the basement studio that was Good Earth. He was wearing a long camel-coloured trench coat that seemed a little too large for him; it was wrapped around his slim frame and tied, not buckled, with the belt. He had the air, still, of a teenager, displaying no sense of world-weariness or superiority. He greeted me with a huge smile, leaning back a little to appraise me as he shook my hand. I introduced myself and he just said, 'Hi Chris – David.' As if I might not have known!

Every overdub added to the songs would be accompanied by much discussion and cultural cross-referencing, not only to other artists, but also authors, poets, mathematicians and film directors. It was an attempt, I think, to ensure that we in the studio understood the songs' intent and direction of travel. I quite often felt out of my depth, as the names of philosophers and playwrights were thrown into the creative and inspiring maelstrom.

As far as backing vocals were concerned, David and Tony loved the vitality and freshness of vocal groups like The Shangri-Las and Martha And The Vandellas. They also admired Phil Spector's 'Wall of Sound' recordings. Tony, David and I arranged ourselves around one microphone and worked out the balance between ourselves. We worked out a rough routine with the track in the control room beforehand, then we sang it till we got it right. There was considerable vibrato involved! It was the best fun! To be honest, I don't remember Lynn Maitland being there...

David seemed very relaxed throughout the sessions I worked on. He was working simultaneously on a horror film – *The Hunger* – and Susan Sarandon accompanied him to the studio on a couple of occasions. He appeared to cope with the pressures of making both the album and the film, interspersed admirably with a fair amount of clubbing. He was never bad-tempered or impatient, and he indulged all the guest musicians and session musicians, famous or not. He listened to their stories and their opinions and generally made the sessions seem both enjoyable and consequential. David didn't play any instruments during those London sessions, but, memorably, most of the lead vocals were recorded during that period. I was struck by how David acted out the songs as he sang them. His body shape seemed to change and morph into different characters – one minute sinewy ingénue, next swaggering soul singer...

Tony and David had worked together a lot by this time and, having already cut the basic tracks together in New York, seemed totally in tune with each other concerning the way the songs might progress. They also had the ability to embrace the extra dimension brought to the sessions, especially by Robert Fripp. I did become chief engineer briefly towards the end of my time at Good Earth but, at this point, I was only Tony's assistant engineer. However, I did work on all the sessions, including those with Pete Townshend and Robert Fripp. It was a pleasure to meet Pete Townshend and to watch and listen to him play, but it was Mr Fripp who stole the show for me. His work on the album was, quite literally, transformative. I only ask you to imagine 'Fashion' or 'Scary Monsters' without his guitar parts! Here is the perfect example of allowing a musician the space and freedom to create, and fully embracing and adopting their contribution. (2018)

TONY VISCONTI

David desperately wanted a Wurlitzer stereo electric piano on the track that would develop into 'Ashes To Ashes' – he also needed someone to play it. We had a stereo Wurlitzer delivered and David popped into Springsteen's session and came back with their keyboardist Roy Bittan. David explained to him the concept of the now famous piano intro to the song and then the light chording he wanted for the verses. Unfortunately when we powered up the Wurlitzer we discovered only one side worked and even then not very well. We were impatient to use the talented Bittan and it was too late in the evening to order a replacement, so I suggested that we use a normal piano and I would attempt to make it sound like a stereo Wurlitzer. Back in London I had recently acquired a new piece of gear called the Instant Flanger[30]; luckily the Power Station had one too. I soon got a decent moving stereo image to emulate a Wurlitzer, but I couldn't resist playing with it further, and then got a ridiculous shaking sound – which everyone in the studio instantly loved. That's the piano sound in the intro and outro of 'Ashes To Ashes', a grand piano played by Roy Bittan going through an Instant Flanger in a way it was never meant to be used.

I don't know how intentional it was at this point but, like *Sgt. Pepper* we reprised the opening song at the end of the album[31]. This was actually the same exact backing track and a great example of how mixing and different overdubs can change the nature of a track completely. The opener version was a fiery affair but, as a closer it was now gentle and let the listener down easily. This version was completely in English, as it was originally conceived. As the album opened with a recording of my 24-track machine starting up, the album closes with the sound of the tape running out and the reel slowing down to a complete stop. (2007)

MARK RAVITZ

In 1980, David Bowie didn't go on tour, but he still gave a lot of importance to each small appearance he made, especially on television. We'd met again once or twice after the Diamond Dogs tours, but we weren't close or anything. So I was pleasantly surprised when he got in touch again for his appearance on *Saturday Night Live*, which he really wanted to stage. It's also funny that the exhibition *David Bowie Is* will soon be in Brooklyn, and it's so close to my house that I'll be able to walk there! I even received a VIP invitation for the opening night. I'm eager to see it; I understand that the outfits from the show will be on display. I built the dog you see at his feet during 'TVC 15'; a cousin of mine helped me put the little video monitor in there... My wife made the papier mâché puppet for 'Boys Keep Swinging' after some drawings I had done. She put a lot of effort into the nipples! Most of the outfits came from a theatre costume shop. I remember Klaus Nomi well. He was definitely a trip and left us too soon.

Another funny thing was that, before starting the work, David had sent me a personal note that I still have to this day. He was asking me to go easy on the money because he was paying everything himself! At the time, that sounded very English to me. Still, the show was a big success and whenever I come across it, I still find it surreal. (2018)

HAZEL O'CONNOR

I followed Bowie's career but, at the time, I was being sucked into my own spiral. The news I had of him came in bursts, mainly from Tony Visconti, because I'd remained friends with him after he produced my first album[32]. Like when he chose to work with Nile Rodgers over Tony... I always thought his brief association with the New Romantics was surprising, as well as the fact that he asked Steve Strange to appear in the video of 'Ashes To Ashes'. Of course Steve was a Bowie super-fan so he was thrilled. He died not long before his hero...

David gave good advice from our first meeting. Tony knew I was a big fan and he phoned me while I was shooting *Breaking Glass*: 'If you want to see David, come to the studio tonight, he'll be there!' He had to record a version of 'Space Oddity' for *The Kenny Everett Show*. It was brilliant; I got to watch my hero sing a hit that I loved!

So we chatted and the first thing David did was talk to me about the film I was acting in. As a joke, he asked me if the title was inspired by his song[33]. I said no, and going off on a tangent, he said, 'Tony told me you used to cut hair – would you cut mine?' And I did! I have to say I was rather intimidated: not only was I cutting David Bowie's hair, but Coco, his assistant, was also there! Like everyone else, I'd heard a lot of stories about her and I thought that at the slightest wrong move, she would have cut my head off! What struck me that day was that he didn't have a huge ego. I didn't have my scissors with me and I had to manage with a pair we found in the studio office. But that didn't bother him and he said, laughing, 'Please, do what I asked.'

He also wanted to know the date of my next concert and I said I was going to open for Iggy Pop at the Music Machine. He said he'd be there. I saw him again at a screening of *Breaking Glass*. I arrived late, because I'm never early, and when I went to sit down, I tripped and ended up on someone's lap: what a coincidence, it was him! To be honest, I didn't think he'd be at Iggy's concert, but he was definitely there the second night. He was a man of his word!

When I started having problems dealing with fame, he was very helpful when he said, 'Don't forget: everyone thinks they know you and, in a way, that's true. They know certain facts, because they read things and hear about you on the radio. In terms of human relationships, this doesn't work in your favour. The only way to face this situation is to know at least one thing about the people you interact with, even if it's someone who's harassing you. One simple thing and you'll be on an equal footing. After that, it's easy.'

Whether he fell to Earth or not, Bowie deeply loved people. He wasn't cold but, in his relations with others, he gave the impression that he followed a sort of code: something basic that should exist between all human beings, but that they've had a tendency to forget. On a personal level, that's what gave him a better grasp of fame. When they become stars, many artists lose their humanity, but that never happened to him! (2017)

ZAINE GRIFF

The first time I spoke to David Bowie was in 1977, in a club in Mayfair, London. We talked about music a lot; he was very relaxed and particularly interested in what I was doing. He was the one who started the conversation and it was weird because he sometimes whispered a few words to his bodyguard or to the intellectuals sitting at his table. I thought he was very friendly.

Two years later, I was finishing my album *Ashes And Diamonds* with Tony Visconti producing it and he asked me if he could use my musicians to record some songs with David for a television show. I obviously agreed and Tony explained that he wanted stripped-down versions of the songs. We recorded with Andy Duncan[34] on drums, Steve Bolton on guitar, Andy Clark on keyboards and I played bass. At the start of the session, David sat cross-legged on the floor of the studio and he played the songs for us on his 12-string guitar. And we went from there.

When it was time to do the vocals, it was simple: he went into the booth and it only took him one take! We also got the chance to attend the mix. David was there and he looked like a member of the band. He was curious about everything; he talked to us about art and wanted to know about the latest hairstyles! Having lived in Berlin for several months, he had to catch up on lost time and stay up-to-date on the latest London fashions. I never saw him again after that day. David Bowie left us far too soon, just as he was moving into a new creative phase. (2018)

JOE JACKSON

Oh yeah, my cover of 'Scary Monsters' surprised everyone last night at La Cigale. You know, I've already sung 'Life On Mars?' and one or two other songs of his... But I wanted to do something different this time. Actually, I wanted it to sound even more 'scary'! But I ruined the effect a bit by announcing the song twice. (2008)

JOHN CALE

You think there's a bit of Bowie in *blackAcetate*[35]? I started recording long before him, didn't I? But yes, I see what you mean. Musicians often borrow from each other! (2005)

CHRIS FRANTZ

I remember that concert at Radio City Hall in New York, in November 1980, which was very impressive for us, because it was a big stage. And David was there on the side, hidden from the audience, watching us. At one point, because he wasn't David Bowie for nothing, he started dancing. He shot me a look and gave me a thumbs up to show me that it was great. We felt like he was curious about everything that was happening... He came backstage after the show but, unfortunately, he locked himself in David Byrne's dressing room. It's the type of thing singers do when they meet up!

Two years later we were playing at the Montreux festival and David came backstage to meet us. It was the first time we met him in person. He was really sweet and nice. He was all by himself and was wearing a dark green anorak, and he wasn't acting much like a star. Tom Tom Club was actually opening for Talking Heads! We were our own opening act! Bowie was very classy, polite and, at one point, he was looking at the buffet backstage and asked, 'Are you gonna eat that cheese?' We said, 'Well, probably not...' To be honest, we'd taken something; we were already pretty high and didn't have much of an appetite. He asked, 'May I have it?' And we said, 'Sure!' So he wrapped the cheese up in a napkin and put it in the pocket of his anorak! After that, we talked some more and before we got on stage, he said, 'How about those nuts? Are you gonna eat those?' And we said, 'No, you can have them.' So he wrapped them up in another napkin and put them in another pocket. Honestly, we thought that was so amusing! Nobody comes backstage and asks for your food! They might ask for a glass of beer or champagne, but anyway... It was nice to think that we were able to give him a little snack, to feed the hero! (2018)

FRANK DARCEL

At the end of 1980, I was still playing guitar with Marquis de Sade and I ended up in New York the night they reopened the Peppermint Lounge[36]. So I was chilling upstairs, leaning on the balcony of the mezzanine watching Wilson Pickett's show, holding my beer with a finger in the neck of the bottle. Suddenly, I felt someone lightly push me from my right. Then I saw this guy next to me who was doing the exact same thing, his finger in the bottleneck. It was David Bowie! I'd imagined him taller, but it was really him... We watched the show without saying a word for half an hour.

At one point, someone came over to talk to him and three big black bodyguards stood behind him. John Lennon had just been killed and the mood was rather paranoid. In the end, this girl who I later learned was his manager tapped on my shoulder and asked me to leave. Bowie looked at me, the only time he ever did, still without saying a word. Okay, I made a bit of a scene on principle, but I wasn't going to be a smart ass either. The funny thing was that three years later, I opened for him at Auteuil with my band Octobre... (2018)

KENT

I'd been wanting to cover a Bowie song live for a while. Ever since he died in fact. Before then, I wasn't brave enough. Or it was too much of a fan thing. And this tour, I thought it might be the last one. If I didn't do a Bowie cover now, I'd never do one. I've been playing Bowie at home for a long time. Often to understand how this or that song was made.

For the show, I didn't want to play an obvious hit. I'd initially thought of a song from *Blackstar*, but that risked spoiling the mood. I tried 'Ashes To Ashes'. Too complicated. Then 'Absolute Beginners'. I love singing it for the Bm-Amaj7-Edim chord progression in the verse and the riff coming out of the chorus. But it didn't fit in with my current repertoire. So I chose 'Scary Monsters' with a Johnny Cash-style acoustic guitar intro. I'd heard an 'unplugged' version by Bowie and Gabrels, who played it like that. My whole band comes in on the chorus. It's a stubborn, crazy song. The lyrics are as deviant as one can wish for.

Actually, I love the whole album, Fripp's guitars, the structures of the songs. I can't get enough. It's hit material and experimental at the same time. A great lesson in *savoir faire*. (2018)

BRIAN MOLKO

The first time I heard David, I was eight years old and his video for 'Ashes To Ashes' was playing on the TV. My mother was standing in the living room staring at the screen, aghast but captivated, which intrigued me. She recoiled in horror, mumbling something akin to, 'This is disgraceful!'... But by then I was transfixed.

First there's David as Pierrot, who will later drown, but finds the time to lead a psychedelic funeral procession and discuss something very important with a lady twice his age, who has always represented the matriarchal figure for me. Then David's in a padded cell, with a grey pallor I would later identify as the look of withdrawal. Then he's a spaceman, stuck in a chair in an exploding 50s-style kitchen. The video ends with David underwater, looking barely alive. I'd never seen imagery so unsettling in a music video – plus, what did it all mean?

I was equally taken in by the video's colours, that neon nectarine that was familiar, but completely otherworldly in this context – a very fine and daring use of the primitive video effects of the time. And this song was a chart hit? How could that be possible when the music itself was so unashamedly strange?

Many people discredit the 80s, saying it was a terrible decade for music, but I adore it. A huge proportion of my influences come from this decade, from David Bowie to Sonic Youth. Not only was the underground very fertile, but mainstream pop had a very visible avant-garde streak to it. One has only to look at David's contemporaries, such as Kate Bush or Peter Gabriel, who were fearlessly producing otherworldly music that embraced emerging technology and having chart success in the process. David, of course, had already embraced emerging technology in his work with Eno and Visconti. Though he wasn't the first, such an attitude towards change and progress, which had already marked most of David's career, was inescapable, somewhat predestined, and hugely influential.

I would later steal the phrase 'valuable friend' from 'Ashes To Ashes' to use on

Placebo's second album[37]. It never occurred to me at the time to ask him if I could. I presented it to him as a *fait accompli* and he didn't seem to mind. I stole it because, by then, I was acutely aware of what 'Ashes To Ashes' was about and I wanted listeners to make the connection, to understand I was referring to addiction, the phrase perfectly and poetically capturing the warped psychodynamics of a person in the throes of narcotic dependence. (2017)

CHRIS MARTIN

I'd love it if in ten years time, people were still discovering new things when listening to *X&Y*. I hear something new each time I play my favourite records. Combining exploration and immediacy is really what we try to do. *Scary Monsters* by David Bowie is our reference for that. On a first listen, this album is far from obvious, but it contains 'Ashes To Ashes', the greatest song ever written. (2005)

SOPHIE SOLIGNY

'Ashes To Ashes' is a photograph of a time when we danced to Bowie in nightclubs, and to original songs, not remixes! It's a model of perfection. Not only is Tony Visconti's production out of this world, but there are so many different melodies, all fabulous, in this one song. So absolutely modern that it manages to unite all the Bowies we've loved over the decades and, especially, it allows us to go back to the most legendary of all, the 'Life On Mars?' Bowie. 'Ashes To Ashes', for me, has the beauty, power, mystery and emotion of a Kubrick film, in this case *2001: A Space Odyssey*. It has something that goes beyond us, that is full of genius… David doesn't look divine here, he is! (2018)

1. This rather harsh song by viola player and founding member of The Velvet Underground, John Cale, will appear on *Sabotage/Live*, his concert album recorded in June that same year at CBGB (released in December). Apparently, the afternoon of the show, John Cale taught David Bowie a relatively simple viola part and, that evening, he played it to a very respectable standard. (David would also 'play' violin on *The Kenny Everett Video Show* the following month.) In October 1979, in New York, Cale and Bowie will record (at least) two demos, 'Piano-La' and 'Velvet Couch', which will surface on various bootleg records. According to both artists, they were never meant to become real songs. It has been said again and again that these recordings took place at the Ciarbis Studio (sometimes spelled Clarbis), but this studio's existence has never been confirmed. It might have been a modest rehearsal location or even a fictional place. Towards the end of David Bowie's career, one of the studios mentioned on the jacket of one of his albums will turn out to be pure fabrication.

2. David Bowie will keep in touch with Iggy Pop for many years. When Iggy performs at the Metropol in Berlin in late April 1980, in their old neighbourhood of Schöneberg, Bowie will pop over to Germany and join him on stage for two songs.

3. Opened in 1965 in Monmouth, Rockfield was the first residential studio. Like at the Château d'Hérouville a little later, the staff and the artists lived and ate there. It has sometimes been written that the place belonged to British musician-producer Dave Edmunds, but this was not the case. However, he did record there from his first hit 'I Hear You Knocking' in 1970. Queen also used Rockfield, among other studios (but not Trident), to work on 'Bohemian

Rhapsody'. Hence, contrary to myth and rumour, the piano used by Freddie Mercury on this epic song was not the C. Bechstein that can be heard on 'Life on Mars?' or 'Hey Jude' by The Beatles.

4. In the late 1980s, Tony Visconti will sell Good Earth, which in 2007 will be taken over by Jasmin Lee, the daughter of Ten Years After's guitarist. She'll rename it Dean Street Studios. Its central location continues to make it a popular recording space in London. Alvin Lee is the author's guitar hero. They met in 2008 and Lee confessed he hated glam rock.

5. It will be officially released in 1992 on the Rykodisc reissue of *Scary Monsters* (the other bonus tracks will be the sparse version of 'Space Oddity', 'Crystal Japan' and 'Alabama Song'). Then, in 2002, it will come out as a bonus track on the double-CD edition of *Heathen*.

6. He will be on the show again in November 1991 with Tin Machine.

7. The last to play John Merrick will be Bradley Cooper in 2015.

8. French television presenter Yves Mourousi – a super fan – will send a television crew to the US to make a report with journalist Patrice Drevet.

9. In that same studio, the year before, Ian Hunter and Mick Ronson (with Roy Bittan on piano) recorded *You're Never Alone With A Schizophrenic*, Ian's fourth solo album.

10. The backing tracks for the song will end up on bootleg records but, if it was ever finished, the official version remains unreleased. 'I Feel Free' will be re-recorded in 1992 for *Black Tie White Noise*.

11. Tom Verlaine produced his first album but, according to his label – Elektra – his mix was not good enough. The record, as it was sold in 1979, was in fact mixed by Bob Clearmountain, one of the best soundscapers of his generation, with whom Bowie will work many times in the 1980s and 1990s.

12. It's not the best known part of his career but, in the early 1980s, Pete Townshend was a book publisher. His company – Eel Pie Publishing – issued many biographies of musicians, including the very informative *Bowie: An Illustrated Record*, written with style by Roy Carr and Charles Shaar Murray in 1981.

13. It's clear that, like a good number of other British musicians of his generation, David Bowie was passionate about vocal ensembles. In 1967, the title of his song 'Please Mr Gravedigger' recalled 'Please Mr Postman', a hit by The Marvelettes and, back when he was playing in bands, they sometimes covered hits by these mostly female groups. During their joint performance on American television in 1975, it was probably Bowie who suggested to Cher that they use bits of 'Maybe' and 'Da Doo Ron Ron', made popular by The Chantels and The Crystals respectively. He also loved Ronnie Spector's version of 'Try Some, Buy Some', a George Harrison song he had considered for a *Pin Ups II* that never happened, but which he will end up recording in 2003 for *Reality*. During *Young Americans* and the tour that followed, David Bowie had put a lot of emphasis on the vocal harmonies but, in 1973, those on 'Drive-In Saturday' and 'The Prettiest Star' (on *Aladdin Sane*) already showed the same inclination. In 1984, the backing vocals on 'Absolute Beginners' will also be very 1960s and, the following year, his cover of 'Dancing In The Street' (a hit for Martha And The

Vandellas) as a duet with Mick Jagger, will be a sort of climax. At the dawn of the 1970s, Bowie's friend Marc Bolan had worked with Flo & Eddie, whose high voices could emulate those of girl bands, and Bolan's meeting with African-American singer Gloria Jones, who sang on T. Rex's last records, will be the cherry on the cake for him. Gloria Jones and Marc Bolan will record 'To Know You Is To Love You' together, a personal version of the classic track written by Phil Spector for The Teddy Bears.

14. Referred to as a 'casual friend' by Tony Visconti in his autobiography, Lynn is the wife of Graham Maitland, a Scottish musician who played with the Southampton band Fleur De Lys in the 1960s, then in Five Day Rain, a cult psychedelic band. His album recorded in 1970 didn't officially come out until 2006! Graham Maitland passed away several years ago.

15. This fashion designer had a shop – Modern Classics – in Shoreditch in London, where the New Romantics stocked up on their eccentric outfits. David Bowie went to the London premiere of *Just A Gigolo* in February 1979 with Vivienne Lynn, a model and the girlfriend of Willie Brown. The dress code was 1920s Germany, so he wore a kimono!

16. Because 2019 will mark the 50th anniversary of *Space Oddity*, it will be a big year in terms of 'derivative' records. On 15 November, Parlophone will release *Conversation Piece*, a five-CD box set (available in digital form) including demos, BBC sessions and rare and unreleased recordings from 1968–1969. The song that gives its name to this rather controversial box set (a good part of its contents will be sold on vinyl throughout the year) will also appear on a new version of the album remixed by Tony Visconti (available on vinyl and digital). It will take its original spot on the album, from where it was bumped due to lack of space. *Conversation Piece* will come with a 120-page book with (mostly) exclusive photos and liner notes. Many fans on social media will criticize the exploitation of David Bowie's catalogue and boycott the box set.

17. Since Tony Visconti's autobiography came out, all writers of articles about *Scary Monsters* or books on David Bowie have repeated that Michi Hirota, the voice on 'It's No Game (Part 1)', was an actress from the musical *The King And I*, which was playing at the Palladium Theatre in London (from June 1979 to September 1980). Hirota must have been standing in for someone else, because her name does not appear on the official programme. When contacted for this book, she did not respond. In the mid-1970s her husband – composer and percussionist Joji Hirota – worked with Lindsay Kemp.

18. The working title of the song was 'Cameras In Brooklyn' (which sounds very Eno), while 'Ashes To Ashes' was once called 'People Are Turning To Gold'.

19. The overuse of the device (now often a plug-in), also known as noise gate (whose main purpose is to eliminate unwanted noise), can emphasize the mechanical sound in some instruments.

20. Played on a DX-7 (Yamaha) or a Jupiter 8 (Roland) according to Tony Visconti.

21. The exhibition was called *Larger Than Life*, Edward Bell's first and also the first in this gallery, which opened in 1980.

22. David Bowie and Edward Bell spent some time together in the early 1980s. In *Unmade Up...* (Unicorn), a book of his memories of the musician, published in 2017, Bell says that they regularly saw Derek Boshier (who gave Bowie painting lessons). Edward Bell also mentions meeting filmmaker Derek Jarman to talk about a Bowie film project that was at a very advanced stage. Scored by Brian Eno and featuring Lindsay Kemp (as a cabaret performer), Jarman's punk fantasy (*Jubilee*) came out in 1978.

23. Welshman Stephen Harrington, known as Steve Strange, was a music lover, occasional singer and cult figure on the London scene in the late 70s and early 80s. He rose to fame in 1980 as the main performer of the hit 'Fade To Grey' by Visage, written by Midge Ure and Billy Currie from Ultravox, and Chris Payne, who played keyboards and viola with Gary Numan. Before then, Strange and his friend Rusty Egan (also a member of Visage, whose girlfriend at the time was Brigitte Arens, from Luxembourg, who sings the French lines in 'Fade To Grey') had become well known as hosts and DJs for Bowie nights (and Roxy Music nights) held at Billy's, a club in Soho, then at Blitz in Covent Garden. With its colourful and androgynous clientele, this former wine bar became the hub of the New Romantic movement. Strange was on the door of the club and, not long after turning away Mick Jagger (for security reasons, as the club was chock full the night he came), he let David Bowie in through a back door. The two will get on and the idol will ask his fan to appear in the video of 'Ashes To Ashes' (and to bring three friends). He will also 'borrow' Richard Sharah, the Australian make-up artist responsible for his Pierrot face (the following year, Sharah will do Gary Numan's make-up). Steve Strange and Egan went on hosting parties at Club For Heroes on Baker Street, and others at Camden Palace. In 2002, Strange will publish *Blitzed!* (Orion), a rollercoaster-like autobiography. He will die of a heart attack in early 2015 while putting the finishing touches to *Demons To Diamonds*, Visage's fifth album. His version of 'Loving The Alien', Eurodisco and quite queasy, is not the best song on this record.

24. In June 2001, 'Crystal Japan' will be released again with 'Abdulmajid' and 'All Saints' on *All Saints: Collected Instrumentals 1977–1999*. 'Abdulmajid', conceived by Bowie and Eno, probably dates back to the Berlin sessions, but it was given a significant revamp (and renamed – Abdulmajid is Iman's last name; she was introduced to David Bowie in 1990). Philip Glass will revisit this track in the second movement of his *'Heroes' Symphony* in 1997. All Saints is the ambient label Dominic Norman-Taylor founded in 1991, after the closure of Brian Eno's Opal.

25. On *The Tonight Show*, David Bowie appears with a number of musicians Carlos Alomar plays with regularly or knows well: bass player John Kumnick, G.E. Smith on guitar, Steve Goulding on drums and Gordon Grody on piano (and second voice). Carlos Alomar also plays keyboards on the first song ('Life On Mars?') and a multi-neck guitar on 'Ashes To Ashes', the second. Some of them will also appear in the 'Fashion' video. Rehearsals for the show took place at RCA studios (in the D) and everyone enjoyed David Bowie's company. They found him funny, charming and professional – he hit the high notes in the chorus of 'Life On Mars?', but the song was played a tone lower than it was on *Hunky Dory*. For this book, John Kumnick confirmed the identity of all the musicians. He told the author that, after the show, the Los Angeles to New York flight was full, so they were asked to put their instruments in the hold. Since they didn't have flight cases to protect them, they asked Bowie's tour manager to talk to the airline personnel, to request they keep their instruments with them. When he saw that the manager was getting nowhere, David chipped in: 'Hello! Excuse me, I'm David Bowie. I'm travelling with some guitars that Elvis gave me. Could I please put them next to me in the plane because I care about them very much and I wouldn't want them to be ruined?' In under 30 seconds, without even having to drop the name 'Presley', the guitars were in the cabin. G.E. Smith played with Hall & Oates for a decade before becoming the musical director for *Saturday Night Live*. Steve Goulding was the drummer of The Rumour then, the band that accompanied Graham Parker, and he co-wrote Nick Lowe's 'I Love The Sound Of Breaking Glass'. At the time, before becoming a vocal coach, Gordon Grody was a popular backing vocalist and worked regularly with Robin Clark and Tawatha Agee (both interviewed for this book). He released *Exclusively Yours* in 1977, an excellent disco album. As for John Kumnick, he will play with many famous musicians, including Iggy Pop and Serge Gainsbourg, at the Casino de Paris in 1985.

26. As he explained in an interview with radio presenter Tim Rice, David Bowie got the idea for the album title by reading the phrase 'Scary Monsters and Super Heroes' on a cereal box.

27. The name of this criminal, who is still behind bars, is well known. Since John Lennon's death, some authors and journalists have decided that he does not deserve to appear in their work, so they refuse to mention his name. Out of respect for Lennon's memory, the author sticks to this convention.

28. In fact, the basic tracks of these two versions are identical. The tempo is 103bpm.

29. This guitar synthesizer by Japanese manufacturer Roland was one of the first to hit the market, in 1977. Robert Fripp and Adrian Belew are two other David Bowie guitarists who used it extensively.

30. Another Eventide machine, released in 1976, which can be heard very clearly on *Physical Graffiti*, Led Zeppelin's album. As with other legendary 'vintage' sound processors, the Instant Flanger FL 201 is now available as a plug-in.

31. Actually, on *Sgt. Pepper*, there's another song – one of the best – after the reprise of the title song: 'A Day In The Life'.

32. Tony Visconti produced two of Hazel O'Connor's first three albums: *Breaking Glass* (1980), which is the soundtrack to the eponymous film by Brian Gibson, and *Cover Plus* (1981). Since Edward Bell did the cover of *Cover Plus*, which has the same feel as *Scary Monsters*, O'Connor has sometimes been accused of copying but, in fact, she'd already worked with Bell for *Sons And Lovers*, her second album also released in 1980. Hazel O'Connor still makes music and her back catalogue was recently reissued by Cherry Red. One of the bonus tracks on the expanded edition of *Sons And Lovers* is a cover of 'Suffragette City', recorded live at the Dominion Theatre in London in 1980 (featuring backing vocalist Simon Le Bon, as Duran Duran were her support act at the time).

33. 'Breaking Glass' is the second song on the A-side of *Low*. It was co-written by Bowie, Murray and Davis.

34. In 1980, Andy Duncan produced *Bright As Fire*, an album by avant-garde jazz musician Mike Westbrook (under the name The Westbrooke Blake) and asked Tony Visconti to mix the album at Good Earth. On the back of the original sleeve, it says, 'Produced by Tony Visconti, Andy Duncan and Mike Westbrook.'

35. These words come from an interview John Cale will give the author in 2005. Under the name Davie Jones (with The King Bees), Bowie, who was five years younger than him, taped his first single three years before Cale started recording with The Velvet Underground.

36. Located at 128 West 45th Street, near Times Square, the Peppermint Lounge has had many iterations, including its first during the twist craze from the late 50s to the mid-60s. The club reopened under its original name in the early 1980s, and became a new wave hot spot. It then changed location and closed for good in 1986.

37. In 'My Sweet Prince' on *Without You I'm Nothing*, in 1998.

DISCOGRAPHY
(1967–1980)

Below is a list of official albums David Bowie released in the UK between 1967 and 1980. The main British and American singles are mentioned in the book along with the most notable of those released in other countries. The Rykodisc/EMI reissues from the 1990s, and those from EMI/Warner in the 2000s, are also mentioned in the relevant chapters.

David Bowie (1967)
(Deram)
A-SIDE
'Uncle Arthur'
'Sell Me A Coat'
'Rubber Band'
'Love You Till Tuesday'
'There Is A Happy Land'
'We Are Hungry Men'
B-SIDE
'Little Bombardier'
'Silly Boy Blue'
'Come And Buy My Toys'
'Join The Gang'
'She's Got Medals'
'Maid Of Bond Street'
'Please Mr Gravedigger'

David Bowie (1969)
**Reissued with the title *Space Oddity*
in 1972**
(Philips-RCA)
A-SIDE
'Space Oddity'
'Unwashed And Somewhat Slightly
Dazed'
'Letter To Hermione'
'Cygnet Committee'
B-SIDE
'Janine'
'An Occasional Dream'
'Wild Eyed Boy From Freecloud'
'God Knows I'm Good'
'Memory Of A Free Festival'

The Man Who Sold The World (1971)
(Mercury)

A-SIDE

'The Width Of A Circle'
'All The Madmen'
'Black Country Rock'
'After All'

B-SIDE

'Running Gun Blues'
'Saviour Machine'
'She Shook Me Cold'
'The Man Who Sold The World'
'The Supermen'

Hunky Dory (1971)
(RCA)

A-SIDE

'Changes'
'Oh! You Pretty Things'
'Eight Line Poem'
'Life On Mars?'
'Kooks'
'Quicksand'

B-SIDE

'Fill Your Heart' (Rose-Williams)
'Andy Warhol'
'Song For Bob Dylan'
'Queen Bitch'
'The Bewlay Brothers'

*The Rise And Fall Of Ziggy Stardust
And The Spiders From Mars* (1972)
(RCA)

A-SIDE

'Five Years'
'Soul Love'
'Moonage Daydream'
'Starman'
'It Ain't Easy' (Davies)

B-SIDE

'Lady Stardust'
'Star'
'Hang On To Yourself'
'Ziggy Stardust'
'Suffragette City'
'Rock'n'Roll Suicide'

Aladdin Sane (1973)
(RCA)

A-SIDE

'Watch That Man'
'Aladdin Sane (1913–1938–197?)'
'Drive-In Saturday'
'Panic In Detroit'
'Cracked Actor'

B-SIDE

'Time'
'The Prettiest Star'
'Let's Spend The Night Together'
(Jagger-Richards)
'The Jean Genie'
'Lady Grinning Soul'

Pin Ups (1973)
(RCA)

A-SIDE

'Rosalyn' (Duncan-Farley –
original version: The Pretty Things)
'Here Comes The Night' (Berns –
original version: Them)
'I Wish You Would' (Arnold –
original version: The Yardbirds)
'See Emily Play' (Barrett –
original version: Pink Floyd)
'Everything's Alright' (Crouch-
Konrad-Stavely-James-Karlson –
original version: The Mojos)
'I Can't Explain' (Townshend –
original version: The Who)

B-SIDE

'Friday On My Mind' (Young-Harry
Vanda – original version:
The Easybeats)
'Sorrow' (Feldman-Goldstein-
Gottehrer – original version:
The Merseys)
'Don't Bring Me Down' (Dee –
original version: The Pretty Things)
'Shapes Of Things' (Samwell-Smith-
McCarty-Relf – original version:
The Yardbirds)
'Anyway, Anyhow, Anywhere'
(Daltrey-Townshend – original
version: The Who)
'Where Have All The Good Times
Gone' (Davies – original version:
The Kinks)

Diamond Dogs (1974)
(RCA)

A-SIDE

'Future Legend'
'Diamond Dogs'
'Sweet Thing'
'Candidate'
'Sweet Thing (Reprise)'
'Rebel Rebel'

B-SIDE

'Rock'n'roll With Me' (Bowie-Peace)
'We Are The Dead'
'1984'
'Big Brother'
'Chant Of The Ever Circling Skeletal
Family'

David Live (1974)
(RCA)

A-SIDE

'1984'
'Rebel Rebel'
'Moonage Daydream'
'Sweet Thing'

B-SIDE

'Changes'
'Suffragette City'
'Aladdin Sane (1913–1938–197?)'
'All The Young Dudes'
'Cracked Actor'

C-SIDE

'Rock'n'roll With Me' (Bowie-Peace)
'Watch That Man'
'Knock On Wood' (Floyd-Cropper)
'Diamond Dogs'

D-SIDE
'Big Brother'
'The Width Of A Circle'
'The Jean Genie'
'Rock'n'Roll Suicide'

Young Americans (1975)
(RCA)
A-SIDE
'Young Americans'
'Win'
'Fascination' (Bowie-Vandross)
'Right'
B-SIDE
'Somebody Up There Likes Me'
'Across The Universe' (Lennon-McCartney)
'Can You Hear Me'
'Fame' (Bowie-Alomar-Lennon)

Station To Station (1976)
(RCA)
A-SIDE
'Station To Station'
'Golden Years'
'Word On A Wing'
B-SIDE
'TVC 15'
'Stay'
'Wild Is The Wind' (Washington-Tiomkin)

Low (1977)
(RCA)
A-SIDE
'Speed Of Life'
'Breaking Glass' (Bowie-Davis-Murray)
'What In The World'
'Sound And Vision'
'Always Crashing In The Same Car'
'Be My Wife'
'A New Career In A New Town'
B-SIDE
'Warszawa' (Bowie-Eno)
'Art Decade'
'Weeping Wall'
'Subterraneans'

"Heroes" (1977)
(RCA)
A-SIDE
'Beauty And The Beast'
'Joe The Lion'
"Heroes" (Bowie-Eno)
'Sons Of The Silent Age'
'Blackout'
B-SIDE
'V-2 Schneider'
'Sense Of Doubt'
'Moss Garden' (Bowie-Eno)
'Neuköln' (Bowie-Eno)
'The Secret Life Of Arabia' (Bowie-Eno-Alomar)

Stage (1978)
(RCA)

A-SIDE
'Hang On To Yourself'
'Ziggy Stardust'
'Five Years'
'Soul Love'
'Star'

B-SIDE
'Station To Station'
'Fame' (Bowie-Alomar-Lennon)
'TVC 15'

C-SIDE
'Warszawa' (Bowie-Eno)
'Speed Of Life'
'Art Decade'
'Sense Of Doubt'
'Breaking Glass' (Bowie-Davis-Murray)

D-SIDE
"Heroes" (Bowie-Eno)
'What In The World'
'Blackout'
'Beauty And The Beast'

Lodger (1979)
(RCA)

A-SIDE
'Fantastic Voyage' (Bowie-Eno)
'African Night Flight' (Bowie-Eno)
'Move On'
'Yassassin'
'Red Sails' (Bowie-Eno)

B-SIDE
'DJ' (Bowie-Eno-Alomar)
'Look Back In Anger' (Bowie-Eno)
'Boys Keep Swinging' (Bowie-Eno)
'Repetition'
'Red Money' (Bowie-Alomar)

Scary Monsters (And Super Creeps)
(1980)
(RCA)

A-SIDE
'It's No Game (No 1)' (Bowie-Miura)
'Up The Hill Backwards'
'Scary Monsters (And Super Creeps)'
'Ashes To Ashes'
'Fashion'

B-SIDE
'Teenage Wildlife'
'Scream Like A Baby'
'Kingdom Come' (Verlaine)
'Because You're Young'
'It's No Game (No 2)'

INDEX

Assad, Bashar al- 575
Astley, Jon 356, 364–5
The Astronettes 217, 218, 317, 339, 348, 364, 382,
    406, 645
Atkins, Chet 244
Atlantic Crossing 498
Average White Band 392, 481
Ayers, Roy 414
Ayres, Tom 140

B

Baal 382, 524
Baby's Got A Gun 579
Bach, J.S. 250, 332
Bacharach, Burt 60
Bacon, Francis (painter) 580
Bacon, Sir Francis (scientist and philosopher) 437
Bad Company 494, 511, 512, 527–8, 529, 530, 532
Bad Reputation 551–2
Badfinger 363
Badger 455
Badham, John 392
Baez, Joan 121
Bailey, David 525
Baker, Josephine 341
Baker, Ronnie 422, 423
Baldry, Long John 229
Ball, Hugo 636
Balthus 487
The Band 100, 129, 264, 350
Bangs, Lester 351
Barjavel, René 276
Barnbrook, Jonathan 382, 647
Barnum & Bailey 594
Barrault, Jean-Louis 82
Barre, Martin 312
Barrett, Eric 455, 459, 469, 482, 617
Barrett, Syd 12, 61, 102, 238, 311, 325, 330, 332,
    478, 485
Barrie, Jack 40, 159
Bart, Lionel 37, 97
Bartók, Béla 142
Basil, Toni 346, 356, 374–6, 384, 387, 426, 427,
    436, 439
Bass, Billy 261
Battisti, Lucio 342
Baumann, Peter 548, 579
The Beach Boys 36, 128, 249, 306, 315, 443
The Beastie Boys 361
The Beat Room 33
The Beatles 11, 32, 34, 41, 50, 52, 53, 54, 60, 62–4,
    65, 70, 81, 86, 89, 90, 93, 102, 109, 110, 117,
    121, 128, 129, 130, 134, 161, 168, 175, 191,
    192, 193, 203, 209, 215, 244, 250, 251, 258,
    261, 269, 278, 295, 305, 313, 324, 328, 331,
    338, 383, 402, 403, 405, 406, 408, 422, 435–6,
    437, 443, 539, 599, 603, 614, 627, 630, 639, 667
The Beatstalkers 59, 70, 84, 89, 117, 182
Beausoleil, Bobby 451, 481
Beck, Jeff 3–4, 134, 135, 141, 143, 161, 179, 264,
    278, 280, 281, 293, 304, 320, 325, 382, 452
The Bee Gees 123, 312, 412, 438, 522, 542, 581

Beefheart, Captain 572
Beethoven, Ludwig van 250
Before And After Science 494, 572
Beggars Opera 496
Belafonte, Harry 394
Belew, Adrian 249, 591, 592, 593, 597, 601, 602,
    603, 608, 610–11, 612, 616, 618–19, 640, 671
Bell, Edward 646, 647, 669, 671
Bell, Thom 393, 424, 481
Bellotte, Pete 494
Bennett, Cliff 476
Bennett, Michael 374, 387
Benson, Gerard 92
Bergier, Jacques 481
Berlin, Brigid 171
Berns, Bert 333
Berry, Chuck 48, 215, 249, 265, 271, 328, 465
Best of Bowie 581
Bethell, Barry 277
Beuselinck, Oscar 59
Bewlay Bros. 550, 626
Bingenheimer, Rodney 140, 141, 160, 448
Birch, Ian 549
Birkett, Jack 67, 82, 87, 90, 217
Bittan, Roy 383, 452–3, 456, 457, 471, 482, 580,
    639, 645, 660, 667
Black And Blue 564
Black, Cilla 438
Black, Robin 312
Black Sabbath 89, 141, 143, 160, 480, 581
Black Tie White Noise 19, 667
Blackburn, Tony 202
Blackmore, Ritchie 260, 445, 480, 498
Blackstar 27, 161, 386, 401, 446, 501, 542, 551,
    581, 598, 600, 612, 615, 629, 664
Blackwell, Chris 160, 628
Blah-Blah-Blah 234, 521, 589
Blake, George 59
Bland, Bobby 'Blue' 34
Blavatsky, Helena 481
Blazer, Sam 375
Blondie 386, 549, 629, 636
Bloom, John 32, 44
Bluck, Roger 32
The Blue Dukes 385
Blue Mink 127, 155, 192, 301, 339, 357–8
Bluesology 121
Blur 536
Bob Marley And The Wailers 385
Bolan, Marc 32, 50, 52, 53, 68, 70, 81, 97, 100,
    102, 103, 109, 110, 111, 123, 130, 138, 142,
    148, 166, 168, 169, 173, 193, 204, 205, 206,
    210, 213, 225, 226, 233, 235, 239, 240, 247,
    257–8, 263, 272, 286, 311, 341, 384, 462,
    517–18, 525, 538, 548, 550, 553–4, 558, 580,
    588, 668
Bolan, Rolan 554
Bolder, Trevor 134, 142, 154, 156, 169, 170, 172,
    178, 179–80, 181, 192, 195, 203, 209, 213, 214,
    220, 221, 222, 227, 264, 271, 278, 280, 281,
    282, 283, 285, 287, 289, 304, 313, 314, 317,
    318, 319, 320, 323, 324, 339, 342, 383, 386

ACKNOWLEDGEMENTS

Thanks go to Sophie Soligny and...

...Tony Visconti, Mike Garson, Hermione Farthingale, Reeves Gabrels and Alain Lahana, as well as Mark Adams, Kevin Cann, Éric Dahan, Eileen Darcy (and Isolar), Alan Edwards, EMI, Nicolas Godin, Yves Guillemot, Harper Collins Publishers, Rémi Hurel, Eric Jean-Jean, Buford Jones, Christian Lebrun, Robin Lumley, Philippe Manœuvre, Philippe Marie, RCA, Mick Rock, Rock&Folk, Aurélien Masson, Alain de la Mata, Laurence Patrice, Corinne 'Coco' Schwab, Clifford Slapper, Leila Soligny, Thomas Soligny, Sony, Julian Stockton, les Éditions de la Table Ronde, les Éditions Tournon, Universal, Verycords and Warner.

Thank you to everyone at Gallimard.

Thank you to all the interviewees in the book and to those, colleagues, friends or family members who helped me access them. Thank you to those interviewees who pre-empted me and reached out before I did.

Thank you to Mary Finnigan, Geoffrey MacCormack, Tony Visconti and their editors for having authorized the inclusion of a few passages in their books (mentioned in the notes). Thank you to Pat Metheny for authorizing the inclusion of a few lines from his website.

Thank you to Ian Hunter for authorizing the publication of the lyrics to his song 'Dandy', from *Fingers Crossed* (Proper Records, 2016). ASCAP 2016.

Thank you to Anil and Jonathan Barnbrook, Mick Rock, Lisa and Margaux Chetteau (my Pink Fairies).

Thank you to Pink Floyd, Carole King and the Pet Shop Boys for writing the soundtrack to the making of this book. For their aptly named albums *The Endless River* (Warner, 2014), *Rhymes & Reasons* (A&M, 1972) and *Behaviour* (Parlophone, 1990). Thank you to Dave Stewart and Ebony McQueen for the support when it was needed most.

WITH THANKS TO...

John 'Twink' Alder, Tawatha Agee, Anthony Agnello, Air, Damon Albarn, Alex Alexander, Zachary Alford, Carlos Alomar, Ian Anderson, Laurie Anderson, Janet Armstrong, Kevin Armstrong, Ian Astbury, Jon Astley, Jonathan Barnbrook, Toni Basil, Jeff Beck, Robin Beck, Adrian Belew, Poogie Bell, Trevor Bolder, Boz Boorer, Patrick Boutoille, Derek Bramble, Patti Brett, Phill Brown, Carla Bruni, Robbie Buchanan, Paul Buckmaster, David Cage, Pierre Calamel, John Cale, John Cambridge, Kevin Cann, Ian 'Knox' Carnochan, Sophia Anne Caruso, Matt Chamberlain, Chanchan Von Shoeshine, Eugene Chaplin, Michael Chapman, Gerald Chevin, Leee Black Childers, Alan Childs, Keith Christmas, Robin Clark, Eddie Clarke, Bob Clearmountain, Rod Clements, Rob Clydesdale, John Conte, Neil Conti, Tom Conti, Jason Cooper, Elvis Costello, Terry Cox, Steve Crow, Cherie Currie, Roger Daltrey, Frank Darcel, Gail Davies, Carl Davis, Brent DeBoer, Tim Delaughter, Paul Dempsey, Vernon Dewhurst, Donovan, Gail Ann Dorsey, Gus Dudgeon, Aynsley Dunbar, Alan Edwards, Steve Elson, Jennifer Elster, Michael Esper, Marc Exiga, Hermione Farthingale, Larry Fast, Marla Feldstein, Bryan Ferry, Sammy Figueiroa, Yossi Fine, Jean Fineberg, Mary Finnigan, Matthew Fisher, Ken Fordham, Robert Fox, Chris Frantz, Robert Fripp, Martin Fry, Reeves Gabrels, Dave Gahan, Ricky Gardiner, Laurent Garnier, Mike Garson, Claude Gassian, Rob Gentry, Lisa Germano, Barry Gibb, Dana Gillespie, David Gilmour, Philip Glass, Jay Glennie, Roger Glover, Nicolas Godin, Jon Goldberger, Mac Gollehon, Martin Gore, Glenn Goring, Nicky Graham, Zaine Griff, Emm Gryner, Steve Guest, Mark Guiliana, Mick Haggerty, Page Hamilton, Chuck Hammer, Gijsbert Hanekroot, Steve Harley, Stan Harrison, Chris Haskett, Laurie Heath, Des Henly, Henry Hey, Stacy Heydon, Tom Hingston, Clare Hirst, Tim Hollier, Peter Holmström, Mary Hopkin, Harry Hughes, Peter Humphreys, Ian Hunter, John 'Hutch' Hutchinson, Chrissie Hynde, Joe Jackson, Eric Stephen Jacobs,

Eddie Jobson, Jay-Jay Johanson, Buford Jones, Dennis Katz, Kent, Pete Keppler, Chris Kimsey, Erdal Kizilcay, Markus Klinko, Albert Koski, Lenny Kravitz, Emir Ksasan, John Kumnick, Alain Lahana, Clive Langer, Chris Langhart, Amanda Lear, David Lebolt, Louise Lecavalier, Will Lee, Tim Lefebvre, Gerry Leonard, Mike Levesque, Linda Lewis, Jason Lindner, Nick Lowe, Robin Lumley, Geoff MacCormack, Ralph Mace, Dennis 'Blackeye' MacKay, Russell Mael, Alan Mair, Phil Manzanera, Michel Marie, Chris Martin, Giles Martin, Harry Maslin, Aurélien Masson, Sylvia Massy, Brian May, Phil May, Robin Mayhew, Paddy McAloon, Jim McCarty, Donald McCaslin, Ian McCulloch, Roger McGough, Ewan McGregor, Henry McGroggan, Greg McLeod, Mario J McNulty, Pat Metheny, Eduard 'Edu' Meyer, Marc Minelli, Moby, Brian Molko, Ben Monder, Jean-Baptiste Mondino, Martha Mooke, Jacqui Moore, Mike Moran, Andrew Morris, Toby Mountain, Elliott Murphy, George Murray, Tony Newman, Andy Newmark, Kuêlan Nguyen, Steve Nieve, Cécile Nougaro, Hazel O'Connor, Terry O'Neill, Mat Osman, Hugh Padgham, Holly Palmer, Norma Palmer, Phil Palmer, Tim Palmer, Alan Parker, Kevin Paul, Guy Peellaert, Jean-Hervé Péron, Lenny Pickett, Mark Plati, Malcolm Pollack, Iggy Pop, Chris Porter, Roger Powell, Sonjay Prabhakar, Mark Pritchett, Michael Prowda, Marcel Rapp, Mark Ravitz, Lou Reed, Tim Renwick, Gilles Riberolles, Michael Riesman, William Riley, Catherine Ringer, Michel Ripoche, Billy Ritchie, Mick Rock, Nile Rodgers, Paul Rodgers, Hans-Joachim Roedelius, Carmine Rojas, Mick Ronson, Mike Ross-Trevor, Michael Rother, Jordan Rudess, Catherine 'Cat' Russell, Phillipe Saisse, Ryuichi Sakamoto, Hunt Sales, Tony Sales, David Sanborn, Edward Sanders, Craig San Roque, Margo Sappington, Mark Saunders, Eric Schermerhorn, Irmin Schmidt, Thilo Schmied, Maria Schneider, Peter Schwartz, Ken Scott, Bobbie Seagroatt, Matthew Seligman, Justin Shirley-Smith, Bill Siddons, George Simms, Chris Simpson, Gerald Simpson, David Sitek, Clifford Slapper, Earl Slick, Sophie Soligny, Jack Spann, Dave Stewart, Michael Stipe, Bridget St John, Guy St-Onge, Richard Strange, Masayoshi Sukita, Dominik Tarqua, Joe Tarsia, Mike Tarsia, Courtney Taylor-Taylor, Neil Tennant, Laurent Thibault, Gary Tole, Erin Tonkon, David Torn, Franz Treichler, Steven Tyler, George Underwood, Midge Ure, Ivo van Hove, Dave Vanian, Mike Vernon, Simon Vinestock, Tony Visconti, Klaus Voorman, Cuong Vu, Enda Walsh, Lloyd Watson, Paul Wertico, Jonathan Weston, Paul Westwood, James Williamson, Woody Woodmansey, Roger Wootton, Jonathan Wyner, Kristeen Young and Roy Young.

Picture Credits

Chapter images:

56, 94, 132, 164, 198, 256, 308, 334, 388, 440, 486, 544, 584, 632 © Jérôme Soligny/ Truant Songs.

Inset images

1 courtesy of Robin Lumley; 2 © Alister McDonald/Leemage; 3 (above) © CA/ Redferns/Getty Images; 3 (below) © The Rudy Calvo Collection/Cache Agency/ DALLE; 4 © Archives Tony Visconti; 4 (above) © David Bebbington/RetnaUK Credit/DALLE; 5 (below) © Vernon Dewhurst; 6 © PICTORIAL/DALLE; 7 © Rolf Adlercreutz/Alamy/DALLE; 8 © Michael Putland/Getty Images; 9, 11 (above), 13, 14 (below) © MickRock; 10; 20 © Sukita; 11 (below) © Gijsbert Hanekroot; 12 © Debi Doss/Redferns/Getty Images; 14 (above), 16, 17 (above) © Terry O'Neill/Iconic Images/Getty Images; 15 © Gijsbert Hanekroot/Redferns/ Getty Images; 17 (below), 18 (above) Steve Schapiro/Corbis via Getty Images; 18 (below) © Gijsbert Hanekroot; 19 (above), 22 (above) © Claude Gassian; 19 (below), 21 (above), 22 (below) © Christian Simonpiétri/Sygma via Getty Images; 21 (below) © Larry Hulst/Michael Ochs Archives/Getty Images; 23 (above) © STILLS/Gamma-Rapho via Getty Images; 23 (below) © Ron Tom/ NBC/NBCU Photo Bank via Getty Images; 24 courtesy of Robin Lumley.

First published by Editions Gallimard Loisirs, Paris © Editions Gallimard Loisirs 2019

First published in Great Britain in 2023 by Monoray, an imprint of
Octopus Publishing Group Ltd
Carmelite House
50 Victoria Embankment
London EC4Y oDZ
www.octopusbooks.co.uk

An Hachette UK Company
www.hachette.co.uk

Text copyright © Jérôme Soligny 2023

Distributed in the US by Hachette Book Group
1290 Avenue of the Americas
4th and 5th Floors
New York, NY 10104

Distributed in Canada by Canadian Manda Group
664 Annette St. Toronto, Ontario, Canada M6S 2C8

ISBN 978 1 80096 063 3

A CIP catalogue record for this book is available from the British Library.

Printed and bound in UK

1 3 5 7 9 10 8 6 4 2

This FSC® label means that materials used for the
product have been responsibly sourced.